W9-BIK-243

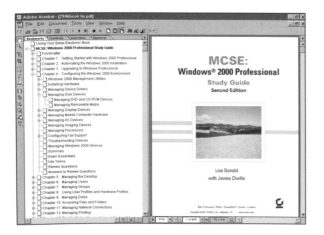

Search through two complete books in PDF!

✔ Access the entire *MCSE: Windows 2000 Professional Study Guide*, complete with figures and tables, in electronic format.

✔ Search the *MCSE: Windows 2000 Professional Study Guide* chapters to find information on any topic in seconds.

✔ Look up any networking term in the *Dictionary of Networking*.

Use the Electronic Flashcards for PCs or Palm devices to jog your memory and prep last-minute for the exam!

✔ Reinforce your understanding of key concepts with these hardcore flashcard-style questions.

✔ Download the Flashcards to your Palm device, and go on the road. Now you can study anywhere, any time.

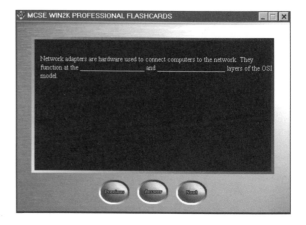

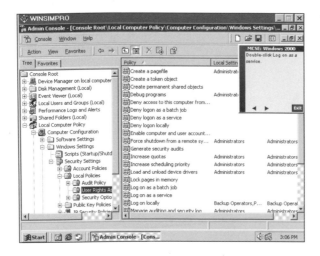

Prepare for Microsoft's tough simulation questions with the WinSim 2000 program!

✔ Use the simulators to guide you through real-world tasks step-by-step, or watch the movies to see the "invisible hand" perform the tasks for you.

SYBEX

MCSE: Windows 2000 Professional Study Guide
Exam 70-210: Objectives

SYBEX

NOTE   Exam objectives are subject to change at any time without prior notice and at Microsoft's sole discretion. Please visit Microsoft's Training & Certification Web site (www.microsoft.com/Train_Cert) for the most current listing of exam objectives.

SYBEX

MCSE:
Windows 2000 Professional
Study Guide
Second Edition

MCSE:
Windows® 2000 Professional
Study Guide
Second Edition

Lisa Donald

with James Chellis

San Francisco • Paris • Düsseldorf • Soest • London

SYBEX

Associate Publisher: Neil Edde
Contracts and Licensing Manager: Kristine O'Callaghan
Acquisitions and Developmental Editor: Jeff Kellum
Editors: Carol Henry, Suzanne Goraj, Linda Orlando, Marilyn Smith
Production Editor: Shannon Murphy
Technical Editors: Michelle A. Roudebush, Donald Fuller
Book Designer: Bill Gibson
Graphic Illustrator: Tony Jonick
Electronic Publishing Specialist: Nila Nichols
Proofreaders: Judith Hibbard, Emily Hsuan, Nelson Kim, Laurie O'Connell, Yariv Rabinovitch, Nancy Riddiough
Indexer: Ted Laux
CD Coordinator: Christine Harris
CD Technician: Kevin Ly
Cover Designer: Archer Design
Cover Photographer: Natural Selection

Library of Congress Card Number: 2001088246

ISBN: 0-7821-2946-3

SYBEX

To Our Valued Readers:

When Sybex published the first editions of the four core Windows® 2000 MCSE Study Guides, Windows® 2000 had been out for only six months, and the MCSE exams had just been released. In writing the Study Guides, the authors brought to the table their experience with Windows® 2000 as well as insights gained from years of classroom teaching. With the official Microsoft exam objectives as their guides, the authors set out to write comprehensive, yet ultimately clear, concise, and practical courseware. And we believe they succeeded.

Over the past year, however, our authors have learned many new things about how Windows® 2000 works and have received significant and useful feedback about how Microsoft is testing individuals on the vast array of topics encompassed by the four core exams. We at Sybex have also received a tremendous amount of invaluable feedback—both praise and criticism—regarding the four core Windows® 2000 Study Guides. The second edition that you hold in your hand is the product of the feedback that readers such as yourself have provided to us.

So what "new and improved" material will you find in this new edition? We have confidence in the core instructional material in the books, so the authors have made only minor modifications to this content. They have, however, made the chapter review questions and bonus exam questions more challenging, to better reflect the type of questions you'll encounter on the actual exams. We've also added Real World Scenarios throughout the book. This new feature allowed the authors to add critical context and perspective on Windows® 2000 technologies that wasn't available when Microsoft first released the products. Finally, we've added Exam Essentials to the end of each chapter. These re-emphasize those subject areas that are most important for success on the exams.

We believe you'll find this Study Guide to be an indispensable part of your exam prep program. As always, your feedback is important to us. Please send comments, questions, or suggestions to support@sybex.com. At Sybex we're continually striving to meet and exceed the needs of individuals preparing for IT certification exams. Readers like you are critical to these efforts.

Good luck in pursuit of your MCSE!

Neil Edde
Associate Publisher—Certification
Sybex, Inc.

SYBEX Inc. 1151 Marina Village Parkway, Alameda, CA 94501
Tel: 510/523-8233   Fax: 510/523-2373   HTTP://www.sybex.com

Software License Agreement: Terms and Conditions

The media and/or any online materials accompanying this book that are available now or in the future contain programs and/or text files (the "Software") to be used in connection with the book. SYBEX hereby grants to you a license to use the Software, subject to the terms that follow. Your purchase, acceptance, or use of the Software will constitute your acceptance of such terms.

The Software compilation is the property of SYBEX unless otherwise indicated and is protected by copyright to SYBEX or other copyright owner(s) as indicated in the media files (the "Owner(s)"). You are hereby granted a single-user license to use the Software for your personal, noncommercial use only. You may not reproduce, sell, distribute, publish, circulate, or commercially exploit the Software, or any portion thereof, without the written consent of SYBEX and the specific copyright owner(s) of any component software included on this media.

In the event that the Software or components include specific license requirements or end-user agreements, statements of condition, disclaimers, limitations or warranties ("End-User License"), those End-User Licenses supersede the terms and conditions herein as to that particular Software component. Your purchase, acceptance, or use of the Software will constitute your acceptance of such End-User Licenses.

By purchase, use or acceptance of the Software you further agree to comply with all export laws and regulations of the United States as such laws and regulations may exist from time to time.

Software Support

Components of the supplemental Software and any offers associated with them may be supported by the specific Owner(s) of that material but they are not supported by SYBEX. Information regarding any available support may be obtained from the Owner(s) using the information provided in the appropriate read.me files or listed elsewhere on the media. Should the manufacturer(s) or other Owner(s) cease to offer support or decline to honor any offer, SYBEX bears no responsibility. This notice concerning support for the Software is provided for your information only. SYBEX is not the agent or principal of the Owner(s), and SYBEX is in no way responsible for providing any support for the Software, nor is it liable or responsible for any support provided, or not provided, by the Owner(s).

Warranty

SYBEX warrants the enclosed media to be free of physical defects for a period of ninety (90) days after purchase. The Software is not available from SYBEX in any other form or media than that enclosed herein or posted to www.sybex.com. If you discover a defect in the media during this warranty period, you may obtain a replacement of identical format at no charge by sending the defective media, postage prepaid, with proof of purchase to:

SYBEX Inc.
Customer Service Department
1151 Marina Village Parkway
Alameda, CA 94501
(510) 523-8233
Fax: (510) 523-2373
e-mail: info@sybex.com
WEB: HTTP://WWW.SYBEX.COM

After the 90-day period, you can obtain replacement media of identical format by sending us the defective disk, proof of purchase, and a check or money order for $10, payable to SYBEX.

Disclaimer

SYBEX makes no warranty or representation, either expressed or implied, with respect to the Software or its contents, quality, performance, merchantability, or fitness for a particular purpose. In no event will SYBEX, its distributors, or dealers be liable to you or any other party for direct, indirect, special, incidental, consequential, or other damages arising out of the use of or inability to use the Software or its contents even if advised of the possibility of such damage. In the event that the Software includes an online update feature, SYBEX further disclaims any obligation to provide this feature for any specific duration other than the initial posting. The exclusion of implied warranties is not permitted by some states. Therefore, the above exclusion may not apply to you. This warranty provides you with specific legal rights; there may be other rights that you may have that vary from state to state. The pricing of the book with the Software by SYBEX reflects the allocation of risk and limitations on liability contained in this agreement of Terms and Conditions.

Shareware Distribution

This Software may contain various programs that are distributed as shareware. Copyright laws apply to both shareware and ordinary commercial software, and the copyright Owner(s) retains all rights. If you try a shareware program and continue using it, you are expected to register it. Individual programs differ on details of trial periods, registration, and payment. Please observe the requirements stated in appropriate files.

Copy Protection

The Software in whole or in part may or may not be copy-protected or encrypted. However, in all cases, reselling or redistributing these files without authorization is expressly forbidden except as specifically provided for by the Owner(s) therein.

For Kevin. You are the best!

Acknowledgments

This book is the result of a great team. First, I'd like to thank Carol Henry (on the second edition) and Marilyn Smith (on the first edition), who both did a tremendous job of translating my writing into a form that is very readable. Marilyn and Carol put in countless hours and worked through my many revisions as the book evolved. In addition, they were both super people to work with.

I'd also like to thank the team that made this book possible. Thanks to James Chellis for allowing me to work on the MCSE series. James is a visionary and is my business idol. Neil Edde, the Associate Publisher for this series, has nurtured the MCSE since the early days. Jeff Kellum, the Acquisitions and Developmental Editor, is always fun to work with (even though he can be a slave driver at times). Shannon Murphy, the Production Editor, somehow managed to keep this project on track, which was not always an easy task.

Michelle Roudebush and Donald Fuller worked as the Technical Editors. They did a great job of keeping me honest and minimizing any errors within the book. Any errors missed by the editor and technical editors were caught by the book's proofreaders: Judith Hibbard, Emily Hsuan, Nelson Kim, Laurie O'Connell, Yariv Rabinovitch, and Nancy Riddiough. Tony Jonick developed the artwork from my drawings. Nila Nichols worked as the Electronic Publishing Specialist. Christine Harris and Kevin Ly managed and created content for the accompanying CD. Matthew Sheltz worked very hard on the CD test engine and is also very appreciated. Without the great work of the team, this book would not have been possible.

On the local front, I'd like to thank Martina Fiserova, who keeps my life sane. Without her, I'd never get anything done. I'd also like to thank my family for always supporting me.

Contents at a Glance

Contents

Chapter 15 Performing System Recovery Functions 705

Table of Exercises

Introduction

Microsoft's Microsoft Certified Systems Engineer (MCSE) track for Windows 2000 is the premier certification for computer industry professionals. Covering the core technologies around which Microsoft's future will be built, the MCSE Windows 2000 program is a powerful credential for career advancement.

This book has been developed to give you the critical skills and knowledge you need to prepare for one of the core requirements of the new MCSE certification program: *Installing, Configuring, and Administering Microsoft Windows 2000 Professional* (Exam 70-210).

The Microsoft Certified Professional Program

Since the inception of its certification program, Microsoft has certified over one million people. As the computer network industry grows in both size and complexity, these numbers are sure to grow—and the need for *proven* ability will also increase. Companies rely on certifications to verify the skills of prospective employees and contractors.

Microsoft has developed its Microsoft Certified Professional (MCP) program to give you credentials that verify your ability to work with Microsoft products effectively and professionally. Obtaining your MCP certification requires that you pass any one Microsoft certification exam. Several levels of certification are available based on specific suites of exams. Depending on your areas of interest or experience, you can obtain any of the following MCP credentials:

Microsoft Certified System Engineer (MCSE)   This certification track is designed for network and systems administrators, network and systems analysts, and technical consultants who work with Microsoft Windows 2000 client and server software. You must take and pass seven exams to obtain your MCSE.

Since this book covers one of the Core MCSE exams, we will discuss the MCSE certification in detail in this Introduction.

Microsoft Certified Solution Developer (MCSD)   This track is designed for software engineers and developers and technical consultants who primarily use Microsoft development tools. Currently, you can take exams on Visual Basic, Visual C++, and Visual FoxPro. However, with Microsoft's pending release of Visual Studio 7, you can expect the requirements for this track to change by the end of 2001. You must take and pass four exams to obtain your MCSD.

Microsoft Certified Database Administrator (MCDBA)   This track is designed for database administrators, developers, and analysts who work with Microsoft SQL Server. As of this printing, you can take exams on either SQL Server 7 or SQL Server 2000, but Microsoft is expected to announce the retirement of SQL Server 7. You must take and pass four exams to achieve MCDBA status.

Microsoft Certified Trainer (MCT)   The MCT track is designed for any IT professional who develops and teaches Microsoft-approved courses. To become an MCT, you must first obtain your MCSE, MCSD, or MCDBA; then you must take a class at one of the Certified Technical Training Centers. You will also be required to prove your instructional ability. You can do this in various ways: by taking a skills-building or train-the-trainer class; by achieving certification as a trainer from any of a number vendors; or by becoming a Certified Technical Trainer through the Chauncey Group (www.chauncey.com/ctt.html). Last of all, you will need to complete an MCT application.

As of March 1, 2001, Microsoft no longer offers MCSE NT 4 required exams. Those who are certified in NT 4 have until December 31, 2001, to upgrade their credentials to Windows 2000. Also, Microsoft has retired three other certification tracks: MCP+Internet, MCSE+Internet, and MCP+Site Builder. The topics and concepts that are tested in these certifications have been incorporated into the MCSE and MCSD exams.

Windows 2000

Over the next few years, companies around the world will deploy millions of copies of Windows 2000 as the central operating system for their mission-critical networks. This will generate an enormous need for qualified consultants and personnel who can design, deploy, and support Windows 2000 networks.

Because Windows 2000 is such a vast product, its administrators must have a wealth of professional skills. As an example of Windows 2000's complexity, consider it has more than 35 million lines of code as compared with Windows NT 4's 12 million! Much of this code is needed to support the wide range of functionality that Windows 2000 offers.

The Windows 2000 line comprises several versions:

Windows 2000 Professional This is the client edition of Windows 2000, which is comparable to Windows NT Workstation 4 but also includes the best features of Windows 98, as well as many new features.

Windows 2000 Server/Windows 2000 Advanced Server A server edition of Windows 2000, this version is for small to midsized deployments. Advanced Server supports more memory and processors than Server does.

Windows 2000 Datacenter Server This is a server edition of Windows 2000 for large, widescale deployments and computer clusters. Datacenter Server supports the most memory and processors of the three versions.

Companies implementing the expansive Windows 2000 operating system want to be certain that you are the right person for the job being offered. The MCSE track is designed to help you prove that you are.

How Do You Become an MCSE?

Attaining MCSE certification has always been a challenge. In the past, students have been able to acquire detailed exam information—even most of the exam questions—from online "brain dumps" and third-party "cram" books or software products. For the new MCSE exams, this is simply not the case.

Microsoft has taken strong steps to protect the security and integrity of the new MCSE track. Now, prospective MCSEs must complete a course of study that develops detailed knowledge about a wide range of topics. It supplies them with the true skills needed, derived from working with Windows 2000 and related software products.

The new MCSE program is heavily weighted toward hands-on skills and experience. Microsoft has stated that "nearly half of the core required exams' content demands that the candidate have troubleshooting skills acquired through hands-on experience and working knowledge."

Fortunately, if you are willing to dedicate the time and effort to learn Windows 2000, you can prepare yourself well for the exams by using the proper tools. By working through this book, you can successfully meet the exam requirements.

This book is part of a complete series of Sybex MCSE Study Guides, published by Sybex Inc., that together cover the core Windows 2000 requirements as well as the new Design exams needed to complete your MCSE track. Study Guide titles include the following:

- *MCSE: Windows 2000 Professional Study Guide,* Second Edition, by Lisa Donald with James Chellis (Sybex, 2001)

- *MCSE: Windows 2000 Server Study Guide,* Second Edition, by Lisa Donald with James Chellis (Sybex, 2001)

- *MCSE: Windows 2000 Network Infrastructure Administration Study Guide,* Second Edition, by Paul Robichaux with James Chellis (Sybex, 2001)

- *MCSE: Windows 2000 Directory Services Administration Study Guide,* Second Edition, by Anil Desai with James Chellis (Sybex, 2001)

- *MCSE: Windows 2000 Network Security Design Study Guide,* by Gary Govanus and Robert King (Sybex, 2000)

- *MCSE: Windows 2000 Network Infrastructure Design Study Guide,* by Bill Heldman (Sybex, 2000)

- *MCSE: Windows 2000 Directory Services Design Study Guide,* by Robert King and Gary Govanus (Sybex, 2000)

Exam Requirements

Candidates for MCSE certification in Windows 2000 must pass seven exams, including four core operating system exams, one design exam, and two electives, as described in the sections that follow.

Core Requirements

Windows 2000 Professional (70-210)

Windows 2000 Server (70-215)

Windows 2000 Network Infrastructure Administration (70-216)

Windows 2000 Directory Services Administration (70-217)

Design Requirement

Designing a Windows 2000 Directory Services Infrastructure (70-219)

Plus one of the following

Designing Security for a Windows 2000 Network (70-220)

Designing a Windows 2000 Network Infrastructure (70-221)

Designing Web Solutions with Windows 2000 Server Technologies (70-226)

Electives

Any of the Design exams not taken for the Design requirement

Plus two of the following

Any current Elective exam. Topics include Exchange Server, SQL Server, and ISA Server.

For a more detailed description of the Microsoft certification programs, including a list of current and future MCSE electives, check Microsoft's Training and Certification Web site at www.microsoft.com/trainingandservices.

The *Installing, Configuring, and Administering Microsoft Windows 2000 Professional* Exam

The Windows 2000 Professional exam covers concepts and skills related to installing, configuring, and managing Windows 2000 Professional computers. It emphasizes the following elements of Windows 2000 Professional support:

- Installing Windows 2000 Professional

- Implementing and administering resources

- Implementing, managing, and troubleshooting resources

- Monitoring and optimizing system performance and reliability

- Configuring and troubleshooting the Desktop environment

- Implementing, managing, and troubleshooting network protocols and services

- Implementing, monitoring, and troubleshooting security

This exam is quite specific regarding Windows 2000 Professional requirements and operational settings, and it can be particular about how administrative tasks are performed within the operating system. It also focuses on fundamental concepts of Windows 2000 Professional's operation. Careful study of this book, along with hands-on experience, will help you to prepare for this exam.

Microsoft provides exam objectives to give you a very general overview of possible areas of coverage on the Microsoft exams. For your convenience, this Study Guide includes objective listings positioned within the text at points where specific Microsoft exam objectives are discussed. Keep in mind, however, that exam objectives are subject to change at any time without prior notice and at Microsoft's sole discretion. Please visit Microsoft's Training and Certification Web site (www.microsoft.com/trainingandservices) for the most current listing of exam objectives.

Types of Exam Questions

In an effort to both refine the testing process and protect the quality of its certifications, Microsoft has focused its Windows 2000 exams on real experience and hands-on proficiency. There is a higher emphasis on your past working environments and responsibilities, and less emphasis on how well you can memorize. In fact, Microsoft says an MCSE candidate should have at least one year of hands-on experience.

Microsoft will accomplish its goal of protecting the exams' integrity by regularly adding and removing exam questions, limiting the number of questions that any individual sees in a beta exam, limiting the number of questions delivered to an individual by using adaptive testing, and adding new exam elements.

Exam questions may be in a variety of formats: Depending on which exam you take, you'll see multiple-choice questions, as well as select-and-place and prioritize-a-list questions. Simulations and case study–based formats are included, as well. You may also find yourself taking what's called an *adaptive format exam.* Let's take a look at the types of exam questions and examine the adaptive testing technique, so that you'll be prepared for all of the possibilities.

With the release of Windows 2000, Microsoft has stopped providing a detailed score breakdown. This is mostly because of the various and complex question formats. Previously, each question focused on one objective. The Windows 2000 exams, however, contain questions that may be tied to one or more objectives from one or more objective sets. Therefore, grading by objective is almost impossible.

For more information on the various exam question types, go to www.microsoft.com/trainingandservices/default.asp?PageID=mcp&PageCall=tesinn&SubSite=examinfo.

MULTIPLE-CHOICE QUESTIONS

Multiple-choice questions come in two main forms. One is a straightforward question followed by several possible answers, of which one or more is correct. The other type of multiple-choice question is more complex and based on a specific scenario. The scenario may focus on a number of areas or objectives.

SELECT-AND-PLACE QUESTIONS

Select-and-place exam questions involve graphical elements that you must manipulate in order to successfully answer the question. For example, you might see a diagram of a computer network, as shown in the following graphic taken from the select-and-place demo downloaded from Microsoft's Web site.

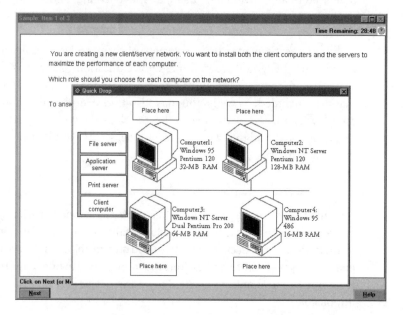

A typical diagram will show computers and other components next to boxes that contain the text "Place here." The labels for the boxes represent various computer roles on a network, such as a print server and a file server. Based on information given for each computer, you are asked to select each label and place it in the correct box. You need to place *all* of the labels correctly. No credit is given for the question if you correctly label only some of the boxes.

In another select-and-place problem you might be asked to put a series of steps in order, by dragging item from boxes on the left to boxes on the right, and placing them in the correct order. One other type requires that you drag an item from the left and place it under an item in a column on the right.

SIMULATIONS

Simulations are the kinds of questions that most closely represent actual situations and test the skills you use while working with Microsoft software interfaces. These exam questions include a mock interface on which you are asked to perform certain actions according to a given scenario. The simulated interfaces look nearly identical to what you see in the actual product, as shown in this example:

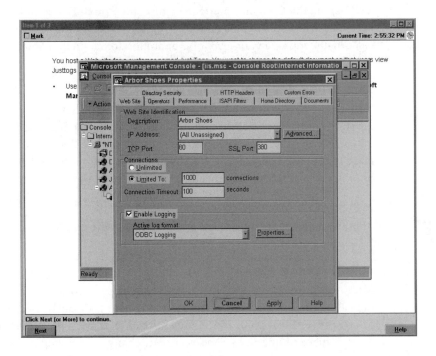

Because of the number of possible errors that can be made on simulations, be sure to consider the following recommendations from Microsoft:

- Do not change any simulation settings that don't pertain to the solution directly.

- When related information has not been provided, assume that the default settings are used.

- Make sure that your entries are spelled correctly.

- Close all the simulation application windows after completing the set of tasks in the simulation.

The best way to prepare for simulation questions is to spend time working with the graphical interface of the product on which you will be tested.

We recommend that you study with the WinSim 2000 product, which is included on the CD that accompanies this study guide. By completing the exercises in this study guide and working with the WinSim 2000 software, you will greatly improve your level of preparation for simulation questions.

CASE STUDY–BASED QUESTIONS

Case study–based questions first appeared in the MCSD program. These questions present a scenario with a range of requirements. Based on the information provided, you answer a series of multiple-choice and select-and-place questions. The interface for case study–based questions has a number of tabs, each of which contains information about the scenario.

At present, this type of question appears only in most of the Design exams.

ADAPTIVE EXAM FORMAT

Microsoft presents many of its exams in an *adaptive* format. This format is radically different from the conventional format previously used for Microsoft certification exams. Conventional tests are static, containing a fixed number of questions. Adaptive tests change depending on your answers to the questions presented.

The number of questions presented in your adaptive test will depend on how long it takes the exam to ascertain your level of ability (according to the statistical measurements on which exam questions are ranked). To determine a test-taker's level of ability, the exam presents questions in an increasing or decreasing order of difficulty.

Unlike the earlier test format, the adaptive test does *not* allow you to go back to see a question again. The exam only goes forward. Once you enter your answer, that's it—you cannot change it. Be very careful before entering your answers. There is no time limit for each individual question (only for the exam as a whole). Your exam may be shortened by correct answers (and lengthened by incorrect answers), so there is no advantage to rushing through questions.

Microsoft will regularly add and remove questions from the exams. This is called *item seeding*. It is part of the effort to make it more difficult for individuals to merely memorize exam questions that were passed along by previous test-takers.

Exam Question Development

Microsoft follows an exam-development process consisting of eight mandatory phases. The process takes an average of seven months and involves more than 150 specific steps. The MCP exam development consists of the following phases:

Phase 1: Job Analysis Phase 1 is an analysis of all the tasks that make up a specific job function, based on tasks performed by people who are currently performing that job function. This phase also identifies the knowledge, skills, and abilities that relate specifically to the performance area being certified.

Phase 2: Objective Domain Definition The results of the job analysis phase provide the framework used to develop objectives. Development of objectives involves translating the job-function tasks into a comprehensive package of specific and measurable knowledge, skills, and abilities. The resulting list of objectives—the *objective domain*—is the basis for the development of both the certification exams and the training materials.

Phase 3: Blueprint Survey   The final objective domain is transformed into a blueprint survey in which contributors are asked to rate each objective. These contributors may be MCP candidates, appropriately skilled exam-development volunteers, or Microsoft employees. Based on the contributors' input, the objectives are prioritized and weighted. The actual exam items are written according to the prioritized objectives. Contributors are queried about how they spend their time on the job. If a contributor doesn't spend an adequate amount of time actually performing the specified job function, his or her data are eliminated from the analysis. The blueprint survey phase helps determine which objectives to measure, as well as the appropriate number and types of items to include on the exam.

Phase 4: Item Development   A pool of items is developed to measure the blueprinted objective domain. The number and types of items to be written are based on the results of the blueprint survey.

Phase 5: Alpha Review and Item Revision   During this phase, a panel of technical and job-function experts review each item for technical accuracy. The panel then answers each item and reaches a consensus on all technical issues. Once the items have been verified as being technically accurate, they are edited to ensure that they are expressed in the clearest language possible.

Phase 6: Beta Exam   The reviewed and edited items are collected into beta exams. Based on the responses of all beta participants, Microsoft performs a statistical analysis to verify the validity of the exam items and to determine which items will be used in the certification exam. Once the analysis has been completed, the items are distributed into multiple parallel forms, or *versions*, of the final certification exam.

Phase 7: Item Selection and Cut-Score Setting   The results of the beta exams are analyzed to determine which items will be included in the certification exam. This determination is based on many factors, including item difficulty and relevance. During this phase, a panel of job-function experts determine the *cut score* (minimum passing score) for the exams. The cut score differs from exam to exam because it is based on an item-by-item determination of the percentage of candidates who answered the item correctly and who would be expected to answer the item correctly.

Phase 8: Live Exam   In the final phase, the exams are given to candidates. MCP exams are administered by Prometric and Virtual University Enterprises (VUE).

Tips for Taking the Windows 2000 Professional Exam

Here are some general tips for achieving success on your certification exam:

- Arrive early at the exam center so that you can relax and review your study materials. During this final review, you can look over tables and lists of exam-related information.

- Read the questions carefully. Don't be tempted to jump to an early conclusion. Make sure you know *exactly* what the question is asking.

- Answer all questions. Remember that the adaptive format does *not* allow you to return to a question. Be very careful before entering your answer. Because your exam may be shortened by correct answers (and lengthened by incorrect answers), there is no advantage to rushing through questions.

- On simulations, do not change settings that are not directly related to the question. Also, assume default settings if the question does not specify or imply which settings are used.

- For questions you're not sure about, use a process of elimination to get rid of the obviously incorrect options first. This improves your odds of selecting the correct answer when you need to make an educated guess.

Exam Registration

You may take the Microsoft exams at any of more than 1,000 Authorized Prometric Testing Centers (APTCs) and VUE Testing Centers around the world. For the location of a testing center near you, call Prometric at 800-755-EXAM (755-3926), or call VUE at 888-837-8616. Outside the United States and Canada, contact your local Prometric or VUE registration center.

Find out the number of the exam you want to take, and then register with the Prometric or VUE registration center nearest to you. At this point, you will be asked for advance payment for the exam. The exams are $100 each and you must take them within one year of payment. You can schedule exams up to six weeks in advance or as late as one working day prior to the date of the exam. You can cancel or reschedule your exam if you contact the center at least two working days prior to the exam. Same-day registration is available in some locations, subject to space availability. Where same-day registration is available, you must register a minimum of two hours before test time.

You may also register for your exams online at www.prometric.com or www.vue.com.

When you schedule the exam, you will be provided with instructions regarding appointment and cancellation procedures, ID requirements, and information about the testing center location. In addition, you will receive a registration and payment confirmation letter from Prometric or VUE.

Microsoft requires certification candidates to accept the terms of a Non-Disclosure Agreement before taking certification exams.

Is This Book for You?

If you want to acquire a solid foundation in Windows 2000 Professional, and your goal is to prepare for the exam by learning how to use and manage the new operating system, this book is for you. You'll find clear explanations of the fundamental concepts you need to grasp, and plenty of help to achieve the high level of professional competency you need to succeed in your chosen field.

If you want to become certified as an MCSE, this book is definitely for you. However, if you just want to attempt to pass the exam without really understanding Windows 2000, this Study Guide is *not* for you. It is written for people who want to acquire hands-on skills and in-depth knowledge of Windows 2000.

How to Use This Book

What makes a Sybex Study Guide the book of choice for over 100,000 MCSEs? We took into account not only what you need to know to pass the exam, but what you need to know to take what you've learned and apply it in the real world. Each book contains the following:

Objective-by-objective coverage of the topics you need to know   Each chapter lists the objectives covered in that chapter, followed by detailed discussion of each objective.

Assessment Test   Directly following this Introduction is an Assessment Test that you should take. It is designed to help you determine how much you already know about Windows 2000. Each question is tied to a topic discussed in the book. Using the results of the Assessment test, you can figure out the areas where you need to focus your study. Of course, we do recommend you read the entire book.

Exam Essentials   To highlight what you learn, you'll find a list of Exam Essentials at the end of each chapter. The Exam Essentials section briefly highlights the topics that need your particular attention as you prepare for the exam.

Key Terms and Glossary   Throughout each chapter, you will be introduced to important terms and concepts that you will need to know for the exam. These terms appear in italic within the chapters, and a list of the Key Terms appears just after the Exam Essentials. At the end of the book, a detailed Glossary gives definitions for these terms, as well as other general terms you should know.

Review questions, complete with detailed explanations   Each chapter is followed by a set of Review Questions that test what you learned in the chapter. The questions are written with the exam in mind, meaning that they are designed to have the same look and feel of what you'll see on the exam. Question types are just like the exam, including multiple choice, exhibits, select-and-place, and prioritize-a-list.

Hands-on exercises   In each chapter, you'll find exercises designed to give you the important hands-on experience that is critical for your exam preparation. The exercises support the topics of the chapter, and they walk you through the steps necessary to perform a particular function.

Real World Scenarios   Because reading a book isn't enough for you to learn how to apply these topics in your everyday duties, we have provided Real World Scenarios in special sidebars. These explain when and why a particular solution would make sense, in a working environment you'd actually encounter.

Interactive CD Every Sybex Study Guide comes with a CD complete with additional questions, flashcards for use with a palm device, a Windows simulation program, and two complete electronic books. Details are in the following section.

The topics covered in this Study Guide map directly to Microsoft's official exam objectives. Each exam objective is covered completely.

What's on the CD?

With this new member of our best-selling MCSE Study Guide series, we are including quite an array of training resources. The CD offers numerous simulations, bonus exams, and flashcards to help you study for the exam. We have also included the complete contents of the Study Guide in electronic form. The CD's resources are described here:

The Sybex Ebook for Windows 2000 Professional Many people like the convenience of being able to carry their whole Study Guide on a CD. They also like being able to search the text via computer to find specific information quickly and easily. For these reasons, the entire contents of this Study Guide are supplied on the CD, in PDF format. We've also included Adobe Acrobat Reader, which provides the interface for the PDF contents as well as the search capabilities.

WinSim 2000 We developed the WinSim 2000 product to allow you to experience the multimedia and interactive operation of working with Windows 2000 Professional. WinSim 2000 provides both audio/video files and hands-on experience with key features of Windows 2000 Professional. Built around the Study Guide's exercises, WinSim 2000 will help you attain the knowledge and hands-on skills that you must have in order to understand Windows 2000 Professional (and pass the exam). Here is a sample screen from WinSim 2000:

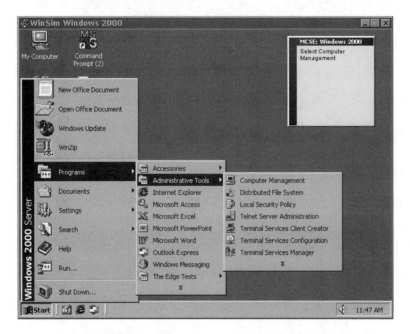

The Sybex MCSE EdgeTests The EdgeTests are a collection of multiple-choice questions that will help you prepare for your exam. The questions are grouped into seven sets:

- The Assessment Test.

- Two bonus exams designed to simulate the actual live exam.

- All the questions from the Study Guide organized by chapter for your review.

- All the questions from the Study Guide, plus the two bonus exams, organized by objective area for your review.

- A random test generator that selects up to 75 questions from all of the questions listed above.

- An adaptive test simulator that will give you the feel for how adaptive testing works.

Here is a sample screen from the Sybex MCSE EdgeTests:

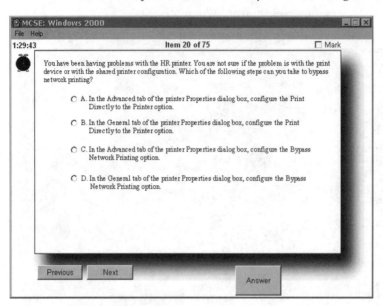

Sybex MCSE Flashcards for PCs and Palm Devices The "flashcard" style of question offers an effective way to quickly and efficiently test your understanding of the fundamental concepts covered in the exam. The Sybex MCSE Flashcards set consists of more than 150 questions presented in a special engine developed specifically for this Study Guide series. Here's what the Sybex MCSE Flashcards interface looks like:

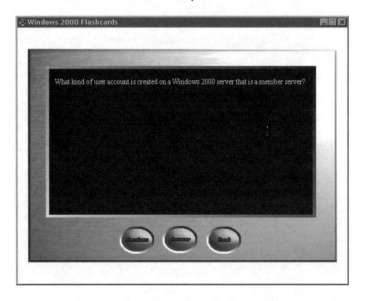

Because of the high demand for a product that will run on palm devices, we have also developed, in conjunction with Land-J Technologies, a version of the flashcard questions that you can take with you on your Palm OS PDA (including the PalmPilot and Handspring's Visor).

How Do You Use This Book?

This book provides a solid foundation for the serious effort of preparing for the exam. To best benefit from this book, you may wish to use the following study method:

1. Take the Assessment Test to identify your weak areas.

2. Study each chapter carefully. Do your best to fully understand the information.

3. Complete all the hands-on exercises in the chapter, referring back to the text as necessary so that you understand each step you take. If you don't have access to a lab environment in which you can complete the exercises, install and work with the exercises available in the Win-Sim 2000 software included with this Study Guide.

To do the exercises in this book, your hardware should meet the minimum hardware requirements for Windows 2000 Professional. See Chapter 1 for the minimum and recommended system requirements.

4. Read over the Real World Scenarios to improve your understanding of how to use what you learn in the book.

5. Study the Exam Essentials and Key Terms to make sure you are familiar with the areas you need to focus on.

6. Answer the review questions at the end of each chapter. If you prefer to answer the questions in a timed and graded format, install the EdgeTests from the book's CD and answer the chapter questions there instead of in the book.

7. Take note of the questions you did not understand, and study the corresponding sections of the book again.

8. Go back over the Exam Essentials and Key Terms.

9. Go through the Study Guide's other training resources, which are included on the book's CD. These include WinSim 2000, electronic flashcards, the electronic version of the chapter review questions (try taking them by objective), and the two bonus exams.

To learn all the material covered in this book, you will need to study regularly and with discipline. Try to set aside the same time every day to study, and select a comfortable and quiet place in which to do it. If you work hard, you will be surprised at how quickly you learn this material. Good luck!

Contacts and Resources

To find out more about Microsoft Education and Certification materials and programs, to register with Prometric or VUE, or to obtain other useful certification information and additional study resources, check the following resources:

Microsoft Training and Certification Home Page
www.microsoft.com/trainingandservices

This Web site provides information about the MCP program and exams. You can also order the latest Microsoft Roadmap to Education and Certification.

Microsoft TechNet Technical Information Network
www.microsoft.com/technet
800-344-2121

Use this Web site or phone number to contact support professionals and system administrators. Outside the United States and Canada, contact your local Microsoft subsidiary for information.

Palm Pilot Training Product Development: Land-J
www.land-j.com
407-359-2217

Land-J Technologies is a consulting and programming business currently specializing in application development for the 3Com PalmPilot Personal Digital Assistant. Land-J developed the Palm version of the Flashcards, which is included on the CD that accompanies this Study Guide.

Prometric

www.prometric.com

800-755-3936

Contact Prometric to register to take an MCP exam at any of more than 800 Prometric Testing Centers around the world.

Virtual University Enterprises (VUE)

www.vue.com

888-837-8616

Contact the VUE registration center to register to take an MCP exam at one of the VUE Testing Centers.

MCP Magazine Online

www.mcpmag.com

Microsoft Certified Professional Magazine is a well-respected publication that focuses on Windows certification. This site hosts chats and discussion forums, and tracks news related to the MCSE program. Some of the services cost a fee, but they are well worth it.

Windows 2000 Magazine

www.windows2000mag.com

You can subscribe to this magazine or read free articles at the Web site. The study resource provides general information on Windows 2000.

Cramsession on Brainbuzz.com

cramsession.brainbuzz.com

Cramsession is an online community focusing on all IT certification programs. In addition to discussion boards and job locators, you can download one of a number of free cramsessions, which are nice supplements to any study approach you take.

Assessment Test

1. What extension is applied by default to custom consoles that are created for the MMC?

   A. .mmc

   B. .msc

   C. .con

   D. .mcn

2. Which users are able to manage mandatory profiles on Windows 2000 Professional computers?

   A. The user who uses the profile

   B. Server Operators

   C. Power Users

   D. Administrators

3. Which MMC snap-in would you load to access System Monitor?

   A. System Monitor

   B. Performance Monitor

   C. ActiveX Control

   D. Performance Logs and Alerts

4. If you wanted only users with valid usernames and passwords to have access to a specific resource, to which of the following groups would you assign permissions?

   A. Domain Users

   B. Users

   C. Everyone

   D. Authenticated Users

5. Which of the following options cannot be configured as a part of an answer file?

   A. Display settings

   B. Network settings

   C. Time zone

   D. Screen saver

6. Which of the following print permissions are applied to the Power Users group by default on shared Windows 2000 Professional printers? Choose all that apply.

   A. No permissions are granted automatically

   B. Print

   C. Manage Printers

   D. Manage Documents

7. Which accessibility utility is used to read aloud screen text, such as the text in dialog boxes, menus, and buttons?

   A. Read-Aloud

   B. Orator

   C. Dialog Manager

   D. Narrator

8. Which option within the Windows 2000 Professional upgrade process gives a summary of likely problems with the upgrade?

   A. The Troubleshooting Guide

   B. The Compatibility Issues Report

   C. The Upgrade Report

   D. The Professional Upgrade Status Report

9. Which utility is used to track performance in Windows 2000?

    A. Performance Monitor

    B. System Monitor

    C. Event Viewer

    D. Process Manager

10. What utility is used to set processor affinity if you have multiple processors installed on your Windows 2000 Professional computer?

    A. Control Panel, Processors

    B. System Monitor

    C. System Manager

    D. Task Manager

11. What icon do you use in Control Panel in Windows 2000 Professional to set locale settings?

    A. Regional Options

    B. Locale Settings

    C. Geographical Settings

    D. Multinational Support

12. Susan is a member of the Sales and Managers groups. The Managers group has been allowed the Full Control permission to the D:\DATA folder. The Sales group has been allowed the Read & Execute permission to D:\DATA but has been denied the Full Control permission. What are Susan's effective rights?

    A. Full Control

    B. Read & Execute

    C. Read

    D. No permissions

13. Which utility can you use to install a non–Plug and Play network adapter in Windows 2000 Professional?

A. Control Panel, Network icon

B. Control Panel, Network and Dial-up Connections icon

C. Control Panel, Network Adapters icon

D. Control Panel, Add/Remove Hardware icon

14. You want Linda to be able to create users and groups on your Windows 2000 Professional computer. Linda says she is not able to create new users after she logs on. When you change Linda's group memberships, which groups can you make her a member of in order to allow her the necessary permissions for creating new users? Choose two answers.

A. Admins

B. Administrators

C. Power Users

D. Server Operators

15. Which option allows you to configure Windows 2000 Professional computers to use a hardware profile?

A. Hardware Profile Editor

B. Control Panel, System

C. Computer Management utility

D. MMC Computer Manager utility

16. Which separator page file would you use if you want to set up a separator page on a Windows 2000 Professional computer and you're using a PostScript print device that did not support dual-mode printing?

A. `pcl.sep`

B. `pscript.sep`

C. `sysprint.sep`

D. `sysprintj.sep`

17. Which option would you use if you wanted to access network files from your laptop while traveling and then have the file resynchronize with the network when you reattached the laptop to the network?

    A. Synchronized folders

    B. Managed folders

    C. Roaming folders

    D. Offline files and folders

18. Which command can you use to verify the IP configuration being used by your computer?

    A. IPCONFIG

    B. TESTIP

    C. PING

    D. GROPE

19. What information must be configured on a VPN client so that it can access a VPN server? Choose two answers.

    A. IP address

    B. MAC address

    C. Domain name

    D. Connection address

20. Which of the following statements is true regarding the creation of a group?

    A. Only members of the Administrators group can create users on a Windows 2000 Professional computer.

    B. Group names can be up to 64 characters.

    C. Group names can contain spaces.

    D. Group names can be the same as usernames, but not the same as other group names on the computer.

21. Which of the following statements is/are true concerning spanned volumes? Choose all that apply.

A. Spanned volumes can contain space from 2 to 32 physical drives.

B. Spanned volumes can contain space from 2 to 24 physical drives.

C. Spanned volumes can be formatted as FAT16, FAT32, or NTFS partitions.

D. Spanned volumes can only be formatted as NTFS partitions.

22. Which of the following user rights is required to install computers through RIS? Choose two answers.

A. Join a Computer to the Domain

B. Remotely Install Windows 2000

C. Log On as a Batch Job

D. Authorize the RIS Server

23. What process should you use to configure your computer to dual-boot Windows 2000 Professional and Window 98, and to use the features of NTFS?

A. Install Windows 98 first and Windows 2000 Professional last. Create two partitions. Install Windows 98 on the first partition and format the partition as FAT32. Put Windows 2000 on the second partition and format the partition as NTFS.

B. Install Windows 2000 Professional first and Windows 98 last. Create two partitions. Install Windows 98 on the first partition and format the partition as FAT32. Put Windows 2000 on the second partition and format the partition as NTFS.

C. Install Windows 2000 Professional first and Windows 98 last. Create two partitions. Install Windows 2000 on the first partition and format the partition as NTFS. Put Windows 98 on the second partition and format the partition as FAT.

D. You cannot dual-boot between Windows 98 and Windows 2000 Professional.

24. How do you start the Windows 2000 Recovery Console if you cannot start your Windows 2000 Professional operating system?

   A. Use the Windows 2000 Professional Setup Disks.

   B. Start it through WINNT32 /RC.

   C. Press F8 during the boot sequence.

   D. Boot with the Windows 2000 boot disk; then type **WINNT /CMDCONS**.

25. Which of the following will prevent a Windows 2000 Professional upgrade from successfully installing? Choose all that apply.

   A. A drive that was compressed with DoubleSpace

   B. A drive that was compressed with DriveSpace

   C. A computer that has only 64MB of RAM

   D. A computer that has only a Pentium 133MHz processor

26. You have a remote user who would like to be able to send print jobs to a network printer from an Internet connection using a URL. Which of the following protocols allows Windows 2000 to support this option?

   A. IPP

   B. RPP

   C. MPP

   D. IIP

27. How do you access advanced startup options in Windows 2000 during the boot process?

   A. Press the spacebar.

   B. Press F6.

   C. Press F8.

   D. Press F10.

28. You want to install Windows 2000 Professional on a computer that has no operating system installed, but the computer will not boot to the CD-ROM drive. Which of the following actions is the best solution to your problem?

   A. Create Windows 2000 Professional Setup Boot Disks using the Windows 2000 Professional CD on another computer. Use these disks on your computer, so you can start the installation process.

   B. Create the Emergency Startup disks using the Windows 2000 Professional CD on another computer. Use these disks on your computer, so you can start the installation process.

   C. Upgrade your computer.

   D. Install Windows 98 on the computer; then upgrade it to Windows 2000 Professional.

29. Which utility is used to upgrade a FAT16 or FAT32 partition to NTFS?

   A. UPFS

   B. UPGRADE

   C. Disk Manager

   D. CONVERT

30. Which of the following audit policy options allows you to track events related to file and print object access?

   A. File and Object Access

   B. Audit Object Access

   C. Audit File and Print Access

   D. Audit All File and Print Events

Answers to Assessment Test

1. **B.** When you create a custom console for the MMC, the `.msc` file-name extension is automatically applied. See Chapter 4 for more information.

2. **D.** Only members of the Administrators group can manage mandatory profiles. See Chapter 8 for more information.

3. **C.** Select ActiveX Control in the Add/Remove Snap-in dialog box (Console ➢ Add/Remove Snap-in). Then, from the Insert ActiveX Control dialog box, select System Monitor Control to access the System Monitor utility. See Chapter 14 for more information.

4. **D.** You would assign permissions to the Authenticated Users group if you wanted only users with valid usernames and passwords to access a specific resource. See Chapter 7 for more information.

5. **D.** You can't configure user preference items, such as screen saver options, in an answer file. See Chapter 2 for more information.

6. **B, C, D.** By default, the Power Users group is allowed Print, Manage Printers, and Manage Documents permissions. See Chapter 12 for more information.

7. **D.** The Narrator utility uses a sound output device to read on-screen text. See Chapter 5 for more information.

8. **C.** Sometimes the answer is so obvious that it doesn't appear to be correct. This is the case here. The report that shows you any potential problems with the upgrade process is simply named Upgrade Report. See Chapter 3 for more information.

9. **B.** In Windows NT 4, Performance Monitor is used to track system performance. In Windows 2000, System Monitor is used for this task. See Chapter 14 for more information.

10. D. You can set processor affinity for Windows 2000 processes through the Task Manager utility. Processor affinity is the ability to assign a processor to a dedicated process (program). This feature is only available when multiple processors are installed. See Chapter 4 for more information.

11. A. Of the four options given, only Regional Options appears in Control Panel. Through Regional Options, you can configure multilingual support and locale information. See Chapter 5 for more information.

12. B. Susan is not allowed the Full Control permission because it was explicitly denied through her membership in the Sales group. She is allowed the Read & Execute permission. See Chapter 10 for more information.

13. D. In Windows 2000, you add hardware through the Add/Remove Hardware option in Control Panel. You can manage existing network adapters through Network and Dial-up Connections. See Chapter 11 for more information.

14. B, C. On Windows 2000 Professional computers, members of the Administrators and Power Users groups are able to create new users. See Chapter 6 for more information.

15. B. You configure hardware profiles through the System icon in Control Panel. You can also access this dialog box by right-clicking My Computer and selecting Properties. There is no "Hardware Profile Editor" or "MMC Computer Manager" utility. The Computer Management utility is used to manage system tools, storage, services, and applications. See Chapter 8 for more information.

16. C. You would use the `sysprint.sep` separator page if you have a PostScript print device that does not support dual-mode printing. If you want to use separator pages on a print device that does support dual-mode printing, you would use the `pcl.sep` separator page. See Chapter 12 for more information.

17. **D.** You would use offline files and folders to take data offline and then resynchronize data when you reattached the laptop to the network. See Chapter 10 for more information.

18. **A.** The IPCONFIG command displays a computer's IP configuration. See Chapter 11 for more information.

19. **A, C.** When you configure a VPN connection, you see the Destination Address dialog box. There you must specify the IP address or host domain name of the computer to which you'll connect. See Chapter 13 for more information.

20. **C.** Administrators and members of the Power Users local groups can create new groups. Group names can contain up to 256 characters and can contain spaces. Group names must be unique to the computer, different from all the other usernames and group names that have been specified on that computer. See Chapter 7 for more information.

21. **A, C.** You can create a spanned volume from free space that exists on a minimum of 2 to a maximum of 32 physical drives. When the spanned volume is initially created, it can be formatted with FAT16, FAT32, or NTFS. If you extend a volume that already contains data, however, the partition must be NTFS. See Chapter 9 for more information.

22. **A, C .** In order to install an image through RIS, the user who is installing the RIS client must have the Join a Computer to the Domain user right and the Logon as a Batch Job right. See Chapter 2 for more information.

23. **A.** Install Windows 98 first and Windows 2000 Professional last. Otherwise, your boot loader menu will not work properly. Create two partitions, and then install Windows 98 on the first partition and format it as FAT32. Put Windows 2000 on the second partition and format the partition as NTFS. When you boot to Windows 2000, you will be able to see both partitions. When you boot to Windows 98, you will only see the first partition. See Chapter 1 for more information.

24. A. Start the Recovery Console through the Windows 2000 Professional Setup Disks, or by installing the Recovery Console using the WINNT32/ CMDCONS command prior to failure. See Chapter 15 for more information.

25. A, B. You can upgrade a computer that only has 64MB of RAM or a Pentium 133MHz processor, but you can't upgrade drives that have DoubleSpace or DriveSpace installed. See Chapter 3 for more information.

26. A. The Internet Printing Protocol (IPP) allows users to print to a URL.

27. C. During the boot process, you are prompted to press F8 to access the Advanced Options menu. See Chapter 15 for more information.

28. A. The Windows 2000 Professional Setup Boot Disks can be used to start a Windows 2000 Professional installation on a computer that does not support booting to a CD-ROM drive. You can also upgrade the computer, but that is not the best solution. See Chapter 1 for more information.

29. D. The CONVERT utility is used to convert a FAT16 or FAT32 partition to NTFS. See Chapter 9 for more information.

30. B. Though all four options seem plausible, only the Audit Object Access option actually exists. Audit Object Access is used to enable auditing of access to files, folders, and printers. Once you enable auditing of object access, you must enable file auditing through NTFS security, or enable print auditing through printer security. See Chapter 6 for more information.

Chapter

1

Getting Started with Windows 2000 Professional

MICROSOFT EXAM OBJECTIVES COVERED IN THIS CHAPTER:

✓ Perform an attended installation of Windows 2000 Professional.

✓ Troubleshoot failed installations.

Windows 2000 Professional is not just an upgraded version of Windows 98 or Windows NT 4. Instead, it integrates the best features of both of those operating systems and adds other features, such as more hardware support and reduced cost of ownership. You should evaluate the features that Windows 2000 Professional offers to determine if it meets your requirements.

After you decide that Windows 2000 Professional is the operating system for you, your next step is to install it. This process is fairly easy if you have prepared for the installation, know what the requirements are, and have met the prerequisites for a successful installation.

Preparing for an installation involves making sure that your hardware meets the minimum requirements and that Windows 2000 Professional supports your hardware. When you install Windows 2000 Professional, you should also decide if you are upgrading or installing a clean copy on your computer. An upgrade preserves existing settings; a clean install puts a fresh copy of the operating system on your computer. Installation preparation also involves making choices about your system's configuration, such as selecting a file system and a disk-partitioning scheme.

Once you've completed all the planning, you are ready to install Windows 2000 Professional. This is a straightforward process that involves running a Setup program, running a Setup Wizard, and installing Windows 2000 Networking.

If you have any problems with the installation, you will need to trouble-shoot them. Some problems that you might encounter are media defects or hardware that doesn't meet the minimum requirements.

When you install Windows 2000, you should also consider if the computer will be used for dual-boot or multi-boot purposes. Dual-booting or multi-booting allows you to have your computer boot with operating systems other than Windows 2000 Professional.

The first section of this chapter covers the design goals of Windows 2000 Professional. Then you will learn how to prepare for Windows 2000 Professional installation, perform the installation, troubleshoot any installation problems, and set up for dual-booting or multi-booting.

The Design Goals of Windows 2000 Professional

In order to develop Windows 2000 Professional, Microsoft devised the following design goals:

- Integrate the best features of Windows 98
- Integrate the best features of Windows NT Workstation 4
- Provide a wide range of support for hardware
- Make the operating system easier to use
- Reduce the cost of ownership

The Windows 2000 Professional features associated with these design goals are covered in the following sections.

Features from Windows 98

Windows 98 offers a variety of features that were not integrated into Windows NT Workstation 4. The following Windows 98 features are included in Windows 2000 Professional:

- Support for *Plug and Play*, which allows the operating system to recognize and configure hardware without any user intervention.
- Added support for the *Advanced Configuration and Power Interface (ACPI),* considered to be the next generation of power management for Plug and Play technology. Features of ACPI include:
  - The automatic and dynamic detection of hardware that is installed

- The ability to determine what hardware resources (such as IRQs and I/O ports) are required by the new device, and whether other devices need to be automatically reconfigured to accommodate the new device

- The ability to load the appropriate driver automatically (if the driver is available)

- Added support for the *Universal Serial Bus (USB),* which is an external serial bus standard that allows a single USB port to support up to 127 devices. Common USB devices include mice, modems, and keyboards. USB supports hot-plug (which allows you to add devices to the computer without powering down the computer) and Plug and Play technology.

- New support for the *Institute of Electrical and Electronic Engineers (IEEE) 1394 standard,* which supports data transfer at speeds up to 400Mbps. Trademark names for this standard are FireWire, I-link, and Lynx.

- The use of the Active Desktop, which integrates the user's browser and shell into a single integrated Desktop.

Features from Windows NT Workstation 4

Windows NT Workstation 4 is the foundation upon which Windows 2000 Professional is built. The following features that made Windows NT Workstation 4 a powerful operating system are included in Windows 2000 Professional:

- An operating system with a high degree of reliability. Windows 2000 Professional is more robust and less likely to crash than Windows *9x* operating systems.

- Local security that is built into the operating system. Windows 2000 Professional requires that users be authenticated with a valid logon name and password before they can access the computer. Support is also included for the NTFS file system, which allows you to set local security for the file system.

- A high-performance operating system, with true 32-bit processing.

Hardware Support

The ability to support a wide range of hardware was a major design goal for Windows 2000 Professional. The operating system provides drivers for many types of peripherals, including monitors, sound cards, digital cameras, printers, scanners, DVD drives, CDRW (CD Read/Write) drives, and network cards.

Ease of Use

When you use Windows 2000 Professional for the first time, you will notice that the user interface is not exactly the same as the Windows 9x or NT 4 interface. The operating system is designed so that users who need to perform a specific task can intuitively figure out how to accomplish that task. Following are some of the features that make Windows 2000 Professional easier to use:

- The installation process is simpler than the process for Windows NT installations and requires less user input.

- The user shell (interface) is more logically organized and offers more customization options.

- Users can easily add hardware. Windows 2000 Professional supports self-repairing applications, Plug and Play, and ACPI. These features reduce the possibility of system downtime when new hardware is installed.

Lower Cost of Ownership

Windows 2000 Professional reduces the cost of ownership by minimizing the maintenance and rollout costs associated with installing, upgrading, and maintaining the operating system. Windows 2000 Professional comes with many deployment options, such as support for remote installations and automated unattended installations. Through Remote Installation Services (RIS), you can easily install the Windows 2000 operating system and applications.

RIS and automated installations are covered in Chapter 2, "Automating the Windows 2000 Installation."

New Features of Windows 2000

There are a host of new features created for Windows 2000 Professional to set it aside from all its competitors. The following are some of the new features:

- Disk quota support

- Inherited and uninherited permissions

- Internet printing support

- The ability to configure printer drivers for additional operating systems that will connect to your print server

- The Encrypting File System (EFS), which uses public and private encryption, allowing a user to transparently encrypt files

- A highly integrated Wizard technology to make configuration tasks easier

- Enhanced virtual private networking support (previous versions have VPN support; Windows 2000 Professional adds IPSec and L2TP support)

Why Do You Really Want to Use Windows 2000 Professional?

Now that Windows 2000 Professional has been out for over one year, has the new operating system been widely implemented? Are people happy with the updates? The answer to both questions is yes. By selecting Windows 2000 over Windows 95, 98, or NT, companies and users have seen better application performance, improved support for mobile users (which is extremely important in today's business environment), and better cost efficiency (in terms of less IT support required).

Preparing to Install Windows 2000 Professional

As mentioned in the previous section, Windows 2000 Professional is easy to install. But this doesn't mean you don't need to prepare for the installation process. Before you begin the installation, you should know what is required for a successful installation and have all of the pieces of information you'll need to supply during the installation process. In preparing for the installation, you should make sure you have the following information:

- The hardware requirements for Windows 2000 Professional

- How to use the Hardware Compatibility List (HCL) to determine if your hardware is supported by Windows 2000 Professional

- The difference between a clean install and an upgrade

- The installation options suitable for your system, including which disk-partitioning scheme and file system you should select for Windows 2000 Professional to use

The following sections describe the hardware requirements and installation considerations.

Hardware Requirements

In order to install Windows 2000 Professional successfully, your system must meet certain hardware requirements. Table 1.1 lists the minimum requirements as well as the more realistic recommended requirements.

The minimum requirements specify the minimum hardware required before you should even consider installing Windows 2000 Professional. These requirements assume that you are installing only the operating system and not running any special services or applications. For example, you may be able to get by with the minimum requirements if you are just installing the operating system to learn the basics of the software.

The recommended requirements are what Microsoft suggests to achieve what would be considered "acceptable performance" for the most common configurations. Since computer technology and the standard for acceptable performance are constantly changing, the recommendations are somewhat subjective. However, the recommended hardware requirements are based on the standards at the time that Windows 2000 Professional was released.

The hardware requirements listed in Table 1.1 were those specified at the time this book was published. Check Microsoft's Web site at http://www.microsoft.com/windows2000/guide/professional/sysreq/default.asp for the most current information.

TABLE 1.1 Hardware Requirements

Component	Minimum Requirement	Recommended Requirement
Processor	Intel Pentium 133MHz or higher	Intel Pentium 133MHz or higher
Memory	64MB	132MB
Disk space	2GB hard disk with 650MB of free disk space	1GB or more of free disk space
Network	None	Network card and any other hardware required by your network topology (if you want to connect to a network)
Display	Video adapter and monitor with VGA resolution	Video adapter and monitor with VGA resolution or higher

 Real World Scenario

Deciding on Minimum Hardware Requirements

The company you work for has decided that everyone will have their own laptop running Windows 2000 Professional. You need to decide on the new computers' specifications for processor, memory, and disk space.

The first step is to determine what applications will be used. Typically most users will work with an e-mail program, a word processor, a spreadsheet, presentation software, and maybe a drawing or graphics program. Under these demands, a low-end Pentium processor and 64MB of RAM will make for a very slow-running machine with a real likelihood of memory errors. So for this usage, you can assume that the minimum baseline configuration would be a Pentium III processor with 132MB of RAM.

Based on your choice of baseline configuration, you should then fit a test computer with the applications that will be used on it, and test the configuration in a lab environment simulating normal use. This will give you an idea if the RAM and processor calculations you have made for your environment are going to provide suitable response.

Today's disk drives have become capable of much larger capacity, while dropping drastically in price. So for disk space, the rule of thumb is to buy whatever is the current standard. Hard drives are currently shipping in the GB range, which is sufficient for most users. If users plan to store substantial graphics or video files, you may need to consider buying larger-than-standard drives.

Also consider what the business requirements will be over the next 12 to 18 months. If you will be implementing applications that are memory or processor intensive, you may want to spec out the computers initially with hardware sufficient to support upcoming needs, to avoid costly upgrades in the near future.

Depending on the installation method you choose, other devices may be required, as follows:

- If you are installing Windows 2000 Professional from the CD, you should have at least a 12x CD-ROM drive.

- To start the installation locally and to create an Emergency Repair Disk, you need a high-density floppy drive.

- If you choose to install Windows 2000 Professional from the network, you need a network connection and a server with the distribution files.

Windows 2000 Professional supports computers with one or two processors.

Measurement Units Used in Hardware Specifications

Computer processors are typically rated by speed. The speed of the processor, or *central processing unit (CPU),* is rated by the number of clock cycles that can be performed in one second. This measurement is typically expressed in *megahertz (MHz).* One MHz is one million cycles per second.

Hard disks are commonly rated by capacity. The following measurements are used for disk space and memory capacity:

1*MB (megabyte)* = 1024KB (kilobytes)

1*GB (gigabyte)* = 1024MB

1*TB (terabyte)* = 1024GB

1*PB (petabyte)* = 1024TB

1*EB (exabyte)* = 1024PB

The Hardware Compatibility List (HCL)

Along with meeting the minimum requirements, your hardware should appear on the *Hardware Compatibility List (HCL).* The HCL is an extensive list of computers and peripheral hardware that have been tested with the Windows 2000 Professional operating system.

The Windows 2000 Professional operating system requires control of the hardware for stability, efficiency, and security. The hardware and supported drivers on the HCL have been put through rigorous tests to ensure their compatibility with Windows 2000 Professional. Microsoft guarantees that the items on the list meet the requirements for Windows 2000 and do not have any incompatibilities that could affect the stability of the operating system.

If you call Microsoft for support, the first thing a Microsoft support engineer will ask about is your configuration. If you have any hardware that is not on the HCL, you won't be able to get support from Microsoft.

To determine if your computer and peripherals are on the HCL, check the most up-to-date list at www.microsoft.com/hwtest/hcl.

As I learned from my own mistake, you shouldn't just assume that a hardware item is on the HCL. I recently purchased a computer manufactured by a well-known, brand-name company. Because it was a higher-end Pentium with all the bells and whistles and came with Windows 98 preinstalled, I assumed that it would support Windows NT and Windows 2000. The salesperson said it would. When I got home and opened the box, I couldn't find any documentation about loading Windows NT or Windows 2000. A check of the vendor's Web site and a call to their technical support hotline verified that the computer did not support either operating system. I had to return the computer and argue with the store manager to get my money back.

Clean Install or Upgrade?

Once you've determined that your hardware not only meets the minimum requirements but also is on the HCL, you need to decide whether you want to do a *clean install* or an *upgrade*.

The only operating systems that can be upgraded to Windows 2000 Professional are Windows 95, Windows 98, and Windows NT 3.51 or 4. Any other operating system cannot be upgraded, but it may be able to coexist with Windows 2000 in a dual-boot environment. Dual-booting is covered in the "Supporting Multiple-Boot Options" section later in this chapter.

If you don't have an operating system that can be upgraded, or if you want to keep your previous operating system intact, you need to perform a clean install. A clean install puts Windows 2000 Professional operating system into a new folder and uses its default settings the first time the operating system is loaded. The process for a clean installation is described in the "Running the Windows 2000 Professional Installation Process" section later in this chapter.

Installation Options

There are many choices that you will need to make during the Windows 2000 Professional installation process. Following are some of the options that you will configure:

- How your hard disk space will be partitioned

- The file system your partitions will use

- Whether the computer will be a part of a workgroup or a domain

- The language and locale for the computer's settings

Before you start the installation, you should know which choices you will select. The following sections describe the options and considerations for picking the best ones for your installation.

Partitioning of Disk Space

Disk partitioning is the act of taking the physical hard drive and creating logical partitions. A *logical drive* is how space is allocated to the drive's primary and logical partitions. For example, if you have a 5GB hard drive, you might partition it into two logical drives: a C: drive, which might be 2GB, and a D: drive, which might be 3GB.

The following are some of the major considerations for disk partitioning:

- The amount of space required

- The location of the system and boot partition

- Any special disk configurations you will use

- The utility you will use to set up the partitions

These considerations are covered in detail in the following sections.

Partition Size

One important consideration in your disk-partitioning scheme is determining the partition size. You need to consider the amount of space taken up by your operating system, the applications that will be installed, and the amount of stored data. It is also important to consider the amount of space required in the future.

Just for Windows 2000, Microsoft recommends that you allocate at least 1GB of disk space. This allows room for the operating system files and for future growth in terms of upgrades and installation files that are placed with the operating system files.

The System and Boot Partitions

When you install Windows 2000, files will be stored in two locations: the system partition and the boot partition.

The *system partition* contains the files needed to boot the Windows 2000 Professional operating system. The files stored on the system partition do not take any significant disk space. By default, the system partition uses the computer's active partition, which is usually the C: drive.

The *boot partition* contains the files that are the Windows operating system. By default, the Windows operating system files are located in a folder named WINNT. You can, however, specify the location of this folder during the installation process. Microsoft recommends that the boot partition be at least 1GB.

Special Disk Configurations

Windows 2000 Professional supports several disk configurations. Options include simple, spanned, and striped volumes. These configuration options are covered in detail in Chapter 9, "Managing Disks."

Windows 2000 Server also includes options for mirrored and RAID 5 volumes.

Disk Partition Configuration Utilities

If you are partitioning your disk prior to installation, you can use several utilities, such as the DOS or Windows FDISK program or a third-party utility such as PowerQuest's Partition Magic. You might want to create only the first partition where Windows 2000 Professional will be installed. You can then use the Disk Management utility in Windows 2000 to create any other partitions you need. The Windows 2000 Disk Management utility is covered in Chapter 9.

You can get more information about FDISK and other disk utilities from your DOS or Windows documentation. Also, basic DOS functions are covered in *MCSE 2000 JumpStart: Computer and Network Basics* by Lisa Donald (Sybex, 2000).

File System Selection

Another factor that determines your disk-partitioning scheme is the type of file system you use. Windows 2000 supports three file systems:

- *File Allocation Table (FAT16)*

- *FAT32*

- *New Technology File System (NTFS)*

The following sections briefly describe these three file systems. See Chapter 9 for more details about the features of FAT, FAT32, and NTFS.

FAT16

FAT16 (originally just FAT) is the 16-bit file system widely used by DOS and Windows 3.*x*. FAT16 tracks where files are stored on a disk using a file allocation table and a directory entry table. The disadvantages of FAT16 are that it only supports partitions up to 2GB and it does not offer the security features of NTFS. The advantage of FAT is that it is backward compatible, which is important if the computer will be dual-booted with another operating system, such as DOS, Unix, Linux, OS/2, or Windows 3.1. Almost all PC operating systems read FAT16 partitions.

FAT32

FAT32 is the 32-bit version of FAT, which was first introduced in 1996 with Windows 95, with OEM (original equipment manufacturer) Service Release 2 (OSR2). With FAT32, disk partitions can be as large as 2TB (terabytes). It has more fault-tolerance features than FAT16, and also improves disk-space usage by reducing the size of clusters. However, it lacks several of the features offered by NTFS for a Windows 2000 system, such as local security, file encryption, disk quotas, and compression.

If you choose to use FAT, Windows 2000 will automatically format the partition with FAT16 if the partition is less than 2GB. If the partition is over 2GB, it will be automatically partitioned as FAT32.

Windows NT 4 and earlier releases of NT do not support FAT32 partitions.

NTFS

NTFS is a file system designed to provide additional features for Windows NT and Windows 2000 computers. Some of the features NTFS offers include the following:

- The ability to set local security on files and folders.

- The option to compress data. This feature reduces disk-storage requirements.

- The flexibility to assign disk quotas. Disk quotas are used to limit the amount of disk space a user can use.

- The option to encrypt files. Encryption offers an additional level of security.

Unless you are planning on dual-booting your computer to an operating system other than Windows NT, Microsoft recommends using NTFS.

Membership in a Domain or Workgroup

One Windows 2000 Professional installation choice is whether your computer will be installed as a part of a *workgroup* or as part of a *domain*.

You should install as part of a workgroup if you are a part of a small, decentralized network or if you are running Windows 2000 on a computer that is not part of a network. To join a workgroup, you simply choose that workgroup.

Domains are part of larger, centrally administered networks. You should install as part of a domain if any Windows 2000 servers on your network are configured as domain controllers with the Microsoft Active Directory installed. There are two ways to join a domain. You can preauthorize a computer before installation, through Active Directory Users and Computers utility. The second way is done during the Windows 2000 Professional installation, when you specify an Administrator name and password (or other user who has rights to add computers to the domain). In order to successfully join a domain, a domain controller for the domain and a DNS server must be available to authenticate the request to join the domain.

Language and Locale

Language and locale settings are used to determine the language the computer will use. Windows 2000 supports many languages for the operating system interface and utilities.

Locale settings are used to configure the locality for items such as numbers, currencies, times, and dates. An example of a locality is that English for United States specifies a short date as *mm/dd/yyyy* (month/day/year), and English for South Africa specifies a short date as *yyyy/mm/dd* (year/month/day).

Choosing Your Installation Method

You can install Windows 2000 Professional either by using the distribution files on the Windows 2000 Professional CD, or by using files that have been copied to a network share point. The following sections discuss both installation methods.

Installing Windows 2000 from the CD

When you install Windows 2000 from the Windows 2000 Professional CD, you have several options for starting the installation:

- You can boot to another operating system, access your CD-ROM drive, and run WINNT.EXE or WINNT32.EXE (depending on the operating system you are using, as explained in the next section).

- If your computer is able to boot to the CD, you can insert the Windows 2000 Professional CD into its CD-ROM drive and restart your computer.

- If your computer has no operating system installed and does not support booting from the CD-ROM drive, you can use the Windows 2000 Professional Setup Boot Disks.

Installing from Another Operating System

If your computer already has an operating system installed and you want to upgrade your operating system or dual-boot your computer, you boot your computer to the operating system that is currently installed, then start the Windows 2000 Professional installation process. Depending on the operating system that is running, you start the installation by using one of the following commands from the I386 folder:

- From Windows 9x or Windows NT, use WINNT32.EXE.

- From any other operating system, use WINNT.EXE.

Installing by Booting from the Windows 2000 CD

If your computer can boot from the CD-ROM drive, then all you need to do is insert the Windows 2000 Professional CD and restart your computer. When the computer boots, the Windows 2000 Professional installation process will start automatically.

Installing from Setup Boot Disks

If your computer cannot boot from the CD-ROM drive, you can create floppy disks that can boot to the Windows 2000 Professional operating system. These disks are called the *Windows 2000 Professional Setup Boot Disks*. From these floppy disks, you can install or reinstall the Windows 2000 operating system. The Windows 2000 Professional Setup Boot Disks are not specific to a computer; they can be used by any computer running Windows 2000 Professional.

To create the Windows 2000 Professional Setup Boot Disks, you need four high-density floppy disks. They should be labeled Windows 2000 Professional Setup Boot Disk, Windows 2000 Professional Setup Disk #2, Windows 2000 Professional Setup Disk #3, and Windows 2000 Professional Setup Disk #4.

The command to create boot disks from a Windows 2000 or Windows NT computer is MAKEBT32.EXE. The command to make boot disks from Windows 9*x* or any other operating system is MAKEBOOT.EXE. These utilities are located on the Windows 2000 Professional CD in the BOOT-DISK folder.

The Windows 2000 Professional Setup Boot Disks are also used for the Recovery Console and the Emergency Repair Disk (disaster recovery methods), which are covered in Chapter 15, "Performing System Recovery Functions." You will create Windows 2000 Professional Setup Boot Disks in an exercise in Chapter 15.

Installing Windows 2000 over a Network

If you are installing Windows 2000 Professional from the network, you need a *distribution server* and a computer with a network connection. A distribution server is a server that has the Windows 2000 Professional distribution files copied to a shared folder. The following steps are used to install Windows 2000 Professional over the network:

1. Boot the target computer.

2. Attach to the distribution server and access the share that has the \WINNT folder shared.

3. Launch WINNT or WINNT32 (depending on the computer's current operating system).

4. Complete the Windows 2000 Professional installation.

You can also install Windows 2000 Professional through an unattended process, which is covered in greater detail in Chapter 2, "Automating the Windows 2000 Installation."

Running the Windows 2000 Professional Installation Process

This section describes how to run the Windows 2000 Professional installation process. As explained in the previous section, you can run the installation from the CD or over a network. The only difference in the installation procedure is your starting point: from your CD-ROM drive or from a network share. The steps in the following sections assume that the disk drive is clean and that you are starting the installation using the Windows 2000 Professional CD.

Microsoft
✓ *Exam*
Objective

Perform an attended installation of Windows 2000 Professional.

There are three main steps in the Windows 2000 Professional installation process:

- Run the Setup program. If you boot from DOS or Windows 9x, the Setup program will be DOS based. If you boot from Windows NT, Setup will be GUI based.

- Run the Setup Wizard.

- Install Windows 2000 Networking.

Each of these steps is covered in detail in the following sections.

The following sections give the details of the installation process to show how the process works. But you should not actually install Windows 2000 Professional until you reach Exercise 1.1. In that exercise, you'll set up your computer to complete the rest of the exercises in this book.

Running the Setup Program

The Setup program starts the Windows 2000 installation. In this stage of the installation, you start the installation program, choose the partition where Windows 2000 Professional will be installed, and then copy files.

The following steps are involved in running the Setup program:

1. On an Intel computer, access your CD-ROM drive and open the I386 folder. This folder contains all of the installation files for an Intel-based computer.

2. Start the Setup program.

   - If you are installing Windows 2000 from an operating system other than Windows 9*x* or Windows NT, launch WINNT.

   - If you are installing Windows 2000 from 32-bit mode Windows 9*x* or Windows NT, launch WINNT32.

3. The Windows 2000 Setup dialog box appears. Your first choice is to specify the location of the distribution files. By default, this is where you executed the WINNT program. Normally, you just accept the default path and press Enter.

4. The Setup files are copied to your disk. If the SMARTDRV program is not loaded on your computer, you will see a message recommending that you load SMARTDRV. This is a disk-cacheing program that speeds up the process of copying files. SMARTDRV ships with DOS and Windows.

NOTE With SMARTDRV, it usually takes a few minutes to copy the files. Without SMARTDRV, it can take more than an hour.

5. Once the files have been copied, you are prompted to remove any floppy disks and to restart the computer.

6. The opening Windows 2000 Setup dialog box appears. At this point, you can set up Windows by pressing Enter, repair a Windows 2000 installation by pressing R, or quit the setup process by pressing F3.

7. The Windows 2000 License Agreement dialog box appears. You can accept the License Agreement by pressing F8, or you can disagree by pressing Esc (or F3 if you are in DOS mode). If you press Esc, the installation program will terminate, and your name and address will be sent directly to Microsoft for further analysis (just kidding about that second part).

8. The next dialog box asks you which partition you want to use to set up Windows 2000. You can pick a partition that already exists, or you can choose free space and a partition will be created for you. Whichever partition you choose must have at least 1GB of free space. The default folder name will be WINNT. At this point, you can create or delete partitions and the file systems the partitions will use.

After you indicate the partition that will be used as the Windows 2000 boot partition, the Windows installation files will be copied to the installation folders. Then the computer automatically reboots.

Running the Windows 2000 Setup Wizard

Once your computer finishes with the Setup program, the computer will restart, and the Windows 2000 Setup Wizard will start automatically. The Setup Wizard begins by detecting and installing device drivers. This process will take several minutes, and your screen may flicker during this process.

Then the Setup Wizard will gather information about your locale, name, and product key, as follows (you click Next after completing each dialog box):

1. The Regional Settings dialog box appears. From this dialog box, you choose your locale and keyboard settings. Locale settings are used to configure international options for numbers, currencies, times, and dates. Keyboard settings allow you to configure your keyboard to support different local characters or keyboard layouts. For example, you can choose Danish or United States-Dvorak through this option.

2. In the Personalize Your Software dialog box, you fill in the Name and Organization boxes. This information is used to personalize your operating system software and the applications that you install. If you install Windows 2000 Professional in a workgroup, the Name entry here is used for the initial user.

3. The Product Key dialog box appears. In the boxes at the bottom of this dialog box, you type in the 25-character product key, which can be found on the back of your Windows 2000 CD case.

4. The Computer Name and Administrator Password dialog box appears. Here, you specify a name that will uniquely identify your computer on the network. Your computer name can be up to 15 characters. The Setup Wizard suggests a name, but you can change it to another name. Through this dialog box, you also type and confirm the Administrator password. An account called Administrator will automatically be created as a part of the installation process.

WARNING Be sure that the computer name is a unique name within your network. If you are part of a corporate network, you should also verify that the computer name follows the naming convention specified by your Information Services (IS) department.

5. If you have a Plug and Play modem installed, you will see the Modem Dialing Information dialog box. Here, you specify your country/region, your area code (or city code), whether you dial a number to get an outside line, and whether the telephone system uses tone dialing or pulse dialing.

6. The Date and Time Settings dialog box appears. In this dialog box, you specify date and time settings and the time zone in which your computer is located. You can also configure the computer to automatically adjust for daylight savings time.

7. The Network Settings dialog box appears. This dialog box is used to specify how you want to connect to other computers, networks, and the Internet. You have two choices:

   - Typical Settings installs network connections for Client for Microsoft Networks, as well as File and Print Sharing for Microsoft Networks. It also installs the TCP/IP protocol with an automatically assigned address.

   - Custom Settings allows you to customize your network settings. You can choose whether or not you want to use Client for Microsoft Networks, File and Print Sharing for Microsoft Networks, and the TCP/IP protocol. You should use the custom settings if you need to specify particular network settings, such as a specific IP address and subnet mask (rather than using an automatically assigned address).

8. In the next dialog box, Workgroup or Computer Domain, you specify whether your computer will be installed as a part of a local workgroup or as a part of a domain. (See the "Membership in Domain or Workgroup" section earlier in this chapter for details about these choices.)

9. The computer will perform some final tasks, including installing Start menu items, registering components, saving settings, and removing any temporary files. This will take several minutes. After the final tasks are complete, you will see the Completing the Windows 2000 Setup Wizard dialog box. Remove the CD from your computer and then click the Finish button to restart your computer.

Installing Windows 2000 Networking

Once your computer finishes with the Setup Wizard and the computer restarts, the Network Identification Wizard starts automatically. The Network Identification Wizard is responsible for the network component installation.

Depending on your computer's configuration, you may see a dialog box that deals with how users will log on to the computer. This dialog box offers two choices:

- The Users Must Enter a User Name and Password to Use This Computer option does just what it says. If you select this option, users must enter a username and password to log on to the computer.

- The Windows Always Assumes the Following User Has Logged On option sets up Windows 2000 so that the user does not need to enter a username or password to use the computer. If you are the only person using the computer in a secure, non-networked environment, you might choose this option. However, in a networked, business environment, you do not want to allow such a security risk.

Next, the Network Identification Wizard prompts you to finish the wizard. If you chose the Users Must Enter a User Name and a Password to Use This Computer option, you need to provide a valid Window 2000 username and password in the Windows logon dialog box. At this point, the only users defined on the system are Administrator and the *initial user* (which is the username you entered for identification).

The installation is complete. You are logged on and greeted with the Windows 2000 Professional Getting Started Wizard, which helps new users navigate the operating system.

Setting Up Your Computer for Hands-on Exercises

The exercises in this book assume that your computer is configured in a specific manner. Your computer should have at least a 3GB drive that is configured with the minimum space requirements and partitions. Other exercises in this book make assumptions that your computer is configured as follows:

- 2GB (about 2000MB) C: primary partition with the FAT file system

- 250MB D: extended partition with the FAT file system

- 250MB of free space

Of course, you can allocate more space to your partitions if it is available.

You are probably wondering why we are not using any NTFS partitions. The reason is that you will convert a FAT partition to NTFS and use the features of NTFS in Chapter 9. You will also use the features of NTFS in Chapter 10, "Accessing Files and Folders." You are probably also wondering about the free space requirement. You need free space because you will create partitions in Chapter 9. If no free space exists, you won't be able to complete that exercise.

Exercise 1.1 assumes that you are not currently running Windows NT and that you are performing a clean installation and not an upgrade. Your partitions should be created and formatted, and SMARTDRV should be loaded. Also, before you begin, make sure that your hardware meets the requirements listed in Table 1.1.

As noted earlier in this chapter, you can set up your partitions through the DOS or Windows FDISK utility or a third-party program. For example, if you have a Windows 98 computer, you can use it to create a Windows 98 boot disk. Set up the disk with FDISK and FORMAT, and manually copy the SMARTDRV utility from the Windows folder on the Windows 98 computer to the Windows 98 boot disk. Then you will be able to boot your computer and see your CD-ROM drive.

You should make a complete backup of your computer before repartitioning your disk or installing new operating systems. All data will be lost during this process!

EXERCISE 1.1

Installing Windows 2000 Professional

In this exercise, you will install Windows 2000 Professional, which is a three-part process.

Running the Setup Program

1. Boot your computer and insert the Windows 2000 CD into your CD-ROM drive.

2. From the DOS prompt on your computer, access your CD-ROM drive. If you have configured your computer to our recommended specifications, your CD-ROM drive should be E:.

3. From the CD-ROM drive prompt, change to the I386 directory by typing **CD I386** and pressing Enter.

4. From the \I386> prompt, type **WINNT** and press Enter.

5. From the Windows 2000 Setup dialog box, press Enter to accept the default path location for the Windows 2000 distribution files. It will take a few minutes to copy the files.

6. Remove any floppy disks from the computer and press Enter to restart the computer.

7. The computer restarts, and the Welcome to Setup screen appears. Press Enter to set up Windows 2000.

8. The License Agreement dialog box appears. Scroll down to the bottom of the page. Press F8 to agree to the license terms if you wish to continue.

9. In the next dialog box, specify the C: partition as the one you want to use to set up Windows 2000. Then press Enter.

10. In the next dialog box, choose to leave the current file system intact (no changes). Press Enter to continue.

Setup now examines your disks. The Windows installation files will be automatically copied to the installation folder, which will take a few minutes. After the files are copied, the computer will automatically reboot. After the computer reboots, the Welcome to the Setup Wizard dialog box will appear. You are prompted to click Next to continue. If you do not make a selection within 10 seconds, the installation will continue automatically. The Windows 2000 Professional Setup program will automatically detect and install drivers on your computer. This process will take a few minutes.

EXERCISE 1.1 *(continued)*

Running the Windows 2000 Setup Wizard

11. The Regional Settings dialog box appears. Click Next to accept the default settings and continue.

12. In the Personalize Your Software dialog box, type your name and organization. Click the Next button.

13. In the Product Key dialog box, type the 25-character product key (this key can be found on a sticker on the CD case). Click the Next button.

14. The Computer Name and Administrator Password dialog box appears. Type in the computer name. You can also specify an Administrator password (since this computer will be used for practice, you can leave the Password field blank if you want to). Click the Next button.

15. If you have a Plug and Play modem installed, the Modem Dialing Information dialog box appears. Specify the settings for your environment and click the Next button.

16. The Date and Time Settings dialog box appears. Verify that all of the settings are correct and click the Next button.

17. After the Networking component files are copied (which takes a few minutes), the Network Settings dialog box appears. Confirm that the Typical Settings button is selected. Then click the Next button.

18. In the Workgroup and Computer Domain dialog box, confirm that the option No, This Computer Is Not on a Network, or Is on a Network without a Domain, is selected to indicate that you don't want to put the computer in a domain. In this dialog box, you can accept the default workgroup name, WORKGROUP, or you can specify a unique workgroup name. Since this is a practice computer, the workgroup name is not important. Click the Next button. The Setup components are installed, which takes several minutes.

EXERCISE 1.1 *(continued)*

19. When the Completing the Windows 2000 Setup Wizard appears, remove the CD from the drive and click the Finish button. The computer will restart.

20. When the computer reboots, choose Microsoft Windows 2000 from the boot selection options by pressing Enter. (This is the default selection if no choice is made.)

Running the Network Identification Wizard

21. Windows 2000 Professional starts and displays the Welcome to the Network Identification Wizard dialog box. Click the Next button to continue.

22. In the Users of This Computer dialog box, click to turn on the Users Must Enter a User Name and Password to Use This Computer option. Click the Next button to continue.

23. In the Completing the Network Identification Wizard dialog box, click the Finish button.

Windows 2000 Professional is now installed, and you should be logged on to Windows 2000 and see the Getting Started with Windows 2000 dialog box.

Troubleshooting Installation Problems

The Windows 2000 installation process is designed to be as simple as possible. The chances for installation errors are greatly minimized through the use of wizards and the step-by-step process. However, it is possible that errors may occur.

Microsoft ✔ ***Exam Objective***   **Troubleshoot failed installations.**

The following are some possible installation errors you might encounter:

Media errors	Media errors are caused by defective or damaged CDs. To check the CD, put it into another computer and see if you can read it. Also check your CD for scratches or dirt—it may just need to be cleaned.
Insufficient disk space	Windows 2000 needs at least 1GB of free space for the installation program to run properly. If the Setup program cannot verify that this space exists, the program will not let you continue.
Not enough memory	Make sure that your computer has the minimum amount of memory required by Windows 2000 Professional (64MB). Having insufficient memory may cause the installation to fail or blue-screen errors to occur after installation.
Not enough processing power	Make sure that your computer has the minimum processing power required by Windows 2000 Professional (Pentium 133MHz). Having insufficient processing power may cause the installation to fail or blue-screen errors to occur after installation.
Hardware that is not on the HCL	If your hardware is not on the HCL, Windows 2000 may not recognize the hardware, or the device may not work properly.
Hardware with no driver support	Windows 2000 will not recognize hardware without driver support.
Hardware that is not configured properly	If your hardware is Plug and Play compatible, Windows should configure it automatically. If your hardware is not Plug and Play compatible, you will need to manually configure the hardware per the manufacturer's instructions.
Incorrect CD key	Without a valid CD key, the installation will not go past the Product Key dialog box. Make sure that you have not typed in an incorrect key (check the back of your CD case for this key).

Failure to access TCP/IP network resources	If you install Windows 2000 with typical settings, the computer is configured as a DHCP client. If there is no DHCP server to provide IP configuration information, the client will be unable to access network resources through TCP/IP.
Failure to connect to a domain controller when joining a domain	Make sure that you have specified the correct domain name. If your domain name is correct, verify that your network settings have been set properly and that a domain controller and DNS server are available. If you still can't join a domain, install the computer in a workgroup, then join the domain after installation.

When you install Windows 2000 Professional, several log files are created by the Setup program. You can view these logs to check for any problems during the installation process. Two log files are particularly useful for troubleshooting:

- The action log includes all of the actions that were performed during the setup process and a description of each action. These actions are listed in chronological order. The action log is stored as *Windir*\setupact.log.

- The error log includes any errors that occurred during the installation. For each error, there is a description and an indication of the severity of the error. This error log is stored as *Windir*\setuperr.log.

In Exercise 1.2, you will view the Windows 2000 setup logs to determine if there were any problems with your Windows 2000 installation.

EXERCISE 1.2

Troubleshooting Failed Installations with Setup Logs

1. Select Start ➢ Programs ➢ Accessories ➢ Windows Explorer.

2. In Windows Explorer, double-click My Computer, double-click Local Disk (C:), and double-click WINNT (this is the default *Windir* folder, set up in Exercise 1.1).

---

3. Since this is the first time you have opened the WINNT folder, click the Show All Files option to display all the files that it contains.

4. In the WINNT folder, double-click the setupact file to view your action log in Notepad. When you are finished viewing this file, close Notepad.

5. Double-click the setuperr file to view your error file in Notepad. If no errors occurred during installation, this file will be empty. When you are finished viewing this file, close Notepad.

6. Close Windows Explorer.

Supporting Multiple-Boot Options

You may want to install Windows 2000 Professional but still be able to run other operating systems. *Dual-booting* or *multi-booting* allows your computer to boot multiple operating systems. Your computer will be automatically configured for dual-booting if there was a supported operating system on your computer prior to the Windows 2000 Professional installation (and you didn't upgrade from that operating system).

One reason for dual-booting is to test various systems. If you have a limited number of computers in your test lab, and you want to be able to test multiple configurations, you dual-boot. For example, you might configure one computer to multi-boot with Windows NT Workstation 4, Windows NT Server 4 configured as a Primary Domain Controller (PDC), Windows 2000 Professional, and Windows 2000 Server.

Another reason to set up dual-booting is for software backward compatibility. For example, you may have an application that works with Windows 95 but not under Windows 2000 Professional. If you want to use Windows 2000 but still access your legacy application, you can configure a dual-boot.

Here are some keys to successful dual-boot configurations:

- Make sure you have plenty of disk space. It's a good idea to put each operating system on a separate partition, although this is not required.

- Put the simplest operating systems on first. If you want to support dual-booting with DOS and Windows 2000 Professional, DOS must be installed first. If you install Windows 2000 Professional first, you cannot install DOS without ruining your Windows 2000 configuration. This requirement also applies to Windows 9*x*.

- Never, ever, upgrade to Windows 2000 dynamic disks. Dynamic disks are seen only by Windows 2000 and are not recognized by any other operating system, including Windows NT.

- Do not convert your file system to NTFS if you are planning a dual-boot with any operating system except Windows NT or Windows 2000. These operating systems are the only ones that recognize NTFS.

- If you will dual-boot with Windows NT 4, you must turn off disk compression, or Windows 2000 will not be able to read the drive properly.

If you are planning on dual-booting with Windows NT 4, you should upgrade it to NT 4 Service Pack 4 (or higher), which provides NTFS version 5 support.

Once you have installed each operating system, you can choose the operating system that you will boot to during the boot process. You will see a boot selection screen that asks you to choose which operating system you want to boot.

Summary

In this chapter, you learned how to install Windows 2000 Professional. We covered the following topics:

- The design goals of Windows 2000 Professional, which include taking the best features of Windows 98 and Windows NT 4, providing a wide range of support for hardware, making the operating system easy to use, and lowering the cost of ownership.

- Installation preparation, which begins with making sure that your computer meets the minimum system requirements and that all of your hardware is on the Hardware Compatibility List (HCL). Then you need to decide whether you will perform a clean install or an upgrade. Finally, you should plan which options you will select during installation. Options include method of partitioning your disk space, selecting a file system, whether the computer will be installed as a part of a workgroup or a domain, and your language and locale settings.

- The methods you can use for installation, which include using the distribution files on the Windows 2000 Professional CD or using files that have been copied to a network share point. If you will be installing Windows 2000 from the CD, you can start the installation by booting from another operating system, booting from the CD, or using the Windows 2000 Professional Setup Boot Disks.

- How to install Windows 2000 Professional, which proceeds in three main installation phases: running the Setup program, running the Setup Wizard, and installing Windows 2000 Networking.

- How to troubleshoot installation problems. Common errors are caused by media problems, lack of disk space or memory, and hardware problems. You can view Setup log files to check for problems that occurred during the installation.

- Information about supporting dual-boot or multi-boot environments. Dual-booting and multi-booting allow you to boot to a choice of two or more operating systems.

Exam Essentials

Be able to tell if a computer meets minimum hardware requirements for Windows 2000 Professional.   Windows 2000 has minimum hardware requirements that must be met. In addition, the hardware must be on the HCL, and Windows 2000 drivers must be available for all devices.

Understand the different methods that can be used for Windows 2000 Professional installation.   Be able to specify the steps and setup involved in installing Windows 2000 through options such as local CD (with or without the Setup Boot Disks) and through network installation.

Understand the reasons why a Windows 2000 installation would fail.
You should be able to list common reasons for failure of a Windows 2000
Professional installation and be able to offer possible fixes or solutions.

Specify what is required to support multiple-boot configurations.   If
you plan to install Windows 2000 Professional on the same computer that
is running other operating systems, be able to specify what must be configured to support dual- or multiple-boot configurations.

Key Terms

Before taking the exam, you should be familiar with the following terms:

Advanced Configuration and
Power Interface (ACPI)

Institute of Electrical and
Electronic Engineers (IEEE)
1394 standard

boot partition

logical drive

central processing unit (CPU)

MB (megabyte)

clean install

multi-boot

disk partitioning

NTFS (New Technology File
System)

distribution server

PB (petabyte)

domain

Plug and Play

dual-boot

system partition

EB (exabyte)

TB (terabyte)

FAT32

Universal Serial Bus (USB)

File Allocation Table (FAT16)

Windows 2000 Professional Setup
Boot Disks

GB (gigabyte)

Workgroup

Hardware Compatibility
List (HCL)

Review Questions

1. James has decided to install Windows 2000 on a test computer in the lab. He can choose among several computers. When making his selection, what is the minimum processor required for an Intel-based computer to install and run Windows 2000 Professional?

   A. 80486

   B. A Pentium with a 133MHz or better processor

   C. A Pentium II with a 166MHz or better processor

   D. A Pentium III with a 333MHz or better processor

2. Martina wants to install Windows 2000 on a computer that is already running Windows NT 4 Workstation. She has an extra 4GB partition that can be used. What is the minimum free disk space required to install Windows 2000 Professional on the extra partition?

   A. 500MB

   B. 650MB

   C. 1GB

   D. 1.2GB

3. Dionne is purchasing 12 new computers for the training room. She needs to make sure that the computers will support Windows 2000 Professional. What is the name of the list that shows the computers and peripheral hardware that have been extensively tested with the Windows 2000 Professional operating system?

   A. The Windows Compatibility List

   B. The W2K Compatibility List

   C. The Microsoft Compatibility List

   D. The Hardware Compatibility List

4. Selecting file systems is a very important part of the Windows 2000 configuration. What three file systems supported by Windows 2000 Professional can you consider?

   A. FAT16

   B. HPFS

   C. FAT32

   D. NTFS

5. Mike is installing a Windows 2000 Professional machine. He has decided that he wants the computer to be a part of the Active Directory within SJ.MASTERMCSE.COM. Which of the following options should he choose for computer membership?

   A. Workgroup

   B. Active Directory

   C. Domain

   D. MDS

6. John is installing Windows 2000 Professional. He has a good understanding of the installation process. Which of the following is *not* a major step in the Windows 2000 Professional installation process?

   A. Running the Configuration Setup Wizard

   B. Running the Setup program

   C. Running the Setup Wizard

   D. Installing Windows 2000 Networking

7. Tom has machines running DOS, Windows 95, Windows 98, and Windows NT 4 Workstation that he needs to upgrade to Windows 2000 Professional. He is not sure if he should use WINNT or WINNT32. From which of the following operating systems would you run the WINNT32 command? Choose all that apply.

   A. DOS

   B. Windows 95

   C. Windows 98

   D. Windows NT

8. Sean has four computers in the test lab. He wants to install Windows 2000 Professional. The configurations for each of his computers are listed in the exhibit below. Place a mark on the computer that does *not* meet the minimum requirements for Windows 2000 Professional.

	Computer A	Computer B	Computer C	Computer D
Processor	PII/266	PIII/450	PII/166	Pentium/133
Memory	64MB	64MB	32MB	64MB
Free Disk Space	2GB	750GB	650GB	1GB

9. James is installing a Window 2000 Professional computer in the Sales.ABCCorp.com domain. Select and place the servers that must be available on the network to support the addition of James' computer to the domain.

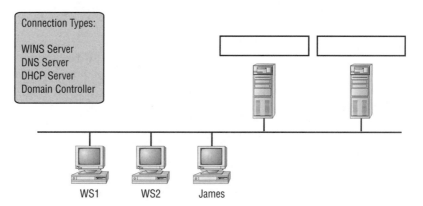

Connection Types:

WINS Server
DNS Server
DHCP Server
Domain Controller

WS1   WS2   James

10. Your computer is configured with two hard drives. You have decided to configure logical drive C: on disk 0, and logical disk D: on disk 1. You want to run Windows 98 for backward compatibility with some applications that will not run under Windows 2000. However, you also want to run Windows 2000 Professional to take advantage of the Windows 2000 features. On drive D:, you want to store files that should have a high level of security. You will install Windows 98 on drive C: and Windows 2000 Professional on drive D:. How should the drives on this computer be configured?

   A. Configure both logical drives as FAT32.

   B. Configure both logical drives with NTFS.

   C. Configure logical drive C: as FAT32 and logical drive D: as NTFS.

   D. Configure logical drive C: as NTFS and logical drive D: as FAT32.

11. You have a computer that will dual-boot between Windows NT 4 and Windows 2000 Professional. Which of the following statements reflects proper configuration?

   A. You should turn off disk compression on the Windows NT 4 configuration.

   B. You should enable dynamic disks on the Windows 2000 Professional configuration.

   C. You should install both operating systems into the same Windir directory so you will be able to access applications under both operating systems.

   D. You should edit the Registry on the Windows 2000 computer for HKEY_LOCAL_MACHINE\DualBoot to a value of 1 so that you will be able to access applications under both operating systems.

12. You have a computer that is on the HCL. The hard drive was erased and you are unable to access the CD-ROM drive. Where can you find the 32-bit command to create the Windows 2000 Professional Setup Boot Disks on the Windows 2000 Professional CD? The computer that will create the disks is already running Windows 2000 Professional.

    A. \I386\MAKEBOOT

    B. \I386\MAKEBT32

    C. \BOOTDISK\MAKEBOOT

    D. \BOOTDISK\MAKEBT32

13. Catherine wants to be able to install Windows 2000 Professional over the network on 20 computers. What folder must be copied from the Windows 2000 Professional CD?

    A. \OEM

    B. \I386

    C. \Intel

    D. \$WINI386

14. Eammon installed a computer with Windows 2000 Professional. The network card was not recognized. Eammon needs to troubleshoot the computer. Which of the following steps should he take? Choose all that apply.

    A. Make sure the network card is on the HCL.

    B. Check to see if the network card is Plug and Play compatible or if it needs to be manually configured.

    C. Make sure the network card is compatible with the other network cards on the network.

    D. Make sure you have the latest driver for the network card.

15. You are in the process of troubleshooting a Windows 2000 Professional installation. You want to verify all of the actions that were taken during the Setup phase. Where can you find a log file that will tell you this information?

A. *Windir*\verify.log

B. \Logfiles\verify.log

C. *Windir*\setupact.log

D. \Logfiles\setup.log

Answers to Review Questions

1. B. The processor must be at least a Pentium 133MHz or better.

2. B. You must have a minimum of a 2GB drive with at least 650MB of free space to install Windows 2000 Professional.

3. D. The Hardware Compatibility List (HCL) shows the computers and components that have been tested to work with Windows 2000.

4. A, C, D. Windows 2000 supports the FAT16, FAT32, and NTFS file systems. Windows NT 3.51 was the last version of NT to support the HPFS file system.

5. C. You can install your computer as a part of a workgroup or as a part of the domain. Domains are part of the Active Directory, but you install computers into domains, not directly into the Active Directory. There is no such thing as MDS within the context of Windows 2000.

6. A. Option A does not exist.

7. B, C, D. You can run WINNT32 only from Windows NT or Windows 2000.

8. You should have placed a mark on Computer C. Computers A, B, and D meet the minimum requirements of a Pentium 133MHz or higher processor, 64MB of memory, and at least 650MB of free disk space. Computer C does not.

9. You should have dragged and dropped a DNS Server and a domain controller.

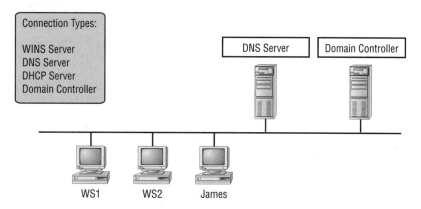

You must have a domain controller and a DNS server running in your domain in order to add a computer to the domain.

10. C. You should configure logical drive C: as FAT32 because Windows 98 will not read NTFS partitions. Logical drive D: should be configured as NTFS because you want to implement local security.

11. A. You should turn off disk compression before you dual-boot. Windows 2000 does not support the disk compression that was used by Windows NT 4. There is no way to configure the operating systems to recognize applications under both platforms.

12. D. If you are creating Windows 2000 Professional Setup Boot Disks from a computer that is running Windows 2000, Windows NT, or Windows 9x, you use the MAKEBT32.EXE command. If you are making the boot disks from a 16-bit operating system, you use the MAKEBOOT .EXE command. These commands can be found in the BOOTDISK folder on the Windows 2000 Professional CD.

13. B. You must copy the \I386 folder and share the folder to install Windows 2000 Professional over a network.

14. A, B, D. If your computer will not recognize your network card, you should ensure that the network card is on the HCL and make sure you have the latest driver. You can check for the latest driver on the vendor's Web site. Even if the card is not on the HCL and is not Plug and Play compatible, it may work if it is properly configured.

15. C. You can find the log file that details Setup actions in *Windir*\setupact.log.

Chapter

2

Automating the Windows 2000 Installation

MICROSOFT EXAM OBJECTIVES COVERED IN THIS CHAPTER:

✓ **Perform an unattended installation of Windows 2000 Professional.**

- Install Windows 2000 Professional by using Windows 2000 Server Remote Installation Services (RIS).

- Install Windows 2000 Professional by using the System Preparation Tool.

- Create unattended answer files by using Setup Manager to automate the installation of Windows 2000 Professional.

✓ **Manage applications by using Windows Installer packages.**

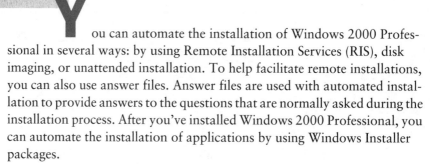

You can automate the installation of Windows 2000 Professional in several ways: by using Remote Installation Services (RIS), disk imaging, or unattended installation. To help facilitate remote installations, you can also use answer files. Answer files are used with automated installation to provide answers to the questions that are normally asked during the installation process. After you've installed Windows 2000 Professional, you can automate the installation of applications by using Windows Installer packages.

This chapter begins with an overview of the three automated deployment options. Next, it details the use of unattended answer files, RIS, and disk images. Finally, you will learn how to automate application installation through the use of Windows Installer packages.

Choosing Automated Deployment Options

If you need to install Windows 2000 Professional on multiple computers, you could manually install the operating system on each computer, as described in Chapter 1, "Getting Started with Windows 2000 Professional." However, automatic deployment will make your job easier, more efficient, and more cost effective.

The following sections contain overviews of these options for automated deployment:

- Remote installation

- Disk imaging (cloning)

- Unattended installation

An Overview of Remote Installation

Remote Installation Services (RIS) is a new technology introduced with Windows 2000 to allow *remote installation* of Windows 2000 Professional.

A RIS server installs Windows 2000 Professional on RIS clients, as illustrated in Figure 2.1. The RIS server must have the RIS server software installed and configured. RIS clients are computers that have a *Pre-Boot Execution Environment (PXE)* network card or use a RIS boot disk with a PXE-compatible network card. The RIS clients access RIS servers through Dynamic Host Configuration Protocol (DHCP) to remotely install the operating system from the RIS server. No other software is required to connect to the RIS server. Remote installation is a good choice for automatic deployment when you need to be able to deploy large numbers of computers and your clients are PXE compliant.

FIGURE 2.1 Remote Installation Services (RIS) uses a RIS server and RIS clients.

RIS Server

RIS Client

Stores:
• RIS server software
• Windows 2000 Professional,
  CD-based, or RIPrep images
• Answer files (optional)

Requires:
• PXE-based boot ROM, or
• RIS boot disk with a network adapter that
  supports PXE, or
• Net PC computer

The RIS server can be configured with either of two types of images:

- A CD-based image contains only the Windows 2000 Professional operating system. You can create answer files for CD-based images to respond to the Setup program's configuration prompts.

- A Remote Installation Preparation (RIPrep) image can contain the Windows 2000 operating system and applications. This type of image is based on a preconfigured computer.

RIS installation is discussed in the "Using Remote Installation Services" section later in this chapter.

An Overview of Disk Imaging

Disk imaging, or disk duplication, is the process of creating a reference computer for the automated deployment. The reference, or source, computer has Windows 2000 Professional installed and is configured with the settings and applications that should be installed on the target computers. Disk imaging is a good choice for automatic deployment when you have the hardware that supports disk imaging and you have a large number of computers with similar configuration requirements. For example, education centers that re-install the same software every week might use this technology.

You use the *System Preparation Tool (Sysprep)* utility to prepare the disk image. Then you remove the drive that has the disk image and insert it into a special piece of hardware, called a disk duplicator, to copy the image. The copied disks are inserted into the target computers. After you add the hard drive that contains the disk image to the target computers, you can complete the installation from those computers. Figure 2.2 illustrates the disk-imaging process. You can also copy disk images by using special third-party software.

You can also configure disk imaging so that the drive is not removed. The reference computer is booted to an image boot disk. The image is labeled and uploaded to a remote server. When the image is required, you boot the computer with the image boot disk and download the selected image from a menu.

FIGURE 2.2 Disk imaging uses a reference computer for configuring target computers.

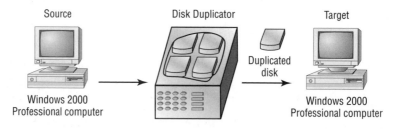

The process for creating disk images is covered in detail in the "Using Disk Images" section later in this chapter.

An Overview of Unattended Installation

Unattended installation is a practical method of automatic deployment when you have a large number of clients to install and the computers are not PXE compliant. With an unattended installation, you use a distribution server to install Windows 2000 Professional on a target computer.

The distribution server contains the Windows 2000 Professional operating system files and possibly an answer file to respond to installation configuration queries. The target computer must be able to connect to the distribution server over the network. After the distribution server and target computers are connected, you can initiate the installation process. Figure 2.3 illustrates the unattended installation process.

FIGURE 2.3 Unattended installation uses a distribution server and a target computer.

Distribution Server

Target

Stores:
• Windows 2000 Professional
  operating system files
• Answer files (optional)

Requires:
• Enough software to
  connect to the
  distribution server

 The process for unattended installations is covered in *Mastering Windows 2000 Server*, by Mark Minasi (Sybex, 2000).

Using Setup Manager to Create Answer Files

Answer files are automated installation scripts used to answer the questions that appear during a normal Windows 2000 Professional installation. You can use answer files with Windows 2000 unattended installations, Sysprep (disk images), or RIS installations. Setting up answer files allows you to easily deploy Windows 2000 Professional to computers that may not be configured in the same manner, with little or no user intervention.

Microsoft ✓ *Exam* *Objective*

Perform an unattended installation of Windows 2000 Professional.

- Create unattended answer files by using Setup Manager to automate the installation of Windows 2000 Professional.

You create answer files through the *Setup Manager (SETUPMGR)* utility. There are several advantages to using Setup Manager to create answer files:

- You can easily create answer files through a graphical interface, which reduces syntax errors.

- The utility simplifies the addition of user-specific or computer-specific configuration information.

- With Setup Manager, you can include application setup scripts within the answer file.

- The utility creates the distribution folder that will be used for installation files.

In order to access the Setup Manager utility, you must extract the *Windows 2000 Deployment Tools* from the Windows 2000 Professional CD. The following sections explain how to access the Setup Manager utility and how to use Setup Manager to create an unattended answer file. You will also learn how to customize answer files by directly editing them.

Extracting the Windows 2000 Deployment Tools

The Windows 2000 Deployment Tools include the Setup Manager utility for creating unattended answer files, as well as the System Preparation Tool utility for creating disk images. The Deployment Tools are stored on the Windows 2000 Professional CD, in the \Support\Tools folder, in the Deploy.cab file. You can extract these files by using the File ➢ Extract command in Windows Explorer.

In Exercise 2.1, you will extract the Windows 2000 Deployment Tools.

EXERCISE 2.1

Extracting the Windows 2000 Deployment Tools

1. Log on to your Windows 2000 computer as Administrator.

EXERCISE 2.1 *(continued)*

2. Use Windows Explorer to create a folder named **Deployment Tools** on the root folder of your C: drive.

3. Insert the Windows 2000 Professional CD. Using Windows Explorer, copy the \Support\Tools\Deploy file (the .cab extension is hidden by default) to the C:\Deployment Tools folder.

4. Double-click the Deploy.cab file to display its contents.

5. In Windows Explorer, select Edit ➢ Select All. Then select File ➢ Extract.

6. The Browse for Folder dialog box appears. Select Local Disk (C:) and then Deployment Tools. Click the OK button to extract the files to the specified folder.

7. Verify that the Deployment Tools were extracted to C:\Deployment Tools. There should be eight items (including the Deploy.cab file).

Unattended Answer Files

After you have extracted the Windows 2000 Deployment Tools from the Windows 2000 Professional CD, you can run the Setup Manager utility to create a new answer file, create an answer file that duplicates the current computer's configuration, or edit existing answer files.

An answer file can be used to provide answers to a CD-based installation. Simply create a new answer file named winnt.sif and copy it to a floppy. Insert the Windows 2000 Professional CD and set the BIOS to boot from CD. As the installation begins, Windows 2000 will look for winnt.sif and use it as the answer file.

The following steps describe how to create a new installation script. In this example, the instructions are for creating an answer file for a RIS installation. This answer file provides default answers, uses the default display configuration, configures typical network settings, and does not edit any additional options.

1. Select Start ➤ Run and click the Browse button in the Run dialog box. Double-click the Deployment Tools folder, double-click the SETUPMGR program, and then click the OK button.

2. The Windows 2000 Setup Manager Wizard starts. Click the Next button.

3. The New or Existing Answer File dialog box appears, as shown in Figure 2.4. This dialog box provides choices for creating a new answer file, creating an answer file that duplicates this computer's configuration, or modifying an existing answer file. Select the option Create a New Answer File, and click the Next button.

FIGURE 2.4   The New or Existing Answer File dialog box

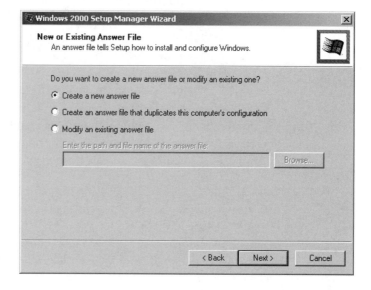

4. The Product to Install dialog box appears, as shown in Figure 2.5. You can choose Windows 2000 Unattended Installation, Sysprep Install, or Remote Installation Services. Select Remote Installation Services and click the Next button.

FIGURE 2.5 The Product to Install dialog box

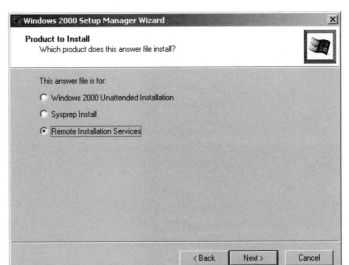

5. The User Interaction Level dialog box appears, as shown in Figure 2.6. This dialog box offers the following options:

   - Provide Defaults allows you to configure default answers that will be displayed. The user is prompted to review the default answer and can change the answer if desired.

   - Fully Automated uses all the answers in the answer file and will not prompt the user for any interaction.

   - Hide Pages lets you hide the wizard page from the user, if you have supplied all of the answers on the Windows Setup Wizard page.

   - The Read Only option allows the user to see the Setup Wizard display page, but not to make any changes to it (this option is used if the Setup Wizard display page is shown to the user).

   - The GUI Attended option allows only the text-mode portion of the Windows Setup program to be automated.

   Select the Provide Defaults option and click the Next button to continue.

FIGURE 2.6 The User Interaction Level dialog box

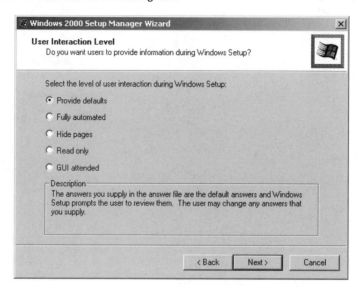

6. Next up is the Administrator Password dialog box (Figure 2.7). You can choose to prompt the user for a password, or you can specify the Administrator password. You can also specify that when the computer starts, the Administrator will automatically be logged on. Enter and confirm an Administrator password. Then click the Next button.

FIGURE 2.7 The Administrator Password dialog box

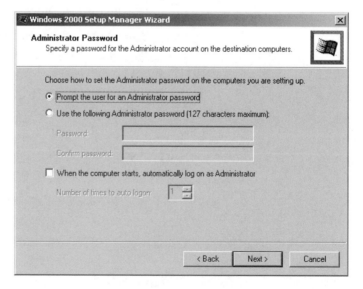

7. Next, from the Display Settings dialog box (Figure 2.8), you can configure the following settings:

- For the Colors option, set the display color to the Windows default, 16 colors, 256 colors, high color (16 bit), high color (24 bit), or high color (32 bit).

- The Screen Area option allows you to set the screen area to the Windows default, or to one of the following: 640x480, 800x600, 1024x768, 1280x1024, or 1600x1200.

- The Refresh Frequency option (the number of times the screen is updated) allows you to set the refresh frequency to the Windows default or to 60Hz, 70Hz, 72Hz, 75Hz, or 85Hz.

- The Custom button displays a dialog box in which you can further customize display settings for the color, screen area, and refresh frequency.

For this example, click Next to accept the default configuration and continue.

FIGURE 2.8 The Display Settings dialog box

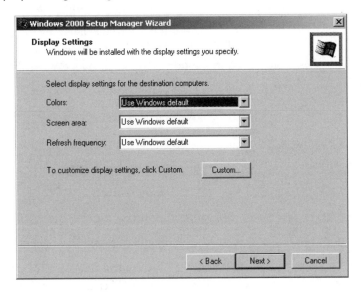

8. In the Network Settings dialog box, Figure 2.9, choose Typical Settings (installs TCP/IP, enables DHCP, and installs Client for Microsoft Networks) or Custom Settings (allows you to customize the computer's network settings). Select the Typical Settings option and click the Next button.

FIGURE 2.9   The Network Settings dialog box

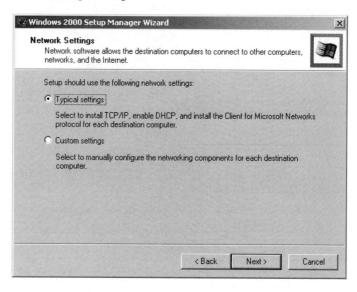

9. The Time Zone dialog box appears. Select your computer's time zone from the drop-down list and click the Next button.

10. The Additional Settings dialog box appears, as shown in Figure 2.10. If you select to edit additional settings, you can configure the following options:

   - Telephony settings

   - Regional settings

   - Languages

   - Browser and shell settings

   - Installation folder

   - Install printers

   - A command that will run once the first time a user logs on

   Click the Next button to accept the default selection of No, Do Not Edit the Additional Settings.

FIGURE 2.10 The Additional Settings dialog box

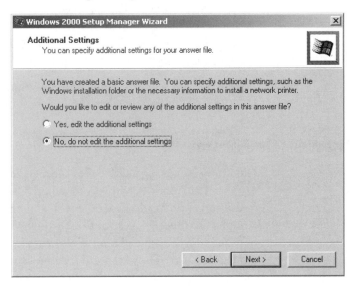

11. The Setup Information File Text dialog box appears, as shown in Figure 2.11. This dialog box allows you to give the answer file a descriptive name and help text. Enter the name in the Description String text box, and the help text in the Help String text box. Click Next to continue.

FIGURE 2.11 The Setup Information File Text dialog box

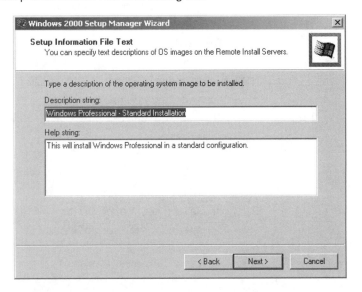

12. The Answer File Name dialog box appears. Click the Browse button. Select Local Disk (C:) and click the Create New Folder icon. Create a new folder for the answer files and click the Open button. In the Save As dialog box, specify a filename (the default is `remboot.sif`) and click the Save button. Then click the Next button.

13. When you see the Completing the Windows 2000 Setup Manager Wizard dialog box, click the Finish button.

Answer File Format

In addition to creating answer files through Setup Manager, you can edit or create your answer files with any text editor (such as Notepad). Answer files consist of section headers, parameters, and values for the parameters. You do not have to specify every option through your answer file if the option is not required by the installation. Following is a sample answer file, `Unattended.txt`. The next section defines some of the options that are configured through the answer file.

```
;SetupMgrTag
[Data]
    AutoPartition=1
    MsDosInitiated="0"
    UnattendedInstall="Yes"

[Unattended]
    UnattendMode=ProvideDefault
    OemPreinstall=Yes
    TargetPath=\WINNT

[GuiUnattended]
    AdminPassword=abc
    OEMSkipRegional=1
    TimeZone=4

[UserData]
    FullName="Test User "
    OrgName="ABC Corp"
    ComputerName=SJ-UserTest
```

```
[TapiLocation]
    CountryCode=1
    AreaCode=408

[SetupMgr]
    DistFolder=C:\win2000dist
    DistShare=win2000dist

[Identification]
    JoinDomain=SJ-CORP
    DomainAdmin=administrator
    DomainAdminPassword=test

[Networking]
    InstallDefaultComponents=Yes
```

Options that can be configured through the answer file include the following:

- Providing support for hardware devices, including storage devices, hardware abstraction layers (HALs), and Plug and Play devices

- Setting passwords for local user accounts, or forcing users to change their password if they are upgrading their operating system

- Setting options for language and multilingual support, and time zone configuration

- Configuring display settings

- Configuring file systems, including the ability to convert FAT16 or FAT32 partitions to NTFS during the install

- Installing applications during the GUI mode phase of Setup or when the user logs on the first time using Windows Installer service

Adding Hardware

If you have hardware that is Plug and Play compatible but the Windows 2000 Professional CD does not provide a driver for your hardware, you can still configure the hardware through the unattended installation. In this section you will learn how to configure settings for

- Mass storage devices

- Plug and Play devices

- HALs

Mass Storage Devices

If you have a mass storage device on the remote computer that is recognized and supported by Windows 2000, you need not specify anything in the answer file for mass storage devices. However, if the device has a driver that is not shipped with the Windows 2000 Professional CD, possibly because the device is brand-new, you can configure the device through mass storage devices.

Here are the steps to configure mass storage devices:

1. The distribution folder that contains the remote image files (all the files that will be used by the remote installation) contains a folder called \\OEM. Within this folder, create a folder called **Textmode** and copy into it the Windows 2000 mass storage device driver. These driver files should contain files with extensions of `*.sys`, `*.dll`, `*.inf`, `*.cat`, and the `Txtsetup.oem` file. Also, copy the files to the [PnPdrvrs] location within the distribution folder.

2. Within your answer file, create a **[MassStorageDrivers]** section. The parameters and values to be set within the `Txtsetup.oem` file should be provided by the manufacturer of the mass storage device.

3. Within your answer file, create a section named **[OEMBootFiles]** that includes a list of all of the driver files that are in the \\OEM\ Textmode folder. For example, a device named driver might be configured as follows:

```
[OEMBootFiles]
driver.sys
driver.dll
driver.inf
Txtsetup.oem
```

Plug and Play Devices

If you have a Plug and Play device that does not have a driver included on the Windows 2000 Professional CD, you can add the driver to the unattended installation as follows:

1. Within the \$OEM$\$1 subfolder, create a folder that will be used to store the Plug and Play drivers; for example, \$OEM$\$1\PnPdrivers. You may even want to create subdirectories for specific devices; for example, \$OEM$\$1\PnPdrivers\Modems.

2. In the answer file, edit the [Unattended] section heading to reflect the location of your Plug and Play drivers. For example, if you installed your Plug and Play modem in \$OEM$\$1\PnPdrivers\Modems and your sound card in \$OEM$\$1\PnPdrivers\SoundCards, your answer file would have the following line:

```
[Unattended]
    OEMPnPDriversPath=PnPdrivers\Modems;
PnPdrivers\SoundCards
```

If the drivers you are installing are not digitally signed, you will have to configure the driver-signing policy within the [Unattended] section of the answer file as DriverSigningPolicy=Ignore. Use unsigned drivers with caution.

HALs

If you want to use alternate HALs, follow these steps:

1. Create a folder called \OEM\Textmode (or verify that one exists).

2. Copy any files that are provided by the HAL vendor into the Textmode folder.

3. Edit the [Unattended] section of the answer file based on the instructions from the HAL manufacturer.

Setting Passwords

If you are upgrading a Windows 95 or Windows 98 computer to Windows 2000 Professional, you can customize the answer file to set passwords for the user accounts. You can also opt to force users to change their passwords during the first logon.

Table 2.1 explains the options that can be configured for passwords.

TABLE 2.1 Password Options for Answer Files

Answer File Section	Key	Usage	Example
[Win9xUpg]	DefaultPassword	Sets a password to whatever you specify, for all computers that are upgraded from Windows 95 or Windows 98 to Windows 2000 Professional.	DefaultPassword=*password*
[Win9xUpg]	ForcePassword	Forces all users who have upgraded from Windows 95 or Windows 98 to change their password the first time they log on.	ForcePasswordChange=Yes
[Win9xUpg]	UserPassword	Forces specific users to change their passwords on their local accounts when they log on to Windows 2000 Professional for the first time after upgrading from Windows 95 or Windows 98.	UserPassword=*user*, *password*,*user*,*password*
[GuiUnattended]	AdminPassword	Sets the local Administrator password.	AdminPassword=*password*

Language, Regional, and Time Zone Settings

The [RegionalSettings] section heading is used to set language and regional settings. Time zone settings are in the [GUIUnattended] section.

In order to set regional settings for answer files, you must copy the appropriate language files to the computer's hard disk. This can be accomplished by using the /copysource:*lang* switch with WINNT32, or the /rx:*lang* switch with WINNT. Following are the options that can be set for the [RegionalSettings] section:

- **InputLocale** specifies the input locale and the keyboard layout for the computer.

- **Language** specifies the language and locale that will be used by the computer.

- **LanguageGroup** specifies default settings for the SystemLocale, InputLocale, and UserLocale keys.

- **SystemLocale** allows localized applications to run and to display menus and dialog boxes in the language selected.

- **UserLocale** controls settings for numbers, time, and currency.

To set the time zone, you edit the [GuiUnattended] section of the answer file as follows:

```
[GuiUnattended]
    TimeZone=TimeZone
```

Display Settings

The [Display] section of the answer file is normally used to customize the display settings for portable computers. You should verify that you know what proper settings are before you set this option. Following are the options that can be set in this section of the answer file:

- **BitsPerPel** specifies the number of valid bits per pixel for the graphics device.

- **Vrefresh** sets the refresh rate for the graphics device that will be used.

- **Xresolution** specifies the horizontal resolution for the graphics device that will be used.

- **Yresolution** specifies the vertical resolution for the graphics device that will be used.

Converting to NTFS

You can configure the answer file to automatically convert FAT16 or FAT32 partitions during the installation. To convert the drives, you add the following entry:

```
[Unattended]
    FileSystem=ConvertNTFS
```

Installing Applications

You can install applications through unattended installations in a variety of ways. Following are some of the options you can choose:

- Use the Cmdlines.txt file to add applications during the GUI portion of Setup.

- Within the answer file, configure the [GuiRunOnce] section to install an application the first time a user logs on.

- Create a batch file.

- Use the Windows Installer (discussed in the last part of this chapter).

- Use the Sysdiff tool to install applications that do not have automated installation routines. To use the Sysdiff method, install Windows 2000 Professional on a reference computer and take a snapshot of the base configuration. Then add your applications and take another snapshot of the reference computer with the differences. The difference file can then be applied to computers that are being installed through unattended installations.

Using Remote Installation Services (RIS)

You can remotely install Windows 2000 Professional through RIS. A variety of installation options are available through the *Windows 2000 Client Installation Wizard (CIW)*. For RIS installation, you need a RIS server that stores the Windows 2000 Professional operating system files in a shared image folder, and clients that can access the RIS server. Depending on the type of image you will distribute, you may also want to configure answer files so that users need not respond to any Windows 2000 Professional installation prompts. (Answer files are described in the preceding section.)

Microsoft
Exam
Objective

Perform an unattended installation of Windows 2000 Professional.

- Install Windows 2000 Professional by using Windows 2000 Server Remote Installation Services (RIS).

Following are some of the advantages of using RIS for automated installation:

- You can remotely install Windows 2000 Professional.

- The procedure simplifies management of the server image by allowing you to access Windows 2000 distribution files and use Plug and Play hardware detection during the installation process.

- You can quickly recover the operating system in the event of a computer failure.

- Windows 2000 security is retained when you restart the destination computer.

Here are the basic steps of the RIS process:

1. The RIS client initiates a special boot process through the PXE network card (and the computer's BIOS configured for a network boot), or through a special remote boot disk. On a PXE client, the client presses F12 to boot to PXE.

2. The client computer sends out a DHCP discovery packet that requests an IP address for the client and the IP address of a RIS server. Within the discovery packet, the client also sends its Globally Unique Identifier (GUID).

3. If the DHCP server and RIS server are on the same computer, the information requested in the discovery packet is returned. If the DHCP server and the RIS server are on separate networks, the DHCP server will return the client information for IP configuration. Then the client will send out another broadcast to contact the RIS server.

4. The client contacts the RIS server using the Boot Information Negotiation Layer (BINL) protocol. The RIS server contacts Active Directory to see if the client is a "known client" and whether it has already been authorized through Active Directory. The authorization process is discussed later in this section.

5. If the client is authorized to access the RIS server, BINL provides to the client the location of the RIS server and the name of the *bootstrap image* (enough software to get the client to the correct RIS server).

6. The RIS client accesses the bootstrap image via the *Trivial File Transfer Protocol (TFTP)*, and the Windows 2000 Client Installation Wizard is started.

7. The RIS client is prompted for a username and password.

8. Depending on the user or group credentials, the user sees a menu offering the operating systems that can be installed. The user sees only the options for the installs determined by the parameters defined on the RIS server.

The following sections describe how to set up the RIS server and the RIS clients, and how to install Windows 2000 Professional through RIS.

RIS Client Options

RIS offers several client installation options. This allows administrators to customize remote installations based on organizational needs. When the client accesses the Windows 2000 Client Installation Wizard (CIW), they see the installation options that have been defined by the administrator. Remote installation options include the following:

Automatically setting up the computer   When you automatically set up the computer, the user sees the option of which operating system will be installed but is not prompted for any configuration settings. If only one operating system is offered, the user does not even have to make any selections and the entire installation process is automatic.

Customizing the setup of the computer   If you configure RIS to support customizing the setup of the computer, then Administrators who install computers within the enterprise can override the RIS settings to specify the name and location of the computer being installed within Active Directory.

Restarting a previous setup attempt   The option to restart a previous setup attempt is used when a remote installation fails prior to completion. The operating system installation will restart when this option is selected from the CIW.

Performing maintenance or troubleshooting   The maintenance and troubleshooting option provides access to third-party troubleshooting and maintenance tools. Examples of tasks that can be completed through this option include updating flash BIOS and using PC diagnostic tools.

Preparing the RIS Server

The RIS server is used to manage and distribute the Windows 2000 Professional operating system to RIS client computers. As explained earlier in this chapter, RIS servers can distribute CD-based images or *RIPrep images*. A CD-based image contains the operating system installation files and can be customized for specific computers through the use of answer files. RIPrep images are based on a preconfigured computer and can contain applications as well as the operating system. RIPrep images are used to deploy Windows 2000 Professional to computers that are configured with typical settings.

The RIS server is configured to specify how client computers will be installed and configured. The Administrator can configure the following options for client computers:

- Define the operating system installation options that will be presented to the user. Based on access permissions from Access Control Lists (ACLs), Administrators can define several installation options, and then allow specific users to select an option based on their specific permissions.

- Define an automatic client-computer naming format, which bases the computer name on a custom naming format. For example, the computer names might be a combination of location and username.

- Specify the default Active Directory location for client computers that are installed through remote installation.

- Pre-stage client computers through Active Directory so that only authorized computers can access the RIS server. This option requires a specified computer name, a default Active Directory location, and identification of RIS servers and the RIS clients they will service.

- Authorize RIS servers so that unauthorized RIS servers can't offer RIS services to clients.

The following steps for preparing the RIS server are discussed in the sections coming up:

1. Make sure that the server meets the requirements for running RIS.

2. Install RIS.

3. Configure and start RIS.

4. Authorize the RIS server through DHCP Manager.

5. Grant users who will perform RIS installations the user right to create computer accounts.

6. Grant users who will perform the RIS installation the Log On as a Batch Job user right.

7. Configure the RIS server to respond to client computers (if this was not configured when RIS was installed).

8. Configure RIS template files (if you wish to customize installation options for different computers or groups).

There is a hands-on exercise to create a RIS server in *MCSE: Windows 2000 Server Study Guide*, 2nd ed., by Lisa Donald with James Chellis (Sybex, 2001).

Meeting the RIS Server Requirements

In order for RIS to work, the computer acting as the RIS server must be a Windows 2000 domain controller or member server. The server on which you will install RIS must meet the hardware requirements for RIS and be able to access the required network services.

Hardware Requirements

The RIS server must meet the following hardware requirements:

- Minimum processor (Pentium 133MHz or higher) and memory (128MB) required for Windows 2000 Server.

- At least two disk partitions, one for the operating system and one for RIS images. The partition that will hold the RIS images should be at least 2GB and be formatted as NTFS.

- A network adapter installed.

Network Services

The following network services must be running on the RIS server or be accessible to the RIS server from another network server:

- TCP/IP must be installed and configured.

- A Dynamic Host Configuration Protocol (DHCP) server, which is used to assign DHCP addresses to RIS clients. (Make sure that your DHCP scope has enough addresses to accommodate all the RIS clients that will need IP addresses.)

- A Domain Name System (DNS) server, which is used to locate the Active Directory controller.

- Active Directory, which is used to locate RIS servers and RIS clients, as well as to authorize RIS clients and manage RIS configuration settings and client installation options.

Installing the RIS Server

You add the RIS server components through the Add/Remove Programs icon in Control Panel. To install the RIS server components on the RIS server, take the following steps:

1. Select Start ➢ Programs ➢ Administrative Tools ➢ Configure Your Server.

2. The Windows 2000 Configure Your Server dialog box appears. Click the Advanced option in the panel on the left, and select Optional Components.

3. Click the Start the Windows Components Wizard option.

4. When the Wizard starts, select the Remote Installation Services option and click the Next button.

5. The Insert Disk dialog box prompts you to insert the Windows 2000 Server CD so that the proper files can be copied. Insert the CD and click the OK button.

6. After the process is complete, you'll see the Completing the Windows Components Wizard dialog box. Click the Finish button.

7. When you see the System Settings Change dialog box, click the Yes button to restart your computer.

As part of the RIS installation, the following services are loaded on the server. These services are required for the RIS server to function properly.

BINL   The *Boot Information Negotiation Layer (BINL)* protocol is used to respond to client requests for DHCP and the CIW.

SIS   The *Single Instance Store (SIS)* manages duplicate copies of images by replacing duplicate images with a link to the original files. The main purpose of this service is to reduce disk space.

SIS Groveler   The *SIS Groveler service* scans the SIS volume for files that are identical. If identical files are found, this service creates a link to the duplicate files instead of storing duplicate files.

TFTP   The *Trivial File Transfer Protocol (TFTP)* is a UDP-based file transfer protocol that is used to download the CIW from the RIS server to the RIS clients.

Configuring and Starting RIS with a CD-Based Image

After you have the RIS server components installed on the RIS server, you can use the RISETUP utility to configure the RIS installation. This utility performs the following actions:

- Locates an NTFS partition that will be used to store the remote image(s)

- Creates the directory structure that will be used for the remote images

- Copies all the files that are required to install Windows 2000 Professional

- Copies the Client Installation Wizard files and screens

- Configures the Remote Installation Service

- Starts the services that are required by RIS, which include BINL, TFTP, and the SIS Groveler service

- Creates a share named Reminist that provides the share for the root of the RIS directory structure

- Creates the appropriate IntelliMirror management *Service Control Point (SCP)* object that is used within Active Directory to support RIS

- Creates the SIS common store directory and the related files that are required to support SIS on the RIS server

With RIS installed, you can configure the RIS server through the following steps:

1. Select Start ➤ Run, type **RISETUP** in the Run dialog box, and click the OK button.

2. When the Remote Installation Services Setup Wizard starts, click the Next button to continue.

3. The Remote Installation Folder Location dialog box appears next. The remote installation folder must be on an NTFS version 5 (or later) partition and must not reside on the same partition as the system or boot partition. Specify the path of the remote installation folder and click the Next button.

4. Next up is the Initial Settings dialog box. Here you configure client support during server configuration. You can specify that the server should respond to client computers requesting service, and that the server should not respond to unknown client computers. You can select one or both options, or leave them both unchecked and configure client support later. Make your selection(s) and click the Next button.

The instructions in this section describe how to use a CD-based image. To create a RIPrep image, run the Remote Installation Service Setup Wizard on a Windows 2000 Professional computer that has been configured to be used as an image.

5. In the Installation Source Files Location dialog box that appears next, specify the location of the Windows 2000 Professional distribution files and click the Next button.

6. In the Windows Installation Image Folder Name dialog box, specify the name of the folder to be used for the Windows 2000 Professional distribution files and click the Next button.

7. The Friendly Description and Help Text dialog box appears next. Here you specify a friendly name and help text to help users select the Windows installation image. Enter a name and text, and click Next to continue.

8. The Review Settings dialog box appears next, where you confirm your installation choices. If all of the settings are correct, click the Finish button.

9. The installation files will be copied, which can take several minutes. When the process is complete, click the Done button.

Authorizing the RIS Server through DHCP Manager

In order for a RIS server to respond to client requests, the DHCP server must be authorized through the Active Directory. By authorizing DHCP servers, you ensure that rogue DHCP servers do not assign client IP addresses. You'll learn more about DHCP in Chapter 11, "Managing Network Connections." To authorize the DHCP server, take the following steps:

1. Select Start ➤ Programs ➤ Administrative Tools ➤ DHCP.

2. In the left pane of the DHCP window, right-click your DHCP server. From the pop-up menu, select Authorize, as shown in Figure 2.12.

FIGURE 2.12 Authorizing a DHCP server

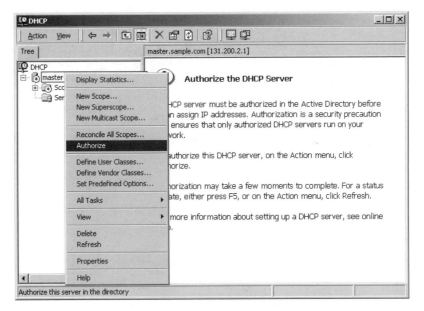

3. Close the DHCP console.

 Use this same process to authorize the RIS server.

Granting the User Right to Create Computer Accounts

In order to install an image using RIS, users must have the user right to create a computer account in the Active Directory. You can specify that users can create accounts anywhere in the domain, or that users can create computer accounts only in specific organizational units.

To grant the user right to create computer accounts, take the following steps:

1. Select Start ➢ Programs ➢ Administrative Tools ➢ Active Directory Users and Computers.

2. The Active Directory Users and Computers window appears, as shown in Figure 2.13. Right-click the domain or organizational unit where you want to allow users to create computer accounts and select Delegate Control from the pop-up menu.

FIGURE 2.13 The Active Directory Users and Computers window

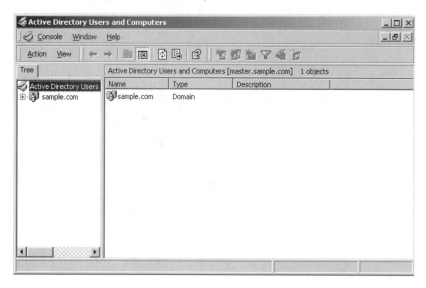

3. The Delegation of Control Wizard starts. Click the Next button to continue.

4. In the Users or Groups dialog box (Figure 2.14), click the Add button.

FIGURE 2.14 The Users or Groups dialog box

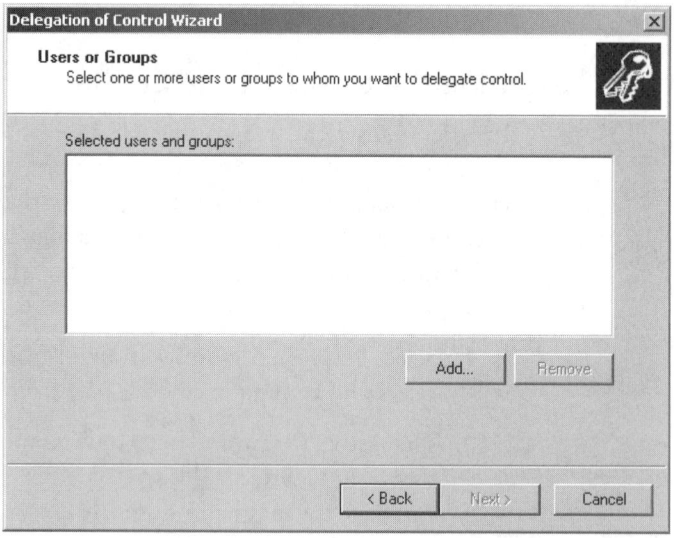

5. The Select Users, Computers, or Groups dialog box appears next, as shown in Figure 2.15. Select the users or groups that will use RIS to install Windows 2000 Professional, click the Add button, and click OK.

FIGURE 2.15   The Select Users, Computers, or Groups dialog box

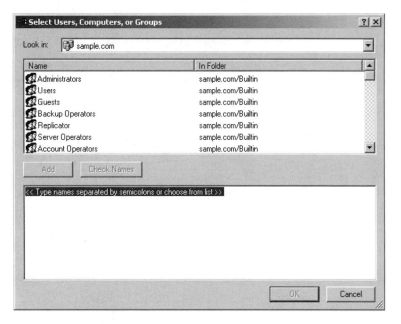

6. When you return to the Users or Groups dialog box, click the Next button to continue.

7. In the Tasks to Delegate dialog box, select the check box Join a Computer to the Domain and then click the Next button.

8. In the Completing the Delegation of Control dialog box, verify that all the configuration options are correct and click the Finish button.

9. Close the Active Directory Users and Computers window.

Active Directory is covered in detail in *MCSE: Windows 2000 Directory Services Administration Study Guide,* 2nd ed., by Anil Desai with James Chellis (Sybex, 2001).

Granting the User Right to Log On as a Batch Job

The user account that will perform the remote installation must have the user right that allows logging on as a batch job. By default, the Administrators group does not have this user right. To assign the Log On as a Batch Job user right, take the following steps:

1. Add the Group Policy snap-in to the MMC administrator console. (The MMC and snap-ins are covered in Chapter 4, "Configuring the Windows 2000 Environment." Adding the Group Policy snap-in and assigning user rights are covered in Chapter 6, "Managing Users.")

2. Expand Local Computer Policy, then Computer Configuration, then Windows Settings, then Security Settings, then Local Policies, and User Rights Assignment.

3. Double-click the Log On as a Batch Job user right.

4. The Local Security Policy Setting dialog box appears, as shown in Figure 2.16. Click the Add button.

5. The Select Users or Groups dialog box appears. Click the user or group to which you want to assign this permission, click the Add button, and then click the OK button.

6. You will return to the Local Security Policy Setting dialog box. Click the OK button.

FIGURE 2.16   The Local Security Policy Setting dialog box

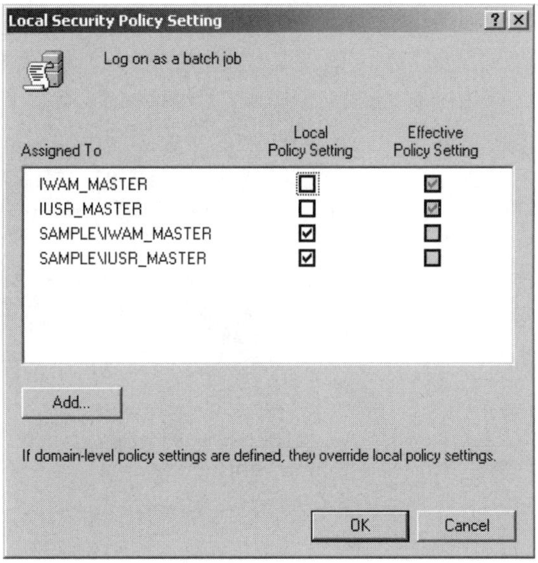

Configuring the RIS Server to Respond to Client Requests

The RIS server must be configured to respond to client requests. You can configure the server response as a part of the RIS server installation or do it later, after the RIS server is installed and ready for client requests. Take the following steps to configure the RIS server to respond to client requests:

1. Select Start ➢ Programs ➢ Administrative Tools ➢ Active Directory Users and Computers.

2. The Active Directory Users and Computers window appears (shown earlier in Figure 2.13). Expand your domain and select Computers or Domain Controllers to access the computer that acts as your RIS server. Right-click the RIS server, and select Properties from the pop-up menu.

3. In the computer's Properties dialog box, select the Remote Install tab to see the dialog box shown in Figure 2.17.

FIGURE 2.17 The Remote Install tab of the computer's Properties dialog box

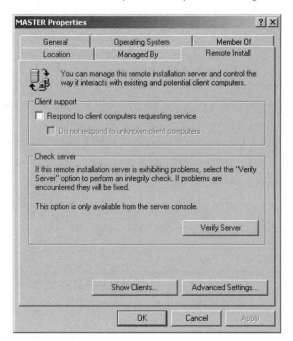

4. Check the Respond to Client Computers Requesting Service check box. Click the OK button.

5. Close the Active Directory Users and Computers window.

Using RIS Template Files

RIS template files are used to specify the installation parameters for your client computers. When you use the RISETUP utility, a standard template called Ristndrd.sif is automatically created. You can have as many template files as you need in order to perform custom installations for different computers, or for groups that require custom configurations such as Sales and Marketing. Template files must have an .sif filename extension.

Preparing the RIS Client

The RIS client is the computer on which Windows 2000 Professional will be installed. RIS clients rely on a technology called PXE (Pre-Boot Execution Environment), which allows the client computer to remotely boot and connect to a RIS server.

In order to act as a RIS client, the computer must meet all the hardware requirements for Windows 2000 Professional (see Chapter 1) and have a network adapter installed. In addition, the RIS client must support one of the following configurations:

- Use a PXE-based boot ROM (a boot ROM is a special chip that uses read-only memory) with a BIOS that supports starting the computer with the PXE-based boot ROM (as opposed to booting from the hard disk).

- Follow the *Net PC* standard for PCs, which uses industry-standard components for the computer. This includes processor, memory, hard disk, video, audio, and an integrated network adapter and modem, in a locked case with limited expandability capabilities. The primary advantages of Net PCs are that they are less expensive to purchase and to manage.

- Have a network adapter that supports PXE and that can be used with a RIS boot disk.

- Follow the Net PC standard, which supports the ability to boot to the network, manage upgrades, and prevent users from changing hardware and operating system configurations.

To create a RIS boot disk, take the following steps:

1. On a Windows 2000 Professional computer that is connected to the same network as the RIS server, select Start ≻ Run. In the Run dialog box, type the following command and click the OK button:

   `\\RIS_Server\Reminst\Admin\I386\Rbfg.exe`

2. The Windows 2000 Remote Boot Disk Generator dialog box appears, as shown in Figure 2.18. Insert a blank floppy disk in your computer, select the appropriate destination drive, select the installed network card from the Adapter List, and click the Create Disk button.

FIGURE 2.18 The Windows 2000 Remote Boot Disk Generator dialog box

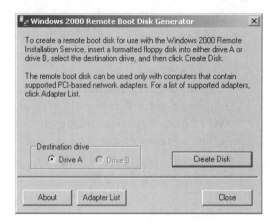

3. You see a message verifying that the boot floppy was created and asking whether you want to create another disk. You can click Yes and repeat the procedure to create another boot disk, or click No. After you are finished creating RIS boot disks, click the Close button.

Installing Windows 2000 Professional through RIS

After the RIS server has been installed and configured, you can install Windows 2000 Professional on a RIS client that uses either a PXE-compliant network card or a RIS boot disk with a network card that supports PXE.

To install Windows 2000 Professional on the RIS client, take the following steps:

1. Start the computer. When prompted, press F12 for a network service boot.

2. The Client Installation Wizard starts. Press Enter to continue.

3. The Windows 2000 Logon dialog box appears. Specify the domain to which you will log on, and enter a valid domain username and password.

4. A menu appears with the options Automatic Setup, Custom Setup, Restart a Previous Setup Attempt, and Maintenance and Troubleshooting. Select Automatic Setup.

If you have only one RIS image, it will automatically be installed. If you have multiple RIS images, the user will see a menu of RIS images. After you select a RIS image, the remote installation process will start. What happens next depends on the image type and whether you have configured answer files.

Using Disk Images

You can use disk images to install Windows 2000 Professional on several computers that have the same configuration. Also, if a computer is having technical difficulties, you can use a disk image to quickly restore it to a baseline configuration.

Microsoft ✔ *Exam Objective*	**Perform an unattended installation of Windows 2000 Professional.** • Install Windows 2000 Professional by using the System Preparation Tool.

In order to create a disk image, you install Windows 2000 Professional on the source computer with the configuration that you want to copy. The source computer's configuration should also include any applications that should be installed.

Once you have your source computer configured, you use the System Preparation Tool (Sysprep) to prepare the disk image for disk duplication. After you've created the disk image, you can copy the image to destination computers through third-party software or through hardware disk duplication.

Preparing for Disk Duplication

In order to use a disk image, the source and target computers must meet the following requirements:

- Both the source and destination computers must have the same type of mass-storage controller (SCSI or IDE).

- Both the source and destination computers must have the same HAL (Hardware Abstraction Layer). This means the processor type must be the same on both computers.

- The size of the destination computer's hard drive must be at least as large as the source computer's hard drive.

- Plug and Play devices on the source and destination computers do not need to match, as long as the drivers for the Plug and Play devices are available.

Using the System Preparation Tool

The System Preparation Tool is included on the Windows 2000 Professional CD in the \Support\Tools folder, in the `Deploy.cab` file. When you run this utility on the source computer, it strips out information from the master copy that must be unique for each computer, such as the security ID (SID).

After you install the copied image on the target computer, a Mini-Setup Wizard runs. This Wizard automatically creates a unique computer SID and then prompts the user for computer-specific information, such as the product ID, regional settings, and network configuration. The required information can also be supplied through an automated installation script.

Following are some of the command switches that you can use to customize the System Preparation Tool's operation:

`-quiet`	Runs the installation with no user interaction
`-pnp`	Forces Setup to run Plug and Play detection of hardware
`-reboot`	Restarts the target computer
`-nosidgen`	Doesn't create an SID on the destination computer (used with disk cloning)

After you run the System Preparation Tool on a computer, you need to run the Setup Manager Wizard to reconfigure all of the unique information for the computer. Run this utility only on source reference computers that will be used for disk duplication purposes.

Creating a Disk Image

To run the System Preparation Tool and create a disk image, take the following steps:

1. Install Windows 2000 Professional on a source computer. (See Chapter 1 for instructions on installing Windows 2000 Professional.)

2. Log on to the source computer as Administrator and, if desired, install and configure any applications that also should be installed on the target computer.

3. Extract the `Deploy.cab` file from the Windows 2000 Professional CD. (See "Extracting Windows 2000 Deployment Tools" earlier in this chapter for instructions on extracting this file.)

4. Select Start ➤ Run and click the Browse button in the Run dialog box. Select Local Drive (C:), Deployment Tools, double-click Sysprep, and click the OK button.

5. The Windows 2000 System Preparation Tool dialog box appears, as shown in Figure 2.19. This dialog box warns you that the execution of this program will modify some of the computer's security parameters. Click the OK button.

FIGURE 2.19   The Windows 2000 System Preparation Tool dialog box

6. You will be prompted to turn off your computer.

In Exercise 2.2, you will use the System Preparation Tool to prepare the computer for disk imaging. In Exercise 2.3, you will complete the Windows 2000 Professional installation on the target computer. These exercises assume that you have completed Exercise 2.1.

EXERCISE 2.2

Using the System Preparation Tool

1. Log on to the source computer as Administrator and, if desired, install and configure any applications that also should be installed on the target computer.

2. Select Start ➤ Run and click the Browse button. Select Local Drive (C:), Deployment Tools. Double-click Sysprep and click the OK button.

3. In the Windows 2000 System Preparation Tool dialog box, click the OK button.

4. When prompted, turn off your computer.

Copying and Installing from a Disk Image

After you've run the System Preparation Tool on the source computer, you can copy the image and then install it on the target computer.

If you are using special hardware (a disk duplicator) to duplicate the disk image, shut down the source computer and remove the disk. Copy the disk and install the copied disk into the target computer. If you are using special software, copy the disk image per the software vendor's instructions.

After the image is copied, turn on the destination computer. The Mini-Setup Wizard runs and prompts you as follows (if you have not configured an answer file):

- Accept the End User License Agreement.

- Specify regional settings.

- Enter a name and organization.

- Specify your product key.

- Specify the computer name and Administrator password.

- Specify dialing information (if a modem is detected).

- Specify date and time settings.

- Specify which networking protocols and services should be installed.

- Join a workgroup or a domain.

If you have created an answer file for use with disk images, as described in the earlier section "Using Setup Manager to Create Answer Files," the installation will run without requiring any user input.

In Exercise 2.3, you will use the stripped image that was created in Exercise 2.2 to simulate the process of continuing an installation from a disk image.

EXERCISE 2.3

Installing Windows 2000 Professional from a Disk Image

1. Turn on your computer. The Windows 2000 Setup Wizard will start. Click the Next button to continue (this will happen automatically if you don't click the Next button after about 10 seconds).

2. In the License Agreement dialog box, click the I Accept This Agreement option and click the Next button.

3. In the Regional Settings dialog box, click Next to accept the default settings and continue.

4. In the Personalize Your Software dialog box, enter your name and organization. Then click the Next button.

5. In the Your Product Key dialog box, type the 25-character product key and click the Next button.

6. In the Computer Name and Administrator Password dialog box, specify the computer name and an Administrator password (if desired). Then click the Next button.

7. If you have a modem installed, the Modem Dialing Information dialog box appears. Specify your dialing configuration and click the Next button.

8. In the Date and Time Settings dialog box, specify the date, time, and time zone. Then click the Next button.

9. In the Network Settings dialog box, verify that Typical Settings is selected and click the Next button.

10. In the Workgroup or Computer Domain dialog box, verify that the No, This Computer Is Not on a Network, or Is on a Network without a Domain Controller option is selected and click the Next button.

11. When the Completing the Windows 2000 Setup Wizard dialog box appears, click the Finish button.

12. When the computer restarts, start Windows 2000 Professional.

13. When the Network Identification Wizard starts, click the Next button.

14. In the Users of This Computer dialog box, select the Users Must Enter a User Name and Password to Use This Computer option and click the Next button.

15. When the Completing the Network Identification Wizard dialog box appears, click the Finish button.

16. Log on to the computer as Administrator.

Installing Applications with Windows Installer Packages

With Windows 2000, you can easily distribute new applications through *Windows Installer packages*, which are special application distribution files. In order to use Windows Installer packages, you must have a Windows 2000 server configured as a domain controller (so that Active Directory is running).

Microsoft
Exam
Objective

Manage applications by using Windows Installer packages.

Windows Installer packages work with applications that are one of the following file types:

- *Microsoft Installer (MSI)* format files, which are usually provided by the software vendor. They support components such as on-demand installation of features as they are accessed by users.

- Repackaged applications (MSI files) that do not include the native Windows Installer packages. Repackaged applications are used to provide users with applications that can be cleanly installed, are easily deployed, and can perform self-diagnosis and repair.

- ZAP files, which are used if you do not have MSI files. ZAP files are used to install applications using their native Setup program.

If your application includes a modification tool, you can create customized application installations that include specific features of the application through the use of modification (.mst) files.

Windows Installer packages work as *published applications* or *assigned applications*. When you publish an application, users can choose whether or not they will install the application through the Control Panel Add/Remove Programs icon. When you assign an application to users or computers, the package is automatically installed when the user selects the application on the Programs menu or via document invocation (by the document extension).

The primary steps for using Windows Installer packages to distribute applications are as follows, and are discussed in the sections coming up:

1. Copy the MSI application to a network share.

2. Create a Group Policy object (GPO) for the application.

3. Filter the GPO so only authorized users can access the application.

4. Add the package to the GPO.

5. If it is a published application, install it through the Control Panel Add/Remove Programs icon.

Copying the MSI Application to a Share

As noted earlier, Windows Installer works with MSI applications. Applications that use the MSI standard will include a file with an .msi extension on the application's distribution media. Create a network share that will be used to store the application, and copy the .msi file to the network share. For example, suppose Windows 2000 Server Administrative Tools is the sample application that you want to distribute. You would copy the application file named Adminpak.msi from the Windows 2000 Server CD \I386 folder to the D:\Packages\AdminTools folder on the Windows 2000 Server domain controller.

 If you have an application that does not use MSI, you can still deploy the program by creating your own MSI file. To help you create your own MSI file, Microsoft provides VERITAS Software Console and WinINSTALL LE Discover. This software is available in the *Microsoft Windows 2000 Server Resource Kit* (Microsoft Press, 2000).

Creating a Group Policy Object

Your next step in preparing an application for distribution is to create a GPO on a Windows 2000 Server domain controller. To create a GPO, take the following steps:

1. Select Start ➢ Programs ➢ Administrative Tools ➢ Active Directory Users and Computers.

2. Right-click your domain name and select Properties from the pop-up menu. Click the Group Policy tab.

3. In the Group Policy tab (Figure 2.20), click the New button.

FIGURE 2.20 The Group Policy tab of the domain Properties dialog box

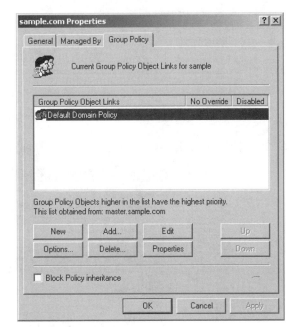

4. A new Group Policy Object will be created. Specify the new GPO name (for this example, type **AdminTools**).

Filtering the Group Policy Object

After you've created the GPO, you must filter it so that only authorized users will be able to install the application. To filter a GPO, take the following steps:

1. In the Group Policy tab of the domain Properties dialog box (see Figure 2.20), highlight the group policy (AdminTools) you created and click the Properties button.

2. The GPO's Properties dialog box appears. Click the Security tab (see Figure 2.21).

   a. Remove permissions from all groups except Domain Admins and SYSTEM, by highlighting the group and clicking the Remove button.

   b. For the Domain Admins group, click the Allow boxes to set these permissions: Read, Write, Create All Child Objects, Delete All Child Objects, and Apply Group Policy.

FIGURE 2.21 The Security tab of the GPO's Properties dialog box, with default settings

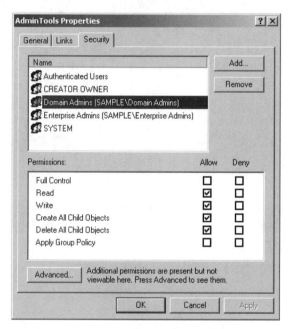

3. Click the OK button to close the GPO's Properties dialog box.

Adding the Package to the Group Policy Object

The next step in preparing to use a Windows Installer is to add the package (.MSI) to the GPO you created for it. You can configure the package so that it is published or assigned to a user or a computer. Published applications are advertised through the Add/Remove Programs utility. Assigned applications are advertised through the Programs menu.

If you are configuring the package for a user, you add the package to the User Configuration\Software Settings\Software installation. If the package is for a computer, you add it to the Computer Configuration\Software Settings\Software installation. In this example, the application will be published for users. To publish an application, take the following steps:

1. In the Group Policy tab of the domain Properties dialog box (see Figure 2.20), highlight the group policy (AdminTools) and click the Edit button.

2. The Group Policy window appears, as shown in Figure 2.22. Expand User Configuration, then Software Settings.

FIGURE 2.22 The Group Policy window

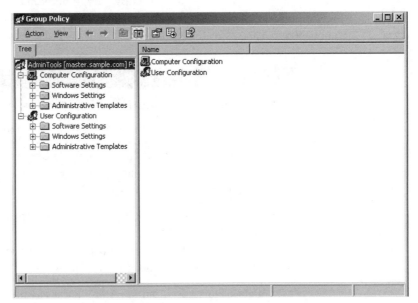

3. Right-click Software Installation and select New ➢ Package. Specify the location of the software package and click the Open button.

4. The Deploy Software dialog box appears next, as shown in Figure 2.23. Here, you'll specify the deployment method. The options are Published, Assigned, and Advanced Published or Assigned. For this example, select Published and click the OK button.

FIGURE 2.23 Specifying the deployment method

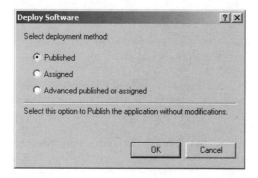

If you have access to a Windows 2000 domain controller, you can complete the steps in Exercise 2.4 to publish an application. You will also need to have access to the Windows 2000 Server CD.

EXERCISE 2.4

Publishing an Application with Windows Installer

1. Select Start ➢ Programs ➢ Accessories ➢ Windows Explorer.

2. In Windows Explorer, double-click My Computer and double-click Local Disk (C:). Select File ➢ New ➢ Folder and type in the name **AdminTools**.

3. Insert the Windows 2000 Server CD and copy the application file named I386\Adminpak.msi from the CD to the C:\AdminTools folder. Right-click the AdminTools folder and select Sharing. Select the Share This Folder option and click the OK button.

4. Select Start ➢ Programs ➢ Administrative Tools ➢ Active Directory Users and Computers.

5. In the Active Directory Users and Computers window, right-click your domain name and select Properties. Click the Group Policy tab. Click the New button and enter the name **AdminTools**.

6. Highlight the AdminTools package and click the Properties button. Click the Security tab. Remove permissions from all groups except Domain Admins and SYSTEM by highlighting each group and clicking the Remove button. For the Domain Admins group, check the Allow boxes to allow the Read, Write, Create All Child Objects, Delete All Child Objects, and Apply Group Policy permissions. Click the OK button.

7. Highlight the AdminTools package and click the Edit button. Expand User Configuration, then Software Settings. Right-click Software Installation and select New ➤ Package.

8. Specify the network location (based on your computer name and the share name) of the software package and click the Open button.

9. In the Deploy Software dialog box, specify the deployment method Published, then click the OK button.

Installing a Published Application

After the application (package) has been published, users who have permission to access the application can install it on a Windows 2000 Professional computer that is a part of the same domain that contains the application. The published application is available through the Add/Remove Programs icon in Control Panel. In the Add/Remove Programs utility, click the Add New Programs option, and you will see the published application listed in the dialog box. Select the application and click the Add button to install it.

Real World Scenario

Publishing Software Applications

Your company uses a variety of applications. You only want to install the applications on computers where a particular application will actually be used, so that you can manage your costs for software licensing. However, you don't want the IT staff running around constantly installing applications all over the enterprise.

You decide to use Windows Installer packages to automatically install applications when users try to access files with filename extensions matching applications associated with Windows Installer packages. The first application you installed was ABC.MSI version 1.0. When the new version, ABC.MSI 2.0, became available, you added the upgraded software to the list of published applications. However, users are complaining that when they invoke ABC files, the older version of the software is being installed.

To correct this problem, you need to edit the order of software listed within the GPO so that the newer version of ABC.MSI is listed before the older version of the software. You should also configure the upgrade to be mandatory so that all of your users will be using the same version of the software.

If you completed Exercise 2.4, you can follow the steps in Exercise 2.5 to install the published application.

EXERCISE 2.5

Installing a Published Application

1. Log on to a Windows 2000 Professional computer that is a part of the domain that contains the published application. Log on as a user who has permission to access the application.

2. Select Start ➢ Settings ➢ Control Panel. Double-click the Add/Remove Programs icon, then click the Add New Programs option.

3. The published application (AdminTools) is listed in the dialog box. To install the application, highlight it and click the Add button.

Summary

In this chapter, you learned how to install Windows 2000 Professional through automated installation. We covered the following topics:

- An overview of the three common methods for automated installation, which include remote installation, disk imaging, and unattended installations

- Using unattended answer files to automatically respond to the queries that are generated during a normal installation process

- How to use RIS, including installing and configuring the RIS server as well as the requirements for the RIS clients

- Creating disk images using the System Preparation Tool (Sysprep)

- Installing applications through Windows Installer packages

Exam Essentials

Know the difference between unattended installation methods. Understand the various options available for unattended installations of Windows 2000 Professional and when it is appropriate to use each installation method.

Know how to use Setup Manager to create answer files. Understand how to access and use Setup Manager to create answer files. Be able to edit the answer files and know the basic options that can be configured for answer files.

Understand the features and uses of RIS. Know when it is appropriate to use RIS to manage unattended installations. Be able to list the requirements for setting up RIS servers and RIS clients. Be able to complete an unattended installation using RIS.

Be able to use Disk Images for unattended installations. Know how to perform unattended installations of Windows 2000 Professional using disk images.

Be able to install applications using Windows Installer packages.
Know the requirements for installing applications using Windows
Installer packages, and understand how to successfully deploy those
packages.

Key Terms

Before taking the exam, you should be familiar with the following
terms:

answer file	Remote Installation Services (RIS)
assigned applications	Setup Manager (SETUPMGR)
Boot Information Negotiation Layer (BINL)	Single Instance Store (SIS)
bootstrap image	SIS Groveler Service
Client Installation Wizard (CIW)	System Preparation Tool (Sysprep)
disk imaging	Trivial File Transfer Protocol (TFTP)
Microsoft Installer (MSI)	unattended installation
Net PC	Windows Installer packages
Pre-Boot Execution Environment (PXE)	Windows 2000 Deployment Tools
published applications	ZAP files
remote installation	
Remote Installation Preparation (RIPrep) image	

Review Questions

1. Your company has decided to use RIS services to install 100 client computers. You have set up the RIS server and now want to test a single RIS client to make sure that the installation will go smoothly. In the following diagram, select and place the servers that need to be on the network in order to support the RIS installation.

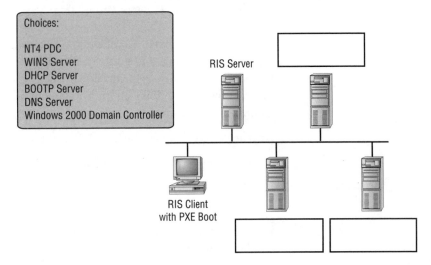

Choices:

NT4 PDC
WINS Server
DHCP Server
BOOTP Server
DNS Server
Windows 2000 Domain Controller

RIS Server

RIS Client
with PXE Boot

2. You want to use RIS to install 50 client computers. Half of the clients are PXE compliant, and the other half are not. The computers that are not PXE compliant are listed on the HCL and have network cards, which can work with a RIS boot disk. What command should you run to create a RIS boot disk?

   A. RBFG

   B. PXEBOOT

   C. RIPREP

   D. RISBOOT

3. You are in charge of developing a plan to install 200 Windows 2000 Professional computers in your company's data center. You decide to use RIS. What command should you use to configure the RIS server?

   A. RIPREP

   B. RISCONFIG

   C. RISETUP

   D. The RIS icon in Control Panel

4. Your company has a variety of client computers that are running Windows 98. You want to upgrade these machines to Windows 2000 using RIS. What requirement must be met on a client computer in order to install Windows 2000 Professional from a RIS server? Choose two answers.

   A. The computer must use a PXE-based boot ROM.

   B. The computer must use a RIPrep-based boot ROM.

   C. The computer must use a RIS boot disk with any network adapter that supports RIPrep.

   D. The computer must use a RIS boot disk with a network adapter that supports PXE.

5. You are creating an UNATTENDED.TXT file that will be used in conjunction with unattended installations. The computers on which Windows 2000 Professional will be installed currently have FAT32 partitions. You want to convert the partitions to NTFS during the unattended installation. Which of the following options should you use in the file?

   A. [Unattended]
      FileSystem=ConvertNTFS

   B. [FileSystem]
      FileSystem=ConvertNTFS

   C. [Unattended]
      FileSystem=NTFS

   D. [FileSystem]
      FileSystem=NTFS

6. Curtis wants to use RIS to install 25 Windows 2000 Professional computers. He does not want to create the answer files with a text editor. What other program can he use to create unattended answer files?

A. UAF

B. Answer Manager

C. Setup Manager

D. SYSPREP

7. Mike recently published a software upgrade of the ABC.MSI program through Windows Installer packages using a group policy. When users invoke documents associated with this application, they are still installing the older version of the application. What does Mike need to do to ensure that the latest version of the software is installed on all of the client computers? Select two answers.

A. Specify that the upgrade is mandatory.

B. Configure the newer version of the application with high priority.

C. Make sure that the newest version of the application is listed at the top of the GPO.

D. Configure the newest version of the application with a .ZAP extension.

8. Bob is using RIS to install 100 clients that are identically configured. The first 65 computers are installed with no problems. When he tries to install the other 35, he receives an error and the installation process will not begin. Which of the following would cause this failure?

A. The RIS server has been authorized to serve only 65 clients.

B. The WINS server is no longer available.

C. The DHCP server does not have enough IP addresses to allocate to the RIS clients.

D. The network bandwidth has become saturated.

9. Mike wants to use Windows Installer packages to install the ABC.MSI application. Which of the following services must be running on the network in order to support the use of Windows Installer packages?

   A. DHCP

   B. WINS

   C. Installer

   D. Active Directory

10. You run a training department that needs the same software installed from scratch on the training computers each week. You decide to use third-party software to deploy disk images. Which Windows 2000 utility can you use in conjunction with third-party imaging software to create these disk images?

    A. UAF

    B. Answer Manager

    C. Setup Manager

    D. Sysprep

11. You are trying to decide whether or not you want to use RIS as a method of installing Windows 2000 Professional within your company. Which of the following options is *not* an advantage of using a RIS automated installation?

    A. The Windows 2000 security is retained when you restart the computer.

    B. Plug and Play hardware detection is used during the installation process.

    C. Unique information is stripped out of the installation image so that it can be copied to other computers.

    D. You can quickly recover the operating system in the event of a system failure.

12. You want to install a RIS server to be used in deploying Windows 2000 Professional. Which of the following is *not* a requirement for configuring the RIS server?

   A. The remote installation folder must be NTFS version 5 or later.

   B. The remote installation folder must reside on the system partition.

   C. You need to configure the RIS server through the RISETUP command.

   D. The DHCP server must be authorized through the Active Directory.

13. You are using RIS to install 20 Windows 2000 Professional computers. When the clients attempt to use RIS, they are not able to complete the unattended installation. You suspect that the RIS server has not been configured to respond to client requests. Which one of the following utilities would you use to configure the RIS server to respond to client requests?

   A. Active Directory, Users and Computers

   B. Active Directory, Users and Groups

   C. RIS Manager

   D. RISMAN

14. You want to install a group of 25 computers using disk images created through Sysprep. Your plan is to clone a reference computer and then copy the clone to all the machines. You do not want to create a SID on the destination computer when you use the image. Which Sysprep command-line switch should you use to set this up?

   A. -nosid

   B. -nosidgen

   C. skipsid

   D. -quiet

15. You are attempting to install an application through the Microsoft Installer program. You realize that the application you want to install does not have Microsoft Installer files. What types of file can you use with this application to install it through Windows Installer packages?

A. ZAW files

B. ZIP files

C. ZAP files

D. MSI files

Answers to Review Questions

1.

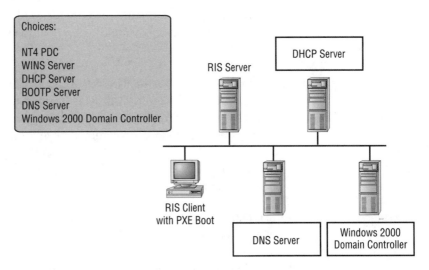

Choices:

NT4 PDC
WINS Server
DHCP Server
BOOTP Server
DNS Server
Windows 2000 Domain Controller

DHCP Server

RIS Server

RIS Client
with PXE Boot

DNS Server

Windows 2000
Domain Controller

DNS, DHCP, and the Active Directory must be properly configured and running in order for RIS to work.

2. A. You can create a RIS boot disk from any Windows 2000 computer by attaching to *RIS_Server*\REMINST\ADMIN\i386 and running the Rbfg.exe command.

3. C. The RISETUP command is used to configure the RIS server.

4. A, D. In order to act as a RIS client, the client computer must have either a PXE-based boot ROM, or a RIS boot disk with a network adapter that supports PXE.

5. A. You can configure the answer file to automatically convert FAT16 or FAT32 partitions during the installation. To convert the drives, you add the following entry to the UNATTENDED.TXT:

```
[Unattended]
    FileSystem=ConvertNTFS
```

6. C. Setup Manager (SETUPMGR) is used to create unattended answer files.

7. A, C. If you want to require all users to use the most updated software, you should configure the upgrade as mandatory. The newest version of the software should be listed at the top of the GPO.

8. C. In order to access the RIS server, the RIS clients must be able to access the DHCP server. Each RIS client will use an IP address from the DHCP server's scope, so you should ensure that the DHCP server has enough addresses to accommodate all of the RIS clients.

9. D. You must have the Active Directory installed to use Windows Installer packages.

10. D. Once you have a reference computer installed, you can use the Sysprep utility to prepare the computer to be used with disk imaging.

11. C. Unique information is stripped out of the installation image when you use the System Preparation Tool to create a disk image.

12. B. When you configure your RIS server, the remote installation folder can't be on the system partition.

13. A. You enable RIS servers to respond to client requests through the Active Directory Users and Computers utility. In the Remote Install tab of the RIS server Properties dialog box, enable the option Respond to Client Computers Requesting Service.

14. B. The -nosidgen switch prevents SID generation.

15. C. ZAP files are used if you don't have MSI files. ZAP files are used to install applications using their native setup programs.

Chapter

3

Upgrading to Windows 2000 Professional

MICROSOFT EXAM OBJECTIVES COVERED IN THIS CHAPTER:

✓ **Upgrade from a previous version of Windows to Windows 2000 Professional.**

- Apply update packs to installed software applications.
- Prepare a computer to meet upgrade requirements.

Before you attempt to upgrade Windows 2000 Professional, you need to understand the difference between an upgrade and a clean installation. If your previous operating system can be upgraded to Windows 2000 Professional and you want to retain your system settings, then you choose to perform an *upgrade*. If your operating system does not support a Windows 2000 upgrade or if you want to start from scratch, then you choose to perform a *clean installation*. Client upgrade paths and requirements are used to determine if your operating system can be upgraded to Windows 2000 Professional. In order to upgrade, you must be running Windows 9*x* or Windows NT 3.51 or 4, and your hardware must meet the minimum requirements. This chapter covers the requirements for upgrading to Windows 2000 Professional.

You also should consider possible upgrade problems or known issues. This is especially important if you are upgrading from Windows 9*x*, because the upgrading process is not as smooth as it is when you are starting from a Windows NT system. An example of an upgrade issue is lack of support in Windows 2000 for applications or utilities that use virtual device drivers. You'll find a discussion of these issues in this chapter.

There are several tasks you should perform to prepare your computer before you start the upgrade process. This chapter provides an upgrade checklist to help you plan your upgrade strategy. The checklist includes items such as deleting any unnecessary files or applications and taking an inventory of your computer's configuration.

Finally, after you've made your preparations, you are ready for the big moment. Here, you will learn about all of the steps involved in the Windows 2000 upgrade process.

Upgrade packs are used to make any changes to your Windows 9*x* or Windows NT applications that are required to make the application work properly in Windows 2000. The final section of this chapter describes how to apply upgrade packs.

The upgrade processes for Windows 2000 Professional and Server are extremely similar. The major differences involve the client upgrade paths and hardware requirements.

Deciding Whether to Upgrade

An upgrade allows you to preserve existing settings. A *clean install* places Windows 2000 in a new folder. After a fresh install, you need to reinstall all of your applications and reset your preferences.

You should perform an upgrade if the following conditions are true:

- You are running Windows 9*x* or Windows NT Workstation 3.51 or 4.

- You want to keep your existing applications and preferences.

- You want to preserve any local users and groups you've created under Windows NT.

- You want to upgrade your current operating system with the Windows 2000 operating system.

You should perform a clean install if any of the following conditions are true:

- There is no operating system currently installed.

- You have an operating system installed that does not support an upgrade to Windows 2000 (such as DOS or Windows 3.*x*).

- You want to start from scratch, without keeping any existing preferences.

- You want to be able to dual-boot between Windows 2000 and your previous operating system.

Performing a clean install and dual-booting are covered in detail in Chapter 1, "Getting Started with Windows 2000 Professional."

Preparing to Upgrade to Windows 2000 Professional

Like any other major change to your computer, upgrading to Windows 2000 Professional requires some preparatory steps.

Microsoft ✓ *Exam* *Objective*	**Upgrade from a previous version of Windows to Windows 2000 Professional.** • Apply update packs to installed software applications. • Prepare a computer to meet upgrade requirements.

Getting ready to upgrade to Windows 2000 Professional involves the following steps:

- Make sure that your system meets the operating system and hardware requirements.

- Consider upgrade issues, particularly if you're upgrading from Windows 95 or 98.

- Use an upgrade checklist to plan for the upgrade.

These preparations are discussed in detail in the following sections.

Client Upgrade Paths and Requirements

In order to upgrade to Windows 2000 Professional, you must follow a particular path. Only the following operating systems can be directly upgraded to Windows 2000 Professional:

- Windows 95 (all releases)

- Windows 98 (all releases)
- Windows NT Workstation 3.51
- Windows NT Workstation 4

There is no upgrade path from Windows NT Server to Windows 2000 Professional.

If you are running a version of Windows NT Workstation prior to 3.51, you first need to upgrade to Windows NT Workstation 3.51 or Windows NT Workstation 4. Then you can upgrade to Windows 2000 Professional. You cannot upgrade to Windows 2000 Professional from any version of Windows NT Server.

The hardware requirements for upgrading are the same as those for a clean installation. In order to upgrade to Windows 2000 Professional, your computer hardware must meet the following requirements:

- Pentium 133MHz or higher processor
- 64MB of RAM (more memory is recommended)
- 2GB hard drive with at least 650MB of free disk space
- VGA or better resolution monitor

Along with meeting these requirements, your hardware should be listed on the Hardware Compatibility List (HCL). See Chapter 1 for more information about the HCL.

The hardware requirements listed here were those specified at the time this book was published. Check Microsoft's Web site at http://www.microsoft .com/windows2000/upgrade for the most current information.

Upgrade Considerations for Windows 9*x*

The upgrade to Windows 2000 Professional from Windows NT is a smoother process than it is from Windows 9*x*. This is because the Windows NT and Windows 2000 structures have more in common than the Windows 9*x* and Windows 2000 structures do. Therefore, upgrading from Windows 9*x* requires more planning and testing than upgrading from Windows NT.

Compatibility Problems

To assist you in the upgrade process, the Windows 2000 Setup program provides a "report-only" mode, which generates compatibility reports and stores them in a central location. You can then analyze these reports to determine whether your hardware or software applications will port properly from Windows 9*x* to Windows 2000 Professional.

You can generate the Windows 2000 compatibility report in two ways:

- Run `Winnt32/checkupgradeonly`, which will launch the Windows 2000 Setup program, but will only run enough of the Setup procedure to generate the compatibility report.

- Run the Windows 2000 Readiness Analyzer. The Readiness Analyzer can be found at `www.microsoft.com/windows2000/upgrade/compat/default.asp`. After the download, run Chkupgrd.exe.

A compatibility report is automatically generated as part of the Windows 2000 upgrade process. If any of your applications are not compatible with Windows 2000, you may be able to obtain software written by the software vendor to make the application work. This software is in the form of a migration DLL (dynamic link library), which is implemented in an upgrade pack. Upgrade packs are discussed in more detail later in this chapter, in the "Applying Update Packs" section. If an upgrade pack is not available, you will need to get a version of the application that will work with Windows 2000 Professional.

Unsupported Options

Although Windows 9*x* can be upgraded to Windows 2000 Professional, you should be aware that the following options are not supported through the upgrade process:

Applications that use file-system filters   This includes third-party antivirus software and disk-quota management software. These types of file-system filters won't work under Windows 2000. You should contact vendors who use file-system filters for upgraded software supported by Windows 2000 Professional. One example of an error you might see is an MBR (Master Boot Record) error when Windows 2000 reboots during the upgrade. In this case you should verify that the virus checker is disabled.

Any custom power-management solutions or tools   Custom power-management solutions are no longer used, because these features are added through Windows 2000 Advanced Configuration and Power Interface (ACPI) and Advanced Power Management (APM). You should remove any custom power-management solutions or tools prior to running the upgrade process. (The ACPI and APM are covered in Chapter 4, "Configuring the Windows 2000 Environment.")

Any custom Plug and Play solutions   Custom Plug and Play solutions are no longer used, because Windows 2000 has a full set of Plug and Play features. You should remove any custom Plug and Play solutions before starting the upgrade process.

Third-party applications for Windows 9x that support compressed drives, disk defragmenters, and disk utilities   These are not supported by Windows 2000 because it offers native support for disk compression and disk defragmentation (which are discussed in Chapter 9, "Managing Disks"). If you want to use third-party utilities, contact the vendor to get an upgrade of your application that has been written specifically for Windows 2000. If the application can't be upgraded to a Windows 2000–specific version, you should remove the utility prior to running the upgrade process.

Any applications or utilities that use virtual device drivers (VxDs) or 386 drivers   Older 16-bit drivers for Windows 9x were based on VxDs (virtual device drivers). VxDs are not compatible with the Windows 2000 operating system. You can find out if you are using these drivers by checking the [386Enh] section of the System.ini file. Some device drivers use VxDs to provide property pages in property dialog boxes. If you want to continue to use these applications or utilities, you should contact the vendor to get an upgrade of your application or utility that has been written specifically for Windows 2000.

An Upgrade Checklist

Once you have made the decision to upgrade, you should develop a plan of attack. The following upgrade checklist (valid for upgrading from both

Windows 9x and NT) will help you plan and implement a successful upgrade strategy.

- Back up your data and configuration files. Before you make any major changes to your computer's configuration, you should back up your data and configuration files and then verify that you can successfully restore your backup. Chances are if you have a valid backup, you won't have any problems. Chances are if you *don't* have a valid backup, you will have problems.

- Delete any unnecessary files or applications, and clean up any program groups or program items you don't use. Theoretically, you want to delete all the junk on your computer before you upgrade. Think of this as the spring-cleaning step.

- Verify that there are no existing problems with your drive prior to the upgrade. Perform a disk scan, a current virus scan, and defragmentation. These, too, are "spring-cleaning" chores. This step just prepares your drive for the upgrade.

- Uncompress any partitions that have been compressed with DriveSpace or DoubleSpace. You cannot upgrade partitions that are currently compressed.

- Verify that your computer meets the minimum hardware requirements for Windows 2000 Professional. Be sure that all of your hardware is on the HCL.

- Once you verify that your computer and components are on the HCL, make sure you have the Windows 2000 drivers for the hardware. You can verify this with the hardware manufacturer.

- Make sure that your BIOS (Basic Input/Output System) is current. Windows 2000 requires that your computer have the most current BIOS. If it does not, the computer may not be able to use advanced power-management features or device configuration features. In addition, your computer may cease to function during or after the upgrade.

- Take an inventory of your current configuration. This inventory should include documentation of your current network configuration, the applications that are installed, the hardware items and their configuration, the services that are running, and any profile and policy settings.

- Perform the upgrade. In this step, you upgrade from your previous operating system to Windows 2000 Professional.

- Verify your configuration. After Windows 2000 Professional has been installed, use your inventory to verify that the upgrade was successful.

 Real World Scenario

Handling an Upgrade Application Failure

You have a laptop that is running Windows NT 4.0 Workstation. You upgrade the laptop to Windows 2000 Professional and add it to a Windows 2000 Organizational Unit that has default security applied. Your laptop uses an application called XYZ.EXE, which worked perfectly under NT 4.0. After the upgrade, however, you find that you can no longer run XYZ.EXE and suspect that the problem is related to the security settings.

In this case, Windows 2000 provides a template called Compatws.inf, which can be used within the Security Templates utility. (The Security Templates utility is discussed in detail in *MCSE: Windows 2000 Server Study Guide*, 2nd ed., by Lisa Donald with James Chellis, Sybex 2001.) By default, the Windows 2000 permissions are fairly restrictive, which can cause older applications to fail because they were not designed to run under the Windows 2000 environment. The Compatws.inf file corrects this problem by loosening the default permissions so that older applications are more likely to run successfully. However, this environment is not considered a secure one, and an updated application that supports Windows 2000 should be used when available.

The Contingency Plan

Before you upgrade, you should have a contingency plan in place. Your plan should assume the worst-case scenario. For example, what happens if you upgrade and the computer doesn't work anymore? It is possible that, after checking your upgrade list and verifying that everything should work, your attempt at the actual upgrade may not work. If this happens, you may want to return your computer to the original, working configuration.

Indeed, I have made these plans, created my backups (two, just in case), verified my backups, and then had a failed upgrade anyway—only to discover that I had no clue where to find my original operating system CD. A day later, with the missing CD located, I was able to get up and running again. My problem was an older BIOS, and the manufacturer of my computer did not have an updated BIOS.

Performing the Windows 2000 Upgrade

As you would expect, the process of upgrading to Windows 2000 is much simpler than performing a clean installation (as we did in Chapter 1). You pick the system from which you are upgrading, and then follow the Setup Wizard's instructions to provide the information the Setup program needs. The final steps in the upgrade process are automatic.

Exercise 3.1 gives the steps used in the Windows 2000 Professional upgrade process.

To set up your computer to be used for the exercises in this book, in Chapter 1 you installed Windows 2000 Professional from scratch. You would follow the steps in Exercise 3.1 if you were upgrading from your current operating system, and you had not yet performed the clean install procedure outlined in Exercise 1.2.

For the purpose of studying for the MSCE exam with this book, it is recommended that you install Windows 2000 Professional as outlined in Exercise 1.2. If you perform an upgrade instead, you may not be able to complete some of the other exercises in this book successfully.

EXERCISE 3.1

Upgrading to Windows 2000 Professional

1. Insert the Windows 2000 Professional CD into your CD-ROM drive. When the upgrade dialog box appears, click Yes to upgrade. If necessary, select Start ➢ Run ➢ Browse (from Windows NT Workstation 3.51, open Program Manager and select File ➢ Run ➢ Browse), select your CD-ROM drive, open the I386 folder, and launch WINNT32 to bring up the upgrade dialog box.

2. In the Welcome to the Windows 2000 Setup Wizard dialog box, click the Upgrade to Windows 2000 (Recommended) option. Click the Next button to continue.

3. In the License Agreement dialog box, click the option to accept the agreement.

4. In the Product Key dialog box, type in your 25-character product key. Then click the Next button.

5. In the Preparing to Upgrade to Windows 2000 dialog box, click Next to continue.

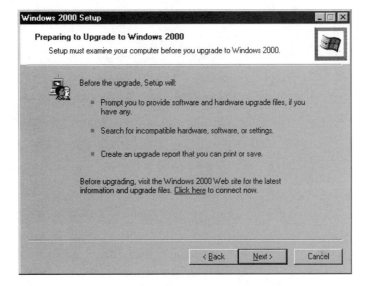

6. In the Provide Upgrade Packs dialog box, select the Yes, I Have Upgrade Packs option if you have obtained upgrade packs for any third-party software applications. Otherwise, select No, I Don't Have Any Upgrade Packs. Then click the Next button.

7. The Upgrading to the Windows 2000 NTFS File System dialog box appears if your computer has FAT16 or FAT32 partitions. Select the No, Do Not Upgrade My Drive option. (You will upgrade to NTFS in an exercise in Chapter 9.) Then click the Next button.

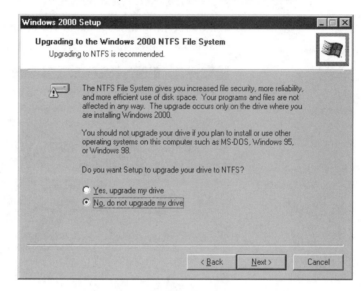

8. The *Upgrade Report* dialog box appears. If this upgrade report shows that errors were found, click the Save As button and specify the filename and location for saving the information. Click the Next button to continue.

EXERCISE 3.1 *(continued)*

9. In the Ready to Install Windows 2000 dialog box, click the Next button. The upgrade process continues automatically, and Windows 2000 Professional will be installed on your computer.

Note: The actual amount of time taken for the upgrade process varies with specific hardware and software configurations. For example, in my test lab, the installation took about 45 minutes.

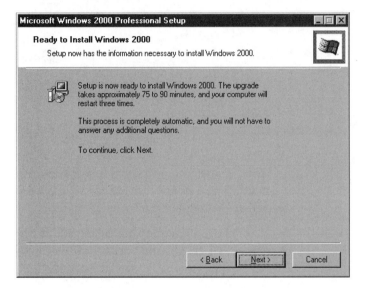

After you install the Windows 2000 Professional upgrade, you can just sit back and relax while the Setup program performs the rest of the upgrade automatically. When the process is complete, Windows 2000 Professional will be installed on your computer. At this point, it's a good idea to verify that everything was upgraded properly. Using the inventory you made before upgrading (see the "Upgrade Checklist" section earlier in the chapter), check to see that your hardware and software have made it through the transition and are working properly.

Applying Update Packs

Theoretically, any applications that you had installed on your previous operating system should work with the upgraded operating system. The upgrade process is supposed to keep all the program groups, and you shouldn't need to reinstall applications to have them work.

Microsoft *Exam* *Objective*	**Upgrade from a previous version of Windows to Windows 2000 Professional.** • Apply update packs to installed software applications. • Prepare a computer to meet upgrade requirements.

In the real world, however, it's possible that some applications will not upgrade properly. In the worst case, the application will disappear after the upgrade, and you will need to reinstall it (as sometimes occurred with Windows NT upgrades). Reasons for an application's not upgrading properly include the following:

- The configuration information must be stored in a part of the Registry different from that used for Windows NT or Windows 9*x*.

- The Registry values used by Windows NT or Windows 9*x* are different from the Registry values that are required by Windows 2000.

- Different versions of files (for example, .dll or .exe) may be required for the application to work properly in Windows 2000.

- The application may make calls specific to the Windows 9*x* operating system that are not supported in Windows 2000.

WARNING If a Windows 9*x* application makes direct calls to the hardware, it may have to be rewritten to work properly with Windows 2000. Windows NT and Windows 2000 do not allow applications to access the hardware directly.

Microsoft recommends that application developers test their applications for Windows 2000 upgrade compatibility. Some applications will upgrade without any problems, but other applications will need help. For third-party software, this help comes in the form of a migration DLL, which is implemented as the upgrade pack in Windows 2000. Third-party vendors may supply migration DLLs through their company's Web site or by distributing disks or CDs to registered users of the applications.

When you run the upgrade process, Windows 2000 should detect any applications that are installed. If any migration DLLs have been installed, they will be applied automatically. You can also specify that upgrade packs be applied during the upgrade process, as seen in Figure 3.1.

FIGURE 3.1   The Provide Upgrade Packs dialog box

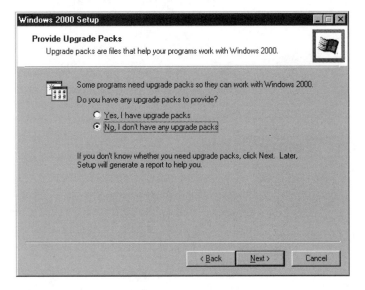

Summary

In this chapter, you learned how to upgrade to Windows 2000 Professional. We covered the following topics:

- Guidelines for when you should upgrade and when you should install a fresh copy of Windows 2000 Professional

- The client upgrade paths that can upgrade to Windows 2000 Professional and the minimum hardware requirements to perform an upgrade

- Upgrade considerations and potential problems with the Windows 2000 Professional upgrade process

- An upgrade checklist with steps to help ensure a successful upgrade

- All of the steps in the Windows 2000 Professional upgrade process

- How to apply update packs to software applications so that they work under Windows 2000 Professional

Exam Essentials

Be able to list the requirements for a Windows 2000 Professional upgrade. Know the requirements for upgrading a computer to Windows 2000 Professional, including what operating systems can be upgraded, what the hardware requirements are, and the steps for completing an upgrade.

Know all the possible issues that may arise during a Windows 2000 Professional upgrade. Be aware of possible upgrade problems. This includes application compatibility, and the fact that other system configurations may work with Windows 9x but will be incompatible with Windows 2000 Professional.

Understand the purpose of an update pack and how it is applied. Know how to apply upgrade packs to change Windows 9x or Windows NT applications in order to make them work properly in Windows 2000.

Key Terms

Before you take the exam, be sure you're familiar with the following key terms:

clean installation or clean install	upgrade pack
upgrade	Upgrade Report

Review Questions

1. Gabriella is in charge of upgrading her office computers to Windows 2000 Professional. Currently the office uses a variety of desktop operating systems. Which of the following operating systems can be upgraded to Windows 2000 Professional? Choose all that apply.

    A. Windows NT Workstation 3.5

    B. Windows NT Workstation 3.51

    C. Windows NT Workstation 4

    D. Windows 95

2. Martina is considering upgrading her Windows 95 computer to Windows 2000. Which of the following three configuration options would cause the most serious difficulties for her upgrade? (Choose all that apply.)

    A. She has applications that are running under Windows 95 and are not specifically written for Windows 2000 Professional.

    B. She has third-party drivers that support compressed drives.

    C. She has third-party applications that use virtual device drivers (VxDs).

    D. She uses custom power-management solutions and tools.

3. Rick wants to upgrade his Windows 95 computer to Windows 2000 Professional. His computer does not have auto-run enabled. Which command would he use to initiate the upgrade?

    A. WIN2K

    B. INSTALL

    C. WINNT

    D. WINNT32

4. Corrine is running an application called ABC.EXE on her Windows 95 computer. The application is configured based on Corrine's preferences. She wants to upgrade her computer to Windows 2000 Professional. The developer of the application has provided a migration option for Windows 2000. During the upgrade process, which option should Corrine use so that the ABC.EXE application will work properly with Windows 2000 Professional after the upgrade?

A. DLL packs

B. Upgrade packs

C. Application packs

D. UPG packs

5. Serena wants to upgrade her Windows 95 computer to Windows 2000. What is the minimum amount of memory required so that her computer can be upgraded to Windows 2000 Professional?

A. 16MB

B. 32MB

C. 64MB

D. 128MB

6. Cindy has a computer that currently has a FAT16 partition, an HPFS partition, an NTFS partition (from NT 4.0 Workstation), and a FAT32 partition (from Windows 98). Which of the following partitions will Windows 2000 recognize during an upgrade? Choose all that apply.

A. FAT16

B. HPFS

C. NTFS

D. FAT32

7. The computers at the XYZ Corporation all use a specialized program called XYZ.EXE. All of the computers are being upgraded to Windows 2000 Professional. The developer of XYZ.EXE has provided update packs to facilitate the upgrade. Which of the following operating systems would most likely require the use of update packs during the upgrade to Windows 2000 Professional? Choose all that apply.

   A. Windows 95

   B. Windows 98

   C. Windows NT Workstation 3.51

   D. Windows NT Workstation 4

8. Dan has several computers that he would like to upgrade to Windows 2000 Professional. He is trying to determine what factors go into determining when an upgrade is appropriate. In which of the following cases would he choose *not* to upgrade to Windows 2000 Professional?

   A. He is currently running Windows 95 and wants to take advantage of the new features of Windows 2000 Professional.

   B. He wants to keep his existing applications and preferences.

   C. He wants to preserve any local users and groups created with Windows NT Workstation.

   D. He wants his computer to be able to dual-boot between his current operating system and Windows 2000 Professional.

9. Catherine has four computers that she wants to upgrade to Windows 2000 Professional. Without doing any hardware upgrades, which of the following computers can she upgrade to Windows 2000 Professional? Choose all that apply.

Computer	Operating System	Processor	Memory	Available Disk Space
Computer A:	Windows 95	Pentium 133MHz	32MB	750MB
Computer B:	Windows NT Workstation 3.5	Pentium 433MHz	64MB	2GB
Computer C:	Windows 95	Pentium 266MHz	64MB	1GB
Computer D:	Windows 98	Pentium 133MHz	128MB	650MB

    A. Computer A

    B. Computer B

    C. Computer C

    D. Computer D

10. Todd is about to upgrade his computer to Windows 2000 Professional. Which of the following tasks should *not* be completed prior to a Windows 2000 upgrade?

    A. Back up all of your data and configuration files.

    B. Perform a virus scan on your computer.

    C. Compress any files that are not frequently used.

    D. Take an inventory of your current configuration.

11. Otto wants to upgrade his computer from Windows NT Workstation 3.5 to Windows 2000 Professional. Which of the following options should he use?

    A. Run WINNT.

    B. Run WINNT32.

    C. Run Upgrade.

    D. First, upgrade to Windows NT 3.51 or Windows NT 4.

12. Which of the following options are features found in Windows update packs? Choose three answers.

    A. Update packs can be used to modify the Registry so that an application will work properly with Windows 2000.

    B. Update packs can be used with computers that dual-boot between different operating systems, so that applications will be recognized by both operating systems.

    C. Update packs are used to update files that must be upgraded to work properly with Windows 2000.

    D. The application may need modification by an update pack so that the application does not make direct calls to the system hardware.

13. Caitlin plans to upgrade her Windows 98 computer to Windows 2000 Professional. She wants to ensure that the upgrade will work as smoothly as possible. Which program should she use to check for compatibility problems prior to a Windows 2000 upgrade?

    A. WINNT with /Checkupgradeonly

    B. WINNT with /Upgrdrpt

    C. WINNT with /Upgradecomp

    D. WINNT with /Chkcomp

14. Kevin wants to upgrade his Windows 95 computer to Windows 2000 Professional. He has read that Windows 2000 does not support VxD drivers and wants to verify that these are not used in his current configuration. How can he tell if the Windows 95 computer is using VxDs, prior to a Windows 2000 upgrade?

   A. Check the `System.ini` file

   B. Check the `Config.ini` file

   C. Check the `Report.ini` file

   D. Check the `Program.ini` file

15. You have Windows 95 installed in your C:\Windows folder. You install Windows 2000 Professional to the C:\WINNT folder. What is the result of this configuration?

   A. You have upgraded to Windows 2000 Professional and will be able to dual-boot to Windows 95.

   B. You have upgraded to Windows 2000 Professional and won't be able to access your Windows 95 operating system.

   C. You have configured your computer to dual-boot and will be able to access the Windows 95 settings, since both installation folders are on the same partition.

   D. You have configured your computer to dual-boot, but you won't be able to access the Windows 95 settings because the operating system files are in different installation folders.

Answers to Review Questions

1. B, C, D. You can upgrade to Windows 2000 Professional from Windows 95, Windows 98, Windows NT 3.51, and Windows NT 4. If you want to upgrade from Windows NT 3.5, you must first upgrade to Windows NT 3.51 or Windows NT 4.

2. B, C, D. Applications that run under Windows 95 will probably work with Windows 2000. The exceptions are applications that use VxDs or disk filters.

3. D. Windows 2000 does not use an Install program for the installation or upgrade. You use WINNT32 to start an upgrade from Windows 9*x*, or Windows NT 3.51 or 4. There is no command called WIN2K.

4. B. The Windows 2000 upgrade process will ask you if you want to provide any upgrade packs. Upgrade packs are used to specify how applications that are upgraded should be configured.

5. C. The memory requirements for an installation and an upgrade are the same. Your computer must have a minimum of 64MB of memory to install or upgrade to Windows 2000 Professional.

6. A, C, D. Windows 2000 will recognize only FAT16, FAT32, and NTFS partitions.

7. A, B. Windows 95 and 98 are more likely to require the use of update packs than Windows NT because Windows 2000 Professional is much more compatible with Windows NT than with Windows 95/98. Windows NT applications will therefore probably upgrade more successfully than will Windows 95 and Windows 98 applications.

8. D. If Dan wants his computer to dual-boot, he should install a clean copy of Windows 2000 Professional instead of upgrading to Windows 2000 Professional.

9. C, D. Computers C and D, with Windows 95 and 98, meet the minimum requirements of upgrading to the Windows 2000 Professional operating system. You must also have a Pentium 133MHz processor or higher, 64MB (or more) of memory, and at least 650MB of free disk space.

10. C. You should not compress any infrequently used files because Windows 2000 will not upgrade a partition that is currently compressed.

11. D. There is no direct upgrade path from Windows NT Workstation 3.5 to Windows 2000 Professional. In order to upgrade from Windows NT 3.5, Otto must first upgrade to Windows NT 3.51 or Windows NT 4.

12. A, C, D. Windows update packs are used to upgrade applications so that they will work properly with Windows 2000. Windows update packs may modify the Registry, update application files, and update calls so that they do not directly access system hardware.

13. A. To test a computer for compatibility issues without actually performing an upgrade, use the `WINNT` command with the `/checkupgradeonly` switch.

14. A. You can determine if you are using VxD or 386 drivers by looking at the `[386Enh]` section of the `System.ini` file.

15. D. If you put the installation files in separate folders, you will create a computer that dual-boots. There will be no sharing of configuration information in this case.

Chapter
4

Configuring the Windows 2000 Environment

MICROSOFT EXAM OBJECTIVES COVERED IN THIS CHAPTER:

✓ **Implement, manage, and troubleshoot disk devices.**
  - Install, configure, and manage DVD and CD-ROM devices.
  - Monitor and configure removable media, such as tape devices.

✓ **Implement, manage, and troubleshoot display devices.**
  - Configure multiple-display support.
  - Install, configure, and troubleshoot a video adapter.

✓ **Implement, manage, and troubleshoot mobile computer hardware.**
  - Configure Advanced Power Management (APM).
  - Configure and manage card services.

✓ **Implement, manage, and troubleshoot input and output (I/O) devices.**
  - Monitor, configure, and troubleshoot I/O devices, such as printers, scanners, multimedia devices, mouse, keyboard, and smart card reader.
  - Monitor, configure, and troubleshoot multimedia hardware, such as cameras.
  - Install, configure, and manage Infrared Data Association (IrDA) devices.
  - Install, configure, and manage wireless devices.
  - Install, configure, and manage USB devices.

✓ **Update drivers.**

✓ **Manage and troubleshoot driver signing.**

✓ **Monitor and configure multiple processing units.**

✓ **Configure and troubleshoot fax support.**

After you've installed Windows 2000 Professional, you will need to install and configure your hardware. The easiest hardware devices to install are those that follow the Plug and Play standard. However, it's not that difficult to install non–Plug and Play hardware through the Add/Remove Hardware utility in Control Panel.

To configure your hardware, you generally use the Computer Management utility or Control Panel. You can also create custom administrative consoles through the Microsoft Management Console (MMC).

In this chapter, you will examine the process of configuring the Windows 2000 environment, beginning with an overview of the main configuration utilities. Then you will learn how to update drivers and manage driver signing. Next, you will see how to configure many different types of hardware, including disk devices, display devices, mobile computer hardware, I/O devices, imaging devices, multiple processors, and fax support. Finally, you will learn how to configure and manage Windows 2000 services.

Windows 2000 Management Utilities

Windows 2000 Professional includes several utilities for managing various aspects of the operating system configuration:

- In Control Panel, you can configure a wide range of options, such as your display, mouse, and system properties.

- The Computer Management utility provides tools for managing common system functions, the computer's storage facilities, and the computer's services.

- The Microsoft Management Console (MMC) provides a common environment for administrative tools.

- The Registry Editor allows you to edit the Registry for advanced system configuration.

Each of these utilities is covered in detail in the following sections.

Control Panel

Control Panel is the main utility for configuring your computer's setup. You can access Control Panel by selecting Start ➢ Settings ➢ Control Panel or by opening My Computer and selecting Control Panel. The Control Panel window contains icons for its various options, as shown in Figure 4.1. Table 4.1 provides brief descriptions of the Control Panel options.

FIGURE 4.1 The Control Panel window

TABLE 4.1   Control Panel Options

Option	Description
Accessibility Options	Options that make Windows 2000 more accessible to users with limited sight, hearing, or mobility
Add/Remove Hardware	Install, remove, and troubleshoot your hardware (primarily used for non–Plug and Play hardware)
Add/Remove Programs	Change or remove programs that are currently installed on your computer, add new programs, and add or remove Windows 2000 components
Administrative Tools	Provides access to Windows 2000 administrative utilities, including Component Services, Computer Management, Data Sources (ODBC), Event Viewer, Local Security Policy, Performance, Services, and Telnet Server Administration
Date/Time	Set the date, time, and time zone for your computer
Display	Configure your computer's display, including background, screen saver, appearance, Active Desktop, and visual effects
Folder Options	Configure folder options, such as general folder properties, file associations, and offline files and folders
Fonts	Manage the fonts installed on your computer
Game Controllers	Add, remove, and configure game controllers, including joysticks and game pads
Internet Options	Configure Internet connection properties, including security, content settings, and Internet programs

TABLE 4.1   Control Panel Options *(continued)*

Option	Description
Keyboard	Configure keyboard settings, including speed, input locales (language and keyboard layout), and the keyboard driver
Mouse	Configure mouse settings, including button configuration, mouse pointers, motion settings, and the mouse driver
Network and Dial-up Connections	Settings for network and dial-up connections, and a Wizard to create new connections
Phone and Modem Options	Configure telephone dialing options and modem properties
Power Options	Configure power schemes, hibernation, APM, and UPS options
Printers	Install and manage printers
Regional Options	Set regional options, including numbers, currency, time, date, and input locales
Scanners and Cameras	Configure cameras and scanners
Scheduled Tasks	Configure tasks to be run at specific times or intervals
Sounds and Multimedia	Configure sound devices and assign sounds to system events
System	Configure system properties, including network identification, hardware, user profiles, and advanced settings
Users and Passwords	A simple tool for managing users and passwords (the Local Users and Groups utility is used for advanced user management, as described in Chapter 6, "Managing Users")

The Control Panel options for configuring hardware devices are described in this chapter. The other options are covered throughout the book. For example, you will learn how to use Accessibility Options, Regional Options, and Display settings in Chapter 5, "Managing the Desktop."

Computer Management

Computer Management provides a single, consolidated tool for managing common management tasks. The interface is organized into three areas:

System Tools   Provides access to utilities for managing the computer, such as Event Viewer and System Information.

Storage   Provides access to utilities for managing the computer's storage, such as Disk Management and Disk Defragmenter.

Services and Applications   Provides access to utilities for managing the computer's services, such as WMI (Windows Management Instrumentation) Control and Indexing Service.

You can access Computer Management by right-clicking the My Computer icon on your Desktop and selecting Manage from the pop-up menu. The main Computer Management window is shown in Figure 4.2. The following sections provide an overview of the utilities that can be accessed through Computer Management.

FIGURE 4.2   The Computer Management window

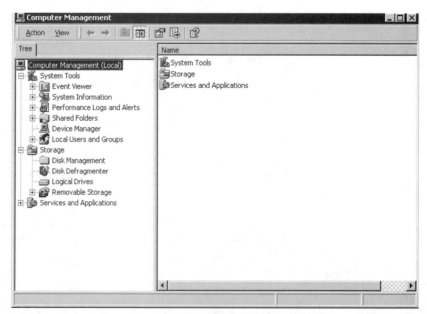

System Tools

System Tools includes six utilities that are used to manage common system functions:

- Event Viewer
- System Information
- Performance Logs and Alerts
- Shared Folders
- Device Manager
- Local Users and Groups

Event Viewer

The *Event Viewer* utility tracks information about your hardware and software. You can also monitor Windows 2000–related security events. The Event Viewer tracks information through three log files:

- The Application log includes events related to applications that are running on the computer, such as SQL Server or Outlook Express application errors.
- The Security log includes events related to security, such as the success or failure of actions monitored through auditing.
- The System log includes events related to the operating system, such as failure to load a device driver.

Using the Event Viewer utility is discussed in detail in Chapter 15, "Performing System Recovery Functions."

System Information

The *System Information* utility is used to collect and display information about the computer's current configuration. This information can be used to troubleshoot your computer's configuration. It can also be printed and kept for reference.

In System Information, the data are organized into five categories by default: System Summary, Hardware Resources, Components, Software Environment, and Internet Explorer 5. Figure 4.3 shows the System Summary folder open, with its contents displayed in the panel on the right.

FIGURE 4.3   The System Information tool in Computer Management

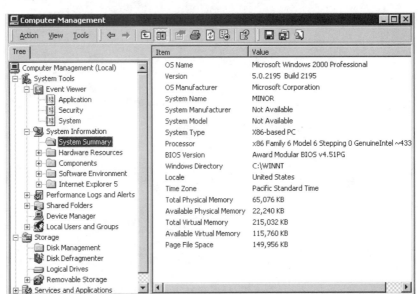

Performance Logs and Alerts

Through the *Performance Logs and Alerts* utility, you can configure logs of performance-related data (called counter logs and trace logs) and generate alerts based on performance-related data. You can view these logs through the Windows 2000 System Monitor utility or through database and spreadsheet applications.

Using the Performance Logs and Alerts utility is discussed in detail in Chapter 14, "Optimizing Windows 2000."

Shared Folders

Through the *Shared Folders* utility, you can create and manage shared folders on the computer. This utility displays the following information:

- All of the shares that have been created on the computer

- The user sessions that are open on each share

- The files that are currently open, listed by user

Chapter 10, "Accessing Files and Folders," includes a discussion of using Shared Folders.

Device Manager

The *Device Manager* utility provides information about all the devices currently recognized by your computer. For each device, Device Manager shows the following information:

- Whether or not the hardware on your computer is working properly
- Settings for the device
- Resources used by the device

From Device Manager, you can load, unload, and update device drivers. You also can print a summary of all the device information for your computer.

Using the Device Manager utility is discussed in the "Installing Non–Plug and Play Hardware," "Updating Drivers," "Managing Disk Devices," and "Troubleshooting Devices" sections later in this chapter.

Local Users and Groups

The *Local Users and Groups* utility is used to manage users and groups on a Windows 2000 Professional computer or on a Windows 2000 Server running as a member server. Chapter 6 discusses working with the Local Users and Groups utility.

Storage

Storage contains four utilities that are used to manage the computer's storage facilities: Disk Management, Disk Defragmenter, Logical Drives, and Removable Storage.

Disk Management

Disk Management is the Windows 2000 graphical interface for managing disks, volumes, partitions, logical drives, and dynamic volumes.

Chapter 9, "Managing Disks," discusses usage of the Disk Management utility.

Disk Defragmenter

The *Disk Defragmenter* utility helps you to analyze and defragment your disk. The purpose of disk defragmentation is to optimize disk access by rearranging existing files so that they are stored contiguously.

The Disk Defragmenter utility is discussed in Chapter 9.

Logical Drives

The *Logical Drives* utility lists all of the logical drives that exist on your computer. Through this utility, you can manage the properties of each logical drive.

Removable Storage

The *Removable Storage* utility provides information about your computer's removable storage media, including CD-ROMs, DVDs, tapes, and jukeboxes containing optical discs.

Services and Applications

Through the Services and Applications utility, you can manage all of the *services* installed on your computer. The services are grouped in three categories: WMI Control, Services, and Indexing Services.

WMI Control

WMI (Windows Management Instrumentation) Control provides an interface for monitoring and controlling system resources. Through WMI Control, you can view WMI status and manage Windows 2000 operations and configuration settings.

Services

Services lists all of the services on your computer. Through Services, you can manage general service properties, the logon account the service uses, and the computer's recovery response if the service fails. This utility also shows any dependencies that the service requires.

Using the Services utility is covered in more detail in the "Managing Windows 2000 Services" section later in this chapter.

Indexing Service

The *Indexing Service* is used to create an index based on the contents and properties of files stored on your local hard drive. A user can then use the Windows 2000 Search function to search through or query the index for specific keywords.

The Indexing Service is not started by default on a Windows 2000 Professional computer. This service is required for successful indexing and query support.

Details on using the Indexing Service are in Chapter 10.

Microsoft Management Console

The *Microsoft Management Console (MMC)* is the console framework for management applications. The MMC provides a common environment for snap-ins, which are administrative tools developed by Microsoft or third-party vendors. The MMC offers many benefits, including the following:

- The MMC console is highly customizable—you add only the snap-ins you need.

- Snap-ins use a standard, intuitive interface, so they are easier to use than previous versions of administrative utilities.

- MMC consoles can be saved and shared with other administrators.

- You can configure permissions so that the MMC runs in authoring mode, which an administrator can manage, or in user mode, which limits what users can access.

- Most snap-ins can be used for remote computer management.

As shown in Figure 4.4, the MMC console contains two panes: a console tree on the left and a details pane on the right. The console tree lists the hierarchical structure of all snap-ins that have been loaded into the console. The details pane contains a list of properties or other items that are part of the snap-in that is highlighted in the console tree.

FIGURE 4.4 The MMC console tree and details pane

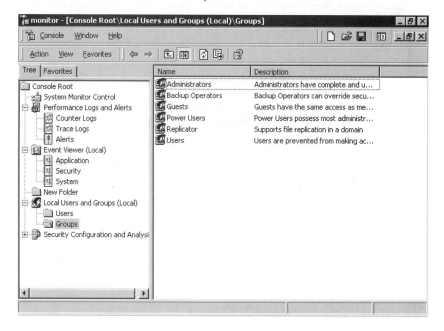

On a Windows 2000 Professional computer, there is no item created for the MMC by default. To open the console, select Start ≻ Run and type **MMC** in the Run dialog box. When you first open the MMC, it contains only the Console Root folder, as shown in Figure 4.5. The MMC does not have any default administrative functionality. It is simply a framework used to organize administrative tools through the addition of snap-in utilities.

FIGURE 4.5 The opening MMC window

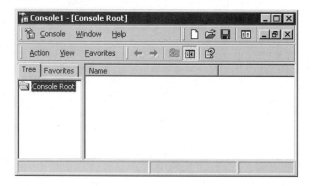

Configuring MMC Modes

You can configure the MMC to run in author mode, for full access to the MMC functions, or in one of three user modes, which have more limited access to the MMC functions. To set a console mode, select Console ➢ Options to open the Options dialog box. In this dialog box, you can select from the console modes listed in Table 4.2.

TABLE 4.2 MMC Console Modes

Console Mode	Description
Author mode	Allows use of all the MMC functions.
User mode–full access	Allows users full access to window management commands, but they cannot add or remove snap-ins.
User mode–limited access, multiple window	Allows users to create new windows, but they can access only the areas of the console tree that were visible when the console was last saved.
User mode–limited access, single window	Allows users to access only the areas of the console tree that were visible when the console was last saved, and they cannot create new windows.

Adding Snap-Ins

To add snap-ins to the MMC console and save it, take the following steps:

1. From the main console window, select Console ➢ Add/Remove Snap-in to open the Add/Remove Snap-in dialog box.

2. Click the Add button to open the Add Standalone Snap-in dialog box.

3. Highlight the snap-in you wish to add, and click the Add button.

4. If prompted, specify whether the snap-in will be used to manage the local computer or a remote computer. Then click the Finish button.

5. Repeat steps 3 and 4 to add each snap-in you want to include in your console.

6. When you are finished adding snap-ins, click the Close button.

7. Click the OK button to return to the main console screen.

8. After you have added snap-ins to create a console, you can save it by selecting Console ➢ Save As and entering a name for your console. You can save the console to a variety of locations, including a program group or the Desktop. By default, custom consoles have an .msc extension.

In exercises in later chapters, you will add MMC snap-ins to create different custom consoles and save them in various locations. This will give you an idea of the flexibility of the MMC and how you can set up custom consoles for your administrative tasks.

Registry Editor

The *Registry* is a database used by the operating system to store configuration information. The Registry Editor program is used to edit the Registry. This utility is designed for advanced configuration of the system. Normally, when you make changes to your configuration, you use other utilities, such as Control Panel.

Only experienced administrators should use the Registry Editor. It is intended for making configuration changes that can only be made directly through the Registry. For example, you might edit the Registry to specify an alternate location for a print spool folder. Improper changes to the Registry can cause the computer to fail to boot. Use the Registry Editor with extreme caution.

Windows 2000 ships with two Registry Editor utilities:

- The *REGEDT32* program is the primary utility for Registry editing in Windows 2000. It supports full editing of the Registry. To use REGEDT32, select Start ➢ Run and type **REGEDT32** in the Run dialog box.

- The *REGEDIT* program is included with Windows 2000 because it has better search capabilities than REGEDT32. However, it is lacking some of the options available with REGEDT32. For example, you can't set security for Registry keys through REGEDIT, and you can't use REGEDIT in read-only mode. To run REGEDIT, select Start ➢ Run and type **REGEDIT** in the Run dialog box.

The Registry is organized in a hierarchical tree format of keys and subkeys that represent logical areas of computer configuration. By default, when you open the Registry Editor, you see five Registry key windows, as shown in Figure 4.6 and described in Table 4.3.

FIGURE 4.6   The Registry Editor windows

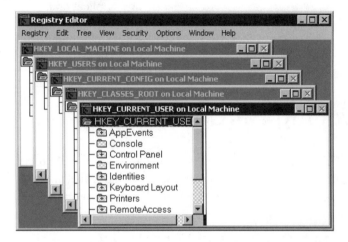

TABLE 4.3   Registry Keys

Registry Key	Description
HKEY_CURRENT_USER	Configuration information for the user who is currently logged on to the computer. This key is a subkey of the HKEY_USERS key.
HKEY_USERS	Configuration information for all users of the computer.
HKEY_LOCAL_MACHINE	Computer hardware configuration information. This computer configuration is used regardless of the user who is logged in.

TABLE 4.3 Registry Keys *(continued)*

Registry Key	Description
HKEY_CLASSES_ROOT	Configuration information used by Windows Explorer to properly associate file types with applications.
HKEY_CURRENT_CONFIG	Configuration of the hardware profile that is used during system startup.

Installing Hardware

If you buy new hardware, it will probably be Plug and Play. If you use older hardware, you will most likely need to configure the hardware to be properly recognized by the operating system.

Installing Plug and Play Devices

Plug and Play technology uses a combination of hardware and software that allows the operating system to automatically recognize and configure new hardware without any user intervention. Windows 2000 Plug and Play support includes the following features:

- Automatic and dynamic recognition of hardware that is installed

- Automatic resource allocation (or reallocation, if necessary)

- Determination of the correct driver that needs to be loaded for hardware support

- Support for interaction with the Plug and Play system

- Support for power management features

To test Plug and Play device installation, I installed a second EIDE drive on my computer, upgraded my CD-ROM drive, and added a Zip drive. Each time I added a device, Windows 2000 Professional automatically recognized it, and I did not need to set any configuration options.

Installing Non–Plug and Play Hardware

Legacy or older hardware is also supported by Windows 2000 Professional. When you install this type of hardware, you need to configure it just as you did before Plug and Play technology was introduced.

First, you need to configure the hardware device's resources manually on the device or through a software configuration program. Hardware resources include the device's interrupt request (IRQ), I/O port address, memory address, and Direct Memory Access (DMA) settings. Before you configure the resources for the new device, determine which resources are available. You can view a listing of the currently allocated resources in the Device Manager utility, as follows:

1. Right-click My Computer and select Manage. In the Computer Management window, select System Tools and then Device Manager.

2. Select View ➤ Resources by Connection.

3. Device Manager displays a list of the current resources. Click a resource to see all of the allocated resources of that type. Figure 4.7 shows an example of an IRQ listing in Device Manager.

FIGURE 4.7   Viewing resource allocation in Device Manager

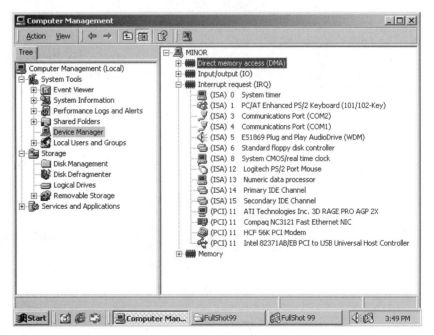

After you've configured the hardware resources, you can use the Add/Remove Hardware utility in Control Panel to add the new device to Windows 2000 Professional and install the device driver. If the device is not listed, you will need a manufacturer-provided driver. Insert the disk that contains the driver and click the Have Disk button in Add/Remove Hardware.

Managing Device Drivers

A *device driver* is software that allows a specific piece of hardware to communicate with the Windows 2000 operating system. Most of the devices on the Microsoft Hardware Compatibility List (HCL) have drivers that are included on the Windows 2000 Professional distribution CD. Managing device drivers involves updating them when necessary and deciding how to handle drivers that may not have been properly tested.

Updating Drivers

Device manufacturers periodically update device drivers to add functionality or enhance driver performance. The updated drivers are typically posted on the manufacturer's Web site.

Microsoft ✓ *Exam* *Objective*	**Update drivers.**

Exercise 4.1 takes you through the steps to update a device driver. In order to complete this exercise, you need to have an updated driver for one of your hardware devices.

EXERCISE 4.1

Updating a Device Driver

1. From the Desktop, right-click My Computer and select Manage from the pop-up menu.

2. The Computer Management window opens (see Figure 4.2 earlier in this chapter). Select System Tools, then Device Manager.

3. The right side of the window lists all the devices that are installed on your computer. Select the device whose driver you want to update.

4. The device Properties dialog box appears. Click the Driver tab.

5. The Driver tab contains information about the driver, including the provider, date, version, and digital signer. The three buttons at the bottom of this dialog box allow you to see more details, uninstall the driver, or update the driver. Click the Update Driver button in the lower-right corner.

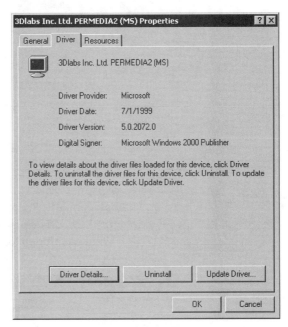

6. The Upgrade Device Driver Wizard starts. Click the Next button.

7. The Install Hardware Device Drivers dialog box appears. You can choose to have the Wizard search for a suitable driver, which is recommended, or you can have the Wizard display a list of known drivers for the device so you can choose a specific driver. Make your selection and click the Next button.

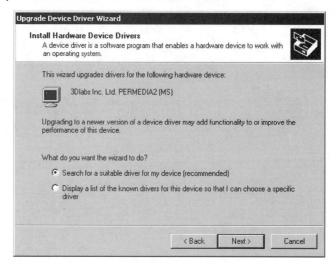

8. The Locate Driver Files dialog box appears. Here you specify the location of the driver files. You can have the Wizard look on your floppy disk or CD-ROM drive, or you can specify a location, or use the Microsoft Windows Update utility. Once you make your selection, click the Next button.

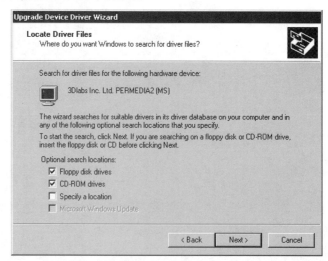

EXERCISE 4.1 *(continued)*

9. The Driver Files Search Results dialog box appears next. If a suitable driver for your device was found, click the Next button. Otherwise you can manually specify the location of a driver you want to use.

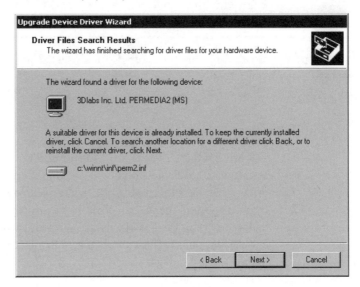

10. The files will be installed for your driver. Then you will see the Completing the Upgrade Device Driver Wizard dialog box. Click the Finish button to close this dialog box.

11. You may see a dialog box indicating that you must restart your computer before the change can be successfully implemented. If necessary, restart your computer.

The Microsoft Windows Update utility connects your computer to Microsoft's Web site and checks for driver and other updates. This utility is discussed in Chapter 14.

Managing Driver Signing

In the past, poorly written device drivers have caused problems in Windows operating systems. Microsoft is now promoting a mechanism called *driver signing* as a way of ensuring that drivers are properly tested before they are released to the public.

<table>
<tr><td>*Microsoft*
✓ *Exam*
Objective</td><td>**Manage and troubleshoot driver signing.**</td></tr>
</table>

Through the Driver Signing Options dialog box, you can specify how Windows 2000 Professional will respond if you select to install an unsigned driver. To access this dialog box, right-click My Computer, select Properties from the pop-up menu, and click the Hardware tab in the System Properties dialog box. This tab has Hardware Wizard, Device Manager, and Hardware Profiles options, as shown in Figure 4.8. Clicking the Driver Signing button in the Device Manager section opens the Driver Signing Options dialog box, as shown in Figure 4.9.

FIGURE 4.8 The Hardware tab of the System Properties dialog box

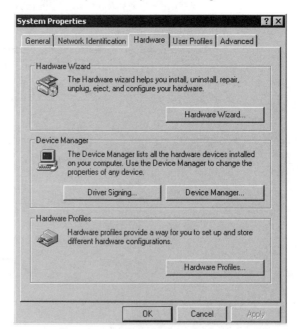

FIGURE 4.9 Driver signing options

In the Driver Signing Options dialog box, you can select from three options for file system verification:

- The Ignore option has Windows 2000 install all of the files, whether or not they are signed. You will not see any type of message about driver signing.

- The Warn option has Windows 2000 display a warning message before installing an unsigned file. You can then choose to continue with the installation or cancel it. This is the default setting.

- The Block option has Windows 2000 prevent the installation of any unsigned file. You will see an error message when you attempt to install the unsigned driver, and you will not be able to continue.

If you check the Apply Setting As System Default option, the settings that you apply will be used by all users who log on to the computer.

In Exercise 4.2, you will check the system's setting for driver signing.

EXERCISE 4.2

Managing Driver Signing

1. From the Desktop, right-click My Computer and select Properties.

2. In the System Properties dialog box, click the Hardware tab, then click the Driver Signing button.

EXERCISE 4.2 *(continued)*

3. In the Driver Signing Options dialog box, verify that the Warn radio button is selected and the Apply Setting As System Default check box is checked.

4. Click the OK button to close the dialog box.

Managing Disk Devices

You can manage disk devices through the Device Manager utility. The following sections describe how to manage CD-ROM, *DVD*, and removable media devices. Managing disks is covered in Chapter 9.

Microsoft ✓ Exam Objective	**Implement, manage, and troubleshoot disk devices.** • Install, configure, and manage DVD and CD-ROM devices. • Monitor and configure removable media, such as tape devices.

Managing DVD and CD-ROM Devices

DVDs and CD-ROMs are listed together under DVD/CD-ROM Drives in Device Manager. Double-click DVD/CD-ROM Drives, then double-click the device you wish to manage. This brings up the device Properties dialog box, which has three tabs:

- The General tab, shown in Figure 4.10, lists the device type, manufacturer, and location. It also shows the device status, which indicates whether the device is working properly. If the device is not working properly, you can click the Troubleshooter button at the lower-right of the dialog box to get some help with resolving the problem.

- The Properties tab, shown in Figure 4.11, allows you to set options such as volume and playback settings.

- The Driver tab, shown in Figure 4.12, shows information about the currently loaded driver, as well as buttons that allow you to see driver details, uninstall the driver, or update the driver. (See the "Updating Drivers" section earlier in the chapter for details on updating a driver.)

FIGURE 4.10   The General tab of a CD-ROM Properties dialog box

FIGURE 4.11   The Properties tab of a CD-ROM Properties dialog box

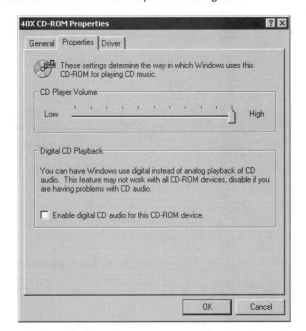

FIGURE 4.12 The Driver tab of a CD-ROM Properties dialog box

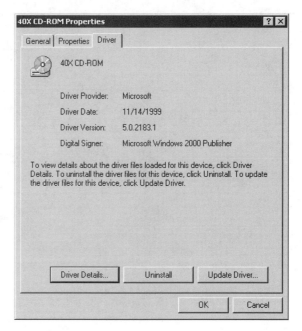

In Exercise 4.3, you will manage disk devices.

EXERCISE 4.3

Managing Disk Devices

1. From the Desktop, right-click My Computer and select Manage. In Computer Management, select System Tools, then Device Manager.

2. Double-click DVD/CD-ROM Drives, then double-click the DVD or CD-ROM device you wish to manage.

3. In the General tab of the device Properties dialog box, verify that your device is working properly. If the device is not working properly, click the Troubleshooter button. The Troubleshooter Wizard will ask you a series of questions and attempt to help you resolve the problem.

4. Click the Properties tab, and configure the options to suit your personal preferences.

5. Click the Driver tab. Note the information about the currently loaded driver.

6. Click the OK button to save your settings and close the dialog box.

Managing Removable Media

Removable media are devices such as tape devices and Zip drives. Like DVD and CD-ROM devices, removable media can also be managed through Device Manager.

Removable media are listed under Disk Drives in Device Manager. Double-click Disk Drives, then double-click the removable media device you wish to manage. This brings up the device Properties dialog box. The General and Driver tabs are similar to those for CD-ROM and DVD devices, as described in the preceding section. The Disk Properties tab contains options for the specific removable media device. For example, for an IOMEGA Zip 250, you can enable or disable the write cache, as shown in Figure 4.13.

FIGURE 4.13 The Disk Properties tab of a Zip disk Properties dialog box

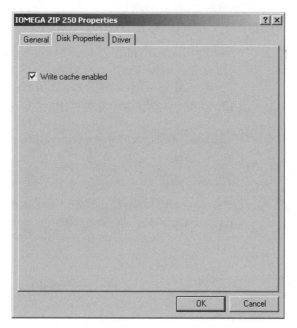

Managing Display Devices

A *video adapter* is the device that outputs the display to your monitor. You install a video adapter in the same way that you install other hardware. If it is a Plug and Play device, all you need to do is shut down your computer, add the video adapter, and turn on your computer. Windows 2000 Professional will automatically recognize the new device.

Microsoft
Exam
Objective

Implement, manage, and troubleshoot display devices.

- Configure multiple-display support.

- Install, configure, and troubleshoot a video adapter.

You can configure several options for your video adapters, and if you have multiple monitors with their own video adapters, you can configure multiple-display support. The following sections describe video adapter configuration, and how to configure your computer to support multiple monitors.

Configuring Video Adapters

The options for video adapters are on the Settings tab of the Display Properties dialog box, as shown in Figure 4.14. To access this dialog box, select the Display icon in Control Panel, or right-click an empty area on your Desktop and select Properties from the pop-up menu.

The Colors option in the Settings tab sets the color depth for your video adapter. The Screen Area option allows you to set the resolution for your video adapter.

The other tabs in the Display Properties dialog box allow you to customize the appearance of your Desktop. These options are discussed in Chapter 5.

FIGURE 4.14   The Settings tab of the Display Properties dialog box

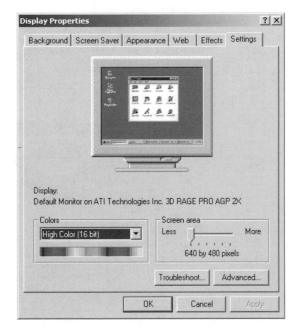

To configure advanced settings for your video adapter, click the Advanced button in the lower-right corner of the Settings tab. This brings up the Properties dialog box for the monitor, as shown in Figure 4.15. There are five tabs with options for your video adapter and monitor:

- The General tab allows you to configure the font size for the display. You can also specify what action Windows 2000 will take after you change your display settings.

- The Adapter tab allows you to view and configure the properties of your video adapter.

- In the Monitor tab, you can view and configure the properties of your monitor, including the refresh frequency (how often the screen is redrawn).

WARNING   A lower refresh frequency setting can cause your screen to flicker. Setting the refresh frequency too high can damage some hardware.

- The Troubleshooting tab allows you to configure how Windows 2000 uses your graphics hardware. For example, you can configure hardware acceleration settings.

- Use the Color Management tab to select color profiles (the colors that are displayed on your monitor).

FIGURE 4.15 The Properties dialog box for a display monitor

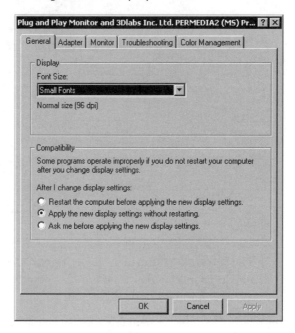

In Exercise 4.4, you will view the properties of your video adapter.

WARNING Normally, the video adapter is configured for typical use. Be careful if you change these settings, because improper settings may cause your display to be unreadable.

EXERCISE 4.4

Managing Your Video Adapter

1. Right-click an empty area on the Desktop, choose Properties, and select the Settings tab.

2. Click the Advanced button at the bottom of the Settings tab. Note your current settings in the General tab.

3. Click the Adapter tab. Note your current settings.

4. Click the Monitor tab. Note your current settings.

5. Click the Troubleshooting tab. Note your current settings.

6. Click the OK button to close the monitor Properties dialog box.

7. Click the OK button to close the Display Properties dialog box.

Setting the Video's Resolution, Color Selection, and Refresh Rate

Depending on your video adapter, you can configure a monitor's resolution, color selection, and refresh rate. *Resolution* specifies how densely packed the pixels are. The more pixels, or dots per inch (dpi), the clearer the image. The SVGA (super video graphics adapter) standard is 1024x768, but high-end models can display higher resolution, for example 1600x1200. The *color* selection specifies how many colors are supported by your video adapter; for example, the monitor may be displaying 16 colors or 256 colors. *Refresh rate* indicates how many times per second the screen is refreshed (redrawn). In order to avoid flickering, this rate should be set to at least 72Hz.

Certain applications require specific configurations based on graphics used. If you run across an application that requires a specific resolution, color selection, or refresh rate, or if a user makes a request based on personal preferences, you can easily determine what options are supported by the video adapter. In Control Panel, select Display Properties ➢ Settings ➢ Advanced ➢ Adapter ➢ List All Modes.

Using Multiple-Display Support

Windows 2000 Professional allows you to extend your Desktop across a maximum of 10 monitors. This means you can spread your applications across multiple monitors.

To set up multiple-display support, you must have a video adapter installed for each monitor, and you must use either Peripheral Connection Interface (PCI) or Accelerated Graphics Port (AGP) video adapter cards. In order to use the video adapter that is built into the system board for multiple-display support, the chip set must use the PCI or AGP standard.

If your computer has the video adapter built into the system board, you should install Windows 2000 Professional before you install the second video adapter. This is because Windows 2000 will disable the video adapter that is built into the system board if it detects a second video adapter. When you add a second video adapter after Windows 2000 is installed, it will automatically become the primary video adapter.

In Exercise 4.5, you will configure multiple-display support.

EXERCISE 4.5

Configuring Multiple-Display Support

1. Turn off your computer and install the PCI or AGP adapters. Plug your monitors into the video adapters and turn on your computer. Assuming that the adapters are Plug and Play, Windows 2000 will automatically recognize your new adapters and load the correct drivers.

2. Open the Display Properties dialog box (right-click an empty area on your Desktop and select Properties) and click the Settings tab. You should see an icon for each of the monitors.

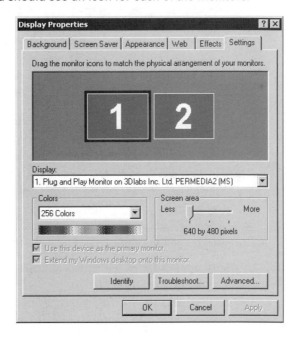

3. Click the number of the monitor that will act as your additional display. Then select the Extend My Windows Desktop onto This Monitor check box. Repeat this step for each additional monitor you wish to configure.

   You can arrange the order in which the displays are arranged by dragging and dropping the monitor icons in the Settings tab of the Display Properties dialog box.

4. When you are finished configuring the monitors, click OK to close the dialog box.

Troubleshooting Multiple-Display Support

If you are having problems with multiple-display support, use the following troubleshooting guidelines:

The Extend My Windows Desktop onto This Monitor option isn't available.   If the Settings tab of the Display Properties dialog box doesn't give you the option Extend My Windows Desktop onto This Monitor, confirm that your secondary adapter is supported for multiple-display support. Confirm that Windows 2000 is able to detect the secondary video adapter. Try selecting the secondary adapter rather than the primary adapter in the Display Properties dialog box.

No output appears on the secondary display.   Confirm that your secondary adapter is supported for multiple-display support, especially if you are using the built-in motherboard video adapter. Confirm that the correct video driver has been installed for the secondary display. Restart the computer to see if the secondary video driver is initialized. Check the status of the video adapter in Device Manager. Try switching the order of the video adapters in the computers slots. See if the system will recognize the device as the primary display.

An application is not properly displayed.   Disable the secondary display to determine if the problem is specific to multiple-display support. Run the application on the primary display. If you are running MS-DOS applications, try running the application in full-screen mode. For Windows applications, try running the application in a maximized window.

Managing Mobile Computer Hardware

Windows 2000 Professional includes several features that are particularly useful for laptop computers. For example, through Power Options in Control Panel, you can set power schemes and enable power management features with Windows 2000.

Microsoft ✓ *Exam* *Objective*	**Implement, manage, and troubleshoot mobile computer hardware.** · Configure Advanced Power Management (APM). · Configure and manage card services.

In Windows 2000, ACPI specifies six different levels of power states, including

- Complete shutdown of PC
- Hibernation
- Standby (three levels)
- Fully active PC

The similarity between hibernation and standby is that they both allow you to avoid shutting down your computer in order to save power. The key difference is in your computer's state of shutdown.

Hibernation falls short of a complete shutdown of the computer. With hibernation, the computer saves all of your desktop state as well as any open files. In order to use the computer again, press the power button. The computer starts more quickly than from a complete shutdown because it does not have to go through the complete startup process. You will have to again log on to the computer. You will also notice that all the documents that were open when the computer went into hibernation are still available. With hibernation you can easily resume work where you left off. You can configure your computer to hibernate through Power Options, or by entering Start ➢ Shut Down and then selecting Hibernate from the drop-down menu. This option will only appear if hibernation has been enabled through Power Options.

Standby does not save data automatically as hibernation does. With standby you can access your computer more quickly than a computer that is in hibernation, usually through a mouse click or keystroke, and the desktop appears as it was prior to the standby. The response time depends on the level of your computer's standby state. On an ACPI compliant computer, there are three levels of standby, each level putting the computer into a deeper sleep. The first level turns off power to the monitor and hard drives. The second level turns off power to the CPU and cache. The third level supplies power to RAM only and preserves the desktop in memory. You will only see an option to configure standby on Windows 2000 computers in which a battery has been detected. You can configure your computer for standby through Power Options, or through Start ➤ Shut Down and then selecting Standby from the drop-down menu. This option will only appear if standby has been enabled through Power Options.

Put your computer in standby mode if you will be away for a few minutes. Use hibernation mode if you will be away for a more extended period of time.

To determine whether Windows 2000 is running in ACPI mode:

1. Click Start ➤ Settings ➤ Control Panel.

2. Double-click Administrative Tools, and click Computer Management.

3. Click Device Manager, then click System devices.

If Microsoft ACPI-Compliant System is listed under System Devices, as shown in Figure 4.16, then the computer is operating in ACPI mode. During Windows 2000 Setup, ACPI is installed only on systems that have an ACPI-compatible BIOS.

FIGURE 4.16 ACPI-compliant computer

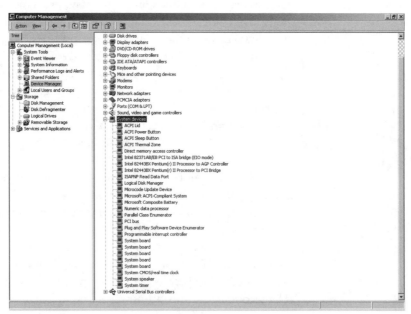

You may be able to upgrade your computer's BIOS to make it ACPI capable. Check with your computer's manufacturer for upgrade information.

The following sections describe the power management and card service options.

Managing Power Options

You configure power options through the Power Options Properties dialog box, as shown in Figure 4.17. To access this dialog box, select the Power Options icon in Control Panel. This dialog box has five tabs: Power Schemes, Alarms, Power Meter, Advanced, and Hibernate. The options on these tabs are described in the following sections.

FIGURE 4.17   The Power Options Properties dialog box

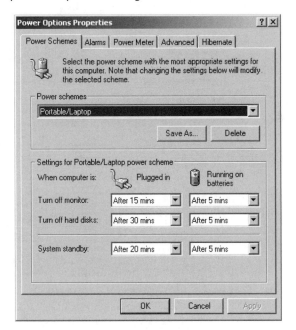

Configuring Power Schemes

The Power Schemes tab (see Figure 4.17) helps you select the most appropriate power scheme for your computer. Power schemes control automatic turn-off of the monitor and hard disks, based on a specified period of inactivity. This feature allows you to conserve your laptop's battery when the computer isn't being used. From the drop-down list, you can select one of the preconfigured power schemes listed in Table 4.4. Alternatively, you can create a custom power scheme by clicking the Save As button, giving the power scheme a new name, and choosing power scheme options.

TABLE 4.4   Windows 2000 Power Schemes

Power Scheme	Turn Off Monitor	Turn Off Hard Disks
Home/Office Desk	After 20 minutes	Never
Portable/Laptop	After 15 minutes	After 30 minutes
Presentation	Never	Never
Always On	After 20 minutes	Never
Minimal Power Management	After 15 minutes	Never
Max. Battery	After 15 minutes	Never

Configuring Alarms

The Alarms dialog box, shown in Figure 4.18, allows you to specify what type of alarm should be given when the battery capacity reaches a specified level. There are two types of alarms: low battery alarm and critical battery alarm. Low battery alarm gives you a chance to plug your computer into a power source or to perform an orderly shutdown of the computer. By default, a low battery alarm occurs when the battery is at 10 percent capacity. A critical battery alarm is used to alert you that battery shutdown is imminent. By default, this alarm occurs when the battery is at 3 percent capacity.

With each type of alarm, you can specify an alarm action that will occur when the alarm has been triggered. This can be a simple alert, a power-level specification, and/or the running of a program. For an alarm alert, a sound is made or a text message is displayed. A power-level specification is used to automatically trigger the computer to power off or into standby. If you run a program, it can be any program you specify, perhaps one that saves and closes all open documents.

FIGURE 4.18 The Alarms tab of Power Options Properties

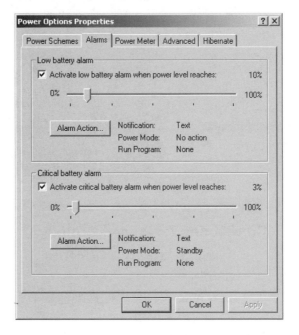

Configuring Power Meter

The Power Meter tab (Figure 4.19), shows the power status of your battery or batteries. It will show you the current power source—AC power or battery—and the percentage of charge in the battery.

FIGURE 4.19   Power Meter properties

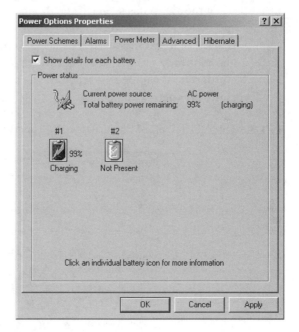

Configuring Advanced Options

Among the advanced options (Figure 4.20), you can configure several power options, including

- Whether the Power Management icon will be displayed on the Taskbar

- Whether the user will be prompted for a Windows 2000 password when the computer goes into standby

- What happens when power buttons are used for closing the portable computer's lid, pressing the power button, or pressing the sleep button

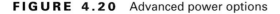

FIGURE 4.20 Advanced power options

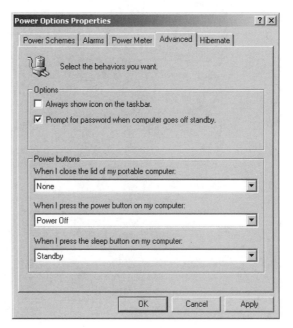

Configuring Hibernation

Hibernation for a computer means that anything stored in memory is also stored on your hard disk. This ensures that when your computer is shut down, you do not lose any of the information that is stored in memory. When you take your computer out of hibernation, it returns to its previous state.

To configure your computer to hibernate, use the Hibernate tab of the Power Options Properties dialog box, as shown in Figure 4.21. Simply select the Enable Hibernate Support check box.

FIGURE 4.21 The Hibernate tab of the Power Options Properties dialog box

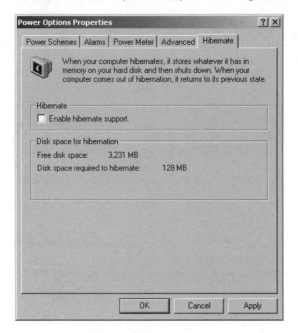

If you have a laptop running Windows 2000 Professional, you can complete the steps in Exercise 4.6 to configure the laptop to support ACPI.

EXERCISE 4.6

Configuring Power Management Support

1. Select Start ≻ Settings ≻ Control Panel and double-click the Power Options icon.

2. In the Power Options Properties dialog box, click the Power Schemes tab.

3. Configure the Power Schemes for your computer based on your personal preferences, and click OK.

4. Close Control Panel.

If you are using APM on your Windows 2000 computer and your BIOS does not support APM, you may experience problems such as the computer's not being able to shut down. In this case you should upgrade your computer with a BIOS that supports APM, or you can disable APM support on the computer.

Managing Card Services

In order to add devices to a laptop computer, you use special credit-card sized devices called *PCMCIA* (Personal Computer Memory Card International Association) cards, or more simply, PC Cards. PC Cards have three different standards:

- Type I cards can be up to 3.3 mm thick. These cards are primarily used for adding memory to a computer.

- Type II cards can be up to 5.5 mm thick. These cards are typically used for modem and network cards.

- Type III cards can be up to 10.5 mm thick. These cards are typically used for portable disk drives.

Windows 2000 Professional allows you to exchange PC Cards on-the-fly (called hot swapping). However, you should make sure that your laptop supports hot-swap technology before you try to remove a card from or add a card to a running computer.

As with any Plug and Play device, when you add a PC Card to a Windows 2000 Professional computer, the card will be recognized automatically. You can view and manage PC Cards through Device Manager.

Managing I/O Devices

Your input/output (I/O) devices are the ones that allow you to get information into and out of your computer. Examples of I/O devices are keyboards, mice, printers, and scanners. Your devices may be connected to your computer by standard cabling, or they may use wireless technology (such as IrDA or RF) or be connected through a USB port.

Microsoft Exam Objective

Implement, manage, and troubleshoot input and output (I/O) devices.

- Monitor, configure, and troubleshoot I/O devices, such as printers, scanners, multimedia devices, mouse, keyboard, and smart card reader.

- Install, configure, and manage Infrared Data Association (IrDA) devices.

- Install, configure, and manage wireless devices.

- Install, configure, and manage USB devices.

The subobjective "Install, configure, and manage modems" for the objective "Implement, manage, and troubleshoot input and output (I/O) devices" is covered in Chapter 13, "Dial-Up Networking and Internet Connectivity."

The following sections describe how to manage your keyboard, mouse, wireless devices, and USB devices. Scanners are covered in the next section. You will learn how to install and configure printers in Chapter 12, "Managing Printing."

Configuring the Keyboard

You can configure keyboard options through the Keyboard Properties dialog box, shown in Figure 4.22. To access this dialog box, select the Keyboard icon in Control Panel.

You must have a keyboard attached to your computer before you can install Windows 2000 Professional.

FIGURE 4.22   The Keyboard Properties dialog box

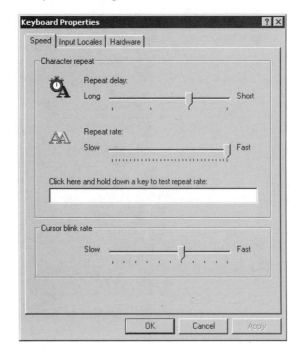

This dialog box has three tabs with options that control your keyboard's behavior:

- The Speed tab lets you configure how quickly characters are repeated when you hold down a key. You can also specify the cursor blink rate.

- In the Input Locales tab you specify the keyboard layout based on your input locale (for example, English United States or United States-Dvorak).

- The Hardware tab specifies the device settings for your keyboard.

Configuring the Mouse

You can configure your mouse through the Mouse Properties dialog box, shown in Figure 4.23. To access this dialog box, select the Mouse icon in Control Panel.

FIGURE 4.23 The Mouse Properties dialog box

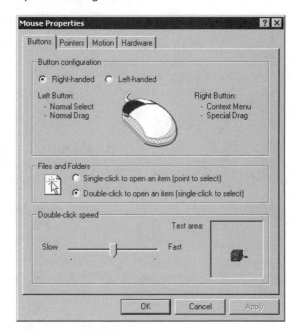

The Mouse Properties dialog box has four tabs with options that control your mouse's behavior:

- The Buttons tab allows you to configure the mouse properties for right-handed or left-handed use and choose whether you use a single-click to open an item (point to select) or double-click to open an item (single-click to select). You can also configure the speed that is used to indicate a double-click.

- The Pointers tab lets you select the pointer scheme that is used by your mouse.

- The Motion tab lets you specify how fast your mouse pointer moves. You can also configure the snap-to-default feature, which automatically moves the pointer to a default button in a dialog box when new dialog boxes are opened.

- The Hardware tab specifies the device settings for your mouse.

In Exercise 4.7, you will configure your keyboard and mouse I/O devices.

EXERCISE 4.7

Configuring I/O Devices

1. Select Start ➤ Settings ➤ Control Panel and double-click the Keyboard icon.

2. In the Speed tab, set the Repeat Delay and Repeat Rate options based on your personal preferences. Also adjust the Cursor Blink Rate if you want to change it. Click the OK button.

3. In Control Panel, double-click the Mouse icon.

4. In the Motion tab, set the Speed, Acceleration, and Snap-to-Default options as you prefer. Click the OK button.

5. Close Control Panel.

Configuring Wireless Devices

Wireless devices use wireless transmission rather than transmitting over cable. Following are two of the technologies used for wireless transmission:

- Infrared Data Association (IrDA), which is a standard for transmitting data through infrared light waves

- RF (Radio Frequency), which is a standard for transmitting data through radio waves

Common examples of wireless devices include keyboards, mice, and network cards. You should follow the vendor's instructions to install wireless devices. Wireless devices are configured in the same manner as other devices on your computer. For example, you can set options for a wireless keyboard through the Keyboard Properties dialog box.

Configuring USB Devices

Universal Serial Bus (USB) is an external bus standard that allows you to connect USB devices through a USB port. USB supports transfer rates up to

12Mbps. A single USB port can support up to 127 devices. Examples of USB devices include modems, printers, and keyboards.

If your computer supports USB, and USB is enabled in the BIOS, you will see Universal Serial Bus Controller listed in Device Manager. Double-click your USB controller to see the dialog box shown in Figure 4.24.

FIGURE 4.24 The USB controller Properties dialog box

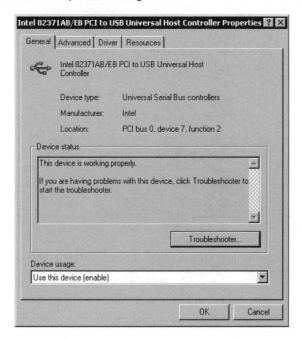

The USB controller Properties dialog box has four tabs with options and information for your USB adapter:

- The General tab lists the device type, manufacturer, and location. It also shows the device status, which indicates whether or not the device is working properly. If the device is not working properly, you can click the Troubleshooter button in the lower-right area of the dialog box.

- The Advanced tab allows you to configure how much of the bandwidth each device that is connected to the USB adapter can use.

- The Driver tab shows driver properties and lets you uninstall or update the driver.

- The Resources tab shows all of the resources that are used by the USB adapter.

After the USB adapter is configured, you can attach USB devices to the adapter in a daisy-chain configuration.

 If your computer has a built-in USB device and your computer does not detect the device through Device Manager, confirm that the USB is enabled in the computer's BIOS and that the BIOS supports USB devices.

Managing Imaging Devices

A scanner is a device that can read text or graphics that are on paper and translate the information to digital data that the computer can understand. Digital cameras take pictures in a digital format that can be read by the computer.

Microsoft *Exam* *Objective*	**Implement, manage, and troubleshoot input and output (I/O) devices.**
	- Monitor, configure, and troubleshoot I/O devices, such as printers, scanners, multimedia devices, mouse, keyboard, and smart card reader.
	- Monitor, configure, and troubleshoot multimedia hardware, such as cameras.

After you install a scanner or digital camera on a Windows 2000 Professional computer, you can manage the device through the Scanners and Cameras Properties dialog box, shown in Figure 4.25. You access this dialog box by selecting the Cameras and Scanners icon in Control Panel.

FIGURE 4.25 The Scanners and Cameras Properties dialog box

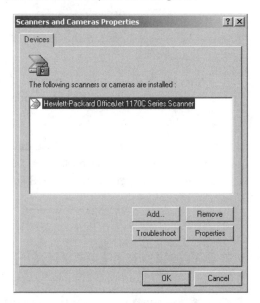

The Scanners and Cameras Properties dialog box lists the devices that are recognized by your computer. You can click the Add button to add a scanner or camera, the Remove button to remove the selected device, or the Troubleshooter button to run a Troubleshooter Wizard. Clicking the Properties button displays a dialog box with additional options, as shown in Figure 4.26.

FIGURE 4.26 A scanner's Properties dialog box

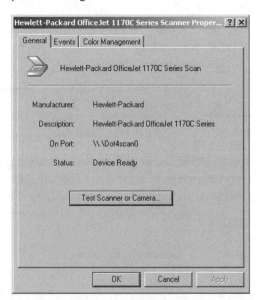

The scanner or camera Properties dialog box has three tabs with options and information about the device:

- The General tab lists the manufacturer, description, port, and status of the device. It also contains a button that you can click to test the scanner or camera.

- The Events tab allows you to associate an event with an application. For example, you can specify that when you scan a document, it should be automatically linked to the imaging program, and the imaging program will start and display the document you just scanned.

- The Color Management tab allows you to associate a color profile with the scanner or camera.

If you have a scanner or digital camera installed on your computer, you can complete the steps in Exercise 4.8 to view and configure its properties.

EXERCISE 4.8

Managing and Monitoring Imaging Devices

1. Select Start ➢ Settings ➢ Control Panel and double-click the Scanners and Camera icon.

2. In the Scanners and Cameras Properties dialog box, click the Properties button.

3. In the General tab of the scanner or camera Properties dialog box, click the Test Scanner or Camera button to make sure the device is working properly.

4. Click the Events tab. Set any associations based on your computer's configuration and your personal preferences.

5. Click the Color Management tab. If desired, associate a color profile with the scanner or camera.

6. Click the OK button to close the scanner or camera Properties dialog box.

EXERCISE 4.8 *(continued)*

7. Click the OK button to close the Scanner and Camera Properties dialog box.

8. Close Control Panel.

Managing Processors

Normally, multiple processors are associated with servers. However, Windows 2000 Professional can support up to two processors. If your computer is capable of supporting multiple processors, you should follow the computer manufacturer's instructions for installing the second processor. This usually involves updating the processors driver to a driver that supports multiple processors through the Upgrade Device Driver Wizard.

Microsoft ✓ *Exam* *Objective*	**Monitor and configure multiple processing units.**

Once you install a second processor, you can monitor the processors through the System Monitor utility. You can verify that multiple processors are recognized by the operating system, as well as configure multiple processors, through the Task Manager utility. Chapter 14 discusses the System Monitor and Task Manager utilities in detail.

To configure multiple processors, you can associate each processor with specific processes that are running on the computer. This is called *processor affinity*. Once you have two processors installed on your computer, you can set processor affinity. You'll do this in Exercise 4.9.

EXERCISE 4.9

Configuring Multiple Processors

1. Press Ctrl+Alt+Del and click the Task Manager button.

2. In the Task Manager dialog box, click the Processes tab.

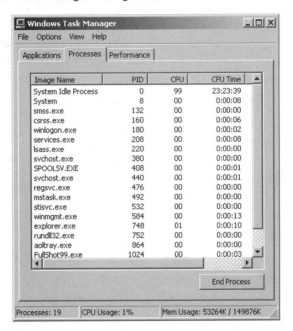

3. In the Processes tab, right-click the explorer.exe process and select Processor Affinity.

EXERCISE 4.9 *(continued)*

4. In the Processor Affinity dialog box, check the CPU 1 check box and click the OK button.

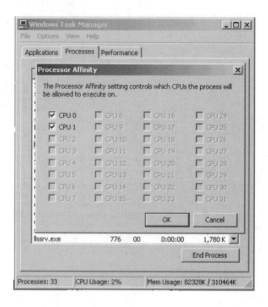

5. Close the Task Manager utility.

Configuring Fax Support

Windows 2000 Professional allows you to add and configure fax support. In order to add fax support, you must have a device connected to your computer that can send and receive faxes. The most common example of a fax device is a fax modem.

Microsoft ✓ *Exam* *Objective*	**Configure and troubleshoot fax support.**

You configure fax support through the Fax icon in Control Panel and start the Fax Service through the Computer Management utility, as described in the following sections.

Setting Fax Properties

To configure fax support and set fax properties, take the following steps:

1. Select Start ➤ Settings ➤ Control Panel and double-click the Fax icon.

2. You see the Fax Properties dialog box, as shown in Figure 4.27. In the User Information tab, you can fill in the information you want to appear on your cover page. You can set other cover page options on the Cover Pages tab, and specify notification options on the Status Monitor tab.

FIGURE 4.27 The User Information tab of the Fax Properties dialog box

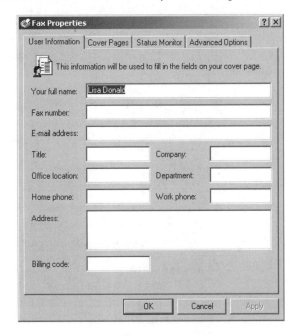

3. Click the Advanced Options tab to configure fax support. You have options for managing the fax service and adding a fax printer, as shown in Figure 4.28. Click the Add a Fax Printer button.

FIGURE 4.28 The Advanced Options tab of the Fax Properties dialog box

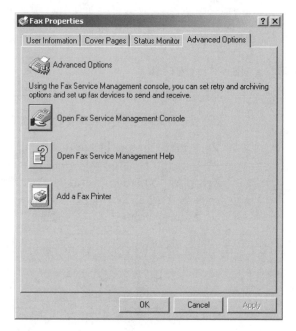

4. If a device that supports faxing capabilities is attached to your computer, you will see a message indicating that the fax printer was created successfully. Click the OK button.

5. You return to the Advanced Options tab. Click the Open Fax Service Management Console button.

6. The Fax Service Management window appears (Figure 4.29). Click Devices in the right-hand pane to list the fax devices. Double-click the fax device you want to configure.

7. The fax device's Properties dialog box appears, as shown in Figure 4.30. Here you can configure Send and Receive properties. If you want to receive faxes, you configure their properties through the Received Faxes tab. When you are finished setting the fax device properties, click the OK button.

8. Close the Fax Service Management window.

FIGURE 4.29 The Fax Service Management window

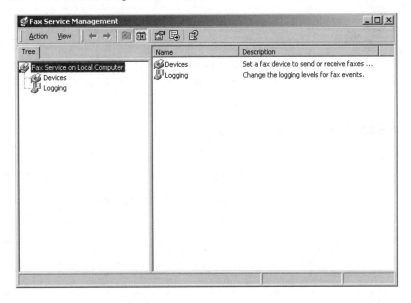

FIGURE 4.30 The Properties dialog box for a fax device

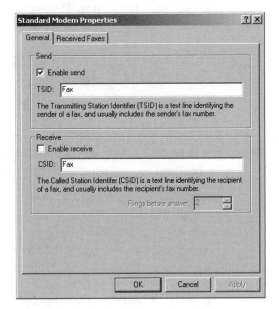

You can also configure the Fax Queue, Fax Service Management, My Faxes, and Send Cover Page Fax options through the Fax Service Management utility. To access this utility, select Start ➢ Programs ➢ Accessories ➢ Communications ➢ Fax.

Starting the Fax Service

After you configure fax support, you need to start the Fax Service in Windows 2000 Professional. To start the service, take the following steps:

1. Right-click My Computer on the Desktop and select Manage from the pop-up menu.

2. Expand Services and Applications, then Services.

3. Double-click Fax Service and click the Start button.

4. Select Automatic as the Startup Type and click the OK button.

5. Close the Computer Management window.

Starting and configuring Windows 2000 Professional services are discussed in more detail in the next section.

 Real World Scenario

Setting Up Send and Receive Fax Support

Your boss asks you to configure fax support on a computer for a user in the Sales department. After you configure the fax support, the user complains that the computer will send faxes but not receive faxes.

To correct the situation so that the computer can receive faxes, you will need to do two things. First, verify that a fax printer has been created through Control Panel (click the Fax icon, then Advanced Options, then Add a Fax Printer). Also, verify that the Fax Service Management is configured to receive faxes. Access the Fax Properties Advanced Properties tab, select Fax Service Management Console, then Devices, and expand Devices. Find out if the fax is configured for both send and receive options. If the computer is *not* configured to receive, double-click on your fax device. This brings up a dialog box in which you can specify that the fax should also receive faxes.

If you are having trouble with your fax device, use the Troubleshooter Wizard available through the Device Manager utility, as described for sound cards in the next section.

Troubleshooting Devices

When Device Manager does not properly recognize a device, it reports the problem by displaying an exclamation point icon next to the device. To troubleshoot a device that is not working properly, double-click the device to open its Properties dialog box. Figure 4.31 shows an example of the Properties dialog box for a device that does not have the proper driver loaded.

FIGURE 4.31 The device's Properties dialog box reports that the device is not configured correctly.

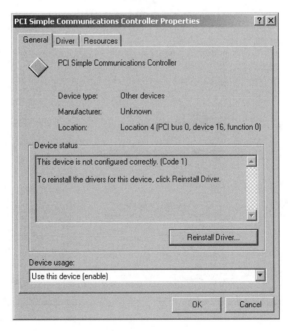

If a device connected to your computer doesn't appear in Device Manager, you can get some hints on troubleshooting through the Troubleshooter

Wizard. As an example, if your sound card is not working properly and is not listed in Device Manager, you can use the Troubleshooter Wizard, as shown in Exercise 4.10.

EXERCISE 4.10

Using the Troubleshooter Wizard

1. From the Desktop, right-click My Computer and select Manage. In Computer Management, select System Tools, then Device Manager.

2. In Device Manager, double-click Computer and double-click Standard PC.

3. The computer Properties dialog box appears. Click the Troubleshooter button.

4. The Windows 2000 Help window opens, with the Hardware Troubleshooter section displayed in the right pane. You can choose from a wide range of situations. For this exercise, select My Sound Card Doesn't Work and click the Next button.

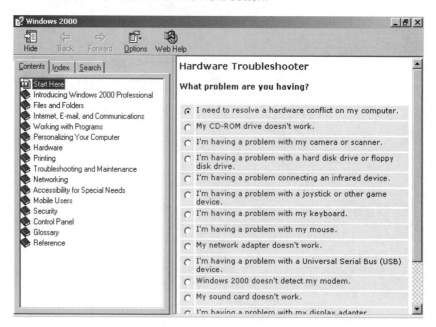

5. In the next Troubleshooter Wizard window, specify whether or not you have a PCI sound card. In this exercise, select Yes, I Have a PCI Sound Card and click the Next button.

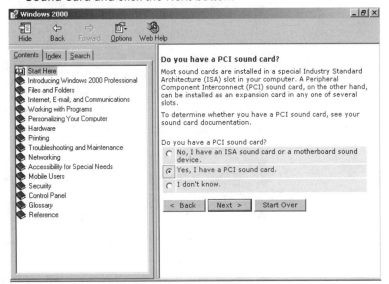

6. Next, the wizard asks if your sound card is compatible with Windows 2000. If your sound card is not on the HCL, the wizard directs you to the card manufacturer for assistance. In this example, select Yes, Windows 2000 Supports My Sound Card and click the Next button.

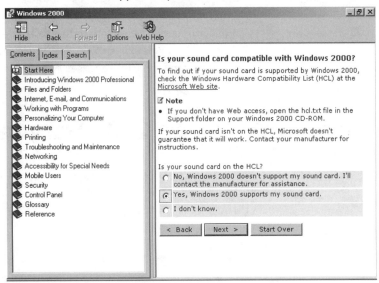

7. The Troubleshooter Wizard identifies a possible problem and solution—in this case, it suggests that your PCI card might be in a faulty slot. You are advised to move the card to a different slot to see if this corrects the problem. (You may prefer to have this tested at a computer repair center.)

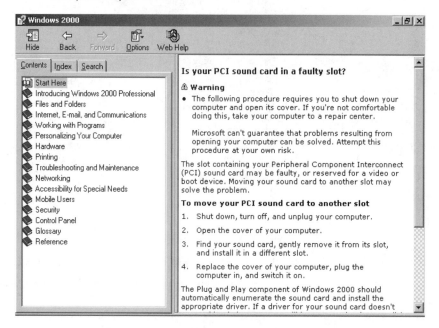

8. After you follow the suggested procedure, the wizard asks you if your problem is corrected. In this example, the problem is fixed, but if your device still isn't working, the Troubleshooter Wizard will suggest other possible courses of action.

Managing Windows 2000 Services

A service is a program, routine, or process that performs a specific function within the Windows 2000 operating system. You can manage services through the Services window (Figure 4.32), which can be accessed in a variety of ways. If you go through the Computer Management utility, right-click My Computer, select Manage, expand Services and Applications, and then expand Services. You can also go through Administrative Tools, or set up the Services manager as an MMC snap-in.

FIGURE 4.32   The Services window

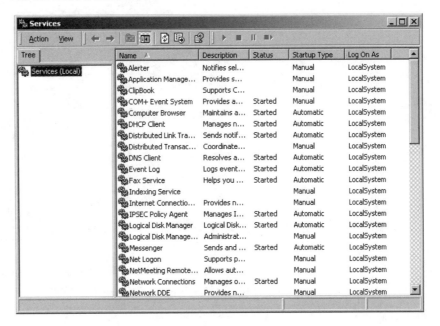

For each service, the Services window lists the name, a short description, the startup type, and the logon account that is used to start the service. To configure the properties of a service, double-click it to open its Properties dialog box, shown in Figure 4.33. This dialog box contains four tabs of options for services: General, Log On, Recovery, and Dependencies.

FIGURE 4.33 Service Properties dialog box

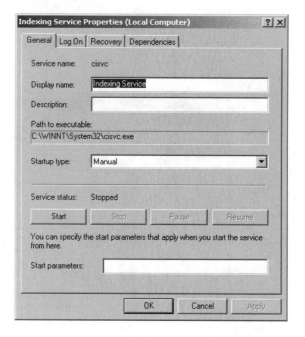

The General tab of the service Properties dialog box (see Figure 4.33), allows you to view and configure the following options:

- The service display name

- A description of the service

- The path to the service executable

- The startup type, which can be automatic, manual, or disabled

- The current service status

- Startup parameters that can be applied when the service is started

In addition, the buttons across the lower part of the dialog box allow you to start, stop, pause, or resume the service.

In the Log On tab of the service Properties dialog box, Figure 4.34, you configure the logon account that will be used to start the service. Choose the local system account or specify another logon account. At the bottom, you can select hardware profiles with which to associate the service. For each hardware profile, you can set the service as enabled or disabled.

FIGURE 4.34   The Log On tab of the service Properties dialog box

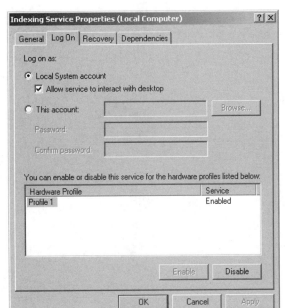

The Recovery tab, Figure 4.35, allows you to designate what action will be taken if the service fails to load. For the first, second, and subsequent failures, you can select from the following actions:

- Take no action

- Restart the service

- Run a file

- Reboot the computer

If you choose to run a file, specify it along with any command-line parameters. If you choose to reboot the computer, you can configure a message that will be sent to users who are connected to the computer before it is restarted.

FIGURE 4.35 The Recovery tab of the service Properties dialog box

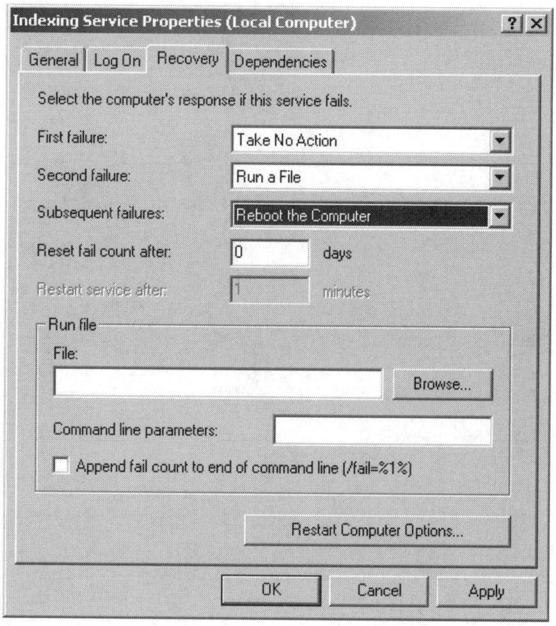

The Dependencies tab, Figure 4.36, lists any services that must be running in order for the specified service to start. If a service fails to start, you can use this information to examine the dependencies and then make sure each one is running. In the bottom panel, you can verify if any other services depend on this service before you decide to stop.

FIGURE 4.36 The Dependencies tab of the service Properties dialog box

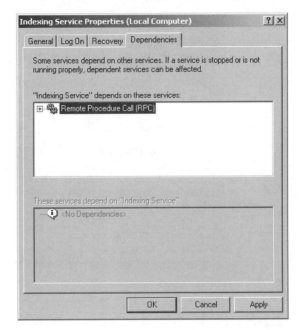

Summary

In this chapter, you learned about configuring the Windows 2000 Professional environment. We covered the following topics:

- Utilities used to manage configuration, which include Control Panel, Computer Management, the Microsoft Management Console (MMC), and the Registry Editor

- Installing hardware, including Plug and Play and non–Plug and Play devices

- Managing device drivers, including how to update drivers and set options for driver signing

- Managing disk devices, including CD-ROM devices, DVD devices, and removable media

- Managing display devices, including video adapters and multiple displays

- Managing mobile computer hardware, including how to set power options and configure card services

- Managing I/O devices, including keyboards, mice, wireless devices, and USB devices

- Managing imaging devices, including scanners and digital cameras

- Managing processors, including how to set processor affinity in a multiple-processor computer

- Configuring fax support and starting the Fax Service

- Using the Windows 2000 Troubleshooter Wizard to troubleshoot problems with devices

- Managing Windows 2000 Professional services

Exam Essentials

Understand how to install new hardware on your computer. Be able to successfully install hardware that is Plug and Play compatible, as well as hardware that is not Plug and Play compatible.

Manage and update device drivers. Be able to successfully upgrade device drivers. Understand and be able to configure your computer to use different levels of driver signing.

Manage display devices. Understand how to configure your computer with a single monitor or multiple monitors. Be able to list the requirements for installing and configuring multiple monitors.

Support mobile computers through power management features. Understand the features that are available through ACPI, and be able to configure a laptop computer to use these features.

Know the configuration requirements to support multiple processors. Windows 2000 Professional can support up to two processors. Be able to specify what options must be configured when upgrading to the second processor.

Key Terms

Before taking the exam, you should be familiar with the following terms:

Advanced Power Management (APM)	PCMCIA (PC Card)
Computer Management	Plug and Play
Control Panel	processor affinity
device driver	REGEDIT
Device Manager	REGEDT32
Disk Defragmenter	Registry
Disk Management	Removable Storage
driver signing	service
DVD (Digital Versatile Disc)	Shared Folders
Event Viewer	System Information
hibernation	System Tools
Indexing Service	uninterruptible power supply (UPS)
Local Users and Groups	Universal Serial Bus (USB)
Logical Drives	video adapter
Microsoft Management Console (MMC)	WMI (Windows Management Instrumentation) Control
Performance Logs and Alerts	

Review Questions

1. Michelle wants to create a customized administrative interface using snap-ins based on the utilities that she commonly uses. Which of the following Windows 2000 configuration utilities should she use?

   A. Control Panel

   B. Computer Management

   C. Microsoft Management Console

   D. Registry Editor

2. The system administrator of the XYZ network wants to edit the Registry, including setting security on the Registry keys. What primary utility that supports full editing of the Windows 2000 Registry should the system administrator use?

   A. REGEDIT

   B. REDIT

   C. REGEDIT32

   D. REGEDT32

3. Jim has an XYZ-manufactured modem installed in his computer. The XYZ Corporation released a new driver for the modem. Jim is slightly worried that the driver may not have been fully tested and may cause his computer to work improperly. What is the process that Microsoft uses with Windows 2000 to ensure that the drivers you install on your computer are properly tested and verified?

   A. Driver confirmation

   B. Driver optimization

   C. Driver signing

   D. Driver verification

4. Tracey is setting up two monitors for her Windows 2000 computer. Which of the following statements are true regarding configuration of multiple displays? Choose two answers.

    A. You need a special cable that allows you to connect two monitors to a video adapter.

    B. You must install an adapter for each monitor that you will configure.

    C. You must use PCI or AGP adapters.

    D. Windows 2000 allows you to extend your Desktop across up to eight monitors.

5. Jack's laptop computer battery only lasts for about two hours, so he wants to configure the computer to turn off the monitor and disk drives if the computer hasn't been accessed for five minutes. Which Windows 2000 feature will allow Jack to conserve power on his laptop?

    A. ACPI

    B. UPS

    C. HPS

    D. HPM

6. Todd has a new device that connects to his computer through either the serial port or the USB port. He wants to connect it through the USB port but does not know what is included in USB support and asks you about it. Which of the following statements regarding USB devices is *not* true?

    A. USB supports transmission speeds up to 20Mbps.

    B. You can connect up to 127 devices through a single USB port.

    C. You can configure your USB adapter properties through Device Manager.

    D. Common examples of USB devices include modems, printers, and keyboards.

7. Tina is dissatisfied with the configuration of her keyboard and mouse. She wants to reset the keyboard speed and the mouse pointer rate. Which utility should she use to configure the keyboard and mouse properties?

   A. Control Panel

   B. Computer Management

   C. Microsoft Management Console

   D. Registry Editor

8. Cam is trying to install a network card that is not Plug and Play compatible. When she restarts the computer, the card is not recognized. She has a Windows 2000 driver for the device and wants to manually configure the network card. Which utility should she use to install the network card?

   A. Device Manager

   B. Computer Manager

   C. Control Panel, Add/Remove Hardware

   D. MMC

9. Elena is using a laptop computer that uses ACPI. She wants to see what percentage of the battery power is still available. She also wants to know if hibernation has been configured. Which of the following utilities should she use?

   A. Device Manager

   B. Computer Manager

   C. Control Panel, Power Management

   D. MMC

10. Fred does not have a separate fax machine and wants to be able to use the fax support included in Windows 2000 in conjunction with his modem. Which utility should he use to configure fax support in Windows 2000?

   A. Device Manager

   B. Computer Manager

   C. Control Panel, Fax

   D. MMC

11. Jason has a computer that can support two processors. Currently his computer is configured with a single processor, but he is planning on adding a second processor. Which of the following steps would you need to take in Windows 2000 Professional so that the second processor will be recognized when it is installed?

   A. Update the driver to support multiple processors.

   B. Through Device Manager, access the computer's properties and enable the Allow Multiple Processors option.

   C. Through Control Panel, access System Properties, open the Advanced tab, and enable the Allow Multiple Processors option.

   D. Do nothing; this is enabled by default.

12. Jose has inherited a Windows 2000 laptop from work; it was originally licensed to Bill Gates. He wants to change that name to Jose Gonzales. He wants to change the value of this specification within the Registry, but doesn't know the name of the key that is used set the license name. When he goes into the registry with the REGEDT32 command, he can only access the information shown in the following illustration. Which command-line utility should Jose use that would offer better search capabilities for the Registry?

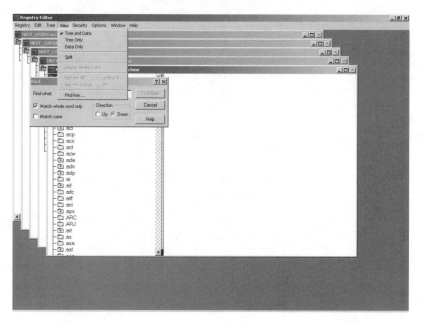

A. REGEDIT

B. REDIT

C. REGEDIT32

D. EDTREG32

13. In the past, you have had problems with users updating drivers that have caused their computers to work improperly. You want to prevent this from happening in your Windows 2000 system. To accomplish this, which option should you configure in the Driver Signing Options dialog box shown here?

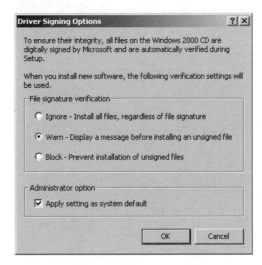

A. Configure driver signing for Ignore

B. Configure driver signing for Warn

C. Configure driver signing for Block

14. Kim is installing an application that requires the screen area be configured for 1024x768. How can she verify or make this setting?

A. Through Control Panel, Monitor Settings

B. Through Device Manager, Monitor

C. Through Control Panel, Display Properties, Settings

D. Through Device Manager, Display Properties, Settings

15. You have configured your computer for multiple-display support. Everything works properly when you run Windows applications. However, you do not see your MS-DOS application properly displayed. What can you do?

A. Try running the application in full-screen mode.

B. Restart the computer and see if the secondary video adapter is initialized.

C. Increase the screen area on both displays to 1024x768.

D. Set the colors to 256 Colors.

Answers to Review Questions

1. C. The Microsoft Management Console (MMC) is a console framework that uses snap-ins. Administrators can create custom consoles for administrative tasks.

2. D. In Windows 2000, you can edit the Registry with REGEDIT or REGEDT32. REGEDIT includes more advanced search capabilities, but REGEDT32 supports full editing.

3. C. Microsoft uses driver signing to verify that drivers have been properly tested before they are installed on a Windows 2000 computer. By default, you will see a warning message when you try to install a driver that has not been signed.

4. B, C. If you want to configure multiple displays in Windows 2000, you need a PCI or an AGP video adapter for each monitor that will be connected. Windows 2000 allows you to extend your Desktop across up to 10 monitors.

5. A. ACPI (Advanced Computer Power Management) is the technology that is used to reduce the power consumption of a computer.

6. A. USB supports transmission speeds up to 12Mbps.

7. A. You configure keyboard and mouse properties through their respective icons in Control Panel.

8. C. The Add/Remove Hardware icon in Control Panel starts the Add/Remove Hardware Wizard to install hardware that is not Plug and Play compatible.

9. C. The Power Management icon in Control Panel can be used to configure options such as power schemes, advanced options, hibernation, APM, and UPS properties.

10. C. You configure fax support in Windows 2000 through the Fax icon in Control Panel.

11. A. When you upgrade your computer from a single processor to a multiple-processor configuration, you must update the processor's driver to support this configuration.

12. A. In Windows 2000, you can edit the Registry with REGEDIT or REGEDT32. REGEDIT includes more advanced search capabilities, but REGEDT32 supports full editing.

13. C. Driver signing verifies that drivers have been thoroughly tested and verified by Microsoft. When you set driver signing to Block, only signed drivers can be installed.

14. C. You can set your display's colors and screen area through Control Panel, by clicking the Display icon and opening the Settings tab of the Display Properties dialog box.

15. A. If you are running a MS-DOS application with multiple-display support and you do not see the application properly, try running the application in full-screen mode. If the problem is occurring with a Windows application, try running the application in a maximized window. You could also try disabling the secondary display to determine whether the problem was specific to multiple-display support.

Chapter

5

Managing the Desktop

MICROSOFT EXAM OBJECTIVES COVERED IN THIS CHAPTER:

✓ **Configure and troubleshoot desktop settings.**

✓ **Configure support for multiple languages or multiple locations.**

  ▪ Enable multiple-language support.

  ▪ Configure multiple-language support for users.

  ▪ Configure local settings.

  ▪ Configure Windows 2000 Professional for multiple locations.

✓ **Configure and troubleshoot accessibility services.**

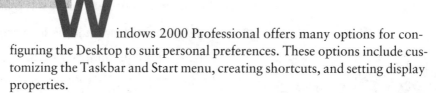

Windows 2000 Professional offers many options for configuring the Desktop to suit personal preferences. These options include customizing the Taskbar and Start menu, creating shortcuts, and setting display properties.

Windows 2000 Professional also includes support for multiple languages and regional settings. The support that comes with localized versions of Windows 2000 Professional allows users to view, edit, and print multilingual documents. You can also specify locale settings for the Desktop to customize items such as the date and currency for your geographical location.

Accessibility options are used to support users with limited sight, hearing, or mobility. You can configure the Desktop and use Windows 2000 Professional utilities to provide a higher degree of accessibility.

This chapter describes how to manage Desktop settings, multilanguage support, and accessibility options.

Managing Desktop Settings

The *Desktop*, shown in Figure 5.1, appears after a user has logged on to a Windows 2000 Professional computer. Users can configure their Desktops to suit their personal preferences and to work more efficiently. As an administrator, you may need to troubleshoot an improperly configured Desktop.

The items listed in Table 5.1 appear on the Desktop by default.

Microsoft
Exam
Objective

Configure and troubleshoot desktop settings.

FIGURE 5.1 The Windows 2000 Desktop

TABLE 5.1 Default Desktop Items

Item	Description
My Documents	By default, stores the documents that are created. Each user has a unique My Documents folder, so even if a computer is shared, each user will have unique personal folders.

TABLE 5.1 Default Desktop Items *(continued)*

Item	Description
My Computer	Provides access to all local and network drives, as well as Control Panel. My Computer is used to view and manage the computer.
My Network Places	Provides access to shared resources. My Network Places is used to connect to resources such as local network resources and Web resources.
Recycle Bin	Holds files and folders that have been deleted. Files can be retrieved or cleared from (for permanent deletion) the Recycle Bin.
Internet Explorer	The built-in Web browser. Along with an Internet connection, Internet Explorer provides an interface for accessing the Internet or a local intranet.
Taskbar	Contains the Start button to open the Start menu, and buttons for any programs, documents, and windows that are running on the computer. You can easily switch between open items by clicking the item in the Taskbar.
Connect to the Internet	Starts a Wizard to configure your Internet connection.

You can configure the Desktop by customizing the Taskbar and Start menu, adding shortcuts, and setting display properties. These configurations are described in the following sections.

Customizing the Taskbar and Start Menu

Users can customize the Taskbar and *Start menu* through the Taskbar and Start Menu Properties dialog box, shown in Figure 5.2. The easiest way to access this dialog box is to right-click a blank area in the Taskbar and choose Properties from the pop-up menu.

FIGURE 5.2 The General tab of the Taskbar and Start Menu Properties dialog box

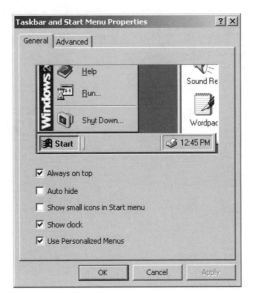

The Taskbar and Start Menu Properties dialog box has two tabs: General and Advanced, containing the options described in the following sections.

Configuring General Properties

Through the General tab of the Taskbar and Start Menu Properties dialog box (see Figure 5.2), you can specify Taskbar and Start menu features such as whether the Taskbar is always visible and whether small or large icons are used on the Start menu. Table 5.2 lists the properties on the General tab.

TABLE 5.2 General Taskbar and Start Menu Properties

Property	Description
Always on Top	Specifies that the Taskbar will always be displayed, even if you maximize another window. This option is enabled by default.

TABLE 5.2 General Taskbar and Start Menu Properties *(continued)*

Property	Description
Auto Hide	Hides the Taskbar. This option is disabled by default. When it is enabled, you show the Taskbar by clicking the area of the screen where the Taskbar appears.
Show Small Icons in Start Menu	Reduces the size of the icons that are displayed on the Start menu. This option is disabled by default. You might enable it if you have many icons and want to display more options without needing to scroll.
Show Clock	Displays a digital clock in the right corner of the Taskbar. By right-clicking the clock, you can adjust the computer's date and time. This option is enabled by default.
Use Personalized Menus	Hides applications that have not been recently used. You can access the hidden applications by clicking the arrow at the bottom of the Programs menu. This option is enabled by default.

Configuring Advanced Properties

The Advanced tab of the Taskbar and Start Menu Properties dialog box, shown in Figure 5.3, allows you to customize your Start menu. You can add or remove items from the Start menu, remove records of recently accessed items, and specify which options are displayed.

FIGURE 5.3   The Advanced tab of the Taskbar and Start Menu Properties dialog box

To add an option to the Start menu, click the Add button in the upper-right corner of the Advanced tab. This starts a Wizard that guides you through the process of creating a shortcut that will be placed on the Start menu. To delete a Start menu option, click the Remove button. If you want to remove the records that Windows 2000 Professional keeps of recently accessed documents, programs, and Web sites, click the Clear button. The Advanced button allows you to add or remove items from the Start menu through Windows Explorer. If you want to return to the defaults for the Program menu, click the Re-sort button.

The Start Menu Settings section of the Advanced tab allows you to configure various Start menu features (listed in Table 5.3). By default, all of these options are disabled for new users.

TABLE 5.3   The Start Menu Settings

Setting	Description
Display Administrative Tools	Specifies whether Administrative Tools appears on the Programs menu.

TABLE 5.3 The Start Menu Settings *(continued)*

Setting	Description
Display Favorites	Specifies whether the Favorites menu appears on the Start menu.
Display Logoff	Specifies whether the Logoff menu appears on the Start menu.
Expand Control Panel	Specifies that you want the contents of Control Panel to be displayed in a menu instead of a window.
Expand My Documents	Specifies that you want the contents of My Documents to be displayed in a menu instead of a window.
Expand Network and Dial-Up Connections	Specifies that you want the contents of Network and Dial-Up Connections to be displayed in a menu instead of a window.
Expand Printers	Specifies that you want the contents of Printers to be displayed in a menu instead of a window.
Scroll the Programs Menu	Specifies that you want the contents of Programs to be displayed in a scrolling menu instead of listed in columns.

In Exercise 5.1, you will check your current Taskbar and Start menu configuration and then set general and advanced Taskbar and Start menu properties.

EXERCISE 5.1

Configuring Taskbar and Start Menu Options

1. Select Start ➤ Programs. Note the size of the icons in the Start menu. Notice that there is no Programs menu item for Administrative Tools or Windows Explorer.

2. Select Start ➤ Settings ➤ Control Panel. A window with all of the Control Panel contents appears.

3. Right-click an empty space on the Taskbar and choose Properties.

4. In the General tab of the Taskbar and Start Menu Properties dialog box, select the Show Small Icons in Start Menu check box.

5. Click the Advanced tab. Click the Add button. In the Create Shortcut dialog box, type **Explorer** in the Type the Location of the Item text box and click the Next button. In the Select Program Folder dialog box, accept the default folder of Programs and click the Next button. In the Select a Title for the Program dialog box, edit the name for the shortcut to **Windows Explorer** and click the Finish button.

6. In the Start Menu Settings section of the Advanced tab, check the Display Administrative Tools and Expand Control Panel check boxes. Click the Apply button, then click the OK button.

7. Select Start ➤ Programs and note the size of the icons in the Start menu. Notice that the Programs menu lists Administrative Tools and Windows Explorer.

8. Select Start ➤ Settings ➤ Control Panel. Notice that the Control Panel contents are displayed in a menu.

9. Edit the Taskbar and Start Menu properties as you like, or return them to their default settings.

Using Shortcuts

Shortcuts are links to items that are accessible from your computer or network. You can use a shortcut to quickly access a file, program, folder, printer, or computer from your Desktop. Shortcuts can exist in various locations, including on the Desktop, on the Start menu, and within folders.

To create a shortcut from Windows Explorer, just right-click the item for which you want to create a shortcut and select Create Shortcut from the pop-up menu. Then you can click the shortcut and drag it to where you want it to appear.

In Exercise 5.2, you will create a shortcut and place it on the Desktop.

EXERCISE 5.2

Creating a Shortcut

1. Select Start ➢ Programs ➢ Accessories ➢ Windows Explorer to start Windows Explorer.

2. Expand My Computer, then Local Disk, then WINNT, then System32.

3. Right-click calc.exe and select Create Shortcut. You see an icon labeled Shortcut to calc.exe.

4. Click the Shortcut to calc.exe icon and drag it to the Desktop.

Setting Display Properties

The options in the Display Properties dialog box, shown in Figure 5.4, allow you to customize the appearance of your Desktop. You can access this dialog box by right-clicking an empty area on the Desktop and selecting Properties from the pop-up menu. Alternatively, you can select Start ➢ Settings ➢ Control Panel ➢ Display. The Display Properties dialog box has six tabs with options that control various aspects of your display:

- The Background tab lets you pick your Desktop background, which uses a picture or an HTML document as wallpaper.

- The Screen Saver tab lets you select a screen saver that will start after the system has been idle for a specified amount of time. You can also specify a password that must be used to reaccess the system after it has been idle. When the idle time has been reached, the computer will be locked, and you must enter the password of the user who is currently logged on to access the computer.

- The Appearance tab has choices for the color scheme used for the Desktop.

- The Web tab lets you select whether or not you want to use the *Active Desktop*, which makes your Desktop look and work like a Web page.

- The Effects tab lets you set special visual effects for the Desktop.

 The Settings tab is used to configure display properties, which are not related to user preferences. Configuring the display is covered in Chapter 4, "Configuring the Windows 2000 Environment."

FIGURE 5.4 The Display Properties dialog box

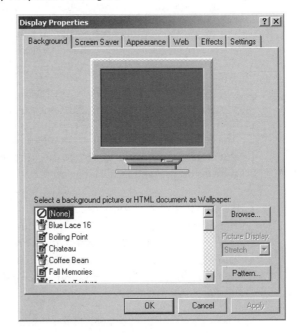

In Exercise 5.3, you will configure display options.

EXERCISE 5.3

Configuring Display Options

1. Right-click an unoccupied area on the Desktop and select Properties to open the Display Properties dialog box.

2. In the Background tab, select Prairie Wind as wallpaper. From the Picture Display drop-down list, select Stretch.

3. Click the Screen Saver tab, select the Starfield Simulation screen saver, and specify a wait of five minutes.

4. Click the Appearance tab, select the Red, White, and Blue (VGA) Scheme. Click the OK button to see your new display settings.

5. Set the display properties to suit your personal preferences, or reset them to their default values.

Configuring Personal Preferences

The most common configuration change made by users is to configure their Desktop. This lets them use the computer more efficiently, and the customization makes them more comfortable with it.

To help users work more efficiently with their computer, you should determine what applications or files are frequently and commonly used, and verify that shortcuts or Start menu items are added for those elements. You can also remove shortcuts or Start menu items for elements that are used seldom or not at all, helping to make the work area less cluttered and less confusing.

Less-experienced users will feel more comfortable with their computer if they have a Desktop personalized to their preferences. This might include their choice of Desktop and a screen saver.

Through the Mouse and Keyboard icons in Control Panel, you can specify your personal preferences for mouse and keyboard settings. Mouse and keyboard properties are covered in Chapter 4.

Managing Multiple Languages and Regional Settings

Windows 2000 Professional supports multiple languages through the use of multilanguage technology. Multilanguage technology is designed to meet the following needs:

- Provide support for multilingual editing of documents
- Provide support for various language interfaces in your environment
- Allow users who speak various languages to share the same computer

<table>
<tr><td>Microsoft
Exam
Objective</td><td>Configure support for multiple languages or multiple locations.
• Enable multiple-language support.
• Configure multiple-language support for users.
• Configure local settings.
• Configure Windows 2000 Professional for multiple locations.</td></tr>
</table>

Multilingual Technology

Windows 2000 supports user options to view, edit, and process documents in multiple languages. These options are provided through Unicode support, National Language Support API, Multilingual API, Resource Files, and Multilingual developer support.

Unicode is an international standard that allows character support for the common characters used in the world's most common languages.

The National Language Support API is used to provide information for locale, character mapping, and keyboard layout. *Locale settings* are used to set local information such as date and time format, currency format, and country names. Character mapping arranges the mapping of local character encodings to Unicode. Keyboard layout settings include character typing information and sorting information.

The Multilingual API is used to set up applications to support keyboard input and fonts from various language versions of applications. For example, Japanese users will see vertical text, and Arabic users will see right-to-left ligatures. This technology allows users to create mixed-language documents.

Windows 2000 stores all language-specific information, such as text for help files and dialog boxes, in files separate from the operating system files. System code can thus be shared by all language versions of Windows 2000, while using the specific files of the currently selected language.

Multilingual developer support is a special set of APIs that enables developers to create generic code and then provide support for multiple languages.

Choosing Windows 2000 Multiple-Language Support

Multilanguage support consists of two technologies:

- Multilingual editing and viewing, which supports multiple languages while a user is viewing, editing, and printing documents

- Multilanguage user interfaces, so that the Windows 2000 Professional user interface can be presented in different languages

Depending on the level of language support required by your environment, you may use either a localized version of Window 2000 Professional or the multilanguage version of Windows 2000 Professional. The following sections describe these versions and how to configure multilanguage support.

Using Localized Windows 2000

Microsoft provides localized editions of Windows 2000 Professional. For example, users in the United States will most likely use the English version, and users in Japan will most likely use the Japanese version. Localized versions of Windows 2000 Professional include fully localized user interfaces for the language that was selected. In addition, localized versions allow users to view, edit, and print documents in more than 60 different languages. However, localized versions do not support multilanguage user interfaces.

Using Windows 2000 Multilanguage Version

Windows 2000 Multilanguage Version provides user interfaces in a number of different languages. This version is useful in multinational corporations where users speak several languages and must share computers. It is also appropriate when administrators want to deploy a single version of Windows 2000 Professional worldwide. You can manage multiple users who share a single computer and speak different languages through user profiles (covered in Chapter 8, "Using User Profiles and Hardware Profiles") or through group policies (covered in Chapter 7, "Managing Groups").

Two sets of files are necessary to support Windows 2000 Multilanguage Version:

- Language groups, which contain the fonts and files required to process and display the specific languages

- Windows 2000 Professional Multilanguage Version files, which contain the language content required by the user interface and help files

When you install Windows 2000 Multilanguage Version, you select the initial language that will be installed on the computer. For each language that you wish to use, you must also have the appropriate language group installed. For example, if you want to use the Japanese user interface, you must also install the Japanese language group. If you want to install other language support after installation, you can install and remove Windows 2000 Multilanguage Version files and language groups through Regional Options in Control Panel. Each instance of Multilanguage Version files will use approximately 45MB of disk space. You can set the default user interface (UI) language, or add/remove UI languages through the `Muisetup.exe` file.

Windows 2000 Multilanguage Version allows users to select the User Interface in any of the following languages:

Arabic	Finnish	Korean
Brazilian	French	Norwegian
Chinese (Simplified)	German	Portuguese
Chinese (Traditional)	Greek	Russian
Czech	Hebrew	Polish
Danish	Hungarian	Spanish
Dutch	Italian	Swedish
English	Japanese	Turkish

Windows 2000 Multilanguage Version is not available through retail stores. You order this version of Windows 2000 Professional through Microsoft Volume Licensing Programs. For more information about the multilanguage version, go to www.microsoft.com/licensing.

Enabling and Configuring Multilingual Support

On a localized version of Windows 2000 Professional, you enable and configure multilingual editing and viewing through *Regional Options* in Control Panel. To access the Regional Options dialog box (Figure 5.5), select Start ➢ Settings ➢ Control Panel ➢ Regional Options.

In the list box at the bottom of the Regional Options dialog box, check the language settings that you wish to support on the computer. After you click OK, you may be prompted to insert the Windows 2000 Professional CD to copy the distribution files required for multiple-language support. Then you will need to restart your computer for the new changes to take effect. After the restart, you will notice a new icon on the Taskbar that shows the current locale and keyboard inputs that are being used. You can switch to another supported language by clicking this icon and selecting the locale input you wish to use.

FIGURE 5.5 The Regional Options dialog box

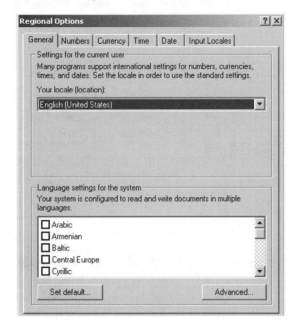

Configuring Locale Settings

For localized Windows 2000 Professional as well as the Multilanguage Version, you can also configure locale settings for number, currency, time, and date formats, and for input locales (which allows you to select the input language you will use). Like multilingual support, these settings are made through the Regional Options dialog box (see Figure 5.5). Simply select the locale (location) for the regional settings that you want to use from the drop-down list at the top of the dialog box.

In Exercise 5.4, you will configure the locale settings on your computer.

EXERCISE 5.4

Configuring Locale Settings

1. Select Start ➢ Settings ➢ Control Panel ➢ Regional Options. In the Regional Options dialog box, note your current locale.

EXERCISE 5.4 *(continued)*

2. One by one, click the Numbers, Currency, Time, and Date tabs and note the configurations in each tab.

3. Click the General tab, and select the Danish locale (location) from the drop-down list at the top. Then click the Apply button.

4. Again, open the Numbers, Currency, Time, and Date tabs and note the changed configurations.

5. Return to the General tab, reset your locale to the original configuration, and click the Apply button.

Real World Scenario

Supporting Multilingual Environments

Your company has an office in Tokyo. Computers are shared by users there who require both English and Japanese language support, for document management as well as the user interface (UI). Your CIO has asked you to set up a system that lets users in the Tokyo office use Windows 2000 in any language.

To do this, you must use Windows 2000 Multilanguage Version. Each user of a computer can select the preferred UI and specify locale information. This is stored as part of the user's profile. When you log on as a specific user, you see the linguistic and locale information that has been configured.

Configuring Accessibility Features

Through its accessibility options and accessibility utilities, Windows 2000 Professional supports users with limited sight, hearing, or mobility. The following sections describe how to use these accessibility features.

Microsoft
Exam
Objective

Configure and troubleshoot accessibility services.

Setting Accessibility Options

Through *Accessibility Options* in Control Panel, you can configure keyboard, sound, display, mouse, and general properties of Windows 2000 Professional for users with special needs. To access the Accessibility Options dialog box (Figure 5.6), select Control Panel ➢ Accessibility Options. This dialog box has five tabs with options to configure special behavior for your computer:

- The Keyboard tab contains settings for using StickyKeys, FilterKeys, and ToggleKeys. StickyKeys allows the use of the Shift, Ctrl, or Alt key in conjunction with another key, one key at a time. FilterKeys ignores brief or repeated keystrokes. ToggleKeys makes a noise whenever you press the Caps Lock, Num Lock, or Scroll Lock key.

- The Sound tab allows you specify whether you want to use SoundSentry, which generates a visual warning whenever the computer makes a sound, and ShowSounds, which displays captions for speech and sounds on your computer.

- The Display tab contains high-contrast settings for Windows colors and fonts.

- The Mouse tab lets you enable use of MouseKeys, which allows you to control the mouse pointer through the keyboard.

- The General tab contains several maintenance and administrative options. You can choose to automatically reset accessibility features after these features have been idle for a specified amount of time, and to use notification features to notify you when accessibility features are turned on or off. You can also configure SerialKey devices to provide alternative access to keyboard and mouse features. Administrative options allow you to apply accessibility options to the logon Desktop and to defaults for new users.

FIGURE 5.6 The Accessibility Options dialog box

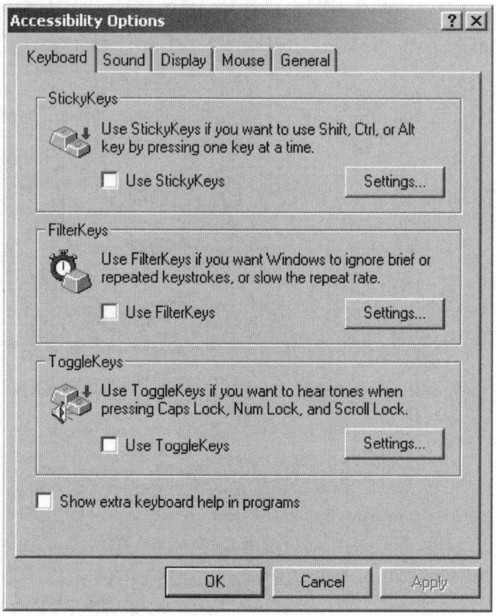

Using Accessibility Utilities

Windows 2000 provides several accessibility utilities. These utilities include the Accessibility Wizard, Magnifier, Narrator, On-Screen Keyboard, and Utility Manager.

The Accessibility Wizard

The *Accessibility Wizard* configures a computer based on the user's vision, hearing, and mobility needs. While working through the Accessibility Wizard, the user selects the text size that is the easiest to read. The wizard also collects input to determine if the user has vision, hearing, or mobility challenges.

Through the Accessibility Wizard, you can also configure the option, "I want to set administrative options." This lets you configure accessibility options for all of a computer's new user accounts or only for the current user profile. You can also create an .acw file (Accessibility Wizard Settings) that can then be copied to another user's profile folder. This can be on the same computer or a different one; it allows the new user to have the same accessibility configuration.

The Magnifier Utility

The *Magnifier utility* creates a separate window to magnify a portion of your screen, as shown in Figure 5.7. This option is useful for users who have poor vision. To access Magnifier, select Start ➤ Programs ➤ Accessories ➤ Accessibility ➤ Magnifier.

FIGURE 5.7   The Magnifier utility

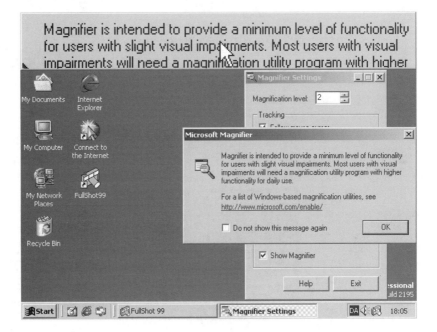

The Narrator Utility

The *Narrator utility* can read aloud on-screen text, dialog boxes, menus, and buttons. This utility requires that you have some type of sound output device installed and configured. To access Narrator, select Start ➤ Programs ➤ Accessories ➤ Accessibility ➤ Narrator. This brings up the dialog box shown in Figure 5.8.

FIGURE 5.8 The Narrator dialog box

The On-Screen Keyboard

The *On-Screen Keyboard* displays a keyboard on the screen, as shown in Figure 5.9. Users can use the On-Screen Keyboard keys through a mouse or another input device as an alternative to the keys on the regular keyboard. To access the On-Screen Keyboard, select Start ≻ Programs ≻ Accessories ≻ Accessibility ≻ On-Screen Keyboard.

FIGURE 5.9 The On-Screen Keyboard

The Utility Manager

The *Utility Manager* allows you to start and stop the Windows 2000 Professional accessibility utilities. You can also specify whether these utilities are automatically started when Windows 2000 Professional starts or when the Utility Manager is started. To access the Utility Manager, select Start ≻ Programs ≻ Accessories ≻ Accessibility ≻ Utility Manager. Figure 5.10 shows the Utility Manager.

FIGURE 5.10   The Utility Manager

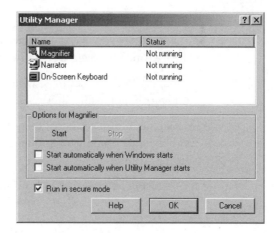

In Exercise 5.5, you will use the Windows 2000 Professional accessibility features.

EXERCISE 5.5

Using Accessibility Features

1. Select Start ➢ Programs ➢ Accessories ➢ Accessibility ➢ Magnifier.

2. Experiment with the Magnifier utility. When you are finished, click the Exit button in the Magnifier Settings dialog box.

3. Select Start ➢ Programs ➢ Accessories ➢ Accessibility ➢ On-Screen Keyboard.

4. Select Start ➢ Programs ➢ Accessories ➢ Notepad to open Notepad.

5. Create a text document using the On-Screen Keyboard. When you are finished, close the Notepad document without saving it.

6. Close the On-Screen Keyboard.

Summary

In this chapter, you learned about managing the Windows 2000 Professional Desktop. We covered the following topics:

- Managing Desktop settings, which include customizing the Taskbar and Start menu, using shortcuts, and setting display properties

- Managing multiple languages and regional settings, which include enabling and configuring multilingual support and choosing locale settings

- Configuring accessibility options and using accessibility utilities

Exam Essentials

Be able to configure and troubleshoot desktop settings.   Understand how to customize and configure the Windows 2000 desktop settings, and be able to troubleshoot desktop settings that have been misconfigured.

Configure the computer for multiple language support.   Be able to define the language features that are available in various versions of Windows 2000. Know how to configure locale information and support multiple-language requirements for document processing and the User Interface on a single computer.

Set accessibility options for users with special needs.   Be able to list the accessibility options and their capabilities. Know how to use the Accessibility Manager and Utility Manager, and be able to specify the administrative tasks that can be performed through each utility.

Key Terms

Before taking the exam, you should be familiar with the following terms:

Accessibility options	My Network Places
Accessibility Wizard	Narrator utility
Active Desktop	On-Screen Keyboard
Desktop	Recycle Bin
Internet Explorer	Regional Options
locale settings	shortcut
Magnifier utility	Start menu
My Computer	Taskbar
My Documents	Utility Manager

Review Questions

1. You have recently hired three employees who need to use Windows 2000 accessibility features. All of the users need the same configuration. You want to configure these options on one computer and copy them to the other computers. Which utility do you use to create the accessibility file and what extension should the file have?

   A. Accessibility Wizard, .acw file

   B. Accessibility Wizard, .acc file

   C. Utility Manager, .acw file

   D. Utility Manager, .acc file

2. Dan is using Windows 2000 on his laptop computer. Programs he frequently uses are not on the Taskbar or Start menu, and programs he has never used are still listed from the manufacturer's initial install. Which of the following methods should Dan use to configure the Taskbar and Start menu in Windows 2000 Professional?

   A. Right-click an empty space on the Taskbar and choose Properties from the pop-up menu.

   B. Select Control Panel ➢ Menu Settings.

   C. Right-click My Computer and choose Manage from the pop-up menu.

   D. Right-click My Computer and choose Properties from the pop-up menu.

3. Vince likes the idea of using shortcuts to quickly access files and applications. He wants to create shortcuts on his computer and wants to know which of the following locations can contain a shortcut. Choose all that apply.

   A. Start menu

   B. MMC

   C. Desktop

   D. Folder

4. Barbara has a laptop that is using Windows 2000 Professional localized version for English. She is spending the summer in Mexico City and wants to configure the user interface so that it is displayed in Spanish. How should she configure her computer?

   A. Configure Regional Options to add Spanish language support.

   B. Through Control Panel, Add/Remove Software icon, add Spanish language support.

   C. Configure Regional Options to add Spanish language support, then set the locale settings for Mexico.

   D. None of the above.

5. Bob has impaired vision and is having trouble reading documents on his Windows 2000 laptop. Which accessibility utility can Bob use to enlarge a portion of the screen for better visibility?

   A. Enlarger

   B. Expander

   C. Magnifier

   D. Microscope

6. You are supporting Windows 2000 computers used by a variety of employees from several countries. When they visit your location, each employee would like their desktop to appear as it would in their native country. Which of the following locale options can you configure for these users through Windows 2000? Choose all that apply.

   A. The format of the date displayed on the computer

   B. The language that is used to display the GUI

   C. The currency symbol used by default on the computer

   D. The format of the time displayed on the computer

7. You have just accidentally deleted your C:\Documents\ Timesheet.xls file. What is the easiest way to recover this file?

   A. In Folder Options, click the Show Deleted Files option.

   B. In Folder Options, click the Undo Deleted Files option.

   C. Click the Recycle Bin icon on the Desktop and restore the deleted file.

   D. Restore the file from your most recent tape backup.

8. You are a member of a workgroup environment consisting of computers running Windows 2000 Professional. You log on as user Kasia, who is a member of the Administrators group. When you select Start ➤ Programs, you do not see Administrative Tools. How do you correct this problem?

   A. Log on as the user Administrator.

   B. Add Administrative Tools through the Taskbar and Start Menu Properties dialog box, General tab.

   C. Add Administrative Tools through the Taskbar and Start Menu Properties dialog box, Advanced tab.

   D. Add Administrative Tools through the Taskbar and Start Menu Properties dialog box, Management tab.

9. Jeff has a new display adapter and monitor. He wants to set display properties for his Desktop. Which of the following options are *not* set through the Display Properties dialog box?

   A. Desktop background

   B. Screen saver

   C. Special visual effects for your Desktop

   D. Contrast and brightness of the monitor

10. You sit in a busy area of the office. Sometimes, you forget to log off or lock the computer when you leave your desk. How can you configure your computer so that it will become password protected if it is idle for more than 10 minutes?

    A. Through Control Panel, Logon/Logoff icon

    B. Through Display Properties, Screen Saver tab

    C. Through Control Panel, Security icon

    D. Through Local Users and Groups, Security properties

11. Brett is using a laptop computer that has Windows 2000 Multi-language Version installed. The computer is configured for English and Spanish, with English as the default language. Brett has been assigned to work in Mexico City for a year and now wants his default user interface to be in Spanish. Through which file can you edit the default language interface?

    A. `Muisetup.exe`

    B. `MLsetup.exe`

    C. `Langsetup.exe`

    D. `Muiconfig.exe`

12. You are planning to install Windows 2000 Multilanguage Version in your environment. Maria has requested that you install user interfaces on her computer for Russian, Polish, and English. When determining the resources required for this configuration, how much disk space should be allocated for each language?

    A. 10MB

    B. 20MB

    C. 45MB

    D. 85MB

13. Cindy has just installed Windows 2000 Professional on her home computer. The Windows 2000 version she is using is a localized English version. Cindy would also like to be able to use Simplified Chinese to create documents to send to her friends in Taiwan. How can she configure the computer to support Simplified Chinese language settings?

    A. Through Control Panel, Language icon

    B. Through Control Panel, Regional Options icon

    C. Through Control Panel, Multilanguage Support icon

    D. Only by upgrading to Windows 2000 Multilanguage Version

14. Ken configured his computer with the accessibility options StickyKeys and ToggleKeys. Everything was working properly. Then Ken went to a meeting. When he returned after 30 minutes, his accessibility options were no longer working. What is most likely the problem?

    A. The accessibility options are configured to be automatically reset if the computer remains idle for a specified amount of time.

    B. Ken needs to log on again to enable the accessibility features.

    C. Ken needs to restart his computer to enable the accessibility features.

    D. The accessibility settings have become corrupt and need to be reset.

15. Meredith is a user with limited mobility. She wants to use an alternative pointing device instead of a regular mouse pointer. You install the device and load the appropriate driver. What additional step should you take?

    A. Configure SerialKey Devices through Accessibility Options.

    B. Configure Disable Serial Devices through Accessibility Options.

    C. Configure Alternative Serial Devices through Accessibility Options.

    D. Configure ParallelKey Devices through Accessibility Options.

Answers to Review Questions

1. A. You can copy a user's accessibility settings by using the administrative options in the Accessibility Wizard. After you create the desired configuration, you can save it as an .acw file, which can then be copied to the target user's profile folder.

2. A. The easiest way to configure the Taskbar and Start menu properties is by right-clicking an open area of the Taskbar and choosing Properties. There is no Menu Settings option in Control Panel.

3. A, C, D. You can put shortcuts in the Start menu, on the Desktop, or in a folder. You can't put a shortcut in the Microsoft Management Console (MMC).

4. D. Localized versions of Windows 2000 Professional do not support multilanguage user interfaces. Localized versions support only the ability to view, edit, and print documents in other languages. Language support for the GUI is provided in Windows 2000 Multilanguage Version.

5. C. The Magnifier utility creates a separate window that magnifies the portion of the screen that is being used.

6. A, C, D. Locale settings are used to configure regional settings for numbers, currency, time, date, and input locales.

7. C. The easiest way to recover a deleted file is to restore it from the Recycle Bin. The Recycle Bin holds all of the files and folders that have been deleted, as long as there is space on the disk. From this utility, you can retrieve or permanently delete files.

8. C. You can specify options such as Display Administrative Tools, Display Logoff, and Display Favorites through the Advanced tab of the Taskbar and Start Menu Properties dialog box.

9. D. Through the Display Properties dialog box, you can set your Desktop background, the screen saver to be used by your computer, and any special visual effects for your Desktop. Contrast and brightness of the monitor are typically set through the monitor's controls.

10. B. The Screen Saver tab of the Display Properties dialog box allows you to select a screen saver that will start after the computer has been idle for a specified amount of time. You can configure the screen saver to require the user's password in order to resume the computer's normal function. When the password is invoked, the computer will be locked. To access the locked computer, you must enter the password of the user who is currently logged on.

11. A. You can edit the default user language interface or add or remove user interface languages through the `Muisetup.exe` file.

12. C. Each instance of Multilanguage Version files will use approximately 45MB of disk space.

13. B. Localized versions of Windows 2000 Professional include fully localized user interfaces for the language that was selected. In addition, localized versions include the ability to view, edit, and print documents in more than 60 different languages. On a localized version of Windows 2000 Professional, you enable and configure multilingual editing and viewing through the Regional Options icon in Control Panel.

14. A. Through the Accessibility Options icon of Control Panel, you can control how long the accessibility options will be active if the computer is idle. A setting on the General tab allows you to turn off accessibility options if the computer has been idle for a specified number of minutes. You should check this setting if working accessibility options unexpectedly become disabled.

15. A. In the General tab of the Accessibility Options dialog box, you can select the Support SerialKey Devices option to allow alternative access to keyboard and mouse features.

Chapter 6

Managing Users

MICROSOFT EXAM OBJECTIVES COVERED IN THIS CHAPTER:

✓ **Implement, configure, manage, and troubleshoot local security policy.**

✓ **Implement, configure, manage, and troubleshoot local user accounts.**

- Implement, configure, manage, and troubleshoot auditing.
- Implement, configure, manage, and troubleshoot account settings.
- Implement, configure, manage, and troubleshoot account policy.
- Create and manage local users and groups.
- Implement, configure, manage, and troubleshoot user rights.

✓ **Implement, configure, manage, and troubleshoot local user authentication.**

- Configure and troubleshoot local user accounts.
- Configure and troubleshoot domain user accounts.

✓ **Implement, configure, manage, and troubleshoot a security configuration.**

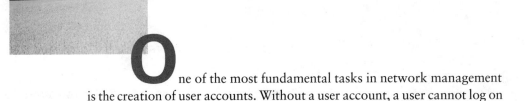

One of the most fundamental tasks in network management is the creation of user accounts. Without a user account, a user cannot log on to a computer, server, or network.

When users log on, they supply a username and password. Then their user accounts are validated by some security mechanism. In Windows 2000 Professional, users can log on to a computer locally, or they can log on through Active Directory.

When you first create users, you assign them usernames, passwords, and password settings. After a user is created, you can change these settings and select other options for that user through the user Properties dialog box.

You can also set up policies to help manage user accounts. Account policies are used to control the logon environment for the computer, such as password and logon restrictions. Local policies specify what users are able to do once they log on and include auditing, user rights, and security options.

In this chapter, you will learn about user management at the local level, including creating user accounts, managing user properties, setting account and local policies, and troubleshooting user account authentication. We'll begin with an overview of the types of Windows 2000 user accounts and how the logon process works.

Windows 2000 User Accounts

When you install Windows 2000 Professional, several user accounts are created automatically. You can then create new user accounts. On Windows 2000 Professional computers, you can create local user accounts. If your network has a Windows 2000 Server domain controller, your network can have domain user accounts, as well.

Built-in Accounts

By default, a computer that is installed with Windows 2000 Professional in a workgroup has three user accounts:

Administrator   The *Administrator account* is a special account that has full control over the computer. You provide a password for this account during Windows 2000 Professional installation. The Administrator account can perform all tasks, such as creating users and groups, managing the file system, and setting up printing.

Guest   The *Guest account* allows users to access the computer even if they do not have a unique username and password. Because of the inherent security risks associated with this type of user, the Guest account is disabled by default. When this account is enabled, it is usually given very limited privileges.

Initial user   The *initial user* account uses the name of the registered user. This account is created only if the computer is installed as a member of a workgroup, rather than as part of a domain. By default, the initial user is a member of the Administrators group.

By default, the name Administrator is given to the account with full control over the computer. You can increase the computer's security by renaming the Administrator account and then creating an account named Administrator without any permissions. This way, even if a hacker is able to log on as Administrator, the intruder won't be able to access any system resources.

Local and Domain User Accounts

Windows 2000 supports two kinds of users: local users and domain users. A computer that is running Windows 2000 Professional has the ability to store its own user accounts database. The users stored at the local computer are known as *local user accounts*.

The *Active Directory* is a directory service that is available with the Windows 2000 Server platform. It stores information in a central database that allows users to have a single user account for the network. The users stored in the Active Directory's central database are called *domain user accounts*.

Microsoft Exam Objective

Implement, configure, manage, and troubleshoot local user authentication.

- Configure and troubleshoot local user accounts.
- Configure and troubleshoot domain user accounts.

If you use local user accounts, they are required on each computer that the user needs access to within the network. For this reason, domain user accounts are commonly used to manage users on large networks.

On Windows 2000 Professional computers and Windows 2000 member servers, you create local users through the Local Users and Groups utility, as described in the "Working with User Accounts" section later in the chapter. On Windows 2000 Server domain controllers, you manage users with the Microsoft Active Directory Users and Computers utility.

> Active Directory is covered in detail in *MCSE: Windows 2000 Directory Services Administration Study Guide*, 2nd ed., by Anil Desai with James Chellis (Sybex, 2001).

Logging On and Logging Off

Users must log on to a Windows 2000 Professional computer before they can use that computer. When you create user accounts, you set up the computer to accept the logon information provided by the user.

When users are ready to stop working on a Windows 2000 Professional computer, they should log off. Logging off is accomplished through the Windows Security dialog box.

The following sections describe the *logon* and *logoff* processes and the options in the Windows Security dialog box.

Local User Logon Authentication

When you log on to a Windows 2000 Professional computer locally, you must present a valid username and password (ones that exist within the local accounts database). As part of a successful *authentication*, the following steps take place:

1. At system startup, the user is prompted to press Ctrl+Alt+Delete to access the logon dialog box. The user types in a valid logon name and password, and then clicks the OK button.

The Ctrl+Alt+Delete sequence was originally used for security purposes. Security violations occurred when programs were written to mimic the logon process, but were actually copying out the username and password. If a rogue password program were running and you pressed Ctrl+Alt+Delete, it would cause the computer to reboot or the Windows Security dialog box to appear.

2. The local computer compares the user's logon credentials with the information in the local security database.

3. If the information presented matches the account database, an *access token* is created. Access tokens are used to identify the user and the groups of which that user is a member.

Access tokens are created only when you log on. If you change group memberships, you need to log off and log on again to update the access token.

Figure 6.1 illustrates the three main steps in the logon process.

FIGURE 6.1 The logon process

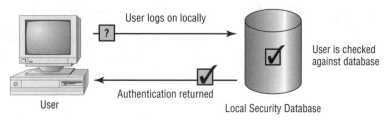

Other actions that take place as part of the logon process include the following:

- The system reads the part of the Registry that contains user configuration information.

- The user's profile is loaded. (User profiles are discussed briefly in the "Setting Up User Profiles, Logon Scripts, and Home Folders" section later in this chapter and in more detail in Chapter 8, "Using User Profiles and Hardware Profiles.")

- Any policies that have been assigned to the user through a user or group policy are enforced. (Policies for users are discussed later in this chapter, in the "Using Account Policies" and "Using Local Policies" sections. Group policies are covered in Chapter 7, "Managing Groups.")

- Any logon scripts that have been assigned are executed. (Assigning logon scripts to users is discussed in the "Setting Up User Profiles, Logon Scripts, and Home Folders" section.)

- Persistent network and printer connections are restored. (Network connections are discussed in Chapter 11, "Managing Network Connections," and printer connections are covered in Chapter 12, "Managing Printing.")

Through the logon process, you can control what resources a user can access by assigning permissions. Permissions are granted to either users or groups. Permissions also determine what actions a user can perform on a computer. In Chapter 10, "Accessing Files and Folders," you will learn more about assigning resource permissions.

Logging Off Windows 2000 Professional

You normally log off Windows 2000 Professional via the Windows Security dialog box, shown in Figure 6.2. (Another way to log off is to use Start ➤ Shutdown ➤ Logoff.) You access the Windows Security dialog box by pressing Ctrl+Alt+Delete.

FIGURE 6.2 The Windows Security dialog box

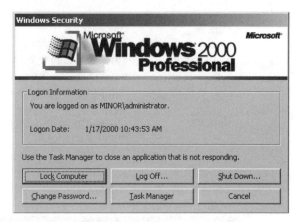

The Windows Security dialog box shows which user is currently logged on, as well as the logon date and time. From this dialog box, you can just log off the current user (and leave the computer running) or you can log off and shut down the computer. In addition, there are a few other tasks you can perform using the Windows Security dialog box. Table 6.1 lists the options in the Windows Security dialog box.

TABLE 6.1 The Windows Security Dialog Box Options

Option	Description
Lock Computer	Leaves the current user logged on while securing the computer from other access. To unlock the computer, you type in the password of the user who locked it.
Change Password	Allows users to change their own password. The user must enter the old password and then type in and confirm the new password.
Log Off	Logs off the active user but leaves the Windows 2000 Professional computer running. This allows other users to access services and shares that have been created on that computer.
Task Manager	Brings up the Task Manager utility.

TABLE 6.1 The Windows Security Dialog Box Options *(continued)*

Option	Description
Shut Down	Forces all files to be closed, saves all changes that have been made to the operating system, and prepares the computer to be shut down.
Cancel	Closes the Windows Security dialog box without making any changes.

In Exercise 6.1, you will use the options in the Windows Security dialog box.

EXERCISE 6.1

Using the Windows Security Dialog Box

1. You should already be logged on as Administrator before you begin this exercise. Press Ctrl+Alt+Delete to access the Windows Security dialog box.

2. Click the Lock Computer button to lock the computer.

3. Press Ctrl+Alt+Delete. Supply the Administrator password to unlock the computer.

4. Click the Change Password button to access the Change Password dialog box. You can change the password or click the Cancel button to keep your current password.

5. Click the Task Manager button. Click each tab in the Task Manager window to get a general idea of the features that Task Manager offers. (See Chapter 14, "Optimizing Windows 2000," for details on using the Task Manager.)

6. When you're finished exploring, close the Task Manager window. You return to the Desktop.

Working with User Accounts

To set up and manage users, you use the *Local Users and Groups* utility. With Local Users and Groups, you can create, delete, and rename user accounts, as well as change passwords.

Microsoft Exam Objective

Implement, configure, manage, and troubleshoot local user accounts.

- Implement, configure, manage, and troubleshoot account settings.
- Create and manage local users and groups.

The procedures for many basic user management tasks—such as creating, disabling, deleting, and renaming user accounts—are the same for both Windows 2000 Professional and Server.

Using the Local Users and Groups Utility

The first step to working with Windows 2000 Professional user accounts is to access the Local Users and Groups utility. There are two common methods for accessing this utility:

- You can load Local Users and Groups as a Microsoft Management Console (MMC) snap-in. (See Chapter 4, "Configuring the Windows 2000 Environment," for details on the MMC and the purpose of snap-ins.)

- You can access the Local Users and Groups utility through the Computer Management utility.

In Exercise 6.2, you will use both methods for accessing the Local Users and Groups utility.

EXERCISE 6.2

Accessing the Local Users and Groups Utility

In this exercise, you will first add the Local Users and Groups snap-in to the MMC. Next, you will add a shortcut to your Desktop that will take you to the MMC. Finally, you will use the other access technique of opening the Local Users and Groups utility from the Computer Management utility.

Adding the Local Users and Groups Snap-in to the MMC

1. Select Start ≻ Run. In the Run dialog box, type MMC and press Enter.

2. Select Console ≻ Add/Remove Snap-in.

3. In the Add/Remove Snap-in dialog box, click the Add button.

4. In the Add Standalone Snap-in dialog box, select Local Users and Groups and click the Add button.

5. In the Choose Target Machine dialog box, click the Finish button to accept the default selection of Local Computer.

6. Click the Close button in the Add Standalone Snap-in dialog box. Then click the OK button in the Add/Remove Snap-in dialog box.

7. In the MMC window, expand the Local Users and Groups folder to see the Users and Groups folders.

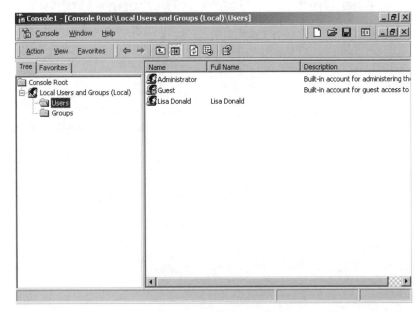

Adding the MMC to Your Desktop

8. Select Console ➢ Save. Click the folder with the up arrow icon until you are at the root of the computer.

9. Select the Desktop option and specify **Admin Console** as the file-name. The default extension is .msc. Click the Save button.

Accessing Local Users and Groups through Computer Management

10. Right-click My Computer and select Manage.

11. In the Computer Management window, expand the System Tools folder and then the Local Users and Groups folder.

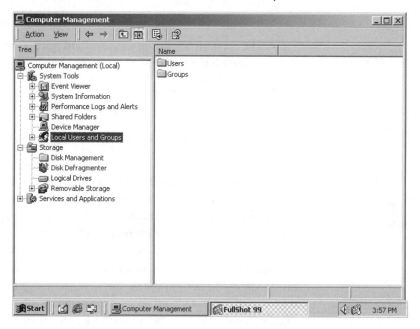

If your computer doesn't have the MMC configured, the quickest way to access the Local Users and Groups utility is through the Computer Management utility.

Creating New Users

To create users on a Windows 2000 Professional computer, you must be logged on as a user with permissions to create a new user, or you must be a member of the Administrators group or Power Users group. (Groups are covered in Chapter 7.)

Username Rules and Conventions

The only real requirement for creating a new user is that you must provide a valid username. "Valid" means that the name must follow the Windows 2000 rules for usernames. However, it's also a good idea to have your own rules for usernames, which form your naming convention.

The following are the Windows 2000 rules for usernames:

- A username must be between 1 and 20 characters.

- The username must be unique to all other user and group names stored on the specified computer.

- The username cannot contain the following characters:

    * / \ [ ] : ; | = , + * ? < > "

- A username cannot consist exclusively of periods or spaces.

Keeping these rules in mind, you should choose a naming convention (a consistent naming format). For example, consider a user named Kevin Donald. One naming convention might use the last name and first initial, for the username DonaldK. Another naming convention might use the first initial and last name, for the username KDonald. Other user-naming conventions are based on the naming convention defined for e-mail names, so that the logon name and e-mail name match. You should also provide a mechanism that would accommodate duplicate names. For example, if you had a user named Kevin Donald and a user named Kate Donald, you might use a middle initial, for usernames such as KLDonald and KMDonald.

Naming conventions should also be applied to objects such as groups, printers, and computers.

Usernames and Security Identifiers

When you create a new user, a *security identifier*, or *SID*, is automatically created on the computer for the user account. The username is a property of the SID. For example, a user SID might look like this:

S-1-5-21-823518204-746137067-120266-629-500

It's apparent that using SIDs for user identification would make administration a nightmare. Fortunately, for your administrative tasks, you see and use the username instead of the SID.

SIDs have several advantages. Because Windows 2000 uses the SID as the user object, you can easily rename a user while still retaining all the properties of that user. SIDs also ensure that if you delete and re-create a user account with the same username, the new user account will not have any of the properties of the old account, because it is based on a new, unique SID. Renaming and deleting user accounts are discussed later in this chapter.

Make sure that your users know that usernames are not case sensitive, but passwords are.

In Exercise 6.3, you will use the New User dialog box to create several new local user accounts. We will put these user accounts to work in subsequent exercises in this chapter. Table 6.2 describes all the options available in the New User dialog box.

Before you start this exercise, make sure that you are logged on as a user with permissions to create new users and have already added the Local Users and Groups snap-in to the MMC (see Exercise 6.2).

EXERCISE 6.3

Creating New Local Users

1. Open the Admin MMC shortcut that was created in Exercise 6.2 and expand the Local Users and Groups snap-in.

EXERCISE 6.3 *(continued)*

2. Highlight the Users folder and select Action ➢ New User. The New User dialog box appears.

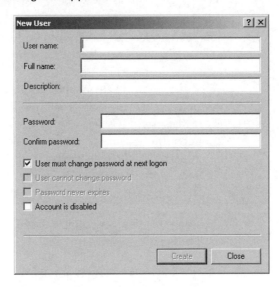

3. In the User Name text box, type **Cam**.

4. In the Full Name text box, type **Cam Presely**.

5. In the Description text box, type **Sales Vice President**.

6. Click the Create button to add the user. (Leave the Password and Confirm Password text boxes empty and accept the defaults for the check boxes.)

7. Use the New User dialog box to create six more users, filling out the fields as follows:

   Name: **Kevin**; Full Name: **Kevin Jones**; Description: **Sales-Florida**; Password: (blank)

   Name: **Terry**; Full Name: **Terry Belle**; Description: **Marketing**; Password: (blank)

   Name: **Ron**; Full Name: **Ron Klein**; Description: **PR**; Password: **superman**

Name: **Wendy**; Full Name: **Wendy Smith**; Description: **Sales-Texas**; Password: **supergirl**

Name: **Emily**; Full Name: **Emily Buras**; Description: **President**; Password: **peach**

Name: **Michael**; Full Name: **Michael Phillips**; Description: **Tech Support**; Password: **apple**

8. After you've finished creating all of the users, click the Close button to exit the New User dialog box.

TABLE 6.2   User Account Options Available in the New User Dialog Box

Option	Description
User name	Defines the username for the new account. Choose a name that is consistent with your naming convention (e.g., WSmith). This is the only required field. Usernames are not case sensitive.
Full name	Allows you to provide more detailed name information. This is typically the user's first and last name (e.g., Wendy Smith). By default, this field contains the same name as the User Name field.
Description	Typically used to specify a title and/or location (e.g., Sales-Texas) for the account, but it can be used to provide any additional information about the user.
Password	Assigns the initial password for the user. For security purposes, avoid using readily available information about the user. Passwords can be up to 14 characters and are case sensitive.
Confirm password	Confirms that you typed the password the same way two times to verify that you entered the password correctly.

TABLE 6.2 User Account Options Available in the New User Dialog Box *(continued)*

Option	Description
User must change password at next logon	If enabled, forces the user to change the password the first time they log on. This is done to increase security. By default, this option is selected.
User cannot change password	If enabled, prevents a user from changing their password. It is useful for accounts such as Guest and accounts that are shared by more than one user. By default, this option is not selected.
Password never expires	If enabled, specifies that the password will never expire, even if a password policy has been specified. For example, you might enable this option if this is a service account and you do not want the administrative overhead of managing password changes. By default, this option is not selected.
Account is disabled	If enabled, specifies that this account cannot be used for logon purposes. For example, you might select this option for template accounts or if an account is not currently being used. It helps keep inactive accounts from posing security threats. By default, this option is not selected.

You can also create users through the command-line utility NET USER. For more information about this command, type **NET USER /?** from a command prompt.

Disabling User Accounts

When a user account is no longer needed, the account should be disabled or deleted. After you've disabled an account, you can later enable it again to restore it with all of its associated user properties. An account that is deleted, however, can never be recovered.

User accounts that are not in use pose a security threat because an intruder could access your network though an inactive account. For example, after inheriting a network, I ran a network security diagnostic and noticed several accounts for users who no longer worked for the company. These accounts had Administrative rights, including dial-in permissions. This was a very risky situation, and the accounts were deleted on the spot.

You might disable an account because a user will not be using it for a period of time, perhaps because that employee is going on vacation or taking a leave of absence. Another reason to disable an account is that you're planning to put another user in that same function. For example, suppose that Rick, the engineering manager, quits. If you disable his account, when your company hires a new engineering manager, you can simply rename Rick's user account (to the username for the new manager) and enable that account. This ensures that the user who takes over Rick's position will have all the same user properties and own all the same resources.

Disabling accounts also provides a security mechanism for special situations. For example, if your company were laying off a group of people, a security measure would be to disable their accounts at the same time the layoff notices were given out. This prevents those users from inflicting any damage to the company's files on their way out. (Yes, this does seem cold-hearted, and other employees are bound to fear for their jobs any time the servers go down and they aren't able to log on, but it does serve the purpose.)

In Exercise 6.4, you will disable a user account. Before you follow this exercise, you should have already created new users (see Exercise 6.3).

EXERCISE 6.4

Disabling a User

1. Open the Admin MMC shortcut that was created in Exercise 6.2 and expand the Local Users and Groups snap-in.

2. Open the Users folder. Double-click user Kevin to open his Properties dialog box.

EXERCISE 6.4 *(continued)*

3. In the General tab, check the Account Is Disabled box. Click the OK button.

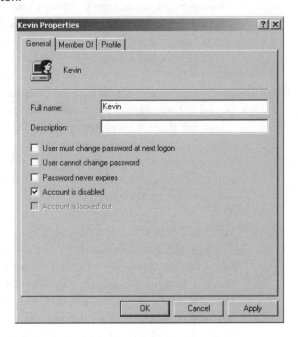

4. Log off as Administrator and attempt to log on as Kevin. This should fail, since the account is now disabled.

5. Log on as Administrator.

 You can also access a user's Properties dialog box by highlighting the user and right-clicking (clicking the secondary mouse button).

Deleting User Accounts

As noted in the preceding section, you should delete a user account if you are sure that the account will never be needed again.

To delete a user, open the Local Users and Groups utility, highlight the user account you wish to delete, and click Action to bring up the menu shown in Figure 6.3. Then select Delete.

FIGURE 6.3 Deleting a user account

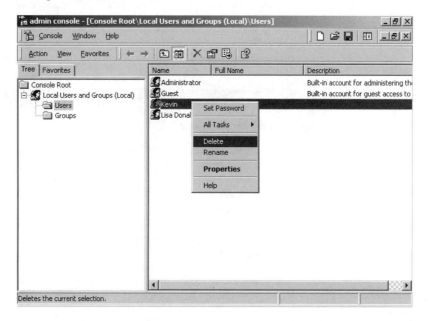

Because user deletion is a permanent action, you will see the dialog box shown in Figure 6.4, asking you to confirm that you really wish to delete the account. After you click the Yes button here, you will not be able to re-create or reaccess the account (unless you restore your local user accounts database from a backup).

FIGURE 6.4 Confirming user deletion

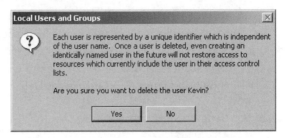

In Exercise 6.5, you will delete a user account. This exercise assumes that you have completed the previous exercises in this chapter.

EXERCISE 6.5

Deleting a User

1. Open the Admin MMC shortcut that was created in Exercise 6.2 and expand the Local Users and Groups snap-in.

2. Expand the Users folder and single-click on user Kevin to select his user account.

3. Select Action ➢ Delete. The dialog box for confirming user deletion appears.

4. Click the Yes button to confirm that you wish to delete this user.

The Administrator and Guest accounts cannot be deleted. The *initial user* account can be deleted.

Renaming Users

Once an account has been created, you can rename the account at any time. Renaming a user account allows the user to retain all of the associated user properties of the previous username. As noted earlier in the chapter, the name is a property of the SID.

You might want to rename a user account because the user's name has changed (for example, the user got married) or because the name was spelled incorrectly. Also, as explained in the "Disabling User Accounts" section, you can rename an existing user's account for a new user, such as someone hired to take an ex-employee's position, when you want the new user to have the same properties.

In Exercise 6.6, you will rename a user account. This exercise assumes that you have completed all of the previous exercises in this chapter.

EXERCISE 6.6

Renaming a User

1. Open the Admin MMC shortcut that was created in Exercise 6.2 and expand the Local Users and Groups snap-in.

2. Open the Users folder and highlight user Terry.

3. Select Action ➢ Rename.

4. Type in the username **Taralyn** and press Enter. Notice that the Full Name retained the original property of Terry in the Local Users and Groups utility.

 Renaming a user does not change any "hard-coded" names, such as the user's home folder. If you want to change these names as well, you need to modify them manually.

Changing a User's Password

What do you do if user Terry forgot her password and can't log on? You can't just open a dialog box and see her old password. However, as the Administrator, you can change Terry's password, and then she can use the new one.

In Exercise 6.7, you will change a user's password. This exercise assumes that you have completed all of the previous exercises in this chapter.

EXERCISE 6.7

Changing a User's Password

1. Open the Admin MMC shortcut that was created in Exercise 6.2 and expand the Local Users and Groups snap-in.

2. Open the Users folder and highlight user Ron.

3. Select Action ➢ Set Password. The Set Password dialog box appears.

4. Type in the new password and then confirm the password. Click the OK button.

Managing User Properties

For more control over user accounts, you can configure user properties. Through the user Properties dialog box, you can change the original password options, add the users to existing groups, and specify user profile information.

Microsoft
✔ *Exam*
Objective

Implement, configure, manage, and troubleshoot local user accounts.

- Implement, configure, manage, and troubleshoot account settings.
- Create and manage local users and groups.

To open the user Properties dialog box, access the Local Users and Groups utility, open the Users folder, and double-click the user account. The user Properties dialog box has tabs for the three main categories of properties: General, Member Of, and Profile.

The General tab (shown in Exercise 6.4 earlier in the chapter) contains the information that you supplied when you set up the new user account, including any Full Name and Description information, the password options you selected, and whether the account is disabled. (See "Creating a New User" earlier in this chapter.) If you want to modify any of these properties after you've created the user, simply open the user Properties dialog box and make the changes on the General tab.

The Member Of tab is used to manage the user's membership in groups. The Profile tab lets you set properties to customize the user's environment. These properties are discussed in detail in the following sections.

Managing User Group Membership

The Member Of tab of the user Properties dialog box displays all the groups that the user belongs to, as shown in Figure 6.5. From this tab, you can add the user to an existing group or remove that user from a group. To add a user to a group, click the Add button and select the group that the user should belong to. If you want to remove the user from a group, highlight the group and click the Remove button.

FIGURE 6.5   The Member Of tab of the user Properties dialog box

Groups are used to logically organize users who have similar resource access requirements. Managing groups is much easier than managing individual users. Chapter 7 discusses the process of creating and managing groups.

The steps used to add a user to an existing group are shown in Exercise 6.8. This exercise assumes that you have completed all of the previous exercises in this chapter.

EXERCISE 6.8

Adding a User to a Group

1. Open the Admin MMC shortcut that was created in Exercise 6.2 and expand the Local Users and Groups snap-in.

2. Open the Users folder and double-click user Wendy. The user Properties dialog box appears.

3. Select the Member Of tab and click the Add button. The Select Groups dialog box appears.

4. Highlight the Power Users group and click the Add button. Then click the OK button.

5. Click the OK button to close the user Properties dialog box.

Setting Up User Profiles, Logon Scripts, and Home Folders

The Profile tab of the user Properties dialog box, shown in Figure 6.6, allows you to customize the user's environment. Here, you can specify the following items for the user:

- User profile path
- Logon script
- Home folder

The following sections describe how these properties work and when you might want to use them.

FIGURE 6.6 The Profile tab of the user Properties dialog box

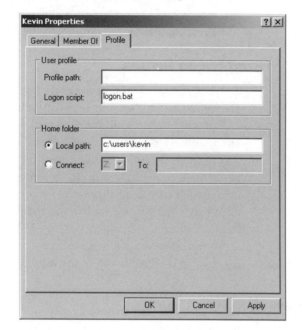

Setting a Profile Path

User profiles contain information about the Windows 2000 environment for a specific user. For example, profile settings include the Desktop arrangement, program groups, and screen colors that users see when they log on.

By default, when a user logs on, a profile is opened for a user. Any changes the user makes to the Desktop are stored on the local computer when the user logs off. For example, suppose user Rick logs on, picks his wallpaper, creates shortcuts, and customizes the Desktop to his personal preference. When he logs off, his profile is stored locally. If another user logs on at the same computer, that user's profile—not Rick's—will be loaded.

See Chapter 8, "Using User Profiles and Hardware Profiles," for a full discussion of profiles.

The Profile Path option in the Profile tab is used to point to another location for profile files other than the default local location. This allows users to access profiles that have been stored in a shared network folder. Profiles can thus be used for an individual user or shared by a group of users. To specify a path, just type it in the Profile Path text box.

Using Logon Scripts

Logon scripts are files that run every time a user logs on to the network. They are usually batch files, but they can be any type of executable file.

You might use logon scripts to set up drive mappings or to run a specific executable file each time a user logs on to the computer. For example, you could run an inventory management file that collects information about the computer's configuration and sends that data to a central management database. Logon scripts are also useful for compatibility with non–Windows 2000 clients that want to log on but still maintain consistent settings with their native operating system.

To run a logon script for a user, enter the script name in the Logon Script text box in the Profile tab of the user Properties dialog box.

Logon scripts are not commonly used in Windows 2000 networks. Windows 2000 automates much of the user's configuration. This isn't the case in (for example) older NetWare environments, and administrators use logon scripts to configure the users' environment.

Setting Up Home Folders

Users normally store their personal files and information in a private folder called a *home folder*. In the Profile tab of the user Properties dialog box, you can specify the location of a home folder as a local folder or a network folder.

To specify a local path folder, choose the Local Path option and type the path in the text box next to that option. To specify a network path for a folder, choose the Connect option and specify a network path using a UNC (Universal Naming Convention) path. A UNC consists of the computer name and the share that has been created on the computer. In this case, a network folder should already be created and shared. For example, if you wanted to connect to a share called \Users\Wendy on a server called SALES, you'd choose the Connect option and select a drive letter that would be mapped to the home directory, and then type \\SALES\Users\Wendy in the To box.

If the home folder that you are specifying does not exist, Windows 2000 will attempt to create the folder for you. You can also use the variable %username% in place of a specific user's name.

In Exercise 6.9, you will assign a home folder to a user. This exercise assumes that you have completed all of the previous exercises in this chapter.

EXERCISE 6.9

Assigning a Home Folder to a User

1. Open the Admin MMC shortcut that was created in Exercise 6.2 and expand the Local Users and Groups snap-in.

2. Open the Users folder and double-click user Wendy. The user Properties dialog box appears.

3. Select the Profile tab and click the Local Path radio button to select it.

4. Specify the home folder path by typing **C:\Users\Wendy** in the text box for the Local Path option. Then click the OK button.

5. Use Windows Explorer to verify that this folder was created.

 Real World Scenario

Using Home Folders

You are the administrator for a 100-user network. One of your primary responsibilities is to make sure that all data is backed up daily. This has become difficult because daily backup of each user's local hard drive is impractical. You have also had problems with employees' deleting important corporate information as they are leaving the company.

After examining the contents of a typical user's local drive, you realize that most of the local disk space is taken by the operating system and the user's stored applications. This information does not change and does not need to be backed up. What you are primarily concerned with is backing up the user's data.

To more effectively manage this data and accommodate the necessary backup, you should create home folders for each user, stored on a network share. This allows the data to be backed up daily, to be readily accessible should a local computer fail, and to be easily retrieved if the user leaves the company.

Here are the steps to create a home folder that resides on the network: Decide which server will store the users' home folders, and create a directory structure that will store the home folders efficiently (for example, C:\HOME) and create a single share to the home folder. Then use NTFS and share permissions to ensure that only the specified user has permissions to their home folder. Setting permissions is covered in Chapter 10, "Accessing Files and Folders." After you create the share and assign permissions, you can specify the location of the home folder through the Profile tab of User Properties.

Using Account Policies

*A*ccount policies are used to specify the user account properties that relate to the logon process. They allow you to configure computer security settings for passwords and account lockout specifications.

Microsoft
✔ *Exam*
Objective

Implement, configure, manage, and troubleshoot local security policy.

Implement, configure, manage, and troubleshoot local user accounts.

- Implement, configure, manage, and troubleshoot account policy.

Microsoft ✓ *Exam* *Objective* **Implement, configure, manage, and troubleshoot a security configuration.**

If security is not an issue—perhaps because you are using your Windows 2000 Professional computer at home—then you don't need to bother with account policies. On the other hand, if security is important—for example, because your computer provides access to payroll information—then you should set very restrictive account policies.

Loading the Local Computer Policy Snap-In

To implement account policies, you first need to add the *Local Computer Policy* snap-in to the MMC, as demonstrated in Exercise 6.10.

 You can also access the account policies and local policies by opening Control Panel and selecting Administrative Tools ➢ Local Security Policy.

EXERCISE 6.10

Adding the Local Computer Policy Snap-in to the MMC

1. Open the Admin MMC shortcut that was created in Exercise 6.2 and expand the Local Users and Groups snap-in.

2. From the main menu, select Console ➢ Add/Remove Snap-in.

3. In the Add/Remove Snap-in dialog box, click the Add button.

4. Highlight the Group Policy option and click the Add button.

5. The Group Policy object specifies Local Computer by default. Click the Finish button.

6. Click the Close button.

7. In the Add/Remove Snap-in dialog box, click the OK button.

From the MMC, follow this path of folders to access the Account Policies folders: Local Computer Policy, Computer Configuration, Windows Settings, Security Settings, Account Policies. Figure 6.7 shows the Account Policies folders: Password Policy and Account Lockout Policy. These represent the two types of account policies, which are covered in the following sections.

FIGURE 6.7 Accessing the Account Policies folders

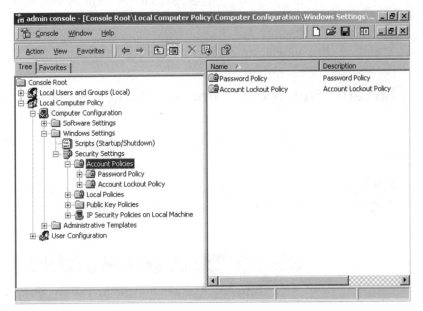

Setting Password Policies

Password policies ensure that security requirements are enforced on the computer. It is important to understand that the password policy is set on a per-computer basis; it cannot be configured for specific users. Figure 6.8 shows the password policies, which are described in Table 6.3.

FIGURE 6.8   The password policies

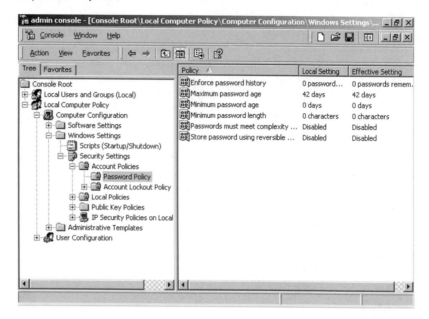

TABLE 6.3   Password Policy Options

Policy	Description	Default	Minimum	Maximum
Enforce Password History	Keeps track of user's password history	Remember 0 passwords	Same as default	Remember 24 passwords
Maximum Password Age	Determines maximum number of days user can keep valid password	Keep password for 42 days	Keep password for 1 day	Keep password for up to 999 days

TABLE 6.3   Password Policy Options *(continued)*

Policy	Description	Default	Minimum	Maximum
Minimum Password Age	Specifies how long password must be kept before it can be changed	0 days (password can be changed immediately)	Same as default	999 days
Minimum Password Length	Specifies minimum number of characters password must contain	0 characters (no password required)	Same as default	14 characters
Passwords Must Meet the Complexity Requirements of the Installed Password Filters	Allows you to install password filter	Disabled	Same as default	Enabled
Store Password Using Reversible Encryption for All Users in the Domain	Specifies higher level of encryption for stored user passwords	Disabled	Same as default	Enabled

The password policies in Table 6.3 are used as follows:

- Enforce Password History is used so that users cannot use the same password. Users must create a new password when their password expires or is changed.

- Maximum Password Age is used so that after the maximum password age is exceeded, users are forced to change their password.

- Minimum Password Age prevents users from changing their password several times in rapid succession in order to defeat the purpose of the Enforce Password History policy.

- Minimum Password Length ensures that users create a password and specifies the length requirement for that password. If this option isn't set, users are not required to create a password at all.

- The option Passwords Must Meet the Complexity Requirements of the Installed Password Filters is used to prevent users from using as passwords items found in a dictionary of common names.

- The option to Store Password Using Reversible Encryption for All Users in the Domain provides a higher level of security for user passwords.

In Exercise 6.11, you will configure password policies for your computer. This exercise assumes that you have added the Local Computer Policy snap-in to the MMC (see Exercise 6.10).

EXERCISE 6.11

Setting Password Policies

1. Open the Admin MMC shortcut that was created in Exercise 6.2 and expand the Local Computer Policy Snap-in.

2. Expand the folders as follows: Computer Configuration, Windows Settings, Security Settings, Account Policies, Password Policy.

3. Open the Enforce Password History policy. In the Effective Policy Setting field, specify that **5** passwords will be remembered. Click the OK button.

4. Open the Maximum Password Age policy. In the Local Policy Setting field, specify that the password expires in **60** days. Click the OK button.

Setting Account Lockout Policies

The *account lockout policies* are used to specify how many invalid logon attempts should be tolerated. You configure the account lockout policies so that after x number of unsuccessful logon attempts within y number of minutes, the account will be locked for a specified amount of time or until the Administrator unlocks the account.

Account lockout policies are similar to a bank's arrangements for ATM access code security. You have a certain number of chances to enter the correct PIN. That way, anyone who steals your card can't just keep guessing your access code until they get it right. Typically, after three unsuccessful attempts, the ATM machine takes the card. Then you need to request a new card from the bank.

Figure 6.9 shows the account lockout policies, which are described in Table 6.4.

FIGURE 6.9 The account lockout policies

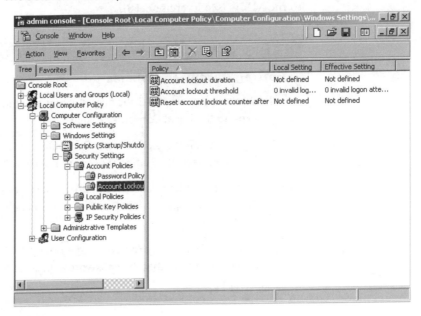

TABLE 6.4 Account Lockout Policy Options

Policy	Description	Default	Minimum	Maximum	Suggested
Account Lockout Threshold	Specifies number of invalid attempts allowed before account is locked out	0 (disabled, account will not be locked out)	Same as default	999 attempts	5 attempts
Account Lockout Duration	Specifies how long account will remain locked if Account Lockout Threshold is exceeded	0; but if Account Lockout Threshold is enabled, 30 minutes	Same as default	99,999 minutes	5 minutes
Reset Account Lockout Counter After	Specifies how long counter will remember unsuccessful logon attempts	0; but if Account Lockout Threshold is enabled, 5 minutes	Same as default	99,999 minutes	5 minutes

In Exercise 6.12, you will configure account lockout policies and test their effects. This exercise assumes that you have completed all of the previous exercises in this chapter.

EXERCISE 6.12

Setting Account Lockout Policies

1. Open the Admin MMC shortcut that was created in Exercise 6.2 and expand the Local Computer Policy snap-in.

2. Expand the folders as follows: Computer Configuration, Windows Settings, Security Settings, Account Policies, Account Lockout Policy.

3. Open the Account Lockout Threshold policy. In the Local Policy Setting field, specify that the account will lock after **3** invalid logon attempts. Click the OK button.

EXERCISE 6.12 *(continued)*

4. Open the Account Lockout Duration policy. In the Local Policy Setting field, specify that the account will remain locked for **5** minutes. Click the OK button.

5. Log off as Administrator. Try to log on as Emily with an incorrect password three times.

6. After you see the error message stating that account lockout has been enabled, log on as Administrator.

7. To unlock Emily's account, open the Local Users and Groups snap-in in the MMC, expand the Users folder, and double-click user Emily.

8. In the General tab of Emily's Properties dialog box, click to remove the check from the Account Is Locked Out check box. Then click OK.

Using Local Policies

As you learned in the preceding section, account policies are used to control logon procedures. When you want to control what a user can do *after* logging on, you use *local policies*. With local policies, you can implement auditing, specify user rights, and set security options.

Microsoft ✓ ***Exam Objective***

Implement, configure, manage, and troubleshoot local security policy.

Implement, configure, manage, and troubleshoot local user accounts.

- Implement, configure, manage, and troubleshoot auditing.
- Implement, configure, manage, and troubleshoot user rights.

To use local policies, first add the Local Computer Policy snap-in to the MMC (see Exercise 6.10). Then, from the MMC, follow this path of folders to access the Local Policies folders: Local Computer Policy, Computer Configuration, Windows Settings, Security Settings, Local Policies. Figure 6.10

shows the three Local Policies folders: Audit Policy, User Rights Assignment, and Security Options, covered in the following sections.

FIGURE 6.10   Accessing the Local Policies folders

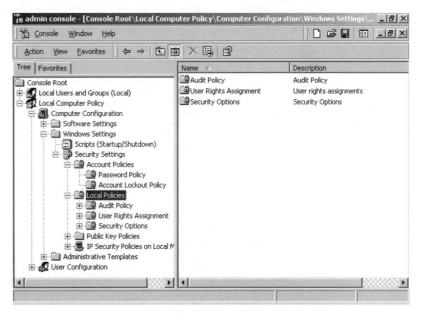

Setting Audit Policies

My mother once told me to trust no one. *Audit policies* reinforce this thinking. By implementing auditing, you can watch what your users are doing.

You audit events that pertain to user management through the audit policies. By tracking certain events, you can create a history of specific tasks, such as user creation and successful or unsuccessful logon attempts. You can also identify security violations that arise when users attempt to access system management tasks for which they do not have permission.

Users who try to go to areas for which they do not have permission usually fall into two categories: hackers, and people who are just curious to see what they can get away with. Both are very dangerous.

When you define an audit policy, you can choose to audit success or failure of specific events. The success of an event means that the task was successfully accomplished. The failure of an event means that the task was not successfully accomplished.

By default, auditing is not enabled, and it must be manually configured. Once auditing has been configured, you can see the results of the audit through the Event Viewer utility, Security log. (The Event Viewer utility is covered in Chapter 15.)

Auditing too many events can degrade system performance due to its high processing requirements. Auditing can also use excessive disk space to store the audit log. You should use this utility judiciously.

Figure 6.11 shows the audit policies, which are described in Table 6.5.

FIGURE 6.11 The audit policies

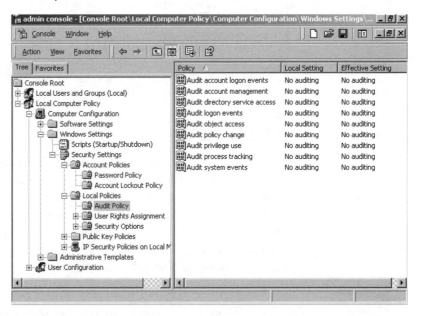

TABLE 6.5   Audit Policy Options

Policy	Description
Audit Account Logon Events	Tracks when a user logs on, logs off, or makes a network connection
Audit Account Management	Tracks user and group account creation, deletion, and management actions
Audit Directory Service Access	Tracks directory service accesses
Audit Logon Events	Audits events related to logon, such as running a logon script or accessing a roaming profile
Audit Object Access	Enables auditing of access to files, folders, and printers
Audit Policy Change	Tracks any changes to the audit policy
Audit Privilege Use	Tracks any changes to who can or cannot define or see the results of auditing
Audit Process Tracking	Tracks events such as activating a program, accessing an object, and exiting a process
Audit System Events	Tracks system events such as shutting down or restarting the computer, as well as events that relate to the Security log in Event Viewer

After you set the Audit Object Access policy to enable auditing of object access, you must enable file auditing through NTFS security, or print auditing through printer security.

In Exercise 6.13, you will configure audit policies and view their results. This exercise assumes that you have completed all previous exercises in this chapter.

EXERCISE 6.13

Setting Audit Policies

1. Open the Admin MMC shortcut that was created in Exercise 6.2 and expand the Local Computer Policy snap-in.

2. Expand the folders as follows: Computer Configuration, Windows Settings, Security Settings, Local Policies, Audit Policy.

3. Open the Audit Account Logon Events policy. In the Local Policy Setting field, specify Audit These Attempts. Check the boxes for Success and Failure. Click the OK button.

4. Open the Audit Account Management policy. In the Local Policy Setting field, specify Audit These Attempts. Check the boxes for Success and Failure. Click the OK button.

5. Log off as Administrator. Attempt to log on as Kevin. The logon should fail (because there is no user account with the username Kevin).

6. Log on as Administrator. Select Start ➢ Settings ➢ Control Panel ➢ Administrative Tools ➢ Event Viewer to open Event Viewer.

7. From Event Viewer, open the Security log. You should see the audited events listed in this log.

Assigning User Rights

The *user right policies* determine what rights a user or group has on the computer. User rights apply to the system. They are not the same as permissions, which apply to a specific object (permissions are discussed in Chapter 10).

An example of a user right is the Back Up Files and Directories right. This right allows a user to back up files and folders, even if the user does not have permissions through the file system. The other user rights are similar in that they deal with system access as opposed to resource access.

Figure 6.12 shows the user right policies, which are described in Table 6.6.

FIGURE 6.12 The user right policies

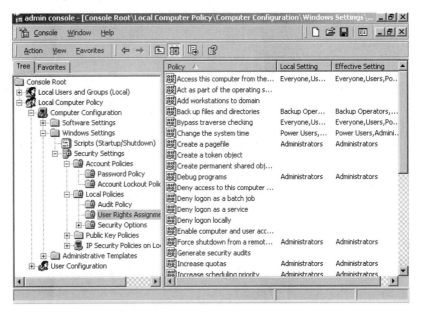

TABLE 6.6 User Rights Assignment Policy Options

Right	Description
Access This Computer from the Network	Allows a user to access the computer from the network
Act as Part of the Operating System	Allows low-level authentication services to authenticate as any user
Add Workstations to the Domain	Allows a user to create a computer account on the domain
Back Up Files and Directories	Allows a user to back up all files and directories, regardless of how the file and directory permissions have been set

T A B L E 6.6 User Rights Assignment Policy Options *(continued)*

Right	Description
Bypass Traverse Checking	Allows a user to pass through and traverse the directory structure, even if that user does not have permissions to list the contents of the directory
Change the System Time	Allows a user to change the internal time of the computer
Create a Pagefile	Allows a user to create or change the size of a page file
Create a Token Object	Allows a process to create a token if the process uses the NtCreateToken API
Create Permanent Shared Objects	Allows a process to create directory objects through the Windows 2000 Object Manager
Debug Programs	Allows a user to attach a debugging program to any process
Deny Access to This Computer from the Network	Allows you to deny specific users or groups access to this computer from the network
Deny Logon as a Batch File	Allows you to prevent specific users or groups from logging on as a batch file
Deny Logon as a Service	Allows you to prevent specific users or groups from logging on as a service
Deny Logon Locally	Allows you to deny specific users or groups access to the computer locally
Enable Computer and User Accounts to Be Trusted by Delegation	Allows a user or group to set the Trusted for Delegation setting for a user or computer object

TABLE 6.6 User Rights Assignment Policy Options *(continued)*

Right	Description
Force Shutdown from a Remote System	Allows the system to be shut down by a user at a remote location on the network
Generate Security Audits	Allows a user, group, or process to make entries in the Security log
Increase Quotas	Allows a user to manipulate how processes are served by manipulating the processor quota
Increase Scheduling Priority	Specifies that a process can increase or decrease the priority that is assigned to another process
Load and Unload Device Drivers	Allows a user to dynamically unload and load Plug-and-Play device drivers
Lock Pages in Memory	No longer used in Windows 2000 (it was originally intended to force data to be kept in physical memory and not allow the data to be paged to the page file)
Log On as a Batch Job	Allows a process to log on to the system and run a file that contains one or more operating system commands
Log On as a Service	Allows a service to log on in order to run the specific service
Log On Locally	Allows a user to log on at the computer where the user account has been defined
Manage Auditing and Security Log	Allows a user to manage the Security log
Modify Firmware Environment Variables	Allows a user or process to modify the system environment variables

TABLE 6.6 User Rights Assignment Policy Options *(continued)*

Right	Description
Profile Single Process	Allows a user to monitor nonsystem processes through tools such as the Performance Logs and Alerts utility
Profile System Performance	Allows a user to monitor system processes through tools such as the Performance Logs and Alerts utility
Remove Computer from Docking Station	Allows a user to undock a laptop through the Windows 2000 user interface
Replace a Process Level Token	Allows a process to replace the default token that is created by the subprocess with the token that the process specifies
Restore Files and Directories	Allows a user to restore files and directories, regardless of file and directory permissions
Shut Down the System	Allows a user to shut down the local Windows 2000 computer
Synchronize Directory Service Data	Allows a user to synchronize data associated with a directory service
Take Ownership of Files or Other Objects	Allows a user to take ownership of system objects

In Exercise 6.14, you will apply a user right policy. This exercise assumes that you have completed all of the previous exercises in this chapter.

EXERCISE 6.14

Setting User Rights

1. Open the Admin MMC shortcut that was created in Exercise 6.2 and expand the Local Computer Policy snap-in.

2. Expand folders as follows: Computer Configuration, Windows Settings, Security Settings, Local Policies, User Rights Assignment.

3. Open the Log On as a Service user right. The Local Security Policy Setting dialog box appears.

4. Click the Add button. The Select Users or Groups dialog box appears.

5. Select user Emily. Click the Add button. Then click the OK button.

6. In the Local Security Policy Setting dialog box, click the OK button.

Defining Security Options

Security option policies are used to configure security for the computer. Unlike user right policies, which are applied to a user or group, security option policies apply to the computer. Figure 6.13 shows the security option policies, which are described briefly in Table 6.7.

Microsoft
✓ Exam
Objective

Implement, configure, manage, and troubleshoot a security configuration.

FIGURE 6.13 The security option policies

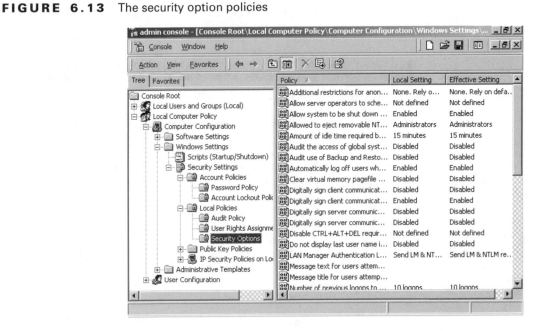

TABLE 6.7 Security Options

Option	Description	Default
Additional Restrictions for Anonymous Users	Allows you to impose additional restrictions on anonymous connections	None (rely on default permissions)
Allow Server Operators to Schedule Tasks (domain controllers only)	Allows server operators to schedule specific tasks to occur at specific times or intervals	Not defined

TABLE 6.7 Security Options *(continued)*

Option	Description	Default
Allow System to Be Shut Down Without Having to Log On	Allows the user to shut down the system without logging on	Enabled (but the local policy settings are overridden if the domain-level policy settings are defined)
Allowed to Eject Removable NTFS Media	Allows removable NTFS media to be ejected	Administrators
Amount of Time Idle Before Disconnecting Session	Allows sessions to be disconnected when they are idle	15 minutes
Audit the Access of Global System Objects	Allows access of global system objects to be audited	Disabled
Audit Use of All User Rights including Backup and Restore Privilege	Allows all user rights, including backup and restore, to be audited	Disabled
Automatically Log Off Users When Logon Time Expires	Automatically logs off users if they have limited logon hours and their logon time has expired	Enabled
Clear Virtual Memory Pagefile When System Shuts Down	Specifies that the page file should be cleared when the system is shut down	Disabled
Digitally Sign Client Communication (always)	Specifies that the server should always digitally sign client communication	Disabled

TABLE 6.7 Security Options *(continued)*

Option	Description	Default
Digitally Sign Client Communication (when possible)	Specifies that the server should digitally sign client communication when possible	Enabled
Digitally Sign Server Communication (always)	Ensures that server communications will always be digitally signed	Disabled
Digitally Sign Server Communication (when possible)	Specifies that server communications should be signed when possible	Disabled
Disable CTRL+ALT+DEL Requirement for Logon	Allows the Ctrl+Alt+Delete requirement for logon to be disabled	Not defined
Do Not Display Last User Name in Logon Screen	Prevents the last user-name in the logon screen from being displayed	Disabled
LAN Manager Authentication Level	Specifies the LAN Manager Authentication Level	Send LAN Manager and NTLM (NT LAN Manager) responses
Message Text for Users Attempting to Log On	Displays message text for users trying to log on	Text space is blank
Message Title for Users Attempting to Log On	Displays a message title for users trying to log on	Title space is blank

TABLE 6.7 Security Options *(continued)*

Option	Description	Default
Number of Previous Logon Attempts to Cache (in case domain controller is not available)	Specifies the number of previous logon attempts stored in the cache	10
Prevent System Maintenance of Computer Account Password	Prevents the system maintenance of computer account passwords	Disabled
Prevent Users from Installing Print Drivers	Prevents users from installing print drivers	Disabled
Prompt User to Change Password Before Expiration	Prompts the user to change the password before expiration	14 days before password expiration
Recovery Console: Allow Automatic Administrative Logon	Specifies that when the Recovery Console is loaded, Administrative logon should be automatic, as opposed to a manual process	Disabled
Recovery Console: Allow Floppy Copy and Access to All Drives and Folders	Allows you to copy files from all drives and folders when the Recovery Console is loaded	Disabled
Rename Administrator Account	Allows the Administrator account to be renamed	Not defined
Rename Guest Account	Allows the Guest account to be renamed	Not defined

TABLE 6.7 Security Options *(continued)*

Option	Description	Default
Restrict CD-ROM Access to Locally Logged-On Users Only	Restricts CD-ROM access to users who are logged on locally	Disabled
Restrict Floppy Access to Locally Logged-On Users Only	Restricts floppy disk drive access to users who are logged on locally	Disabled
Secure Channel: Digitally Encrypt or Sign Secure Channel Data (always)	Specifies that secure channel data is always digitally encrypted or signed	Disabled
Secure Channel: Digitally Encrypt Secure Channel Data (when possible)	Specifies that secure channel data is digitally encrypted when possible	Disabled
Secure Channel: Digitally Sign Secure Channel Data (when possible)	Specifies that secure channel data is digitally signed when possible	Enabled
Secure Channel: Require Strong (Windows 2000 or later) Session Key	Provides a secure channel and requires a strong (Windows 2000 or later) session key	Disabled
Send Unencrypted Passwords to Connect to Third-Party SMB Servers	Allows unencrypted passwords to connect to third-party SMB servers	Disabled

TABLE 6.7 Security Options *(continued)*

Option	Description	Default
Shut Down System Immediately If Unable to Log Security Audits	Specifies that the system shuts down immediately if it is unable to log security audits	Disabled
Smart Card Removal Behavior	Changes the smart card removal behavior	No action
Strengthen Default Permissions of Global System Objects (e.g., Symbolic Links)	Strengthens the default permissions of global system objects	Enabled
Unsigned Driver Installation Behavior	Controls the behavior of the unsigned driver installation	Warn but allow installation
Unsigned Non-Driver Installation Behavior	Controls the behavior of the unsigned non-driver installation	Silently succeed

In Exercise 6.15, you will define some security option policies and see how they work. This exercise assumes that you have completed all of the previous exercises in this chapter.

EXERCISE 6.15

Defining Security Options

1. Open the Admin MMC shortcut that was created in Exercise 6.2 and expand the Local Computer Policy snap-in.

2. Expand folders as follows: Computer Configuration, Windows Settings, Security Settings, Local Policies, Security Options.

3. Open the policy Message Text for Users Attempting to Log On. In the Local Policy Setting field, type **Welcome to all authorized users**. Click the OK button.

EXERCISE 6.15 *(continued)*

4. Open the policy Prompt User to Change Password Before Expiration. In the Local Policy Setting field, specify **3** days. Click the OK button.

5. Log off as Administrator and log on as Michael (with the password **apple**).

6. Log off as Michael and log on as Administrator.

Troubleshooting User Accounts Authentication

When a user attempts to log on through Windows 2000 and is unable to be authenticated, you will need to track down the reason for the problem. The following sections offer some suggestions that can help you troubleshoot logon authentication errors for local and domain user accounts.

Microsoft
✓ *Exam*
Objective

Implement, configure, manage, and troubleshoot local user authentication

- Configure and troubleshoot local user accounts.
- Configure and troubleshoot domain user accounts.

Troubleshooting Local User Account Authentication

If a local user is having trouble logging on, the problem may be with the username, password, or the user account itself. The following are some common cause of local logon errors:

Incorrect username   You can verify that the username is correct by checking the Local Users and Groups utility. Verify that the name was spelled correctly.

Incorrect password   Remember that passwords are case sensitive. Is the Caps Lock key on? If you see any messages relating to an expired password or locked-out account, the reason for the problem is obvious. If necessary, you can assign a new password through the Local Users and Groups utility.

Prohibitive user rights   Does the user have permission to log on locally at the computer? By default, the Log On Locally user right is granted to the Users group, so all users can log on to Windows 2000 Professional computers. However, if this user right was modified, you will see an error message stating that the local policy of this computer does not allow interactive logon. The terms *interactive logon* and *local logon* are synonymous and mean that the user is logging on at the computer where the user account is stored on the computer's local database.

A disabled or deleted account   You can verify whether an account has been disabled or deleted by checking the account properties through the Local Users and Groups utility.

A domain account logon at the local computer   If a computer is a part of a domain, the logon dialog box has options for logging on to the domain or to the local computer. Make sure that the user has chosen the correct option.

Domain User Accounts Authentication

Troubleshooting a logon problem for a user with a domain account involves checking the same areas as you do for local account logon problems, as well as a few others.

The following are some common causes of domain logon errors:

Incorrect username   You can verify that the username is correct by checking the Microsoft Active Directory Users and Computers utility to verify that the name was spelled correctly.

Incorrect password   As with local accounts, check that the password was entered in the proper case (and the Caps Lock key isn't on), the password hasn't expired, and the account has not been locked out. If the password still doesn't work, you can assign a new password through the Local Users and Groups utility.

Prohibitive user rights   Does the user have permission to log on locally at the computer? This assumes that the user is attempting to log on to the domain controller. Regular users do not have permission to log on locally at the domain controller. The assumption is that users will log on to the domain from network workstations. If the user has a legitimate reason to log on locally at the domain controller, that user should be assigned the Log On Locally user right.

A disabled or deleted account   You can verify whether an account has been disabled or deleted by checking the account properties through the Microsoft Active Directory Users and Computers utility.

A local account logon at a domain computer   Is the user trying to log on with a local user account name instead of a domain account? Make sure that the user has selected to log on to a domain in the Logon dialog box.

The computer is not part of the domain   Is the user sitting at a computer that is a part of the domain to which the user is trying to log on? If the Windows 2000 Professional computer is not a part of the domain that contains the user account or does not have a trust relationship defined with the domain that contains the user account, the user will not be able to log on.

Unavailable domain controller   Is the domain controller available to authenticate the user's request? If the domain controller is down for some reason, the user will not be able to log on until it comes back up (unless the user logs on using a local user account).

Use of the Microsoft Active Directory Users and Computers utility is covered in *MCSE: Windows 2000 Directory Services Administration Study Guide*, 2nd ed., by Anil Desai with James Chellis (Sybex, 2001).

In Exercise 6.16, you will propose solutions to user authentication problems.

EXERCISE 6.16

Troubleshooting User Authentication

1. Log on as user Emily with the password **peach** (all lowercase). You should see a message indicating that the system could not log you on. The problem is that Emily's password is Peach, and passwords are case sensitive.

2. Log on as user Bryan with the password **apple**. You should see the same error message that you saw in step 1. The problem is that the user Bryan does not exist.

3. Log on as Administrator. Right-click My Computer and select Manage. Double-click Local Users and Groups.

4. Right-click Users and select New User. Create a user named **Gus**. Type in and confirm the password **abcde**. Deselect the User Must Change Password at Next Logon option and check the Account Is Disabled option.

5. Log off as Administrator and log on as Gus with no password. You will see a message indicating that the system could not log you on because the username or password was incorrect.

6. Log on as Gus with the password **abcde**. You will see a different message indicating that your account has been disabled.

7. Log on as Administrator.

Summary

In this chapter, you learned about user management features in Windows 2000 Professional. We covered the following topics:

- The types of accounts supported by Windows 2000 Professional. You can set up local user accounts and domain user accounts. Windows 2000 also comes with three built-in system accounts: Administrator, Guest, and initial user.

- The user logon and logoff processes. To log on to a Windows 2000 Professional computer, the user must supply a username and password, with which the system authenticates the user. The Log Off option is in the Windows Security dialog box.

- The procedures for creating and managing user accounts. You create user accounts and manage them through the Local Users and Groups utility.

- The user properties. You can set these to manage user accounts. Through the Member Of tab of the user Properties dialog box, you can add users to groups or remove them from group membership. Through the Profile tab, you can set a profile path, logon script, and home folder for the user.

- Account policies, which control the logon process. The two types of account policies are password and account lockout policies.

- Local policies, which control what a user can do at the computer. The three types of local policies are audit, user rights, and security options policies.

- Troubleshooting user logon and authentication problems. Some of the problems you may encounter are incorrect usernames or passwords, prohibitive user rights, and disabled or deleted accounts.

Exam Essentials

Create and manage user accounts.   When creating user accounts, be aware of the requirements for doing so. Know how to rename and delete user accounts. Be able to manage all user properties.

Configure and manage local user authentication.   Understand the options that can be configured to manage local user authentication and when these options would be used to create a more secure environment. Be able to specify where local user authentication options are configured.

Set up a security configuration based on network requirements.   Define the options that can be configured for secure network environments. Know where to configure each option.

Key Terms

Before you take the exam, be sure you're familiar with the following key terms:

access token	local logon
account lockout policies	local policies
account policies	local user account
Active Directory	Local Users and Groups
Administrator account	logon
audit policies	logon script
authentication	password policies
domain user account	security identifier (SID)
Guest account	security option policies
home folder	user profile
interactive logon	user rights
Local Computer Policy	

Review Questions

1. Your network's security has been breached. You are trying to redefine security so that a user cannot repeatedly attempt user logon with different passwords. To accomplish this, which of the following items (in the Local Security Settings dialog box shown here) should you define?

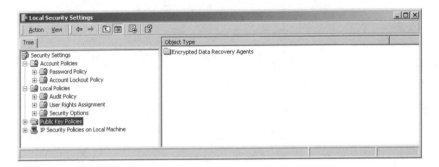

   A. Password policy

   B. Account lockout policy

   C. Audit policy

   D. Security options

2. Jim is managing his Windows 2000 Professional computer so that it can be used by multiple users, each with different security requirements. He wants to create a unique user account for each user. Which MMC snap-in should he use?

   A. User Manager

   B. User Manager for Professional

   C. Local Users and Groups

   D. Professional Users and Groups

3. Your network has experienced security breaches because users have been selecting simple passwords. You want to prevent this from happening in the future. Which password policy should you implement if you do not want your users to use passwords consisting of simple words?

   A. Passwords Must Be Advanced

   B. Passwords Must Contain Non-alphanumeric Characters

   C. Passwords Must Be Unique

   D. Passwords Must Meet the Complexity Requirements of the Installed Password Filters

4. Cam has just installed Windows 2000 Professional. No changes have been made to the default user accounts. She is trying to determine if any of the default account assignments poses a security threat. Which of the following statements are true regarding the built-in accounts? (Choose all that apply.)

   A. By default, the Administrator account cannot be deleted.

   B. By default, the Guest account can be deleted.

   C. By default, the Administrator account is enabled.

   D. By default, the Guest account is enabled.

5. Dionne wants to create a home folder that is located on a network share on a server that is backed up daily. Which option should she select within the Profile tab of User Properties to create a home folder that was located on a network path?

   A. Connect

   B. Local path

   C. Network path

   D. Connect path

6. Due to recent security violations, you are requiring all users to change their passwords. Which of the following utilities can users run to change their password on a Windows 2000 Professional computer?

   A. The Change Password button in the Windows Security dialog box

   B. The NET PASS command-line utility

   C. The SETPASS utility

   D. The Local Users and Groups utility

7. Beth has just installed Windows 2000 Professional on her laptop and wants to create a user account for herself. Which of the following usernames is *not* valid?

   A. Beth Johnson

   B. Bethany Johnson-Smith

   C. Beth123

   D. BSmith (Beth)

8. You have a Windows 2000 Professional computer that is located in an unsecured area. You want to track usage of the computer by recording user logon and logoff events. To do this, which of the following auditing policies must be enabled?

   A. Audit Account Logon Events

   B. Audit Process Tracking

   C. Audit Logon Events

   D. Audit System Events

9. Bill is very good at troubleshooting hardware and installing new devices and updating drivers. You want Bill to be able to add and remove hardware as well as update drivers on the Windows 2000 Professional computers in your network. What is the minimum assignment that will allow Bill to complete this task?

    A. Add Bill to the Administrators group.

    B. Add Bill to the Server Operators group.

    C. Add Bill to the Manage Devices group.

    D. Grant Bill the user right Load and Unload Device Drivers on each computer he will manage.

10. You have just decided to install the XYZ Virus Scanner application. The scanner runs as a service. You create a user account called VirScan that will be used to run the service. What user right must be granted for this account?

    A. Log On as a Batch Job

    B. Log On as a Service

    C. Process Service Requests

    D. Manage Services and Security

11. You have a computer that is shared by many users. You want to ensure that when users press Ctrl+Alt+Delete to log on, they do not see the name of the last user. What do you configure?

    A. Set the security option Clear User Settings When Users Log Off

    B. Set the security option Do Not Display Last User Name in Logon Screen

    C. Set the security option Prevent Users from Seeing Last User Name

    D. Configure nothing; this is the default setting

12. You have configured auditing so that you can track events such as account management tasks and system events. Where can you view the results of the audit?

    A. Audit Manager

    B. \Windir\audit.log

    C. Event Viewer, System log

    D. Event Viewer, Security log

13. You have recently hired Al as an assistant for network administration. You have not decided how much responsibility you want Al to have. In the meantime, you want Al to be able to restore files on Windows 2000 Professional computers in your network, but you do not want Al to be able to run the backups. What is the minimum assignment that will allow Al to complete this task?

    A. Add Al to the Administrators group.

    B. Grant Al the Read right to the root of each volume he will back up.

    C. Add Al to the Backup Operators group.

    D. Grant Al the user right Restore Files and Directories.

14. Which password policy would you implement if you want to prevent users from reusing passwords they have used previously?

    A. Passwords Must Be Advanced

    B. Enforce Password History

    C. Passwords Must Be Unique

    D. Passwords Must Meet the Complexity Requirements of the Installed Password Filters

15. Christine wants to connect her home folder to a shared folder that exists in the workgroup SALES, on a computer called DATA, and on a share called Users. Christine has full access to this folder and share. She also wants to use a variable for her username when she specifies the path to the network folder. Which of the following options should Christine use?

A. In the Profiles tab of Christine's User Properties, she should click the Connect button and specify the path as \\SALES\DATA\Users\%logonname%.

B. In the Profiles tab of Christine's User Properties, she should click the Connect button and specify the path as \\SALES\DATA\Users\%username%.

C. In the Profiles tab of Christine's User Properties, she should click the Connect button and specify the path as \\DATA\Users\%logonname%.

D. In the Profiles tab of Christine's User Properties, she should click the Connect button and specify the path as \\DATA\Users\%username%.

Answers to Review Questions

1. **B.** Account lockout policies, a subset of account policies, are used to specify options that prevent a user from attempting multiple failed logon attempts. If the Account Lockout Threshold value is exceeded, the account will be locked.

2. **C.** User Manager was the utility used in Windows NT 4. Local Users and Groups is the utility used by Windows 2000 Professional.

3. **D.** While all of the options sound plausible, the only valid password policy is Passwords Must Meet the Complexity Requirements of the Installed Password Filters.

4. **A, C.** By default, the Administrator and Guest accounts cannot be deleted, although they can both be renamed. The Administrator account is enabled by default, but the Guest account is disabled by default for security reasons. It is strongly recommended that you use a complex password for the Administrator account during the system installation.

5. **A.** All of the options seem plausible, but the only option that appears on the Profile tab of the user Properties dialog box is Connect.

6. **A.** The only way for the users to change their passwords is through the Windows Security dialog box. There is no command-line option. An Administrator can change a user's password through the Local Users and Groups utility.

7. **B.** Bethany Johnson-Smith is not a valid username because it is more than 20 characters. The other names that include spaces and parentheses are valid. Characters not valid for usernames include * / \ [ ] : ; | = , + * ? < > ". A username that consists solely of periods or spaces is also invalid.

8. **A.** Audit Account Logon Events is used to track when a user logs on, logs off, or makes a network connection.

9. D.   The Load and Unload Device Drivers user right allows a user to dynamically unload and load Plug and Play device drivers.

10. B.   The Log On as a Service user right allows a service to log on in order to run the specific service.

11. B.   The security option Do Not Display Last User Name is used to prevent the last username in the logon screen from being displayed in the logon dialog box.

12. D.   Once auditing has been configured, you can see the results of the audit through the Security log in the Event Viewer utility.

13. D.   The Restore Files and Directories user right allows a user to restore files and directories, regardless of file and directory permissions.

14. B.   The Enforce Password History policy allows the system to keep track of a user's password history for up to 24 passwords.

15. D.   In order to connect to a shared network folder for a users home folder, you must use the UNC path to the share. In this case, Christine would specify \\DATA\Users. The variable that can be used is %username%.

Chapter

7

Managing Groups

MICROSOFT EXAM OBJECTIVES COVERED IN THIS CHAPTER:

✓ **Implement, configure, manage, and troubleshoot local user accounts.**

- Implement, configure, manage, and troubleshoot account settings.
- Create and manage local users and groups.

Groups are an important part of network management. Many administrators are able to accomplish the majority of their management tasks through the use of groups; they rarely assign permissions to individual users. Windows 2000 Professional includes built-in local groups, such as Administrators and Backup Operators. These groups already have all the permissions needed to accomplish specific tasks. Windows 2000 Professional also uses default special groups, which are managed by the system. Users become members of special groups based on their requirements for computer and network access.

You create and manage local groups through the Local Users and Groups utility. Through this utility, you can add groups, change group membership, rename groups, and delete groups.

Local group policies allow you to set computer configuration and user configuration options that apply to every user of the computer. Group policies are typically used with Active Directory and are applied as Group Policy Objects (GPOs). Local group policies may be useful for computers that are not part of a network or in networks that don't have a domain controller. Although group policies are not represented in an official test objective, the topic is covered on the exam; you should understand how group policies work. In this chapter, you will learn about all the built-in groups. Then you will learn how to create and manage groups. The final sections in this chapter cover local group policies and GPOs within Active Directory.

This chapter covers the group-related material for the objective, "Implement, configure, and troubleshoot local user accounts." All of the user-related references for this objective are discussed in Chapter 6, "Managing Users."

Using Built-in Groups

On a Windows 2000 Professional computer, default local groups have already been created and assigned all necessary permissions to accomplish basic tasks. In addition, there are built-in special groups that the Windows 2000 system handles automatically. These groups are described in the following sections.

Windows 2000 Professional and Windows 2000 Servers that are installed as member servers have the same default groups.

Default Local Groups

A *local group* is a group that is stored on the local computer's accounts database. These are the groups to which you can add users and manage directly on a Windows 2000 Professional computer. By default, the following local groups are created on Windows 2000 Professional computers:

- Administrators
- Backup Operators
- Guests
- Power Users
- Replicator
- Users

The following sections briefly describe each group, its default permissions, and the users assigned to the group by default.

If possible, you should add users to the built-in local groups rather than creating new groups from scratch. This simplifies administration because the built-in groups already have the appropriate permissions. All you need to do is add the users that you want to be members of the group.

The Administrators Group

The *Administrators group* has full permissions and privileges. Its members can grant themselves any permissions they do not have by default, to manage all the objects on the computer. (Objects include the file system, printers, and account management.) By default, the Administrator and *initial user* account are members of the Administrators local group.

Assign users to the Administrators group with caution.

Members of the Administrators group can perform the following tasks:

- Install the operating system.
- Install and configure hardware device drivers.
- Install system services.
- Install service packs, hot fixes, and Windows updates.
- Upgrade the operating system.
- Repair the operating system.
- Install applications that modify the Windows system files.
- Configure password policies.
- Configure audit policies.
- Manage security logs.
- Create administrative shares.
- Create administrative accounts.
- Modify groups and accounts that have been created by other users.
- Remotely access the Registry.
- Stop or start any service.
- Configure services.
- Increase and manage disk quotas.
- Increase and manage execution priorities.
- Remotely shut down the system.

- Assign and manage user rights.
- Reenable locked-out and disabled accounts.
- Manage disk properties, including formatting hard drives.
- Modify systemwide environment variables.
- Access any data on the computer.
- Back up and restore all data.

The Backup Operators Group

Members of the *Backup Operators group* have permissions to back up and restore the file system, even if the file system is NTFS and they have not been assigned permissions to access the file system. However, the members of Backup Operators can only access the file system through the Backup utility. In order to access the file system directly, Backup Operators must have explicit permissions assigned. There are no default members of the Backup Operators local group.

The Guests Group

The *Guests group* has limited access to the computer. This group is provided so that you can allow people who are not regular users to access specific network resources. As a general rule, most administrators do not allow Guest access because it poses a potential security risk. By default, the Guest user account is a member of the Guests local group.

The Power Users Group

The *Power Users group* has fewer rights than the Administrators group, but more rights than the Users group. There are no default members of the Power Users local group.

Assign users to the Power Users group with caution.

Members of the Power Users group can perform the following tasks:

- Create local users and groups.
- Modify the users and groups that they have created.

- Create and delete network shares (except administrative shares).

- Create, manage, and delete local printers.

- Modify the system clock.

- Stop or start services (except services that are configured to start automatically).

- Modify the program files directory.

Members of the Power Users group cannot access any NTFS resources that they have not been given explicit permissions to use.

The Replicator Group

The *Replicator group* is intended to support directory replication, which is a feature used by domain servers. Only domain users who will start the replication service should be assigned to this group. The Replicator local group has no default members.

The Users Group

The *Users group* is intended for end users who should have very limited system access. If you have installed a fresh copy of Windows 2000 Professional, the default settings for the Users group prohibit its members from compromising the operating system or program files. By default, all users who have been created on the computer, except Guest, are members of the Users local group.

An efficient function for the Users group is to allow users to run but not modify installed applications. Users should not be allowed general access to the file system.

Special Groups

Special groups are used by the system. Membership in these groups is automatic if certain criteria are met. You cannot manage special groups through the Local Users and Groups utility. Table 7.1 describes the special groups that are built into Windows 2000 Professional.

TABLE 7.1 Special Groups in Windows 2000 Professional

Group	Description
Creator Owner	The account that created or took ownership of the object. This is typically a user account. Each object (files, folders, printers, and print jobs) has an owner. Members of the Creator Owner group have special permissions to resources. For example, if you are a regular user who has submitted 12 print jobs to a printer, you can manipulate your print jobs as Creator Owner, but you can't manage any print jobs submitted by other users.
Creator	The group that created or took ownership of the object (rather than an individual user). When a regular user creates an object or takes ownership of an object, the username becomes the Creator Owner. When a member of the Administrators group creates or takes ownership of an object, the group Administrators become the Creator group.
Everyone	The group that includes anyone who could possibly access the computer. Everyone group includes all users who have been defined on the computer (including Guest), plus (if your computer is a part of a domain) all users within the domain. If the domain has trust relationships with other domains, all users in the trusted domains are part of the Everyone group, as well.
Interactive	The group that includes all users who use the computer's resources locally. Local users belong to the Interactive group.
Network	The group that includes users who access the computer's resources over a network connection. Network users belong to the Network group.

TABLE 7.1 Special Groups in Windows 2000 Professional *(continued)*

Group	Description
Authenticated Users	The group that includes users who access the Windows 2000 operating system through a valid username and password. Users who can log on belong to the Authenticated Users group.
Anonymous Logon	The group that includes users who access the computer through anonymous logons. When users gain access through special accounts created for anonymous access to Windows 2000 services, they become members of the Anonymous Logon group.
Batch	The group that includes users who log on as a user account that is only used to run a batch job. Batch job accounts are members of the Batch group.
Dialup	The group that includes users who log on to the network from a dial-up connection. Dial-up users are members of the Dialup group. (Dialup connections are covered in Chapter 13, "Dial-Up Networking and Internet Connectivity.")
Service	The group that includes users who log on as a user account that is only used to run a service. You can configure the use of user accounts for logon through the Services program (discussed in Chapter 4, "Configuring the Windows 2000 Environment"), and these accounts become members of the Service group.
System	When the system accesses specific functions as a user, that process becomes a member of the System group.
Terminal Server User	The group that includes users who log on through Terminal Services. These users become members of the Terminal Server User group.

You can learn more about domains and trust relationships in *MCSE: Windows 2000 Directory Services Administration Study Guide,* 2nd ed., by Anil Desai with James Chellis (Sybex, 2001). Terminal Services are covered in *MCSE: Windows 2000 Server Study Guide,* 2nd ed., by Lisa Donald with James Chellis (Sybex, 2001).

Working with Groups

Groups are used to logically organize users with similar rights requirements. Groups simplify administration because you can manage a few groups rather than many user accounts. For the same reason, groups simplify troubleshooting. Users can belong to as many groups as needed, so it's not difficult to put users into groups that make sense for your organization.

For example, suppose Jane is hired as a data analyst, to join the four other data analysts who work for your company. You sit down with Jane and create an account for her, assigning her the network permissions for the access you think she needs. Later, however, you find that the four other data analysts (who have similar job functions) sometimes have network access Jane doesn't have, and sometimes she has access they don't have. This is happening because all their permissions were assigned individually, and months apart. To avoid such problems and reduce your administrative workload, you can assign all the company's data analysts to a group and then assign the appropriate permissions to that group. Then, as data analysts join or leave the department, you can simply add them to or remove them from the group.

Microsoft ✓ *Exam* *Objective*	**Implement, configure, manage, and troubleshoot local user accounts.** • Implement, configure, manage, and troubleshoot account settings. • Create and manage local users and groups.

This chapter covers the group-related material for the objective "Implement, configure, and troubleshoot local user accounts." All of the user-related sub-objectives for this objective are covered in Chapter 6.

You can create new groups for your users, and you can use the Windows 2000 Professional default local built-in groups that were described in the previous section. In both cases, your planning should include checking to see if an existing local group meets your requirements before you decide to create a new group. For example, if all of the users need to access a particular application, it makes sense to use the default Users group rather than creating a new group and adding all the users to that group.

To work with groups, you use the Local Users and Groups utility. In Chapter 6, you learned how to load and use the Local Users and Groups MMC snap-in to create and manage users. In the following sections, you will learn how to use this snap-in to create and manage groups.

The procedures for many basic group-management tasks—creating, deleting, and renaming groups—are the same for both Windows 2000 Professional and Windows 2000 Server.

Creating Groups

In order to create a group, you must be logged on as a member of the Administrators group or the Power Users group. The Administrators group has full permissions to manage users and groups. The members of the Power Users group can manage only the users and groups that they create.

As you do in your choices for usernames, keep your naming conventions in mind when assigning names to groups. When you create a local group, consider the following guidelines:

- The group name should be descriptive (for example, Accounting Data Users).

- The group name must be unique to the computer, different from all other group names and usernames that exist on that computer.

- Group names can be up to 256 characters. It is best to use alphanumeric characters for ease of administration. The backslash (\ ) character is not allowed.

Creating groups is similar to creating users, and it is a fairly easy process. After you've added the Local Users and Groups snap-in to the MMC, expand it to see the Users and Groups folders. Right-click the Groups folder and select New Group from the pop-up menu. This brings up the New Group dialog box, shown in Figure 7.1.

If your computer doesn't have an MMC configured, you can access the Local Users and Groups utility through the Computer Management utility. Right-click My Computer and select Manage from the pop-up menu to open the Computer Management utility. In the System Tools folder, you will see the Local Users and Groups folder. Expand that folder to access the Users and Groups folders in the utility.

FIGURE 7.1 The New Group dialog box

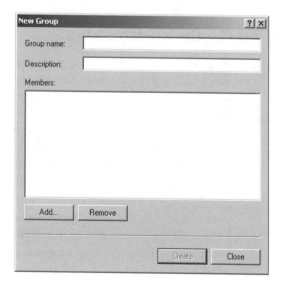

The only required entry in the New Group dialog box is the group name. If appropriate, you can enter a description for the group, and you can add (or remove) group members. When you're ready to create the new group, click the Create button.

In Exercise 7.1, you will create two new local groups. This exercise assumes that you have added the Local Users and Groups snap-in to the MMC (see Exercise 6.2 in Chapter 6).

EXERCISE 7.1

Creating Local Groups

1. Open the MMC and expand the Local Users and Groups snap-in.

2. Right-click the Groups folder and select New Group.

3. In the New Group dialog box, type **Data Users** in the Group Name text box. Click the Create button.

4. Right-click the Groups folder and select New Group.

5. In the New Group dialog box, type **Application Users** in the Group Name text box. Click the Create button.

Managing Group Membership

After you've created a group, you can add members to it. As mentioned earlier, you can put the same user in multiple groups. You can easily add and remove users through the group Properties dialog box, shown in Figure 7.2. To access this dialog box from the Groups folder in the Local Users and Groups utility, double-click the group you want to manage.

From the group's Properties dialog box, you can change the group's description and add or remove group members. When you click the Add button to add members, the Select Users or Groups dialog box appears (Figure 7.3). Here, you select the user accounts you wish to add and click the Add button. Click the OK button to add the selected users to the group. (Although the special groups that were covered earlier in the chapter are listed in this dialog box, you cannot manage the membership of these special groups.)

FIGURE 7.2   The group Properties dialog box

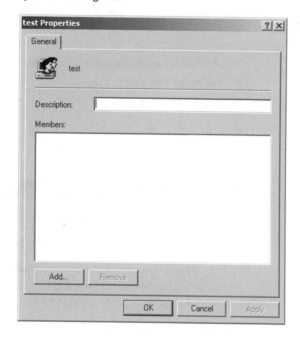

FIGURE 7.3   The Select Users or Groups dialog box

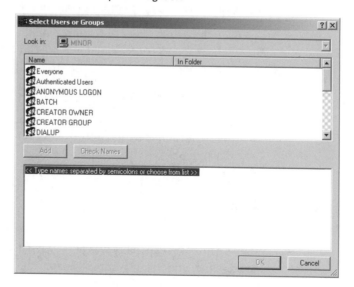

To remove a member from the group, select the member in the Members list of the Properties dialog box, and click the Remove button.

You can select multiple contiguous users for addition to or removal from a group, by Shift+clicking the first and last users. To select multiple noncontiguous users, Ctrl+click each one.

In Exercise 7.2, you will create new user accounts and then add these users to one of the groups you created in Exercise 7.1.

EXERCISE 7.2

Adding Users to a Local Group

1. Open the MMC and expand the Local Users and Groups snap-in.

2. Create four new users: **Bent**, **Claire**, **Patrick**, and **Trina**. (See Chapter 6 for details on creating user accounts.) Deselect the User Must Change Password at Next Logon option for each user.

3. Expand the Groups folder.

4. Double-click the Data Users group (created in Exercise 7.1).

5. In the group Properties dialog box, click the Add button.

6. In the Select Users or Groups dialog box, select Bent, Claire, Patrick, and Trina (hold down the Ctrl key as you click each member).

7. Click the Add button. Then click the OK button.

8. In the group Properties dialog box, you will see that the users have all been added to the group. Click OK to close the group Properties dialog box.

Renaming Groups

Windows 2000 Professional provides an easy mechanism for changing a group's name (this capability was not offered in any versions of Windows NT). For example, you might want to rename a group because its current name does not conform to existing naming conventions.

As happens when you rename a user account, a renamed group keeps all of its properties, including its members and permissions.

To rename a group, right-click the group and choose Rename from the pop-up menu. Enter a new name for the group and press Enter.

In Exercise 7.3, you will rename one of the groups you created in Exercise 7.1.

EXERCISE 7.3

Renaming a Local Group

1. Open the MMC and expand the Local Users and Groups snap-in.

2. Expand the Groups folder.

3. Right-click the Application Users group (created in Exercise 7.1) and select Rename.

4. Rename the group to **App Users** and press Enter.

Deleting Groups

If you are sure that you will never again want to use a particular group, you can delete it. Once a group is deleted, you lose all permissions assignments that have been specified for the group.

To delete a group, right-click the group and choose Delete from the pop-up menu. You will see a warning that once a group is deleted, it is gone for good. Click the Yes button if you're sure you want to delete the group.

If you delete a group and give another group the same name, the new group won't be created with the same properties as the deleted group.

In Exercise 7.4, you will delete one of the groups that you created in Exercise 7.1 and renamed in Exercise 7.3.

EXERCISE 7.4

Deleting a Local Group

1. Open the MMC and expand the Local Users and Groups snap-in.

2. Expand the Groups folder.

3. Right-click the App Users group and choose Delete.

4. In the dialog box that appears, click Yes to confirm that you want to delete the group.

Using Local Group Policies

Group policies allow you to manage various computer and user configuration settings, ranging from IP security to connection sharing. Administrators typically use group policies to manage users' Desktops, controlling the options users will see and are able to change.

 Even though group policies are not represented in an official test objective, this topic is covered on the exam and you should understand how group policies work.

Normally, group policies are applied through Active Directory—but they can also be applied locally. In this section you will examine group policies and how they are applied locally. In the next section, you will learn how group polices can be applied through Active Directory.

When you use *local group policies*, there is only one Group Policy Object, which applies to all of the computer's users. Policies that have been linked though Active Directory will take precedence over any established local group policies. Local group policies are typically applied to computers that are not part of a network or are in a network that does not have a domain controller, and thus do not use Active Directory.

You administer local group policies through the *Local Group Policy snap-in* in the MMC. Group policy settings are organized into two categories:

- Computer configuration policies, which relate to all users of a particular computer

- User configuration policies, which typically deal with options that are specific to users or groups

Use caution in setting local group policies. Any policies you set will be applied to all users of the computer, including the Administrator.

Group Policies within Active Directory

If your Windows 2000 Professional computer is a part of Active Directory, group policies can be applied as *Group Policy Objects (GPOs)*. Group policies contain configuration settings for the following options:

Software   Software policies are used to configure system services, the appearance of the desktop, and application settings.

Scripts   Scripts are special instructions that can be configured to run when the user logs on or off at the computer, or when the computer is started or shut down.

Security   Security policies define how security is configured and applied at the local computer or through Active Directory.

Application and File Deployment   Application and file deployment policies are used to assign and publish applications, or to place files in the user's desktop or within a specific folder (for example, the Start menu) or within Favorites.

Quick Overview of Active Directory

Within Active Directory, you have several levels of hierarchical structure. A typical structure will consist of domains and organizational units. Other levels exist within Active Directory, but this section focuses on *domains* and *Organizational Units (OUs)* in the context of using GPOs.

The domain is the main unit of organization within Active Directory. Within a domain are many domain objects (including users, groups, and GPOs). Each domain object can have security applied that specifies who can access the object and the level of access they have.

Within a domain, you can further subdivide and organize domain objects through the use of Organizational Units. This is one of the key differences between Windows NT domains and Windows 2000 domains: The NT domains were not able to store information hierarchically. Windows 2000 domains, through the use of OUs, allow you to store objects hierarchically, typically based on function or geography. For example, assume that your company is called ABCCORP. You have locations in New York, San Jose, and Belfast. You might create a domain called ABCCORP.COM with OUs called NY, SJ, and Belfast. In a very large corporation, you might also organize the OUs based on function. For example, the domain could be ABC-CORP.COM and the OUs might be SALES, ACCT, and TECHSUPP. Based on the size and security needs of your organization, you might also have OUs nested within OUs. As a general rule, however, you will want to keep your Active Directory structure as simple as possible.

Group Policy Objects and Active Directory

The default location for GPOs within Active Directory on all domain controllers is the \%SystemRoot%\Sysvol folder. Within each root folder, there is a policy file called `gpt.ini` that contains information about the group policy.

When GPOs are created within Active Directory, there is a specific order of inheritance. That is, the polices are applied in a specific order within the hierarchical structure of Active Directory. When a user logs onto Active Directory, depending on where within the hierarchy GPOs have been applied, the order of application is as follows:

1. Local computer

2. Site (group of domains)

3. Domain

4. OU

What this means is that the local policy is by default applied first when a user logs on. Then the site policies are applied, and if the site policy contains settings that the local policy doesn't have, they are added to the local policy. If there are any conflicts, the site policy overrides the local policy. Then the domain policies are defined. Again, if the domain policy contains additional settings, they are incorporated. When settings conflict, the domain policy overrides the site policy. Next, the OU policies are applied. Additional settings are incorporated; for conflicts, the OU policy overrides the domain policy. If conflicts occur between computer and user policy settings, the user policy setting is applied.

The following options are available for overriding the default behavior of GPO execution:

No Override   The No Override option is used to specify that child containers can't override the policy settings of higher-level GPOs. In this case, the order of precedence would be that site settings override domain settings, and domain settings override OU settings. The No Override option would be used if you wanted to set corporate-wide policies without allowing administrators of lower-level containers to override your settings. This option can be set per-container, as needed.

Block Inheritance   The Block Inheritance option is used to allow the child container to block GPO inheritance from parent containers. This option would be used if you did not want to inherit GPO settings from parent containers and only wanted the GPO you had set for your container to be applied.

If there is a conflict between the No Override and the Block Inheritance settings, then the No Override option would be applied.

Usage of Group Policy Objects is covered in greater detail in *MCSE: Windows 2000 Server Study Guide,* 2nd ed., by Lisa Donald with James Chellis (Sybex, 2001).

🌐 **Real World Scenario**

Applying GPOs

You manage a network that consists of 500 computers all running Windows 2000 Professional. You are already using Active Directory and have logically defined your OUs based on function. One OU, called Sales, has 50 users. Your task is to configure the Sales computers so that they all have a consistent desktop that can't be modified. You also need to add the new Sales Management software to each computer.

It would take days for you to manually configure each computer with a local group policy and then add the software. In this case, GPOs are a real benefit. As the Administrator of the Sales OU, you can create a single GPO that will be applied to all users of the container. You can specify the desktop settings and publish the application. Next time the Sales users log on, the group policies will be applied, and the users' Registries will be updated to reflect the changes. In addition, through the automated publishing of the application, it can be configured to be automatically loaded on each of the Sales users' computers.

By using GPOs, you can add new software, configure computers, and accomplish other tasks from your computer that would normally require you to physically visit each machine.

Summary

In this chapter, you learned about group management with Windows 2000 Professional. We covered the following topics:

- The Windows 2000 Professional built-in groups, which include default local groups such as Administrators and Power Users, and default special groups such as Everyone and Network. You can manage the default local groups, but the special groups are managed by the system.

- The procedure for creating groups. You create groups through the Local Users and Groups utility.

- The procedure for adding users to groups and removing users from groups. You perform these tasks through the group's Properties dialog box.

- Renaming and deleting groups, both of which are performed by right-clicking the group in the Groups folder of the Local Users and Groups utility, and selecting the appropriate option from the pop-up menu.

- The purpose of group policies and the options that you can configure for local group policies.

- How Group Policy Objects are applied through Active Directory.

Exam Essentials

Be able to manage local groups.   Know the local groups that are created on Windows 2000 Professional computers by default, and understand what rights each group has. Know how to create and manage new groups.

Know how to set local group policies.   Understand the purpose of local group policies. Be aware of the options that can be configured through local group policies.

Understand how group policies are used within Active Directory. Know what options can be configured through Group Policy Objects within Active Directory, and the order of inheritance.

Key Terms

Before you take the exam, be sure you're familiar with the following key terms:

Administrators group	Batch group
Anonymous Logon group	Creator group
Authenticated Users group	Creator Owner group
Backup Operators group	Dialup group

domain

Everyone group

Group Policy Object (GPO)

Guests group

Interactive group

local groups

Local Group Policy snap-in

Network group

Organizational Unit (OU)

Power Users group

Replicator group

Service group

special groups

System group

Terminal Server User group

Users group

Review Questions

1. Prioritize-a-list: As network administrator, you have configured GPOs for your local computers, domains, sites, and OUs. Your GPOs are not being applied as you expected they would be. You have not set any filter or inheritance settings. What is the default order of inheritance that will be applied to the GPOs?

Local Computer	
Domain	
Site	
OU	

2. Sean works in the IT unit and needs to be able to manage the Sales Organizational Unit (OU). You want him to be able to create users and groups, but not to manage properties of users and groups that he did not create. To which of the following groups should you add Sean?

   A. Administrators

   B. Power Users

   C. Server Operators

   D. Power Operators

3. A user in your San Jose domain is attempting to install an updated modem driver. They report that they can't get the driver to update properly. You log on to the user's computer with administrative rights to the San Jose domain and attempt to update the driver. When you check the driver through Device Manager, you notice that the old driver is still installed. In Control Panel, you open the System icon and see that driver signing is configured with Ignore for the driver signing verification. You suspect that the problem may be with the GPO's configuration. Which of the following actions should you take that will make the least impact on the GPO for Active Directory?

   A. Configure the domain GPO for the Warn file signature verification, and then attempt to update the driver.

   B. For the Sales domain, set the No Override option.

   C. For the Sales domain, set the Block Inheritance option.

   D. Configure the local computer for the Warn file signature verification, and then attempt to update the driver.

4. You want to make Brett a member of the Backup Operators group. Which of the following statements about the Backup Operators group is true?

   A. By default, only Administrators and Power Users can be members of the Backup Operators group.

   B. Backup Operators do not require any additional permissions to NTFS file systems in order to back up and restore the file system.

   C. Backup Operators have full access to the NTFS file system.

   D. Backup Operators can modify any services that relate to system backup.

5. Linda installs her Windows 2000 Professional computer as a member of a workgroup. Which types of groups can she create on her computer?

   A. Security group

   B. Distribution group

   C. Source group

   D. Local group

6. You are considering adding the user Rick to the Power Users group. If you add him to this group, what tasks will he be able to perform? (Choose all that apply.)

   A. Create local users and groups.

   B. Create and delete all network shares.

   C. Stop and start all network services.

   D. Create, manage, and delete local printers.

7. If you log on as user Brad to a Windows 2000 Professional computer that contains the user account Brad, which of the following groups will you belong to by default? (Choose all that apply.)

   A. Users

   B. Authenticated Users

   C. Everyone

   D. Interactive

8. Your Active Directory structure consists of a domain called CCCUSA, which is a part of a site called CCCCORP. There is an OU called Sales, and each computer within Sales has a local policy set. You have configured all of the GPOs with the No Override option. Which of the following policies will be applied in the event of conflict?

   A. Domain

   B. Site

   C. OU

   D. Local computer

9. You have a logon script that is used to partially configure the Windows Explorer interface. You want to ensure that the entire script is processed before the Windows Explorer interface is run. What group policy setting should you use to arrange this?

    A. Run Logon Scripts Synchronously

    B. Run Startup Scripts Asynchronously

    C. Minimum Wait Time for Group Policy Scripts

    D. Wait for Logon Scripts to Complete

10. You want to configure your computer so that test.samplecorp.com is the primary DNS suffix that will be used for DNS name registration and DNS name resolution. What group policy setting can be used to configure this option?

    A. Set DNS Suffix

    B. Enable DNS Name Resolution

    C. Apply DNS Configuration

    D. Primary DNS Suffix

11. You want to configure a Windows 2000 computer so that all users see an option for logoff on the Start menu. Which of the following actions will set this configuration?

    A. Create custom logon scripts.

    B. Create a custom local group policy.

    C. Set this option in the Profile tab of the user Properties dialog box.

    D. Create a custom local group object that is configured with this attribute.

12. Rick has been added to the Administrators group, but you suspect that he is abusing his administrative privileges. All he really needs permission for is creating and managing local user accounts. You do not want Rick to be able to look at any NTFS folders or files to which he has not explicitly been granted access. To which group should you add Rick so that he can do his job but will have the minimum level of administrative rights?

A. Administrators

B. Power Users

C. Account Operators

D. Server Operators

13. You are logged on as John, who is a member of the Power Users group. When John accesses the Printers folder, he does not see an Add Printer option. What is the most likely reason for this?

A. There are no Plug and Play printers attached to the computer.

B. There are no LPT ports defined in the computer's BIOS.

C. In the group policy settings, addition of printers is disabled.

D. Members of the Power Users group do not have permissions to create new printers.

14. When you change group policies, what configuration information is edited on a Windows 2000 Professional computer when a user logs on and the group policy is applied?

A. The Registry

B. .ini files

C. .inf files

D. .cfg files

15. You have created a GPO for the domain ACCT. In what folder will the group policy files be stored by default?

A. In the \%SystemRoot%\GPO folder

B. In the \%SystemRoot%\GPT folder

C. In the \%SystemRoot%\SYSVOL folder

D. In the \%SystemRoot%\POL folder

Answers to Review Questions

1.

Local Computer
Site
Domain
OU

By default GPOs are applied in the order of local computer, site, domain, and OU. The policies will be combined unless conflicting settings are applied, in which case the last policy that is applied contains the effective setting.

2. B. Members of the Power Users group can create users and groups, but they can manage only the users and groups they themselves have created. Administrators can manage all users and groups. The Server Operators group exists only on Windows 2000 domain controllers. The Power Operators group does not exist by default on Windows 2000 computers.

3. A. You should just configure a specific GPO so that the file signature verification is set to Warn as opposed to Block, which will refuse upgrading of the driver if it is unsigned without any user notification. The last GPO applied is the domain's, so you should edit the Sales domain's GPO for this arrangement.

4. B. There are no default members of the Backup Operators group. Members of this group have access to the file system during the backup process, but they do not have normal file access. Backup Operators group members have no special permissions to modify system services.

5. D. The only type of group that can exist on a Windows 2000 Professional computer is a local group.

6. A, D. Members of the Power Users group can create local users and groups, but they can only manage the users and groups that they have created. Power Users can create and delete network shares, *except* administrative shares. Power Users can stop and start network services, *except* services that are configured to start automatically. Power Users can create, manage, and delete local printers.

7. A, B, C, D. By default, all users who exist on a Windows 2000 Professional computer are added to the computer's Users group. Users who log on with a valid username and password automatically become a member of the Authenticated Users special group. By default, anyone who can use the computer becomes a member of the special group Everyone. Since Brad works at the computer where his user account actually resides, he automatically becomes a member of the special group Interactive.

8. B. The No Override option is used to specify that child containers can't override the policy settings of higher-level GPOs. In this case, the order of precedence would be as follows: Site would override Domain, and Domain would override OU. The No Override option can be used if you want to set corporatewide policies and do not want to give administrators of lower-level containers the capability to override your settings. This option can be set on a per container basis, as needed.

9. A. Run Logon Scripts Synchronously is an option in the system policy for computer configuration, which specifies that logon scripts should finish running before the Windows Explorer interface is run. Configuring this option can cause the display of the Desktop to be delayed.

10. D. Primary DNS Suffix is the local group policy setting that is used to specify the primary Domain Name Service (DNS) suffix that will be used for both DNS name registration and DNS name resolution.

11. B. Start menu and Taskbar local group policies allow you to configure options such as whether users see a Logoff option on the Start menu.

12. B. The members of the Power Users group have the rights to create and manage the local users and groups that they create, without being able to look at NTFS folders and files that they have not been given access to. Account Operators and Server Operators are not built-in groups on Windows 2000 Professional computers.

13. C. Members of the Power Users group can create new printers. The most likely reason John doesn't have the Add Printer option is that the option to add new printers has been disabled in the group policy settings. You do not need a Plug and Play printer attached to the computer; nor do you need to have LPT ports configured in order to create a printer.

14. A. When you edit group policies, you edit the configuration settings that are stored in the Windows 2000 Registry.

15. C. On all domain controllers, GPOs are automatically stored within Active Directory in the \%SystemRoot%\SYSVOL folder. Within each root folder, there is a policy file called `gpt.ini` that contains information about the group policy.

Chapter

8

Using User Profiles and Hardware Profiles

MICROSOFT EXAM OBJECTIVES COVERED IN THIS CHAPTER:

- ✓ Configure and manage user profiles.
- ✓ Manage hardware profiles.

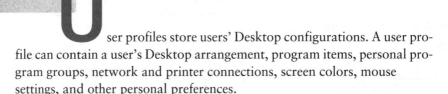

ser profiles store users' Desktop configurations. A user profile can contain a user's Desktop arrangement, program items, personal program groups, network and printer connections, screen colors, mouse settings, and other personal preferences.

User profiles are stored locally by default, but they can be accessed through the network if you configure roaming profiles. If you don't want users to be able to change their user profiles, you can configure mandatory profiles.

Hardware profiles store different hardware configurations for a computer. Hardware profiles are useful when a single computer has multiple hardware configurations.

This chapter covers creation and management of user profiles and hardware profiles. We will begin with an overview of the configuration information stored in user profiles.

User Profile Configuration Options

User profiles store many of the personal configuration options for Windows 2000 Professional. For example, say user Kevin has logged on and customized his Desktop by changing the wallpaper, adding shortcuts, adding items to the Startup folder, and changing the mouse pointer. All of this information will be saved in Kevin's user profile when he logs off. The next time he logs on, his Desktop customizations will be restored.

If a configuration option is a personal preference, it is most likely a part of the user profile. Configuration options that relate to the computer itself are not a part of the user profile. For example, the mouse driver is not a part of a user profile. However, the properties of the mouse configuration—such as its speed, the pointer, and the mouse button settings—reflect the user's personal preferences and are a part of a user profile. Table 8.1 lists some of the settings saved in user profiles.

TABLE 8.1   User Preferences Saved in User Profiles

Settings	Preferences Stored in User Profile
Windows Explorer	View of Windows Explorer, mapped network drives, types of files that are displayed
Control Panel	Screen appearance, accessibility options, mouse and keyboard preferences
Printer settings	Network printer connections
Taskbar	All settings, including program items and their properties
Accessories	Preferences for programs such as Calculator, Command Prompt, and Notepad
Online Help bookmarks	Any bookmarks that the user has set in the Windows 2000 Help program
Windows 2000–based applications	User configuration settings for applications that support such settings

Creating and Managing User Profiles

User profiles are particularly useful when multiple users share the same computer. If each user has a profile, his or her Desktop preferences will be maintained and loaded when that user logs on to the computer.

Microsoft ✓ *Exam* *Objective*	**Configure and manage user profiles.**

User profiles can be used by a single user or by a group of users. If you assign a user profile to a group of users, you can ensure that all users in the group maintain a consistent Desktop. This makes it easier to train users and to troubleshoot problems.

By default, user profiles are created locally on the computer to which the user account logs on, but you can create roaming profiles that are available from the network. Roaming profiles allow users to access their customized Desktop from any computer they log on to within the network.

By default, users can change their own profiles, but Administrators can create and assign mandatory, or read-only, profiles. Users cannot modify mandatory profiles.

The following sections describe how to create local, roaming, and mandatory user profiles.

Local User Profiles

Each time you log on to a Windows 2000 Professional computer, the system checks to see if you have a *local user profile* in the Documents and Settings folder, which was created on the boot partition when you installed Windows 2000 Professional.

If your computer was upgraded from Windows NT 4.0 to Windows 2000 Professional, the default location for user profiles is \WINNT\Profiles\ %UserName%. If you install Windows 2000 Professional from scratch, the default location for user profiles is %systemdrive%\Documents and Settings\ %UserName%.

The first time users log on, they receive a default user profile. A folder that matches the user's logon name is created for the user in the Documents and Settings folder. The user profile folder that is created holds a file called *NTUSER.DAT*, as well as subfolders that contain directory links to the user's Desktop items.

In Exercise 8.1, you will create new users and set up local user profiles.

EXERCISE 8.1

Using Local Profiles

1. Using the Local Users and Groups utility, create two new users: **Liz** and **Tracy**. (See Chapter 6, "Managing Users," for details on creating user accounts.) Deselect the User Must Change Password at Next Logon option for each user.

2. Select Start ➢ Programs ➢ Accessories ➢ Windows Explorer. Expand My Computer, then Local Disk (C:), then Documents and Settings. Notice that this folder does not contain user profile folders for the new users.

3. Log off as Administrator and log on as Liz. When the Getting Started with Windows 2000 dialog box appears, deselect the Show This Screen at Startup option and then click the Exit button.

4. Right-click an open area on the Desktop and select Properties. In the Display Properties dialog box, click the Appearance tab. Select the color scheme Red, White, and Blue (VGA), click the Apply button, and then click the OK button.

5. Right-click an open area on the Desktop and select New ➢ Shortcut. In the Create Shortcut dialog box, type **CALC**. Accept CALC as the name for the shortcut and click the Finish button.

EXERCISE 8.1 *(continued)*

6. Log off as Liz and log on as Tracy. Notice that user Tracy sees the Desktop configuration stored in the default user profile.

7. Log off as Tracy and log on as Liz. Notice that Liz sees the Desktop configuration you set up in steps 3, 4, and 5.

8. Log off as Liz and log on as Administrator. Select Start ➤ Programs ➤ Accessories ➤ Windows Explorer. Expand My Computer, then Local Disk (C:), then Documents and Settings. Notice that this folder now contains user profile folders for Liz and Tracy.

If you need to reapply the default user profile for a user, you can delete the user's profile through the System icon in Control Panel, User Profiles tab.

The drawback of local user profiles is that they are available only on the computer where they were created. For example, suppose all of your Windows 2000 Professional computers are a part of a domain and you use only local user profiles. User Rick logs on at Computer A and creates a customized user profile. When he logs on to Computer B for the first time, he will receive the default user profile rather than the customized user profile he created on Computer A. For users to be able to access their user profile from any computer they log on to, you need to use roaming profiles, as described in the next section.

Roaming Profiles

A *roaming profile* is stored on a network server and allows users to access their user profile, regardless of the client computer to which they're logged on. Roaming profiles provide a consistent Desktop for users who move around, no matter which computer they access. Even if the server that stores the roaming profile is unavailable, the user can still log on using a local profile.

In Exercise 8.2, you will simulate the process of creating a roaming profile. This is just a simulation because, in order for roaming profiles to work on a Windows 2000 Professional computer, roaming profiles must be configured on a Windows 2000 Server computer.

EXERCISE 8.2

Using Roaming Profiles

In this exercise, you will set up a roaming profile, which is a four-part process. Then you will test the profile.

Creating a Profile

1. Using the Local Users and Groups utility, create a user named **Tester**. Deselect the User Must Change Password at Next Logon option.

2. Log on as Tester. Right-click an open area on the Desktop and select New ➢ Shortcut. In the Create Shortcut dialog box, type **EXPLORER**. Accept EXPLORER as the name for the shortcut and click the Finish button.

3. Right-click an open area on the Desktop and select Properties. In the Display Properties dialog box, click the Appearance tab. Select the color scheme Maple, click the Apply button, and then click the OK button.

Creating a Network Share for User Profiles

4. Log off as Tester and log on as Administrator.

5. Select Start ➢ Programs ➢ Accessories ➢ Windows Explorer. Expand My Computer, then Local Disk (C:).

6. Select File ➢ New ➢ Folder. Name the new folder **Profiles**.

7. Right-click the Profiles folder and select Sharing. In the Sharing dialog box, click the Share This Folder radio button and leave all of the other values at their default settings. Click the OK button.

Copying the User Profile to the Network Share Folder

8. Select Start ➢ Settings ➢ Control Panel ➢ System and click the User Profiles tab.

EXERCISE 8.2 *(continued)*

9. In the User Profiles tab of the System Properties dialog box, high-light the *computername*\Tester profile and click the Copy To button.

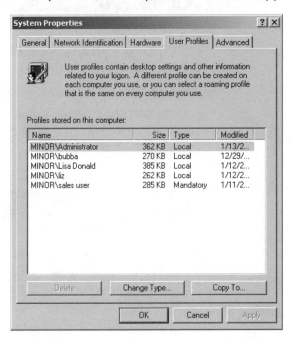

Note: When you go through the Copy To button in the User Profiles tab of the System Properties dialog box, the process copies the NTUSER.DAT file, as well as all of the folders associated with the pro-file. You should always use this method to copy a profile to a net-work share, rather than using other file-copying options.

10. In the Copy To dialog box, specify **C:\Profiles\Tester** and click the OK button. Click the OK button to close the System Properties dia-log box.

Configuring the User Properties to Use a Roaming Profile

11. Open the Local Users and Groups utility and expand the Users folder.

EXERCISE 8.2 *(continued)*

12. Double-click user Tester to open the user Properties dialog box and click the Profile tab.

13. In the Profile Path text box, type ***computername*\profiles\tester**, replacing *computername* with the unique name of your computer. Click the Apply button and then click the Close button.

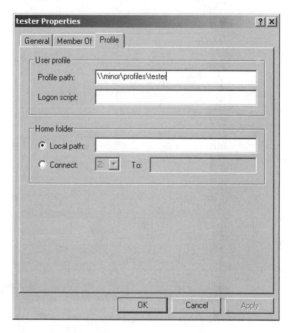

Testing the Roaming Profile

14. Log off as Administrator and log on as Tester. You should see the profile that was created for Tester.

15. Log off as Tester and log on as Administrator.

 Normally you would configure roaming profiles for users who are part of an Active Directory domain. In this case, you would use the Active Directory Users and Computers utility to specify the location of a user's roaming profile.

Using Mandatory Profiles

A *mandatory profile* is a profile that can't be modified by the user. Only members of the Administrators group can manage mandatory profiles. You might consider creating mandatory profiles for users who should maintain consistent Desktops. For example, suppose that you have a group of 20 salespeople who know enough about system configuration to make changes, but not enough to fix any problems they create. For ease of support, you could use mandatory profiles. This way, all of the salespeople will always have the same profile and will not be able to change their profiles.

You can create mandatory profiles for a single user or a group of users. The mandatory profile is stored in a file named *NTUSER.MAN*. A user with a mandatory profile can set different Desktop preferences while logged on, but those settings will not be saved when the user logs off.

Only roaming profiles can be used as mandatory profiles. Mandatory profiles do not work for local user profiles.

In Exercise 8.3, you will simulate the process of creating a mandatory profile. As with the sample roaming profile you created in Exercise 8.2, the mandatory profile will not actually work because you have not first configured roaming profiles on a Windows 2000 Server computer.

EXERCISE 8.3

Using Mandatory Profiles

In this exercise, you will set up a mandatory profile, which is a four-part process. Then you will test the profile.

Creating a Profile

1. Using the Local Users and Groups utility, create a user named **Sales User**. Deselect the User Must Change Password at Next Logon option.

2. Log off as Administrator and log on as Sales User.

3. Select Start ➢ Settings ➢ Control Panel ➢ Mouse. Click the Pointers tab and select Conductor from the Scheme drop-down list. Click the Apply button, then click the OK button.

4. In Control Panel, select Sounds and Multimedia. In the Sounds tab, select Utopia from the Scheme drop-down list; then click the OK button.

5. Right-click an open area on the Desktop and select Properties. In the Display Properties dialog box, click the Effects tab. Under Visual Effects, select the Use Large Icons option. Click the Apply button, then click the OK button.

Renaming the NTUSER.DAT File

6. Log off as Sales User and log on as Administrator.

7. Select Start ➢ Programs ➢ Accessories ➢ Windows Explorer.

8. In Windows Explorer, select Tools ➢ Folder Options and click the View tab. Click the Show Hidden Files and Folders radio button and uncheck the Hide File Extensions for Known File Types check box. Click the Apply button, then click the OK button.

9. In Windows Explorer, expand My Computer, then Local Disk (C:), then Documents and Settings, then Sales User.

10. Right-click the NTUSER.DAT file and rename the file to NTUSER.MAN. Close Windows Explorer.

Copying the User Profile to the Network Share Folder

11. Select Start ➢ Settings ➢ Control Panel ➢ System and click the User Profiles tab in the System Properties dialog box.

12. Highlight the *computername*\Sales User profile and click the Copy To button.

13. In the Copy To dialog box, specify **C:\Profiles\Sales User** and click the OK button. Click the OK button to close the System Properties dialog box.

Configuring the User Properties to Use a Mandatory Profile

14. Open the Local Users and Groups utility and expand the Users folder.

15. Double-click user Sales User to open the user Properties dialog box and click the Profile tab.

EXERCISE 8.3 *(continued)*

16. In the Profile Path text box, type ***computername*\Profiles\Sales User**, replacing ***computername*** with the unique name of your computer. Click the Apply button, then click the Close button.

Note: If the client accessing the mandatory profile is a Windows NT 4 or Windows 2000 computer, you do not need to include the user profile name in the Profile Path setting in the user Properties dialog box. For example, you could specify \\Server1\Profiles\Tester. However, if the client is a Windows NT 3.*x* computer, you must include the user profile name in the Profile Path setting. For example, you would specify \\Server\Profiles\Tester\NTUSER.MAN.

Testing the Mandatory Profile

17. Log off as Administrator and log on as Sales User.

18. Select Start ➤ Settings ➤ Control Panel ➤ Mouse. Click the Pointers tab and choose Dinosaur from the Scheme drop-down list. Click the Apply button, then click the OK button.

19. Log off as Sales User and log on again as Sales User.

20. Log off as Sales User and log on as Administrator.

 Real World Scenario

Copying User Profiles

Within your company you have a user, Sharon, who logs in with two different user accounts. One account is a regular user account, and the other is an Administrator Account used for administration tasks only.

When Sharon established all her desktop preferences and installed the computer's applications, they were installed with the Administrator account. Now when she logs in with the regular user account, she can't access the Desktop and profile settings that were created for her as an administrative user.

To solve this problem, you can copy a local user profile from one user to another. When you copy a user profile, the following items are copied: Favorites, Cookies, My Documents, Start menu items, and other unique user registry settings.

Creating and Managing Hardware Profiles

*H*ardware profiles store hardware configurations for a computer. Using hardware profiles allows you to manage multiple hardware configurations for a single computer. For example, suppose you have a laptop computer that can be used with a docking station that attaches to the network. If the computer is configured for network connectivity and the computer is not docked, you will see error messages at startup. To avoid this, you can create hardware profiles for this laptop computer: one hardware profile (with network settings) to load when the computer is docked, and another hardware profile (without network settings) to load when the computer is undocked.

Microsoft **Manage hardware profiles.**
Exam
Objective

When you set up hardware profiles, you specify hardware configurations that can be accessed when Windows 2000 Professional is started. You manage hardware profiles through the Hardware Profiles dialog box, shown in Figure 8.1. To access this dialog box, select Start ➤ Settings ➤ Control Panel ➤ System. (You can also access the System Properties dialog box by right-clicking My Computer and selecting Properties.) In the System Properties dialog box, click the Hardware tab and then click the Hardware Profiles button. The options in the Hardware Profiles dialog box are described in Table 8.2.

FIGURE 8.1 The Hardware Profiles dialog box

TABLE 8.2 Hardware Profile Options

Option	Description
Available Hardware Profiles	Lists all the hardware profiles that have been created. If only one profile is listed, you will not see hardware profile selection options when Windows 2000 is started. If there is only one profile, it can't be deleted. You can change the order of the profiles in the Available Hardware Profiles list by selecting a profile and clicking the up- or down-arrow button to the right of the list.

TABLE 8.2 Hardware Profile Options *(continued)*

Option	Description
Properties	Opens a dialog box where you can specify whether the computer is portable. A portable computer usually has two profiles: one for when the computer is docked, and another for when the computer is undocked. You can also specify whether the profile will appear in the hardware profile selection options when Windows 2000 is started.
Copy	Opens a dialog box that lets you copy an existing hardware profile. You can then edit the copied profile.
Rename	Allows you to give your hardware profile a different name. For example, you might rename Profile 1 to Docked Portable.
Delete	Deletes the hardware profile that is currently highlighted. This option is not active if only one hardware profile is listed.
Hardware Profiles Selection	Specifies how the hardware profile selection options should be configured for Windows 2000 startup. You can specify that the computer boot process stop until a selection is made, or you can configure the computer to select the first profile that is listed (the list is in the order shown in the Available Hardware Profiles list box) if no choice has been made within x number of seconds.

Every computer has at least one hardware profile. The default profile that is created when you install Windows 2000 Professional is called Profile 1.

If you are going to create a profile for a portable computer that will be docked, you should have the portable computer in the docking station when you create the profile.

In Exercise 8.4, you will configure two hardware profiles for your computer.

EXERCISE 8.4

Managing Hardware Profiles

1. Select Start ➢ Settings ➢ Control Panel ➢ System, click the Hardware tab, and click the Hardware Profiles button. This brings up the Hardware Profiles dialog box.

2. Click the Copy button to copy Profile 1. Name the copy **Undocked** and click the OK button.

3. Highlight Undocked and click the Properties button. In the undocked Properties dialog box, select the This Is a Portable Computer check box, and the radio button for The Computer Is Undocked. Click the OK button.

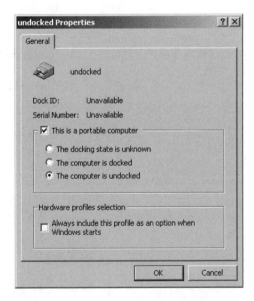

4. In the Hardware Profiles dialog box, highlight Profile 1 (Current) and click the Rename button. Rename the profile to **Docked** and click the OK button.

5. Highlight Docked and click the Properties button. Select the This is a Portable Computer option. Select the radio button for The Computer Is Docked. Click the OK button.

6. Click the OK button to close the Hardware Profiles dialog box. Close any other dialog boxes that are open.

7. Shut down and restart your computer. When the computer restarts, you will see the hardware profile selection options. Select a profile to load it.

Once you have created a hardware profile, you can further customize it by booting to the appropriate profile and making changes to it through Device Manager. None of your alterations will be associated with any other hardware profiles that have been created.

Summary

This chapter described how to create and manage user profiles and hardware profiles. We covered the following topics:

- The configurations stored in user profiles, which include most user preference settings
- How to create local user profiles, roaming profiles, and mandatory profiles
- How to configure hardware profiles, which are used to manage a single computer that has more than one hardware configuration

Exam Essentials

Be able to configure and manage user profiles.   Understand how to create and configure local user profiles, roaming user profiles, and mandatory user profiles.

Be able to configure and manage hardware profiles.   Be able to create and manage hardware profiles for various hardware configurations on the same computer. This is especially important for laptop computers.

Key Terms

Before taking the exam, you should be familiar with the following terms:

hardware profile	NTUSER.MAN
local user profile	roaming profile
mandatory profile	user profile
NTUSER.DAT	

Review Questions

1. You have a computer that was installed with Windows 2000 Professional. Where are user profiles stored by default on this computer?

   A. \WINNT\Profiles

   B. \Documents and Settings

   C. \WINNT\User Profiles

   D. \User Profiles

2. Bill uses two different Windows 2000 computers. He wants to be able to use his user profile from either computer. Which of the following steps would you need to take in order to specify that a user profile is available over the network for a Windows 2000 client?

   A. In Control Panel, in the User Profiles tab of the System Properties dialog box, specify that the profile is a roaming profile.

   B. Rename the user profile to NTUSER.NET.

   C. Use Windows Explorer to copy the user profile to a network share.

   D. In the Local Users and Groups utility, in the Profile tab of the user Properties dialog box, specify a UNC path for the roaming profile.

3. Lori wants to know which of the following configuration items are specific to her user account and which are configured for all users of the computer. Choose all of the options that would be stored within a user profile.

   A. The mouse driver that the user will use

   B. The mouse pointer that the user will use

   C. The keyboard layout that the user will use

   D. The screen saver that the user will use

4. Rob has been having problems because users in the Sales group are changing their profiles so that they are no longer using the corporate defined standard. Which of the following steps should Rob take to create a mandatory profile in Windows 2000 Professional? (Choose all that apply.)

   A. In Control Panel, in the User Profiles tab of the System Properties dialog box, specify that the profile is a mandatory profile.

   B. Rename the user profile to NTUSER.MAN.

   C. Copy the profile to a network share using the User Profiles tab of the System Properties dialog box in Control Panel.

   D. In the Local Users and Groups utility, in the Profile tab of the user Properties dialog box, specify a UNC path for the roaming profile.

5. Which of the following options can be configured when you edit hardware profile properties? Choose all that apply.

   A. Whether or not the computer is portable

   B. The software profile that will be used

   C. Whether or not the computer uses different hot-plug devices

   D. Whether or not the hardware profile is included in the hardware profile selection options when Windows 2000 is booted

6. Following is the Profile tab of the Properties dialog box for user Liz. What user profile will Liz use based on this information?

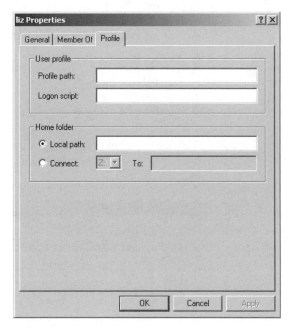

A. Since Liz has no user profile specified, she will access the default profile each time she logs on.

B. The Profile Path box is blank because Liz has never logged on to the computer.

C. Since the Profile Path box is blank, Liz will use her locally stored profile.

D. Liz will access the All_Users default profile each time she logs on.

7. You have decided to store the roaming profile for user Rick on the domain SALES, computer SERVER, share PROFILES, subfolder RICK. What path should you specify for Rick's profile path?

   A. \\SALES\SERVER\PROFILES\RICK

   B. \\SERVER\PROFILES\RICK

   C. \\SALES\PROFILES\RICK

   D. \\SERVER\PROFILES

8. You are trying to create a mandatory profile for user Brett. When you look in Brett's profile folder, you see the following. What is the most likely explanation?

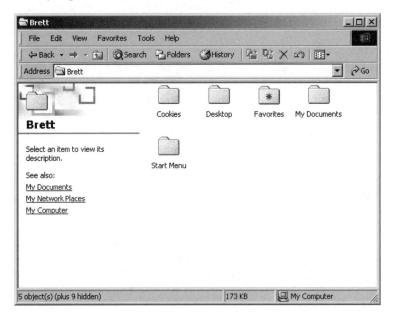

   A. Brett has never logged on to the computer, so his profile has not been created.

   B. You are not in the correct folder for user Brett.

   C. Brett is using a roaming profile.

   D. By default, the NTUSER.DAT file is hidden, and you need to configure Folder Options to allow you to view hidden files.

9. Everything has been working properly on your computer. You have just edited your hardware profiles named Docked (which is on the network) and Undocked (which is not on the network). You reboot your computer and take a coffee break. When you return, you realize you can't access any network resources. What is the most likely problem?

    A. Your IP configuration is not properly set.

    B. You pulled the network cable from your computer.

    C. Your network card is failing.

    D. The hardware profile for Undocked has been set as the default profile.

10. You have created two hardware profiles for your laptop, named Docked and Undocked. How do you specify which of the hardware profiles will be used?

    A. Press F8 during the computer startup and select the profile that will be used.

    B. Press F6 during the computer startup and select the profile that will be used.

    C. Select the profile that will be used by clicking the profile's icon that appears on the Taskbar.

    D. Select the profile from the menu that appears during the computer startup by default.

11. When Kalea logs on to the Windows 2000 Professional computer W2KSales1, she sees her normal Desktop. When Kalea logs on to the Windows 2000 Professional computer W2KSales2, she does not see her normal Desktop. What is the most likely cause?

    A. A roaming user profile is not configured for Kalea.

    B. Kalea does not have permissions to access her user profile from W2KSales2.

    C. Kalea has a mandatory profile configured in W2KSales2.

    D. The computer at which Kalea is logging on is a Windows NT 4 computer.

12. You want to allow Sarah to be able to create and manage the mandatory profiles that are used by the Sales department. Which of the following group memberships would allow her to manage mandatory user profiles?

A. The user to whom the profile is assigned

B. The Administrators group

C. The Power Users group

D. The Server Operators group

13. Nicky and Jaime share the same Windows 2000 Professional computer. Nicky has configured a Desktop that Jaime would like to use. How can you configure Jaime's user profile so that it will initially match Nicky's settings?

A. Copy the NTUSER.DAT file from Nicky's folder to Jaime's folder.

B. Configure a roaming profile that will be used by both users.

C. Copy Nicky's user profile to Jaime's folder in the Documents and Settings folder (using Control Panel ➢ System and selecting the User Profiles tab). Configure the profile so that Jaime is permitted to use the copied profile.

D. Copy Nicky's user profile to Jaime's folder in the Profiles folder using Control Panel ➢ System ➢ User Profiles tab.

14. You want to create a mandatory profile for Rob. Which of the following steps is *not* required to configure a mandatory profile?

A. Create the profile that will be used.

B. Rename the NTUSER.DAT file to NTUSER.MAN.

C. Specify that the user will use a mandatory profile in Control Panel, System, User Profiles tab.

D. Configure the profile as a roaming profile.

15. Bette has completely mucked up her user profile. What is the easiest way to restore her Desktop to the original configuration?

   A. Copy the default user profile to Bette's folder in the Documents and Settings folder.

   B. Delete Bette's user profile through Control Panel ➢ System ➢ User Profiles tab.

   C. Delete user Bette and re-create user Bette.

   D. Create a new user, then copy the new user's user profile to Bette's folder in the Profiles folder.

Answers to Review Questions

1. B. The default location for user profiles is the \Documents and Settings folder in Windows 2000. In Windows NT 4, the default location for user profiles was \WINNT\Profiles.

2. D. After you create the profile that will be used as the roaming profile, you create a folder and share on the network location where the roaming profile will be stored. You use the User Profiles tab of the System Properties dialog box in Control Panel to copy the local profile to the network share. Finally, you specify that the user is using a roaming profile by configuring the user's properties through the Local Users and Groups utility. In the Profile tab, you specify a UNC path for the roaming profile.

3. B, C, D. User profiles generally contain user preference items, which include mouse pointers, keyboard layout, and screen saver settings. User profiles do not contain computer configuration settings (mouse drivers, for instance).

4. B, C, D. Creating a mandatory profile involves three main steps. First, rename the user profile from `NTUSER.DAT` to `NTUSER.MAN`. Second, copy the profile to a network share using the User Profiles tab of the System Properties dialog box in Control Panel. Third, in the Local Users and Groups utility, access the properties of the user who will be assigned the roaming profile, and specify the location of the mandatory profile. This path must be a UNC path for the mandatory profile to work.

5. A, D. The only options that can be configured when you set hardware profile properties are whether or not the computer is portable and whether or not the hardware profile will be included in the hardware profile selection options when Windows 2000 Professional is booted.

6. C. If the Profile Path box is blank, then the user will use a locally stored profile by default.

7. B. You use a UNC path to specify the location of roaming profiles. UNC paths always start with two backslashes \\, followed by the computer name, followed by the share name. If there are any subfolders under the share, then they can be a part of the UNC path. In this example, the correct UNC path to find Rick's profile is \\SERVER\ PROFILES\RICK.

8. D. If Brett had never logged on to the computer, he would not have a folder. You can assume that you are in the correct folder since the window shows the folders associated with user profiles. If Brett has a folder, he is using a local profile, or at some point he had a local profile. The most logical explanation is that since the NTUSER.DAT file is hidden, you need to configure Folder Options to display hidden files.

9. D. When you configured your two hardware profiles, it is possible that the Undocked profile was set as the default selection if no choice was made within a set amount of seconds.

10. D. When you have multiple hardware profiles, by default, you see a menu during the computer startup that allows you to select the hardware profile that will be used. Through this menu, you can select from the docked or undocked profile.

11. A. By default, profiles are only configured to be used locally. In this case, it is likely that no roaming profile has been configured for Kalea.

12. B. Only members of the Administrators group can create and assign mandatory user profiles.

13. C. You can copy Nicky's user profile so that Jaime can use it initially by copying Nicky's user profile to Jaime's folder in the Document and Settings folder. You can perform this copy operation through Control Panel ➤ System ➤ User Profiles tab.

14. C. You specify the profile, in this case mandatory, that the user will use through the user's properties in the Local Users and Groups utility.

15. B. You can replace an existing user profile with the default user profile by deleting the user profile through Control Panel ➤ System ➤ User Profiles tab.

Chapter

9

Managing Disks

MICROSOFT EXAM OBJECTIVES COVERED IN THIS CHAPTER:

✓ **Monitor, manage, and troubleshoot access to files and folders.**

- Configure, manage, and troubleshoot file compression.
- Control access to files and folders by using permissions.
- Optimize access to files and folders.

✓ **Configure and manage file systems.**

- Convert from one file system to another file system.
- Configure file systems by using NTFS, FAT32, or FAT.

✓ **Implement, manage, and troubleshoot disk devices.**

- Install, configure, and manage DVD and CD-ROM devices.
- Monitor and configure disks.
- Monitor, configure, and troubleshoot volumes.
- Monitor and configure removable media, such as tape devices.

✓ **Encrypt data on a hard disk by using Encrypting File System (EFS).**

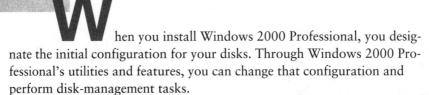

hen you install Windows 2000 Professional, you designate the initial configuration for your disks. Through Windows 2000 Professional's utilities and features, you can change that configuration and perform disk-management tasks.

For file system configuration, you can choose FAT, FAT32, or NTFS. You can also update a FAT or FAT32 partition to NTFS. This chapter covers the features of each file system and how to use the CONVERT utility to upgrade to NTFS.

Another factor in disk management is choosing the configuration for your physical drives. Windows 2000 supports basic storage and dynamic storage. When you install Windows 2000 Professional or upgrade from Windows NT, the drives are configured as basic storage. Dynamic storage is new to Windows 2000 and allows you to create simple volumes, spanned volumes, and striped volumes.

Once you decide on how your disks should be configured, you implement the disk configurations through the Disk Management utility. This utility helps you view and manage your physical disks and volumes. In this chapter, you will learn how to manage both types of storage and to upgrade from basic storage to dynamic storage.

The other disk-management features covered in this chapter are data compression, disk quotas, data encryption, disk defragmentation, disk cleanup, and disk error checking.

The procedures for many disk-management tasks are the same for both Windows 2000 Professional and Server. The main difference is that Windows 2000 Server also supports mirrored and RAID 5 volumes.

Configuring File Systems

Each partition (each logical drive that is created on your hard drive) you create under Windows 2000 Professional must have a file system associated with it.

Microsoft
✓ *Exam*
Objective

Configure and manage file systems.

- Convert from one file system to another file system.
- Configure file systems by using NTFS, FAT32, or FAT.

Monitor, manage, and troubleshoot access to files and folders.

- Optimize access to files and folders.

You configure file systems by using NTFS, FAT32, or FAT. You choose the file system you will use when you create and format the partition. If you have a FAT or FAT32 partition and want to update it to NTFS, you can use the CONVERT utility. The features of each file system and the procedure for converting file systems are covered in the following sections.

In this book, the terms FAT and FAT16 are used synonymously.

File System Selection

Your file system is used to store and retrieve the files stored on your hard drive. One of the most fundamental choices associated with file management is the choice of your file system's configuration. As explained in Chapter 1, "Getting Started with Windows Professional," Windows 2000 Professional supports the FAT16, FAT32, and NTFS file systems. You should choose FAT16 or FAT32 if you want to dual-boot your computer, because these file systems are backward compatible with other operating systems. Choose NTFS, however, if you want to take advantage of features such as local security, file compression, and file encryption.

Table 9.1 summarizes the capabilities of each file system, and they are described in more detail in the following sections.

TABLE 9.1 File System Capabilities

Feature	FAT16	FAT32	NTFS
Supporting operating systems	Most	Windows 95 OSR2, Windows 98, and Windows 2000	Windows NT and Windows 2000
Long filename support	Yes	Yes	Yes
Efficient use of disk space	No	Yes	Yes
Compression support	No	No	Yes
Quota support	No	No	Yes
Encryption support	No	No	Yes
Support for local security	No	No	Yes
Support for network security	Yes	Yes	Yes
Maximum volume size	2GB	32GB	2TB

Windows 2000 Professional also supports *CDFS* (*Compact Disk File System*). However, CDFS cannot be managed. It is only used to mount and read CDs.

FAT16

FAT16 was first used with DOS 3.0 (Disk Operating System) in 1981. With FAT16, the directory-entry table keeps track of the location of the file's first block, the filename and extension, the date- and timestamps on the file, and any attributes associated with the file. FAT16 is similar in nature to a card catalog at a library—when the operating system needs a file, the FAT listing is consulted.

The main advantage of FAT16 is that almost all operating systems support this file system. This makes FAT16 a good choice if the computer will dual-boot with other operating systems (see Chapter 1 for more information about dual-booting). FAT16 is also a good choice for small partitions (FAT16 partitions can only be up to 2GB in size). Because FAT16 is a very simple file system, the overhead associated with storing files is much smaller than with NTFS. In addition, FAT16 partitions support disk compression through utilities such as DRVSPACE, although this utility is not supported by Windows 2000.

The problem with using FAT16 is that it was designed to be used as a single-user file system, and thus it does not support any kind of security. Prior to Windows 95, FAT16 did not support long filenames. Other file systems, such as NTFS, offer many more features, including local security, file compression, and encrypting capabilities.

FAT32

FAT32 is an updated version of FAT. FAT32 was first shipped with Windows 95 OSR2 (Operating System Release 2), and it currently ships with Windows 98. It is supported by Windows 2000.

One of the main advantages of FAT32 is its support for smaller cluster sizes, which results in more efficient space allocation than was possible with FAT16. Files stored on a FAT32 partition can use 20 to 30 percent less disk space than files stored on a FAT16 partition. FAT32 supports drive sizes of up to 2TB. Because of the smaller cluster sizes, FAT32 can also load programs up to 50 percent faster than programs loaded from FAT16 partitions.

The main disadvantage of FAT32 is that it is not compatible with previous versions of Windows NT, including NT 4. It also offers no native support for disk compression.

NTFS

NTFS, which was first used with the NT operating system, now offers the highest level of service and features for Windows 2000 computers. NTFS partitions can be up to 2TB.

NTFS offers comprehensive folder- and file-level security. This allows you to set an additional level of security for users who access the files and folders locally or through the network. For example, two users who share the same

Windows 2000 Professional computer can be assigned different NTFS permissions, so that one user has access to a folder, but the other user is denied access to that folder.

NTFS also offers disk management features—such as compression, disk quotas, and encryption services—and data recovery features. The disk management features are covered later in this chapter. The data recovery features are covered in Chapter 15, "Performing System Recovery Functions."

The main drawback of using NTFS is that only the Windows NT and Windows 2000 operating systems recognize the NTFS file system. If your computer dual-boots with other operating systems, such as Windows 98, the NTFS partition will not be recognized.

File System Conversion

In Windows 2000, you can convert both FAT16 and FAT32 partitions to NTFS. File system conversion is the process of converting one file system to another without the loss of data. If you format a drive as another file system, as opposed to converting that drive, all the data on that drive will be lost.

In order to convert a partition, you use the *CONVERT* command-line utility. The syntax for the CONVERT command is:

CONVERT [drive:] /fs:ntfs

For example, if you wanted to convert your D: drive to NTFS, you would type the following from a command prompt:

CONVERT D: /fs:ntfs

When the conversion process begins, it will attempt to lock the partition. If the partition cannot be locked—perhaps because the partition contains the Windows 2000 operating system files or the system's page file—the conversion will not take place until the computer is restarted.

You can use the /v switch with the CONVERT command. This switch specifies that you want to use verbose mode, and all messages will be displayed during the conversion process.

In Exercise 9.1, you will convert your D: drive from FAT16 to NTFS.

EXERCISE 9.1

Converting a FAT16 Partition to NTFS

1. Copy some folders to the D: drive.

2. Select Start ➤ Programs ➤ Accessories ➤ Command Prompt.

3. In the Command Prompt dialog box, type **CONVERT D: /fs:ntfs** and press Enter.

4. After the conversion process is complete, close the Command Prompt dialog box.

5. Verify that the folders you copied in step 1 still exist on the partition.

Configuring Disk Storage

Windows 2000 Professional supports two types of disk storage: basic storage and dynamic storage. Basic storage is backward compatible with other operating systems and can be configured to support up to four partitions. Dynamic storage is a new system that is configured as volumes. The following sections describe the basic storage and dynamic storage configurations.

Basic Storage

Basic storage consists of primary and extended partitions. The first partition that is created on a hard drive is called a *primary partition*. The primary partition uses all of the space that is allocated to the partition. Each physical drive can have up to four partitions. You can set up four primary partitions, or you can have three primary partitions and one extended partition. With *extended partitions*, you can allocate the space however you like. For example, a 500MB extended partition could have a 250MB D: partition and a 250MB E: partition.

At the highest level of disk organization, you have a physical hard drive. You cannot use space on the physical drive until you have logically partitioned the physical drive. A *partition* is a logical definition of hard drive space.

An advantage of using a single partition on a single physical disk is that you can allocate the space however you want. For example, if you had a 1GB physical drive and you created a single primary partition, you could allocate the space on the drive as needed. On the other hand, if you created two 500MB partitions called C: and D:, and if C: were full and D: had space left, you could not take space from the D: drive without deleting the partition first.

One of the advantages of using multiple partitions on a single physical hard drive is that each partition can have a different file system. For example, the C: drive might be FAT32 and the D: drive might be NTFS. Multiple partitions also make it easier to manage security requirements.

Laptop computers support only basic storage.

Dynamic Storage

Dynamic storage is a new Windows 2000 feature that consists of a *dynamic disk* divided into dynamic *volumes*. Dynamic volumes cannot contain partitions or logical drives, and they are not accessible through DOS.

Dynamic storage supports three dynamic volume types: simple volumes, spanned volumes, and striped volumes. These are similar to disk configurations that were used with Windows NT 4. However, if you've upgraded from NT 4, you are using basic storage, and you can't add volume sets. Fortunately, you can upgrade from basic storage to dynamic storage, as explained in the "Upgrading a Basic Disk to a Dynamic Disk" section later in this chapter.

To set up dynamic storage, you create or upgrade a disk to a dynamic disk. Then you create dynamic volumes within the dynamic disk. You create dynamic storage with the Windows 2000 Disk Management utility, which is discussed after the descriptions of the dynamic volume types.

Simple Volumes

A *simple volume* contains space from a single dynamic drive. The space from the single drive can be contiguous or noncontiguous. Simple volumes are used when you have enough disk space on a single drive to hold your entire volume. Figure 9.1 illustrates two simple volumes on a physical disk.

FIGURE 9.1 Two simple volumes

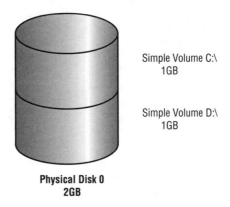

Simple Volume C:\
1GB

Simple Volume D:\
1GB

**Physical Disk 0
2GB**

Spanned Volumes

A *spanned volume* consists of disk space on two or more dynamic drives; up to 32 dynamic drives can be used in a spanned volume configuration. Spanned volume sets are used to dynamically increase the size of a dynamic volume. When you create spanned volumes, the data is written sequentially, filling space on one physical drive before writing to space on the next physical drive in the spanned volume set. Typically, administrators use spanned volumes when they are running out of disk space on a volume and want to dynamically extend the volume with space from another hard drive.

You do not need to allocate the same amount of space to the volume set on each physical drive. This means you could combine a 500MB partition on one physical drive with two 750MB partitions on other dynamic drives, as shown in Figure 9.2.

Because data is written sequentially, you do not see any performance enhancements with spanned volumes as you do with striped volumes (discussed next). The main disadvantage of spanned volumes is that if any drive in the spanned volume set fails, you lose access to all of the data in the spanned set.

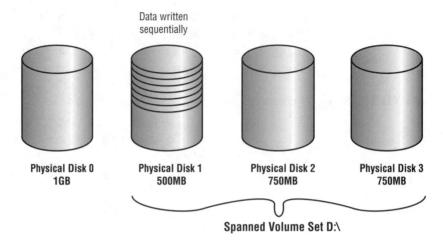

Striped Volumes

A *striped volume* stores data in equal stripes between two or more (up to 32) dynamic drives, as illustrated in Figure 9.3. Since the data is written sequentially in the stripes, you can take advantage of multiple I/O performance and increase the speed at which data reads and writes take place. Typically, administrators use striped volumes when they want to combine the space of several physical drives into a single logical volume and increase disk performance.

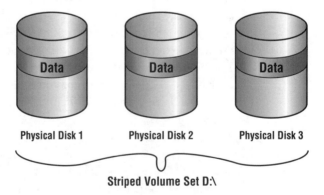

The main disadvantage of striped volumes is that if any drive in the striped volume set fails, you lose access to all of the data in the striped set.

Mirrored volumes and RAID 5 volumes are fault-tolerant dynamic disk configurations. These options are available only with Windows 2000 Server and are covered in detail in *MCSE: Windows 2000 Server Study Guide*, 2nd ed., by Lisa Donald with James Chellis (Sybex, 2001).

Using the Disk Management Utility

The *Disk Management utility* is a graphical tool for managing disks and volumes within the Windows 2000 environment. In this section, you will learn how to access the Disk Management utility and use it to manage basic tasks, basic storage, and dynamic storage.

Microsoft ✓ Exam Objective	**Implement, manage, and troubleshoot disk devices.** • Monitor and configure disks. • Monitor, configure, and troubleshoot volumes.

This chapter covers the material related to managing disks and volumes, for the "Implement, manage, and troubleshoot disk devices" objective. For coverage of the subobjectives concerning management of DVD devices, CD-ROM devices, and removable media, see Chapter 4, "Configuring the Windows 2000 Environment."

In order to have full permissions to use the Disk Management utility, you must be logged on with Administrative privileges. To access the utility, open Control Panel and select Administrative Tools and then Computer Management. Expand the Storage folder to see the Disk Management utility. The

Disk Management utility opening window, shown in Figure 9.4, shows the following information:

- The volumes that are recognized by the computer

- The type of disk, either basic or dynamic

- The type of file system used by each partition

- The status of the partition and whether the partition contains the system or boot partition

- The capacity (amount of space) allocated to the partition

- The amount of free space remaining on the partition

- The amount of overhead associated with the partition

FIGURE 9.4 The Disk Management window

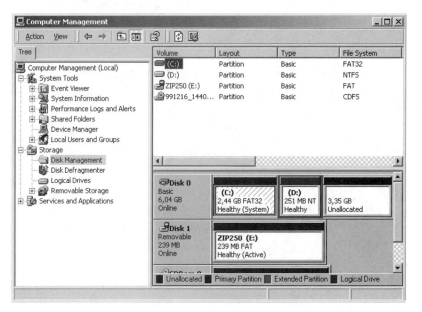

 You can also add Disk Management as a Microsoft Management Console (MMC) snap-in, as described in Chapter 4.

Managing Basic Tasks

With the Disk Management utility, you can perform a variety of basic tasks. These tasks are discussed in the sections that follow:

- View disk and volume properties.
- Add a new disk.
- Create partitions and volumes.
- Upgrade a basic disk to a dynamic disk.
- Change a drive letter and path.
- Delete partitions and volumes.

Viewing Disk Properties

To view the properties of a disk, right-click it in the lower panel of the Disk Management main window (see Figure 9.4) and choose Properties from the pop-up menu. This brings up the Disk Properties dialog box, shown in Figure 9.5, containing the following disk properties:

- The disk number
- The type of disk (basic, dynamic, CD-ROM, removable, DVD, or unknown)
- The status of the disk (online or offline)
- The capacity of the disk
- The amount of unallocated space on the disk
- The hardware device type
- The hardware vendor who produced the drive
- The adapter name
- The logical volumes that have been defined on the physical drive

FIGURE 9.5 The Disk Properties dialog box

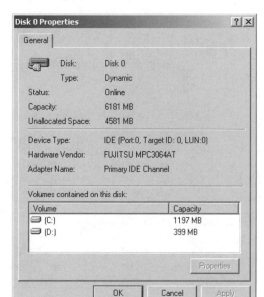

Viewing Volume and Local Disk Properties

On a dynamic disk, you manage volume properties. On a basic disk, you manage local disk properties. Volumes and local disks perform the same function, and the options discussed in the following sections apply to both. (The examples here are based on a dynamic disk using a simple volume. If you are using basic storage, you will view the local disk properties rather than the volume properties.)

To see the properties of a volume, right-click the volume in the upper panel of the Disk Management main window and choose Properties. This brings up the volume Properties dialog box. Volume properties are organized on six tabs: General, Tools, Hardware, Sharing, Security, and Quota. The Security and Quota tabs appear only for NTFS volumes. All these tabs are covered in detail in the following sections.

General

The information on the General tab of the volume Properties dialog box, as seen in Figure 9.6, gives you a general idea of how the volume is configured.

This dialog box shows the label, type, file system, used and free space, and capacity of the volume. The label is shown in an editable text box, and you can change it if desired. The space allocated to the volume is shown in a graphical representation as well as in text form.

FIGURE 9.6   General properties for a volume

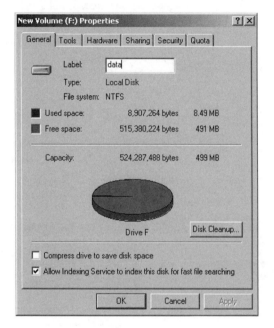

The label on a volume or local disk is for informational purposes only. For example, depending on its use, you might give a volume a label such as "APPS" or "ACCTDB."

The Disk Cleanup button starts the Disk Cleanup utility, with which you can delete unnecessary files and free disk space. This utility is discussed later in this chapter in the "Using the Disk Cleanup Utility" section.

Tools

The Tools tab of the volume Properties dialog box, shown in Figure 9.7, provides access to three tools:

- Click the Check Now button to run the Check Disk utility to check the volume for errors. You would do this if you were experiencing problems accessing the volume, or if the volume had been open during a system restart that did not go through a proper shutdown sequence. This utility is covered in more detail in "Troubleshooting Disk Devices and Volumes" later in this chapter.

- Click the Backup Now button to run the Backup Wizard, which steps you through backing up the files on the volume. Backup procedures are covered in Chapter 15.

- Click the Defragment Now button to run the Disk Defragmenter utility. This utility defragments files on the volume by storing the files contiguously on the hard drive. Defragmentation is discussed later in this chapter, in the "Defragmenting Disks" section.

FIGURE 9.7 The Tools tab of the volume's Properties dialog box

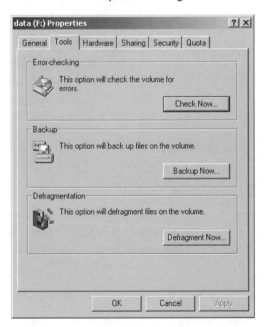

Hardware

The Hardware tab of the volume Properties dialog box, shown in Figure 9.8, lists the hardware associated with the disk drives that are recognized by the Windows 2000 operating system. The bottom half of the dialog box shows the properties of the device that is highlighted in the top half of the dialog box.

FIGURE 9.8 The Hardware tab of the volume Properties dialog box

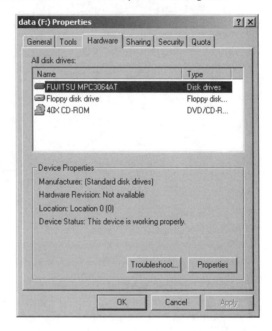

For more details about a hardware item, highlight it and click the Properties button in the lower-right corner of the dialog box. This brings up a Properties dialog box for the item (for example, Figure 9.9). With luck, your Device Status field will report that "This device is working properly." If that's not the case, you can click the Troubleshooter button to get a troubleshooting Wizard that will help you discover what the problem is.

FIGURE 9.9 A disk drive's Properties dialog box accessed through the Hardware tab of the volume Properties dialog box

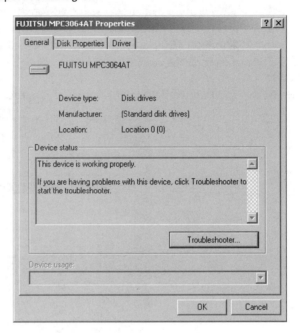

Sharing

In the Sharing tab of the volume Properties dialog box, shown in Figure 9.10, you can specify whether or not the volume is shared. All volumes are shared by default. The share name is the drive letter followed by a $ (dollar sign). The $ indicates that the share is hidden. From this dialog box, you can set the user limit, permissions, and cacheing for the share. Sharing is covered in Chapter 10, "Accessing Files and Folders."

FIGURE 9.10   The Sharing tab of the volume Properties dialog box

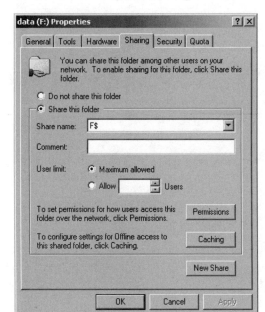

Security

The Security tab of the volume Properties dialog box, shown in Figure 9.11, appears only for NTFS volumes. The Security tab is used to set the NTFS permissions for the volume.

Notice that the default permissions allow the Everyone group Full Control permissions at the root of the volume. This could cause major security problems if any user decides to manipulate or delete the data within the volume. Managing security is covered in Chapter 10.

FIGURE 9.11   The Security tab of the volume Properties dialog box

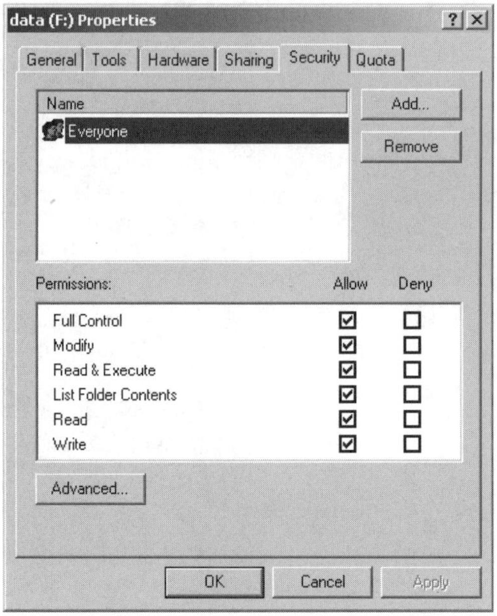

Quota

Like the Security tab, the Quota tab of the volume Properties dialog box appears only for an NTFS volume. Through this tab, you can limit the amount of space available to users within the volume. Quotas are covered in detail in the later section "Setting Disk Quotas."

Adding a New Disk

To increase the amount of disk storage you have, you can add a new disk. This is a fairly common task that you will need to perform as your application programs and files grow larger. How you add a disk depends on whether your computer supports hot swapping of drives. *Hot swapping* is the process of adding a new hard drive while the computer is turned on. Most computers do not support this capability.

Computer doesn't support hot swap   If your computer does not support hot swapping, you must first shut down the computer before you add a new disk. Then add the drive according to the manufacturer's directions. When you're finished, restart the computer. You should find the new drive listed in the Disk Management utility.

Computer supports hot swap   If your computer does support hot swapping, you don't need to turn off your computer first. Just add the drive according to the manufacturer's directions. Then, open the Disk Management utility and select Action ≻ Rescan Disks. You should find the new drive listed in the Disk Management utility.

Creating Partitions and Volumes

Once you add a new disk, the next step is to create a partition (on a basic disk) or a volume (on a dynamic disk). Partitions and volumes fill similar roles in storage of data on disks, and the processes for creating them are similar, as well.

Creating a Volume

The Create Volume Wizard guides you through the process of creating a new volume, as follows:

1. In Disk Management, right-click an area of free storage space and choose Create Volume.

2. The Welcome to the Create Volume Wizard dialog box appears. Click the Next button to continue.

3. The Select Volume Type dialog box appears, as shown in Figure 9.12. In this dialog box, select the type of volume you want to create: simple, spanned, or striped. Only the options supported by your computer's hardware configuration are available. Click the radio button for the type, and then click Next to continue.

FIGURE 9.12   The Select Volume Type dialog box

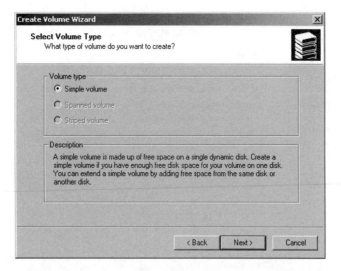

4. The Select Disks dialog box appears, as shown in Figure 9.13. Here, you select the disk and specify the maximum volume size, up to the amount of free disk space that is recognized. Choose the disk that you want the volume to be created on and click the Next button.

FIGURE 9.13 The Select Disks dialog box

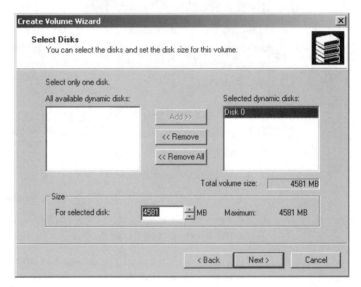

5. Next you see the Assign Drive Letter or Path page of the Wizard, as shown in Figure 9.14. You can specify a drive letter, mount the volume as an empty folder, or choose not to assign a drive letter or drive path. If you choose to mount the volume as an empty folder, you can have an unlimited number of volumes, negating the drive-letter limitation. Make your selections, and click Next to continue.

If you choose not to assign a drive letter or path, users will not be able to access the volume.

FIGURE 9.14 The Assign Drive Letter or Path dialog box

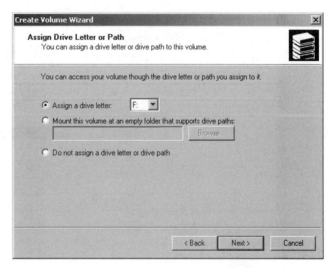

6. The Format Volume dialog box appears, as shown in Figure 9.15. This dialog box allows you to choose whether or not you will format the volume. If you choose to format the volume, you can format it as FAT, FAT32, or NTFS. You can also select the allocation block size, enter a volume label (for information only), specify a quick format, or choose to enable file and folder compression.

Note: Specifying a quick format is risky because this format does not scan the disk for bad sectors, which is done in a normal format operation. After you've made your choices, click the Next button.

FIGURE 9.15   The Format Volume dialog box

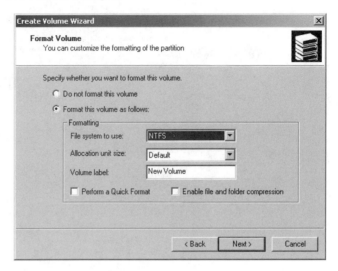

7. The Completing the Create Volume Wizard dialog box appears next (Figure 9.16). Verify your selections. If you need to change any of them, click the Back button to reach the appropriate dialog box. When everything is correctly set, click the Finish button.

FIGURE 9.16   The last page of the Wizard

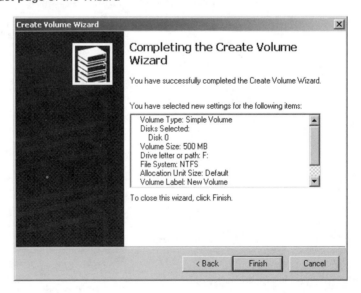

Creating a Partition

The steps to create a logical drive are similar to the steps for creating a volume, which were covered in the preceding section. When you right-click an area of free space in Disk Management and select the Create Logical Drive option, the Create Partition Wizard starts. This wizard displays a series of dialog boxes to guide you through the process of creating a partition:

- In the Select Partition Type dialog box, you select the type of partition you want to create: a primary partition, an extended partition, or a logical drive.

- In the Specify Partition Size dialog box, you specify the maximum partition size, up to the amount of free disk space that is recognized.

- In the Assign Drive Letter or Path dialog box, you assign a drive letter or a drive path. There is also an option to leave the drive letter or path unassigned; but if you enable this option, users will not be able to access the volume. (This "unassigned" option is only used when you have already allocated all 26 drive letters and is not often implemented.)

- The Format Partition dialog box lets you specify whether or not you want to format the partition. If you choose to format the partition, you can select the file system, allocation unit size, and the volume label. You can also choose to perform a quick format and to enable file and folder compression.

The steps to create a logical drive are similar to the steps for creating a volume, which were covered in the previous section. In Exercise 9.2, you will create a partition from the free space that was left on your drive when you installed Windows 2000 Professional (in Exercise 1.1), as specified in Chapter 1.

EXERCISE 9.2

Creating a New Partition

1. Select Start ➤ Settings ➤ Control Panel ➤ Administrative Tools. Expand Computer Management, then Storage, then Disk Management.

2. Right-click an area of free storage and select the Create Partition option.

EXERCISE 9.2 *(continued)*

3. The Create Partition Wizard starts. Click the Next button to continue.

4. The Select Partition Type dialog box appears. Choose Primary Partition and click the Next button.

5. The Specify Partition Size dialog box appears. Specify a partition size of 250MB and click the Next button.

6. The Assign Drive Letter or Path dialog box appears. Click Next to assign the default drive letter shown in this dialog box. If you are using the recommended configuration, C: and D: are assigned as drive letters, E: should be your CD-ROM drive, and the next available drive will be F:.

7. In the Format Partition dialog box, choose to format the drive as NTFS and leave the other settings at their default values. Click the Next button.

8. The Completing the Create Partition Wizard dialog box appears. Click the Finish button.

Upgrading a Basic Disk to a Dynamic Disk

When you install Windows 2000 or upgrade your computer from Windows NT 4.0 to Windows 2000, your drives are configured as basic disks. To take advantage of the features offered by Windows 2000 dynamic disks, you must upgrade your basic disks to dynamic disks.

Upgrading basic disks to dynamic disks is a one-way process and a potentially dangerous operation. If you decide to revert back to a basic disk, you will have to first delete all volumes associated with the drive. Before you do this upgrade (or make any major change to your drives or volumes), create a new backup of the drive or volume and verify that you can successfully restore the backup.

The following steps are involved in the disk-upgrade process:

1. In the Disk Management utility, right-click the drive you want to convert, and select the Upgrade to Dynamic Disk option.

2. In the Upgrade to Dynamic Disk dialog box, check the disk that you want to upgrade and click the OK button.

3. In the Disks to Upgrade dialog box (Figure 9.17), click the Upgrade button.

FIGURE 9.17   The Disks to Upgrade dialog box

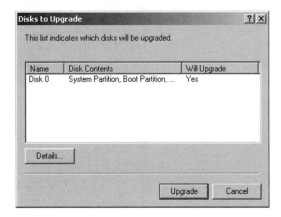

4. A confirmation dialog box warns you that you will no longer be able to boot previous versions of Windows from this disk. Click the Yes button to continue.

5. Another confirmation dialog box warns you that any file systems mounted on the disk will be dismounted. Click Yes to continue.

6. An information dialog box tells you that a reboot is required to complete the upgrade. Click the OK button. Your computer will restart, and the disk-upgrade process is complete.

Changing the Drive Letter and Path

Suppose that you have drive C: assigned as your first partition and drive D: assigned as your CD drive. You add a new drive and partition it as a new volume. By default, the new partition is assigned as drive E:. If you want your logical drives to appear listed before the CD drive, you can use the Disk Management utility's Change Drive Letter and Path option to rearrange your drive letters.

When you need to reassign drive letters, right-click the volume for which you want to change the drive letter and choose Change Drive Letter and Path. This brings up the dialog box shown in Figure 9.18. Click the Edit button to access the Edit Drive Letter or Path dialog box (Figure 9.19). Use the drop-down list next to the Assign a Drive Letter option to select the drive letter you want to assign to the volume.

FIGURE 9.18   The dialog box for changing a drive letter or path

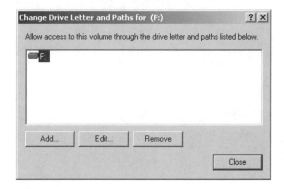

FIGURE 9.19   Editing the drive letter

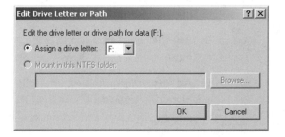

In Exercise 9.3, you will edit the drive letter of the partition you created in Exercise 9.2.

EXERCISE 9.3

Editing a Drive Letter

1. Select Start ➤ Settings ➤ Control Panel ➤ Administrative Tools. Expand Computer Management, then Storage, then Disk Management.

2. Right-click the drive you created in Exercise 9.2 and select Change Drive Letter and Path.

3. In the Change Drive Letter and Paths dialog box, click the Edit button.

4. In the Edit Drive Letter or Path dialog box, select a new drive letter and click the OK button.

5. In the dialog box that appears, click the Yes button to confirm that you want to change the drive letter.

Deleting Partitions and Volumes

You might delete a partition or volume if you wanted to reorganize your disk, or to make sure that data would not be accessed.

Once you delete a partition or volume, it is gone forever.

To delete a partition or volume, in the Disk Management window, right-click the partition or volume and choose the Delete Volume (or Delete Partition) option. You will see a warning that all the data on the partition or volume will be lost. Click Yes to confirm that you want to delete the volume or partition.

Managing Basic Storage

The Disk Management utility offers limited support for managing basic storage. You can create, delete, and format partitions on basic drives. You also can delete volume sets and stripe sets that were created under Windows NT. Most other disk-management tasks require that you upgrade your drive to dynamic disks. (The upgrade process was described in the earlier section, "Upgrading a Basic Disk to a Dynamic Disk.")

Managing Dynamic Storage

As noted earlier in this chapter, a dynamic disk can contain simple, spanned, or striped volumes. Through the Disk Management utility, you can create volumes of each type. You can also create an extended volume, which is the process of adding disk space to a single simple volume. The following sections describe these disk-management tasks.

Creating Simple, Spanned, and Striped Volumes

As explained earlier in "Creating Partitions and Volumes," you use the Create Volume Wizard to create a new volume. To start the Wizard, in the Disk Management utility right-click an area of free space where you want to create the volume. Choose Create Volume. When the Wizard displays the Select Volume Type dialog box, choose the type of volume you want to create.

When you choose to create a spanned volume, you are creating a new volume from scratch that includes space from two or more physical drives, up to a maximum of 32 drives. You can create spanned volumes that are formatted as FAT, FAT32, or NTFS.

When you choose to create a striped volume, you are creating a new volume that combines free space from 2 to 32 drives into a single logical partition. The free space on all drives must be equal in size. Data in the striped volume is written across all drives in 64KB stripes. (Data in spanned and extended volumes is written sequentially.)

Creating Extended Volumes

When you create an extended volume, you are taking a single, simple volume (maybe one that is almost out of disk space) and adding more disk space to the volume, using free space that exists on the same physical hard drive. When the volume is extended, it is seen as a single drive letter. In order to extend a volume, the simple volume must be formatted as NTFS. You cannot extend a system or boot partition.

An extended volume assumes that you are only using one physical drive. A spanned volume assumes that you are using two or more physical drives.

Here are the steps to create an extended volume:

1. In the Disk Management utility, right-click the volume you want to extend and choose Extend Volume.

2. The Extend Volume Wizard starts. Click the Next button.

3. The Select Disks dialog box appears, as shown in Figure 9.20. You can specify the maximum size of the extended volume. The maximum size you can specify is determined by the amount of free space that exists in all of the dynamic drives on your computer.

FIGURE 9.20 The Select Disks dialog box

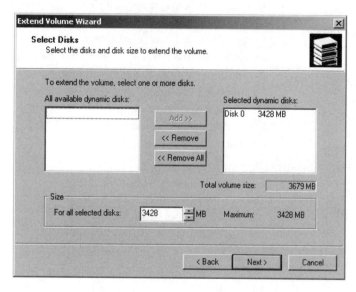

4. The Completing the Extend Volume Wizard dialog box appears. Click the Finish button.

Once a volume is extended, no portion of the volume can be deleted without losing data on the entire set.

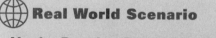

Real World Scenario

You're Running Out of Disk Space

Martha, a user on your network is running out of disk space. The situation needs to be corrected so that she can brought back up and running as quickly as possible. Martha has a 10GB drive (C:) that runs a customer database. She needs additional space added to the C: drive so that the database will recognize the data, since it must be stored on a single drive letter. Martha's computer has a single IDE drive with nothing attached to the second IDE channel.

You have two basic options for managing space in these circumstances. One is to upgrade the disk to a larger disk, but this will necessitate reinstalling the OS and the applications, and restoring the user's data. The other choice is to add a temporary second drive and extend the volume. This will at least allow Martha to be up and running—but it should not be considered a permanent solution. If you do choose to extend the volume, and then either drive within the volume set fails, then the user will lose access to both drives. When Martha's workload allows time for maintenance, you can replace the volume set with a single drive.

Managing Data Compression

*D*ata compression is the process of storing data in a form that takes less space than does uncompressed data. If you have ever "zipped" or "packed" a file, you have used data compression. With Windows 2000, data compression is only available on NTFS partitions.

Microsoft
✓ *Exam*
Objective

Monitor, manage, and troubleshoot access to files and folders.

- Configure, manage, and troubleshoot file compression.

This chapter covers material concerning file compression and (in a later section) optimization of file and folder access, which are subobjectives of the "Monitor, manage, and troubleshoot access to files and folders" objective. A third subobjective, controlling access to files and folders by using permissions, is covered in Chapter 10. That chapter also provides more information about optimizing access to files and folders.

Files as well as folders in the NTFS file system can be either compressed or uncompressed. Files and folders are managed independently, which means that a compressed folder can contain uncompressed files, and an uncompressed folder can contain compressed files.

Access to compressed files by DOS or Windows applications is transparent. For example, if you access a compressed file through Microsoft Word, the file will be uncompressed automatically when it is opened, and then automatically compressed again when it is closed.

Data compression is only available on NTFS partitions. If you copy or move a compressed folder or file to a FAT partition (or a floppy disk), Windows 2000 will automatically uncompress the folder or file.

You cannot have a folder or file compressed and encrypted at the same time. Encryption is discussed in the "Managing Data Encryption with EFS" section later in this chapter.

In Exercise 9.4, you will compress and uncompress folders and files. This exercise assumes that you have completed Exercise 9.1.

EXERCISE 9.4

Compressing and Uncompressing Folders and Files

1. Select Start ➢ Programs ➢ Accessories ➢ Windows Explorer.

2. In Windows Explorer, find and select a folder on the D: drive. The folder you select should contain files.

3. Right-click the folder and select Properties. In the General tab of the folder Properties dialog box, note the value listed for Size on Disk. Then click the Advanced button.

4. In the Advanced Attributes dialog box, check the Compress Contents to Save Disk Space option. Then click the OK button.

EXERCISE 9.4 *(continued)*

5. In the Confirm Attribute Changes dialog box, select the option to Apply Changes to This Folder, Subfolder, and Files. (If this confirmation dialog box does not appear, you can display it by clicking the Apply button in the Properties dialog box.) Click the OK button to confirm your changes.

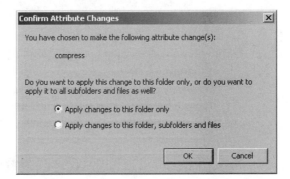

6. In the General tab of the folder Properties dialog box, note the value that now appears for Size on Disk. This size should have decreased because you compressed the folder.

To uncompress folders and files, repeat the steps of this exercise and uncheck the Compress Contents to Save Disk Space option in the Advanced Attributes dialog box.

You can specify that compressed files be displayed in a different color than the uncompressed files. To do so, in Windows Explorer, select Tools ➤ Folder Options ➤ Views. Under Files and Folders, check the Display Compressed Files and Folders with an Alternate Color option.

Setting Disk Quotas

Suppose that you have a server with an 18GB drive that is used mainly for users' home folders, and you start getting "out of disk space" error messages. On closer inspection, you find that a single user has taken up 10GB of space by storing multimedia files that she has downloaded from the Internet. This type of problem can be avoided through the use of disk quotas. *Disk quotas* are used to specify the amount of disk space a user is allowed on specific NTFS volumes. You can specify disk quotas for all users, or you can limit disk space on a per-user basis.

Microsoft
Exam
Objective

Implement, manage, and troubleshoot disk devices.

- Monitor and configure disks.

Before you administer disk quotas, keep in mind the following aspects of disk quota management:

- Disk quotas can be specified only for NTFS volumes.

- Disk quotas apply only at the volume level, even if the NTFS partitions reside on the same physical hard drive.

- Disk usage is calculated on file and folder ownership. When a user creates, copies, or takes ownership of a file, that user is the owner of the file.

- When a user installs an application, the free space that will be seen by the application is based on the disk quota availability, not on the actual amount of free space on the volume.

- The calculation of disk quota space used is based on actual file size. There is no mechanism to support or recognize file compression.

 Disk quotas are not applied to the Administrator account or to members of the Administrators group.

The following sections describe how to set up and monitor disk quotas.

Configuring Disk Quotas

You configure disk quotas through the NTFS volume Properties dialog box (discussed in detail in the earlier section "Managing Basic Tasks"). You learned that you can access the volume's Properties dialog box in the Disk Management utility by right-clicking the drive letter and selecting Properties from the pop-up menu. Another way to access this dialog box is from Windows Explorer—just right-click the drive letter in the Explorer listing and select Properties. In the volume's Properties dialog box, click the Quota tab to see the dialog box shown in Figure 9.21. When you open the Quota tab, you will see that disk quotas are disabled by default.

FIGURE 9.21 The Quota tab of the volume Properties dialog box

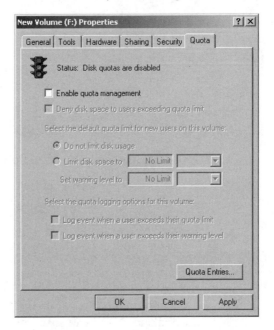

Table 9.2 describes the options that can be configured through the Quota tab.

TABLE 9.2   Disk Quota Configuration Options

Option	Description
Enable quota management	Specifies whether quota management is enabled for the volume.
Deny disk space to users exceeding the quota limit	Specifies that users who exceed their disk quota will not be able to override their disk allocation. Those users will receive "out of disk space" error messages.
Select the default quota limit for new users on this volume	Allows you to define quota limits for new users. Options include not limiting disk space, limiting disk space, and specifying warning levels.
Select the quota logging options for this volume	Specifies whether logged events that relate to quotas will be recorded. You can enable the logging of events for users exceeding quota limits or users exceeding warning limits.

Notice the traffic light icon in the upper-left corner of the Quota tab. It indicates the status of disk quotas, as follows:

- A red light means that disk quotas are disabled.

- A yellow light means Windows 2000 is rebuilding disk quota information.

- A green light means the disk quota system is enabled and active.

The next sections explain how to set quotas for all new users as default quotas, and how to set quotas for a specific user.

Setting Default Quotas

When you set default quota limits for new users on a volume, those quotas apply only to users who have not yet created files on that volume. Users who already own files or folders on the volume will be exempt from the quota policy. Users who have not yet created a file on the volume will be bound by the quota policy.

To set the default quota limit for new users, access the Quota tab of the volume Properties dialog box and check the Enable Quota Management box. Click the Limit Disk Space To radio button, and enter a number in the first box next to the option. In the drop-down list in the second box, specify whether disk space is limited by KB (kilobytes), MB (megabytes), GB (gigabytes), TB (terabytes), PB (petabytes), or EB (exabytes). If you choose to limit disk space, you can also set a warning level, so that users will be warned if they come close to reaching their limit.

If you want to apply disk quotas for all users, apply the quota when the volume is first created. That way, no users will have already created files on the volume and thus will not be exempt from the quota limit.

In Exercise 9.5, you will set a default quota limit on your D: drive. This exercise assumes that you have completed Exercise 9.1.

EXERCISE 9.5

Applying Default Quota Limits

1. Use the Local Users and Groups utility to create three new users: **Shannon**, **Dana**, and **Michelle**. (See Chapter 6, "Managing Users," for details on creating user accounts.) Deselect the User Must Change Password at Next Logon option for each user.

2. Log off as Administrator and log on as Shannon. Drop and drag some folders to drive D:.

3. Log on as Administrator. Select Start ➤ Programs ➤ Accessories ➤ Windows Explorer.

4. In Windows Explorer, expand My Computer. Right-click Local Disk (D:) and select Properties.

5. In the Local Disk Properties dialog box, select the Quota tab.

6. Check the Enable Quota Management check box.

7. Click the Limit Disk Space To radio button. Specify 5MB as the limit. Specify the Set Warning Level To value as 4MB.

8. Click the Apply button, then click the OK button.

9. Log off as Administrator and log on as Dana. Drop and drag some folders to drive D:.

10. Log off as Dana and log on as Administrator.

Setting an Individual Quota

You can also set quotas for individual users. There are several reasons for setting quotas this way:

- You can set restrictions on other users and at the same time allow a user who routinely updates your applications to have unlimited disk space.

- You can set warnings at lower levels for a user who routinely exceeds disk space.

- You can apply the quota to users who already had files on the volume before the quota was implemented and thus have been granted unlimited disk space.

To set an individual quota, click the Quota Entries button in the bottom-right corner of the Quota tab. This brings up the dialog box shown in Figure 9.22. To modify a user's quota, double-click that user. This brings up a dialog box similar to the one shown in Figure 9.23. Here, you can specify whether the user's disk space should be limited, and you can set the limit and the warning level.

FIGURE 9.22 The Quota Entries for volume dialog box

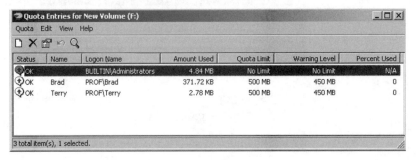

FIGURE 9.23 The quota settings for a user

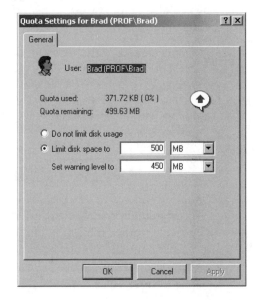

You can also modify the quotas of several users at once by Ctrl+clicking to highlight several users and selecting Quota ➢ Properties.

In Exercise 9.6, you will configure the quotas for individual users. This exercise assumes that you have completed Exercise 9.5.

EXERCISE 9.6

Applying Individual Quota Limits

1. Select Start ➤ Programs ➤ Accessories ➤ Windows Explorer.

2. In Windows Explorer, expand My Computer. Right-click Local Disk (D:) and select Properties.

3. In the Local Disk Properties dialog box, select the Quota tab. Then click the Quota Entries button.

4. Double-click user Dana to bring up his Quota Settings dialog box. Notice that Dana has limited disk space (because he did not create files on the volume before disk quotas were applied). Click the Do Not Limit Disk Usage radio button. Click the Apply button and then click the OK button.

5. Double-click user Shannon to bring up her Quota Settings dialog box. Notice that Shannon does not have her disk space limited (because he had created files on the volume before disk quotas were applied). Click the Limit Disk Space To radio button and specify the limit as 100MB. Set the warning level to 95MB. Click the Apply button and then click the OK button.

Monitoring Disk Quotas

If you implement disk quotas, you will want to monitor the quotas on a regular basis. This allows you to check disk usage by all users who own files on the volume with those quotas applied.

It is especially important to monitor quotas if you have specified that disk space should be denied to users who exceeded their quota limit. Otherwise, some users may not be able to get their work done. For example, suppose that you have set a limit for all users on a specific volume. Your boss tries to save a file she has been working on all afternoon, but she gets an "out of disk space" error message because she has exceeded her disk quota. Although your intentions of setting up and using disk quotas were good, the boss is still cranky.

Disk quota monitoring is accomplished through the Quota Entries dialog box (see Figure 9.22), which appears when you click the Quota Entries button in the Quota tab of the volume Properties dialog box. The dialog box shows the following information:

- The status of the user's disk quota, represented as follows:

  - A green arrow in a dialog bubble means the status is OK.

  - An exclamation point in a yellow triangle means the warning threshold has been exceeded.

  - An exclamation point in a red circle means the user threshold has been exceeded.

- The name and logon name of the user who has stored files on the volume

- The amount of disk space consumed by the user on the volume

- The user's quota limit

- The user's warning level

- The percentage of disk space consumed by the user in relation to their disk quota

Managing Data Encryption with EFS

Data encryption is a way to increase data security. Encryption is the process of translating data into code that is not easily accessible. Once data has been encrypted, you must have a password or key to decrypt the data. Unencrypted data is known as *plain text*, and encrypted data is known as *cipher text*.

Microsoft ✓ *Exam Objective*

Encrypt data on a hard disk by using Encrypting File System (EFS).

The *Encrypting File System (EFS)* is the Windows 2000 technology that is used to store encrypted files on NTFS partitions. Encrypted files add an extra layer of security to your file system. A user with the proper key can transparently access encrypted files. A user without the proper key is denied access. If the user who encrypted the files is unavailable, you can use the *recovery agent* (which by default is the Administrators account) to provide the proper key to decrypt folders or files.

You can encrypt and decrypt files through the volume's Properties dialog box or by using the CIPHER utility, as explained in the following sections.

Encrypting and Decrypting Folders and Files

To use EFS, a user specifies that a folder or file on an NTFS partition should be encrypted. The encryption is transparent to that user, who has access to the file. However, when other users try to access the file, they will not be able to unencrypt the file—even if those users have Full Control NTFS permissions. Instead, they will receive an error message.

To encrypt a folder or a file, take the following steps:

1. Select Start ➢ Programs ➢ Accessories ➢ Windows Explorer.

2. In Windows Explorer, find and select the folder or file you wish to encrypt.

3. Right-click the folder or file and select Properties from the pop-up menu.

4. In the General tab of the folder or file Properties dialog box, click the Advanced button.

5. The Advanced Attributes dialog box appears. Check the Encrypt Contents to Secure Data check box. Then click the OK button.

6. The Confirm Attribute Changes dialog box appears. Specify whether you want to apply encryption only to this folder (Apply Changes to This Folder Only) or to the subfolders and files in the folder, as well (Apply Changes to this Folder, Subfolder, and Files). Then click the OK button.

To decrypt folders and files, repeat these steps, but uncheck the Encrypt Contents to Secure Data option in the Advanced Attributes dialog box.

In Exercise 9.7, you will use EFS to encrypt a folder. This exercise assumes that you have completed Exercise 9.1.

EXERCISE 9.7

Using EFS to Manage Data Encryption

1. Use the Local Users and Groups utility to create the new user **Lauren**. (See Chapter 6 for details on creating user accounts.) Deselect the User Must Change Password at Next Logon option for this user.

2. Select Start ➤ Programs ➤ Accessories ➤ Windows Explorer.

3. In Windows Explorer, find and select a folder on the D: drive. The folder you select should contain files. Right-click the folder and select Properties.

4. In the General tab of the folder Properties dialog box, click the Advanced button.

5. In the Advanced Attributes dialog box, check the Encrypt Contents to Secure Data option. Then click the OK button.

6. In the Confirm Attribute Changes dialog box (if this dialog box does not appear, click the Apply button in the Properties dialog box to display it), select Apply Changes to This Folder, Subfolder, and Files. Then click the OK button.

7. Log off as Administrator and log on as Lauren.

8. Open Windows Explorer and attempt to access one of the files in the folder you encrypted. You should receive an error message stating that the file is not accessible.

9. Log off as Lauren and log on as Administrator.

Using the *CIPHER* Utility

CIPHER is a command-line utility that can be used to encrypt files on NTFS volumes. The syntax for the CIPHER command is as follows:

```
CIPHER /[command parameter] [filename]
```

Table 9.3 lists the command parameters associated with the CIPHER command.

TABLE 9.3 CIPHER Command Parameters

Parameter	Description
/e	Specifies that files or folders should be encrypted.
/d	Specifies that files or folders should be decrypted.
/s:dir	Specifies that subfolders of the target folder should also be encrypted or decrypted based on the option specified.
/I	Causes any errors that occur to be ignored. By default, the CIPHER utility stops whenever an error occurs.
/f	Forces all files and folders to be encrypted or decrypted, regardless of their current state. Normally, if a file is already in the specified state, it is skipped.
/q	Runs CIPHER in quiet mode and only displays the most important information.

In Exercise 9.8, you will use the CIPHER utility to encrypt and decrypt files. This exercise assumes that you have completed Exercise 9.7.

EXERCISE 9.8

Using the CIPHER **Utility**

1. Select Start ➢ Programs ➢ Accessories ➢ Command Prompt.

2. In the Command Prompt dialog box, type **D:** and press Enter to access the D: drive.

3. From the D:\> prompt, type **cipher**. You will see a list of folders and files and the state of encryption. The folder you encrypted in Exercise 9.7 should be indicated by an E.

EXERCISE 9.8 *(continued)*

4. Type **MD TEST** and press Enter to create a new folder named Test.

5. Type **cipher /e test** and press Enter. You will see a message verifying that the folder was encrypted.

Retrieving Encrypted Files

If the user who encrypted the folders or files is unavailable to decrypt the folders or files when they're needed, you can use the recovery agent account to access the encrypted files. On Windows 2000 Professional computers that are not a part of a domain, the default recovery agent is the Administrator. (However, a user who is a member of the Administrators group is not considered a recovery agent and would not have default recovery privileges.)

Here are the steps to recover (retrieve) decrypted files:

1. Back up the encrypted files using the Windows Backup utility. (See Chapter 15 for instructions on backing up and restoring files.)

2. Using the computer where the recovery agent account is located, restore the backup of the encrypted files.

3. In Windows Explorer, access the Properties dialog box for the recovered file. In the General tab, click the Advanced button.

4. In the Advanced tab, uncheck the Encrypt Contents to Secure Data check box.

Because this procedure decrypts the backup copy of the folder or file, the original folder or file remains encrypted. If you don't want to keep the original file encrypted, you could simply decrypt the file with the Recovery Agent without using the Backup and Restore procedure.

Using the Disk Defragmenter Utility

Data is normally stored sequentially on the disk as space is available. *Fragmentation* naturally occurs as users create, delete, and modify files. The access of noncontiguous data is transparent to the user; however, when data is stored in this manner, the operating system must search through the disk to access all the pieces of a file. This slows down data access.

Microsoft
Exam
Objective

Monitor, manage, and troubleshoot access to files and folders.

• Optimize access to files and folders.

Disk defragmentation rearranges the existing files so that they are stored contiguously, which optimizes access to those files. In Windows 2000, you use the *Disk Defragmenter utility* to defragment your disk.

To access the Disk Defragmenter, select Start ➤ Programs ➤ Accessories ➤ System Tools ➤ Disk Defragmenter. The main Disk Defragmenter window (Figure 9.24) lists each volume, the file system used, capacity, free space, and the percentage of free space.

FIGURE 9.24   The main Disk Defragmenter window

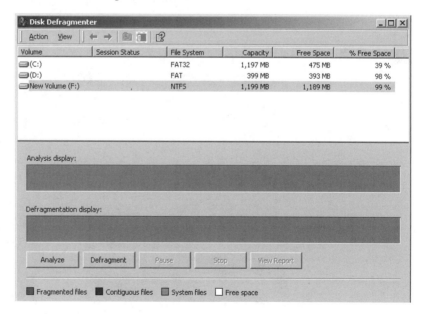

In addition to defragmenting disks, you can also use the Disk Defragmenter to analyze your disk and report on the current file arrangement. The processes of analyzing and defragmenting disks are covered in the following sections.

Analyzing Disks

To analyze a disk, open the Disk Defragmenter utility, select the drive to be analyzed, and click the Analyze button at the bottom-left of the window.

When you analyze a disk, the Disk Defragmenter utility checks for fragmented files, contiguous files, system files, and free space. The results of the analysis are shown in the Analysis display bar (see Figure 9.25). If you chose to defragment your disk, the defragmentation results would be listed in the bottom display bar. Though you can't see it in the figure, on your screen these bars are color-coded as follows:

Fragmented file	Red
Contiguous files	Blue
System files	Green
Free space	White

FIGURE 9.25   The Disk Defragmenter showing the Analysis and Defragmentation display bars

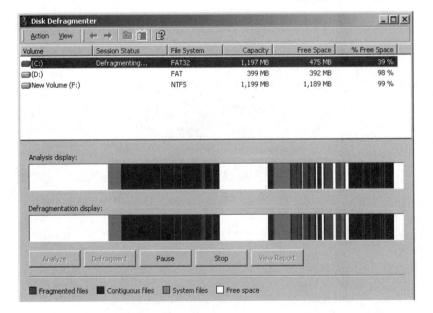

The Disk Defragmenter's analysis also produces a report, which is displayed when you click the View Report button. The report contains the following information:

- An indication of whether the volume needs defragmenting or not

- Volume information, including general volume statistics, volume fragmentation, file fragmentation, page file fragmentation, directory fragmentation, and master file table (MFT) fragmentation

- A list of the most fragmented files

Defragmenting Disks

To defragment a disk, open the Disk Defragmenter utility, select the drive to be defragmented, and click the Defragment button (to the right of the Analyze button at the bottom of the window). Defragmenting causes all files to be stored more efficiently in contiguous space. When defragmentation is complete, you can view a report of the defragmentation process.

You will use the Disk Defragmenter utility in Exercise 9.9 to analyze and defragment a disk.

EXERCISE 9.9

Analyzing and Defragmenting Disks

1. Select Start ➤ Programs ➤ Accessories ➤ System Tools ➤ Disk Defragmenter.

2. Highlight the C: drive and click the Analyze button.

3. When the analysis is complete, click the View Report button to see the analysis report. Record the following information:

   a. Volume size: _____

   b. Cluster size: _____

   c. Used space: _____

   d. Free space: _____

   e. Volume fragmentation-Total fragmentation: _____

   f. Most fragmented file: _____

4. Click the Defragment button.

5. When the defragmentation process is complete, click the Close button.

Using the Disk Cleanup Utility

The *Disk Cleanup utility* identifies areas of disk space that can be deleted to free hard disk space. Disk Cleanup works by identifying temporary files, Internet cache files, and unnecessary program files.

Microsoft ✔ ***Exam*** ***Objective***	**Monitor, manage, and troubleshoot access to files and folders.** • Optimize access to files and folders.

To access this utility, select Start ➤ Programs ➤ Accessories ➤ System Tools ➤ Disk Cleanup. You select the drive you want to clean up, and the Disk Cleanup utility then runs and calculates the amount of disk space you can free up.

In Exercise 9.10, you will use the Disk Cleanup utility.

EXERCISE 9.10

Using the Disk Cleanup Utility

1. Select Start ➤ Programs ➤ Accessories ➤ System Tools ➤ Disk Cleanup.

EXERCISE 9.10 *(continued)*

2. In the Select Drive dialog box, highlight the C: drive and click the OK button.

3. After the analysis is complete, you see the Disk Cleanup dialog box, listing files that are suggested for deletion and showing how much space will be gained by deleting those files. For this exercise, leave all the boxes checked and click the OK button.

4. When you are asked to confirm that you want to delete the files, click the Yes button. The Disk Cleanup utility deletes the files and automatically closes the Disk Cleanup dialog box.

Troubleshooting Disk Devices and Volumes

If you are having trouble with your disk devices or volumes, you can use the Windows 2000 *Check Disk utility*. This utility detects bad sectors, attempts to fix errors in the file system, and scans for and attempts to recover bad sectors.

Microsoft *Exam* *Objective*	**Implement, manage, and troubleshoot disk devices.** • Monitor and configure disks. • Monitor, configure, and troubleshoot volumes.

File system errors can be caused by a corrupt file system or by hardware errors. If you have software errors, the Check Disk utility may help you find them. There is no way to fix hardware errors through software, however. If you have excessive hardware errors, you should replace your disk drive.

In Exercise 9.11, you will run the Check Disk Utility.

EXERCISE 9.11

Using the Check Disk Utility

1. Select Start ➤ Settings ➤ Control Panel ➤ Administrative Tools.

2. Expand Computer Management, then Storage, then Disk Management.

3. Right-click the D: drive and choose Properties.

4. Click the Tools tab, then click the Check Now button.

EXERCISE 9.11 *(continued)*

5. In the Check Disk dialog box, you can choose one or both of the options to automatically fix file system errors, and to scan for and attempt recovery of bad sectors. For this exercise, check both of the disk options check boxes. Then click the Start button.

 If the system cannot gain exclusive access to the partition, the disk will be checked the next time the system is restarted. You cannot gain exclusive access to partitions or volumes that contain the system or boot partition.

Summary

In this chapter, you learned about disk management with Windows 2000 Professional. We covered the following topics:

- File system configuration, which can be FAT16, FAT32, or NTFS. You also learned how to convert a FAT or FAT32 partition to NTFS by using the CONVERT command-line utility.

- Disk storage configuration, which can be basic storage or dynamic storage. Dynamic storage is used to create simple volumes, spanned volumes, and striped volumes.

- Using the Disk Management utility to manage routine tasks, basic storage, and dynamic storage.

- Data compression, which is used to store files in a compressed format that uses less disk space.

- Disk quotas, which are used to limit the amount of disk space users can have on an NTFS partition.

- Data encryption, which is implemented through the Encrypting File System (EFS) and provides increased security for files and folders.

- Disk defragmentation, which is accomplished through the Disk Defragmenter utility and allows you to store files contiguously on your hard drive for improved access speeds.

- The Disk Cleanup utility, which is used to free disk space by removing unnecessary files.

- The Check Disk utility, which can be used to troubleshoot disk errors.

Exam Essentials

Configure and manage file systems. Understand the differences and features of the FAT16, FAT32, and NTFS file systems. Know how to configure options that are specific to the NTFS file system. Understand that you can convert a file system from FAT16 or FAT32 to NTFS, but that you can't convert from NTFS to anything else.

Be able to monitor and configure disks. Use the Disk Management utility to configure disks for simple, spanned, or striped volumes. Be aware of the lack of fault tolerance in disk configurations used by Windows 2000 Professional. Be able to use Disk Management to monitor disks for physical drive and logical drive errors. Be able to use the Disk Cleanup utility and the Disk Defragmenter utility.

Know how to use disk compression. Understand what types of files can benefit from disk compression and be able to configure and manage compressed folders and files.

Be able to use encryption to protect files. Know when it is appropriate to use encryption. Be able to manage compression through Windows Explorer, as well as through the CIPHER command-line utility. Know how to recover encrypted files if the user who encrypted the files is unavailable.

Key Terms

Before you take the exam, be sure you're familiar with the following key terms:

basic storage	dynamic storage
CDFS (Compact Disk File System)	Encrypting File System (EFS)
Check Disk utility	extended partition
CIPHER	FAT16
cipher text	FAT32
CONVERT	hot swapping
data compression	logical drive
data encryption	NTFS
Disk Cleanup utility	partition
disk defragmentation	primary partition
Disk Defragmenter utility	simple volume
Disk Management utility	spanned volume
disk quotas	striped volume
dynamic disk	volume

Review Questions

1. Steve has installed Windows 2000 Professional on his computer. He has FAT16, FAT32, and NTFS partitions. In addition, he boots his computer to Windows NT 4.0 Workstation for testing an application he is writing, checking for compatibility with both operating systems. Which of the following file systems will be seen by both operating systems?

   A. FAT16 and FAT32

   B. FAT32 and NTFS

   C. FAT16 and NTFS

   D. All three file systems will be seen by both operating systems.

2. Jack has an NTFS partition on his Windows 2000 Professional computer. He wants to dual-boot to the Windows 98 operating system to access an application that is not supported by Windows 2000. What command or utility should he use to convert his NTFS partition to FAT?

   A. CONVERT

   B. Disk Administrator

   C. Disk Manager

   D. This operation is not supported

3. Brad is the Payroll manager and stores critical files on his local drive for added security on his Windows 2000 Professional computer. He wants to ensure that he is using the disk configuration with the most fault tolerance and the highest level of consistent availability. Which of the following provisions should he use?

   A. Disk striping

   B. Spanned volumes

   C. Mirrored volumes

   D. Use a good backup scheme

4. Carrie is considering upgrading her basic disk to a dynamic disk on her Windows 2000 Professional computer. She asks you for help in understanding the function of dynamic disks. Which of the following statements is true of dynamic disks in Windows 2000 Professional? Choose all that apply.

   A. Dynamic disks can be recognized by Windows NT 4 or Windows 2000.

   B. Dynamic disks are only supported by Windows 2000.

   C. Dynamic disks support features such as simple volumes, extended volumes, spanned volumes, and striped volumes.

   D. Dynamic disks support features such as simple volumes, extended volumes, spanned volumes, mirrored volumes, and striped volumes.

5. Linda is using Windows 2000 Professional on her laptop computer, and the C: partition is running out of space. You want to identify any areas of free space that can be reclaimed from temporary files. What utility should you use?

   A. Disk Cleanup

   B. Disk Manager

   C. Disk Administrator

   D. Disk Defragmenter

6. Greg is using Windows 2000 Professional to store video files. He doesn't access the files very often and wants to compress the files to utilize disk space. Which of the following options allows you to compress files in Windows 2000 Professional?

   A. COMPRESS.EXE

   B. CIPHER.EXE

   C. PACKER.EXE

   D. Windows Explorer

7. Susan wants the highest level of security possible for her data. She stores the data on an NTFS partition and has applied NTFS permissions. Now she wants to encrypt the files through EFS (Encrypting File System). Which command-line utility can she use to manage data encryption?

   A. ENCRYPT

   B. CIPHER

   C. CRYPTO

   D. EFS

8. You have compressed a 4MB file into 2MB. You are copying the file to another computer that has a FAT32 partition. How can you ensure that the file will remain compressed?

   A. When you copy the file, use the XCOPY command with the /Comp switch.

   B. When you copy the file, use the Windows Explorer utility and specify Keep Existing Attributes.

   C. On the destination folder, make sure that the folder's properties are configured to Compress Contents to Save Disk Space.

   D. You can't maintain disk compression on a non-NTFS partition.

9. Julie is trying to save a file that is 2MB in size, but she's getting an error message that the disk is out of space. When the administrator checks available disk space, he determines that more than 4GB of free disk space remain. What is the most likely cause of the space problem on this computer?

   A. The disk needs to be defragmented.

   B. Julie does not have the NTFS permissions she needs to access the folder where she is trying to save the file.

   C. Julie has exceeded her disk quota.

   D. The folder is encrypted and Julie does not have the key required to write to the folder.

10. Tom is the manager of Human Resources in your company. He is concerned that members of the Administrators group will be able to easily view the contents of the sensitive personnel files. What is the highest level of security that can be applied to the payroll files?

   A. Apply NTFS permissions to the files.

   B. Encrypt the files with EFS.

   C. Secure the files with the Secure.exe command.

   D. Encrypt the files with HSP.

11. Scott frequently works with a large number of files. He is noticing that the larger the files get, the longer it takes to access them. He suspects that the problem is related to the files being spread over the disk. What utility can be used to store the files sequentially on the disk?

   A. Disk Cleanup

   B. Disk Manager

   C. Disk Administrator

   D. Disk Defragmenter

12. What steps do you take to access the Disk Defragmenter utility?

   A. Use Disk Administrator

   B. Use Disk Manager

   C. Through Programs ➢ Accessories ➢ System Tools

   D. Through Programs ➢ Administrative Tools ➢ System Tools

13. Cindy is the payroll manager at your company. The day before the payroll is processed, Cindy is involved in a minor car accident and spends two days in hospital. She has encrypted the payroll files with EFS. How can these files be accessed in her absence?

    A. The Administrator can access the files by backing up the files, restoring the files on the computer where the recovery agent is located, and disabling the files' Encrypt the Contents to Secure Data option.

    B. The Administrator can access the files by using the unencrypt command-line utility.

    C. The Administrator can access the files by using the encrypt -d command-line utility.

    D. The Administrator can access the files by using the access command-line utility.

14. You have an extremely large database that needs to be stored on a single partition. Your boss asks you about the maximum capacity for an NTFS partition. What is the correct answer?

    A. 32GB

    B. 64GB

    C. 132GB

    D. 2TB

15. You have just added a new disk to your computer that supports hot swapping. Your computer now has two physical drives. When you look at Disk Management, you see the screen shown just below. What is the fastest way to allow Windows 2000 Professional to recognize the new disk?

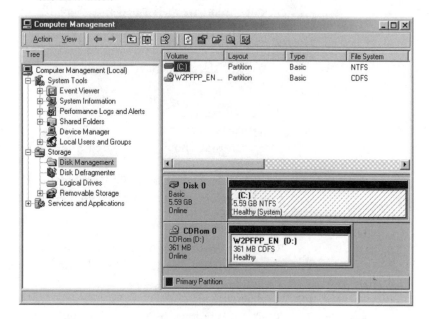

A. Restart the computer.

B. In Disk Manager, select Action ➤ Rescan Disk.

C. In Disk Management, select Action ➤ Rescan Disk.

D. In System Tools, select Update Disks.

Answers to Review Questions

1. C.   Windows NT 4.0 does not recognize FAT32 partitions, so the only file systems that will be recognized by Windows NT 4.0 and Windows 2000 are the FAT16 and NTFS file systems.

2. D.   You can convert from FAT16 or FAT32 to NTFS, but it is a one-way process. You cannot convert from NTFS back to FAT16 or FAT32.

3. D.   Windows 2000 Professional supports simple, spanned, and striped volumes. Mirrored volumes are available with Windows 2000 Server. Brad should make sure he has a good backup for reliability.

4. B, C.   Dynamic disks can only be accessed through Windows 2000. They do not support mirrored volumes in the Professional version of Windows 2000.

5. A.   The Disk Cleanup utility is used to identify areas of space that may be reclaimed through the deletion of temporary files or Recycle Bin files.

6. D.   In Windows 2000, one way you can compress files is through Windows Explorer. Windows 2000 has no programs called COMPRESS or PACKER. The CIPHER program is used to encrypt or decrypt files.

7. B.   The CIPHER utility is used to encrypt or decrypt files. Windows 2000 doesn't have a program called ENCRYPT, CRYPTO, or EFS.

8. D.   Windows 2000 data compression is only supported on NTFS partitions.

9. C.   If Julie experiences "out of space" errors even when the disk has free space, it is likely that the disk has disk quotas applied and Julie has exceeded her quota limitation.

10. B.   You can increase the level of security on folders and files on an NTFS partition by using Encrypting File System (EFS). Only a user with the correct key can access this data.

11. D. The Disk Defragmenter utility is used to rearrange files so that they are stored contiguously on the disk. This optimizes access to those files.

12. C. You access the Disk Defragmenter utility through Start ➢ Programs ➢ Accessories ➢ System Tools ➢ Defragmenter.

13. A. By default, the Administrator is automatically designated as the recovery agent with the ability to access files that have been encrypted. The Administrator can access the files by backing them up, restoring them on the computer where the recovery agent is located, and disabling the Encrypt Contents to Secure Data option in the files' advanced properties.

14. D. You can have NTFS partitions that are up to 2TB in size.

15. C. If your computer supports hot-swapping capability, all you need to do after you add a new disk is select Action ➢ Rescan Disk in the Disk Management utility.

Accessing Files and Folders

MICROSOFT EXAM OBJECTIVES COVERED IN THIS CHAPTER:

✓ **Monitor, manage, and troubleshoot access to files and folders.**

- Configure, manage, and troubleshoot file compression.
- Control access to files and folders by using permissions.
- Optimize access to files and folders.

✓ **Manage and troubleshoot access to shared folders.**

- Create and remove shared folders.
- Control access to shared folders by using permissions.

✓ **Connect to shared resources on a Microsoft network.**

✓ **Manage and troubleshoot the use and synchronization of offline files.**

Administrators must have basic file management skills, including the ability to create a well-defined, logically organized directory structure and maintain that structure. Windows 2000 Professional Folder Options allow you to configure many properties associated with files and folders, such as what you see when you access folders, file type associations, and the use of offline files and folders. Finally, you should know how to search for files and folders.

Local access defines what access a user has to local resources. You can limit local access by applying security for folders and files on NTFS partitions. You should know what NTFS permissions are and how they are applied. You can also optimize local access through the use of the Indexing Service.

A powerful feature of networking is the ability to allow network access to local folders. In Windows 2000 Professional, it is very easy to share folders. You can also apply security to shared folders in a manner that is similar to applying NTFS permissions. Once you share a folder, users with appropriate access rights can access the folders through a variety of methods.

To effectively manage both local and network resource access and troubleshoot related problems, you should understand the resource-access process. Windows 2000 Professional uses access tokens, access control lists, and access control entries to handle resource access.

This chapter covers file and folder management tasks, beginning with the basics of planning and creating a directory structure.

File and Folder Management Basics

Before you perform tasks such as managing NTFS security and network shares, you need to understand how to perform basic file and folder management tasks. The first step in file and folder management is organizing your files and folders. After you have created the structure, you can manage folder options. Another common task is searching for files and folders. These tasks are covered in the following sections.

Organizing Files and Folders

When your files and folders are well organized, you can easily access the information that is stored on your computer. Organizing your files and folders is similar to storing your papers. If you don't have very many papers, the task is easy. The more papers you have, the more challenging the task becomes.

The key to organization is good planning. For example, you might decide to store all of your applications on your C: drive and all of your data on your D: drive. You might organize data by function or by type. Figure 10.1 shows an example of a directory structure that has been logically organized.

FIGURE 10.1 A sample directory structure

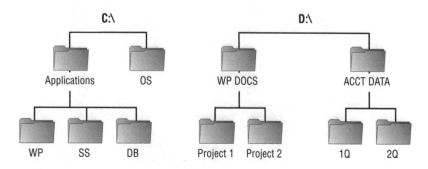

Once you plan your directory structure, you are ready to create the structure on your computer. This involves creating files and folders and may also require you to rename, delete, move, and copy files and folders. These tasks are described in the following sections.

Creating Folders and Files

You can create folders in several ways—through Windows Explorer, the DOS MD command, and through My Computer. The examples in this chapter use Windows Explorer for folder management.

There are many ways to create files, too. The most common way is through applications, including the Windows 2000 Professional WordPad and Notepad utilities. Here are the steps to create a file with Notepad:

1. Select Start ➤ Programs ➤ Accessories ➤ Windows Explorer to open Windows Explorer.

2. Open My Computer and select the drive where the file will be created.

3. Select File ➤ New ➤ Text Document.

4. A new file icon appears in the Windows Explorer window. Type in the name of the new file under the file icon.

5. Double-click the new file to open it in Notepad. Add text to the file, as shown in Figure 10.2.

FIGURE 10.2   Editing a text document with Notepad

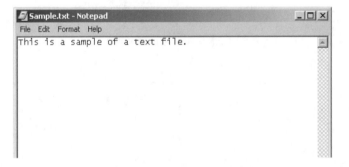

6. Save the file by selecting File ➤ Exit. You will see a dialog box indicating that the contents of the file have changed. Save the changes by clicking the Yes button.

In Exercise 10.1, you will create a simple directory structure and add folders and files. This structure will be used in the other exercises in this chapter.

Creating a Directory and File Structure

1. Select Start ➢ Programs ➢ Accessories ➢ Windows Explorer to start Windows Explorer.

2. Expand My Computer, then Local Disk (D:). Select File ➢ New ➢ Folder.

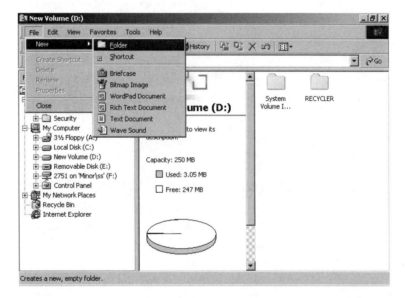

3. Name the new folder **DATA,** and double-click it to open it. Select File ➢ New ➢ Folder again, and name this new folder **WP DOCS**.

4. Confirm that you are in the Data folder. Select File ➢ New ➢ Folder, and name this new folder **SS DOCS**.

5. Confirm that you are still in the DATA folder. Then select File ➢ New ➢ Text Document. Name the file **DOC1.TXT**.

EXERCISE 10.1 *(continued)*

6. Double-click the WP DOCS folder. Select File ➢ New ➢ Text Document. Name the file **DOC2.TXT**.

7. Confirm that you are in the SS DOCS folder. Select File ➢ New ➢ Text Document and name the file **DOC3.TXT**. Your structure should look like the one shown below.

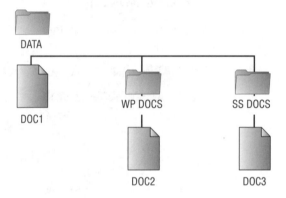

Renaming and Deleting Folders and Files

If you need to rename a folder or a file, right-click the folder or file that you want to rename and select Rename from the pop-up menu. The name will be selected and boxed. Start typing to replace the existing name with your entry, or position the cursor and edit the existing folder name or filename.

To delete a folder or file, right-click the folder or file that you want to remove and select Delete from the pop-up menu. When prompted, click the Yes button to confirm the deletion.

Deleted files or folders are moved to the Recycle Bin, which you can clear periodically to delete files or folders permanently. If you delete a folder or file by accident, you can usually restore the folder or file from the Recycle Bin.

Copying and Moving Folders and Files

You can easily reorganize your directory structure by copying and moving folders and files. When you move a folder or file from its original location (called the *source*) to a new location (called the *destination*), it no longer exists in the source location. When you copy a folder or file, it will exist in both the source and destination locations.

To copy or move a folder or file, right-click the folder or file that you want to copy or move, and drag and drop it into its destination location. When you release the mouse, you will see a pop-up menu that includes the options Copy Here and Move Here, as shown in Figure 10.3. Make the appropriate selection.

FIGURE 10.3   Moving a folder

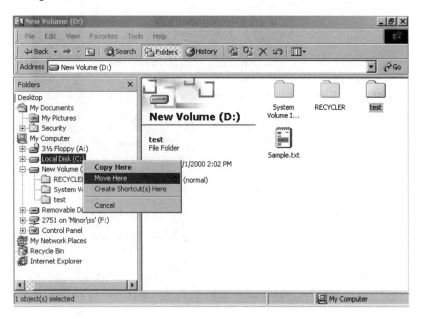

Managing Folder Options

Through the Folder Options dialog box, you can configure options such as the Desktop view and what you see when you open folders. To open the Folder Options dialog box, start Windows Explorer and select Tools ➢

Folder Options. You can also access Folder Options through its icon in Control Panel. The Folder Options dialog box has four tabs: General, View, File Types, and Offline Files. The options on each of these tabs are described in the following sections.

General Folder Options

The General tab of the Folder Options dialog box, shown in Figure 10.4, includes the following options:

- A choice of the Windows classic Desktop or the Active Desktop, which enables Web content on the Desktop

- A choice of using Windows classic folders or enabling Web content in folders

- Whether folders are opened all in the same window when a user is browsing folders, or each folder in a separate window

- Whether a user opens items with a single mouse click or a double-click

FIGURE 10.4 The General tab of the Folder Options dialog box

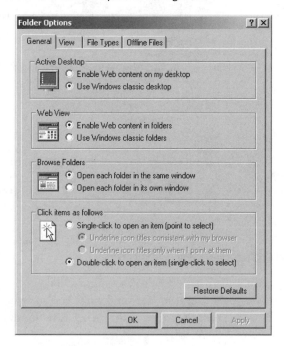

Folder View Options

The options on the View tab of the Folder Options dialog box, shown in Figure 10.5, are used to configure what users see when they open files and folders. For example, you can change the default setting so that hidden files and folders are shown in Windows Explorer and other file lists. The View tab options are described in Table 10.1.

FIGURE 10.5   The View tab of the Folder Options dialog box

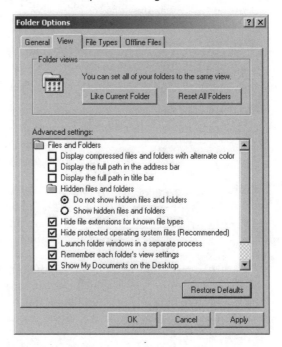

TABLE 10.1   Folder View Options

Option	Description
Display compressed files and folders with an alternate color	By default, compressed files and folders are displayed in the same color as uncompressed files and folders. Enabling this option displays compressed files and folders in an alternate color so that they can be easily identified.

TABLE 10.1 Folder View Options *(continued)*

Option	Description
Display the full path in the address bar	By default, the address bar in the Windows Explorer window shows an abbreviated path of your location, such as Chapter 10 (from the Word Documents folder). Enabling this option displays the full path, such as `C:\Word Documents\Sybex\Prof Book\Chapter 10`.
Display the full path in the title bar	By default, the title bar at the top of the Windows Explorer window shows an abbreviated path of your location. Enabling this option displays the full path.
Hidden files and folders	By default, Do Not Show Hidden Files and Folders is selected, so that files and folders with the Hidden attribute are not listed. Choosing Show Hidden Files and Folders displays these items.
Hide file extensions for known file types	By default, filename extensions, which identify the file type (for example, `.DOC` for Word files and `.XLS` for Excel files), are not shown. Disabling this option displays all filename extensions.
Hide protected operating system files (Recommended)	By default, operating system files are not shown, which protects operating system files from being modified or deleted by a user. Disabling this option displays the operating system files.
Launch folder windows in a separate process	By default, when you open a folder, it shares memory with the previous folders that were opened. Enabling this option opens folders in separate parts of memory, which increases the stability of Windows 2000 but can slightly decrease the performance of the computer.
Remember each folder's view settings	By default, any folder display settings you make are retained each time the folder is reopened. Disabling this option resets the folder display settings to their defaults each time the folder is opened.

TABLE 10.1 Folder View Options *(continued)*

Option	Description
Show my documents on the Desktop	By default, My Documents (a folder created by Windows 2000 for each user who accesses the computer and used as the default location for storing user files) appears on the Desktop. Disabling this option removes My Computer from the Desktop.
Show pop-up description for folder and Desktop options	By default, any summary information configured through file properties (such as title, subject, and author) appears when you click a file. Disabling this option suppresses the display of the summary information.

File Type Options

The File Types tab of the Folder Options dialog box, shown in Figure 10.6, is used to associate filename extensions with application file types. When an extension is associated with a file type, users can double-click the filename in Windows Explorer to open the file in its application. For example, if you have associated .PDF with Adobe Acrobat Reader and you double-click the `Presentation.PDF` file, Acrobat Reader will start and that file will be opened in it.

Through the File Types tab, you can add, delete, and change file-type associations. New filename extensions also may be added automatically when you install new applications on your computer.

FIGURE 10.6 The File Types tab of the Folder Options dialog box

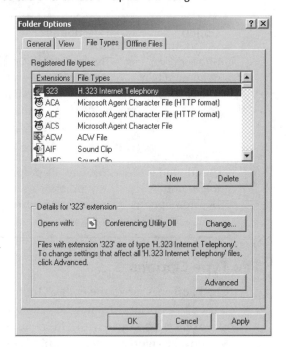

Offline Folder Options

Through the Offline Files tab of the Folder Options dialog box (Figure 10.7), you can configure the computer to use *offline files and folders*. This is a new Windows 2000 Professional feature that allows network folders and files to be stored on Windows 2000 clients. Then if the network location is not available, users can still access network files. In earlier versions of Windows, users who tried to access a network folder would receive an error message. With offline folders, users can still access the network folder even when they are not attached to the network.

Microsoft ✓ *Exam* *Objective*	**Manage and troubleshoot the use and synchronization of offline files.**

FIGURE 10.7 The Offline Files tab of the Folder Options dialog box

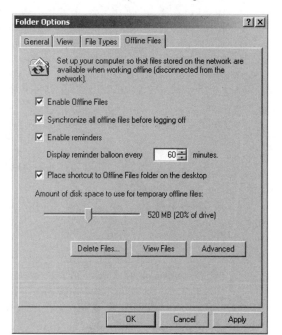

Offline files and folders are particularly useful for mobile users who use the same set of files when they are attached to the network and when they are traveling. Offline files and folders are also useful on networks where users require specific files to perform their jobs, because they will be able to access those files even if the network server goes down (for scheduled maintenance or because of a power outage or another problem). Offline files and folders also increase performance even when the network is available, because users can use the local copy of the file instead of accessing files over the network.

Configuring offline files and folders requires a minimum of two computers:

- The network computer that contains the network version of the folders and files

- The Windows 2000 client computer that will access the network files while they are online or offline

The network computer does not have to be running Windows 2000, but it must use the file and print sharing protocol SMB (Server Message Blocks). All Microsoft operating systems use SMB, but some other operating systems do not. For example, if you were connected to a Novell NetWare share, you would not be able to use offline files and folders, because NetWare uses a protocol called NCP (NetWare Core Protocol) for file and print sharing.

In order to use offline files and folders, you must complete the following tasks:

1. Attach to the shared file or folder that you want to access offline.

2. Configure your computer to use offline files and folders.

3. Make files and folders available for offline access.

4. Specify how offline files and folders will respond to network disconnection.

These tasks are covered in the following sections.

Attaching to the Share

In order to use a file or folder offline, the file or folder must first be made available online. Someone at the server must share the file or folder, and the user must have proper permissions to access the file or folder. Then the user can attach to the shared file or folder. The procedure for sharing files and folders is described in the "Managing Network Access" section later in this chapter.

Configuring Your Computer

You configure your computer to use offline files and folders through the Offline Files tab of the Folder Options dialog box (see Figure 10.7). In this tab, verify that the Enable Offline Files box is checked (this option is enabled by default). To configure automatic synchronization between the offline and online files, make sure that the Synchronize All Offline Files before Logging Off option is checked (this option is also enabled by default).

If you don't configure offline files and folders to be synchronized automatically when you log on to or log off from your computer, you will need to perform the synchronization manually. To manually synchronize a file or folder, right-click the file or folder that has been configured for offline use and select Synchronize from the pop-up menu, as shown in Figure 10.8.

FIGURE 10.8   Manually synchronizing an offline folder

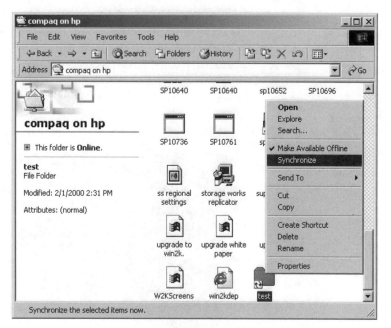

Making Folders or Files Available

To make a file or folder available for offline access, take the following steps:

1. Access the shared file or folder that you wish to use offline. Right-click the file or folder and select Make Available Offline from the pop-up menu (see Figure 10.8).

2. The Welcome to the Offline Files Wizard starts (this Wizard will run only the first time you create an offline file or folder). Click the Next button.

3. As shown in Figure 10.9, a dialog box asks how to synchronize offline files. By default, the option to Automatically Synchronize the Offline Files When I Log On and Log Off My Computer is selected. If you would prefer to manually synchronize files, deselect this option. Click the Next button to continue.

4. The next dialog box, shown in Figure 10.10, allows you to configure reminders and to create a shortcut to the Offline Files folder. Reminders periodically prompt you that you are not connected to the network and are working offline. The Offline Files shortcut is an easy way to access folders that have been configured for offline use. If you are online when you access this folder, you are working online. You can select or deselect either of these options. Then click the Finish button.

FIGURE 10.9 Configuring the synchronization of offline files and folders

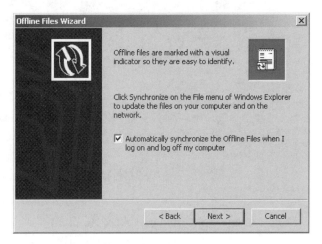

FIGURE 10.10 Configuring reminders and the Offline Files shortcut

5. If the folder you have selected contains subfolders, you will see the Confirm Offline Subfolders dialog box, shown in Figure 10.11. This dialog box allows you to choose whether the subfolders should also be made available offline. Make your selection and click the OK button.

FIGURE 10.11 Configuring offline subfolder availability

The offline files will be copied (synchronized) to the local computer. You can tell that a folder has been configured for offline access by the icon that appears under the folder, as shown in Figure 10.12.

FIGURE 10.12 The icon for offline folders

test

Preventing a Folder from Being Accessed Offline

Once a computer has been configured to support offline folders and files, you can access any share that has been configured with default properties. If you create a share and you do *not* want the files to be accessible offline, you can configure the share properties for offline access through the share's cacheing properties. Shares are discussed in greater detail later in this chapter.

To configure the offline folder's cacheing, access the share's Properties dialog box, as shown in Figure 10.13. Click the Caching button. In the Caching

Settings dialog box (Figure 10.14), uncheck the option to "Allow caching of files in this shared folder." With this option disabled, users can access the data while they are on the network, but they can't use the share offline.

FIGURE 10.13 Sharing properties for a shared folder

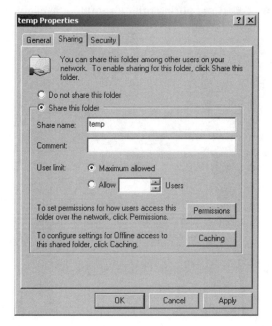

FIGURE 10.14 Caching Settings for a shared folder

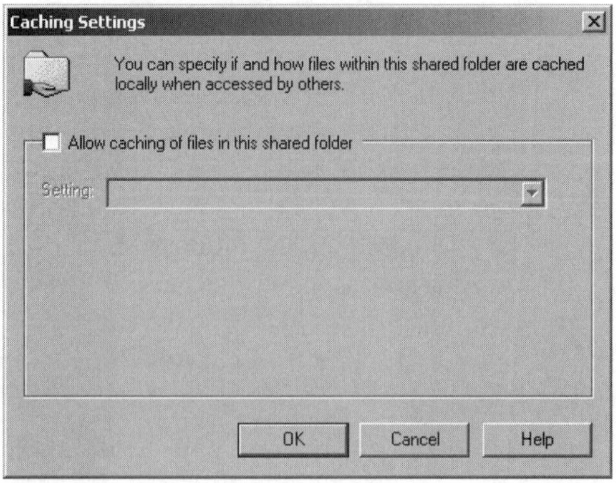

Configuring Your Computer's Behavior after Losing the Network Connection

Through the Offline Files tab of the Folder Options dialog box, you can specify whether or not your computer will begin working offline when a network connection is lost. To make this setting, click the Advanced button in the bottom-right corner of the dialog box. This brings up the Offline Files - Advanced Settings dialog box, as shown in Figure 10.15. Here, you can specify Notify Me and Begin Working Offline (the default selection) or you can select Never Allow My Computer to Go Offline. If you have created offline files and folders for multiple servers, you can use the Exception List portion of the dialog box to specify different behavior for each one.

FIGURE 10.15   The Offline Files - Advanced Settings dialog box

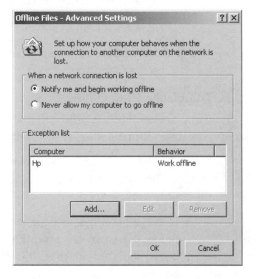

In Exercise 10.2, you will set up your computer to use and synchronize offline files and folders.

Your Windows 2000 Professional computer may be attached to a network that has another computer with shared files or folders. Just as described in the preceding sections, you can also attach to these shared files or folders that you want to access offline, make them available for offline access, and configure how the files will respond to network disconnection.

EXERCISE 10.2

Configuring Offline Files and Folders

1. Select Start ➢ Programs ➢ Accessories ➢ Windows Explorer.

2. In Windows Explorer, select Tools ➢ Folder Options and click the Offline Files tab.

3. In the Offline Files tab of the Folder Options dialog box, make sure that the following options are selected:

   Enable Offline Files

   Synchronize All Offline Files before Logging Off

   Enable Reminders; Display Message Balloon Every 60 Minutes

   Place Shortcut to Offline Files Folder on the Desktop

4. Click the OK button to close the dialog box.

Troubleshooting Offline Files

If you are configuring offline files and folders, and you don't see the Make Available Offline option available as a folder property, check the following:

- Are you connected to a network share on a computer that uses SMB? Offline files and folders won't work from a network computer that does not use SMB.

- Have you configured your computer to use offline files and folders? Before you can make a file or folder available offline, this feature must be enabled through the Offline Files tab of the Folder Options dialog box (select Tools ➢ Folder Options in Windows Explorer).

- Has the folder that you want to access been shared, and do you have proper permissions to access the folder? If you don't see a folder that you want to configure for offline use, it may not be shared or you may not have proper share (and NTFS) permissions to the folder.

Searching for Files and Folders

Windows 2000 Professional offers powerful search capabilities. You can look for a file or folder based on the filename or folder name and also by searching for the text that is contained in the file. This is an extremely useful feature when you know that you have saved a particular file on your computer but you can't find it.

Windows Explorer and My Computer have a Search button on their toolbars. Clicking this button brings up the Search dialog box, shown in Figure 10.16. In this dialog box, you can specify the following options for your search:

- The filename or folder name (the name can contain wildcard characters, such as * or ?)

- The text that you are looking for

- The location that you want to look in

FIGURE 10.16   The Search dialog box

Depending on what you want to find, you might specify the filename or folder name and/or the text that you are looking for. Only one of these fields must be filled in for a search. You must indicate the location that you want to look in; this can be as broad as My Computer or as specific as a particular drive or folder.

Once you have designated your search criteria, click the Search Now button to start the search. The results are displayed in the right side of the window, as shown in Figure 10.17.

The Search Options at the bottom of the Search dialog box allow you to configure more advanced searches by date, type, and size of files. For even more complex searches, you can select Advanced Options and specify subfolders, case sensitivity, and to search slow files (files that reside on removable storage media such as tape or optical drives).

FIGURE 10.17 Search results

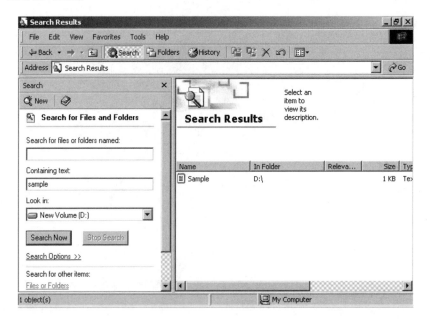

Managing Local Access

The two common types of file systems used by local partitions are FAT (which includes FAT16 and FAT32) and NTFS. (File systems are covered in detail in Chapter 9, "Managing Disks.") FAT partitions do not support local security; NTFS partitions do. This means if the file system on the partition that users access is configured as a FAT partition, you cannot specify any security for the file system once a user has logged on. However, if the partition is NTFS, you can specify the access each user has to specific folders on the partition, based on the user's logon name and group associations.

Microsoft ✓ *Exam* *Objective*	**Monitor, manage, and troubleshoot access to files and folders.** ▪ Control access to files and folders by using permissions. ▪ Optimize access to files and folders.

This chapter covers material related to optimizing access to files and folders and using permissions to control access to files and folders, for the objective "Monitor, manage, and troubleshoot access to files and folders." Using file compression, another subobjective for this objective, is covered in Chapter 9. That chapter also provides more information about optimizing access to files and folders.

The following sections describe how to apply NTFS permissions and some techniques for optimizing local access.

Applying NTFS Permissions

NTFS permissions control access to NTFS folders and files. You configure access by allowing or denying NTFS permissions to users and groups. Normally, NTFS permissions are cumulative, based on group memberships if the user has been *allowed* access. However, if the user had been *denied* access through user or group membership, those permissions override the allowed permissions. Windows 2000 Professional offers five levels of NTFS permissions:

The Full Control permission allows the following rights:

- Traverse folders and execute files (programs) in the folders

- List the contents of a folder and read the data in a folder's files

- See a folder's or file's attributes
- Change a folder's or file's attributes
- Create new files and write data to the files
- Create new folders and append data to files
- Delete subfolders and files
- Delete files
- Change permissions for files and folders
- Take ownership of files and folders

The Modify permission allows the following rights:

- Traverse folders and execute files in the folders
- List the contents of a folder and read the data in a folder's files
- See a folder's or file's attributes
- Change a folder's or file's attributes
- Create new files and write data to the files
- Create new folders and append data to files
- Delete files

The Read & Execute permission allows the following rights:

- Traverse folders and execute files in the folders
- List the contents of a folder and read the data in a folder's files
- See a folder's or file's attributes

The List Folder Contents permission allows the following rights:

- Traverse folders
- List the contents of a folder
- See a folder's or file's attributes

The Read permission allows the following rights:

- List the contents of a folder and read the data in a folder's files
- See a folder's or file's attributes

The Write permission allows the following rights:

- Change a folder's or file's attributes
- Create new files and write data to the files
- Create new folders and append data to files

Any user with Full Control access can manage the security of a folder. By default, the Everyone group has Full Control permission for the entire NTFS partition. However, in order to access folders, a user must have physical access to the computer as well as a valid logon name and password. By default, regular users can't access folders over the network unless the folders have been shared. Sharing folders is covered in the "Managing Network Access" section later in this chapter.

You apply NTFS permissions through Windows Explorer. Right-click the file or folder to which you want to control access, and select Properties from the pop-up menu. This brings up the folder's or file's Properties dialog box. Figure 10.18 shows a folder Properties dialog box.

The process for configuring NTFS permissions for folders and files is the same. The examples in this chapter use a folder, since NTFS permissions are most commonly applied at the folder level.

FIGURE 10.18 The Properties dialog box for a folder

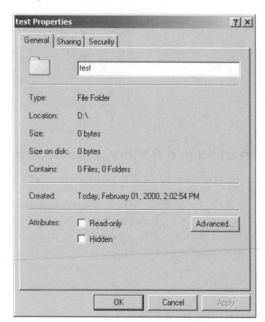

The tabs in the file or folder Properties dialog box depend on the options that have been configured for your computer. For files and folders on NTFS partitions, the dialog box will contain a Security tab, which is where you configure NTFS permissions. (The Security tab is not present in the Properties dialog box for files or folders on FAT partitions, because FAT partitions do not support local security.) The Security tab lists the users and groups that have been assigned permissions to the folder or file. When you click a user or group in the top half of the dialog box, you see the permissions that have been allowed or denied for that user or group in the lower half of the dialog box, as shown in Figure 10.19.

FIGURE 10.19 The Security tab of the folder Properties dialog box

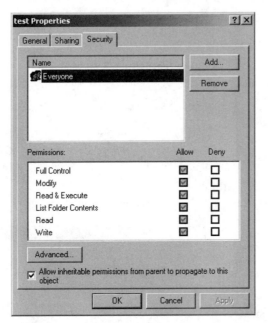

Adding and Removing User and Group NTFS Permissions

To manage NTFS permissions, take the following steps:

1. In Windows Explorer, right-click the file or folder to which you want to control access, select Properties from the pop-up menu, and click the Security tab of the Properties dialog box.

2. Click the Add button to open the Select Users, Computers, or Groups dialog box, as shown in Figure 10.20. You can select users from the computer's local database or from the domain you are in (or trusted domains) from the list box at the top of the dialog box. The list box at the bottom lists all the groups and users for the location that was specified in the top list box.

3. Click the user, computer, or group that you wish to add and click the Add button. That entity appears in the bottom list box. Use Ctrl+click to select noncontiguous users, computers, or groups, and Shift+click to select contiguous users, computers, or groups. Once you have added the user, computer, or group, click the OK button.

4. You return to the Security tab of the folder Properties dialog box. Highlight each user, computer, or group in the top list box individually, and in the Permissions list specify the NTFS permissions to be allowed or denied. When you are finished, click the OK button.

FIGURE 10.20 The Select Users, Computers, or Groups dialog box

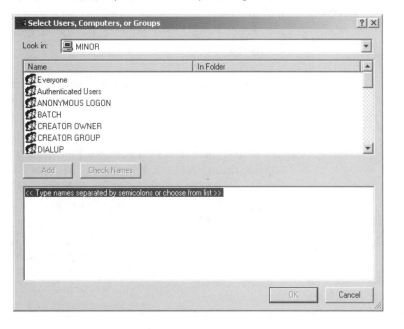

 Through the Advanced button of the Security tab, you can configure more granular NTFS permissions, such as Traverse Folder/ Execute File and Read Attributes permissions.

To remove the NTFS permissions for a user, computer, or group, highlight that entity in the Security tab and click the Remove button.

Be careful when you remove NTFS permissions. You won't be asked to confirm their removal, as you are for deleting most other types of items in Windows 2000 Professional.

Controlling Permission Inheritance

Normally, the directory structure is organized in a hierarchical manner. This means you are likely to have subfolders in the folders to which you apply permissions. In Windows 2000 Professional, by default, the parent folder's permissions are applied to any files or subfolders in that folder. These are called *inherited permissions*.

In Windows NT 4, by default, files in a folder do inherit permissions from the parent folder, but subfolders do not inherit parent permissions. In Windows 2000 Professional, the default is for the permissions to be inherited by subfolders.

You can specify that permissions should not be inherited by subfolders and files through the Security tab of the folder Properties dialog box. If you deselect the Allow Inheritable Permissions from Parent to Propagate to This Object check box at the bottom of the dialog box, you have disabled inherited permissions at this folder level. You are then given a choice of either copying the permissions or removing the permissions from the parent folder.

If an Allow or a Deny check box in the Permissions list in the Security tab has a shaded check mark, this indicates that the permission was inherited from an upper-level folder. If the check mark is not shaded, it means the permission was applied at the selected folder. This is known as an *explicitly assigned* permission. Knowing which permissions are inherited and which are explicitly assigned is useful when you need to troubleshoot permissions.

Determining Effective Permissions

To determine a user's *effective rights* (the rights the user actually has to a file or folder), add all of the permissions that have been allowed through the user's assignments based on that user's username and group associations. After you determine what the user is allowed, you subtract any permissions that have been denied the user through the username or group associations.

As an example, suppose that user Marilyn is a member of both the Accounting and Execs groups. The following assignments have been made to the Accounting Group Permissions:

Permission	Allow	Deny
Full Control		
Modify	X	
Read & Execute	X	
List Folder Contents		
Read		
Write		

The following assignments have been made to the Execs Group Permissions:

Permission	Allow	Deny
Full Control		
Modify		
Read & Execute		
List Folder Contents		
Read	X	
Write		

To determine Marilyn's effective rights, you combine the permissions that have been assigned. The result is that Marilyn's effective rights are Modify, Read & Execute, and Read.

As another example, suppose that user Dan is a member of both the Sales and Temps groups. The following assignments have been made to the Sales Group Permissions:

Permission	Allow	Deny
Full Control		
Modify	X	
Read & Execute	X	
List Folder Contents	X	
Read	X	
Write	X	

The following assignments have been made to the Temps Group Permissions:

Permission	Allow	Deny
Full Control		
Modify		X
Read & Execute		
List Folder Contents		
Read		
Write		X

To determine Dan's effective rights, you start by seeing what Dan has been allowed: Modify, Read & Execute, List Folder Contents, Read, and Write permissions. You then remove anything that he is denied: Modify and Write permissions. In this case, Dan's effective rights are Read & Execute, List Folder Contents, and Read.

In Exercise 10.3, you will configure NTFS permissions based on the preceding examples. This exercise assumes that you have completed Exercise 10.1.

EXERCISE 10.3

Configuring NTFS Permissions

1. Using the Local Users and Groups utility, create two users: **Marilyn** and **Dan**. (See Chapter 6, "Managing Users," for details on creating user accounts.) Deselect the User Must Change Password at Next Logon option.

2. Using the Local Users and Groups utility, create four groups: **Accounting**, **Execs**, **Sales**, and **Temps**. (See Chapter 7, "Managing Groups," for details on creating groups.) Add Marilyn to the Accounting and Execs groups. Add Dan to the Sales and Temps groups.

3. Select Start ➢ Programs ➢ Accessories ➢ Windows Explorer to open Windows Explorer. Expand the DATA folder (on drive D:) that you created in Exercise 10.1.

4. Right-click DATA, select Properties, and click the Security tab.

5. In the Security tab of the folder Properties dialog box, highlight the Everyone group and click the Remove button. You see a dialog box telling you that you cannot remove Everyone because this group is inheriting permissions from a higher level. Click the OK button.

6. In the Security tab, deselect the Allow Inheritable Permissions from Parent to Propagate to This Object. In the dialog box that appears, click the Remove button.

7. Configure NTFS permissions for the Accounting, Execs, Sales, and Temps groups by clicking the Add button. In the Select Users, Computers, or Groups dialog box, highlight the Accounting, Execs, Sales, and Temps groups and click the Add button. Then click OK.

8. In the Security tab, highlight each group and check the Allow or Deny check boxes to add permissions as follows:

   For Accounting, allow Read & Execute (List Folder Contents and Read will automatically be allowed) and Write.

   For Execs, allow Read.

   For Sales, allow Modify (Read & Execute, List Folder Contents, Read, and Write will automatically be allowed).

   For Temps, deny Write.

9. Click the OK button to close the folder Properties dialog box.

10. Log off as Administrator and log on as Marilyn. Access the D:\DATA\DOC1 file, make changes, and then save the changes. Marilyn's permissions should allow these actions.

11. Log off as Marilyn and log on as Dan. Access the D:\DATA\DOC1 file, make changes, and then save the changes. Dan's permissions should allow you to open the file but not to save any changes.

12. Log off as Dan and log on as Administrator.

Determining NTFS Permissions for Copied or Moved Files

When you copy or move NTFS files, the permissions that have been set for those files might change. The following guidelines can be used to predict what will happen:

- If you move a file from one folder to another folder on the same volume, the file will retain the original NTFS permissions.

- If you move a file from one folder to another folder between different NTFS volumes, the file is treated as a copy and will have the same permissions as the destination folder.

- If you copy a file from one folder to another folder on the same volume or on a different volume, the file will have the same permissions as the destination folder.

- If you copy or move a folder or file to a FAT partition, it will not retain any NTFS permissions.

Optimizing Local Access

In order for the data that you store on your computer to be useful, users must be able to access that data easily. One way to optimize local access is to logically organize your directory structure so that users can easily find files. Planning and creating your directory structure were discussed in the "Organizing Files and Folders" section earlier in this chapter.

Another way to optimize local access is to configure the *Indexing Service* to index folders. The Indexing Service is not started by default on Windows 2000 Professional computers. By starting and configuring the Indexing Service, you can speed up searches.

In Exercise 10.4, you will optimize access to folders and files by starting and configuring the Indexing Service.

EXERCISE 10.4

Starting and Configuring the Indexing Service

1. Right-click My Computer and select Manage.

2. Expand Services and Applications, select Services, and double-click Indexing Service.

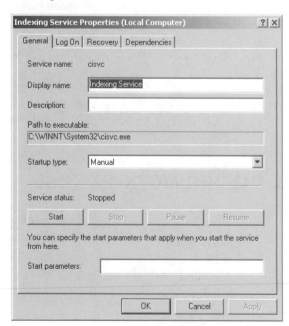

EXERCISE 10.4 *(continued)*

3. In the Indexing Service Properties dialog box, select Automatic from the Startup Type drop-down list. Click the Start button to start the Indexing Service. Click the OK button.

4. Select Start ➢ Programs ➢ Accessories ➢ Windows Explorer to open Windows Explorer. Access the DATA folder (on drive D:).

5. Right-click the folder and select Properties. On the General tab, click the Advanced button at the bottom of the dialog box.

6. In the Advanced Attributes dialog box, verify that the option "For fast searching, allow Indexing Service to index this folder" is enabled. Then click the OK button.

7. Click the OK button to close the folder Properties dialog box.

Managing Network Access

Sharing is the process of allowing network users to access a folder located on a Windows 2000 Professional computer. A network share provides a single location to manage shared data used by many users. Sharing also allows an administrator to install an application once, as opposed to installing it locally at each computer, and to manage the application from a single location.

**Microsoft
Exam
Objective**

Manage and troubleshoot access to shared folders.

- Create and remove shared folders.
- Control access to shared folders by using permissions.

This chapter covers material related to managing shared folders, for the objective "Manage and troubleshoot access to shared folders." Managing Web server resources, a third subobjective for this objective, is covered in Chapter 13, "Dial-Up Networking and Internet Connectivity."

The following sections describe how to create and manage *shared folders*, configure *share permissions*, and provide access to shared resources.

Creating Shared Folders

To share a folder, you must be logged on as a member of the Administrators or Power Users group. You enable and configure sharing through the Sharing tab of the folder Properties dialog box, as shown in Figure 10.21.

FIGURE 10.21   The Sharing tab of the folder Properties dialog box

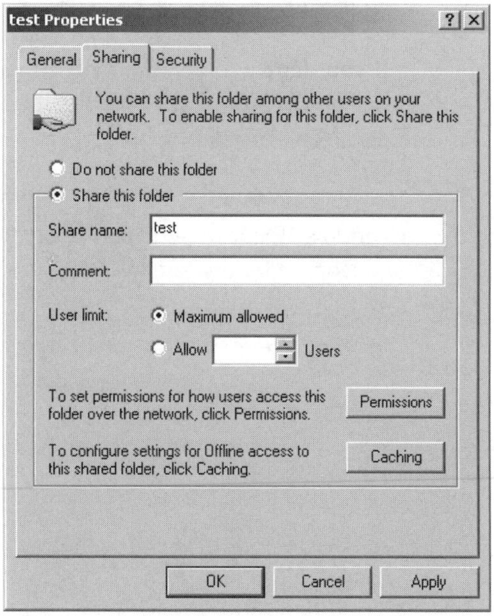

When you share a folder, you can configure the options listed in Table 10.2.

TABLE 10.2 Share Folder Options

Option	Description
Do Not Share This Folder	This folder is only available through local access
Share This Folder	This folder is available through local access and network access
Share Name	A descriptive name by which users will access the folder
Comment	Additional descriptive information about the share (optional)
User Limit	The maximum number of connections to the share at any one time (default is to allow up to 10 users access to a share on a Windows 2000 Professional computer)
Permissions	How users will access the folder over the network
Caching	How folders are cached when the folder is offline

If you share a folder and then decide that you do not want to share it, just select the Do Not Share This Folder radio button in the Sharing tab of the folder Properties dialog box.

In Windows Explorer, you can easily tell that a folder has been shared by the hand icon under the folder.

In Exercise 10.5, you will create a shared folder.

EXERCISE 10.5

Creating a Shared Folder

1. Select Start ➤ Programs ➤ Accessories ➤ Windows Explorer. Expand My Computer, then expand Local Disk (D:).

2. Select File ➤ New ➤ Folder and name the new folder **Share Me**.

3. Right-click the Share Me folder, select Properties, and click the Sharing tab.

4. In the Sharing tab of the folder Properties dialog box, click the Share This Folder radio button.

5. Type **Test Shared Folder** in the Share Name text box.

6. Type **This is a comment for a shared folder** in the Comment text box.

7. Under User Limit, click the Allow radio button and specify 5 users.

8. Click the OK button to close the dialog box.

Configuring Share Permissions

You can control users' access to shared folders by assigning share permissions. Share permissions are less complex than NTFS permissions and can be applied only to folders (unlike NTFS permissions, which can be applied to folders and files).

To assign share permissions, click the Permissions button in the Sharing tab of the folder Properties dialog box. This brings up the Share Permissions dialog box, as shown in Figure 10.22.

FIGURE 10.22 The Share Permissions dialog box

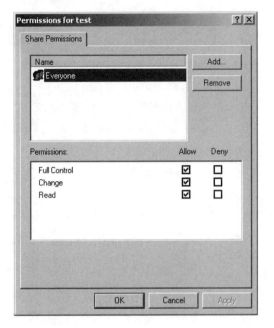

You can assign three types of share permissions:

- The Full Control share permission allows full access to the shared folder.

- The Change share permission allows users to change data within a file or to delete files.

- The Read share permission allows a user to view and execute files in the shared folder.

Full Control is the default permission on shared folders for the Everyone group.

 Shared folders do not use the same concept of inheritance as NTFS folders. If you share a folder, there is no way to block access to lower-level resources through share permissions.

In Exercise 10.6, you will apply share permissions to a folder. This exercise assumes that you have completed Exercises 10.3 and 10.5.

EXERCISE 10.6

Applying Share Permissions

1. Select Start ➢ Programs ➢ Accessories ➢ Windows Explorer. Expand My Computer, then expand Local Disk (D:).

2. Right-click the Share Me folder, select Sharing, and click the Permissions button.

3. In the Share Permissions dialog box, highlight the Everyone group and click the Remove button. Then click the Add button.

4. In the Select Users, Computers, and Groups dialog box, select users Dan and Marilyn, click the Add button, and then click the OK button.

5. Click user Marilyn and check the Allow box for the Full Control permission.

6. Click user Dan and check the Allow box for the Read permission.

7. Click the OK button to close the dialog box.

Managing Shares with the Shared Folders Utility

Shared Folders is a Computer Management utility for creating and managing shared folders on the computer. The Shared Folders window displays all of the shares that have been created on the computer, the user sessions that are open on each share, and the files that are currently open, listed by user.

To access Shared Folders, right-click My Computer on the Desktop and select Manage from the pop-up menu. In Computer Management, expand System Tools and then expand Shared Folders.

You can add the Shared Folders utility as an MMC snap-in. See Chapter 4, "Configuring the Windows 2000 Environment," for information about adding snap-ins to the MMC.

Viewing Shares

When you select Shares in the Shared Folders utility, you see all of the shares that have been configured on the computer. Figure 10.23 shows an example of a Shares listing.

FIGURE 10.23 The Shares listing in the Shared Folders window

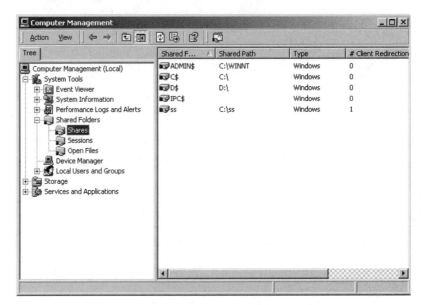

Along with the shares that you have specifically configured, you will also see the Windows 2000 special shares, which are created by the system automatically to facilitate system administration. A share that is followed by a dollar sign ($) indicates that the share is hidden from view when users access utilities such as My Network Places and browse network resources. The following special shares may appear on your Windows 2000 Professional computer, depending on how the computer is configured:

- The *drive_letter*$ share is the share for the root of the drive. By default, the root of every drive is shared. For example, the C: drive is shared as C$.

On Windows 2000 Professional computers and Windows 2000 member servers, only members of the Administrators and Backup Operators group can access the *drive_letter*$ share. On Windows 2000 domain controllers, members of the Administrators, Backup Operators, and Server Operators group can access this share.

- The ADMIN$ share points to the Windows 2000 system root (for example, C:\WINNT).

- The IPC$ share allows remote administration of a computer and is used to view a computer's shared resources. (IPC stands for interprocess communication.)

- The PRINT$ share is used for remote printer administration.

- The FAX$ share is used by fax clients to cache fax cover sheets and documents that are in the process of being faxed.

 Real World Scenario

Managing Remote Computers

Within your organization, you are responsible for managing hundreds of Windows 2000 computers. All of them are installed into Windows 2000 domains. At present, when users have problems accessing a local resource or want to create a share on their computer, an administrator is sent to the local computer. You want to be able to support remote management from a central location, but without adding remote management software to your network.

You can easily access remote computers' local drives through the hidden shares. For example, assume that user Peter has a computer called WS1. When this computer was added to the domain, the Domain Admins group was automatically added to the Administrators group on WS1. Currently no shares have been manually created on Peter's computer, and he wants to create a share on his C:\Test folder. Peter can't share his own folder because he does not have enough rights.

As a member of the Administrators group, you can remotely access Peter's C: drive through the following command: NET USE *x*: \\WS1\C$. Once you've accessed the network drive, you can access the Test folder and create the share remotely. This connection would also allow you to manipulate NTFS permissions on remote computers.

Creating New Shares

In Shared Folders, you can create new shares through the following steps:

1. Right-click the Shares folder and select New File Share from the pop-up menu.

2. The Create Shared Folder Wizard starts, as shown in Figure 10.24. Specify the folder that will be shared (you can use the Browse button to select the folder) and provide a share name and description. Click the Next button.

FIGURE 10.24 The Create Shared Folder Wizard dialog box

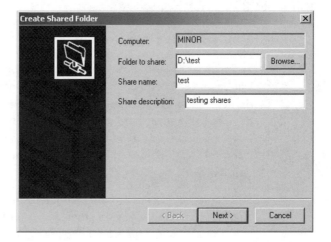

3. The Create Shared Folder Wizard dialog box for assigning share permissions appears next (Figure 10.25). You can select from one of the predefined permissions assignments or you can customize the share permissions. After you specify the permissions that will be assigned, click the Finish button.

FIGURE 10.25   Assigning share permissions

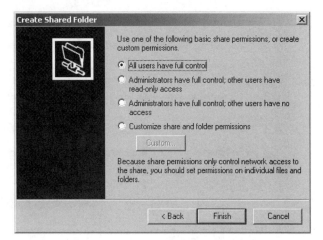

> **4.** The Create Shared Folder dialog box (Figure 10.26) appears, to verify that the folder has been shared successfully. Click the Yes button to create another shared folder, or the No button if you are finished creating shared folders.

FIGURE 10.26   Verifying shared folder creation

> You can stop sharing a folder by right-clicking the share and selecting Stop Sharing from the pop-up menu. You will be asked to confirm that you want to stop sharing the folder.

Viewing Share Sessions

> When you select Sessions in the Shared Folders utility, you see all the users who are currently accessing shared folders on the computer. Figure 10.27 shows an example. The Sessions listing includes the following information:
>
> - The username that has connected to the share
>
> - The computer name from which the user has connected

- The client operating system that is used by the connecting computer

- The number of files that the user has open

- The amount of time for which the user has been connected

- The amount of idle time for the connection

- Whether or not the user has connected through Guest access

FIGURE 10.27 The Sessions listing in the Shared Folders window

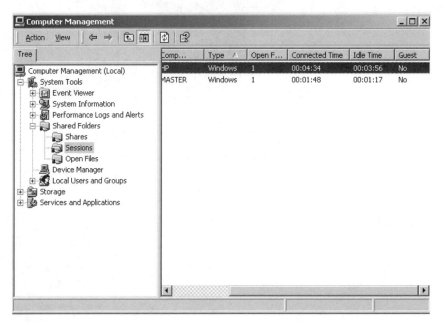

Viewing Open Files in Shared Folders

When you select Open Files in the Shared Folders utility, you see all the files that are currently open from shared folders. Figure 10.28 shows an example. The Open Files listing includes the following information:

- The path and files that are currently open

- The username that is accessing the file

- The operating system of the user who is accessing the file

- Whether or not any file locks have been applied (file locks are used to prevent two users from opening the same file and editing it at the same time)

- The open mode that is being used (such as read or write)

FIGURE 10.28   The Open Files listing in the Shared Folders window

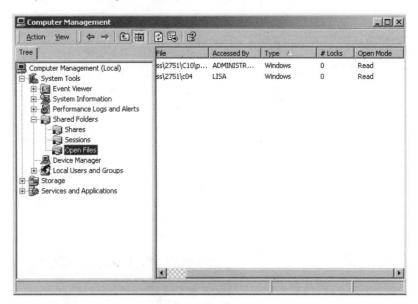

Providing Access to Shared Resources

There are many ways in which a user can access a shared resource. Here, we will look at three common methods:

- Through My Network Places

- By mapping a network drive in Windows Explorer

- Through the NET USE command-line utility

Microsoft
✓ *Exam*
Objective

Connect to shared resources on a Microsoft network.

Accessing a Shared Resource through My Network Places

The advantage of mapping a network location through *My Network Places* is that you do not use a drive letter. This is useful if you have already exceeded the limit of 26 drive letters.

To access a shared resource through My Network Places, take the following steps:

1. Double-click the My Network Places icon on the Desktop.

2. Double-click Add Network Place.

3. The Add Network Place Wizard starts, as shown in Figure 10.29. Type in the location of the Network Place. This can be a UNC path to a shared network folder, an HTTP path to a Web folder, or an FTP path to an FTP site. If you are unsure of the path, you can use the Browse button to search for it. After specifying the path, click the Next button.

4. Enter the name that you want to use for the network location. This name will appear in the computer's My Network Places listing.

FIGURE 10.29 The Add Network Place Wizard dialog box

Network Places are unique for each user and are part of the user's profile. User profiles are covered in Chapter 8, "Using User Profiles and Hardware Profiles."

Mapping a Network Drive through Windows Explorer

Through Windows Explorer, you can map a network drive to a drive letter that appears to the user as a local connection on their computer. Once you create a *mapped drive*, it can be accessed through a drive letter using My Computer.

Here are the steps to map a network drive:

1. Select Start ➤ Programs ➤ Accessories ➤ Windows Explorer to open Windows Explorer.

2. Select Tools ➤ Map Network Drive.

3. The Map Network Drive dialog box appears, as shown in Figure 10.30. Choose the drive letter that will be associated with the network drive.

FIGURE 10.30 Mapping the network drive

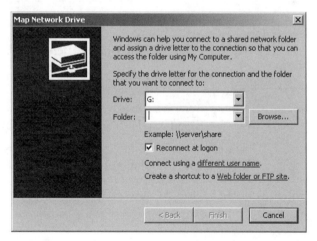

4. From the Folder drop-down list, choose the shared network folder to which you will map the drive.

5. If you want this connection to be persistent (the connection will be saved and used every time you log on), make sure that the Reconnect at Logon check box is checked.

6. If you will be connecting to the share using a different username, click the underlined part of Connect Using a Different User Name. This brings up the Connect As dialog box, shown in Figure 10.31. Fill in the User Name and Password text boxes, then click OK.

7. If you want to create a shortcut to a Web folder, click the underlined part of Create a Shortcut to a Web Folder or FTP Site. This starts the Add Network Place Wizard, which was described in the preceding section.

FIGURE 10.31 The Connect As dialog box

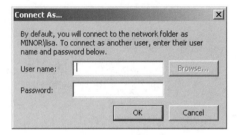

Using the *NET USE* Command-Line Utility

The *NET USE* command-line utility provides a quick and easy way to map a network drive. This command has the following syntax:

```
NET USE x: \\computername\sharename
```

For example, the following command maps drive G: to a share called AppData on a computer named AppServer:

```
NET USE G: \\AppServer\AppData
```

You can get more information about the NET USE command by typing **NET USE /?** from a command prompt.

In Exercise 10.7, you will access shared resources through My Network Places and map a drive in Windows Explorer. This exercise assumes that you have completed Exercise 10.6.

EXERCISE 10.7

Accessing Network Resources

1. Log on as user Marilyn. Double-click the My Network Places icon on the Desktop.

2. Double-click Add Network Place. When the Add Network Place Wizard starts, click the Browse button.

3. Select the workgroup or domain in which your computer is installed. Click your computer name. Select Test Shared Folder and click the OK button. Click the Next button.

4. The Location of Network Place dialog box will appear. Confirm that the path of the share is correct. Click the Next button.

5. Accept the default name for the Network Place. This is the name that will be displayed when you click My Network Places. Click the Finish Button.

6. The folder opens automatically. Close the folder. You will see the new folder in My Network Places.

7. Log off as Marilyn and log on as Dan.

8. Double-click My Network Places. You will not see the Network Place that you created as user Marilyn.

9. Open Windows Explorer and select Tools ➤ Map Network Drive.

10. In the Map Network Drives dialog box, accept the default drive letter and click the Browse button to select the folder. Select the workgroup or domain in which your computer is installed. Click your computer name. Select Test Shared Folder and click the Finish button.

The Flow of Resource Access

Understanding the resource-flow process will help you to trouble-shoot access problems. As you've learned, a user account must have appropriate permissions to access a resource. Resource access is determined through the following steps:

1. At logon, an *access token* is created for the logon account.

2. When a resource is accessed, Windows 2000 Professional checks the *access control list (ACL)* to see if the user should be granted access.

3. If the user is on the list, the ACL checks the *access control entries (ACEs)* to see what type of access the user should be given.

Access tokens, ACLs, and ACEs are covered in the following sections.

Access Token Creation

Each time a user account logs on, an access token is created. The access token contains the *security identifier (SID)* of the currently logged on user. It also contains the SIDs for any groups with which the user is associated. Once an access token is created, it is not updated until the next logon.

Let's assume that user Kevin needs to access the Sales database and that SALESDB is the name of the shared folder that contains the database. Kevin logs on, but he is not able to access the database. You do some detective work and find that Kevin has not been added to the Sales group, which is necessary in order for anyone to have proper access to SALESDB. You add Kevin to the Sales group and let him know that everything is working. Kevin tries again to access SALESDB but is still unable to do so. He logs off and logs on again, and after that he can access the database. This occurs because Kevin's access token is not updated to reflect his new group membership until he logs off and logs back on. When he logs on, a new access token is created, identifying Kevin as a member of the Sales group.

Access tokens are only updated during the logon sequence. They are not updated on-the-fly. So if you add a user to a group, that user needs to log off and log on again in order to have their access token updated.

ACLs and ACEs

Each object in Windows 2000 Professional has an access control list (ACL). An *object* is defined as a set of data that can be used by the system, or a set of actions that can be used to manipulate system data. Examples of objects include folders, files, network shares, and printers. The ACL is a list of user accounts and groups that are allowed to access the resource. Figure 10.32 shows how ACLs are associated with each object.

FIGURE 10.32 Access control lists (ACLs) for network shares

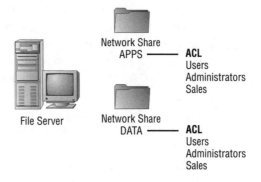

For each ACL, there is an access control entry (ACE) that defines what a user or a group can actually do at the resource. Deny permissions are always listed first. This means that if users have Deny permissions through user or group membership, they will not be allowed to access the object, even if they have explicit Allow permissions through other user or group permissions. Figure 10.33 illustrates the interaction between the ACL and the ACE.

FIGURE 10.33 Access control entries (ACEs) associated with an ACL

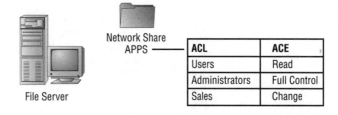

Local and Network Resource Access

Local and network security work together. The most restrictive access will determine what a user can do. For example, if the local folder is NTFS and the default permissions have not been changed, the Everyone group has the Full Control permission. On the other hand, if that local folder is shared and the permissions are set so that only the Sales group had been assigned the Read permission, then only the Sales group can access that shared folder.

Conversely, if the local NTFS permissions allow only the Managers group the Read permission to a local folder, and that folder has been shared with default permissions allowing the Everyone group Full Control permission, only the Managers group can access the folder with Read permissions. This is because Read is the more restrictive permission.

For example, suppose that you have set up the NTFS and share permissions for the DATA folder as shown in Figure 10.34. Jose is a member of the Sales group and wants to access the DATA folder. If he accesses the folder locally, he will be governed by only the NTFS security, so he will have the Modify permission. However, if Jose accesses the folder from another workstation through the network share, he also will be governed by the more restrictive share permission, Read.

As another example, suppose that Chandler is a member of the Everyone group. He wants to access the DATA folder. If he accesses the folder locally, he will have Read permission. If he accesses the folder remotely via the network share, he will still have Read permission. Even though the share permission allows the Everyone group the Change permission to the folder, the more restrictive permission (in this case, the NTFS permission Read) will be applied.

FIGURE 10.34 Local and network security govern access

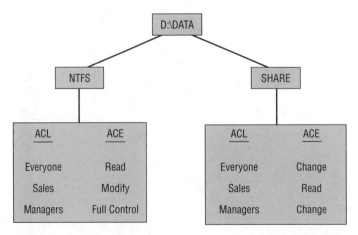

Summary

In this chapter, you learned about managing access to files and folders. We covered the following topics:

- Basic file management, which includes organizing files and folders, creating files and folders, managing folder options, and searching for files and folders

- Local access management, which includes assigning NTFS permissions and optimizing local access

- Network access management, which includes creating shared folders, assigning share permissions, and accessing network resources

- How resources are accessed when local NTFS permissions and network share permissions have been applied

- The flow of resource access, which includes creation of access tokens and controlling access to objects by checking the ACL and ACEs

Exam Essentials

Use offline folders.   Know what offline folders are and how they are used. Be able to configure network folders and Windows 2000 computers to use offline folders.

Be able to manage folder and file properties.   Understand what's needed to manage and configure files and folder properties, including setting overall folder options.

Be able to set folder and file security locally and for network shares. Understand NTFS and share permissions and know how to apply permissions. You should also understand how the permissions work together and be able to troubleshoot permission problems. Also, know how to access network shares via Windows 2000 utilities.

Key Terms

Before you take the exam, be sure you're familiar with the following key terms:

access control list (ACL)	My Network Places
access control entry (ACE)	NET USE
access token	NTFS permissions
effective rights	offline files and folders
Indexing Service	share permissions
inherited permissions	shared folders
mapped drive	

Review Questions

1. Within your company, all users have Windows 2000 Professional laptop computers. The standard configuration is to use NTFS permissions because many users have confidential corporate information on their computers. You want each user to be able to manage the permissions of their computer. Which of the following options would by default allow a user to manage NTFS permissions on NTFS folders? (Choose all that apply.)

    A. Administrators

    B. Power Users

    C. Any user with the Manage NTFS permission

    D. Any user with the Full Control NTFS permission

2. Sam is a member of the Sales group that has Full Control for the Sales share. Sam also has individual permissions to the Sales share set to Read. However, when Sam tries to access the Sales share, he is denied access. Which of the following options would most likely solve Sam's problem?

    A. You should delete Sam's individual permissions.

    B. You should make sure that Sam is not a member of any groups that explicitly have deny permissions.

    C. You should give Sam specific Full Control permission.

    D. You should delete the Sales group's permissions and reapply them.

3. Mary Jane wants to share folders on her Windows 2000 Professional computer. When she tries to create a share, she sees the following Properties dialog box. Which of the following options would allow Mary Jane to see the Sharing tab of this dialog box, containing options to create a share? (Choose all that apply.)

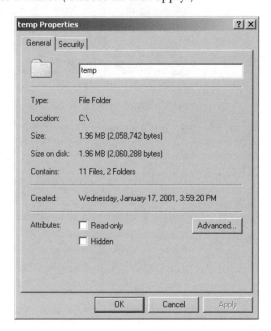

A. Make her a member of the Administrators group.

B. Make her a member of the Power Users group.

C. Assign her Manage NTFS permission to the folders she wants to share.

D. Assign her Full Control NTFS permission to the folders she wants to share.

4. You have just installed Windows 2000 Professional on the Accounting Manager's computer. His C: drive and D: drive have been formatted with NTFS because of his need for robust security. What is the NTFS permission that is applied by default to his computer?

   A. No permissions are assigned

   B. Read

   C. Read & Execute

   D. Full Control

5. Each user within your company uses Windows 2000 Professional and Windows 98 on laptop computers. Many of the users work partly at home or offsite and only occasionally come into the office. These users need a convenient way to manage their folders so that when they are online, their folders are automatically synchronized with the network. You decide to use offline folders. Which of the following options best describes which shares can be used for offline files and folders?

   A. You can use offline files and folders only from shares on Windows 2000 computers.

   B. You can use offline files and folders only from shares on Windows 2000 or Windows 98 clients.

   C. You can use offline files and folders from any share on a computer that uses the SMB protocol.

   D. You can use offline files and folders from any share that is local to your network.

6. You want to improve file access efficiency on your computer by using the Indexing Service. Which of the following statements is true regarding indexing files on Windows 2000 Professional computers?

   A. By default, the Indexing Service is started, and NTFS folders are configured to allow the Indexing Service to index this folder.

   B. By default, the Indexing Service is not started, and NTFS folders are not configured to allow the Indexing Service to index this folder.

   C. By default, the Indexing Service is started, and NTFS folders are not configured to allow the Indexing Service to index this folder.

   D. By default, the Indexing Service is not started, and NTFS folders are configured to allow the Indexing Service to index this folder.

7. Brad, one of your users, wants to be able to use command-line utilities to access shared network folders instead of using GUI utilities. Which command-line utility can be used to map to shared network folders?

   A. MAP

   B. NET SHARE

   C. NET USE

   D. NET ACCESS

8. You have several users who want to access network shared folders. They want to know how they can access the shares. Which of the following options can be used to access shared network folders from a Windows 2000 Professional computer? (Choose all that apply.)

   A. Network Neighborhood

   B. My Network Places

   C. Map a drive in Windows Explorer

   D. Control Panel, Network

9. You have decided to implement compressed folders and files on your D: drive. How can you easily tell which folders and files are compressed?

   A. The folders and files are displayed in an alternate color by default.

   B. Run the `showcomp` command to display folders and files in an alternate color.

   C. In Windows Explorer, access Folder Options, View tab and select the Display Compressed Files and Folders with an Alternate Color option.

   D. In Windows Explorer, access Tools, Advanced Options and select the Display Compressed Files and Folders with an Alternate Color option.

10. Your computer has local C:, D:, and E: drives. You want to see a list of all folders that have been shared on all three local drives. Which utility can you use to quickly see a list of all shares that have been configured on your Windows 2000 Professional computer?

   A. Windows Explorer

   B. Shared Folders

   C. Share Manager

   D. Disk Management

11. Tom needs to create a shared folder to share with other managers. He does not want this share to appear within any browse lists. Which option can he add to the end of the share name to prevent a shared folder from being displayed in users' browse lists?

   A. $

   B. %

   C. *

   D. #

12. Linda has a folder that she would like to share on the network. This folder contains the `salesdata.txt` file. She wants to allow only one user at a time to edit the file, so that one user can't overwrite another user's changes if they open the file at the same time. How should Linda configure this share?

A. She should set the user limit to allow one user.

B. She should configure the file attribute on the `salesdata.txt` file as unshared.

C. She should set a schedule so that users access the file at different times.

D. In Windows Explorer, she should configure the shared folder so that users are not allowed offline access to the folder.

13. You have shared a folder on the network called Customer Contacts. You want this folder to be available to users who are connected to the network, but you don't want the folder to be accessed by users who are offline. What option should you configure to prevent offline access?

A. Within Windows Explorer, set the NTFS permissions of the folder so that it can't be accessed offline.

B. Within Windows Explorer, configure the share properties of the folder so that cacheing of the files in the folder is not allowed.

C. Within Windows Explorer, set the folder's property options so that offline files are not allowed.

D. Within Windows Explorer, uncheck the box to Allow Offline Access in the Sharing properties of the folder that you don't want accessed.

14. Rick has configured his D:\TEST folder so that the Everyone group has Read access to the folder. What will the Everyone group's permissions be for D:\TEST\DATA by default?

A. No permissions

B. Full Control permissions

C. Read permissions

D. Full Access permissions

15. You have a network folder that is also on an NTFS partition. NTFS permissions and share permissions have been applied. Which of the following statements best describes how share permissions and NTFS permissions work together if they have been applied to the same folder?

A. The NTFS permissions will always take precedence.

B. The share permissions will always take precedence.

C. The most restrictive permission within all the share and NTFS permissions will take precedence.

D. The system will look at the cumulative share permissions and the cumulative NTFS permissions. Whichever set is more restrictive will be applied.

Answers to Review Questions

1. A, D. Only members of the Administrators group and users with Full Control NTFS permissions can manage NTFS permissions on NTFS folders. Members of the Power Users group do not have any special access to NTFS folders. There is no "Manage NTFS" permission.

2. B. If a user has been denied permissions through any group membership or user assignment, then it doesn't matter what permissions they are allowed because deny permissions supersede allow permissions.

3. A, B. Only members of the Administrators and Power Users groups can create network shares.

4. D. By default, the Everyone group is assigned Full Control permission for NTFS volumes.

5. C. You can use offline files and folders from any share on a computer that uses the SMB protocol, which is essentially any Microsoft computer with a share.

6. D. By default, the Indexing Service is not started on Windows 2000 Professional computers. However, NTFS folders are configured to allow the Indexing Service to index this folder.

7. C. The NET USE command is used to map shared network folders.

8. B, C. You can access network shares through My Network Places or by mapping a drive in Windows Explorer. Network Neighborhood was in Windows NT 4, and is not in Windows 2000. The Network icon in Control Panel is used to configure network settings, not map network drives.

9. C. In Windows Explorer, you can set the options for viewing folders and files through the View tab of the Folder Options dialog box. This tab includes the Display Compressed Files and Folders with an Alternate Color option.

10. B. The quickest way to see all of the folders that have been shared on a Windows 2000 Professional computer is to open the Shared Folders utility and select the Shares folder.

11. A. If you do not want a folder to be displayed in users' browse lists, you can hide the share by placing a $ at the end of the share name.

12. A. When you configure a share, you can specify a user limit. The Sharing tab of the folder Properties dialog box includes a User Limit option, which you can set to limit access to the folder to one user at a time.

13. B. When you create a share in Windows 2000 Professional, you see a Caching button in the share's Properties dialog box. If you click this button, you can specify that caching of the files in the folder is not allowed. This option is specifically for offline folders and files.

14. C. In Windows 2000 Professional, the default is for the permissions to be inherited by subfolders. This is different from the default in Windows NT 4, where files in a folder inherit permissions from the parent folder, but subfolders do not inherit parent permissions.

15. D. When both NTFS and share permissions have been applied, the system looks at the effective rights for NTFS and share permissions and then applies the most restrictive of the cumulative permissions.

Chapter

11

Managing Network Connections

MICROSOFT EXAM OBJECTIVES COVERED IN THIS CHAPTER:

✓ Install, configure, and troubleshoot network adapters.

✓ Configure and troubleshoot the TCP/IP protocol.

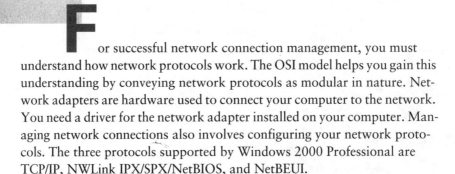

For successful network connection management, you must understand how network protocols work. The OSI model helps you gain this understanding by conveying network protocols as modular in nature. Network adapters are hardware used to connect your computer to the network. You need a driver for the network adapter installed on your computer. Managing network connections also involves configuring your network protocols. The three protocols supported by Windows 2000 Professional are TCP/IP, NWLink IPX/SPX/NetBIOS, and NetBEUI.

This chapter begins with an overview of network protocols, including a discussion of network data flow and the OSI model. Then you will learn how to install and configure network adapters and network protocols.

Reviewing Networking Protocols

Communications over a network are accomplished using networking protocols. To understand the purpose of networking protocols, you should have a basic knowledge of the *OSI (Open Systems Interconnect) model*. The OSI model is not an actual product. It is a theoretical model that describes how networks work. There are several advantages to using the OSI model as a framework for understanding network protocols:

- Breaking down a large concept, such as a network, makes it easier to understand.

- Modularizing network functions allows you to apply specific technologies or protocols at specific layers in a mix-and-match manner.

- Understanding how one network system works and applying it to the OSI model allows you to easily apply that knowledge to other operating systems.

We'll start by looking at an example of how data flows through a network. Then we'll examine how the seven layers of the OSI model work to move data through a network.

Network Data Flow

Figure 11.1 illustrates an example of how data flows from Computer A on one network segment to Computer B on a separate network segment. In this example, the following steps are involved in moving the data from Computer A to Computer B:

1. Starting at Computer A, you create a message (file) using some type of program that offers file services. In this example, the message says "Hello."

2. The computer doesn't understand the characters in "Hello," but it does understand ones and zeros. The message must be translated into ones and zeros through a protocol such as ASCII.

3. At the higher levels of communication, a connection (or session) is established. The connection determines when requests are made so that appropriate responses can be made. Just like human conversations, computer communications are usually a series of requests and responses that must be answered sequentially.

4. Next you must determine if you want the connection to be reliable, called a *connection-oriented service*, or if you want the connection to use less overhead and assume that the connection is reliable, called a *connectionless service*.

5. Because Computer A and Computer B are on separate network segments, you must figure out how to route the message across an internetwork based on the best possible path available.

6. Once the message gets to the correct network segment, it must be delivered to the correct computer on the segment.

7. The message must travel over the physical connection that actually exists between Computer A and Computer B, which is at the lowest level of communication. The data moves through the cabling and network cards that connect the network. At this level, you are sending ones and zeros over the physical network.

FIGURE 11.1 Data flows from Computer A on one network segment to Computer B on another network segment.

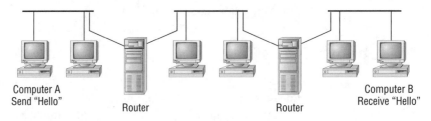

Computer A
Send "Hello"

Router

Router

Computer B
Receive "Hello"

The steps in this data-flow example correlate to the seven layers of the OSI model, discussed in the next section.

The OSI Model Layers

The seven layers of the OSI model are Application, Presentation, Session, Transport, Network, Data Link, and Physical. Each layer has a specific function in providing networking capabilities. Table 11.1 offers a couple of mnemonic phrases to help you remember the order of the layers.

TABLE 11.1 Mnemonics for the OSI Model Layers

Layer	Memory Trick (Read Top to Bottom)	Memory Trick (Read Bottom to Top)
Application	All	Albert
Presentation	People	Prince
Session	Seem	See
Transport	To	To
Network	Need	Need
Data Link	Data	Don't
Physical	Processing	People

The Application Layer

The *Application layer* is used to support the following services:

File services	Store, move, control access to, and retrieve files
Print services	Send data to local or network printers
Message services	Transfer text, graphics, audio, and video over a network
Application services	Process applications locally or through distributed processing
Database services	Allow a local computer to access network services for database storage and retrieval

In addition, the Application layer advertises any services that are being offered and determines whether requests made by the client should be processed locally or remotely (through another network resource).

The Presentation Layer

The *Presentation layer* is used for four main processes:

Character-code translation	Converting symbolic characters such as the letter *h* into ones and zeros, as in 01101000, which is the ASCII code equivalent
Data encryption	Coding data so that it is protected from unauthorized access
Data compression	Reducing the number of packets required for transport
Data expansion	Restoring compressed data to its original format at the receiver's end

The Session Layer

The *Session layer* is responsible for managing communication between a sender and a receiver. Following are some of the communication tasks performed at this layer:

- Establishing connections
- Maintaining connections
- Synchronizing communications

- Controlling dialogues

- Terminating connections

When you create a connection, you authenticate the user account at the sending and receiving computers. Connection creation also involves determining the type of communication that will take place and the protocols that will be used by the lower layers.

Data transfer and dialogue control are used to determine which computer is making requests and which computer is making responses. This also determines whether acknowledgments are required for data transmission.

The Transport Layer

The *Transport layer* is associated with reliable data delivery. With reliable delivery, the sender and receiver establish a connection, and the receiver acknowledges the receipt of data by sending acknowledgment packets to the sender.

Depending on the protocol used, you can send data through the Transport layer using a *connection-oriented service* or a *connectionless service*. A connection-oriented service is like a telephone conversation, where the connection is established and acknowledgments are sent. This type of communication has a high overhead. A connectionless service does not establish a connection and is similar to communicating through the mail. You assume that your letter will arrive, but the communication is not as reliable as a telephone conversation (a connection-oriented service).

The Network Layer

The primary responsibility of the *Network layer* is to move data over an *internetwork*. An internetwork is made up of multiple network segments that are connected with a device, such as a router. Each network segment is assigned a network address. Network layer protocols build routing tables that are used to route packets through the network in the most efficient manner.

The Data Link Layer

The *Data Link layer* is responsible for establishing and maintaining the communication channel, identifying computers on network segments by their physical address, and organizing data into a logical group called a frame. *Frames* are logical groupings of the bits from the Physical layer. Frames contain information about the destination physical address and the source physical address, as well as all the data that has been used at the upper layers of the OSI model.

There are two main sublayers at the Data Link layer: the *Logical Link Control (LLC) sublayer*, which defines flow control, and the *Media Access Control (MAC) sublayer*, which is used for physical addressing.

The communication channel that is established at the Data Link layer is a low-level channel that manages whether or not a communication channel exists. All higher-level communication is handled at the Session layer. Computers are identified by their physical address, which is called the *MAC address*. Ethernet and Token Ring cards have their MAC addresses assigned through a chip on the network card.

The Physical Layer

The details of sending ones and zeros across a cable are handled at the *Physical layer*. The Physical layer is responsible for determining the following information:

- The physical network structure you are using

- The mechanical and electrical specifications of the transmission media that will be used

- How the data will be encoded and transmitted

Installing and Configuring Network Adapters

*N*etwork adapters are hardware used to connect computers (or other devices) to the network. They function at the Physical and Data Link layers of the OSI model, as shown in Figure 11.2.

Microsoft Exam Objective	**Install, configure, and troubleshoot network adapters.**

FIGURE 11.2 Network adapters function at the Physical and Data Link layers of the OSI model.

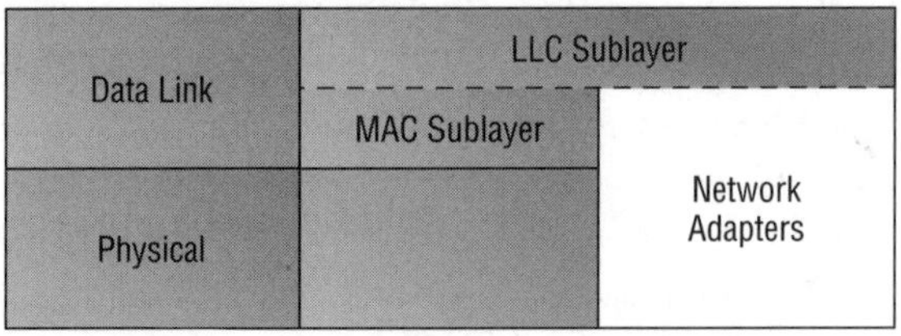

	LLC Sublayer	
Data Link	MAC Sublayer	Network Adapters
Physical		

Network adapters are responsible for providing the physical connection to the network and the physical address of the computer. These adapters (and all other hardware devices) need a *driver* in order to communicate with the Windows 2000 operating system.

In the following sections, you will learn how to install and configure network adapters, as well as how to troubleshoot network adapters that are not working.

Installing a Network Adapter

Before you physically install your network adapter, it's important to read the instructions that came with the hardware. If your network adapter is new, it should be self-configuring, with Plug and Play capabilities. After you install a network adapter that supports Plug and Play, it should work the next time you start up the computer.

New devices will auto-detect settings and be self-configuring. Older devices rely on hardware setup programs to configure hardware. Really old devices require you to manually configure the adapter through switches or jumpers.

When you install a network adapter that is not Plug and Play, the operating system should detect that you have a new piece of hardware and start a Wizard that leads you through the process of loading the adapter's driver. In Exercise 11.1, you will install a network adapter that is not Plug and Play.

EXERCISE 11.1

Installing a Network Adapter

1. If the Add/Remove Hardware Wizard doesn't start automatically, select Start ➢ Settings ➢ Control Panel ➢ Add/Remove Hardware.

2. The Welcome to the Add/Remove Hardware Wizard dialog box appears. Click the Next button to continue.

3. The Choose a Hardware Task dialog box appears. Select the Add/Troubleshoot a Device radio button and click the Next button.

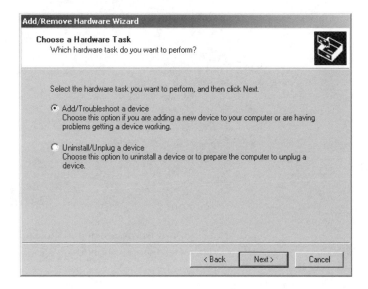

4. Windows 2000 runs the process to detect new hardware and then displays the Choose a Hardware Device dialog box. Choose the Add a New Device option, which is at the top of the Devices list box. Then click the Next button.

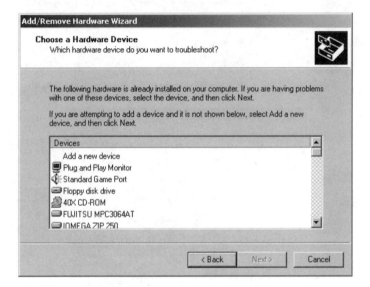

5. The Find New Hardware dialog box appears. Select the Yes, Search for New Hardware option to let Windows 2000 attempt to detect your hardware.

- If the operating system detects the new network adapter, click Next and then skip to step 9.

- If Windows 2000 cannot detect your hardware, select the No, I Want to Select the Hardware from a List radio button, click the Next button and continue with step 6.

EXERCISE 11.1 *(continued)*

6. The Hardware Type dialog box appears. In the Hardware Types list box, select Network Adapters. Then click the Next button.

7. The Select Network Adapter dialog box appears.

- If your manufacturer and network adapter model are listed in this dialog box, select them.

- If your manufacturer and model do not appear, click the Have Disk button and specify the location of the driver's distribution files.

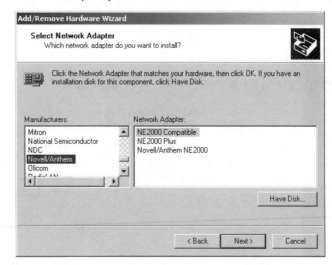

EXERCISE 11.1 *(continued)*

8. In the case that Windows 2000 cannot detect the settings of the device, you will see a warning message. At this point, you will need to refer to the manufacturer's documentation on how to set up the network card. After you configure your device, click the OK button.

9. The Start Hardware Installation dialog box appears. If the driver shown in this dialog box is correct, click the Next button.

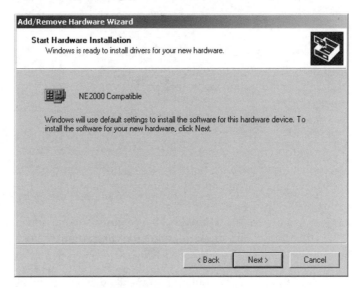

10. The Completing the Add/Remove Hardware Wizard dialog box appears. Click the Finish button.

Configuring a Network Adapter

Once the network adapter has been installed, you can configure it through its Properties dialog box. To access this dialog box, select Start ➢ Settings ➢ Control Panel ➢ Network and Dial-up Connections ➢ Local Area Connection ➢ Properties and click the Configure button. Alternatively, right-click My Network Places and choose Properties, then right-click Local Area Connection, choose Properties, and click the Configure button.

In the network adapter Properties dialog box, the properties are grouped on four tabs: General, Advanced, Driver, and Resources. These properties are explained in the following sections.

General Network Adapter Properties

The General tab of the network adapter Properties dialog box, shown in Figure 11.3, shows the name of the adapter, the device type, the manufacturer, and the location. The Device Status box reports whether or not the device is working properly. If the device is not working properly, you can click the Troubleshooter button to have Windows 2000 display some general troubleshooting tips. You can also enable or disable the device through the Device Usage drop-down list options.

FIGURE 11.3 The General tab of the network adapter Properties dialog box

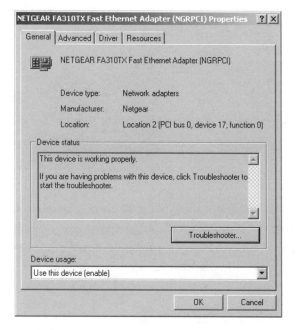

Advanced Network Adapter Properties

The contents of the Advanced tab of the network adapter Properties dialog box vary depending on the network adapter and driver that you are using.

Figure 11.4 shows an example of the Advanced tab for a Fast Ethernet adapter. To configure options in this dialog box, choose the property you want to modify in the Property list box on the left and specify the value for the property in the Value box on the right.

FIGURE 11.4 The Advanced tab of the network adapter Properties dialog box

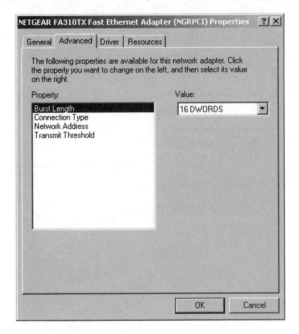

 You should not need to change the settings on the Advanced tab of the network adapter Properties dialog box unless you have been instructed to do so by the manufacturer.

Driver Properties

The Driver tab of the network adapter Properties dialog box, shown in Figure 11.5, provides the following information about your driver:

- The driver provider, which is usually Microsoft or the network adapter manufacturer

- The date that the driver was released

- The driver version, which is useful in determining if you have the latest driver installed

- The digital signer, which is the company that provides the digital signature for driver signing (Driver signing is covered in Chapter 4, "Configuring the Windows 2000 Environment.")

FIGURE 11.5   The Driver tab of the network adapter Properties dialog box

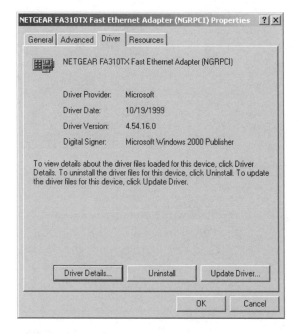

Clicking the Driver Details button at the bottom of the Driver tab brings up the Driver File Details dialog box, as shown in Figure 11.6. This dialog box lists the following details about the driver:

- The location of the driver file, which is useful for troubleshooting

- The original provider of the driver, which is usually the manufacturer

- The file version, which is useful for troubleshooting

- Copyright information about the driver

FIGURE 11.6 The Driver File Details dialog box

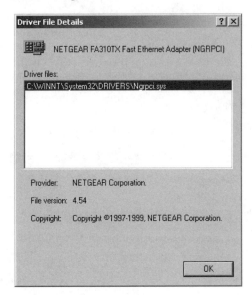

The Uninstall button at the bottom of the Driver tab removes the driver from your computer. You would uninstall the driver if you were going to replace it with a completely new one. Normally, you update the driver rather than uninstalling it.

To update a driver, click the Update Driver button at the bottom of the Driver tab. This starts the Upgrade Device Driver Wizard, which steps you through upgrading the driver for an existing device.

If you cannot find the driver for your network card or the configuration instructions, check the vendor's Web site. Usually, you will be able to find the latest drivers. You also should be able to locate a list of Frequently Asked Questions (FAQs) about your hardware.

Resource Properties

Each device installed on a computer uses computer resources. Resources include interrupt request (IRQ), memory, and I/O (input/output) settings. The Resources tab of the network adapter Properties dialog box lists the resource settings for your network adapter, as shown in Figure 11.7. This information is important for troubleshooting, because if other devices are trying to use the same resource settings, your devices will not work properly. The Conflicting Device List box at the bottom of the Resources tab shows whether any conflicts exist.

FIGURE 11.7 The Resources tab of the network adapter Properties dialog box

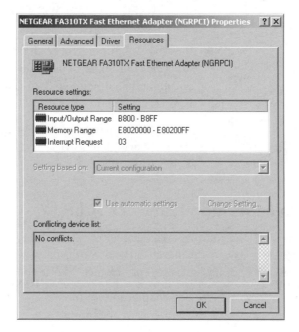

In Exercise 11.2, you will view the properties of your network adapter. This exercise assumes that you have a network adapter installed in your computer.

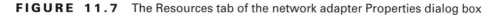

EXERCISE 11.2

Viewing Network Adapter Properties

1. Select Start ➢ Settings ➢ Control Panel ➢ Network and Dial-up Connections ➢ Local Area Connection ➢ Properties and click the Configure button.

2. In the General tab of the connection Properties dialog box, click the Configure button under Connect Using.

EXERCISE 11.2 *(continued)*

3. In the General tab of the network adapter Properties dialog box, verify that the Device Status box shows "This device is working properly."

4. Click the Advanced tab. Note the properties that are available for your driver.

5. Click the Driver tab. Notice the driver date and version information. Click the Driver Details button to see the location of your network adapter's driver file. Click OK to close the Driver File Details dialog box.

6. Click the Resources tab. Note the resources that are being used by your network adapter. Verify that the Conflicting Device List box shows "No conflicts."

Troubleshooting Network Adapters

If your network adapter is not working, the problem may be with the hardware, the driver software, or the network protocols. The following are some common causes for network adapter problems:

Network adapter not on the HCL   If the device is not on the HCL, contact the adapter vendor for advice.

Outdated driver   Make sure that you have the most up-to-date driver for your adapter. You can check for the latest driver on your hardware vendor's Web site.

Network adapter not recognized by Windows 2000   Check Device Manager to see if Windows 2000 recognizes your device. If you do not see your adapter, you will have to manually install it (see "Installing a Network Adapter" earlier in the chapter). You should also verify that the adapter's resource settings do not conflict with the resource settings of other devices (check the Resources tab of the network adapter Properties dialog box).

Hardware that is not working properly   Verify that your hardware is working properly. Run any diagnostics that came with the adapter. If everything seems to work as it should, make sure that the cable is good and that all of the applicable network hardware is installed correctly and is working. This is where it pays off to have spare hardware (such as cables and extra network adapters) that you know works properly.

Improperly configured network protocols   Make sure that your network protocols have been configured properly. Network protocols are covered in detail in the next section of this chapter.

Improperly configured network card   Verify that all settings for the network card are correct.

Bad cable   Make sure that all network cables are good. This can be tricky if you connect to the network through a patch panel.

Bad network connection device   Verify that all network connectivity hardware is properly working. For example, on an Ethernet network, make sure the hub and port that you are using are functioning properly.

Check Event Viewer for any messages that give you a hint about what is causing a network adapter error. See Chapter 15, "Performing System Recovery Functions," for details on using Event Viewer.

 Real World Scenario

Are Ethernet Cards Properly Configured?

You are the network administrator of an Ethernet network. When you purchase Ethernet cards, they are special combo cards that support 10Mbps Ethernet and 100Mbps Ethernet. In addition, the cards have an RJ-45 connector for using unshielded twisted pair (UTP) cables, and a BNC connector for using coaxial cable. Your network is configured to use 100Mbps Ethernet over UTP cabling. Sometimes when you install the new Ethernet cards, they are not able to connect to the network.

A common problem is experienced with the combo Ethernet cards. Even when the hardware configuration for IRQ and base memory are correctly configured and you have the right driver, the correct configuration for speed and cable type may not be detected. Within an Ethernet network, all of the Ethernet cards must transmit at the same speed and be connected to a hub that supports the speed of the cards that you are using. The cards must also be configured to support the cable type that is being used. You can verify these settings through the network adapter's Properties dialog box.

If the configuration is correct and you still can't connect to the network, you should check your network cables. It is estimated that between 70 and 80 percent of all network problems are related to cabling.

Installing and Configuring Network Protocols

Network protocols function at the Network and Transport layers of the OSI model. They are responsible for transporting data across an internetwork. You can mix and match the network protocols you use with Windows 2000 Professional, which supports three protocols: TCP/IP, NWLink IPX/SPX/NetBIOS, and NetBEUI. The following sections describe how to install and configure these protocols.

Using TCP/IP

TCP/IP (Transmission Control Protocol/Internet Protocol) is one of the most commonly used network protocols. TCP/IP evolved during the 1970s. It was originally developed for the Department of Defense (DoD) as a way of connecting dissimilar networks. Since then, TCP/IP has become an industry standard.

Microsoft ✓ *Exam* *Objective*	**Configure and troubleshoot the TCP/IP protocol.**

On a clean installation of Windows 2000 Professional, TCP/IP is installed by default. TCP/IP has the following benefits:

- It is the most common protocol and is supported by almost all network operating systems. It is the required protocol for Internet access.

- TCP/IP is scalable for use in small and large networks. In large networks, TCP/IP provides routing services.

- TCP/IP is designed to be fault tolerant. It is able to dynamically reroute packets if network links become unavailable (assuming alternate paths exist).

- Protocol companions such as Dynamic Host Configuration Protocol (DHCP) and Domain Name System (DNS) offer advanced functionality.

In the next sections, you will learn the basics of using TCP/IP, and then how to configure and test TCP/IP.

Basic TCP/IP Configuration

TCP/IP requires an IP address and a subnet mask. You can also configure many other optional parameters, including the default gateway, DNS server settings, and WINS server settings.

IP Address

The *IP address* uniquely identifies your computer on the network. The IP address is a four-field, 32-bit address, separated by periods. Part of the address is used to identify your network address, and part is used to identify the host (or local) computer's address.

If you use the Internet, then you should register your IP addresses with one of the Internet registration sites. There are three main classes of IP addresses. Depending on the class you use, different parts of the address show the network portion of the address and the host address, as illustrated in Figure 11.8.

FIGURE 11.8 IP class network and host addresses

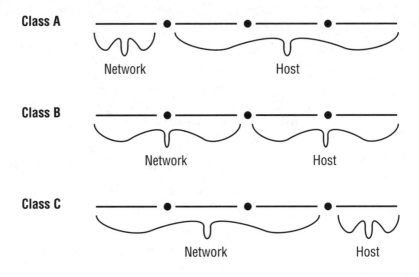

Class A

Network   Host

Class B

Network   Host

Class C

Network   Host

You can find more information about Internet registration at InterNIC's Web site, www.internic.net.

Table 11.2 shows the three classes of network addresses and the number of networks and hosts that are available for each network class.

TABLE 11.2 IP Class Assignments

Network Class	Address Range of First Field	Number of Networks Available	Number of Host Nodes Supported
A	1–126	126	16,777,214
B	128–191	16,384	65,534
C	192–223	2,097,152	254

Subnet Mask

The *subnet mask* is used to specify which part of the IP address is the network address and which part of the address is the host address. By default, the following subnet masks are applied:

Class A	255.0.0.0
Class B	255.255.0.0
Class C	255.255.255.0

By using 255, you are selecting the octet or octets (or, in some cases, the piece of an octet) used to identify the network address. For example, in the class B network address 191.200.2.1, if the subnet mask is 255.255.0.0, then 191.200 is the network address and 2.1 is the host address.

Default Gateway

You configure a *default gateway* if the network contains routers. A *router* is a device that connects two or more network segments together. Routers function at the Network layer of the OSI model.

You can configure a Windows 2000 server to act as a router by installing two or more network cards in the server, attaching each network card to a different network segment, and then configuring each network card for the segment to which it will attach. You can also use third-party routers, which typically offer more features than Windows 2000 servers configured as routers.

As an example, suppose that your network is configured as shown in Figure 11.9. Network A uses the IP network address 131.1.0.0. Network B uses the IP network address 131.2.0.0. In this case, each network card in the router should be configured with an IP address from the segment to which the network card is addressed.

You configure the computers on each segment to point to the IP address of the network card on the router that is attached to their network segment. For example, in Figure 11.9, the computer W2K1 is attached to Network A. The default gateway that would be configured for this computer is 131.1.0.10. The computer W2K2 is attached to Network B. The default gateway that would be configured for this computer is 131.2.0.10.

FIGURE 11.9 Configuring default gateways

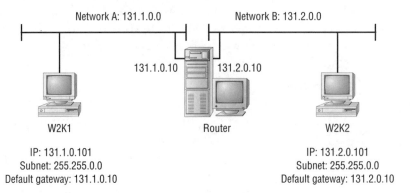

Advanced TCP/IP Configuration

Through TCP/IP, you can also configure advanced TCP/IP options, including

- Dynamic Host Configuration Protocol (DHCP)
- Domain Name System (DNS)
- Windows Internet Name Service (WINS)

Using DHCP

Each device that will use TCP/IP on your network must have a valid, unique IP address. This address can be manually configured or can be automated through DHCP. DHCP is implemented as a DHCP server and a DHCP client (Figure 11.10). The server is configured with a pool of IP addresses and their associated IP configurations. The client is configured to automatically access the DHCP server to obtain its IP configuration.

DHCP works in the following manner:

1. When the client computer starts up, it sends a broadcast DHCP-DISCOVER message, requesting a DHCP server. The request includes the hardware address of the client computer.

2. Any DHCP server receiving the broadcast that has available IP addresses will send a DHCPOFFER message to the client. This message offers an IP address for a set period of time (called a *lease*), a subnet mask, and a server identifier (the IP address of the DHCP server). The address that is offered by the server is marked as unavailable and will not be offered to any other clients during the DHCP negotiation period.

3. The client selects one of the offers and broadcasts a DHCPREQUEST message, indicating its selection. This allows any DHCP offers that were not accepted to be returned to the pool of available IP addresses.

4. The DHCP server that was selected sends back a DHCPACK message as an acknowledgment, indicating the IP address, subnet mask, and the duration of the lease that the client computer will use. It may also send additional configuration information, such as the address of the default gateway or the DNS server address.

FIGURE 11.10 The DHCP lease-generation process

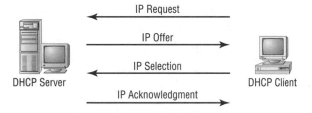

 If you want to use DHCP and there is no DHCP server on your network segment, you can use a DHCP server on another network segment—provided that the DHCP server is configured to support your network segment and a DHCP Relay Agent has been installed on your network router.

 If you are not able to access a DHCP server installed on a Windows 2000 Server within Active Directory, make sure that the DHCP server has been authorized. This is a new feature in Windows 2000.

DNS Servers

DNS servers are used to resolve host names to IP addresses. This makes it easier for people to access domain hosts. For example, do you know what the IP address is for the White House? It's 198.137.240.91. Do you know the domain host name of the White House? It's www.whitehouse.gov. You can understand why many people might not know the IP address but would know the domain host name.

When you access the Internet and type in www.whitehouse.gov, there are DNS servers that resolve the host name to the proper IP address. If you did not have access to a properly configured DNS server, you could configure a HOSTS file for your computer that contains the mappings of IP addresses to the domain hosts that you need to access.

WINS Servers

WINS servers are used to resolve NetBIOS names to IP addresses. Windows 2000 uses NetBIOS names in addition to host names to identify network computers. This is mainly for backward compatibility with Windows NT 4.0, which used this addressing scheme extensively. When you attempt to access a computer using the NetBIOS name, the computer must be able to resolve the NetBIOS name to an IP address. This address resolution can be accomplished by using one of the following methods:

- Through a broadcast (if the computer you are trying to reach is on the same network segment)

- Through a WINS server

- Through an LMHOSTS file, which is a static mapping of IP addresses to NetBIOS computer names

Configuring TCP/IP

Depending on your network setup, TCP/IP configuration is done either manually or dynamically. You can also use advanced TCP/IP options to configure DNS and WINS settings.

Manual IP Configuration

You can manually configure IP if you know your IP address and subnet mask. If you are using optional components such as a default gateway or a DNS server, you need to know the IP addresses of the computers that host these services as well.

In Exercise 11.3, you will manually configure IP. This exercise assumes that you have a network adapter installed in your computer. If you are on a "live" network, check with your network administrator before you make any changes to your IP configuration.

EXERCISE 11.3

Manually Configuring IP

1. From the Desktop, right-click My Network Places and choose Properties.

2. Right-click Local Area Connection and choose Properties.

3. In the Local Area Connection Properties dialog box, highlight Internet Protocol (TCP/IP) and click the Properties button.

4. The Internet Protocol (TCP/IP) Properties dialog box appears. Choose the Use the Following IP Address radio button.

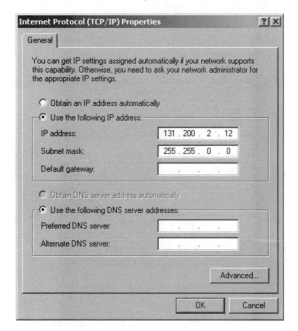

5. In the appropriate text boxes, specify the IP address 131.200.1.1 and subnet mask of 255.255.0.0. Do not specify the default gateway option.

6. Click the OK button to save your settings and close the dialog box.

Advanced Configuration

Clicking the Advanced button in the Internet Protocol (TCP/IP) dialog box opens the Advanced TCP/IP Settings dialog box, shown in Figure 11.11. In this dialog box, you can configure advanced DNS and WINS settings.

FIGURE 11.11 The Advanced TCP/IP Settings dialog box

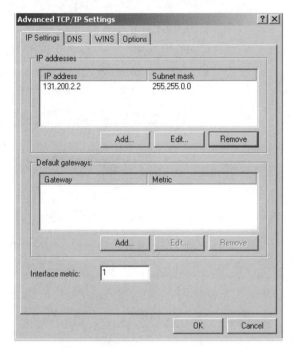

ADVANCED DNS SETTINGS

You can configure additional DNS servers to be used for name resolution and other advanced DNS settings through the DNS tab of the Advanced TCP/IP Settings dialog box, shown in Figure 11.12. The options in this dialog box are described in Table 11.3.

FIGURE 11.12 The DNS tab of the Advanced TCP/IP Settings dialog box

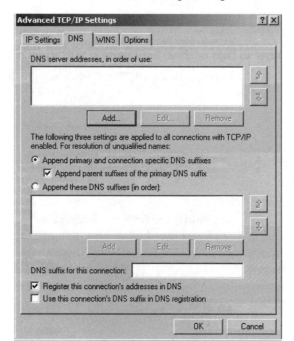

TABLE 11.3 Advanced DNS TCP/IP Settings Options

Option	Description
DNS server addresses, in order of use	Specifies the DNS servers that are used to resolve DNS queries. Use the arrow buttons on the right side of the list box to move a server up or down in the list.
Append primary and connection-specific DNS suffixes	Specifies how unqualified domain names are resolved by DNS. For example, if your primary DNS suffix is TestCorp.com and you type ping lala, DNS will try to resolve the address as lala.TestCorp.com.

TABLE 11.3   Advanced DNS TCP/IP Settings Options *(continued)*

Option	Description
Append parent suffixes of the primary DNS suffix	Specifies whether name resolution includes the parent suffix for the primary domain DNS suffix, up to the second level of the domain name. For example, if your primary DNS suffix is `SanJose.TestCorp.com` and you type `ping lala`, DNS will try to resolve the address as `lala.SanJose.TestCorp.com`. If this doesn't work, DNS will try to resolve the address as `lala.TestCorp.com`.
Append these DNS suffixes (in order)	Specifies the DNS suffixes that will be used to attempt to resolve unqualified name resolution. For example, if your primary DNS suffix is `TestCorp.com` and you type `ping lala`, DNS will try to resolve the address as `lala.TestCorp.com`. If you append the additional DNS suffix `MyCorp.com` and type `ping lala`, DNS will try to resolve the address as `lala.TestCorp.com` and `lala.MyCorp.com`.
DNS suffix for this connection	Specifies the DNS suffix for the computer. If this value is configured by a DHCP server and you specify a DNS suffix, it will override the value set by DHCP.
Register this connection's address in DNS	Specifies that the connection will try to register its address dynamically using the computer name that was specified through the Network Identification tab of the System Properties dialog box (accessed through the System icon in Control Panel).
Use this connection's DNS suffix in DNS registration	Specifies that when the computer registers automatically with the DNS server, it should use the combination of the computer name and the DNS suffix.

ADVANCED WINS SETTINGS

You can configure advanced WINS options through the WINS tab of the Advanced TCP/IP Settings dialog box, shown in Figure 11.13. The options in this dialog box are described in Table 11.4.

FIGURE 11.13 The WINS tab of the Advanced TCP/IP Settings dialog box

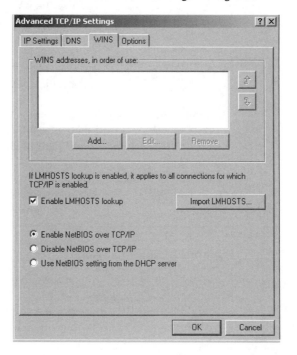

TABLE 11.4 Advanced WINS TCP/IP Settings Options

Option	Description
WINS addresses, in order of use	Specifies the WINS servers that are used to resolve WINS queries. You can use the arrow buttons on the right side of the list box to move a server up or down in the list.

TABLE 11.4 Advanced WINS TCP/IP Settings Options *(continued)*

Option	Description
Enable LMHOSTS lookup	Specifies whether an LMHOSTS file can be used for name resolution. If you configure this option, you can use the Import LMHOSTS button to import an LMHOSTS file to the computer.
Enable NetBIOS over TCP/IP	Allows you to use statically configured IP addresses so that the computer is able to communicate with pre–Windows 2000 computers.
Disable NetBIOS over TCP/IP	Allows you to disable NetBIOS over TCP/IP. Use this option only if your network includes only Windows 2000 clients or DNS-enabled clients.
Use NetBIOS setting from the DHCP server	Specifies that the computer should obtain its NetBIOS-over-TCP/IP and WINS settings from the DHCP server.

Dynamic IP Configuration

Dynamic IP configuration assumes that you have a DHCP server on your network. DHCP servers are configured to automatically provide DHCP clients with all their IP configuration information. By default, when TCP/IP is installed on a Windows 2000 Professional computer, the computer is configured for dynamic IP configuration.

If your computer is configured for manual IP configuration and you want to use dynamic IP configuration, take the following steps:

1. From the Desktop, right-click My Network Places and choose Properties.

2. Right-click Local Area Connection and choose Properties.

3. In the Local Area Connection Properties dialog box, highlight Internet Protocol (TCP/IP) and click the Properties button.

4. The Internet Protocol (TCP/IP) Properties dialog box appears. Select the Obtain an IP Address Automatically radio button. Then click the OK button.

Testing IP Configuration

After you have configured the IP settings, you can test the IP configuration using the IPCONFIG and PING commands.

The IPCONFIG Command

The *IPCONFIG* command displays your IP configuration. Table 11.5 lists the command switches that can be used with the IPCONFIG command.

TABLE 11.5   IPCONFIG Switches

Switch	Description
/all	Shows verbose information about your IP configuration, including your computer's physical address, the DNS server you are using, and whether you are using DHCP
/release	Releases an address that has been assigned through DHCP
/renew	Renews an address through DHCP

In Exercise 11.4, you will verify your configuration with the IPCONFIG command. This exercise assumes that you have a network adapter installed in your computer and have completed Exercise 11.3.

EXERCISE 11.4

Using the IPCONFIG Command

1. Select Start ➢ Programs ➢ Accessories ➢ Command Prompt.

2. In the Command Prompt dialog box, type **IPCONFIG** and press Enter. Note the IP address, which should be the address that you configured in Exercise 11.3.

3. In the Command Prompt dialog box, type **IPCONFIG /all** and press Enter. You now see more information.

The PING Command

The *PING* command is used to send an ICMP (Internet Control Message Protocol) echo request and echo reply to verify whether the remote computer is available. The PING command has the following syntax:

```
PING IP address
```

For example, if your IP address is 131.200.2.30, you would type the following command:

PING 131.200.2.30

PING is useful for verifying connectivity between two hosts. For example, if you were having trouble connecting to a host on another network, PING would help you verify that a valid communication path existed. You would ping the following addresses:

- The loopback address, 127.0.0.1

- The local computer's IP address (you can verify this with IPCONFIG)

- The local router's (default gateway's) IP address

- The remote computer's IP address

If PING failed to get a reply from any of these addresses, you would have a starting point for troubleshooting the connection error.

Using NWLink IPX/SPX/NetBIOS

NWLink IPX/SPX/NetBIOS Compatible Transport is Microsoft's implementation of the Novell IPX/SPX (Internetwork Packet Exchange/Sequenced Packet Exchange) protocol stack. The Windows 2000 implementation of the IPX/SPX protocol stack adds NetBIOS support.

The main function of NWLink is to act as a transport protocol to route packets through internetworks. By itself, the NWLink protocol does not allow you to access NetWare File and Print Services. However, it does provide a method of transporting the data across the network. If you want to access NetWare File and Print Services, you must install NWLink and Client Services for NetWare (software that works at the upper layers of the OSI model to allow access to File and Print Services).

One advantage of using NWLink is that it is easy to install and configure. The following sections describe how to install and configure this protocol.

In Exercise 11.5, you will install the NWLink IPX/SPX protocol. This exercise assumes that you have a network adapter installed in your computer.

EXERCISE 11.5

Installing NWLink IPX/SPX Protocol

1. From the Desktop, right-click My Network Places and choose Properties.

2. Right-click Local Area Connection and choose Properties.

3. In the Local Area Connection Properties dialog box, click the Install button.

4. The Select Network Component Type dialog box appears. Highlight Protocol and click the Add button.

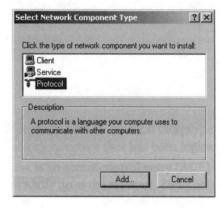

5. The Select Network Protocol dialog box appears. Select NWLink IPX/SPX/NetBIOS Compatible Transport Protocol from the list. Then click the OK button.

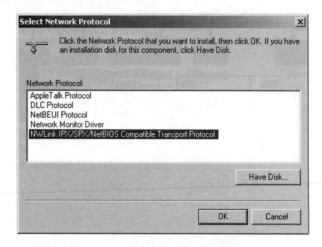

Configuring NWLink IPX/SPX

The only options that you must configure for NWLink are the *internal network number* and the *frame type*. Normally, you leave both settings at their default values.

The internal network number is commonly used to identify NetWare file servers. It is also used when you are running File and Print Services for NetWare or are using IPX routing. Normally, you leave the internal network number at the default setting.

The frame type specifies how the data is packaged for transmission over the network. If the computers that are using NWLink use different frame types, they are not able to communicate with each other. The default setting for frame type is Auto Detect, which will attempt to automatically choose a compatible frame type for your network. If you need to connect to servers that use various frame types, you should configure Manual Frame Type Detection, which will allow you to use a different frame type for each network.

In Exercise 11.6, you will configure the NWLink IPX/SPX protocol.

EXERCISE 11.6

Configuring the NWLink IPX/SPX Protocol

1. From the Desktop, right-click My Network Places and select Properties.

2. Right-click Local Area Connection and select Properties.

3. In the Local Area Connection Properties dialog box, highlight NWLink IPX/SPX/NetBIOS Compatible Transport Protocol and click the Properties button.

EXERCISE 11.6 *(continued)*

4. The NWLink IPX/SPX/NetBIOS Compatible Transport Protocol Properties dialog box appears. In this dialog box, you can configure your internal network number and frame type.

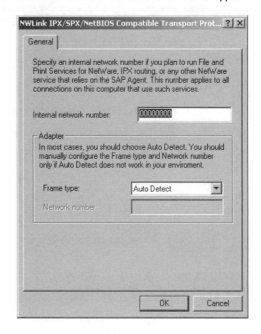

Using NetBEUI

NetBEUI stands for NetBIOS Extended User Interface. It was developed in the mid-1980s to connect workgroups that were running the OS/2 and LAN Manager operating systems. The NetBEUI protocol offers the following advantages:

- It is easy to install.

- There are no configuration requirements.

- It has self-tuning capabilities.

- NetBEUI incurs less overhead than TCP/IP and IPX/SPX and thus offers better performance.

- NetBEUI uses less memory than TCP/IP and IPX/SPX.

NetBEUI's main disadvantage is that it is not routable, so you cannot use it in networks that have more than one network segment. Also, NetBEUI is not as commonly accepted as the TCP/IP protocol.

In Exercise 11.7, you will install NetBEUI.

EXERCISE 11.7

Installing NetBEUI

1. From the Desktop, right-click My Network Places and select Properties.

2. Right-click Local Area Connection and select Properties.

3. In the Local Area Connection Properties dialog box, click the Install button.

4. In the Select Network Component Type dialog box, highlight Protocol and click the Add button.

5. In the Select Network Protocol dialog box, select NetBEUI Protocol from the list and click the OK button.

Managing Network Bindings

Bindings are used to enable communication between your network adapter and the network protocols that are installed. If you have multiple network protocols installed on your computer, you can improve performance by binding the most commonly used protocols higher in the binding order.

To configure network bindings, access the Network and Dial-up Connections window and then select Advanced ➤ Advanced Settings from the main menu bar. The Adapters and Bindings tab of the Advanced Settings dialog box appears, as shown in Figure 11.14. For each local area connection, if there are multiple protocols listed, you can use the arrow buttons on the right side of the dialog box to move the protocols up or down in the binding order.

FIGURE 11.14 The Adapters and Bindings tab of the Advanced Settings dialog box

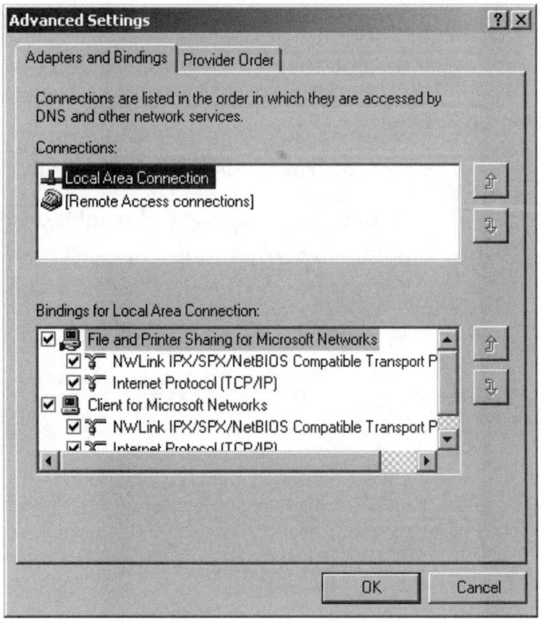

Summary

This chapter described how to manage network connections. We covered the following topics:

- How network protocols are used for network communications, including the movement of data through a network. We examined an overview of the OSI model.

- Installing, configuring, and troubleshooting network adapters. You install adapters that are not Plug and Play compatible through the Add/Remove Hardware Wizard. You configure a network adapter through its Properties dialog box.

- Installing, configuring, and testing network protocols. TCP/IP is the default protocol installed with Windows 2000 Professional. You can also install the NWLink IPX/SPX/NetBIOS and NetBEUI protocols.

Exam Essentials

Be able to install, configure, and troubleshoot network adapters.
Know how to configure Plug and Play and non–Plug and Play network adapters. Know how to troubleshoot network adapter problems that keep a client from attaching to the network.

Be able to configure and troubleshoot TCP/IP.   Know the primary purpose and configuration options for TCP/IP, DHCP, WINS, and DNS. Know how to troubleshoot protocol-related network problems.

Key Terms

Before you take the exam, be sure you're familiar with the following key terms:

Application layer	IP address
connection-oriented service	IPCONFIG
connectionless service	LLC (Logical Link Control) sublayer
Data Link layer	MAC address
default gateway	MAC (Media Access Control) sublayer
DNS (Domain Name System) server	NetBEUI
Driver	network adapter
Frame	Network layer
frame type	NWLink IPX/SPX/NetBIOS Compatible Transport
internal network number	OSI (Open Systems Interconnection) model
Internetwork	Physical layer

PING

Presentation layer

router

Session layer

subnet mask

TCP/IP (Transmission Control Protocol/Internet Protocol)

Transport layer

WINS (Windows Internet Name Service) server

Review Questions

1. You are the network administrator of a very small network. Your network is configured with four computers as shown in the following diagram. When you add WS3, it isn't able to connect to the network. When you type the IPCONFIG command for WS3, you see that an IP address has not been assigned. Which configuration option needs to be corrected?

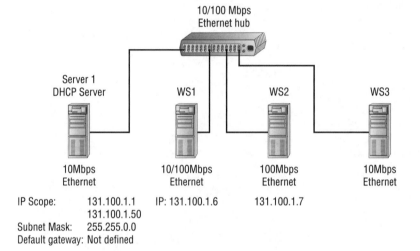

```
                            10/100 Mbps
                            Ethernet hub

     Server 1
     DHCP Server        WS1            WS2            WS3


     10Mbps          10/100Mbps      100Mbps        10Mbps
     Ethernet        Ethernet        Ethernet       Ethernet
IP Scope:    131.100.1.1    IP: 131.100.1.6    131.100.1.7
             131.100.1.50
Subnet Mask:    255.255.0.0
Default gateway: Not defined
```

   A. You need to install in WS3 a card that supports 100Mbps.

   B. The DHCP server needs to be configured with a default gateway.

   C. The DHCP server needs to be authorized.

   D. The Ethernet hub needs to be configured so that it supports 10Mbps Ethernet and 100Mbps Ethernet on the same network.

2. It's Monday morning and you have just plugged your laptop into the corporate network. When you try to access network resources, you are unable to access anything. Your network uses the TCP/IP protocol with a DHCP server. On Friday, you had no problem accessing network resources. What is the first action you should take to determine the problem?

    A. Replace your network cable.

    B. Replace your network card.

    C. Use IPCONFIG to make sure your IP configuration is valid.

    D. Use TCPCONFIG to make sure your IP configuration is valid.

3. You have a very small network consisting of five computers, all attached to the network through a single Ethernet hub. You do not use a Windows 2000 domain but rather are configured as a local workgroup. You do not connect to anything beyond your local network, and you have no special network requirements beyond file and print sharing. In the following exhibit, which network protocol should you choose if you want the fastest service with the simplest configuration?

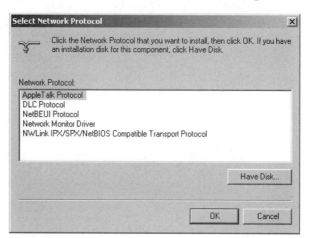

    A. AppleTalk Protocol

    B. DLC Protocol

    C. NetBEUI Protocol

    D. Network Monitor Driver

    E. NWLink IPX/SPX/NetBIOS Compatible Transport Protocol

4. You have a network adapter that is not able to correctly attach to the network. You discover that the driver you are using is outdated and there is an updated driver that will likely solve your problem. In the network adapters Properties dialog box shown here, what tab will you work in to update the network adapter's driver?

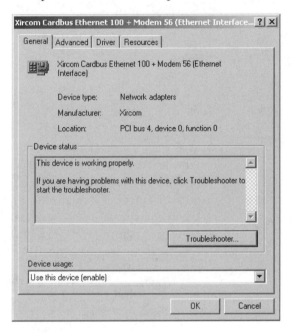

A. General

B. Advanced

C. Driver

D. Resources

5. Your computer is called WS1. You are not able to access any network resources. You know that WS2 can access the network, and you want to test communication between WS1 and WS2. Which command would you use to test communications with another computer based on its IP address?

A. IPCONFIG

B. TESTIP

C. PING

D. GROPE

6. Your network uses the TCP/IP protocol. Julie configures her computer to use TCP/IP. When Julie tries to access network resources, she can't. She checks with you, the network administrator, and you discover that her subnet mask is incorrectly configured. When Julie asks you why the subnet mask is important, what do you tell her is its function?

A. To specify which part of the IP address is the network address and which part of the IP address is the host or client address

B. To specify how packets should be routed through an internetwork

C. To determine the preferred DNS and WINS servers that exist on a network

D. To specify whether you are using a dynamic or static configuration

7. When you try to access the SALES server, which is a Windows NT 4.0 Server, you are able to access it via the IP address but not by its Windows NetBIOS name. In the following exhibit, what IP configuration should you check into?

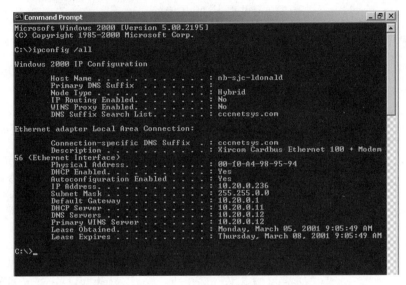

A. IP address

B. Default gateway

C. DNS server

D. Primary WINS server

8. Julie is sitting at computer W2KP1. She wants to be able to access resources on W2KP2. Based on the following diagram, how should Julie configure her default gateway?

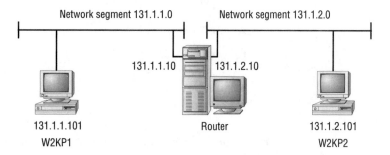

Network segment 131.1.1.0   Network segment 131.1.2.0

131.1.1.10   131.1.2.10

131.1.1.101   Router   131.1.2.101
W2KP1   W2KP2

   A. 131.1.1.0

   B. 131.1.1.10

   C. 131.1.2.0

   D. 131.1.2.10

9. Your primary DNS suffix is configured as `acmetest.com`. You want to access resources on the `acmecorp.com` domain without using fully qualified domain names. Which option should you use?

   A. Append Primary and Connection Specific DNS Suffixes

   B. Append These DNS Suffixes (in order)

   C. Configure This as a HOSTS File

   D. Configure This as an LMHOSTS File

10. When you try to access the `sales.acmecorp.com` server, you can access the server using the server's IP address, but not the fully qualified domain name. Which configuration file can you use to alleviate this problem?

    A. HOSTS

    B. LMHOSTS

    C. dns.txt

    D. wins.txt

11. Your domain suffix is configured as `sanjose.acmecorp.com`. Normally, you access resources from within your domain. Occasionally, you access resources in the `acmecorp.com` domain. You want to be able to access resources in either domain without specifying a fully qualified domain name. Which option should you use?

    A. Append Parent Suffixes of the Primary DNS Suffix

    B. Append Secondary DNS Suffix

    C. Append Child Suffixes of the Primary DNS Suffix

    D. Append Upstream Suffixes of the Primary DNS Suffix

12. Your network consists of Windows 2000 Professional computers and Windows NT 4 Workstation computers. You want to be able to access the Windows NT 4 Workstation computers by using their NetBIOS names. Your network does not have WINS servers configured. Which file should you configure and use?

    A. HOSTS

    B. LMHOSTS

    C. wins.cfg

    D. wins.txt

13. Your network consists of a variety of NetWare servers of many different versions. You have configured your Windows 2000 Professional computer with the NWLink IPX/SPX/NetBIOS Compatible Transport protocol and Client Services for NetWare. You see only some of the NetWare servers, but not the servers you need to access. In the following exhibit, which item is most likely not configured properly?

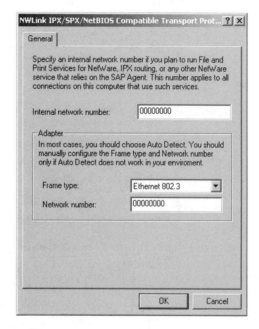

A. Internal network number

B. Frame type

C. Network number

D. Everything is properly configured

14. You have two DHCP servers on your network. Your computer accidentally received the wrong IP configuration from a DHCP server that was misconfigured. The DHCP server with the incorrect configuration has been disabled. What command would you use to release and renew your computer's DHCP configuration?

    A. IPCONFIG

    B. DHCPRECON

    C. RELEASE

    D. IPADJUST

15. Your Windows 2000 Professional computer is configured with TCP/IP, NWLink IPX/SPX/NetBIOS Compatible Transport, and NetBEUI. TCP/IP is your most commonly used network protocol. You want to configure your network bindings so that the TCP/IP protocol is listed first. How do you configure network bindings in Windows 2000?

    A. In the Network and Dial-up Connections window, select Advanced, then Advanced Settings.

    B. In the network adapter Properties dialog box, click the Bindings tab.

    C. In the network adapter Properties dialog box, click the Advanced tab, then click the Bindings button.

    D. This is configurable only through the Registry.

Answers to Review Questions

1. **A.** All Ethernet clients on the same network segment must transmit at the same speed, even if the hub is configured to support both speeds.

2. **C.** If everything worked properly on Friday, then your hardware is most likely in good order. The first thing you should check is your IP configuration, making sure that it was properly set by the DHCP server. You can verify the configuration with the `IPCONFIG` command. If the IP configuration appears to be correct, use the `PING` command to verify that you can communicate with other computers using the TCP/IP protocol.

3. **C.** NetBEUI is the fastest and most efficient protocol, if you do not require routing services.

4. **C.** You use the settings in the Driver tab to uninstall or update a device driver.

5. **C.** The `PING` command is used to send an ICMP echo request and echo reply between two IP hosts to test whether or not a valid communication path exits.

6. **A.** The subnet mask is used to specify which part of the address is the network address and which part of the address is the host or client address.

7. **D.** You use WINS servers to resolve NetBIOS computer names to IP addresses. DHCP servers are used to dynamically assign the IP configuration. DNS servers are used to resolve domain names to IP addresses.

8. **B.** Julie needs to configure the default gateway with the IP address of the router connection that is attached to her subnet, 131.1.1.10.

9. B.   The option to Append These DNS Suffixes (in order), in the DNS tab of the Advanced TCP/IP Settings dialog box, specifies the DNS suffixes that will be used for unqualified name resolution. For example, if your primary DNS suffix is TestCorp.com and you type ping lala, DNS will try to resolve the address as lala.TestCorp.com. If you append the additional DNS suffix MyCorp.com and type ping lala, DNS will try to resolve the address as lala.TestCorp.com and lala.MyCorp.com.

10. A.   If you do not have access to a properly configured DNS server, you can use a HOSTS file to map IP addresses to domain host names.

11. A.   If you use the option to Append Primary and Connection Specific DNS Suffixes (in the DNS tab of the Advanced TCP/IP Settings dialog box), you can also configure the Append Parent Suffixes of the Primary DNS Suffix option. This option specifies whether name resolution includes the parent suffix for the primary domain DNS suffix, up to the second level of the domain name.

12. B.   If your network does not use a WINS server, you can configure an LMHOSTS file to map IP addresses to NetBIOS computer names.

13. B.   The NetWare server you need to connect to may be configured with a different frame type. You should find out what frame type the server is using and configure the Windows 2000 computer with the same frame type.

14. A.   You can release your DHCP configuration with the IPCONFIG /release command, and renew your DHCP configuration with the IPCONFIG /renew command.

15. A.   To configure network bindings, you open the Network and Dial-up Connections window and select Advanced ➢ Advanced Settings. You can specify the binding order in the Adapters and Bindings tab of the Advanced Settings dialog box.

Chapter

12

Managing Printing

MICROSOFT EXAM OBJECTIVES COVERED IN THIS CHAPTER:

✓ **Connect to local and network print devices.**

- Manage printers and print jobs.
- Control access to printers by using permissions.
- Connect to a local print device.

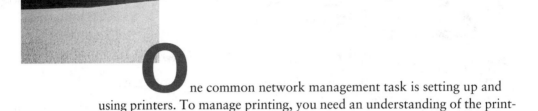

One common network management task is setting up and using printers. To manage printing, you need an understanding of the printing process and the terminology associated with the process.

The process of creating, managing, and deleting printers is fairly easy. When you create printers, you use a Wizard, which leads you through each step of the configuration. Anything that is not configured through the Add Printer Wizard can be configured through the printer's properties. You can also manage printing options such as pausing and deleting print jobs for the entire printer or for specific print documents.

In this chapter, you will learn the basics of Windows 2000 Professional printing, how to set up and configure printers, and how to manage printers and print jobs.

> **NOTE** The printing processes used by Windows 2000 Server and Windows 2000 Professional are the same.

Printing Basics

Before you learn about the specifics of Windows 2000 printing, you should have an understanding of basic network printing principles. Table 12.1 defines the terms that relate to network printing, and the following sections describe the printing process and the roles of print devices and printers.

TABLE 12.1 Windows 2000 Printing Terminology

Term	Definition
Printer	The software interface between the *physical printer* (the print device) and the operating system. This is also referred to as a *logical printer*. You can create printers through the Printers folder.
Print device	The actual physical printer or hardware device that produces the printed output.
Print server	The computer on which the printer has been defined. When you send a job to a network printer, you are actually sending it to the print server first.
Print spooler	A directory or folder on the print server that stores the print jobs until they can be printed. This is also referred to as a *print queue*. Your print server and print spooler must have enough hard disk space to hold all the print jobs that could be pending at any given time.
Print processor	The process that determines whether or not a print job needs further processing once that job has been sent to the spooler. The processing (also called *rendering*) is used to format the print job so that it can print correctly at the print device.
Printer pool	A configuration that allows you to use one printer for multiple print devices. A printer pool is useful when you have multiple printers that use the same print driver and are in the same location. By using printer pools, users can send their print jobs to the first available printer.
Print driver	The specific software that understands your print device. Each print device has its own command set, and each print device has an associated print driver.

TABLE 12.1 Windows 2000 Printing Terminology *(continued)*

Term	Definition
Physical port	The port through which a printer is directly connected to a computer, either a serial (COM) or parallel (LPT) port.
Logical port	The port through which a printer with a network card is attached to a network. *Logical ports* are much faster than *physical ports*. They also are not restricted by parallel and serial cable distance limitations, which apply to printers connected to a PC's parallel or serial port.
Local printer	A printer that uses a physical port and that has not been shared. If a printer is defined as local, the only users who can use it are the local users of the computer to which the printer is attached.
Network printer	A *printer* that is available to local and network users. Network printers can use either a physical or logical port.

The Windows 2000 Printing Process

Printing is a common area of difficulty in many networks. To troubleshoot the problems related to the Windows 2000 printing process, you need to understand the steps involved in the process. A simple overview of the printing process is illustrated in Figure 12.1.

FIGURE 12.1 An overview of the Windows 2000 printing process

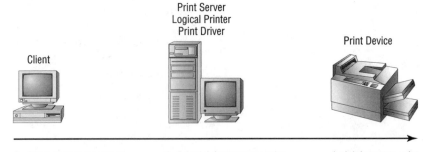

1. Client creates document.

2. Client connects to network printer (downloads print driver).

3. Print job is sent to spooler.

4. Job is sent to print device.

The following steps are involved in the printing process:

1. From the client, the user chooses to print. On any Windows platform, the print request is passed to the *Graphics Device Interface (GDI)*. The GDI calls the *print driver*. If the user is accessing the printer for the first time, the print driver is loaded into the client's memory from the *print server*. The print driver will stay in memory until the computer is turned off or a newer print driver is detected on the print server. The GDI is also responsible for processing print jobs for the appropriate *print device*.

2. The print job is sent to the computer's local *print spooler*, which in turn sends the job over the network to the print server.

3. The router at the print server receives the print job.

4. The router passes the print job to the print spooler on the print server, which spools the print job to a disk.

5. The *print processor* on the spooler analyzes the print job. If the job needs any further processing, the print processor does this so that the job will print correctly.

6. If specified, the separator page processor adds a *separator page* to the front of the print job.

7. The print job is passed to the print manager, which determines when the job should print and directs it to the correct port.

8. The print job goes to the print device, and the job prints.

In order to print to a printer, you must have that printer's driver in place to tell the application how to send the print job. Windows 2000 Professional clients automatically download the print driver from the print server each time they send a print job. If the print driver is updated on the print server, the next time the user sends a job to the printer, the driver is automatically updated.

With Windows 2000 Professional, you can also specify drivers for automatic download for other Windows clients. See the "Configuring Sharing Properties" section later in this chapter for details.

The Roles of Print Devices and Printers

A *print device* is the actual physical printer or hardware device that does the printing. In Windows 2000 terminology, a *printer* is the software interface between the print device and the operating system.

When you set up your computer or your network, you can determine the number of print devices by simply counting the devices you can see and touch. Printers are a bit trickier to enumerate, because you can configure them in several ways:

- One printer per print device

- One printer for multiple print devices, called *printer pooling*

- Multiple printers for a single print device, a configuration usually set up to allow print scheduling

You'll learn how to configure printer pools and set up print scheduling (by configuring the printer's availability) in the "Managing Printer Properties" section later in this chapter.

Setting Up Printers

Before you can access your physical print device under Windows 2000 Professional, you must first create a logical printer. To create a printer, you follow the steps in the Add Printer Wizard. In order to create a new printer in Windows 2000 Professional, you must be logged on as a member of the Administrators or Power Users group.

Microsoft ✓ *Exam* *Objective*	**Connect to local and network print devices.** - Manage printers and print jobs.

This chapter covers the material related to managing printing for the "Connect to local and network print devices" objective. The subobjective for connecting to an Internet printer is covered in Chapter 13, "Dial-Up Networking and Internet Connectivity."

The computer on which you run the Add Printer Wizard and create the printer automatically becomes the print server for that printer. As the print server, the computer must have enough processing power to support incoming print jobs and enough disk space to hold all of the print jobs that will be queued.

In Exercise 12.1, you will create printers using the Add Printer Wizard.

EXERCISE 12.1

Creating Printers

In this exercise, you will create two local printers—one to share, and one that will not be shared. You will manually specify their print device configuration.

Adding the First Printer

1. Select Start ➤ Settings ➤ Printers to open the Printers folder. Then double-click the Add Printer icon.

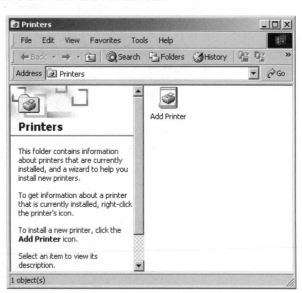

2. The Add Printer Wizard starts. Click the Next button to continue.

3. In the Local or Network Printer dialog box, select the Local Printer radio button. Make sure that the check box for "Automatically detect and install my Plug and Play printer" is not checked (unless you have a print device attached to your computer). Click Next to continue.

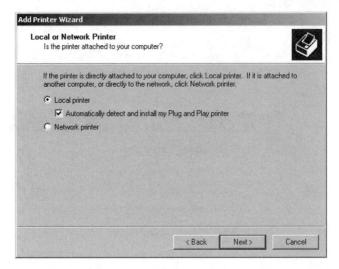

4. In the Select the Printer Port dialog box, select the Use the Following Port radio button, select LPT1 in the list box, and click the Next button.

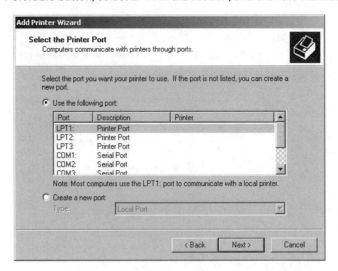

EXERCISE 12.1 *(continued)*

5. Next up is a dialog box that lists printer manufacturers and models. Select the print device manufacturer and model. In this example, choose HP in the Manufacturers list box and HP DeskJet 970Cse in the Printers list box. Then click the Next button.

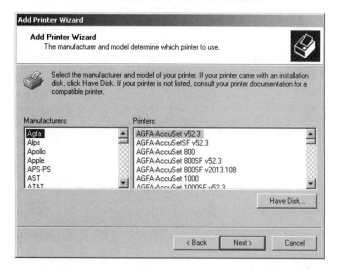

Note: If you have already installed this driver on your computer, this dialog box will also include a Windows Update button next to the Have Disk button.

6. In the Name Your Printer dialog box, leave the default name of HP DeskJet 970Cse and click the Next button.

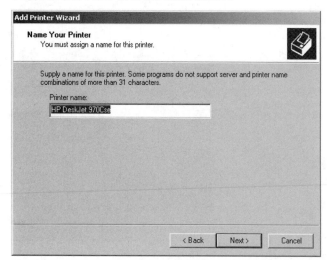

EXERCISE 12.1 *(continued)*

7. In the Printer Sharing dialog box, select the Share As radio button and type **HPDJ970** in the text box. Then click the Next button.

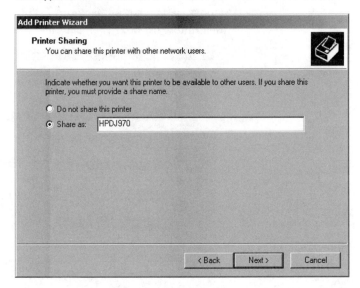

8. In the Location and Comment dialog box, type **Building 6, Room 765** into the Location text box, and **HP DeskJet 970Cse - Color Printer for the Technical Writers Group** into the Comment text box. Click the Next button.

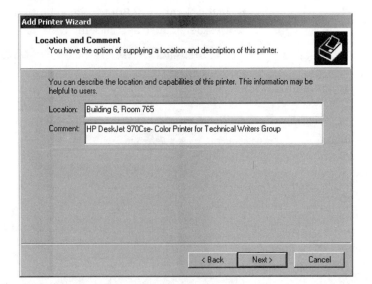

9. In the next dialog box, select the No radio button to skip printing a test page, and click Next to continue.

10. In the Completing the Add Printer Wizard dialog box, click the Finish button.

To complete the printer setup process, the Add Printer Wizard will copy files (if necessary) and create your printer. An icon for your new printer will appear in the Printers folder.

EXERCISE 12.1 *(continued)*

Adding the Second Printer

11. In the Printers folder, double-click the Add Printer icon. When the Add Printer Wizard starts, click the Next button to continue.

12. In the Local or Network Printer dialog box, select the Local Printer radio button. Make sure the check box for "Automatically detect and install my Plug and Play printer" is not checked (unless you have a print device attached to your computer), and click Next to continue.

13. In the Select the Printer Port dialog box, select the Use the Following Port radio button, select LPT2 in the list box, and click the Next button.

14. In next dialog box, choose HP in the Manufacturers list box and HP LaserJet 4 in the Printers list box. Click the Next button.

15. In the Name Your Printer dialog box, leave the default name of HP LaserJet 4 and click the Next button.

16. In the Printer Sharing dialog box, select the Do Not Share This Printer radio button and click the Next button.

17. In the Print Test Page dialog box, select No to skip printing a test page and click the Next button.

18. In the Completing the Add Printer Wizard dialog box, click the Finish button.

If you are creating a printer that is attached to a computer running Windows 2000 Professional, you will most likely be configuring a printer for personal use or limited network access.

Managing Printer Properties

Printer properties allow you to configure options such as the printer name, whether or not the printer is shared, and printer security. To access the printer Properties dialog box, open the Printers folder, right-click the printer you want to manage, and choose Properties from the pop-up menu.

Microsoft Exam Objective

Connect to local and network print devices.

- Manage printers and print jobs.
- Control access to printers by using permissions.

The printer Properties dialog box has six tabs: General, Sharing, Ports, Advanced, Security, and Device Settings. The following sections describe the properties on these tabs.

 The Properties dialog boxes for some printers will contain additional tabs to allow advanced configuration of the printer. For example, if you install an HP DeskJet 970Cse printer, its Properties dialog box will have additional tabs for Color Management and Services.

Configuring General Properties

The General tab of the printer Properties dialog box, shown in Figure 12.2, contains information about the printer. It also lets you set printing preferences and print test pages. The information here (name of the printer, its location, and comments about it) reflects your entries when you set the printer up (as described in the preceding section). You can add or change this information in the text boxes.

FIGURE 12.2 The General tab of the printer Properties dialog box

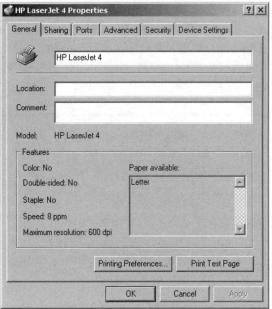

Beneath the Comment box, you see the model of the printer. The items listed in the Features section depend on the model and driver you are using, and may include the following:

- Color printing support

- Double-sided printing support

- Stapling support

- The maximum number of pages that can be printed per minute (ppm)

- The maximum resolution for the printer, in dots per inch (dpi)

At the bottom of the dialog box, you see the Printing Preferences and Print Test Page buttons. Their functions are described in the following sections.

Setting Printing Preferences

Clicking the Printing Preferences button brings up the Printing Preferences dialog box, which allows you to specify the layout of the paper, page order, and paper source. In addition to the Layout and Paper Quality tabs, an Advanced button allows you to configure more printer options.

Layout Settings

The Layout tab of the Printing Preferences dialog box, shown in Figure 12.3, allows you to specify the orientation and page order. Your choices for the Orientation setting are Portrait (vertical) and Landscape (horizontal).

FIGURE 12.3 The Layout tab of the Printing Preferences dialog box

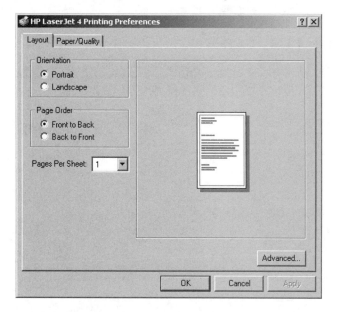

The Page Order setting is new to Windows 2000. It specifies whether you want page 1 of the document to be on the top of the stack (Front to Back) or on the bottom of the stack (Back to Front).

In Windows NT 4, your documents always print back to front, meaning page 1 prints first. At the end of the print job, you have to reorder your pages.

The Pages Per Sheet setting determines how many pages should be printed on a single page. You might use this feature if you were printing a book and wanted two pages to be printed side by side on a single page.

Paper/Quality Settings

The Paper/Quality tab allows you to configure properties that relate to the paper and quality of a print job. Available options depend on the features of your printer. For example, a printer may have only one option, such as Paper Source. For an HP DeskJet 970Cse printer, on the other hand, you can configure Paper Source, Media, Quality Settings, and Color options, as shown in Figure 12.4.

FIGURE 12.4 The Paper/Quality tab of the Printing Preferences dialog box

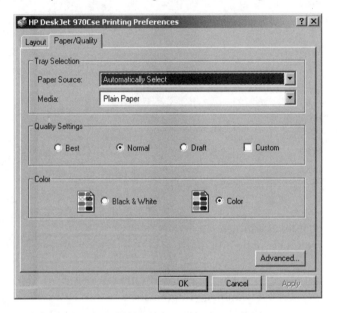

Advanced Settings

Clicking the Advanced button in the lower-right corner of the Printing Preferences dialog box brings up the Advanced Options dialog box, as shown in Figure 12.5. Here, you can configure printer options such as Paper/Output, Graphic, Document Options, and Printer Features. The options available depend on the specific print driver you are using.

FIGURE 12.5 Advanced options for an HP DeskJet 970Cse

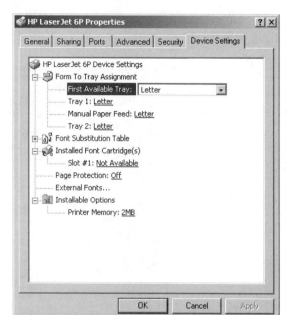

Printing a Test Page

The Print Test Page button at the bottom of the General tab of the printer Properties tab allows you to print a test page. This option is especially useful in troubleshooting printing problems. For example, you might use the Print Test Page option in a situation where no print driver is available for a print device and you want to try to use a compatible print driver. If the print job doesn't print or doesn't print correctly (it might print just one character per page, for example), you will know that the print driver isn't compatible.

Configuring Sharing Properties

The Sharing tab of the printer Properties dialog box, shown in Figure 12.6, allows you to specify whether the computer will be configured as a *local printer* or as a shared *network printer*. If you choose to share the printer, you also need to specify a share name, which will be seen by the network users.

FIGURE 12.6 The Sharing tab of the printer Properties dialog box

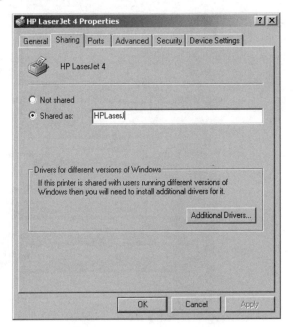

Also available in the Sharing tab is an option for driver support of print clients other than Windows 2000 clients. This is a significant feature of Windows 2000 Professional print support, because you can specify print drivers for other clients to automatically download. The only driver that is loaded by default is the Intel driver for Windows 2000. To provide the additional drivers for the clients, click the Additional Drivers button at the bottom of the Sharing tab. This brings up the Additional Drivers dialog box (Figure 12.7).

FIGURE 12.7 The Additional Drivers dialog box

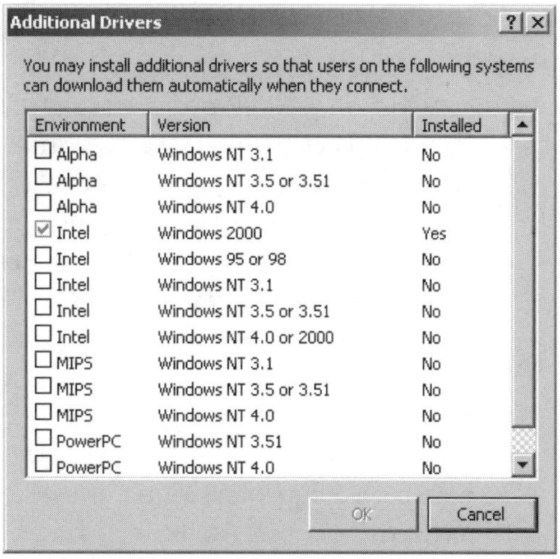

Windows 2000 Professional supports adding print drivers for the following platforms:

- Windows 95 or Windows 98 Intel

- Windows NT 3.1 Alpha, Intel, and MIPS

- Windows NT 3.5 or 3.51 Alpha, Intel, MIPS, and PowerPC

- Windows NT 4.0 Alpha, Intel, MIPS, and PowerPC

In Exercise 12.2, you will share an existing printer. This exercise assumes that you have completed Exercise 12.1.

EXERCISE 12.2

Sharing an Existing Printer

1. Select Start ➢ Settings ➢ Printers to open the Printers folder.

2. Right-click HP LaserJet 4, choose Properties, and click the Sharing tab.

3. Click the Shared As radio button. Type **HPLJ4** in the text box.

4. Click the Apply button, and then click the OK button to close the dialog box.

Configuring Port Properties

A *port* is defined as the interface, which allows the computer to communicate with the print device.

Windows 2000 Professional supports local ports (physical ports) and standard *TCP/IP ports* (logical ports). Local ports are used when the printer attaches directly to the computer. In the case where you are running Windows 2000 Professional in a small workgroup, you would likely run printers attached to the local port LPT1. Standard TCP/IP ports are used when the printer is attached to the network by installing a network card in the printer. The advantage of network printers is that they are faster than local printers and can be located anywhere on the network. When you specify a TCP/IP port, you must know the IP address of the network printer.

In the Ports tab, shown in Figure 12.8, you configure all the ports that have been defined for printer use. Along with deleting and configuring existing ports, you can also set up printer pooling and redirect print jobs to another printer, as described in the next sections.

The Enable Bidirectional Support option on the Ports tab will be available if your printer supports this feature. It allows the printer to communicate with the computer. For example, your printer may be able to send more informative printer errors.

FIGURE 12.8 The Ports tab of the printer Properties dialog box

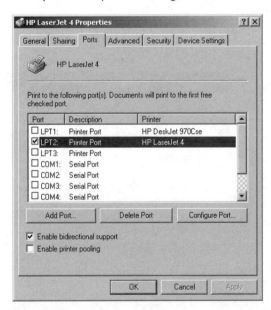

Printer Pooling

Printer pools are used to associate multiple physical print devices with a single logical printer, as illustrated in Figure 12.9. You would use a printer pool if you had multiple physical printers in the same location that were the same type and could use a single print driver. The advantage of using a printer pool is that the first available print device will print your job. This is useful in situations where a group of print devices are shared by a group of users, such as a secretarial pool.

FIGURE 12.9 Printer pooling

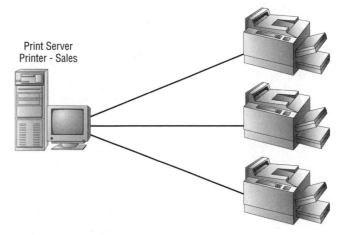

To configure a printer pool, click the Enable Printer Pooling check box at the bottom of the Ports tab, and then check all the ports to which the print devices in the printer pool will attach. If you do not select the Enable Printer Pooling option, you can select only one port per printer.

All of the print devices in a printer pool must be able to use the same print driver.

Redirecting Print Jobs to Another Printer

If your print device fails, you can redirect all the jobs scheduled to be printed at that print device, to another print device that has been configured as a printer. For this redirection to work, the second print device must be able to use the same print driver as the first print device.

To redirect print jobs, click the Add Port button in the Ports tab, highlight New Port, and choose New Port Type. In the Port Name dialog box, type the UNC name of the printer that you want to redirect the jobs to, in the format *computername\printer*.

Configuring Advanced Properties

The Advanced tab of the printer Properties dialog box, shown in Figure 12.10, allows you to control many characteristics of the printer. You can configure the following options:

- The availability of the printer
- The priority of the printer
- The driver the printer will use
- Spooling properties
- How documents are printed
- Printing defaults
- The print processor that will be used
- The separator page

FIGURE 12.10 The Advanced tab of the printer Properties dialog box

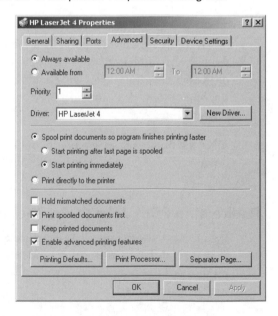

These options are covered in the following sections.

In Windows NT 4, the options now in the Windows 2000 Professional Advanced tab of the printer Properties dialog box were located in the General tab and the Scheduling tab of the printer Properties dialog box.

Printer Availability

Availability, or *scheduling*, specifies when a printer will service jobs. Usually, you control availability when you have multiple printers that use a single print device. For example, you might use this option if you have large jobs that tie up the print device for extended periods of time. You could schedule the large jobs to print only during a specified time, say between 10:00 P.M. and 4:00 A.M.

To set this up, you could create two printers on the same port; perhaps printers named LASER and REPORTS on the LPT1 port. (Both printers are on the same port since the same physical print device services them.) You would configure LASER to always be available, and REPORTS to be available only from 10:00 P.M. to 4:00 A.M. You would then instruct your users to send short jobs to LASER and long jobs to REPORTS, with the understanding that print jobs sent to REPORTS would print only during the specified hours.

By default, the Always Available radio button in the Advanced tab is selected, so that users can use the printer 24 hours a day. To limit the printer's availability, select the Available From radio button and specify the range of time when the printer should be available.

Printer Priority

Priority is another option that you might configure if you have multiple printers that use a single print device. When you set priority, you specify how jobs are directed to the print device. For example, you might use this option when two groups share a printer and you need to control the priority by which the device prints incoming jobs. In the Advanced tab of the printer Properties dialog box, you can set the Priority value to a number from 1 to 99, with 1 as the lowest priority and 99 as the highest priority.

As an example, suppose that the accounting department uses a single print device. The managers there want their print jobs always to print before jobs created by the other accounting department staff. To configure this arrangement, you could create a printer called MANAGERS on port LPT1 with a priority of 99. You would then create a printer on port LPT1 called WORKERS with a priority of 1. Through the Security tab of the printer Properties dialog box, you would allow only managers to use the MANAGERS printer and allow the other accounting users to use the WORKERS printer (Security tab options are covered later in this chapter). When the print manager polls for print jobs, it will always poll the higher-priority printer before the lower-priority printer.

The print manager is responsible for polling the print queue for print jobs and directing the print jobs to the correct port.

Print Driver

The Driver setting in the Advanced tab shows the driver that is associated with your printer. If you have configured multiple printers on the computer, you can select to use any of the installed drivers. Clicking the New Driver button starts the Add Printer Driver Wizard, which allows you to update or add new print drivers.

Spooling

When you configure spooling options, you specify whether print jobs are spooled or sent directly to the printer. *Spooling* means that print jobs are saved to disk in a queue before they are sent to the printer. Consider spooling as the traffic controller of printing—it keeps all the print jobs from trying to print at the same time.

By default, spooling is enabled, with printing beginning immediately. Your other option is to wait until the last page is spooled before printing. An analogy for these choices is the actions you can take in a grocery store's cashier line. Let's say you have an entire cart full of groceries and the guy behind you has only a few things. Even if you've started loading your groceries onto the belt, as long as the cashier hasn't started with your items, you can choose to let the person with fewer items go before you, or you can make him wait. If the cashier has already started totaling your groceries, then you don't have that choice. Windows 2000 Professional spooling options allow you to configure your print environment similarly.

In the Advanced tab, you can leave the Start Printing Immediately option selected, or you can choose the Start Printing After Last Page Is Spooled option. If you choose the latter option, a smaller print job that finishes spooling first will print before your print job, even if your job started spooling before it did. If you specify Start Printing Immediately, the smaller job will have to wait until your print job is complete.

The other spooling option is Print Directly to the Printer, which bypasses spooling altogether. This option doesn't work well in a multiuser environment where multiple print jobs are sent to the same device. However, it is useful in troubleshooting printer problems. If you can print to a print device directly, but you can't print through the spooler, then you know that your spooler is corrupt or has other problems.

 Real World Scenario

Your Print Spooler Runs Out of Room

You have installed a printer on your Windows 2000 Professional computer. Another printer available to your computer is shared by four other users.

Your computer has a C: drive and a D: drive, and the C: drive is running out of space. Spooler errors are occurring because of the large print jobs being sent to the printer. You would like to move the location of the spooler files to the computer's drive D:.

In Windows 2000, you can change the location of your spooler file by accessing the Printers utility (Start ≻ Settings ≻ Printers) and then clicking on File ≻ Server Properties. Then select the Advanced tab, and on the top of the dialog box you can select the location of your spool file. Be aware that this will change the location of the spooler folders for all printers that are located on the computer. You could selectively change spool folder locations per printer, but that can only be done by directly editing the Registry.

Print Options

The Advanced tab contains check boxes for four print options:

- The Hold Mismatched Documents option is useful when you're using multiple forms with a printer. By default, this feature is disabled and jobs are printed on a first-in-first-out (FIFO) basis. You might enable this option if you need to print on both plain paper and certificate forms. Then all the jobs with the same form will print first.

- The Print Spooled Documents First option specifies that the spooler will print jobs that have finished spooling before large jobs that are still spooling, even if that large print job has a higher priority. This option is enabled by default, which increases printer efficiency.

- The Keep Printed Documents option specifies that print jobs should not be deleted from the print spooler (queue) when they are finished printing. By default, this option is disabled. You normally want to delete the print jobs as they print, because saving print jobs can take up substantial disk space.

- The Enable Advanced Printing Features option specifies that any advanced features supported by your printer, such as Page Order and Pages Per Sheet, should be enabled. By default, this option is turned on. You would disable it if compatibility problems occurred. For example, if you are using the driver for a similar print device that does not support all the features of the print device the driver was written for, you should disable the advanced printing features.

Turning on the Keep Printed Documents option can be useful if you need to identify the source or other attributes of a finished print job. In one situation, this option helped track down a person who had been sending nasty notes to a coworker. The staff knew that the notes were being printed on the company laser printer. Since the print queue was on an NTFS volume, the administrator enabled the Keep Printed Documents option and was able to identify the offender through the owner attribute of the file.

Printing Defaults

The Printing Defaults button in the lower-left corner of the Advanced tab (see Figure 12.10) calls up the Printing Preferences dialog box. This is the same dialog box that appears when you click the Printing Preferences button in the General tab of the printer Properties dialog box, and its options were covered in the "Configuring General Properties" section earlier in this chapter.

Print Processor

Print processors are used to specify whether Windows 2000 Professional needs to do additional processing to print jobs. The five print processors supported by Windows 2000 Professional are listed in Table 12.2.

TABLE 12.2 Print Processors Supported by Windows 2000

Print Processor	Description
RAW	Makes no changes to the print document
RAW (FF appended)	Makes no changes to the print document except to always add a formfeed character
RAW (FF Auto)	Makes no changes to the print document except to try to detect if a formfeed character needs to be added
NT EMF	Generally spools documents that are sent from other Windows 2000 clients
TEXT	Interprets all the data as plain text, and the printer will print the data using standard text commands

To modify your Print Processor settings, click the Print Processor button at the bottom of the Advanced tab to open the Print Processor dialog box, shown in Figure 12.11. You will generally leave the default settings as is unless otherwise directed by the print device manufacturer.

FIGURE 12.11 The Print Processor dialog box

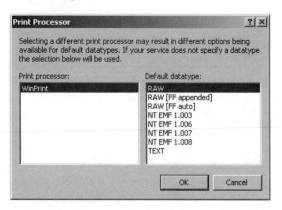

Separator Pages

Separator pages are used at the beginning of each document to identify the user who submitted the print job. If your printer is not shared, a separator page is generally a waste of paper. If the printer is shared by many users, the separator page can be useful for distributing finished print jobs.

To add a separator page, click the Separator Page button in the lower-right corner of the Advanced tab of the printer Properties dialog box. This brings up the Separator Page dialog box (Figure 12.12). Click the Browse button to locate and select the separator page file that you want to use. Windows 2000 Professional supplies the Separator files listed in Table 12.3, which are stored in *Windir*\System32.

FIGURE 12.12 The Separator Page dialog box

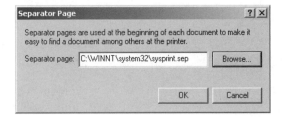

TABLE 12.3 Separator Page Files

Separator Page File	Description
pcl.sep	Used to send a separator page on a dual-language HP printer after switching the printer to PCL (Printer Control Language), which is a common printing standard
pscript.sep	Does not send a separator page, but switches the computer to PostScript printing mode

TABLE 12.3 Separator Page Files *(continued)*

Separator Page File	Description
sysprint.sep	Used by PostScript printers to send a separator page
sysprintj.sep	Same as sysprint.sep, but with support for Japanese characters

You can also create custom separator pages. For more information about creating separator pages, refer to the Windows 2000 Resource Kit.

In Exercise 12.3, you will configure some advanced printer properties. This exercise assumes you have completed Exercise 12.2.

EXERCISE 12.3

Managing Advanced Printer Properties

1. Select Start ➢ Settings ➢ Printers to open the Printers folder.

2. Right-click HP LaserJet 4, choose Properties, and click the Advanced tab.

3. Click the Available From radio button, and specify that the printer is available from 12:00 A.M. to 6:00 A.M.

4. Click the Start Printing After Last Page Is Spooled radio button.

5. Click the Separator Page button. In the Separator Page dialog box, click the Browse button and choose the sysprint.sep file. Click the Open button, then click the OK button in the Separator Page dialog box.

6. Click the OK button to close the printer Properties dialog box.

Security Properties

You can control which users and groups can access Windows 2000 printers by configuring the print permissions. In Windows 2000 Professional, you can allow or deny access to a printer. If you deny access, the user or group will not be able to use the printer, even if their user or group permissions allow such access.

You assign print permissions to users and groups through the Security tab of the printer Properties dialog box, as shown in Figure 12.13. Table 12.4 defines the print permissions that can be assigned.

FIGURE 12.13 The Security tab of the printer Properties dialog box

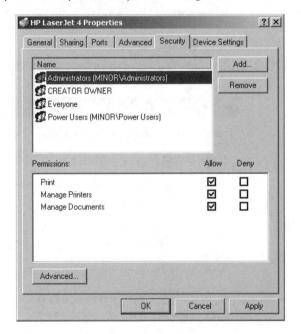

TABLE 12.4   Print Permissions

Print Permission	Description
Print	A user or group can connect to a printer and can send print jobs to the printer.
Manage Printers	Allows administrative control of the printer. With this permission, a user or group can pause and restart the printer, change the spooler settings, share or unshare a printer, change print permissions, and manage printer properties.
Manage Documents	Allows users to manage documents by pausing, restarting, resuming, and deleting queued documents. Users cannot control the status of the printer.

By default, whenever a printer is created, default print permissions are assigned. The default permissions are normally appropriate for most network environments. Table 12.5 shows the default print permissions that are assigned.

TABLE 12.5   Default Print Permissions

Group	Print	Manage Printers	Manage Documents
Administrators	X	X	X
Power Users	X	X	X
Creator Owner			X
Everyone	X		

Print Permission Assignment

Usually, you can accept the default print permissions, but you might need to modify them for special situations. For example, if your company bought an expensive color laser printer for the marketing department, you probably wouldn't want to allow general access to that printer. In this case, you would deselect the Allow check box for the Everyone group, add the Marketing group to the Security tab list, and then allow the Marketing group the Print permission.

To add print permissions, take the following steps:

1. In the Security tab of the printer Properties dialog box, click the Add button.

2. The Select Users, Computers, or Groups dialog box appears. Click the user, computer, or group that you want to assign print permissions to and click the Add button. After you specify all the users you want to assign permissions to, click the OK button.

3. Highlight the user, computer, or group. Select Allow or Deny access for the Print, Manage Printers, and Manage Documents permissions. Click the OK button when you are finished assigning permissions.

To remove an existing group from the permissions list, highlight the group and click the Remove button. That group will no longer be listed in the Security tab and cannot be assigned permissions.

In Exercise 12.4, you will assign print permissions. This exercise assumes that you have completed Exercise 12.1.

EXERCISE 12.4

Assigning Print Permissions

1. Using the Local Users and Groups utility, create two users: **Kim** and **Jennifer**. (See Chapter 6, "Managing Users," for details on creating user accounts.) Deselect the User Must Change Password at Next Logon option.

2. Using the Local Users and Groups utility, create a new group named **Executives**. (See Chapter 7, "Managing Groups," for details on creating groups.) Place Kim in the Execs group.

3. Select Start ➢ Settings ➢ Printers to open the Printers folder.

4. Right-click HP LaserJet 4, select Properties, and click the Security tab. Click the Add button.

5. In the Select Users, Computers, or Groups dialog box, click Execs and click the Add button. Click the OK button to continue.

6. In the Security tab, highlight the Execs group. By default, the Allow check box should be selected for the Print permission. Leave the default setting. Highlight the Everyone group and click the Remove button. Click OK to close the Printer Properties dialog box.

7. Log off as Administrator and log on as Kim.

8. Open the Printers folder and select HP LaserJet 4. Kim should be able to connect to this printer based on her membership in the Execs group.

9. Log off as Kim and log on as Jennifer.

10. Open the Printers folder and select HP LaserJet 4. At the top of the dialog box, you should see the message "HP LaserJet 4 Access denied, unable to connect."

11. Log off as Jennifer and log on as Administrator.

Advanced Settings

The advanced settings accessed from the Security tab allow you to configure permissions, auditing, and owner properties. Clicking the Advanced button in the lower-left corner of the Security tab brings up the Access Control Settings dialog box, shown in Figure 12.14. This dialog box has three tabs that you can use to add, remove, or edit print permissions:

- The Permissions tab lists all the users, computers, and groups that have been given permission to the printer, the permission granted, and whether the permission applies to documents or to the printer.

- The Auditing tab tracks who is using the printer and what type of access is being used. You can track the success or failure of six events: Print, Manage Printers, Manage Documents, Read Permissions, Change Permissions, and Take Ownership.

- The Owner tab shows the owner of the printer (the user or group who created the printer), which you can change if you have the proper permissions. For example, if the print permissions excluded the Administrator from using or managing the printer, and the print permissions needed to be reassigned, an Administrator could take ownership of the printer and then reapply print permissions.

FIGURE 12.14 The Access Control Settings dialog box

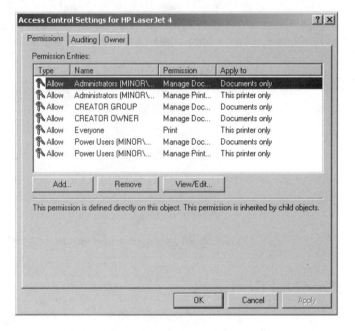

Device Settings Properties

The properties that you see on the Device Settings tab of the printer Properties dialog box depend on the printer and print driver that you have installed. You might configure these properties if you want to manage the associations of forms to tray assignments. For example, you could configure the upper tray to use letterhead and the lower tray to use regular paper. An example of the Device Settings tab for an HP LaserJet 6P printer is shown in Figure 12.15.

FIGURE 12.15 The Device Settings tab of the printer Properties dialog box

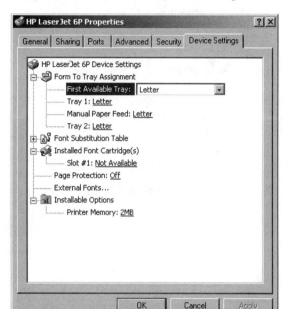

Managing Printers and Print Documents

Administrators or users with the Manage Printers permission can manage the printer's servicing of print jobs and of the print documents in a print queue. When you manage a printer, you manage all the documents in a queue. When you manage print documents, you manage specific documents.

Microsoft
✓ *Exam*
Objective

Connect to local and network print devices.

- Manage printers and print jobs.

As you would expect, you manage printers and print documents from the Printers folder (select Start ➤ Settings ➤ Printers). The following sections describe the printer management and print document management options.

Managing Printers

To manage a printer, right-click the printer you want to manage. From the pop-up menu (Figure 12.16), select the appropriate option for the area you want to manage. Table 12.6 describes these options.

FIGURE 12.16 The printer management options

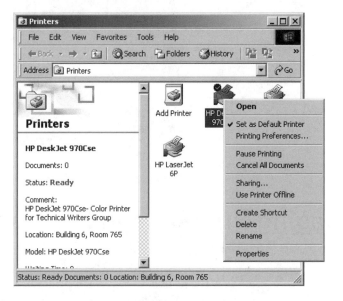

Managing Print Documents

As an Administrator or a user with the Manage Printers or Manage Documents permission, you can manage print documents within a print queue. For example, if a user has sent the same job multiple times, you might need to delete the duplicate print jobs.

To manage print documents, in the Printers folder double-click the printer that contains the documents. This opens a dialog box with information about the documents in its print queue. Select Document from the menu bar

TABLE 12.6 Printer Management Options

Option	Description
Set as Default Printer	Specifies the default printer that will be used when the user does not send a job to an explicit printer (if the computer is configured to access multiple printers).
Printing Preferences	Brings up the Printing Preferences dialog box (see Figures 12.3 and 12.4), which allows you to configure printer settings for page layout and paper quality. You can also access this dialog box through the General tab of the printer Properties dialog box, as described earlier in this chapter.
Pause Printing	While a printer is paused, print jobs can be submitted to the printer, but they will not be forwarded to the print device until you resume printing (by unchecking this option). You might use Pause Printing when you need to troubleshoot the printer or maintain the print device.
Cancel All Documents	Specifies that any jobs currently in the queue will be deleted. You might use this option if the print queue contains jobs that are no longer needed.
Sharing	Allows the printer to be shared or not shared.
Use Printer Offline	Pauses the printer. Print documents will remain in the print queue, even if you restart the computer.
Delete	Removes the printer. You might use this option if you no longer need the printer, if you want to move the printer to another print server, or if you suspect the printer is corrupt and you want to delete and re-create it.

TABLE 12.6 Printer Management Options *(continued)*

Option	Description
Rename	Allows you to rename the printer. You might use this option to give a printer a more descriptive name or a name that follows naming conventions.

to access the pull-down menu of options that you can use to manage documents, as shown in Figure 12.17. These menu options are described in Table 12.7.

FIGURE 12.17 The Document menu options

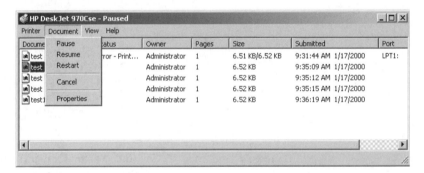

TABLE 12.7 Document Management Options

Option	Description
Pause	Places the printing of this document on hold
Resume	Allows the document to print normally (after it has been paused)
Restart	Resends the job from the beginning, even if it has already been partially printed

TABLE 12.7 Document Management Options *(continued)*

Option	Description
Cancel	Deletes the job from the print spooler
Properties	Brings up the document Properties dialog box, containing options such as user notification when a print job is complete, document priority, document printing time, page layout, and paper quality

In Exercise 12.5, you will manage printers and print documents.

EXERCISE 12.5

Managing Printers and Print Documents

1. Select Start ➤ Settings ➤ Printers to open the Printers folder.

2. Right-click HP LaserJet 4 and select Pause Printing.

3. Select Start ➤ Programs ➤ Accessories ➤ Notepad.

4. Create a new text file and then select File ➤ Save As. In the Save As dialog box, save the file in the default location, My Documents, as `PrintMe.txt`. Click the Save button.

5. While still in Notepad, select File ➤ Print. Select HP LaserJet 4 and click the Print button. Repeat this step two more times so that you have sent a total of three print jobs. Close Notepad.

6. In the Printers folder, double-click HP LaserJet 4. At the top of the window, you will see that the status of the printer is Paused.

7. Right-click one of the print jobs in the print queue and select Cancel. The print job will be deleted.

8. Right-click one of the print jobs in the print queue and select Properties. The print job Properties dialog box appears. Change Notify from Administrator to Emily. Set the Priority from 1 to 99. For Schedule, select Only from 12:00 A.M. to 4:00 A.M. Then click the OK button.

9. Close all of the dialog boxes.

Connecting to Printers

Users can access a local printer or a shared printer. Once a printer has been shared, users with the Print permission can connect to the network printer through their network connection.

Microsoft ✓ *Exam* *Objective*

Connect to local and network print devices.

- Connect to a local print device.

To connect to a network printer, from the Desktop open My Network Places, expand Entire Network, and click View Entire Contents. Expand Microsoft Windows Network, then Workgroup, then *computername*. Finally, double-click the printer to connect to it.

In Exercise 12.6, you will connect to a local network printer.

EXERCISE 12.6

Connecting to a Local Network Printer

1. Double-click My Network Places and then double-click the Entire Network icon.

2. Click View Entire Contents and then double-click Microsoft Windows Network.

3. Double-click Workgroup and then double-click your computer's name. You should see HPDJ970 and HPLJ4. These are the share names for the printers you created in earlier exercises in this chapter.

4. Double-click HPDJ970. At this point, you have a network connection to the HP DeskJet 970Cse printer.

Summary

This chapter explained how to manage printing with Windows 2000 Professional. We covered the following topics:

- Basic printing principles, which included printing terminology, an overview of the Windows 2000 Professional printing process, and how printers and print devices work together

- How to create local and network printers

- Printer properties, including general properties, sharing properties, port properties, advanced properties, security properties, and device settings

- Print management tasks, such as setting default printers and canceling all print documents

- Document management tasks, such as pausing, resuming, and canceling print documents

- Connecting to shared printers

Exam Essentials

Know how to create local and network printers.   Understand what rights are required to create local and network printers, and the process used to create Windows 2000 printers.

Manage network printers.   Know all the options that can be used to manage network printers, including all the printer properties and when they would be used. Be able to set printer priorities and scheduling. Know how to change the location of the spooler file. Set separator files to print or not print based on user preference.

Understand how print permissions are used.   Be able to determine how print permissions are applied based on network requirements.

Be able to connect to print devices as a user.   Know how to connect to and use local and network printers as a user. Be able to manage your own print jobs as a user.

Key Terms

Before taking the exam, you should be familiar with the following terms:

Graphics Device Interface (GDI)

local printer

logical port

logical printer

network printer

physical port

print device

print driver

print processor

print queue

print server

print spooler

printer

printer pool

rendering

separator page

TCP/IP port

Review Questions

1. You want Kevin to be able to manage and create network printers. You do not want him to have administrative rights if they are not required for his printing-related tasks. To which of the following group memberships should you add Kevin?

   A. The Print Operators group

   B. The Power Users group

   C. The Administrators group

   D. The Print Managers group

2. Your network has a variety of network clients. You want to make printing as easy as possible. You have shared a network printer on a Windows 2000 Professional computer. For which of the following clients can you support drivers on the print server? (Choose all that apply.)

   A. Windows 3.1

   B. Windows 95

   C. Windows 98

   D. Windows NT 3.1

3. You have just created a network printer called LASER for a print device that is physically attached to your Windows 2000 Professional computer. You are wondering what print permissions should be applied so that network users can access the new printer. Which of the following print permissions are applied to the Everyone group by default on shared Windows 2000 printers?

   A. No permissions are granted

   B. Print

   C. Manage Printers

   D. Manage Documents

4. Meredith is a member of Everyone, Print Managers, Power Users, and Accounting. The following print permissions have been applied:

Group	Print	Manage Printers	Manage Documents
Everyone	Allow		
Print Managers		Allow	Allow
Accounting	Allow		Deny
Power Users	Allow	Allow	Allow

Based on these assignments, which of the following are Meredith's effective rights?

A. Print

B. Print and Manage Printers

C. Print and Manage Documents

D. Print, Manage Printers, and Manage Documents

5. You have five print devices that are all used by a pool of administrative assistants. You want to configure the printing environment so that print jobs are sent to the first print device that is available. What requirement must be met if you want to use a printer pool?

A. You must use the same print manufacturer and model for all print devices within the printer pool.

B. All of your print devices must be network printers.

C. All of your print devices must be configured to use the same port.

D. All of your print devices must be able to use the same print driver.

6. Dan sits closest to the Accounting printer, and you want him to be able to help manage it. Which of the following options can be managed by Dan if you give him the Manage Documents permission to the printer?

A. Connect and send jobs to a printer

B. Pause a printer

C. Pause a print job

D. Manage the status of a printer

7. You have an Acme laser printer called Acme1, used by 20 network Sales users. The printer has failed and has been sent out for servicing. It is estimated that the printer will be out of service for one week. In the meantime, you want the users to have all their print jobs connected to another Acme laser printer called Acme2, which is used by the Marketing staff. What is the easiest way to have the Sales users send their jobs to Acme2 until the Acme1 printer is back in service?

A. Have the Sales users create a printer for Acme2 and set this printer as their default printer. When Acme1 is back in service, have them reconfigure their default printer as Acme1.

B. Create a new port that will take all the print jobs sent to Acme1 and redirect them to Acme2. After the print device comes back into service, disable the redirection.

C. Rename the Acme2 printer to Acme1.

D. Rename the Acme1 printer to Acme2.

8. You have 10 users who send their print jobs to a Windows 2000 printer called MISLaser. You want to have a custom separator page that identifies the user and the date and time when the job is printed. You have a separator page created called `custom.sep`. Where should this file be stored?

A. *Windir*\Printers

B. *Windir*\Queues

C. *Windir*\System32

D. *Windir*\System32\Printers

9. You have a Windows 2000 printer called ABCLaser that is associated with the ABC laser device. This printer keeps jamming. Tim sits close to the print device and is able to unjam the printer. To perform this maintenance, he needs to be able to pause and restart the printer. What is the minimum permissions that Jim needs to perform this task?

   A. Grant Jim the Manage Documents print permission for the ABCLaser printer.

   B. Grant Jim the Manage Printers print permission for the ABCLaser printer.

   C. Grant Jim the Full Control print permission for the ABCLaser printer.

   D. Make Jim a Printer Operator.

10. Your Windows 2000 Professional computer has an ABC laser printer attached. Five other users in your workgroup want to use your printer. These clients are also running the Windows 2000 Professional operating system. You create a printer called ABCLP and share it. All of the users can attach to the share and use the printer. Six months later, you update the print driver. What do the other users in your group need to do to update the print driver on their computers?

    A. Use the Upgrade Driver Wizard to update the driver on their computers.

    B. Upgrade the print driver through the Printers utility.

    C. Use the Device Manager Wizard to update the driver on their computers.

    D. Do nothing; the next time they attach to the printer, the new print driver will be loaded automatically.

11. You have configured your network printer to be shared. When you configured the printer, you specified that it uses a Windows 2000 print driver. Which of the following clients can use the printer?

    A. Only Windows 2000 clients

    B. Windows NT 4 clients and Windows 2000 clients

    C. Windows 98 clients, Windows NT 4 clients, and Windows 2000 clients

    D. Windows 95 clients, Windows 98 clients, Windows NT 4 clients, and Windows 2000 clients

12. One of your printer devices is attached to the network through a network card that uses the TCP/IP protocol. What do you need to configure for this printer?

    A. A local port

    B. A network port

    C. A TCP/IP port

    D. A URL port

13. You have set up the Accounting and Sales groups to share the same printer device. You want the Sales group's documents to print first. You create an Accounting printer and a Sales printer and assign the respective groups' permissions to their printers. Both printers point to the shared print device. How should you configure the printer priority? (Choose two answers.)

    A. Configure Accounting priority 1

    B. Configure Accounting priority 99

    C. Configure Sales priority 1

    D. Configure Sales priority 99

14. You have been having problems with the HR printer. You are not sure if the problem is with the print device or with the shared printer configuration. Which of the following steps can you take to bypass network spooling?

    A. In the Advanced tab of the printer Properties dialog box, configure the Print Directly to the Printer option.

    B. In the General tab of the printer Properties dialog box, configure the Print Directly to the Printer option.

    C. In the Advanced tab of the printer Properties dialog box, configure the Bypass Network Printing option.

    D. In the General tab of the printer Properties dialog box, configure the Bypass Network Printing option.

15. You want your network printer to service print jobs from 8:00 A.M. to 5:00 P.M. In the Properties dialog shown here, which tab should you click to configure the printer?

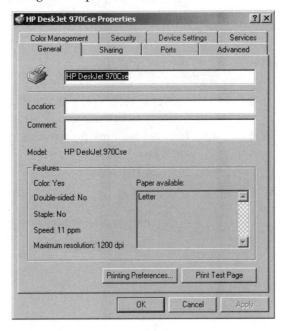

    A. Sharing

    B. Services

    C. Device Settings

    D. Advanced

Answers to Review Questions

1. **B.** In order to create a new printer on a Windows 2000 Professional computer, you must be logged on as a member of the Power Users or Administrators group. Because you want Kevin to have the least amount of administrative rights, however, you should choose the Power Users group for him. Print Operators and Print Managers groups do not exist by default on Windows 2000 Professional computers.

2. **B, C, D.** You can't provide drivers for Windows 3.1 clients. You can provide drivers for the following clients: Windows 95 and Windows 98, Windows NT 3.1 (Alpha, Intel, MIPS, and PowerPC platforms), Windows 3.5 or 3.51 (Alpha, Intel, MIPS, and PowerPC platforms), and Windows NT 4 (Alpha, Intel, MIPS, and PowerPC platforms).

3. **B.** By default, the Everyone group has Print permission to shared printers. Users also have the Manage Documents permission if they are the Creator Owner of a document, but they can't manage other users' documents.

4. **B.** Normally, your print permissions are combined based on group membership. In this case, however, Meredith is a member of a group that has been explicitly denied the Manage Documents permission. Meredith's effective rights are Print and Manage Printers.

5. **D.** In order to use a printer pool, all of your print devices must be able to use the same print driver. When they can use the same print driver, the print devices do not necessarily have to be from the same manufacturer or the same model. Print devices in a pool can be a mixture of local and network printers. They are not configured to use the same port. When you enable printer pooling through the Ports tab of the printer Properties dialog box, you can check multiple ports. You would check each port to which a print device was attached.

6. C. The Manage Documents permission allows a user to manage print documents, including pausing, resuming, and deleting queued documents. A user must have Print permission to connect and send jobs to a printer. In order to pause a printer or manage its status, a user must have the Manage Printers permission.

7. B. If your print device fails, you can redirect all its scheduled print jobs to another print device that has been configured as a printer. For this redirection to work, the new print device must be able to use the same print driver as the old print device. To redirect print jobs, click the Add Port button in the Ports tab, highlight New Port, and choose New Port Type. In the Port Name dialog box, type the UNC name of the printer to which you want to redirect the jobs, in the format *computername**printer*.

8. C. By default, Windows 2000 separator page files are stored in the *Windir*\System32 folder.

9. B. A person or group with the Manage Printers print permission has administrative control of the printer. With this permission, a user or group can pause and restart the printer, change the spooler settings, share and unshare the printer, change print permissions, and manage printer properties.

10. D. Windows 2000 clients automatically download the print driver for a print device when they connect to a network printer. If the print driver is updated on the print server, the driver is automatically updated on the clients the next time they send a print job.

11. A. If you load only Windows 2000 drivers, the other client platforms will not be able to use the printer. In Windows 2000, you can also specify (and provide) print drivers for Windows 95/98 clients, Windows NT 3.1 clients (Alpha, Intel, or MIPS), Windows NT 3.5 and 3.51 clients (Alpha, Intel, MIPS, or PowerPC), and Windows NT 4 clients (Alpha, Intel, MIPS, or PowerPC).

12. C. If you have a print device that attaches to the network with a network card using the TCP/IP protocol, you must configure a TCP/IP port for the printer's use.

13. A, D. You can set printer priority from 1 to 99, with 1 as the lowest priority and 99 as the highest priority.

14. A. The Print Directly to the Printer option, in the Advanced tab of the printer Properties dialog box, bypasses spooling altogether. You can use this setting to troubleshoot printer problems. If you can print to a print device directly, but you can't print through the spooler, then you know that your spooler is corrupt or has other problems.

15. D. The Advanced tab of the printer Properties dialog box includes options for configuring a printer's availability.

Chapter 13

Dial-Up Networking and Internet Connectivity

MICROSOFT EXAM OBJECTIVES COVERED IN THIS CHAPTER:

✓ **Implement, manage, and troubleshoot input and output (I/O) devices.**

- Install, configure, and manage modems.

✓ **Connect to computers by using dial-up networking.**

- Connect to computers by using a virtual private network (VPN) connection.
- Create a dial-up connection to connect to a remote access server.
- Connect to the Internet by using dial-up networking.
- Configure and troubleshoot Internet Connection Sharing.

✓ **Connect to local and network print devices.**

- Connect to an Internet printer.

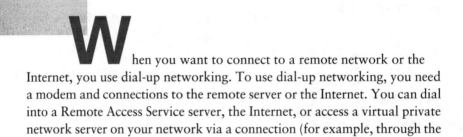

When you want to connect to a remote network or the Internet, you use dial-up networking. To use dial-up networking, you need a modem and connections to the remote server or the Internet. You can dial into a Remote Access Service server, the Internet, or access a virtual private network server on your network via a connection (for example, through the Internet).

With Windows 2000 Professional, you can also configure a feature called *Internet connection sharing*. It allows you to connect a single computer to the network. Then you can enable other users on the same, small network to share the Internet connection. You can also configure printers to be used through the Internet, or to be accessed by local clients through a Web browser.

In this chapter, you will learn how to configure dial-up networking and create dial-up connections on a Windows 2000 Professional client.

The server side of dial-up networking is covered in detail in *MCSE: Windows 2000 Server Study Guide,* 2nd ed., by Lisa Donald with James Chellis (Sybex, 2001).

Setting Up a Modem

D*ial-up networking* allows remote users (for example, a person working from home or someone with a laptop on a business trip) to dial into the network or the Internet. Before you can use dial-up networking, you must have your computer configured to dial out. This requires that you have a modem installed and properly configured.

Microsoft Exam Objective	**Implement, manage, and troubleshoot input and output (I/O) devices.** ▪ Install, configure, and manage modems.

The other subobjectives for the "Implement, manage, and troubleshoot input and output (I/O) devices" objective are covered in Chapter 4, "Configuring the Windows 2000 Environment."

If you install a Plug and Play modem on your Windows 2000 computer, it should be recognized automatically, and an appropriate driver should be loaded.

You can configure and manage the modems installed on your computer through Device Manager. To access Device Manager, right-click My Computer and select Manage from the pop-up menu. Select System Tools, then Device Manager. In the Device Manager window, select Modems and then double-click the modem you want to manage. This brings up the modem's Properties dialog box, as shown in Figure 13.1. This dialog box has six tabs: General, Modem, Diagnostics, Advanced, Driver, and Resources. The options on these tabs are covered in the following sections.

Avoid changing the default modem properties unless advised to by your modem manufacturer or the entity you are connecting to (for example, your Internet service provider). If you make incorrect alterations to the modem configuration, your modem may not work.

Configuring General Modem Properties

The General tab of the modem Properties dialog box (see Figure 13.1) displays the device type, manufacturer, and location. It also shows the device status.

If the modem is not working properly, you can click the Troubleshooter button to start a Troubleshooting Wizard that will help you determine the cause of the problem. See Chapter 4 for more information about troubleshooting devices.

FIGURE 13.1 The General tab of the modem Properties dialog box

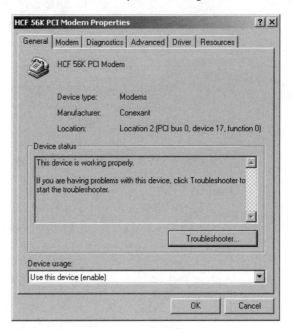

Configuring Modem Properties

The Modem tab, shown in Figure 13.2, shows the port to which the modem is attached. From this tab, you can set the following options:

- The speaker volume for the modem

- The maximum port speed (specified in bits per second)

- Dial control to wait for a dial tone before dialing

FIGURE 13.2   The Modem tab of the modem Properties dialog box

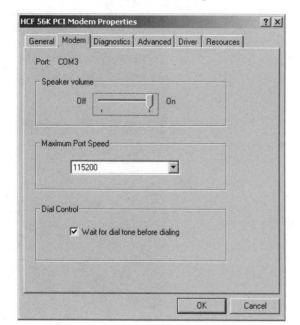

Running Modem Diagnostics

Through the Diagnostics tab, shown in Figure 13.3, you can query the modem. This process can be used in troubleshooting to ensure that the modem is properly responding to requests. Click the Query Modem button, and Device Manager will test the modem by issuing a series of modem commands. These commands and the responses sent back from the modem are listed in the dialog box.

Configuring Advanced Modem Properties

The Advanced tab, shown in Figure 13.4, allows you to specify additional initialization commands. You can also configure advanced port settings and change default preferences, as explained in the following sections.

FIGURE 13.3 The Diagnostics tab of the modem Properties dialog box

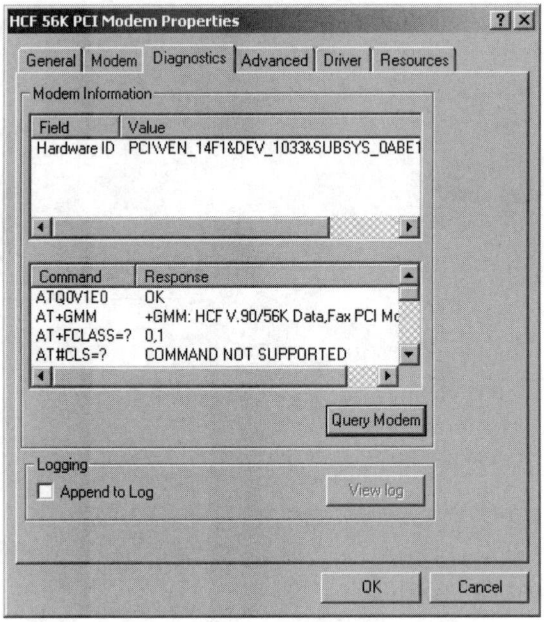

FIGURE 13.4 The Advanced tab of the modem Properties dialog box

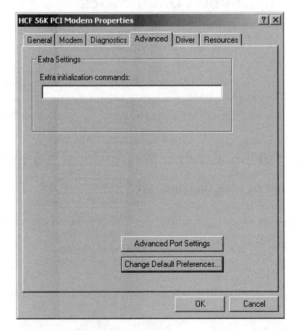

Advanced Port Settings

Clicking the Advanced Port Settings button brings up the Advanced Settings dialog box for your communications (COM) port, as shown in Figure 13.5. Through this dialog box, you can specify whether the port will use FIFO (first in, first out) buffers, as well as the settings that will be used for the receive and transmit buffers. Lower settings can be used to correct connection problems. Higher settings can increase performance.

FIGURE 13.5 Advanced settings for a COM port dialog box

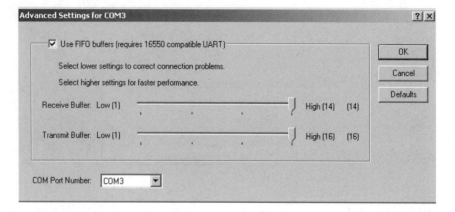

Default Preferences

Clicking the Change Default Preferences button brings up the modem Default Preferences dialog box, as shown in Figure 13.6.

In the General tab, you can set preferences for calls and data connections. The Call Preferences options include settings for disconnecting a call if the connection is idle for more than the specified time, and how long to wait for a connection before canceling a call. The Data Connection Preferences include settings for the port speed, the data protocol, compression (enabled or disabled), and flow control (hardware or software).

Through the Advanced tab (Figure 13.7), you can specify the hardware settings for the port, including data bits, parity, stop bits, and modulation.

FIGURE 13.6 The General tab of the modem Default Preferences dialog box

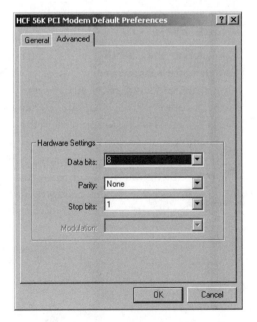

FIGURE 13.7 The Advanced tab of the modem Default Preferences dialog box

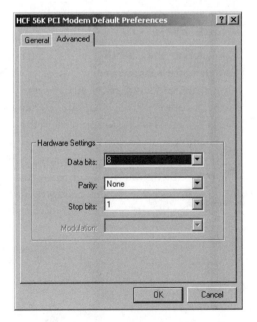

Viewing Driver Details and Updating Drivers

The Driver tab of the modem Properties dialog box, shown in Figure 13.8, displays information about the modem driver that is currently loaded. Clicking the Driver Details button brings up a dialog box with additional information about the modem driver. To uninstall the driver, click the Uninstall button. To update it, click the Update Driver button. See Chapter 4 for details on updating drivers.

FIGURE 13.8   The Driver tab of the modem Properties dialog box

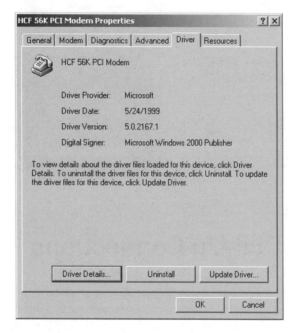

Viewing Modem Resources

The Resources tab, shown in Figure 13.9, lists the resources that are used by your modem. Resources include memory, I/O memory, and interrupt request (IRQ) settings. You can use this information to detect resource conflicts, which may arise if you have non–Plug and Play hardware installed on your computer.

FIGURE 13.9 The Resources tab of the modem Properties dialog box

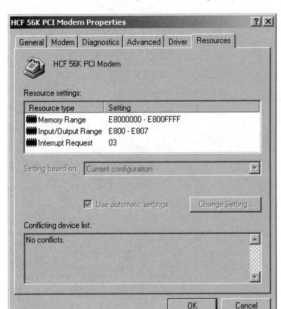

Using Dial-Up Connections

You can use dial-up connections to dial into Remote Access Service (RAS) servers or into the Internet. Windows 2000 also supports virtual private network connections and Internet connection sharing. You will learn how to create these connections in the following sections.

Microsoft ✓ ***Exam*** ***Objective***

Connect to computers by using dial-up networking.

- Connect to computers by using a virtual private network (VPN) connection.

- Create a dial-up connection to connect to a remote access server.

- Connect to the Internet by using dial-up networking.

- Configure and troubleshoot Internet Connection Sharing.

Dialing In to a Remote Access Server

When you dial in to a *Remote Access Service (RAS)* server, you are making a direct connection to an existing RAS server, as illustrated in Figure 13.10. You can connect to the RAS server through a modem connection, an Integrated Services Digital Network (ISDN) connection, or a null-modem cable. The RAS server and the RAS client must use the same connectivity option. They must also use the same protocols as well as compatible security protocols.

FIGURE 13.10 Connecting to a Remote Access Service (RAS) server

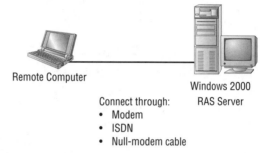

Remote Computer

Windows 2000
RAS Server

Connect through:
• Modem
• ISDN
• Null-modem cable

Creating a RAS Connection

To configure a RAS client, take the following steps:

1. Select Start ➤ Settings ➤ Control Panel and double-click the Network and Dial-up Connections icon.

2. The Network and Dial-up Connections window appears, as shown in Figure 13.11. Double-click the Make New Connection icon.

FIGURE 13.11 The Network and Dial-up Connections window

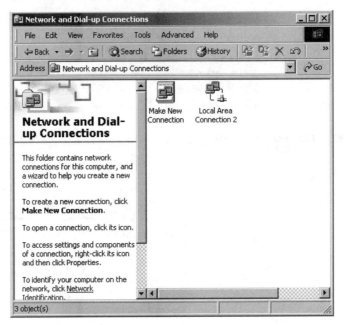

3. When the Network Connection Wizard starts, click the Next button to continue.

4. The Network Connection Type dialog box appears next, as shown in Figure 13.12. Select the Dial-up to Private Network option and click the Next button.

5. Next up is the Phone Number to Dial dialog box. Check the Use Dialing Rules check box (if you don't select this option, you won't be able to access the area code field). Enter the telephone number you wish to dial. If the telephone number is in a different country, enter the associated country code in the Country/Region Code field (for example, the Czech Republic's country code is 420 when you are calling internationally). After you enter the information, click the Next button.

6. In the Connection Availability dialog box that appears next, you can specify that the connection is for all users or only for the current user. If you specify that the connection is for all users, this turns on Internet Connection Sharing. Make your selection and click the Next button.

 **FIGURE 13.12** The Network Connection Type dialog box

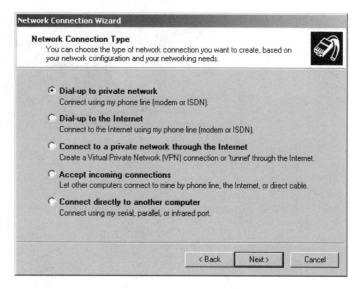

7. In the Completing the Network Connection Wizard dialog box, you can specify the name that will be used for this connection. To save this network connection, click the Finish button.

8. Next you'll see the Connect Dial-up Connection dialog box (Figure 13.13). Here you specify the username and password to be used when dialing into the remote location. You can also specify the number that you will dial and the location you are dialing from. Enter the information and then click the Dial button.

9. When the connection is established, you will see the Connection Complete dialog box. Click the OK button. You are now connected to the RAS server and can use the remote network.

FIGURE 13.13   The Connect Dial-up Connection dialog box

    Configuring a RAS server is covered in *MCSE: Windows 2000 Server Study Guide,* 2nd ed., by Lisa Donald with James Chellis (Sybex, 2001).

Managing the Properties of an RAS Connection

To manage the properties of a RAS connection, open the Network and Dial-up Connections window, right-click the RAS connection, and select Properties from the pop-up menu. This brings up the Dial-up Connection Properties dialog box shown in Figure 13.14. This dialog box has five tabs: General, Options, Security, Networking, and Sharing. The options on these tabs are covered in the following sections.

FIGURE 13.14   The General tab of the Dial-up Connection Properties dialog box

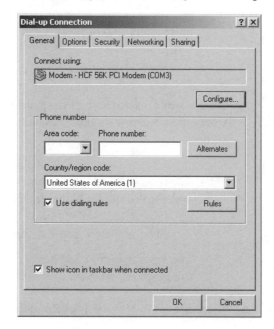

Configuring General RAS Connection Properties

The General tab (see Figure 13.14) includes options for configuring the connection you will use and the telephone number you are dialing. You can also specify whether an icon will be displayed on the Taskbar when a connection is in use.

The Connect Using option specifies the device that will be used to create the connection (for example, a modem or an ISDN adapter). To configure specific properties of the connection device, click the Configure button.

The Phone Number section has text boxes for the area code and telephone number of the connection. To specify alternate telephone numbers to make a connection, click the Alternates button. If you choose to use dialing rules, you can click the Rules button and configure the connection to access an outside line, disable call waiting, or use a calling card.

Configuring RAS Connection Options

The Options tab, shown in Figure 13.15, contains dialing options and re-dialing options. You can configure the following options for dialing:

- The Display Progress While Connecting option displays the progress of the connection attempt.

- The Prompt for Name and Password, Certificate, etc. option specifies that before a connection is attempted, the user will be prompted for a username, password, or (if *smart card* authentication is being used) a certificate.

Smart cards are hardware devices used to provide additional security. They store public and private keys, passwords, and other personal information securely.

- The Include Windows Logon Domain option works in conjunction with the Prompt for Name and Password, Certificate, etc. option. This option specifies that Windows 2000 logon-domain information should be requested prior to initiating a connection.
- The Prompt for Phone Number option allows the telephone number to be viewed, selected, or modified prior to initiating a connection.

FIGURE 13.15 The Options tab of the Dial-up Connection Properties dialog box

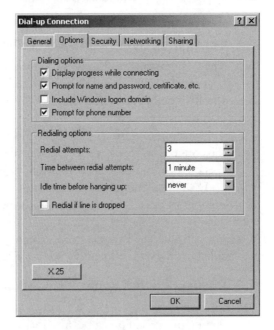

The options for redialing let you specify the number of redial attempts if the connection is not established and the time between the redial attempts. You can also designate how long a connection will remain idle before the computer hangs up. If you want the computer to redial the connection number should the connection be dropped, check the Redial If Line Is Dropped check box.

Configuring RAS Connection Security

Security settings are among the most important options to be configured for dial-up connections. You can set typical or advanced security options in the Security tab of the Dial-up Connection Properties dialog box, as shown in Figure 13.16. This tab also has options for interactive logons and scripting.

FIGURE 13.16   The Security tab of the Dial-up Connection Properties dialog box

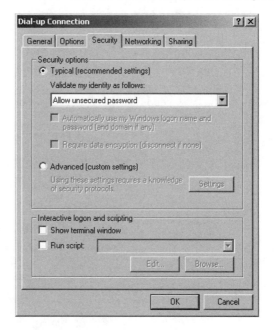

Connections that are more secure require more overhead and are usually slower. Less-secure connections require less overhead and are typically faster.

TYPICAL SECURITY SETTINGS

You generally will configure typical security settings unless you need to use specific security protocols. When you select the Typical radio button, you can then choose to validate the user's identity, to automatically use the Windows logon name and password (and domain if specified), and whether data encryption is required. For validating the user's identity, you can select from the following options:

- Allow Unsecured Password specifies that the password can be transmitted without any encryption.

- Require Secured Password specifies that the password must be encrypted prior to transmission.

- Use Smart Card specifies that you must use a smart card.

ADVANCED SECURITY SETTINGS

If you need to configure specific security protocols, select the Advanced radio button in the Security tab and then click the Settings button. This brings up the Advanced Security Settings dialog box, as shown in Figure 13.17

FIGURE 13.17   The Advanced Security Settings dialog box

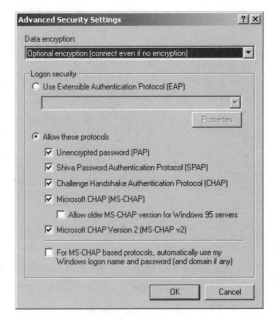

This dialog box allows you to configure the type of data encryption that will be employed. You also specify whether logon security will use the Extensible Authentication Protocol (EAP), which is used in conjunction with other security devices, including smart cards and certificates. In addition, you select from the following protocols for logon security:

- Unencrypted password (PAP), which uses a plain-text password and is the least secure authentication.

- Shiva Password Authentication Protocol (SPAP), which is used to dial in to and be authenticated by Shiva servers.

- Challenge Handshake Authentication Protocol (CHAP), which negotiates a secure form of encrypted authentication.

- Microsoft CHAP (MS-CHAP), which uses the one-way encryption with challenge-response method. This protocol was designed for Windows NT and Windows 2000, but it can also be used by Windows 9x.

- Microsoft CHAP Version 2 (MS-CHAP v2), which is a more secure form of MS-CHAP.

INTERACTIVE LOGON AND SCRIPTING

The Interactive Logon and Scripting options on the Security tab are provided for users who use terminal services for remote access. These options allow you to display a terminal window after dialing, and run a script after dialing.

Scripting features are only supported for serial modems. These features are not available for ISDN devices.

Configuring Networking Options for RAS Connections

The Networking tab, shown in Figure 13.18 contains networking options for the dial-up connection. You can configure the wide area network (WAN) protocol you will use and the network components that will be employed by the network connection.

FIGURE 13.18 The Networking tab of the Dial-up Connection Properties dialog box

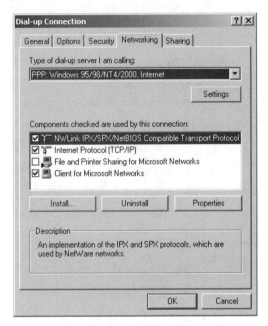

Your choices for the WAN protocol are the Point-to-Point Protocol (PPP) or Serial Line Internet Protocol (SLIP). PPP offers more features and is the WAN protocol used by Windows 9*x*, Windows NT, Windows 2000, and most Internet servers. SLIP is an older protocol that is used with some Unix servers.

The network components used by the connection might include the protocols (such as NWLink IPX/SPX/NetBIOS Compatible Transport Protocol and TCP/IP) and the client software (such as File and Printer Sharing for Microsoft Networks and Client for Microsoft Networks).

Sharing

The Sharing tab of the Dial-up Connection Properties dialog box is used to configure Internet connection sharing. These options are covered in the "Using Internet Connection Sharing" section later in this chapter.

Dialing In to the Internet

When you dial in to the Internet, you use an Internet account, as illustrated in Figure 13.19. The Internet account is obtained through a valid *Internet service provider (ISP)*. There are many ISPs to choose from, and they usually supply software to facilitate your Internet connection through their service. If you do not have software from your ISP, you can set up an Internet connection the first time you click the Internet Explorer icon or the Connect to the Internet icon on the Desktop.

FIGURE 13.19 Making an Internet connection

Remote Computer   Internet Service Provider   Internet

In Exercise 13.1, you will create a new dial-up Internet connection for a new Internet account.

EXERCISE 13.1

Creating a Dial-Up Connection to the Internet

1. Select Start ➢ Settings ➢ Control Panel and double-click the Network and Dial-up Connections icon.

2. In the Network and Dial-up Connections window, double-click the Make New Connection icon.

3. When the Welcome to the Network Connection Wizard starts, click the Next button.

4. In the Network Connection Type dialog box, select the Dial-up to the Internet option and click the Next button.

5. In the Welcome to the Internet Connection Wizard dialog box, you can choose from the following options:

   - The I Want to Sign Up for a New Internet Account option guides you through selecting an ISP and setting up a new account. You can use this option if you do not already have an ISP.

EXERCISE 13.1 *(continued)*

- The I Want to Transfer My Existing Internet Account to This Computer option lets you set up a connection to your ISP. You can use this option if you already have an account with an ISP, but you do not have any software configured on your computer to make a connection to the ISP.

- The I Want to Set Up My Internet Account Manually, or I Want to Connect through a Local Area Network (LAN) option allows you greater control over how your Internet connection is set up.

For this exercise, select the I Want to Sign Up for a New Internet Account option and click the Next button.

6. Microsoft will use the Microsoft Internet Referral Service to provide you with a list of ISPs in your area. When the list of ISPs in your area appears, select an ISP and click the Next button.

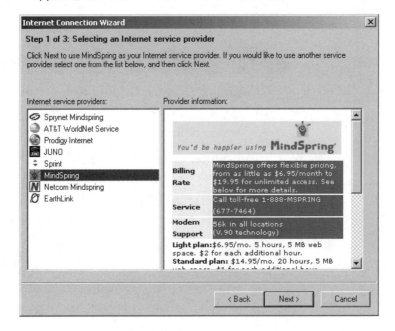

7. Fill in the next dialog box to provide the information for signing up with an ISP. Then click the Next button.

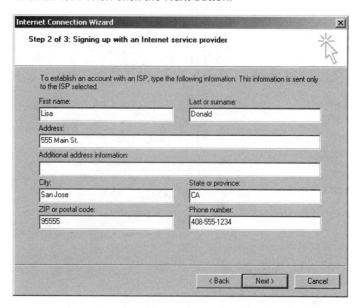

8. Select the billing option you will use and click the Next button.

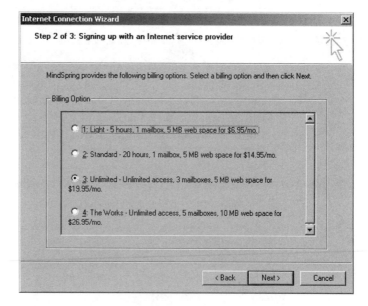

EXERCISE 13.1 *(continued)*

9. Complete the payment information and click the Next button.

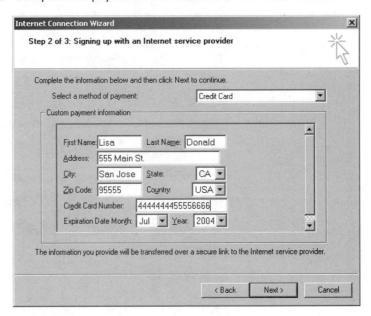

10. When you are connected to the ISP, accept the ISP's service agreement and designate a username and password.

Using Virtual Private Network (VPN) Connections

A *virtual private network (VPN)* is a private network that uses links across private or public networks (such as the Internet). When data is sent over the remote link, it is encapsulated and encrypted and requires authentication services. In order to have a VPN, you must have a Windows 2000 Server computer that has been configured as a VPN server. Figure 13.20 illustrates a VPN.

FIGURE 13.20 Making a virtual private network (VPN) connection

The main advantage of using a VPN rather than an RAS connection is that with an RAS connection, a long-distance call might be required to dial into the RAS server. With a VPN connection, all you need is access to a network such as the Internet.

In Exercise 13.2, you will configure the client for a VPN connection.

EXERCISE 13.2

Configuring a VPN Client

1. Select Start ➢ Settings ➢ Control Panel and double-click the Network and Dial-up Connections icon.

2. In the Network and Dial-up Connections window, double-click the Make New Connection icon.

3. When the Welcome to the Network Connection Wizard starts, click the Next button.

4. In the Network Connection Type dialog box, select the Connect to a Private Network through the Internet option and click the Next button.

5. In the Public Network dialog box, select the Automatically Dial This Initial Connection radio button, make sure Dial-Up Connection is selected in the box below, and click the Next button.

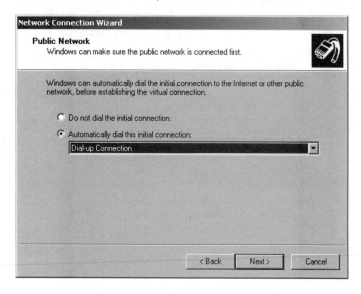

6. In the Destination Address dialog box, enter the host name or the IP address of the computer that you will connect to. Then click the Next button.

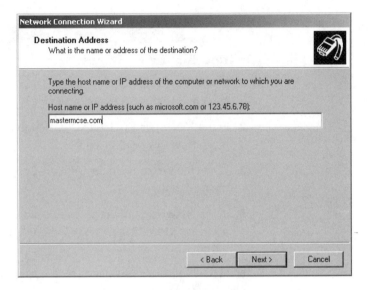

7. In the Connection Availability dialog box, select the For All Users option and click the Next button.

8. In the Completing the Network Connection Wizard dialog box, specify the name that you want to use for the connection and click the Finish button.

9. In the Initial Connection dialog box, click the Yes button to continue.

10. In the Connect Dial-up Connection dialog box, specify the username and password for logging on to the VPN server, and the telephone number of the network that you will dial into. Then click the Dial button.

11. In the dialog box that appears after the connection is established, click the OK button.

Configuring a VPN server is covered in *MCSE: Windows 2000 Server Study Guide,* 2nd ed., by Lisa Donald with James Chellis (Sybex, 2001).

Using Internet Connection Sharing

Internet connection sharing allows you to connect a small network to the Internet through a single connection, as illustrated in Figure 13.21. The computer that dials in to the Internet provides network address translation, addressing, and name resolution services for all of the computers on the network. Through Internet connection sharing, the other computers on the network can use Internet applications such as Internet Explorer and Outlook Express, as well as access Internet resources.

FIGURE 13.21 Internet connection sharing

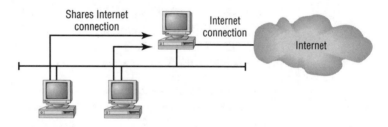

In order to use Internet connection sharing, the following conditions must be met:

- All of the network clients must get their IP addresses automatically through the DHCP allocator.

When Internet connection sharing is enabled, the Internet host computer's address becomes 192.168.0.1 with a subnetmask of 255.255.255.0. The host also becomes the DHCP allocator, which acts as a "baby" DHCP server. The allocator will give out addresses randomly to the clients, in the range 192.168.0.2 through 192.168.0.254 with a subnetmask of 255.255.255.0.

- The host computer must be configured to support Internet connection sharing.

- The client computers must be configured to use Internet connection sharing.

In order to configure Internet connection sharing, you must be a member of the Administrators group.

 Real World Scenario

Using Internet Connection Sharing

You have Windows 2000 Professional on your home computer, which has Internet access. You also have three other computers running Windows 95, Windows 98, and Windows NT 4.0. These computers, used as a part of a home lab for testing and training preparation, are connected through an Ethernet LAN using TCP/IP. They do not have Internet access, and you want to change this so that you can access the Internet from any of your computers.

This alteration is easily accomplished through Internet connection sharing. You will need to enable the Internet Connection Sharing service on the Windows 2000 Professional computer, and configure your client computers to use Internet connection sharing through their Internet browser software.

Configuring Internet Connection Sharing on the Host Computer

The computer that will act as the host computer for Internet connection sharing must be configured to support this option. Following are the options that can be configured:

- Whether Internet connection sharing is enabled. If it is, watch out— local network access may be momentarily disrupted because the IP address will automatically be reassigned to the computers that use Internet connection sharing.

- Whether on-demand dialing is enabled. When it is, if you do not have a permanent connection on the computer that hosts Internet connection sharing, the host computer will automatically dial out whenever a client tries to access the Internet. Enabling Internet Connection Sharing automatically enables on-demand dialing.

- Which applications and services can be used through the shared connection. For example, you could specify that only FTP requests on port 21, Telnet requests on port 23, and HTTP requests on port 80 can be passed through the shared Internet connection.

To configure Internet connection sharing on the host computer, take the following steps:

1. Create an Internet connection or a VPN connection.

2. Verify that the host computer is configured as a DHCP client and that each client (Internet Sharing) computer is also configured as a DHCP client. If the host has a static address, it will be changed to 192.168.0.1 automatically.

3. Select Start ➤ Settings and double-click the Network and Dial-up Connections icon.

4. Right-click the connection you want to share, and select Properties from the pop-up menu.

5. The Properties dialog box for the selected connection appears. Click the Sharing tab and check the Enable Internet Connection Sharing for This Connection check box, as shown in Figure 13.22.

   Enabling Internet Connection Sharing automatically enables on-demand dialing. When on-demand dialing is enabled, if the Internet connection is not active and another computer tries to access Internet resources, a connection will be automatically established.

FIGURE 13.22 The Sharing tab of the Properties dialog box for a VPN connection

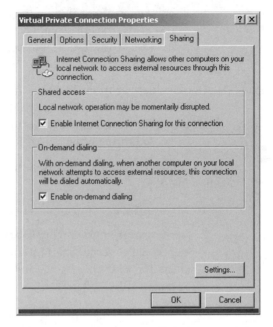

6. Click the Settings button to access the Internet Connection Sharing Settings dialog box (Figure 13.23). This dialog box allows you to specify which applications and services can be serviced through the shared Internet connection. If you leave the blank default settings as is, then all applications and services are supported. However, you may want to limit access to one application—for example, HTTP. If so, you could configure HTTP requests to only be serviced by limited access to HTTP on port 80. When you are done, click the OK button twice to close both open dialog boxes.

FIGURE 13.23 Internet Connection Sharing Settings dialog box

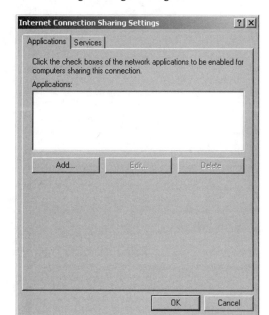

Configuring Internet Connection Sharing on the Network Computers

To configure Internet connection sharing on the network computers, take the following steps:

1. Right-click the Internet Explorer icon on the Desktop and select Properties from the pop-up menu.

2. In the Internet Properties dialog box, click the Connections tab (Figure 13.24) and click the Setup button.

FIGURE 13.24 The Connections tab of the Internet Properties dialog box

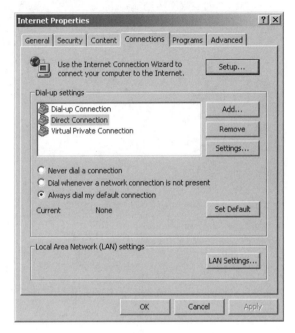

3. The Internet Connection Wizard starts. Select either I Want to Set Up My Internet Connection Manually, or I Want to Connect through a Local Area Network (LAN). Click the Next button.

4. Next you'll see the Setting Up Your Internet Connection dialog box, shown in Figure 13.25. Select the I Connect through a Local Area Network (LAN) option and click the Next button.

5. The Local Area Network Internet Configuration dialog box appears, as shown in Figure 13.26. Here you can choose the Automatic Discovery of Proxy Server option to automatically configure proxy settings, or the Manual Proxy Server option to configure these settings manually. Make your selection and click the Next button.

FIGURE 13.25   The Setting Up Your Internet Connection dialog box

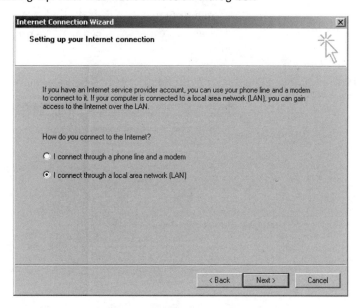

FIGURE 13.26   The Local Area Network Internet Configuration dialog box

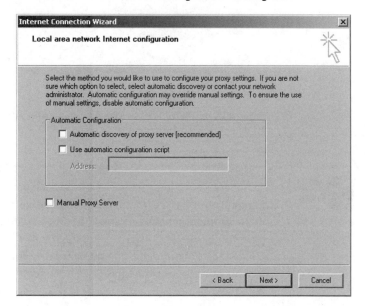

6. The Set Up Your Internet Mail Account dialog box appears next, as shown in Figure 13.27. If desired, you can set up an Internet mail account. In this example, a mail account is not set up. Click the Next button.

FIGURE 13.27   The Set Up Your Internet Mail Account dialog box

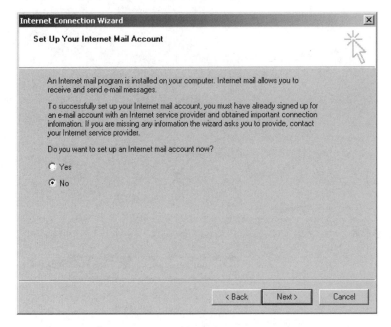

7. In the Completing the Internet Connection Wizard dialog box, click the Finish button.

Do not configure Internet connection sharing on corporate networks with domain controllers, DNS servers, WINS servers, DHCP servers, routers, or other computers that use static IP addresses. When Internet connection sharing is configured, it causes computers that use the shared Internet connection to lose their IP configuration and generates a new IP configuration. Normal network connections then have to be manually reset to access local network resources.

In Exercise 13.3, you will configure the VPN connection you created in Exercise 13.2 to support Internet connection sharing.

EXERCISE 13.3

Configuring Internet Connection Sharing

1. Select Start ➢ Settings and double-click the Network and Dial-up Connections icon. (You can also go to Network and Dial-up Connections through Control Panel.)

2. In the Network and Dial-up Connections window, right-click the connection you want to share and select Properties from the pop-up menu.

3. In the Virtual Private Connections Properties dialog box, click the Sharing tab. Check the Enable Internet Connection Sharing for This Connection check box. Enabling Internet Connection Sharing automatically enables on-demand dialing. Click the OK button.

4. Since your computer is not configured as a DHCP client, you will see a message warning you that the IP address that is assigned to the computer may be lost. Click the Yes button to enable Internet connection sharing.

Managing Internet Printers

Windows 2000 automatically supports *Internet printing* when *Internet Information Services (IIS)* is installed on a Windows 2000 Server or a Windows 2000 Professional client. (Throughout the discussion in this section, the Windows 2000 Server and Windows 2000 Professional client work identically with one exception: A Windows 2000 Professional client cannot support more than 10 concurrent sessions.) Any printers that are shared on the Windows 2000 Server are then automatically made accessible to Internet users through a protocol called *Internet Print Protocol (IPP)*. Windows 2000 clients automatically include IPP print support, and the users can browse and print to *Internet printers* through Internet Explorer 4.01 or higher.

Microsoft ✓ ***Exam*** ***Objective***

Connect to local and network print devices.

- Connect to an Internet printer.

This chapter covers the material related to Internet printing for the "Connect to local and network print devices" objective. The other subobjectives for this objective are covered in Chapter 12, "Managing Printing."

To install a printer from the Internet or an intranet, use the printer's URL as the name of the printer. To support all browsers, an administrator must choose basic authentication. Internet Explorer supports LAN Manager Challenge/Response and Kerberos version 5 authentication.

Adding an Internet Printer

To install an Internet printer on a Windows 2000 Server or Professional client, you must first install IIS. Then you can create a shared printer (see Chapter 12 for details on setting up a shared printer). Then complete the following steps:

1. Select Start ≻ Settings ≻ Printers.

2. In the Printers folder, double-click Add Printer and click the Next button.

3. The Add Printer Wizard starts. Click the Next button.

4. The Local or Network Printer dialog box appears, as shown in Figure 13.28. Select Network Printer and click the Next button.

FIGURE 13.28 The Local or Network Printer dialog box

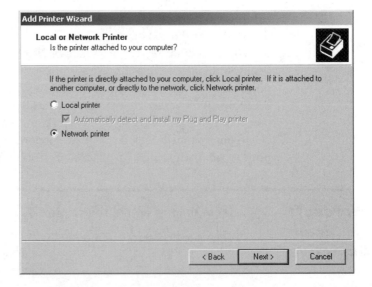

5. The Locate Your Printer dialog box appears, as shown in Figure 13.29. Click the Connect to a Printer on the Internet or on Your Intranet option. In the URL box, type **http://*computername*/printers/ *share_name*/.printer** and click the Next button.

FIGURE 13.29   The Locate Your Printer dialog box

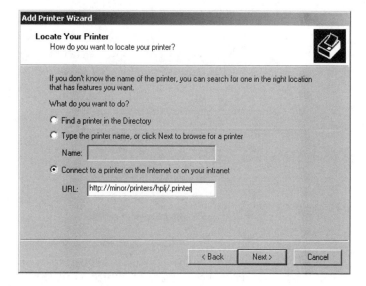

Connecting to an Internet Printer Using a Web Browser

You can manage printers from any browser, but you must use Internet Explorer 4.01 or later to be able to connect to a printer using a browser (the browser must support frames).

To connect to an Internet printer using a Web browser, take the following steps:

1. Open the Web browser, type **http://print_server/printers** in the address bar, and press Enter. If prompted, type your username, domain name, and password.

2. Click the link for the printer you want to connect to.

3. Under Printer Actions, click Connect.

Summary

In this chapter, you learned about dial-up networking and Internet connectivity. We covered the following topics:

- How to configure and manage the modems installed on your computer through Device Manager.

- Using dial-up networking, including creating dial-up connections to RAS servers and to the Internet. You also learned how to configure a VPN connection and how to configure Internet connection sharing.

- The support for Internet printing through IPP.

Exam Essentials

Be able to install a modem.   Be able to install a modem and trouble-shoot any configuration errors.

Be able to configure and support dial-up networking.   Understand the purpose of RAS and VPN connections. Know how to install RAS and VPN clients. Understand the security issues and configure security based on network requirements. Be ready to troubleshoot any connectivity issues. Know how to connect to the Internet, to configure Internet connection sharing, and to define all the options that can be set for Internet connection sharing.

Provide support for Internet connection sharing.   Specify the server requirements for supporting Internet connection sharing. Be able to access and submit print jobs to Internet printers.

Key Terms

Before taking the exam, you should be familiar with the following terms:

dial-up networking

Internet connection sharing

Internet Information Services (IIS)

Internet printer

Internet Print Protocol (IPP)

Internet service provider (ISP)

Remote Access Service (RAS)

smart card

virtual private network (VPN)

Review Questions

1. Your company has branch offices in San Jose and in New York. You also have remote users spread throughout the U.S. Many of the remote users need to access the network eight hours a day and do not want to be connected to the server through a long-distance phone call. You want to configure remote access so that any user with an Internet connection can access the internal network securely. Which of the following network connections should you configure?

   A. RAS connection

   B. RDM connection

   C. VPN connection

   D. DIDO connection

2. Your computer is a part of a very small network. The network administrator recently configured your computer to use Internet connection sharing. After Internet connection sharing was configured, you tested the connection and were able to access the Internet. When you then attempted to access a local resource, you were not able to. What is the most likely problem?

   A. Your IP address was reset through Internet connection sharing.

   B. You need to disconnect any open Internet connections.

   C. Your computer name was reset through Internet connection sharing and needs to be reestablished.

   D. You need to make an entry in the DNS server to reflect the changes made to your computer, to reflect the Internet connection sharing support that was added.

3. You have a small network at home and want to set up Internet connection sharing so that all of your computers can connect to the Internet via a single DSL connection. Which of the following requirements must be met in order to use Internet connection sharing?

   A. You must have a VPN connection.

   B. The network clients must be configured to use WINS.

   C. The network clients must be configured to obtain an IP address automatically.

   D. The network clients must have the ICS service installed.

4. Your company has several remote users. They need to have access to your network printers via an Internet connection. What service must be running on the Windows 2000 Server or Professional client that will host the Internet printers?

   A. IIS

   B. PIP

   C. LIP

   D. PWS

5. You are configuring Internet connection sharing so that users can upload and download files to a central FTP server. Which port should you configure through Internet connection sharing so that FTP is the only service supported?

   A. Port 21

   B. Port 23

   C. Port 80

   D. Port 91

6. You are in the process of configuring Internet connection sharing. How do you set this up on the computer that will act as the host connection?

    A. On the computer that will act as the host, install the ICS service.

    B. On the computer that will act as the host, install the ISC service.

    C. Access the Internet Connections Properties dialog box, click the Advanced tab, and check the Enable Internet Connection Sharing option.

    D. Access the Internet Connections Properties dialog box, click the Sharing tab, and select the option to Enable Internet Connection Sharing.

7. You are using a modem to dial into a VPN server. When you attempt to dial into the VPN server, the connection can't be established. Listening to the connection, you don't hear anything—not even a dial tone. What option should you set so that you can hear what is happening when you try to establish the connection?

    A. In the Modem tab of the modem's Properties dialog box, set the Speaker Volume option using the High setting.

    B. In the Advanced tab of the modem's Properties dialog box, set the speaker volume to high.

    C. In the modem adapter Properties dialog box, select the Audible Connection option.

    D. Use the `volume` command-line utility to adjust the volume.

8. You are having trouble connecting to the Internet and are not sure if the problem is with your modem or with your configuration. How can you determine if the modem is working properly?

    A. Use the `moddiag` command-line utility to run a series of modem diagnostics.

    B. Check the modem diagnostics log that is created in *Windir*\\ System32\\Moddiag.

    C. Use the `testcomm` command-line utility to run a series of modem diagnostics.

    D. In the Diagnostics tab of the modem Properties dialog box, click the Query Modem button.

9. You are configuring a dial-up connection on your Windows 2000 Professional computer. You want the connection to be available only for the user Martha. What should you configure?

    A. Log on as Administrator and create the connection. Then grant to Martha Full Control permission to the dial-up connection.

    B. In the user profile, configure the dial-up connection as nonshared. Specify that only Martha can use the dial-up connection.

    C. Log on as Martha and create the connection. For Connection Availability, specify that the connection is only available for the current user.

    D. In the user profile, configure the dial-up connection as private. Specify that only Martha can use the dial-up connection.

10. You are using a dial-up connection to connect to your company's RAS server. You want to use your company calling card for the connection. How do you configure this?

    A. In the Dial-up Connection Properties dialog box, General tab, select Rules to configure the calling card.

    B. In the modem's Properties dialog box, General tab, select Dialing Properties to configure the calling card.

    C. In the modem's Properties dialog box, use the Configure Calling Cards tab to configure the calling card.

    D. This option can't be configured.

11. Your company has a RAS server set up so that remote salespeople can dial in as necessary. Because of the sensitive information that your company stores on the server, security is a primary concern; so you require remote users to dial in with a smart card. Which protocol for dial-up connection security should you configure if your laptop will use a security device such as a smart card?

    A. EAP

    B. CHAP

    C. PAP

    D. RAP

12. You are configuring a dial-up connection to dial into your company's RAS server. You are using a Windows 2000 Professional computer to access a Windows 2000 RAS server. Which of the following dial-in security protocols offers the highest level of protection?

A. PAP

B. CHAP

C. MS-CHAP

D. MS-CHAP v2

13. You are configuring the networking properties of your dial-up connection. In which of the following situations would you configure a SLIP connection?

A. For dialing in to a Windows 95 computer

B. For dialing in to a Windows NT 4 computer

C. For dialing in to a Windows 2000 computer

D. For dialing in to a Unix server that does not use PPP connections

14. You are considering using a VPN network connection. Which of the following features are offered through VPN connections? (Choose all that apply.)

A. The data will be encapsulated.

B. The data will be encrypted.

C. A username and password will be required.

D. The data will require certificate services.

15. You have a workgroup with five computers, but you have only one telephone line that is dedicated to remote communications. All five users require Internet access to send and receive e-mail. Which option should you configure to support this environment?

A. Dial-up connection sharing

B. Internet connection sharing

C. SLIP connection sharing

D. PPP connection sharing

Answers to Review Questions

1. C.   A virtual private network uses secure links across private or public networks (such as the Internet) to connect a Windows 2000 network to a remote client.

2. A.   When you use Internet connection sharing, it causes computers that use Internet connection sharing to lose their IP configuration. This must be reset so the computer can access local resources.

3. C.   In order to use Internet connection sharing, the network clients must be able to get their IP addresses automatically (through DHCP). The host computer and the client computers must be configured to use Internet connection sharing.

4. A.   In order to support Internet printing, the Windows 2000 Server or Professional client that will host the printers must be running Internet Information Server (IIS).

5. A.   You can control the services available to a user by specifying which ports will be serviced. By default, FTP uses port 21, Telnet uses port 23, and HTTP uses port 80.

6. D.   To configure Internet connection sharing on the computer that will act as the host connection, you create an Internet connection. Then access the Internet connection's Properties dialog box, click the Sharing tab, and select the option to Enable Internet Connection Sharing.

7. A.   In the Modem tab of the modem Properties dialog box, you can set the speaker volume by adjusting a slider between Off and High.

8. D.   The Diagnostics tab of the modem Properties dialog box contains a Query Modem button. Click this button to run a series of modem commands and see how the modem responds.

9. C. To create a dial-up connection, you use the Network Connection Wizard. One of the Wizard's dialog boxes asks you to specify the connection's availability. You can specify that the connection is to be used for all users or only for the current user.

10. A. To configure a connection to use a calling card, access the Dial-up Connection Properties dialog box, General tab, and click the Rules button.

11. A. The Extensible Authentication Protocol (EAP) is used in conjunction with security devices such as smart cards and certificates.

12. D. The MS-CHAP v2 protocol is the most secure form of the Challenge Handshake Authentication Protocol. The PAP protocol uses an unencrypted password.

13. D. Windows 9x, Windows NT, and Windows 2000 use the PPP protocol. You use the SLIP protocol with some Unix servers.

14. A, B, C. When you use virtual private network (VPN) connections, data is encapsulated, is encrypted, and requires authentication services.

15. B. Internet connection sharing allows you to connect a small network to the Internet through a single connection.

Optimizing Windows 2000

MICROSOFT EXAM OBJECTIVES COVERED IN THIS CHAPTER:

✓ **Deploy service packs.**

✓ **Optimize and troubleshoot performance of the Windows 2000 Professional desktop.**

- Optimize and troubleshoot memory performance.
- Optimize and troubleshoot processor utilization.
- Optimize and troubleshoot disk performance.
- Optimize and troubleshoot network performance.
- Optimize and troubleshoot application performance.

✓ **Configure, manage, and troubleshoot the Task Scheduler.**

To have an optimized system, you must monitor its performance. The two tools for monitoring Windows 2000 Professional are System Monitor and Performance Logs and Alerts. With these tools, you can track memory, processor activity, the disk subsystem, the network subsystem, and other computer subsystems.

You can make your administrative tasks easier by automating some of them. You can schedule system tasks by using the Scheduled Task Wizard.

This chapter begins with discussions of the Windows Update utility and service packs. Then you will learn how to monitor and optimize Windows 2000 Professional using the System Monitor, Performance Logs and Alerts, and Task Manager utilities. You will also learn how to optimize application performance.

Keeping Windows 2000 Up-to-Date

An optimal operating system is one that is running the most up-to-date software and has had the most recent service pack installed. Microsoft provides the Windows Update utility to help you obtain updated Windows 2000 software. Microsoft issues service packs as necessary to update the operating system with bug fixes and new features.

Using the Windows Update Utility

The *Windows Update* utility connects your computer to Microsoft's Web site and checks your files to make sure that you have all of the latest and greatest updates.

To use Windows Update, you must first have a valid Internet connection. Then simply choose Start ➢ Windows Update to go to the correct URL for updates.

For product updates, click the Product Updates option on the home page and follow the directions to choose which files you want to update. The files in the update section are arranged by the following categories:

- Critical updates

- Picks of the month

- Recommended updates

- Additional Windows features

- Device drivers

Within each category, you will see the available updates, along with a description, file size, and download time estimate for each update. Just check the files you want to update and click the Download icon to download your selections.

Using Windows Service Packs

Service packs are used to update the Windows operating system, to increase operating system reliability, increase application compatibility, facilitate Windows setup, and address security issues. Windows 2000 offers a new technology for service packs called *slipstream*. With slipstream technology, service packs are applied once, and they are not overwritten as new services are added to the computer. This means you should not need to reapply service packs after new services are added, which sometimes was required when Windows NT 4 service packs were applied.

Microsoft
✓ *Exam*
Objective

Deploy service packs.

You can determine if any service packs have been installed on your computer by using the WINVER command, as shown in Figure 14.1. To issue this command, select Start ≻ Programs ≻ Accessories ≻ Command Prompt. In the Command Prompt dialog box, type **WINVER** and press Enter. You will see a dialog box that shows which service packs are currently installed.

FIGURE 14.1 Response to the WINVER command

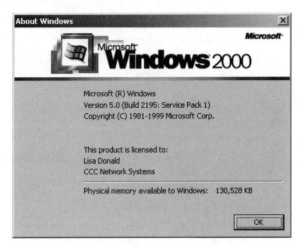

Windows 2000 Service Packs come in two versions:

- Standard, which uses 56-bit encryption.

- High, which uses 128-bit encryption.

The version you install is based on the encryption that is set on your computer. You can determine the encryption that is set on your computer through the command-line utility WINMSD. Then expand Internet Explorer, Summary. As shown in Figure 14.2, the Cipher Strength field will display the level of encryption that is installed on your computer.

FIGURE 14.2 Using WINMSD to determine encryption level

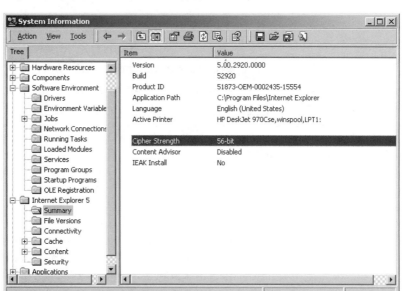

You can find out what the current service pack is from Microsoft's Web site at www.microsoft.com. The current service pack can be downloaded from the Web site or ordered on CD for a minimal charge.

Once you download the proper version of service pack based on your computer's encryption, you click the file to begin the installation process. You will have to agree to the license agreement, and you will have the option to create an Uninstall folder. Then the files will be installed on your computer. If you choose to create an Uninstall folder, it will require about 215 to 315MB of disk space. This Uninstall folder is stored in \%SystemRoot%\$NTServicePackUninstall$.

Using System Monitoring Tools

Before you can optimize the performance of Windows 2000 Professional, you must monitor critical subsystems to determine how your system is currently performing and what (if anything) is causing system bottlenecks. Windows 2000 Professional ships with two tools that you can use to track and monitor system performance: the System Monitor utility and the Performance Logs and Alerts utility.

Microsoft ✓ Exam Objective

Optimize and troubleshoot performance of the Windows 2000 Professional desktop.

- Optimize and troubleshoot memory performance.
- Optimize and troubleshoot processor utilization.
- Optimize and troubleshoot disk performance.
- Optimize and troubleshoot network performance.

You can access the monitoring tools by adding the System Monitor snap-in and the Performance Logs and Alerts snap-in to the MMC. The System Monitor snap-in is added as an ActiveX control.

In Exercise 14.1, you will create a management console for monitoring system performance.

EXERCISE 14.1

Creating a Management Console for Monitoring System Performance

1. Select Start ➢ Run, type MMC in the Run dialog box, and click the OK button.

2. Select Console ➢ Add/Remove Snap-in.

3. In the Add/Remove Snap-in dialog box, click the Add button. In the Add Standalone Snap-in dialog box, select ActiveX Control and click the Add button.

4. In the Insert ActiveX Control dialog box, click the Next button.

5. In the Insert ActiveX Control dialog box, select System Monitor Control and click the Next button. Click the Finish button.

6. In the Add Standalone Snap-in dialog box, click the Close button.

7. In the Add/Remove Snap-in dialog box, click the Add button. In the Add Standalone Snap-in dialog box, select Performance Logs and Alerts and click the Add button, then click the Close button.

8. In the Add/Remove Snap-in dialog box, click the OK button.

9. Select Console ➢ Save As.

10. In the Save As dialog box, select Save in Administrative Tools (the default selection) and save the file as **Monitor**.

You can now access this console by selecting Start ➢ Programs ➢ Administrative Tools ➢ Monitor.

In Windows NT 4, the functions of the System Monitor utility and the Performance Logs and Alerts utility were implemented in the Performance Monitor utility.

Now that you've added the monitoring tools to the MMC, you can use them to monitor and optimize Windows 2000. The following sections describe how to evaluate your system's current performance; how to use System Monitor and Performance Logs and Alerts; and how to monitor and optimize the system memory, processor, disk subsystem, and network subsystem.

Determining System Performance

The monitoring tools allow you to assess your server's current health and determine what it requires to improve its present condition. With System Monitor and Performance Logs and Alerts, you can perform the following tasks:

- Create baselines.

- Identify system bottlenecks.

- Determine trends.

- Create alert thresholds.

Each of these tasks is discussed in the following sections.

Creating Baselines

A *baseline* is a snapshot of how your system is currently performing. Suppose that your computer's hardware has not changed over the last six months, but the computer seems to be performing more slowly now than it did six months ago. If you have been using the Performance Logs and Alerts utility and taking baseline logs, as well as noting the changes in your workload, you can more easily determine what resources are causing the system to slow down.

You should create baselines at the following times:

- When the system is first configured without any load

- At regular intervals of typical usage

- Whenever any changes are made to the system's hardware or software configuration

Baselines are particularly useful for determining the effect of changes that you make to your computer. For example, if you are adding more memory to your computer, you should take baselines before and after you install the memory to determine the effect of the change. Along with hardware changes, system configuration modifications also can affect your computer's performance, so you should create baselines before and after you make any changes to your Windows 2000 Professional configuration.

For the most part, Windows 2000 Professional is a self-tuning system. If you decide to tweak the operating system, you should take baselines before and after each change. If you do not notice a performance gain after the tweak, you should consider returning the computer to its original configuration, because some tweaks may cause more problems than they solve.

You create baselines by using the Performance Logs and Alerts utility to create a baseline counters log file. This process is described in the "Creating Baselines" section later in this chapter.

Identifying System Bottlenecks

A *bottleneck* is a system resource that is inefficient compared with the rest of the computer system as a whole. The bottleneck can cause the rest of the system to run slowly.

You need to pinpoint the cause of a bottleneck in order to correct it. Consider a system that has a Pentium 166 processor with 64MB of RAM. If your applications are memory-intensive, and lack of memory is your bottleneck, then upgrading your processor will not eliminate the bottleneck.

By using System Monitor, you can measure the performance of the various parts of your system, which allows you to identify system bottlenecks in a scientific manner. You will learn how to set counters to monitor your network and spot bottlenecks in the "Using System Monitor" section later in this chapter.

Determining Trends

Many of us tend to manage situations reactively instead of proactively. With reactive management, you focus on a problem when it occurs. With proactive management, you take steps to avoid the problem before it happens. In a perfect world, all management would be proactive.

System Monitor and Performance Logs and Alerts are great tools for proactive network management. If you are creating baselines on a regular basis, you can identify system trends. For example, if you notice average CPU utilization increasing five percent every month, you can assume that within the next six months, you're going to have a problem. Before performance becomes so slow that your system is not responding, you can upgrade the hardware.

Using Alerts for Problem Notification

The Performance Logs and Alerts utility provides another tool for proactive management in the form of *alerts*. Through Performance Logs and Alerts, you can specify alert thresholds (when a counter reaches a specified value) and have the utility notify you when these thresholds are reached.

For example, you could specify that if your logical disk has less than 10 percent of free space, you want to be notified. Once alerted, you can add more disk space or delete unneeded files before you run out of disk space. You will learn how to create alerts in the "Using Performance Logs and Alerts" section later in this chapter.

Using System Monitor

Through *System Monitor*, you can view current data or data from a log file. When you view current activity, you are monitoring real-time activity. When you view data from a log file, you are importing a log file from a previous session.

After you've added the System Monitor snap-in to the MMC (see Exercise 14.1), you can open it by selecting Start ➢ Programs ➢ Administrative Tools ➢ Monitor. Figure 14.3 shows the main System Monitor window when you first open it.

FIGURE 14.3 The main System Monitor window

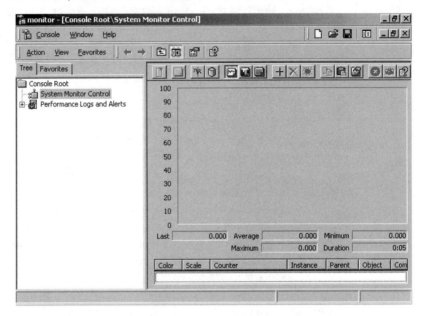

The System Monitor toolbar, shown here, provides access to all of the System Monitor functions:

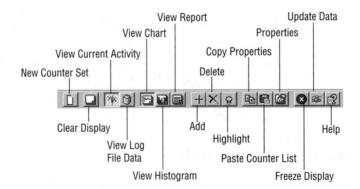

When you first start System Monitor, you will notice that nothing is tracked by default. In order for System Monitor to be useful, you must configure it to track some type of system activity, which is done by adding counters, as described shortly. After you've added counters, they will be listed at the bottom of the System Monitor window. The fields just above the counter list will contain data based on the counter that is highlighted in the list, as follows:

- The Last field displays the most current data.

- The Average field shows the average of the counter.

- The Minimum field shows the lowest value that has been recorded for the counter.

- The Maximum field shows the highest value that has been recorded for the counter.

- The Duration field shows how long the counter has been tracking data.

The following sections describe the three System Monitor views, how to add counters to track data, and how to configure System Monitor properties.

Selecting the Appropriate View

By clicking the appropriate button on the System Monitor toolbar, you can see your data in three views:

Chart view   The chart view, shown in Figure 14.4, is System Monitor's default view. It's useful for viewing a small number of counters in a graphical format. The main advantage of chart view is that you can see how the data has been tracked during the defined time period. This view can be difficult to interpret, however, when you start to track a large number of counters.

Histogram view   The histogram view, shown in Figure 14.5, shows the System Monitor data in a bar graph. This view is useful for examining large amounts of data. However, it only shows performance for the current period. You do not see a record of performance over time, as you do with the chart view.

Report view   The report view, shown in Figure 14.6, offers a logical report of all the counters that are being tracked through System Monitor.

Only the current session's data is displayed. The advantage of report view is that it allows you to easily track large numbers of counters in real time.

FIGURE 14.4 The chart view of System Monitor

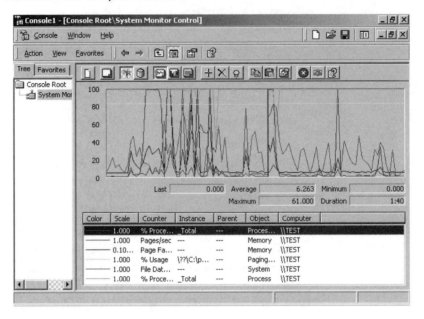

FIGURE 14.5 The histogram view of System Monitor

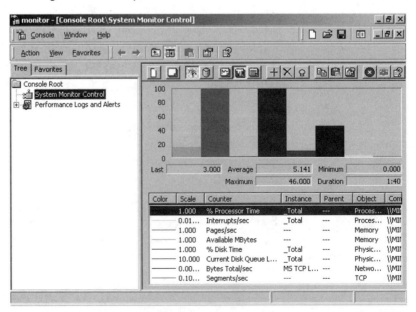

FIGURE 14.6   The report view of System Monitor

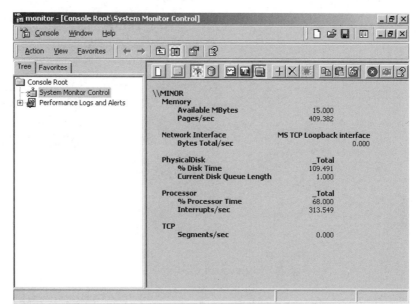

Adding Counters

As mentioned, you must add *counters* to System Monitor in order to track data. To add counters, use the following steps:

1. In System Monitor, click the Add button on the toolbar. This brings up the Add Counters dialog box (Figure 14.7).

To see information about a specific counter, select it and click the Explain button on the right of the Add Counters dialog box. System Monitor will display text regarding the highlighted counter.

FIGURE 14.7 The Add Counters dialog box

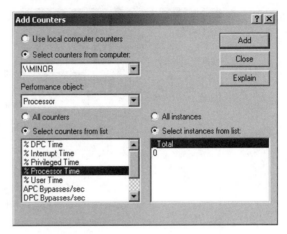

2. In the Add Counters dialog box, select the Use Local Computer Counters (the default) radio button to monitor the local computer. Alternatively, to select counters from a specific computer, choose Select Counters from Computer and pick a computer from the drop-down list.

   You can monitor remote computers if you have Administrative permissions. This option is useful when you do not want the overhead of System Monitor running on the computer you are trying to monitor.

3. Select a performance object from the drop-down list. All Windows 2000 system resources are tracked as performance objects, such as Cache, Memory, Paging File, Process, and Processor.

   All the objects together represents your total system. Some performance objects exist on all Windows 2000 computers; other objects appear only if specific processes or services are running. For example, if you want to track the physical disk's level of activity, choose the PhysicalDisk performance object.

4. Select the All Counters radio button to track all the associated counters, or choose Select Counters from List and pick specific counters from the list box below.

Each performance object has an associated set of counters. Counters are used to track specific information regarding a performance object. For example, the PhysicalDisk performance object has a %Disk Time counter, which will tell you how busy a disk has been in servicing read and write requests. PhysicalDisk also has %Disk Read Time and %Disk Write Time counters, which show you what percentage of disk requests are read requests and what percentage are write requests, respectively.

You can select multiple counters of the same performance object by Shift+clicking contiguous counters or Ctrl+clicking noncontiguous counters.

5. Select the All Instances radio button to track all the associated instances, or choose the Select Instances from List option and pick specific instances from the list box below.

An *instance* is a mechanism that allows you to track the performance of a specific object when you have more than one item associated with a specific performance object. For example, suppose your computer has two physical drives. When you track the PhysicalDisk performance object, you can track both of your drives, or you can track drive 0 and drive 1 separately.

6. Click the Add button to add the counters for the performance object.

7. Repeat steps 2 through 6 to specify any additional counters you want to track. When you are finished, click the Close button.

After you've added counters, you can select a specific counter by highlighting it in System Monitor. To highlight a counter, click it and then click the Highlight button on the System Monitor toolbar, or selecting the counter and press Ctrl+H.

To remove a counter, highlight it in System Monitor and click the Delete button on the toolbar.

Managing System Monitor Properties

To configure the System Monitor properties, click the Properties button on the System Monitor toolbar. The System Monitor Properties dialog box has six tabs: General, Source, Data, Graph, Colors, and Fonts. The properties you can configure on each of these tabs are described in the following sections.

General Properties

The General tab of the System Monitor Properties dialog box (Figure 14.8) contains the following options:

- The view that will be displayed: graph, histogram, or report

- The display elements that will be used: legend, value bar, and/or toolbar

- The data that will be displayed: default (for reports or histograms this is current data; for logs, this is average data), current, average, minimum, or maximum

- The appearance, either flat or 3D

- The border, either none or fixed single

- How often the data is updated, in seconds

- Whether duplicate counter instances are allowed

FIGURE 14.8 The General tab of System Monitor Properties

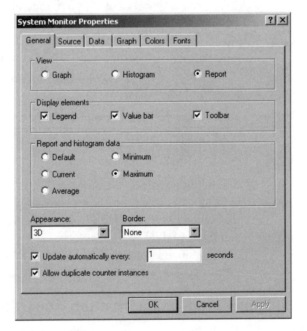

Source Properties

The Source tab, shown in Figure 14.9, allows you to specify the data source. This can be current activity, or it can be data that has been collected in a log file. If you import data from a log file, you can specify the time range that you wish to view.

FIGURE 14.9   The Source tab of the System Monitor Properties dialog box

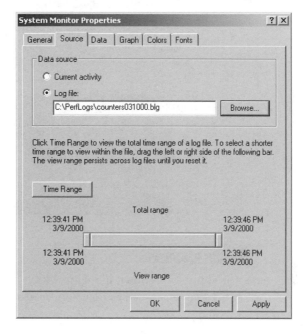

Data Properties

The Data tab, shown in Figure 14.10, lets you specify the counters that you wish to track. You can add and remove counters by clicking the Add and Remove buttons. You can also select a specific counter and define the color, scale, width, and style that is used to represent the counter in the graph.

FIGURE 14.10   The Data tab of the System Monitor Properties dialog box

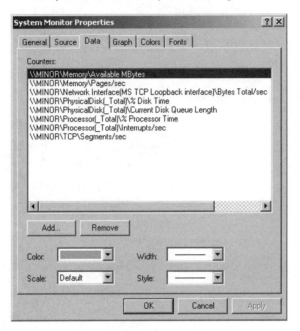

Graph Properties

The Graph tab, shown in Figure 14.11, contains the following options, which can be applied to the chart or histogram view:

- A title

- A vertical axis label

- Whether you will show a vertical grid, a horizontal grid, and/or vertical scale numbers

- The minimum and maximum numbers for the vertical scale

FIGURE 14.11 The Graph tab of the System Monitor Properties dialog box

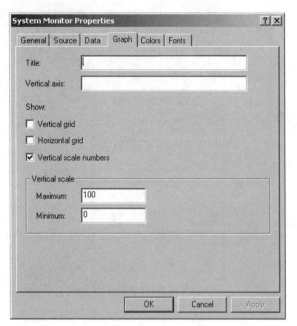

Color and Font Properties

The Colors and Fonts tabs of the System Monitor Properties dialog box have options for customizing the colors and fonts used in the System Monitor display.

Using Performance Logs and Alerts

The *Performance Logs and Alerts snap-in* to the MMC is shown expanded in Figure 14.12. With it, you can create counter logs and trace logs, and you can define alerts. You can view the log files with the System Monitor, as described in the previous section. After you've added the Performance Logs and Alerts snap-in (see Exercise 14.1), open it by selecting Start ➢ Programs ➢ Administrative Tools ➢ Monitor and clicking Performance Logs and Alerts. The following sections describe how to define new counter logs, trace logs, and alerts.

FIGURE 14.12 The expanded Performance Logs and Alerts snap-in

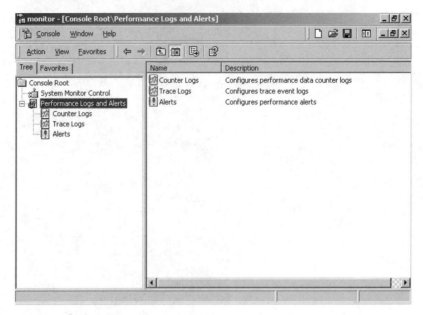

Creating a Counter Log

Counter logs record data about hardware usage and the activity of system services. You can configure logging to occur manually or on a predefined schedule.

To create a counter log, take the following steps:

1. Expand Performance Logs and Alerts, right-click Counter Logs, and select New Log Settings from the pop-up menu.

2. In the New Log Settings dialog box appears, type a name for the log file. For example, you might give the log a name that indicates its type and the date, such as Counter*mmddyy*. Then click the OK button.

3. The counter log file's Properties dialog box appears. You can configure counter log properties as follows:

   - In the General tab, shown in Figure 14.13, specify the counters you want to track in the log and the interval for sampling data. Click the Add button to add counters.

FIGURE 14.13   General properties of the counter log file

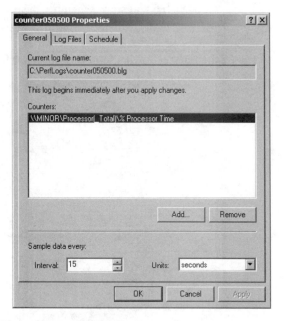

- In the Log Files tab, shown in Figure 14.14, configure the log file's location, filename, type, and size.

FIGURE 14.14   Log Files properties for the counter log file

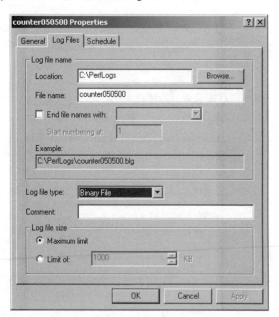

> ▪ In the Schedule tab, shown in Figure 14.15, specify when the log file will start, when it will stop, and what action should be taken, if any, when the log file is closed.

FIGURE 14.15 Schedule properties for the counter log file

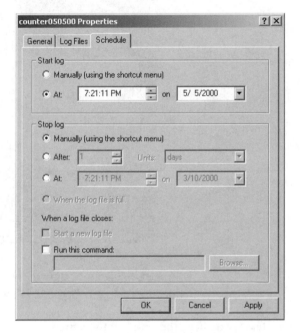

4. When you are finished configuring the counter log file properties, click the OK button. The log will be created and will record the activity for the counters you specified.

Creating a Trace Log

Trace logs measure data continually as opposed to measuring data through periodic samples. Trace logs are also used to track data that is collected by the operating system or programs. For example, you could specify that you want to trace the creation or deletion of processes and threads.

To create a trace log, take the following steps:

1. Expand Performance Logs and Alerts, right-click Trace Logs, and select New Log Settings from the pop-up menu.

2. In the New Log Settings dialog box, type in a name for the log file and click the OK button. For example, you might use the type of log and the date (Trace*mmddyy*).

3. The trace log file's Properties dialog box appears. You can configure trace log properties as follows:

- In the General tab, shown in Figure 14.16, select the check boxes for the system events you want to track—for example, Process Creations/Deletions and Thread Creations/Deletions. You can also specify which system nonproviders you want to track, such as the Active Directory NetLogon process or the Local Security Authority (LSA).

FIGURE 14.16 General properties for the trace log file

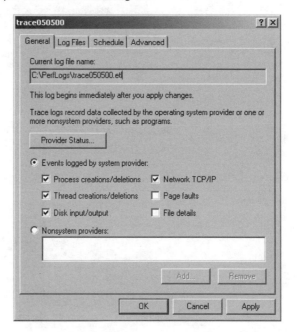

- In the Log Files tab, shown in Figure 14.17, configure the log file's location, filename, type, and size.

FIGURE 14.17 The Log Files properties for the trace log file

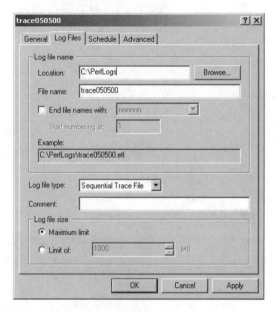

- In the Schedule tab, shown in Figure 14.18, configure when the log file will start, when it will stop, and what action should be taken, if any, when the log file is closed.

FIGURE 14.18 The Schedule properties for the trace log file

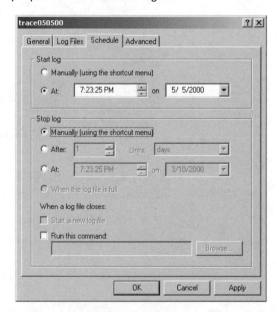

- In the Advanced tab, shown in Figure 14.19, configure the buffer settings for the log file. By default, the log service will save the trace file to memory and then transfer the data to the log file.

FIGURE 14.19   The Advanced properties for the trace log file

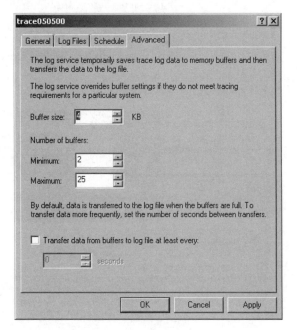

4. When you are finished configuring the trace file properties, click the OK button. The log will be created and will record the activity for the system events you specified.

Creating an Alert

Alerts can be generated when a specific counter exceeds or falls below a specified value. You can configure alerts so that a message is sent, a program is run, or a more detailed log file is generated. Here are the steps to create an alert:

1. Expand Performance Logs and Alerts, right-click Alerts, and select New Alert Settings from the pop-up menu.

2. In the New Alert Settings dialog box, type a name for the alert file and click the OK button.

3. The alert file Properties dialog box appears. You can configure alert properties as follows:

   - In the General tab, shown in Figure 14.20, select the counters you want to track. When you add a counter, you must specify that the alert be generated when the counter is under or over a certain value. You can also set the interval for sampling data.

FIGURE 14.20 The General properties for an alert

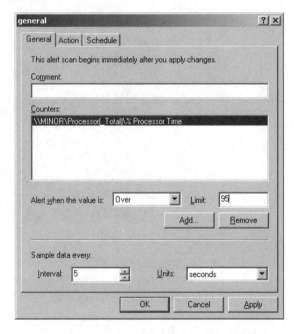

   - In the Action tab, shown in Figure 14.21, specify what action should be taken if an alert is triggered. This can be logging an entry in the application event log, sending a network message, starting another performance data log, and/or running a specific program.

   - In the Schedule tab, shown in Figure 14.22, configure the start and stop dates/times for scans of the counters you have defined.

FIGURE 14.21 The Action properties for an alert

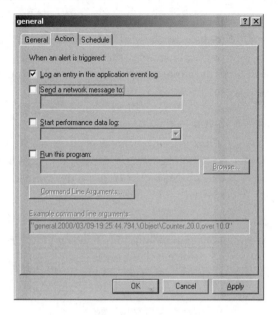

FIGURE 14.22 The Schedule properties for an alert

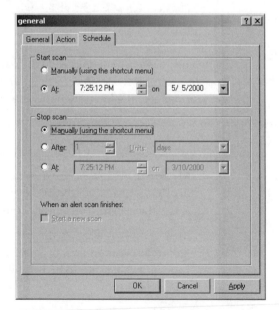

4. When you are finished configuring the alert properties, click the OK button.

Monitoring and Optimizing Memory

When the operating system needs a program or process, the first place it looks is in physical memory. If the required program or process is not in physical memory, the system looks in logical memory (the *page file*). If the program or process is not in logical memory, the system then must retrieve the program or process from the hard disk. It can take thousands of times longer to access information from the hard disk than to get it from physical RAM.

Insufficient memory is the most likely cause of system bottlenecks. If you have no idea what is causing a system bottleneck, memory is usually a good place to start checking. To determine how memory is being used, there are two areas you need to examine:

- Physical memory, which is the physical RAM you have installed on your computer. You can't have too much memory. It's actually a good idea to have more memory than you think you will need just to be on the safe side. As you've probably noticed, each time you add or upgrade applications, you require more system memory.

- The page file, which is logical memory that exists on the hard drive. If you are using excessive paging (swapping between the page file and physical RAM), it's a clear sign that you need to add more memory.

In this book, we use the following format for describing performance object counters: *performance object > counter*. For example, Memory > Available MBytes denotes the Memory performance object and the Available MBytes counter.

Following are the three most important counters for monitoring memory:

- Memory > Available MBytes measures the amount of physical memory that is available to run processes on the computer. If this number is less than 4MB, you should consider adding more memory.

- Memory > Pages/Sec shows the number of times the requested information was not in memory and had to be retrieved from disk. This counter's value should be below 20; for optimal performance, it should be 4 or 5.

- Paging File > %Usage indicates the percentage of the allocated page file that is currently in use. If this number is consistently over 99%, you may need to add more memory.

These counters work together to show what is happening on your system. Use the Paging File > % Usage counter value in conjunction with the Memory > Available MBytes and Memory > Pages/Sec counters to determine how much paging is occurring on your computer.

Some documentation suggests that you can optimize memory by manipulating the page file. This generally applies to servers that use sophisticated disk subsystems. On a regular workstation running Windows 2000 Professional, the best way to optimize memory is to add more physical memory.

 Real World Scenario

Using System Monitor to Identify Bottlenecks

You are the system administrator of a large network. The accounting department has just started using a new accounting application that runs on the department manager's local computer. The manager is complaining about the slowness of this application and says she needs a new computer.

You decide to use System Monitor to find out why her computer is responding so slowly. You see that the processor utilization is at 10% (low). You also can tell that the system is using excessive paging based on the Memory > Pages/Sec counter, currently showing at 25. Considering this information, you determine that for the accounting manager's computer to work efficiently with the application, the computer needs a memory upgrade.

System Monitor helps you measure the performance of various parts of your system, allowing you to identify system bottlenecks scientifically.

In Exercise 14.2, you will monitor your computer's memory subsystem. This exercise assumes that you have completed Exercise 14.1.

EXERCISE 14.2

Monitoring System Memory

1. Select Start ≻ Programs ≻ Administrative Tools ≻ Monitor.

2. In the System Monitor window, click the Add button on the toolbar.

3. In the Add Counters dialog box, specify the following performance objects and counters:

   - Select Memory from the performance object drop-down list, choose Available MBytes in the counter list box, and click the Add button.

   - Select Memory from the performance object drop-down list, choose Pages/Sec in the counter list box, and click the Add button.

   - Select Paging File from the performance object drop-down list, choose %Usage in the counter list box, and click the Add button.

4. Click the Close button. You should see a chart showing how your computer's memory is being used.

5. To generate some activity, select Start ≻ Help. Close Help. Open Help again and then close it. The first time you opened Help, you should have seen a spike in the Memory > Pages/Sec counter, and a much lower spike the second time you accessed Help. This occurs because the Help program must be retrieved from disk the first time you accessed it; the second time you accessed it, it was already in memory.

6. Note the Paging > %Usage counter. If this counter is below 99%, your system is not using excessive paging.

7. Note the Memory > Available MBytes counter. If this counter is above 4MB, you should have sufficient RAM.

Leave System Monitor open, for use again in Exercise 14.3.

Monitoring and Optimizing the Processor

Although processors are usually not the source of bottlenecks, you should still monitor this subsystem to make sure that processor utilization is at an efficient level. Following are the two most important counters for monitoring the system processor:

- Processor > %Processor Time measures the time that the processor spends responding to system requests. If this value is consistently above an average of 80%, you may have a processor bottleneck.

- Processor > Interrupts/Sec shows the average number of hardware interrupts received by the processor each second. If this value is more than 3,500 on a Pentium computer, you might have a problem with a program or hardware that is generating spurious interrupts.

If you suspect that you have a processor bottleneck, you can try the following solutions:

- Use applications that are less processor-intensive.

- Upgrade your processor.

- If your computer supports multiple processors, add one. Windows 2000 Professional can support up to two processors, which will help if you use multithreaded applications.

Beware of running three-dimensional screen savers on your computer. As you will see in Exercise 14.3, they can use quite a bit of the processor's time.

In Exercise 14.3, you will monitor your computer's processor. This exercise assumes that you have completed the other exercises in this chapter.

EXERCISE 14.3

Monitoring the System Processor

1. If System Monitor is not already open, select Start ➢ Programs ➢ Administrative Tools ➢ Monitor.

2. In the System Monitor window, click the Add button on the toolbar.

EXERCISE 14.3 *(continued)*

3. In the Add Counters dialog box, specify the following performance objects and counters:

   - Select Processor from the performance object drop-down list, select %Processor Time in the counter list box, and click the Add button.

   - Select Processor from the performance object drop-down list, select Interrupts/Sec in the counter list box, and click the Add button.

4. Click the Close button. You should see these counters added to your chart.

5. To generate some activity, select Start ➢ Settings ➢ Control Panel ➢ Display. Click the Screen Saver tab. Select 3D FlowerBox (OpenGL) and click the Preview button. Let this process run for about five seconds, and close all of the dialog boxes you opened in this step. You should see that the %Processor Time counter spiked during this process.

6. Note the Processor > %Processor Time counter. If this counter's average is below 80%, you do not have a processor bottleneck.

7. Note the Processor > Interrupts/Sec counter. If this counter is below 3,500 on a Pentium computer, you do not have any processes or hardware that are generating excessive interrupts.

Leave System Monitor open, for use again in Exercise 14.4.

Monitoring and Optimizing the Disk Subsystem

Disk access is the amount of time your disk subsystem takes to retrieve data that is requested by the operating system. The two factors that determine how quickly your disk subsystem will respond to system requests are the average disk access time on your hard drive, and the speed of your disk controller.

You can monitor the PhysicalDisk object, which is the sum of all logical drives on a single physical drive, or you can monitor the LogicalDisk object, which represents a specific logical disk. Following are the most important counters for monitoring the disk subsystem. These counters can be tracked for both the PhysicalDisk object and the LogicalDisk object.

- PhysicalDisk > %Disk Time shows the amount of time the physical disk is busy because it is servicing read or write requests. If the disk is busy more than 90% of the time, you will improve performance by adding another disk channel and splitting the disk I/O requests between the channels.

- PhysicalDisk > %Current Disk Queue Length indicates the number of outstanding disk requests that are waiting to be processed. This value should be less than 2.

When you suspect that you have a disk subsystem bottleneck, the first thing you should check is your memory subsystem. Insufficient physical memory can cause excessive paging, which in turn affects the disk subsystem. If you do not have a memory problem, you can try the following solutions to improve disk performance:

- Use faster disks and controllers.

- Use disk striping to take advantage of multiple I/O channels.

- Balance heavily used files on multiple I/O channels.

- Add another disk controller for load balancing.

NOTE In Windows NT 4, you enabled all disk counters through the DISKPERF –Y command. Physical disk counters are automatically enabled in Windows 2000 Professional. However, you must enable DISKPERF if you want to track the logical disk object and counters.

In Exercise 14.4, you will monitor your disk subsystem. This exercise assumes that you have completed the other exercises in this chapter.

EXERCISE 14.4

Monitoring the Disk Subsystem

1. If System Monitor is not already open, select Start ➢ Programs ➢ Administrative Tools ➢ Monitor.

2. In the System Monitor window, click the Add button on the toolbar.

3. Notice that there is a performance object for PhysicalDisk, but not for LogicalDisk.

4. Select Start ➤ Programs ➤ Accessories ➤ Command Prompt.

5. At the command prompt, type **DISKPERF** **-Y** and press Enter. You see a message stating that performance counters for both the logical and physical disks are set to start when the computer boots. Close the Command Prompt dialog box and restart your computer.

6. Select Start ➤ Programs ➤ Administrative Tools ➤ Monitor.

7. In the System Monitor window, click the Add button on the toolbar.

8. In the Add Counters dialog box, specify the following performance objects and counters:

   - Select PhysicalDisk from the performance object drop-down list, select %Disk Time from the counter list box, and click the Add button.

   - Select PhysicalDisk from the performance object drop-down list, select Current Disk Queue Length from the counter list box, and click the Add button.

   - Select LogicalDisk from the performance object drop-down list, select %Idle Time from the counter list box, and click the Add button.

9. Click the Close button. You should see these counters added to your chart.

10. To generate some activity, open and close some applications and copy some files between the C: drive and D: drive.

11. Note the PhysicalDisk > %Disk Time counter. If this counter's average is below 90%, you are not generating excessive requests to this disk.

12. Note the PhysicalDisk > %Current Disk Queue Length counter. If this counter's average is below 2, you are not generating excessive requests to this disk.

Leave System Monitor open, because you will use this utility again in Exercise 14.5.

You can monitor the amount of free disk space on your logical disk through the LogicalDisk > %Free Space counter. This counter can also be used as an alert. For example, you might set an alert to notify you when LogicalDisk > %Free Space on drive C: is under 10%.

Monitoring and Optimizing the Network Subsystem

Windows 2000 Professional does not have a built-in mechanism for monitoring the entire network. However, you can monitor and optimize the traffic that is generated on the specific Windows 2000 computer. You can monitor the network interface (your network card), and you can monitor the network protocols that have been installed on your computer. The following two counters are useful for monitoring the network subsystem:

- Network Interface > Bytes Total/Sec measures the total number of bytes sent or received from the network interface and includes all network protocols.

- TCP > Segments/Sec measures the number of bytes sent or received from the network interface and includes only the TCP protocol.

Normally, you monitor and optimize the network subsystem from a network perspective rather than from a single computer. For example, you can use a network protocol analyzer to monitor all traffic on the network to determine whether the network bandwidth is acceptable for your requirements or that network bandwidth is saturated.

The following suggestions can help to optimize and minimize network traffic:

- Use only the network protocols you need. For example, use TCP/IP and don't use NWLink and NetBEUI.

- If you need to use multiple network protocols, place the most commonly used protocols higher in the binding order.

- Use network cards that take full advantage of your bus width—for example, 32-bit cards instead of 16-bit cards.

- Use faster network cards—for example, 100Mbps Ethernet instead of 10Mbps Ethernet.

In Exercise 14.5, you will monitor your network subsystem. This exercise assumes that you have completed the other exercises in this chapter.

EXERCISE 14.5

Monitoring the Network Subsystem

1. If System Monitor is not already open, select Start ➢ Programs ➢ Administrative Tools ➢ Monitor.

2. In the System Monitor window, click the Add button on the toolbar.

3. In the Add Counters dialog box, specify the following performance objects and counters:

   - Select Network Interface from the performance object drop-down list, select Bytes Total/Sec in the counter list box, and click the Add button.

   - Select TCP from the performance object drop-down list, select Segments/Sec from the counter list box, and click the Add button.

4. Click the Close button. You should see these counters added to your chart.

5. To generate some activity, copy some files between your C: drive and D: drive.

6. Note the two counters Network Interface > Bytes Total/Sec, and TCP > Segments/Sec. These numbers are cumulative. Use them in your baselines to determine network activity.

Leave your Monitor console open, for use again in Exercise 14.6.

Creating Baseline Reports

As explained earlier in this chapter, baselines show how your server is performing at a certain time. By taking baselines at regular intervals and also whenever you make changes to the system's configuration, you can monitor your server's performance over time.

You can create baselines by setting up a counter log file in the Performance Logs and Alerts utility. After you've created the baseline log file, you can view it in System Monitor, as shown in Figure 14.23.

FIGURE 14.23 Viewing a performance baseline in System Monitor

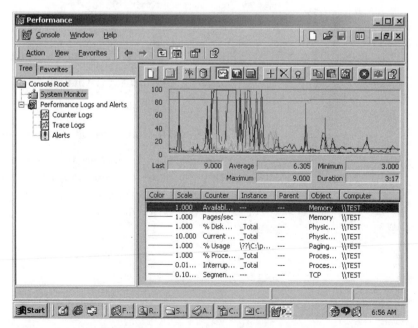

In Exercise 14.6, you will create a baseline report for your computer.

EXERCISE 14.6

Creating a Baseline Report

1. If the Monitor console is not already open, select Start ≻ Programs ≻ Administrative Tools ≻ Monitor.

2. Double-click Performance Logs and Alerts.

3. Right-click Counter Logs and select New Log Settings.

4. In the New Log Settings dialog box, type **Counter*mmddyy*** (replace *mmddyy* with the current month, date, and year) as the log name. The log file will be stored in the C:\PerfLogs folder by default. Click the OK button.

5. In the General tab of the counter log Properties dialog box, click the Add button and add the following counters:

    Memory > Available MBytes

    Memory > Pages/Sec

    Paging File > %Usage

    Processor > %Processor Time

    Processor > Interrupts/Sec

    PhysicalDisk > %Disk Time

    PhysicalDisk > Current Disk Queue Length

    Network Interface > Bytes Total/Sec

    TCP > Segments/Sec

6. Set the interval for sampling data to 5 seconds.

7. Click the Log Files tab. Uncheck the End File Names With check box. This will prevent the appending of *mmddhh* (month/day/hour) to the filename. Click the OK button to close the Properties dialog box and start the log file.

8. Generate some system activity: Start and stop some applications, copy a few files, and run a screen saver for one or two minutes.

9. To view your log file, open System Monitor. Click the View Log File Data button on the toolbar.

10. In the Open File dialog box, select C:\PerfLogs\Counter*mmddyy* and click the Open button.

11. Add the counters from the log file you created to see the data that was collected in your log.

Using Task Manager

The *Task Manager* utility shows the applications and processes that are currently running on your computer, as well as CPU and memory usage information. To access Task Manager, press Ctrl+Alt+Delete and click the Task Manager button. Alternatively, right-click an empty area in the Taskbar and select Task Manager from the pop-up menu.

Microsoft
✓ *Exam*
Objective

Optimize and troubleshoot performance of the Windows 2000 Professional desktop.

- Optimize and troubleshoot processor utilization.
- Optimize and troubleshoot application performance.

Managing Application Tasks

The Applications tab of the Task Manager dialog box, shown in Figure 14.24, lists all of the applications that are currently running on the computer. For each task, you will see the name of the task and the current status (running, not responding, or stopped).

FIGURE 14.24 The Applications tab of the Task Manager dialog box

To close an application, select it and click the End Task button at the bottom of the dialog box. To make the application window active, select it and click the Switch To button. If you want to start an application that isn't running, click the New Task button and specify the location and name of the program you wish to start.

Managing Process Tasks

The Processes tab of the Task Manager dialog box, shown in Figure 14.25, lists all the processes that are currently running on the computer. This is a convenient way to get a quick look at how your system is performing. Unlike System Monitor, Task Manager doesn't require that you first configure the collection of this data; it's gathered automatically.

FIGURE 14.25 The Processes tab of the Task Manager dialog box

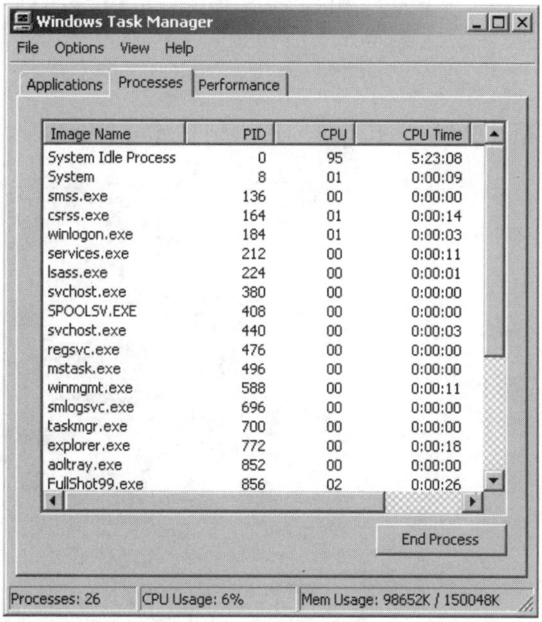

For each process, you will see a unique process ID (PID) that changes each time a process is started. Also displayed are the amount of CPU utilization for the process, and the amount of time the processor spent running the process.

From the Processes tab, you can organize the listing and control processes as follows:

- To organize the processes based on usage, click the column headings. For example, if you click the CPU column, the listing will start with the processes that use the most CPU resources. If you click the CPU column a second time, the listing will be reversed.

- To manage a process, right-click it and choose an option from the pop-up menu. You can choose to end the process, end the process tree, or set the priority of the process (to real time, high, above normal, normal, below normal, or low). If your computer has multiple processors installed, you can also set processor affinity (the process of associating a specific process with a specific processor) for a process. See Chapter 4, "Configuring the Windows 2000 Environment," for details on setting processor affinity.

- To customize the counters that are listed, select View ➤ Select Columns. This brings up the Select Columns dialog box, shown in Figure 14.26, where you can select the information that you want to see listed on the Processes tab.

FIGURE 14.26 Selecting information for the Task Manager Processes tab

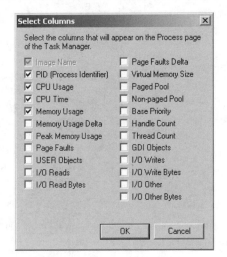

Managing Performance Tasks

The Performance tab of the Task Manager dialog box, shown in Figure 14.27, provides an overview of your computer's CPU and memory usage. This is similar to the information tracked by System Monitor, and you don't have to configure it first as you do with System Monitor.

FIGURE 14.27 The Performance tab of the Task Manager dialog box

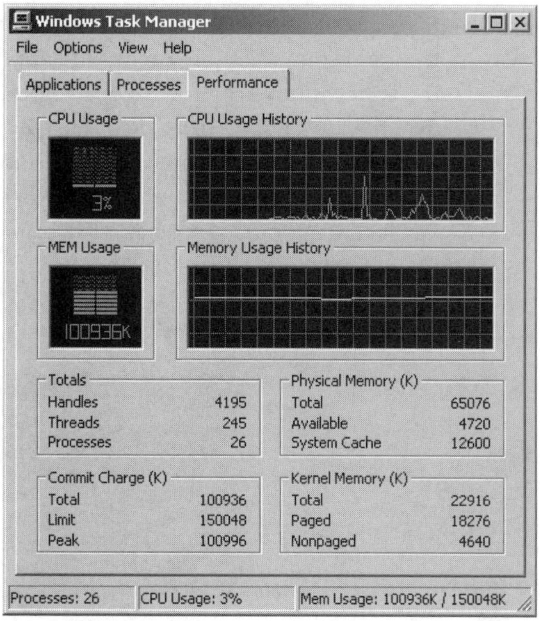

Microsoft ✓ Exam Objective

Optimize and troubleshoot performance of the Windows 2000 Professional desktop.

- Optimize and troubleshoot memory performance

The Performance tab shows the following information:

- CPU usage, in real time and in a history graph
- Memory usage, in real time and in a history graph
- Totals for handles, threads, and processes
- Physical memory statistics
- Commit charge memory statistics
- Kernel memory statistics

Configuring Application Performance

If you run multiple applications concurrently on your Windows 2000 Professional computer, the foreground application is given higher priority when the applications are processed. As noted in the preceding section, you can dynamically change an application's priority through the Processes tab of the Task Manager dialog box. The options for foreground and background application processing are accessed through the System icon in Control Panel. The Advanced tab has a Performance Options button, which displays the Performance Options dialog box shown in Figure 14.28.

FIGURE 14.28 The Performance Options dialog box

This dialog box allows you to configure application response as follows:

- If you select the Applications radio button, foreground applications are always processed at a higher priority than background applications.

- If you select the Background Services radio button, foreground and background applications are processed at the same priority.

In Exercise 14.7, you will configure your computer so that foreground and background applications are processed at the same priority.

EXERCISE 14.7

Optimizing Applications

1. Select Start ➢ Settings ➢ Control Panel and double-click the System icon.

EXERCISE 14.7 *(continued)*

2. In the System Properties dialog box, click the Advanced tab.

3. Click the Performance Options button.

4. In the Performance Options dialog box, click the Background Services radio button. Then click the OK button.

5. In the System Properties dialog box, click the OK button.

Scheduling Tasks

Windows 2000 Professional includes a *Task Scheduler* utility that allows you to schedule tasks to occur at specified intervals. You can set any of your Windows programs to run automatically at a specific time and at a set interval, such as daily, weekly, or monthly. For example, you might schedule your Windows Backup program to run daily at 2:00 A.M.

Microsoft
✓ *Exam*
Objective

Configure, manage, and troubleshoot the Task Scheduler.

In Exercise 14.8, we will create a new task.

EXERCISE 14.8

Creating a New Task

1. Select Start ➢ Settings ➢ Control Panel and double-click the Scheduled Tasks icon.

2. In the Scheduled Tasks window, double-click the Add Scheduled Task icon.

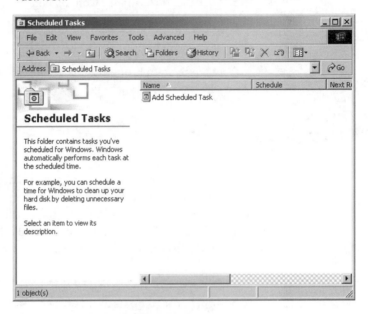

3. When the first page of the Scheduled Task Wizard appears, click the Next button to continue.

4. The first Scheduled Task Wizard dialog box lists applications you can run. You can select an application from the list or click the Browse button to locate any application or program to which your computer has access. After you select an application, click the Next button.

EXERCISE 14.8 *(continued)*

5. The next Wizard dialog box prompts you to select a name for the task and specify when it will be performed. Make your selection and click the Next button.

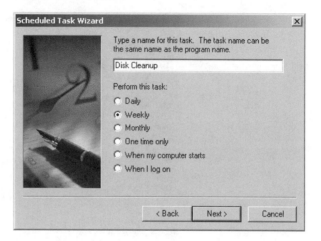

6. Depending on the selection you made for the task's schedule, you may see another dialog box for setting the specific schedule. For example, if you chose to run the task weekly, the next dialog box lets you select the start time for the task, run the task every *x* weeks, and choose the day of the week that the task should be run. Make your selection and click the Next button.

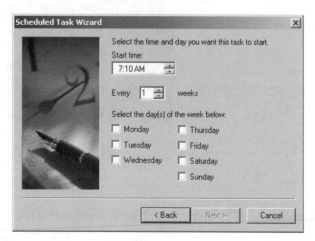

EXERCISE 14.8 *(continued)*

7. Next you are prompted to enter the username and the password that will be used to start the task. After you enter this information, click the Next button.

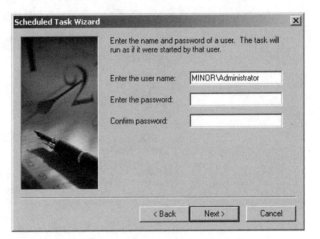

8. The final dialog box shows your selections for the scheduled task. If this information is correct, click the Finish button.

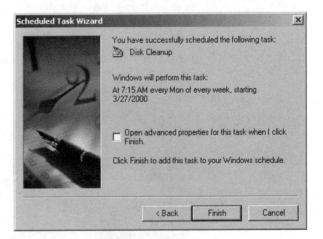

Managing Scheduled Task Properties

You can manage a scheduled task through its properties dialog box; Figure 14.29 shows the properties for the Disk Cleanup job. To access this dialog box, open the Scheduled Tasks window (Start ➢ Settings ➢ Control Panel and double-click the Scheduled Tasks icon). Right-click the task you wish to manage, and choose Properties from the pop-up menu.

The scheduled task properties dialog box has four tabs with options for managing how and when the task is run and who can manage it. These options are described in the following sections.

Task Properties

Through the Task tab (see Figure 14.29), you can configure the following options:

- The command-line program that is used to run the task

- The folders containing related files that might be required to run the specified task (this is the Start In information)

- Any comments that you want to include for informational purposes

- The username and password to be used to run the specified task (this is the Run As information)

- Whether the scheduled task is enabled

FIGURE 14.29 The Task properties for the scheduled task

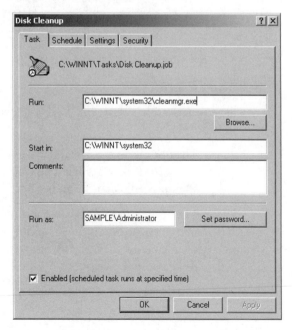

Schedule Properties

The Schedule tab, shown in Figure 14.30, shows the schedule configured for the task. You can change any of these options to reschedule the task.

FIGURE 14.30 The Schedule properties for the scheduled task

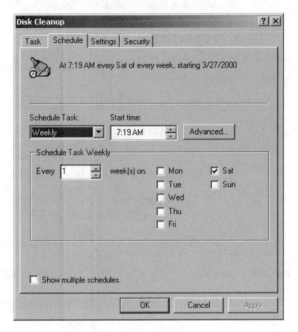

Settings Properties

The Settings tab (Figure 14.31) offers several configuration settings for the scheduled task:

- The options in the Scheduled Task Completed section allow you to delete the task if it will not be run again and specify how long the task should be allowed to run before it is stopped.

- The options in the Idle Time section are useful if the computer must be idle when the task is run. You can specify how long the computer must be idle before the task begins and whether the task should be stopped if the computer ceases to be idle.

- The options in the Power Management section are applicable when the computer on which the task runs may be battery powered. You can specify that the task should not start if the computer is running from batteries and choose to stop the task if battery mode begins.

FIGURE 14.31 The Settings tab of the scheduled task dialog box

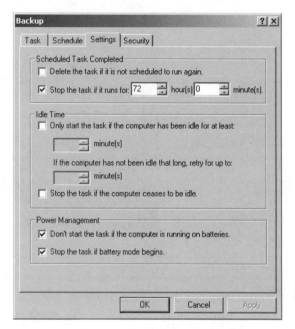

Security Properties

The Security tab, shown in Figure 14.32, allows you to configure the security settings for the scheduled task object.

Normally, only Administrators can manage scheduled tasks. However, you might want to assign this task to other users, who will need the appropriate permissions to manage scheduled tasks. (To assign permissions for a task, click the Add button, select the user or group, and then check the Allow or Deny check boxes for the permissions. See Chapter 10, "Accessing Files and Folders," for more information about assigning permissions to users and groups.)

FIGURE 14.32   The Security tab of the scheduled task dialog box

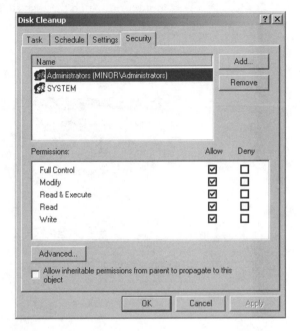

 If you are using Task Scheduler and your jobs are not running properly, make sure that the Task Scheduler service is running and is configured to start automatically. You should also ensure that the user who configured to run the scheduled task has sufficient permissions to run the task.

Summary

In this chapter, you learned about managing Windows 2000 Professional optimization and reliability. We covered the following topics:

- How to keep your operating system up-to-date by using the Windows Update utility and applying Windows 2000 service packs

- How to use the System Monitor utility and the Performance Logs and Alerts utility to track and monitor your system's performance

- How to monitor and optimize memory, the processor, the disk subsystem, and the network subsystem, and how to create a system baseline

- How to use the Task Manager utility to view and manage running applications and processes, and to get an overview of CPU and memory usage

- How to access settings for optimizing application performance through the System icon in Control Panel

- How to automate tasks through the Task Scheduler utility

Exam Essentials

Be able to deploy service packs.   Understand the purpose of service packs. Know how to successfully deploy them and how to verify that they are installed correctly.

Be able to monitor and troubleshoot Windows 2000 Professional performance.   Know which utilities can be used to track Windows 2000 performance events and issues. Know how to track and identify performance problems related to memory, the processor, the disk subsystem, and the network subsystem. Be able to correct system bottlenecks when they are identified.

Know how to use the Task Scheduler to automate system tasks. Understand the purpose of Task Scheduler. Be able to configure Task Scheduler and identify problems that would keep it from running properly.

Key Terms

Before taking the exam, you should be familiar with the following terms:

alert	service pack
baseline	slipstream technology
bottleneck	System Monitor
counter	Task Manager
page file	Task Scheduler
Performance Logs and Alerts	Windows Update

Review Questions

1. Tim is monitoring his computer's performance through Performance Logs and Alerts. One of the counters being monitored is Memory > Available Mbytes. When Tim reads the counter, he sees that it is at 12MB. What should he do?

   A. Add RAM.

   B. Increase the size of the page file.

   C. Split the page file over two physical disk channels.

   D. Take no action.

2. Your accounting department runs a processor-intensive application and you are trying to determine if their current computers need to have the processors upgraded. You load a test computer with a configuration identical to the production computers' and run a program that simulates a typical user's workload. You monitor the Processor > %Processor Time counter. What average value for this counter would indicate a processor bottleneck?

   A. Over 5%

   B. Over 50%

   C. Over 60%

   D. Over 85%

3. Users in the Sales department have been complaining that the Sales application is slow to load. Using Performance Logs and Alerts, you create a baseline report for one of the computers. You notice that the disk subsystem has a high load of activity. What other subsystem should you monitor before you can know for sure whether you have a disk subsystem bottleneck?

   A. Memory

   B. Processor

   C. Network

   D. Application

4. Curtis is trying to load Visio on his computer. Each time he runs this application, it takes between 5 and 10 seconds to load. He uses the Task Manager utility to try and determine if he has a resource bottleneck. Which two of the following subsystems can be easily monitored for performance through Task Manager?

   A. Memory

   B. Processor

   C. Network

   D. Disk

5. As a part of your computer's ongoing system maintenance, you want to run a virus checker on your computer every day at 5:00 p.m. Which Windows 2000 utility allows you to configure automated tasks?

   A. Scheduled Tasks

   B. Automated Scheduler

   C. Task Manager

   D. Task Automater

6. You suspect that your computer has a disk subsystem bottleneck and you want to track disk counters in System Monitor. What must you do in order to enable physical disk counters in System Monitor?

   A. Run DISKPERF -y

   B. Run DISKCOUNT -y

   C. Run PERFMON -y

   D. The counters are enabled by default.

7. You are troubleshooting a Windows 2000 Professional computer in your company. You suspect that the problem is a documented bug that has been fixed with the current service pack. Which command tells you whether any service packs are installed and what versions they are?

A. SERVPACK

B. WINVER

C. CURRENTVER

D. CONFIG

8. You suspect that you have a memory bottleneck on your computer and decide to run System Monitor. You want to track five memory-related counters and monitor the data flows over a specified time period. Which view should you use in System Monitor?

A. Chart

B. Histogram

C. Trace

D. Report

9. You want to create a baseline report for performance monitoring. When you open System Monitor, which of the following counters are active by default?

A. Memory > Pages/Sec

B. Processor > %Processor Time

C. Paging File > %Usage

D. None

10. You are monitoring the Processor > Interrupts/Sec counter through System Monitor. On a Pentium computer, you should suspect that a program or piece of hardware is generating spurious interrupts when this counter reaches which of the following values?

    A. 250

    B. 500

    C. 1,000

    D. 3,500

11. You are monitoring the PhysicalDisk > Current Disk Queue Length counter through System Monitor. You might have a disk subsystem bottleneck when this counter is over which of the following values?

    A. 1

    B. 2

    C. 10

    D. 12

12. An application has stalled and is apparently hung. Which utility will let you view the current status of the application?

    A. Application Manager

    B. Service Manager

    C. Task Manager

    D. Control Panel, Add/Remove Programs

13. When you schedule a task to be run, which of the following task properties *cannot* be configured?

    A. The username and password of the user who will run the task

    B. Power management, so that if the computer is a laptop and is running from the battery, the task will not run

    C. Whether the task will be run once or repeatedly

    D. Whether another task will be run if specific conditions trigger the secondary task

14. You want to track system performance for a baseline over a period of two days. You want the data to be collected every five minutes. What type of log would you create for this monitoring, through Performance Logs and Alerts?

A. Counter log

B. Trace log

C. Monitoring log

D. Baseline log

15. You are monitoring the Memory > Pages/Sec counter through System Monitor. Which of the following statements reflects what is considered optimal performance for this counter?

A. This counter's value should be around 4 to 5.

B. This counter's value should be around 30 to 40.

C. This counter's value should be around 40 to 50.

D. This counter's value should be around 50 to 60.

Answers to Review Questions

1. **D.** As long as the counter for Memory > Available MBytes shows more than 4MB of memory, no bottleneck is indicated and no intervention is needed.

2. **D.** If the average Processor > %Processor Time counter is consistently above 80%, a processor bottleneck may be indicated. (Normally this number will spike up and down over time. If it spikes over 80%, it is not necessarily alarming. If the average is over 80%, then a bottleneck is indicated.)

3. **A.** You should check the memory counters. If your computer does not have enough memory, it can cause excessive paging, which may be perceived as a disk subsystem bottleneck.

4. **A, B.** Through the Performance tab of Task Manager, you can easily monitor your computer's current processor activity and memory utilization.

5. **A.** To automate scheduled tasks, you use the Scheduled Tasks utility.

6. **D.** In Windows 2000, physical disk counters are enabled by default. In order to view Logical Disk counters, you must run `DISKPERF -y`.

7. **B.** The `WINVER` command is used to display the current operating system that is loaded, any service packs that are loaded, and the amount of physical memory that is installed on the computer.

8. **A.** The chart view is used to display a small number of counters in a graphical format. With this view, you can easily track information over a specified time period.

9. **D.** None of System Monitor's counters are on by default.

10. D.   The Processor > Interrupts/Sec counter shows the average number of hardware interrupts the processor receives each second. If this value is more than 3,500 on a Pentium computer, you might have a problem with a program or hardware that is generating spurious interrupts.

11. B.   The PhysicalDisk > Current Disk Queue Length counter indicates the number of outstanding disk requests waiting to be processed. This counter value should be less than 2.

12. C.   The Applications tab of the Task Manager dialog box lists all the applications currently running on the computer. For each task, you will see the name of the task and the current status (running, not responding, or stopped).

13. D.   There are no options to trigger secondary conditional tasks.

14. A.   Counter logs record data about hardware usage and the activity of system services. You can configure logging to occur manually or on a predefined schedule.

15. A.   The Memory > Pages/Sec counter shows the number of times that the requested information was not in memory and had to be retrieved from disk. This counter's value should be below 20. For optimal performance, it should be 4 to 5.

Chapter

15

Performing System Recovery Functions

MICROSOFT EXAM OBJECTIVES COVERED IN THIS CHAPTER:

✓ **Recover system state data and user data.**

- Recover system state data and user data by using Windows Backup.
- Troubleshoot system restoration by using Safe Mode.
- Recover system state data and user data by using the Recovery Console.

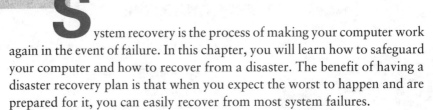

System recovery is the process of making your computer work again in the event of failure. In this chapter, you will learn how to safeguard your computer and how to recover from a disaster. The benefit of having a disaster recovery plan is that when you expect the worst to happen and are prepared for it, you can easily recover from most system failures.

One utility that you can use to diagnose system problems is Event Viewer. Through the Event Viewer utility, you can see logs that list events related to your operating system and applications.

If your computer will not boot, an understanding of the Window 2000 boot process will help you identify the area of failure and correct the problem. You should know the steps in each stage of the boot process, the function of each boot file, and how to edit the BOOT.INI file.

When you have problems starting Windows 2000, you can press F8 when prompted during the boot sequence. This calls up the Windows 2000 Advanced Options menu, which is new to Windows 2000. This menu includes several special boot options, such as Safe Mode and Last Known Good Configuration, that are useful for getting your system started so you can track down and correct problems.

Startup and Recovery options are used to specify how the operating system will react in the event of system failure. For example, you can specify whether or not the system should automatically reboot and whether or not administrative alerts should be sent.

You can use the Dr. Watson utility, which ships with Windows 2000 Professional, to diagnose application errors. When an application error occurs, Dr. Watson starts automatically, displaying information about the error.

If you cannot boot the operating system and your CD-ROM is not accessible, you can recover by using the Windows 2000 Professional Setup Boot Disks. After you've created these setup disks, you can use them to reinstall Windows 2000, start the Recovery Console, or access your Emergency Repair Disk.

Backups are the best protection you can have against system failure. You can create backups through the Windows Backup utility, which offers options to run the Backup Wizard, run the Restore Wizard, and create an Emergency Repair Disk.

Another option that experienced administrators can use to recover from a system failure is the Recovery Console. The Recovery Console boots your computer so that you have limited access to FAT16, FAT32, and NTFS volumes.

In this chapter, you will learn how to use the system recovery functions of Windows 2000 Professional. We'll begin with an overview of techniques to protect your computer and recover from disasters.

Safeguarding Your Computer and Recovering from Disaster

One of the worst events you will experience is a computer that won't boot. An even worse experience is discovering that there is no recent backup for that computer.

Microsoft
Exam
Objective

Recover system state data and user data.

- Recover system state data and user data by using Windows Backup.

- Troubleshoot system restoration by using Safe Mode.

- Recover system state data and user data by using the Recovery Console.

The first step in preparing for disaster recovery is to expect that a disaster will happen at some point, and take proactive steps to plan your recovery before the failure occurs. Following are some of the preparations you can make:

- Perform regular system backups.

- Use virus-scanning software.

- Perform regular administrative functions, such as monitoring the logs in the Event Viewer utility.

In the event that the dreaded day arrives and your system fails, there are several processes you can analyze and Windows 2000 utilities you can use to help get your system up and running again. These options are summarized in Table 15.1.

TABLE 15.1 Windows 2000 Professional Recovery Techniques

Recovery Technique	When to Use
Event Viewer	If the Windows 2000 operating system can be loaded through normal or Safe Mode, one of the first places to look at for hints about the problem is Event Viewer. Event Viewer displays System, Security, and Application logs.
Safe Mode	This is generally your starting point for system recovery. Safe Mode loads the absolute minimum of services and drivers that are needed to boot Windows 2000. If you can load Safe Mode, you may be able to troubleshoot devices or services that keep Windows 2000 from loading normally.
Last Known Good Configuration	This option can help if you made changes to your computer and are now having problems. Last Known Good Configuration is an Advanced Options menu item that you can select during startup. It loads the configuration that was used the last time the computer booted successfully. This option will not help if you have hardware errors.
Windows 2000 Professional Setup Boot Disks	You can use this option if you suspect that Windows 2000 is not loading due to missing or corrupt boot files. Using the Setup Boot Disks allows you to load all the Windows 2000 boot files. If you can boot from a boot disk, you can restore the necessary files from the Emergency Repair Disk.

TABLE 15.1   Windows 2000 Professional Recovery Techniques *(continued)*

Recovery Technique	When to Use
Emergency Repair Disk (ERD)	Try this option when you need to correct configuration errors or to repair system files. The ERD can be used to repair problems that prevent your computer from starting. This disk stores portions of the Registry, the system files, a copy of your partition boot sector, and information that relates to the startup environment.
Dr. Watson	This utility helps when you are experiencing problems with an application. Dr. Watson is used to diagnose and troubleshoot application errors.
Windows Backup	You should use this utility to safeguard your computer. Through the Backup utility, you can create an ERD, back up the system or parts of the system, and restore data from backups that you have made.
Recovery Console	You can use this option if none of the other options or utilities works. The Recovery Console starts Windows 2000 without the graphical interface and allows the administrator limited capabilities, such as adding or replacing files and enabling/disabling services.

All these Windows 2000 Professional recovery techniques are covered in detail in this chapter.

Using Event Viewer

You can use the *Event Viewer* utility to track information about your computer's hardware and software, as well as to monitor security events. All of the traced information is stored in three types of log files:

- The *System log* tracks events related to the Windows 2000 operating system.

- The *Security log* tracks events related to Windows 2000 auditing.

- *The Application log* tracks events related to applications that are running on your computer.

You can access Event Viewer by selecting Start ➢ Settings ➢ Control Panel ➢ Administrative Tools ➢ Event Viewer. Alternatively, right-click My Computer, choose Manage from the pop-up menu, and open Event Viewer under System Tools. From Event Viewer, select the log you want to view. Figure 15.1 shows Event Viewer with the System log displayed.

You can also add Event Viewer as a Microsoft Management Console (MMC) snap-in. Adding MMC snap-ins is covered in Chapter 4, "Configuring the Windows 2000 Environment."

FIGURE 15.1 A System log in Event Viewer

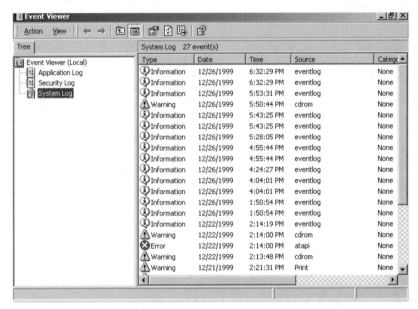

In the log files, you will see all the events that have been recorded. By default, the oldest events are at the bottom of the window and the newest events are at the top. This arrangement can be misleading in troubleshooting, since one error can precipitate other errors. You should always resolve the oldest errors first. To change the default listing order and put the oldest events at the top, click one of the three logs and select View ➤ Oldest First. The following sections describe how to view events and manage logs.

Reviewing Event Types

The Event Viewer logs display five event types, denoted by their icons. Table 15.2 describes each event type.

TABLE 15.2 Event Viewer Log Events

Event Type	Icon	Description
Information	White dialog bubble with blue forward slash (/)	Informs you of the occurrence of a specific action, such as the startup or shutdown of a system. *Information events* are logged for informative purposes.
Warning	Yellow triangle with black exclamation mark (!)	You should be concerned about this event. *Warning events* may not be critical in nature but may be indicative of future errors.
Error	Red circle with white *X*	Indicates the occurrence of an error, such as a driver's failing to load. You should be very concerned about *Error events*.
Success Audit	Yellow key	Indicates the occurrence of an event that has been audited for success. For example, when system logons are being audited, a *Success Audit event* is a successful logon.
Failure Audit	Yellow lock	Indicates the occurrence of an event that has been audited for failure. For example, when system logons are being audited, a *Failure Audit event* is a failed logon due to an invalid username and/or password.

Getting Event Details

Double-clicking an event in an Event Viewer log file brings up the Event Properties dialog box, which shows details about the event. An example of the Event Properties dialog box for an Information event is shown in Figure 15.2. Table 15.3 describes the information that appears in this dialog box.

FIGURE 15.2   The Event Properties dialog box

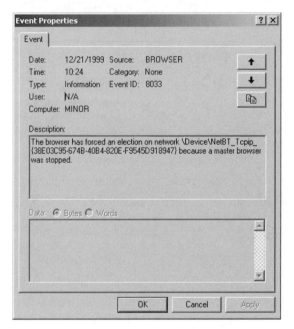

TABLE 15.3   Event Properties Dialog Box Items

Item	Description
Date	The date on which the event was generated
Time	The time at which the event was generated
Type	The type of event that was generated: Information, Warning, Error, Success Audit, or Failure Audit

TABLE 15.3 Event Properties Dialog Box Items *(continued)*

Item	Description
User	The name of the user to whom the event is attributed, if applicable (not all events are attributed to a user)
Computer	The name of the computer on which the event occurred
Source	The software that generated the event (e.g., operating system components or drivers)
Category	The source that logged the event (this field will say "None" until this feature has been fully implemented in Windows 2000)
Event ID	The event number specific to the type of event generated (e.g., a print error event has the event ID 45)
Description	A detailed description of the event
Data	The binary data generated by the event (if any; some events do not generate binary data) in hexadecimal bytes or DWORD format (programmers can use this information to interpret the event)

Managing Log Files

Over time, your log files will grow, and you will need to decide how to manage them. You can clear a log file for a fresh start. You may want to save the existing log file before you clear it, to keep that log file available for reference or future analysis.

To clear all log file events, right-click the log you wish to clear and choose Clear All Events from the pop-up menu. Then specify whether or not you want to save the log before it is cleared.

If you just want to save an existing log file, right-click that log and choose Save Log File As. Then specify the location and name of the file.

To open an existing log file, right-click the log you wish to open and choose Open Log File. Then specify the name and location of the log file and click the Open button.

Setting Log File Properties

Each Event Viewer log has two sets of properties associated with it:

- General properties control items such as the log filename, its maximum size, and the action to take when the log file reaches its maximum size.

- Filter properties specify which events are displayed.

To access the log Properties dialog box, right-click the log you want to manage and select Properties from the pop-up menu. The following sections describe the properties available on the General and Filter tabs of this dialog box.

General Properties

The General tab of the log Properties dialog box, shown in Figure 15.3, displays information about the log file and includes options to control its size. Table 15.4 describes the properties on the General tab.

FIGURE 15.3   The General properties for an Application log

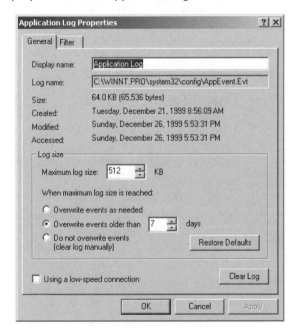

TABLE 15.4 General Log Properties

Property	Description
Display Name	Allows you to change the name of the log file. For example, if you are managing multiple computers and want to distinguish the logs for each computer, you can make the names more descriptive (e.g., DATA-Application and ROVER-Application).
Log Name	Path and filename of the log file.
Size	Current size of the log file.
Created	Date and time when the log file was created.
Modified	Date and time when the log file was last modified.
Accessed	Date and time when the log file was last accessed.
Maximum Log Size	Allows you to specify the maximum size for the log file. You can use this option to prevent the log file from growing too large and taking up excessive disk space.
When Maximum Log Size Is Reached	Allows you to specify what action will be taken when the log file reaches the maximum size (if a maximum size is specified). You can choose to overwrite events as needed (on a first-in-first-out basis), overwrite events that are over a certain age, or prevent events from being overwritten (which means that you would need to clear log events manually).
Using a Low-Speed Connection	Specifies that you are monitoring the log file of a remote computer and that you connect to that computer through a low-speed connection.

The Clear Log button in the General tab of the log Properties dialog box clears all log events.

Filter Properties

The Filter tab of the log Properties dialog box, shown in Figure 15.4, allows you to control the listing of events in the log. For example, if your system generates a large number of logged events, you might want to set the Filter properties so that you can track specific events. You can filter log events based on the event type, source, category, ID, users, computer, or specific time period. Table 15.5 describes the properties on the Filter tab.

FIGURE 15.4 The Filter properties for an Application log

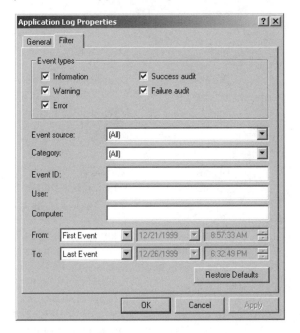

TABLE 15.5 Filter Properties for Logs

Property	Description
Event Type	Allows you to list only the specified event types (Warning, Error, Success Audit, or Failure Audit). By default, all event types are listed.

TABLE 15.5   Filter Properties for Logs *(continued)*

Property	Description
Event Source	Filters events based on the source of the event. The drop-down box lists the software that might generate events, such as Application Popup and DHCP. By default, events triggered by all sources are listed.
Category	Filters events based on the category that generated the event. The drop-down box lists the event categories. By default, events in all categories are listed.
Event ID	Filters events based on a specific event number.
User	Filters events based on the user who caused the event to be triggered.
Computer	Filters events based on the name of the computer that generated the event.
From-To	Filters events based on the date and time when the events were generated. By default, events are listed from the first event to the last event. To specify specific dates and times, select Events On from the drop-down list and select dates and times.

In Exercise 15.1, you will view events in Event Viewer and set log properties.

EXERCISE 15.1

Using the Event Viewer Utility

1. Select Start ➤ Settings ➤ Control Panel ➤ Administrative Tools ➤ Event Viewer.

2. Click System Log in the left pane of the Event Viewer window to display the System log events.

EXERCISE 15.1 *(continued)*

3. Double-click the first event in the right pane of the Event Viewer window to see its Event Properties dialog box. Click the Cancel button to close the dialog box.

4. Right-click System Log in the left pane of the Event Viewer window and select Properties.

5. Click the Filter tab. Clear all the check marks under Event Types except those in the Warning and Error check boxes; then click the OK button. You should see only Warning and Error events listed in the System log.

6. To remove the filter, return to the Filter tab of the log Properties dialog box, click the Restore Defaults button at the bottom, and click the OK button. You should see all of the event types listed again.

7. Right-click System Log and select Clear All Events.

8. You see a dialog box asking if you want to save the System log before clearing it. Click the Yes button. Specify the path and filename for the log file; then click the Save button. All the events should be cleared from the System log.

 Real World Scenario

Using Event Viewer Logs for Problem Resolution

You are a senior network engineer for a company using specialized hardware and software that is run on Windows 2000 Professional computers in the field. One of your junior network engineers is on site in another state. She is reporting errors with your software and hardware but is not able to diagnose the problem.

You want to be able to troubleshoot the problem remotely if possible. One way that you can view a complete history of any informational, warning, or error messages is to have the on-site engineer send the log files to you or to another senior engineer. To do this for both the Application log and System log, the on-site engineer right-clicks on the log, selects Save Log File As, and saves the log file to a file that will automatically be given an .evt extension. These .evt files can then be e-mailed to the more-experienced engineer for problem resolution.

The Event Viewer is a handy utility because it lets you track information about your computer's hardware and software. You can also monitor security events.

The Windows 2000 Boot Process

Some of the problems that cause system failure are related to the Windows 2000 boot process. The boot process starts when you turn on your computer and ends when you log on to Windows 2000.

To identify problems associated with the boot process, you need to understand the steps involved in the process, as well as how the BOOT.INI file controls the process. Also, you should create a Windows 2000 boot disk that you can use to boot the operating system if your computer suffers a boot failure. These topics are covered in the following sections.

The Normal Boot Process

The Windows 2000 boot process consists of five major stages: the preboot sequence, the boot sequence, kernel load, kernel initialization, and logon. Many files are used during these stages. The following sections describe the steps in each stage, the files used, and the errors that might occur.

The Preboot Sequence

A normal boot process begins with the preboot sequence, in which your computer starts up and prepares for booting the operating system.

Finding the Boot Process Files

Most of the boot process files reside in the root of the system partition. In the Windows 2000 Professional documentation, you will see the terms *system partition* and *boot partition*. The system partition is the computer's active partition, which holds the files needed to boot the operating system. This is typically the C: drive. The boot partition refers to the partition where the system files are stored. You can place the system files anywhere. The default folder for the system files is \WINNT and is referred to as the variable *Windir*. The system partition and boot partition can be on the same partition or on different partitions.

If you look for the boot process files but don't see them, they may just be hidden. Among the file attributes used to specify the properties of a file are System (S), Hidden (H), and Read-only (R). This is important to know because, by default, System and Hidden files are not listed in Windows Explorer or through a standard DIR command. You can turn on the display of System and Hidden files in Windows Explorer by selecting Tools ➢ Folder Options and clicking the View tab. Select the Show Hidden Files and Folders option, and uncheck the two options Hide File Extensions for Known File Types, and Hide Protected Operating System Files.

File Accessed in the Preboot Sequence

During the preboot sequence, your computer accesses the NTLDR file. This file is used to control the Windows 2000 boot process until control is passed to the NTOSKRNL file for the boot sequence stage. The NTLDR file is located in the root of the system partition. It has the file attributes of System, Hidden, and Read-only.

Steps in the Preboot Sequence

The preboot sequence consists of the following steps:

1. When the computer is powered on, it runs a *Power On Self-Test (POST)* routine. The POST detects the processor you are using, how much memory is present, what hardware is recognized, and whether the BIOS (Basic Input/Output System) is standard or has Plug and Play capabilities. The system also enumerates and configures hardware devices at this point.

2. The BIOS points to the boot device, and the *Master Boot Record (MBR)* is loaded.

3. The MBR points to the active partition. The active partition is used to specify the partition that should be used to boot the operating system. This is normally the C: drive. Once the MBR locates the active partition, the boot sector is loaded into memory and executed.

4. As part of the Windows 2000 installation process, the NTLDR file is copied to the active partition. The boot sector points to the NTLDR file, and this file executes. The NTLDR file is used to initialize and start the Windows 2000 boot process.

Possible Errors during the Preboot Sequence

If you see errors during the preboot sequence, they are probably not related to Windows 2000 because the operating system has not yet been loaded. The following are some common causes for errors during the preboot stage:

Improperly configured hardware	If the POST cannot recognize your hard drive, the preboot stage will fail. This error is most likely to occur in a computer that is still being initially configured. If everything is working properly, and no changes were made to the configuration and then the hard drive fails, the most probable error is in the hardware.
Corrupt MBR	Viruses that are specifically designed to infect the MBR can corrupt it. You can protect your system from this type of error by using virus-scanning software. Also, most virus-scanning programs can correct an infected MBR.

No partition is marked as active	This can happen if you used the FDISK utility and did not create a partition from all of the free space. If the partition is FAT16 or FAT32 and on a basic disk, you can boot the computer to DOS or Windows 9*x* with a boot disk, run FDISK, and mark a partition as active. If you created your partitions as a part of the Windows 2000 installation and have dynamic disks, an active partition is marked for you during installation.
Corrupt or missing NTLDR file	If the NTLDR file does not execute, it may have been corrupted or deleted (by a virus or malicious intent). You can restore this file through the ERD, which is covered later in this chapter.
SYS program run from DOS or Windows 9*x* after Windows 2000 installation	The NTLDR file may not execute because the SYS program was run from DOS or Windows 9*x* after Windows 2000 was installed. If this has occurred, the only solution is to reinstall Windows 2000.

The Boot Sequence

When the preboot sequence is completed, the boot sequence begins. The phases in this stage include the initial boot loader phase, the operating system selection phase, and the hardware detection phase.

Files Accessed in the Boot Sequence

Along with the NTLDR file, which was described in the Preboot Sequence section, the following files are used during the boot sequence:

- *BOOT.INI* is used to build the operating system menu choices that are displayed during the boot process. It is also used to specify the location of the boot partition. This file is located in the root of the system partition and has the file attributes of System and Hidden.

- *BOOTSECT.DOS* is an optional file that is loaded if you choose to load an operating system other than Windows 2000. It is only used in dual-boot or multi-boot computers. This file is located in the root of the system partition and has the file attributes of System and Hidden.

- *NTDETECT.COM* is used to detect any hardware that is installed and add information about the hardware to the Registry. This file is located in the root of the system partition and has the file attributes of System, Hidden, and Read-only.

- *NTBOOTDD.SYS* is an optional file that is used when you have a SCSI (Small Computer Standard Interface) adapter with the onboard BIOS disabled. (This option is not commonly implemented.) The NTBOOTDD .SYS file is located in the root of the system partition and has the file attributes of System and Hidden.

- *NTOSKRNL.EXE* is used to load the Windows 2000 operating system. This file is located in Windir\System32 and has no file attributes.

Steps in the Boot Sequence

The boot sequence consists of the following steps:

1. For the initial boot loader phase, NTLDR switches the processor from real mode to 32-bit flat memory mode and starts the appropriate mini file system–drivers. Mini file system–drivers are used to support your computer's file systems and include FAT16, FAT32, and NTFS.

2. For the operating system selection phase, the computer reads the BOOT.INI file. If you have configured your computer to dual-boot or multi-boot and Windows 2000 recognizes that you have choices, it builds a menu of operating systems that can be loaded. If you choose an operating system other than Windows 2000, the BOOTSECT.DOS file is used to load the alternate operating system, and the Windows 2000 boot process terminates. If you choose a Windows 2000 operating system, the Windows 2000 boot process continues.

3. If you choose a Windows 2000 operating system, the NTDETECT.COM file is used to perform hardware detection. Any hardware that is detected is added to the Registry, in the HKEY_LOCAL_MACHINE key. Some of the hardware that NTDETECT.COM will recognize includes communication and parallel ports, keyboard, floppy disk drive, mouse, SCSI adapter, and video adapter.

4. Control is passed to NTOSKRNL.EXE to start the kernel load process.

Possible Errors during the Boot Sequence

Following are some common causes for errors during the boot stage:

Missing or corrupt boot files	If NTLDR, BOOT.INI, BOOTSECT.DOS, NTDETECT.COM, or NTOSKRNL.EXE is corrupt or missing (because of a virus or malicious intent), the boot sequence will fail. You will see an error message that indicates which file is missing or corrupt. You can restore these files through the ERD, which is covered later in this chapter.
Improperly configured BOOT.INI file	If you have made any changes to your disk configuration and your computer will not restart, chances are your BOOT.INI file is configured incorrectly. BOOT.INI is covered in an upcoming section.
Unrecognizable or improperly configured hardware	If you have serious errors that cause NTDETECT.COM to fail, you should resolve the hardware problems. If your computer has a lot of hardware, remove all the hardware that is not required to boot the computer. Add hardware one piece at a time and boot the computer after each addition. This will help you identify the hardware component that is bad or is conflicting for a resource with another device.

The Kernel Load Sequence

In the kernel load sequence, the Hardware Abstraction Layer (HAL), computer control set, and low-level device drivers are loaded. The NTOSKRNL .EXE file, which was described in the preceding section, is used during this stage. The kernel load sequence consists of the following steps:

1. The NTOSKRNL.EXE file is loaded and initialized.

2. The HAL is loaded. The HAL is what makes Windows 2000 portable to support platforms such as Intel and Alpha.

3. The control set that the operating system will use is loaded. The control set is used to control system configuration information, such as a list of device drivers that should be loaded.

4. Low-level device drivers, such as disk drivers, are loaded.

If you have problems loading the Windows 2000 kernel, and other recovery options do not solve the problem, you will most likely need to reinstall the operating system.

The Kernel Initialization Sequence

In the kernel initialization sequence, the HKEY_LOCAL_MACHINE\HARDWARE Registry and the Clone Control set are created, device drivers are initialized, and high-order subsystems and services are loaded. The kernel initialization sequence consists of the following steps:

1. Once the kernel has been successfully loaded, the Registry key HKEY_LOCAL_MACHINE\HARDWARE is created. This Registry key is used to specify the hardware configuration of hardware components when the computer is started.

2. The Clone Control set is created. The Clone Control set is an exact copy of the data used to configure the computer and does not include changes made by the startup process.

3. The device drivers that were loaded during the kernel load phase are initialized.

4. Higher-order subsystems and services are loaded.

If you have problems during the kernel initialization sequence, you might try to boot to the Last Known Good Configuration, which is covered in the "Using Advanced Startup Options" section later in this chapter.

The Logon Sequence

In the logon sequence, the user logs on to Windows 2000 and any remaining services are loaded. The logon sequence consists of the following steps:

1. After the kernel initialization is complete, the Log On to Windows dialog box appears. At this point, you type in a valid Windows 2000 username and password.

2. The service controller executes and performs a final scan of HKEY_ LOCAL_MACHINE\SYSTEM\CurrentControlSet\Services to see if there are any remaining services that need to be loaded.

If logon errors occur, they are usually due to an incorrect username or password, or caused by the unavailability of a domain controller to authenticate the request (if the computer is a part of a domain). See Chapter 6, "Managing Users," for more information about troubleshooting user authentication problems.

Errors can also occur if a service cannot be loaded. If a service fails to load, you will see a message in Event Viewer. Using the Event Viewer utility is covered earlier in this chapter.

Editing the BOOT.INI File

The BOOT.INI file is located in the active partition and is used to build the boot loader menu and to specify the location of the Windows 2000 boot partition. This file also specifies the default operating system that should be loaded if no selection is made within the default time allotment. You can open and edit BOOT.INI to add switches or options used in controlling how the operating system is loaded. Figure 15.5 shows a fairly common example of a BOOT.INI file, opened in Notepad.

FIGURE 15.5 A sample BOOT.INI file

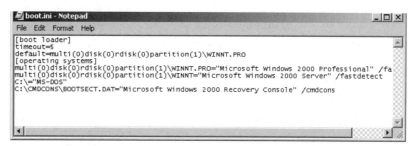

The following sections describe the BOOT.INI ARC (Advanced RISC Computing; RISC stands for Reduced Instruction Set Computing) naming conventions and how to edit the BOOT.INI file.

If you make changes to your disk configuration, you may see a message stating the number of the BOOT.INI file that needs to be changed. This is the ARC number that points to the boot partition. If you try to restart your computer before you edit this file, you will find that the computer will not start.

ARC Naming Conventions

In the BOOT.INI file, the *ARC* path is used to specify the location of the boot partition within the disk channel. ARC names are constructed of the information shown in Table 15.6.

TABLE 15.6 ARC Naming Conventions

ARC Path Option	Description
multi (w) or scsi (w)	Identifies the type of disk controller that is being used by the system. The multi option is used by IDE controllers and SCSI adapters that use the SCSI BIOS. The scsi option is used by SCSI adapters that do not use the SCSI BIOS. The number (w) represents the number of the hardware adapter you are booting from.

TABLE 15.6   ARC Naming Conventions *(continued)*

ARC Path Option	Description
disk (x)	Indicates which SCSI adapter you are booting from if you use the scsi option. If you use multi, this setting is always 0.
rdisk (y)	Specifies the number of the physical disk to be used. In an IDE environment, it is the ordinal of the disk attached to the controller and will always be a 0 or a 1. On a SCSI system, this is the ordinal number of the SCSI drive.
partition (z)	Specifies the partition number that contains the operating system files. The first partition is always 1.

As an example, the BOOT.INI file in Figure 15.5 contains the following line:

multi(0)disk(0)rdisk(0)partition(1)\WINNT.PRO= "Microsoft Windows 2000 Professional"

This indicates that the boot partition is in the following location:

- multi(0) is an IDE controller or a SCSI controller with the BIOS enabled.

- disk(0) is 0 since the multi option was used.

- rdisk(0) specifies that first disk on the controller is being used.

- partition(1) specifies that the system partition is on the first partition.

- \WINNT.PRO indicates the folder that is used to store the system files.

- "Microsoft Windows 2000 Professional" is what the user sees in the boot menu.

BOOT.INI Switches

When you edit your BOOT.INI file, you can add switches or options that allow you to control how the operating system is loaded. Table 15.7 defines the BOOT.INI switches.

TABLE 15.7 BOOT.INI Switches

Switch	Description
/basevideo	Boots the computer using a standard VGA video driver. This option is used when you change your video driver and then cannot use the new driver.
/fastdetect=comx	Keeps the computer from auto-detecting a serial mouse attached to a serial port.
/maxmem:n	Specifies the maximum amount of RAM that is recognized. This option is sometimes used in test environments where you want to analyze performance using different amounts of memory.
/noguiboot	Boots Windows 2000 without loading the GUI. With this option, a command prompt appears after the boot process ends.

BOOT.INI File Access

Because the BOOT.INI file is marked with the System and Hidden attributes, it is not normally seen through Windows Explorer or the DOS DIR command. The following sections explain how to modify the attributes of the BOOT.INI through Windows Explorer and the DOS ATTRIB command.

Changing Attributes through Windows Explorer

To access and change the BOOT.INI attributes through Windows Explorer, take the following steps:

1. Select Start ➤ Programs ➤ Accessories ➤ Windows Explorer.

2. In Windows Explorer, expand My Computer and right-click Local Disk (C:).

3. Select Tools ➢ Folder Options and click the View tab.

4. In the View dialog box, click the Show Hidden Files and Folders radio button. Uncheck the options Hide File Extensions for Known File Types, and Hide Protected Operating System Files (Recommended), as shown in Figure 15.6.

FIGURE 15.6 The View tab of the Folder Options dialog box

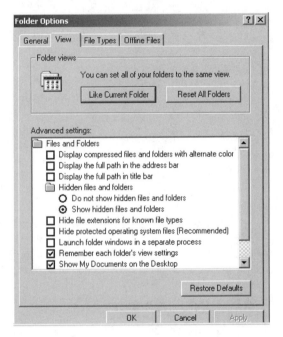

5. You see a dialog box with a warning about displaying protected operating system files. Click the Yes button to display these files. Then click the OK button.

6. You should now see the `BOOT.INI` file in the root of the C: drive. To change the file attributes, right-click the `BOOT.INI` file and select Properties.

7. The boot.ini Properties dialog box appears, as shown in Figure 15.7. Uncheck the Read-only attribute at the bottom of the dialog box and click the OK button.

FIGURE 15.7 General properties for the BOOT.INI file

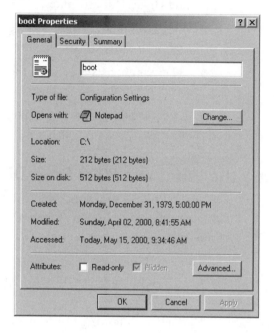

8. Open the BOOT.INI file by double-clicking the file in Windows Explorer.

9. When you're finished editing the BOOT.INI file, you should reset its file attributes to Read-only so that the file is protected from accidental deletion.

Changing Attributes through the ATTRIB Command

The DOS ATTRIB command provides a quick way to access the BOOT.INI file. To use the ATTRIB command, take the following steps:

1. Select Start ➢ Programs ➢ Accessories ➢ Command Prompt.

2. In the Command Prompt dialog box, type **ATTRIB** and press Enter. You should see all of the files that reside at the root of C: and their current file attributes.

3. Type **ATTRIB BOOT.INI −S −H** and press Enter to remove the System and Hidden file attributes.

4. Type **EDIT BOOT.INI** and press Enter to execute the EDIT program and open the BOOT.INI file for editing.

5. When you're finished editing the BOOT.INI file, choose File ➢ Save to save the file and File ➢ Exit to exit the EDIT program.

6. Reset the file attributes by typing **ATTRIB BOOT.INI +S +H** and pressing Enter.

Creating the Windows 2000 Boot Disk

After you create a *Windows 2000 boot disk*, you can use it to boot to the Windows 2000 Professional operating system in the event of a Windows 2000 Professional boot failure. You create a Windows 2000 boot disk through the following process:

1. Format a floppy disk through the Windows 2000 Professional operating system.

2. Copy the following files from the Windows 2000 Professional system partition:

   NTLDR

   NTDETECT.COM

   NTBOOTDD.SYS (if you use SCSI controllers with the BIOS disabled)

   BOOT.INI

3. Test the boot disk by using it to boot to Windows 2000 Professional.

If the BOOT.INI file for the computer has been edited, you will need to update the BOOT.INI file on your Windows 2000 boot disk.

The BOOT.INI file on the Windows 2000 Professional boot disk contains a specific configuration that points to the computer's boot partition. This might keep a Windows 2000 boot disk that was made on one computer from working on another computer.

In Exercise 15.2, you will create a Windows 2000 boot disk.

EXERCISE 15.2

Creating a Windows 2000 Boot Disk

1. Put a blank floppy diskette in your floppy drive.

2. Select Start ➤ Programs ➤ Accessories ➤ Windows Explorer.

3. In Windows Explorer, expand My Computer, right-click 3^1/$_2$ Floppy (A:), and select Format. Accept all of the default options and click the Start button.

4. You see a dialog box warning you that all the data will be lost. Click the OK button.

5. When you see the Format Complete dialog box, click the OK button, and click the Close button to close the Format dialog box.

6. Select Start ➤ Programs ➤ Accessories ➤ Command Prompt.

7. In the Command Prompt dialog box, type **ATTRIB** and press Enter. You see all of the files at the root of the C: drive. Note the file attributes of the NTLDR, NTDETECT.COM, and BOOT.INI files.

8. Type **ATTRIB NTLDR** −S −H −R and press Enter.

9. Type **COPY NTLDR A:** and press Enter.

10. Type **ATTRIB NTLDR** +S +H +R and press Enter.

11. Repeat steps 8 through 10 for the NTDETECT.COM and BOOT.INI files, to remove the file attributes, copy the file, and replace the file attributes. If you have a SCSI adapter with the BIOS disabled, you will also need to copy the NTBOOTDD.SYS file.

12. Verify that all of the files are on the boot disk by typing **DIR A:**.

13. Type **EXIT** to close the Command Prompt dialog box.

14. To test your Windows 2000 boot disk, select Start ➤ Shut Down ➤ Restart and click the OK button.

15. Label your Windows 2000 boot disk and put it in a safe place.

Using Advanced Startup Options

The Windows 2000 advanced startup options can be used to troubleshoot errors that keep Windows 2000 Professional from successfully booting.

Microsoft ✓ ***Exam*** ***Objective***

Recover system state data and user data.

• Troubleshoot system restoration by using Safe Mode.

To access the Windows 2000 advanced startup options, press the F8 key when prompted during the beginning of the Windows 2000 Professional boot process. This will bring up the Windows 2000 Advanced Options menu, which offers the following options for booting Windows 2000:

- Safe Mode
- Safe Mode with Networking
- Safe Mode with Command Prompt
- Enable Boot Logging
- Enable VGA Mode
- Last Known Good Configuration
- Debugging Mode
- Boot Normally

Each of these advanced startup options is covered in the following sections.

Starting in Safe Mode

When your computer will not start, one of the fundamental troubleshooting techniques is to simplify the configuration as much as possible. This is especially important when you do not know the cause of your problem and you have a complex configuration. After you have simplified the configuration, you determine whether the problem is in the basic configuration or is a result of your complex configuration. If the problem is in the basic configuration, you have a starting point for troubleshooting. If the problem is not in the basic configuration, you proceed to restore each configuration option you removed, one at a time. This helps you to identify what is causing the error.

If Windows 2000 Professional will not load, you can attempt to load the operating system through *Safe Mode*. When you run Windows 2000 in Safe Mode, you are simplifying your Windows configuration as much as possible. Safe Mode loads only the drivers needed to get the computer up and running. The drivers that are loaded with Safe Mode include basic files and drivers for the mouse (unless you have a serial mouse), monitor, keyboard, hard drive, standard video driver, and default system services. Safe Mode is considered a diagnostic mode, so you do not have access to all of the features and devices in Windows 2000 Professional that you have access to when you boot normally, including networking capabilities.

A computer booted to Safe Mode will show *Safe Mode* in the four corners of your Desktop, as shown in Figure 15.8.

FIGURE 15.8   A computer running in Safe Mode shows Safe Mode in each corner of the Desktop.

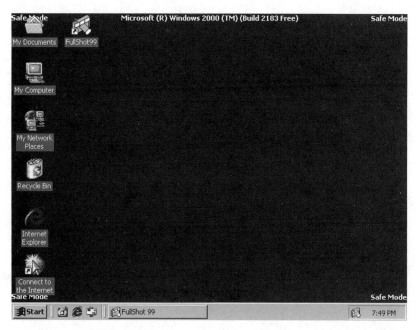

If you boot to Safe Mode, check all of your computer's hardware and software settings in Control Panel and try to determine why Windows 2000 Professional will not boot properly. After you take steps to fix the problem, try to boot to Windows 2000 Professional normally.

In Exercise 15.3, you will boot your computer to Safe Mode.

EXERCISE 15.3

Booting Your Computer to Safe Mode

1. If your computer is currently running, select Start ➢ Shutdown ➢ Restart.

2. During the boot process, press the F8 key to access the Windows 2000 Advanced Options menu.

3. Highlight Safe Mode and press Enter. Then log on as Administrator.

4. When you see the Desktop dialog box letting you know that Windows 2000 is running in Safe Mode, click the OK button.

5. Select My Network Places ➢ Entire Network, then click Microsoft Windows Network. You should get an error message stating that you are unable to browse the network (because you are in Safe Mode). Click OK to close the error dialog box.

6. Select Start ➢ Settings ➢ Control Panel ➢ System ➢ Hardware ➢ Device Manager. Look in Device Manager to see if any devices are not working properly.

Don't restart your computer yet; you will do this as a part of the next exercise.

Enabling Boot Logging

Boot logging creates a log file that tracks the loading of drivers and services. When you choose the *Enable Boot Logging option* from the Advanced Options menu, Windows 2000 Professional loads normally, not in Safe Mode. This allows you to log all of the processes that take place during a normal boot sequence.

This log file can be used to troubleshoot the boot process. When logging is enabled, the log file is written to *Windir*\ntbtlog.txt. A sample of the ntbtlog.txt file is shown in Figure 15.9.

FIGURE 15.9 The Windows 2000 boot log file

```
Microsoft (R) Windows 2000 (R) Version 5.0 (Build 2183)
12 26 1999 19:45:49.500
Loaded driver \WINNT.PRO\System32\ntoskrnl.exe
Loaded driver \WINNT.PRO\System32\hal.dll
Loaded driver \WINNT.PRO\System32\BOOTVID.DLL
Loaded driver pci.sys
Loaded driver isapnp.sys
Loaded driver intelide.sys
Loaded driver \WINNT.PRO\System32\DRIVERS\PCIIDEX.SYS
Loaded driver MountMgr.sys
Loaded driver ftdisk.sys
Loaded driver Diskperf.sys
Loaded driver \WINNT.PRO\System32\Drivers\WMILIB.SYS
Loaded driver dmload.sys
Loaded driver dmio.sys
Loaded driver PartMgr.sys
Loaded driver atapi.sys
Loaded driver disk.sys
Loaded driver \WINNT.PRO\System32\DRIVERS\CLASSPNP.SYS
Loaded driver KSecDD.sys
Loaded driver Ntfs.sys
Loaded driver NDIS.sys
Loaded driver Mup.sys
Loaded driver agp440.sys
Did not load driver Audio Codecs
Did not load driver Legacy Audio Drivers
Did not load driver Media Control Devices
Did not load driver Legacy Video Capture Devices
Did not load driver Video Codecs
Did not load driver WAN Miniport (L2TP)
Did not load driver WAN Miniport (IP)
Did not load driver WAN Miniport (PPTP)
Did not load driver Direct Parallel
Did not load driver Standard PC
Did not load driver Audio Codecs
```

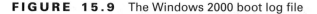

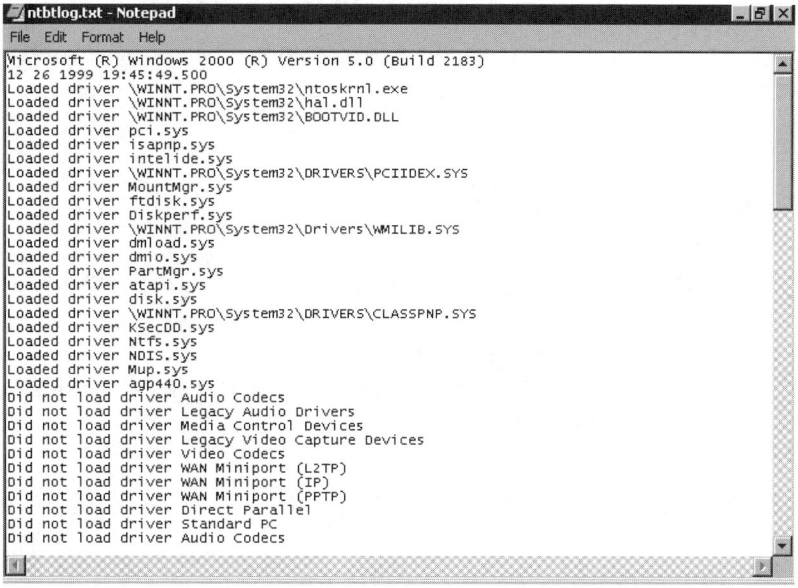

In Exercise 15.4, you will create and access a boot log file.

EXERCISE 15.4

Using Boot Logging

1. Start your computer. If it is already running, select Start ➢ Shutdown ➢ Restart.
2. During the boot process, press the F8 key to access the Windows 2000 Advanced Options menu.
3. Highlight Enable Boot Logging and press Enter. Then log on as Administrator.
4. Select Start ➢ Programs ➢ Accessories ➢ Windows Explorer.
5. In Windows Explorer, expand My Computer, then C:. Open the WINNT folder and double-click `ntbtlog.txt`.

EXERCISE 15.4 *(continued)*

6. Examine the contents of your boot log file.

7. Shut down your computer and restart in normal mode.

The boot log file is cumulative. Each time you boot to any Advanced Options menu mode (except Last Known Good Configuration), you are writing to this file. This allows you to make changes, reboot, and see if you have fixed any problems. If you want to start from scratch, you should manually delete this file and reboot to an Advanced Options menu selection that supports logging.

Using Other Advanced Options Menu Modes

The other selections on the Advanced Options menu work as follows:

- The *Safe Mode with Networking option* is the same as the Safe Mode option, but it adds networking features. You might use this mode if you need networking capabilities in order to download drivers or service packs from a network location.

- The *Safe Mode with Command Prompt option* starts the computer in Safe Mode, but instead of loading the Windows 2000 graphical interface, it loads a command prompt. Experienced troubleshooters use this mode.

- The *Enable VGA Mode option* loads a standard VGA driver without starting the computer in Safe Mode. You might use this mode if you changed your video driver, did not test it, and tried to boot to Windows 2000 with a bad driver that would not allow you to access video. The Enable VGA Mode bails you out by loading a default driver, providing access to video so that you can properly install (and test!) the correct driver for your computer.

When you boot to any Safe Mode, you automatically use VGA Mode.

- The *Last Known Good Configuration option* boots Windows 2000 using the Registry information that was saved the last time the computer was successfully booted. You would use this option to restore configuration information if you have improperly configured the computer and have not successfully rebooted the computer. When you use the Last Known Good Configuration option, you lose any system configuration changes that were made since the computer last successfully booted.

- The *Debugging Mode option* runs the Kernel Debugger, if that utility is installed. The Kernel Debugger is an advanced troubleshooting utility.

- The *Boot Normally option* boots to Windows 2000 in the default manner. This option is on the Advanced Options menu in case you got trigger happy and hit F8 during the boot process, but really wanted to boot Windows 2000 normally.

Windows 2000 handles startup options slightly differently from Windows NT 4. In Windows NT 4, the boot loader menu shows an option to load VGA mode, which appears each time you restart the computer. In Windows 2000, this has been moved to the Advanced Options menu to present the user with a cleaner boot process. Also, in Windows NT 4, you need to press the spacebar as a part of the boot process to access the Last Known Good Configuration option.

Using Startup and Recovery Options

The Startup and Recovery options (see Table 15.8) are used to specify the default operating system that is loaded and to specify which action should be taken in the event of system failure. You can access the Startup and Recovery options from your Desktop by right-clicking My Computer, selecting Properties from the pop-up menu, clicking the Advanced tab, and then clicking the Startup and Recovery button. Alternatively, select Start ≻ Settings ≻ Control Panel ≻ System ≻ Advanced ≻ Startup and Recovery. You will see the dialog box shown in Figure 15.10.

FIGURE 15.10 The Startup and Recovery dialog box

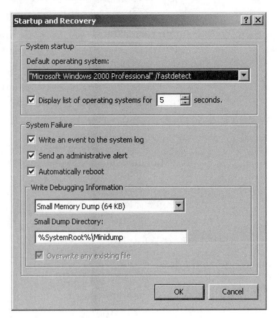

TABLE 15.8 Startup and Recovery Options

Option	Description
Default Operating System	Specifies the operating system that is loaded by default if no selection is made from the operating system selection menu (if your computer dual-boots or multi-boots and an operating system selection menu appears during bootup). The default setting for this option is Microsoft Windows 2000 Professional.

TABLE 15.8 Startup and Recovery Options *(continued)*

Option	Description
Display List of Operating Systems for *x* Seconds	Specifies how long the operating system selection menu is available before the default selection is loaded (if your computer dual-boots or multi-boots and an operating system selection menu appears during bootup). The default setting for this option is 30 seconds.
Write an Event to the System Log	Specifies that an entry is made in the System log any time a system failure occurs. This option is enabled by default, which allows you to track system failures.
Send an Administrative Alert	Specifies that a pop-up alert message will be sent to the Administrator any time a system failure occurs. This option is enabled by default, so the Administrator is notified of system failures.
Automatically Reboot	Specifies that the computer will automatically reboot in the event of a system failure. This option is enabled by default, so the system restarts after a failure without intervention. You would disable this option if you wanted to see the blue screen for analysis.
Write Debugging Information	Specifies that debugging information (a memory dump) is written to a file. You can choose not to create a dump file or to create a small memory dump (64KB) file, a kernel memory dump file, or a complete memory dump file. Complete memory dump files require free disk space equivalent to your memory, and a page file that is at least as large as your memory with an extra 2MB. The default setting is to write debugging information to a small memory dump file.
Overwrite Any Existing File	If you create dump files, this option allows you to create a new dump file that overwrites the old dump file, or to keep all dump files each time a system failure occurs.

In Exercise 15.5, you will access the Startup and Recovery options and make changes to the settings.

Using Startup and Recovery Options

1. From your Desktop, right-click My Computer and choose Properties. Click the Advanced tab and then click the Startup and Recovery button.

2. Change the setting for Display List of Operating Systems from 30 seconds to 10 seconds.

3. In the Write Debugging Information section, choose (None) from the drop-down list.

4. Click the OK button to close the Startup and Recovery dialog box.

Using the Dr. Watson Utility

The *Dr. Watson* utility detects and displays information about system and program failures. When an application error occurs, Dr. Watson will run automatically and you will see a pop-up message letting you know that an application error has occurred. (You can also access Dr. Watson by invoking the *DRWTSN32* command.) Application developers can use the Dr. Watson utility to debug their programs. When an application encounters an error or crashes, Dr. Watson can display the application error and dump the contents of memory into a file.

Although average users will not be able to determine what is wrong with an application by looking at a memory dump file, they might be asked to configure a memory dump so that it can be sent to an application developer for analysis. The information collected by Dr. Watson is stored in a log file that can be viewed at any time.

To access Dr. Watson, select Start ➤ Run and type **DRWTSN32**. The main dialog box for Dr. Watson is shown in Figure 15.11. The Application Errors box at the bottom of the dialog box displays any program errors that Dr. Watson encountered. Above this section are the options that can be configured through Dr. Watson, which are described in Table 15.9.

FIGURE 15.11   The Dr. Watson for Windows 2000 dialog box

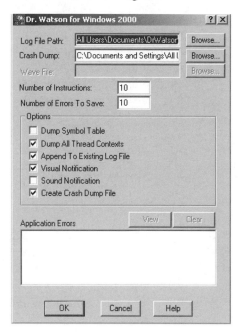

TABLE 15.9   Dr. Watson Configuration Options

Option	Description
Log File Path	Location of the log file that contains application error information.
Crash Dump	Location of the memory dump file that is created when an application crashes (If you choose to create a crash dump file).

TABLE 15.9 Dr. Watson Configuration Options *(continued)*

Option	Description
Wave File	WAV sound file to execute when an error occurs.
Number of Instructions	Maximum number of instructions, or threads, that Dr. Watson can track.
Number of Errors to Save	Maximum number of errors that Dr. Watson can store within the dump file.
Dump Symbol Table	Specifies that the symbol table should be included in the dump file. Symbol files provide more verbose information, which can be used to diagnose system failures. The drawback of this option is that it can cause the log file to grow very quickly.
Dump All Thread Contexts	Specifies whether Dr. Watson will dump all threads to the memory dump, or dump only the thread that caused the application failure.
Append to Existing Log File	Specifies whether Dr. Watson will create a new log file for new program errors or append log information to the existing log file.
Visual Notification	Shows a message box with a program error notification.
Sound Notification	Sounds two beeps when an error occurs. You can also configure a wave file to be used for sound notification.
Create Crash Dump File	Specifies whether you want to create a crash dump file in the event of application failure. If you choose to create a crash dump file, you must also specify a crash dump location.

The difference between setting Startup and Recovery options and running the Dr. Watson utility is that Startup and Recovery options are used to diagnose operating system problems. The Dr. Watson utility, on the other hand, is used to diagnose application errors.

Creating Windows 2000 Professional Setup Boot Disks

You can create floppy disks for use in booting to the Windows 2000 Professional operating system in case your computer will not boot and will not read the CD-ROM drive. These disks are called the *Windows 2000 Professional Setup Boot Disks*. From these diskettes, you can perform the following tasks:

- Reinstall the Windows 2000 operating system if you do not have access to the CD-ROM drive.

- Use the Recovery Console.

- Use an ERD.

Using the Windows 2000 Professional Setup Boot Disks to install Windows 2000 is described in Chapter 1, "Getting Started with Windows 2000 Professional." The Recovery Console and ERD are covered later in this chapter.

Microsoft ✔ *Exam Objective*

Recover system state data and user data.

- Recover system state data and user data by using the Recovery Console.

The Windows 2000 Professional Setup Boot Disks are not specific to a computer. They are general Windows 2000 Professional disks, which can be used by any computer running Windows 2000 Professional.

To create the Windows 2000 Professional Setup Boot Disks, you need four high-density floppy disks, labeled as follows:

- Windows 2000 Professional Setup Boot Disk

- Windows 2000 Professional Setup Disk #2

- Windows 2000 Professional Setup Disk #3

- Windows 2000 Professional Setup Disk #4

The 32-bit command to create boot disks from Windows 2000 or Windows NT is *MAKEBT32.EXE*. The command to make boot disks from Windows 9x or a 16-bit operating system is MAKEBOOT.EXE.

Setup disks created for Windows 2000 Professional will not work with Windows 2000 Server. Vice versa, the Setup disks created for Windows 2000 Server will not work with Windows 2000 Professional.

In Exercise 15.6, you will create Windows 2000 Professional Setup Boot Disks. This exercise requires four high-density floppy disks. You also need the Windows 2000 Professional CD.

EXERCISE 15.6

Creating Windows 2000 Professional Setup Boot Disks

1. Label each of your high-density floppy disks as follows:

   a. **Windows 2000 Professional Setup Boot Disk**

   b. **Windows 2000 Professional Setup Disk #2**

   c. **Windows 2000 Professional Setup Disk #3**

   d. **Windows 2000 Professional Setup Disk #4**

2. Insert the Windows 2000 Professional CD into your CD-ROM drive.

3. Select Start ➢ Run ➢ Browse. Select your CD-ROM drive, then select BOOTDISK, and then select MAKEBT32. Click the OK button.

EXERCISE 15.6 *(continued)*

4. In the command-prompt dialog box, specify the floppy drive to which you want the image copied. This is normally your A: drive.

5. Insert the disk labeled Windows 2000 Professional Setup Boot Disk. The files will be copied.

6. When prompted, insert Windows 2000 Professional Setup Disks #2, #3, and #4, pressing Enter after you insert each one.

7. After the disks have been created, put them in an easily accessible place. You will use them in Exercise 15.8.

Using the Backup Utility

The *Windows 2000 Backup* utility allows you to create and restore backups, and create an *Emergency Repair Disk (ERD)*. Backups protect your data in the event of system failure by storing the data on another medium, such as another hard disk or a tape. If your original data is lost due to corruption, deletion, or media failure, you can restore the data using your backup. The ERD is a subset of a backup that you can use to restore configuration information quickly. System state data includes the Registry, the COM+ registration database, and the system boot files.

Microsoft
Exam
Objective

Recover system state data and user data.

- Recover system state data and user data by using Windows Backup.

To access the Backup utility, select Start ➤ Programs ➤ Accessories ➤ System Tools ➤ Backup. This brings up the Backup window (Figure 15.12).

FIGURE 15.12 The Backup window

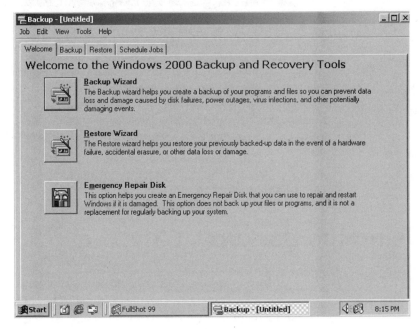

From this window, you can start the Backup Wizard, start the Restore Wizard, or create an ERD. These options are all covered in the following sections.

External tape drives, which attach to your parallel port, are not supported by the Windows 2000 Professional operating system when using the Windows Backup utility. However, you can use third-party backup software to support this configuration.

Creating and Using an ERD

You can use the ERD to repair and restart Windows 2000 in the event that your computer will not start or if the system files have been damaged. You should create an ERD when the computer is installed, and then update the ERD after making any changes to the configuration of your computer. Note that this option does not back up any system data.

You can repair the following items with the ERD:

- The basic system
- System files
- The partition boot sector
- The startup environment
- The Registry (return the Registry to its original configuration)

In the next sections, you will learn how to create and use an ERD.

Preparing an ERD

To create an ERD, click the Emergency Repair Disk button in the opening Backup utility window. This brings up the Emergency Repair Disk dialog box, which asks you to insert a blank, formatted floppy disk into drive A:. At this point, you can also specify whether you want to back up the Registry to the ERD. If the Registry will fit onto your ERD, you should select this option. When you click OK, the system data will be copied to the ERD.

 Update your ERD after you make any major configuration changes to your computer.

You will create an ERD in Exercise 15.7. You will need a blank, formatted, high-density floppy disk for this exercise.

EXERCISE 15.7

Creating an Emergency Repair Disk

1. Select Start ➤ Programs ➤ Accessories ➤ System Tools ➤ Backup.

2. Click the Emergency Repair Disk button.

3. The Emergency Repair Disk dialog box appears. Insert a blank, formatted floppy disk into drive A:.

4. Select the Also Back Up the Registry to the Repair Directory option.

5. Click OK. The system data will be copied to the ERD.

6. A confirmation dialog box appears. Click the OK button to close this dialog box.

Using an ERD

The ERD is not a bootable disk and can only be accessed by using the Windows 2000 Professional Setup CD or setup diskettes that are created from the CD.

In Exercise 15.8, you will restore your system using the ERD. You will need the four Windows Professional Setup Boot Disks you created in Exercise 15.6, and the ERD you created in Exercise 15.7. You will also need the Windows 2000 Professional CD.

EXERCISE 15.8

Restoring Your System with an Emergency Repair Disk

1. Restart your computer using the Windows 2000 Professional Setup Boot Disk.

2. When prompted, insert Windows 2000 Professional Setup Disk #2, #3, and #4, pressing Enter after you insert each one.

3. From the Welcome to Setup dialog box, press the R key to choose to repair a Windows 2000 installation.

4. From the Windows 2000 Repair Options dialog box, press R to repair the Windows 2000 installation using the emergency repair process.

5. Press the M key to choose Manual Repair, or the F key to choose Fast Repair. The Manual Repair option lets you choose to inspect the startup environment, to verify the Windows 2000 system files, and/or to inspect the boot sector. Manual repair does not, however, back up the Registry. The Fast Repair option doesn't require any user input. It attempts to correct problems that relate to system files, the partition boot sector on the system disk, and the startup environment on dual-boot systems.

EXERCISE 15.8 *(continued)*

6. Insert your ERD and press Enter. Then press Enter again in the next dialog box.

7. Press Enter to indicate that you want the Setup program to examine your computer's drives.

8. Insert the Windows 2000 Professional CD into your CD-ROM drive and press Enter. The emergency repair process will examine the files on your drive.

9. When prompted, remove any floppies from your floppy drives and the Windows 2000 Professional CD from the CD-ROM drive. Your computer will restart automatically.

In Windows NT, you create ERDs through the RDISK command. This command is not available in Windows 2000.

Using the Backup Wizard

The *Backup Wizard* takes you through all of the steps that are required for a successful backup. Before you start the Backup Wizard, be sure you are logged on as an Administrator or a member of the Backup Operators group.

In Exercise 15.9, you will use the Backup Wizard to make a sample backup of files. You will need a blank formatted, high-density floppy disk for this exercise.

EXERCISE 15.9

Using the Backup Wizard

1. Create a folder on your D: drive called DATA. Create some small text files in this folder. The size of all of the files combined should not exceed 1MB.

2. Select Start ➢ Programs ➢ Accessories ➢ System Tools ➢ Backup.

3. In the opening Backup window, click the Backup Wizard button.

4. The Welcome to the Windows 2000 Backup and Recovery Tools dialog box appears. Click the Next button.

5. The What to Back Up dialog box appears. This dialog box allows you to select what you will back up. You can choose to back up everything; back up just selected files, drives, or network data; or back up only the system state data. System state data includes the Registry, the COM+ registration database, and the system boot files. For this example, select the Back Up Selected Files, Drives, or Network Data radio button, then click the Next button.

6. The Items to Back Up dialog box appears. Check the items that you want to back up (in this case, select My Computer, expand D:, and check the DATA folder) and click the Next button.

7. The Where to Store the Backup dialog box appears. You can either type in the backup media or filename or click the Browse button to locate it.

8. Click the Browse button, which brings up the Open dialog box. Select the drive (in this case, your floppy drive), give your backup a filename (for example, you might use the date as the filename), and click the Open button.

9. When you return to the Wizard's Where to Store the Backup page, make sure your backup media or filename path is correct, and click the Next button. In the Completing the Backup Wizard page, make sure all the information is correct and click the Finish button. (Clicking the Advanced button in the Completing the Backup Wizard dialog box brings up a dialog box that allows you to specify the type of backup: Normal, Copy, Incremental, Differential, or Daily.)

10. During the backup process, the Wizard displays the Backup Progress dialog box. Once the backup process is complete, you can click the Report button in this dialog box to see details of the backup session. Figure 15.13 is an example of a backup report.

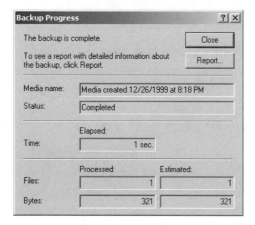

FIGURE 15.13   A sample backup report

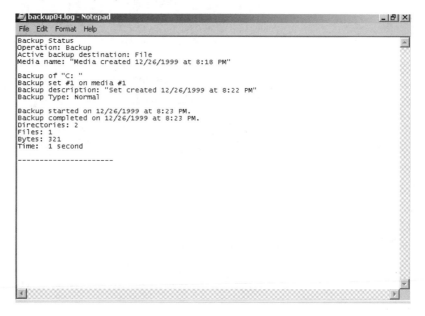

Configuring Backup Options

You can configure specific backup configurations by selecting backup options. To access these options, start the Backup program and select Tools ➢ Options. In the Options dialog box that appears, you'll have five tabs: General, Restore, Backup Type, Backup Log, and Exclude Files. The following sections describe the options of these tabs, used for controlling the backup and restore processes.

Configuring General Backup Options

The General tab, as seen in Figure 15.14, contains options for configuring backup sessions. Table 15.10 describes these options.

FIGURE 15.14 The General tab of the Options dialog box

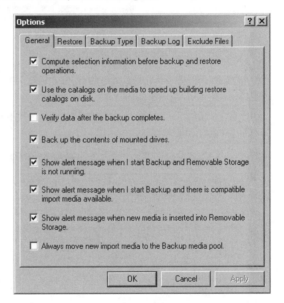

TABLE 15.10   General Backup Options

Option	Description
Compute selection information before backup and restore operations	Estimates the number of files and bytes that will be backed up or restored during the current operation and displays this information prior to the backup or restore operation
Use the catalogs on the media to speed up building restore catalogs on disk	Specifies that you want to use an on-media catalog to build an on-disk catalog, which can be used to select the folders and files to be restored during a restore operation
Verify data after the backup completes	Makes sure that all data has been backed up properly
Back up the contents of mounted drives	Specifies that the data should be backed up on mounted drives; otherwise, only path information on mounted drives is backed up
Show alert message when I start Backup and Removable Storage is not running	Notifies you if Removable Storage is not running (when you are backing up to tape or other removable media)
Show alert message when I start Backup and there is compatible import media available	Notifies you when you start Backup if new media have been added to the Removable Storage import pool.
Show alert message when new media is inserted into Removable Storage	Notifies you when new media are detected by Removable Storage.
Always move new import media to the Backup media pool	Specifies that if new media are detected by Removable Storage, that media should be directed to the Backup media pool.

Configuring Restore Options

The Restore tab of the Options dialog box, shown in Figure 15.15, contains three options that relate to how files are restored when the file already exists on the computer:

- Do not replace the file on my computer (recommended).

- Replace the file on disk only if the file on the disk is older.

- Always replace the file on my computer.

FIGURE 15.15 The Restore tab of the Options dialog box

Selecting a Backup Type

In the Backup Type tab (Figure 15.16) you can specify the default backup type that will be used. You should select this default backup type based on the following criteria:

- How much data you are backing up

- How quickly you wanted to be able to perform the backup

- The number of tapes you are willing to use should you need to perform a restore operation

Table 15.11 describes the backup type options.

FIGURE 15.16 Options for the backup type

TABLE 15.11 Backup Type Options

Option	Description
Normal	Backs up all files, and sets the archive bit as marked for each file that is backed up. Requires only one tape for the restore process.
Copy	Backs up all files, and does not set the archive bit as marked for each file that is backed up. Requires only one tape for the restore process.

TABLE 15.11 Backup Type Options *(continued)*

Option	Description
Differential	Backs up only the files that have not been marked as archived, and does not set the archive bit for each file that is backed up. Requires the last normal backup and the last differential tape for the restore process.
Incremental	Backs up only the files that have not been marked as archived, and sets the archive bit for each file that is backed up. For the restore process, requires the last normal backup and all the incremental tapes that have been created since the last normal backup.
Daily	Backs up only the files that have been changed today and does not set the archive bit for each file that is backed up. Requires each daily backup and the last normal backup for the restore process.

Setting Backup Log Options

The Backup Log tab (Figure 15.17) allows you to specify the amount of information that is logged during the backup process. Select from the following options:

- Detailed, which logs all information, including the names of the folders and files that are backed up

- Summary, which logs only key backup operations such as starting the backup

- None, which specifies that a log file will not be created

Excluding Files

Use the Exclude Files tab of the Options dialog box (Figure 15.18) to explicitly exclude specific files during the backup process. For example, you might choose to exclude the page file or application files.

FIGURE 15.17   Backup Log options

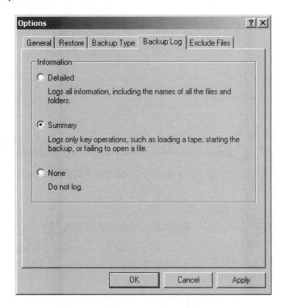

FIGURE 15.18   The Exclude Files tab of backup options

Using the Restore Wizard

Having a complete backup won't help you if your system should fail, unless you can successfully restore that backup. To be sure that you can restore your data, you should test the restoration process before anything goes wrong. You can use the *Restore Wizard* for testing purposes, as well as when you actually need to restore your backup.

In Exercise 15.10, you will use the Restore Wizard.

EXERCISE 15.10

Using the Restore Wizard

1. Select Start ➤ Programs ➤ Accessories ➤ System Tools ➤ Backup.

2. Start the Backup program and click the Restore Wizard button.

3. The Welcome to the Restore Wizard dialog box appears. Click the Next button.

4. The What to Restore dialog box appears next. Click the filename of the backup session that you want to restore (in this case, the file backup session you created in Exercise 15.10). Click the Next button. After you select the backup you want to restore, you can choose to restore the entire session, or you can selectively restore drives, folders, or files from the backup session.

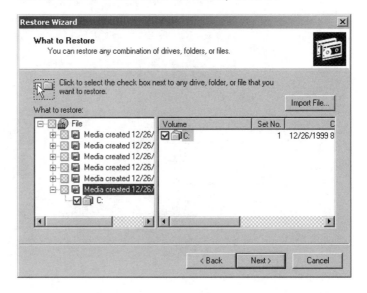

5. The Completing the Restore Wizard dialog box appears. If all of the configuration information is correct, click the Finish button. (Clicking the Advanced button here brings up another dialog box where you can choose a location to which files will be restored. You can choose from the original location, an alternate location, or a single folder.)

6. Next, in the Enter Backup File Name dialog box, verify that the correct filename is specified and click the OK button.

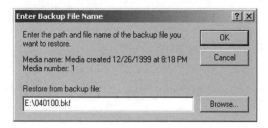

7. During the restoration process, the Wizard displays the Restore Progress dialog box.

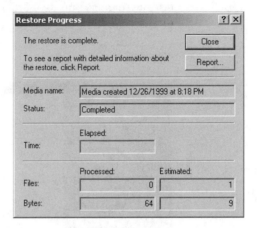

8. Once the restoration process is complete, you can click the Report button in this dialog box to see details of the restore session. Here's an example of a restore report:

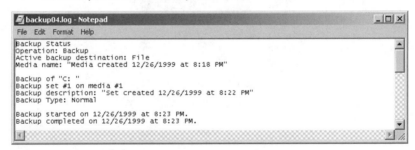

Using the Recovery Console

If your computer will not start, and you have tried to boot to Safe Mode with no luck, there's one more option you can try. The *Recovery Console* is designed for administrators and advanced users. It allows you limited access to FAT16, FAT32, and NTFS volumes without starting the Windows 2000 Professional graphical interface.

Through the Recovery Console, you can perform the following tasks:

- Copy, replace, or rename operating system files and folders. You might have to do this if your boot failure is caused by missing or corrupt files.

- Enable or disable the loading of services when the computer is restarted. If a particular service may be keeping the operating system from booting, you could disable the service. If a particular service is required for successful booting, you want to make sure that service loading was enabled.

- Repair the file system boot sector or the MBR. You might use this option if a virus may have damaged the system boot sector or the MBR.

- Create and format partitions on the drives. You might use this option if your disk utilities will not delete or create Windows 2000 partitions. Normally, you use a disk-partitioning utility for these functions.

In the following sections, you will learn how to access and use the Recovery Console.

Starting the Recovery Console

If you have created the Windows 2000 Professional Setup Disks, you can start the Recovery Console from them. Alternatively, you can add the Recovery Console to the Windows 2000 startup options, but you need to configure this prior to the failure. Each of these options is covered in the following sections.

Starting the Recovery Console with the Windows 2000 Professional Setup Disks

To use the Recovery Console from the Windows 2000 Professional Setup Disks, take the following steps:

1. Restart your computer using the Windows 2000 Professional Setup Boot Disk.

2. Insert each of the other Windows Professional Setup Disks in turn, as prompted.

3. In the Welcome to Setup dialog box, press the R key to repair a Windows 2000 installation.

4. From the Windows 2000 Repair Options menu, press the C key to repair Windows 2000 using the Recovery Console. The Windows 2000 Recovery Console will start.

See the section "Using the Recovery Console," coming up, for details on using the Recovery Console.

Adding the Recovery Console to Windows 2000 Startup

You can add the Recovery Console to the Windows 2000 Professional startup options so it will be available in the event of a system failure. This configuration takes about 7MB of disk space to hold the CMDCONS folder and files. To set up this configuration, take the following steps:

1. Insert the Windows 2000 Professional CD into your CD-ROM drive. You can disable auto-play by pressing the Shift key as the CD is read. From a command prompt, type **cd I386** and press Enter. Then type **WINNT32 /CMDCONS**.

2. The Windows 2000 Setup dialog box appears, asking you to confirm that you want to install the Recovery Console, as shown in Figure 15.19 Click the Yes button.

FIGURE 15.19   The Windows Setup dialog box

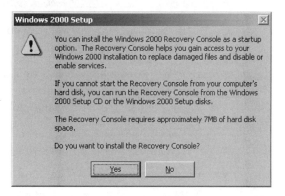

3. The installation files will be copied to your computer. Then you will see a dialog box letting you know that the Recovery Console has been successfully installed. Click the OK button to continue.

The next time you restart your computer, you will see an option for the Microsoft Windows 2000 Recovery Console. You will learn how to use the Recovery Console in the next section.

In Exercise 15.11, you will add the Recovery Console to the Windows 2000 startup options. You will need the Windows 2000 Professional CD for this exercise.

EXERCISE 15.11

Adding Recovery Console to Windows 2000Setup

1. Insert the Windows 2000 Professional CD in your CD-ROM drive. Hold down the Shift key as the CD is read, to prevent auto-play.

2. Select Start ➢ Programs ➢ Accessories ➢ Command Prompt.

3. Change the drive letter to your CD-ROM drive.

4. From the CD drive letter prompt ($x:\>$), type **CD I386** and press Enter.

5. From $x:\I386>$, type **WINNT32 /CMDCONS**.

EXERCISE 15.11 *(continued)*

6. In the Windows 2000 Setup dialog box, click the Yes button to confirm that you want to install the Recovery Console.

7. After the installation files are copied to your computer, a dialog box appears to let you know that the Recovery Console has been successfully installed. Click the OK button.

8. Shut down and restart your computer. In the startup selection screen, select the option for Microsoft Windows 2000 Recovery Console.

9. At the command prompt, type **EXIT** to close the Recovery Console. You return to the Windows Desktop.

Using the Recovery Console

After you add the Recovery Console, you can access it by restarting your computer. In the operating system selection menu, you will see an option for Microsoft Windows 2000 Recovery Console. Select this option to start the Recovery Console.

 Use the Recovery Console with extreme caution. Improper use may cause even more damage than the problems you are trying to fix.

The Recovery Console presents you with a command prompt and very limited access to system resources. This keeps unauthorized users from using the Recovery Console to access sensitive data. Following are the only folders you can access through the Recovery Console:

- The root folder
- The *Windir* folder and the subfolders of the Windows 2000 Professional installation
- The CMDCONS folder
- Removable media drives such as CD-ROM drives

If you try to access any other folders besides the ones listed above, you will receive an "access denied" error message.

In the Recovery Console, you cannot copy files from a local hard disk to a floppy disk. You can only copy files from a floppy disk or CD to a hard disk, or from one hard disk to another hard disk. This is for security purposes.

The first option you must specify is which Windows 2000 operating system you will log on to. Next, you must specify the Administrator password for the system you are logging on to. When the Recovery Console starts, you can use the following commands:

ATTRIB	BATCH	CD	CHDIR
CHKDSK	CLS	COPY	DEL
DELETE	DIR	DISABLE	DISKPART
ENABLE	EXIT	EXPAND	FIXBOOT
FIXMBR	FORMAT	HELP	LISTSVC
LOGON	MAP	MD	MKDIR
MORE	RD	REN	RENAME
RMDIR	SYSTEMROOT	TYPE	

The commands listed just above are explained in more detail in *MSCE: Windows 2000 Server Study Guide*, 2nd ed., by Lisa Donald with James Chellis (Sybex, 2001).

🌐 **Real World Scenario**

Recovery Console to the Rescue

Windows 2000 Professional is currently installed on your home computer. On that computer you want also to work with software that does not run properly on Windows 2000, but runs fine on Windows 98. You decide to install Windows 98 on your computer and dual-boot between the two operating systems. After you've set this up, installing Windows 98 with Windows 2000 already installed, Windows 98 rewrites the master boot record and you no longer see an option to boot Windows 2000.

All is not lost: The Recovery Console can be used to recover in the event of this type of failure, by allowing you to run the `fixmbr` command to rewrite the master boot record to support Windows 2000 again.

Summary

In this chapter, you learned about Windows 2000 Professional's system recovery options and utilities. We covered the following topics:

- Basic techniques that you can use to safeguard your computer and plan for disaster recovery

- The Event Viewer utility, including how to view the details of an event and manage log files

- The Windows 2000 boot process, including the steps in a normal boot; the `BOOT.INI` file; and how to create a Windows 2000 boot disk

- Advanced startup options, including Safe Mode, Enable Boot Logging, Last Known Good Configuration, and other options for booting in special modes

- Startup and Recovery options for specifying what action Windows 2000 should take in the event of system failure

- The Dr. Watson utility, which diagnoses application errors

- Windows 2000 Professional Setup Boot Disks for starting Windows 2000 in the event of system failure and to access the Recovery Console; and the ERD (Emergency Repair Disk), which can be used to repair problems that prevent your computer from starting

- The Windows Backup utility, which includes a Backup Wizard, a Restore Wizard, and an option for creating an ERD

- The Recovery Console, a special boot process that gives you limited access to your file system for replacement of files, or to specify the services that should be started the next time the computer is booted

Exam Essentials

Be able to perform system recovery with Windows Backup.   Understand the options that are supported through Windows Backup and how to use backup and restore procedures. Know how to create Emergency Repair Disks. Understand system state data and how it can be backed up.

Know how to manage system recovery through Safe Mode.   Be able to list the options that can be accessed through Safe Mode, and know when it is appropriate to use each option.

Know how to use the Recovery Console.   Be familiar with the features and purpose of the Recovery Console. Be able to access and use the Recovery Console to facilitate system recovery.

Key Terms

Before you take the exam, be sure you're familiar with the following key terms:

Application log	BOOT.INI
Backup Wizard	BOOTSECT.DOS
Boot Normally	Debugging Mode

Dr. Watson

DRWTSN32

Emergency Repair Disk (ERD)

Enable Boot Logging

Enable VGA Mode

Error event

Event Viewer

Failure Audit event

Information event

Last Known Good Configuration

MAKEBT32.EXE

Master Boot Record (MBR)

NTBOOTDD.SYS

NTDETECT.COM

NTLDR

NTOSKRNL.EXE

POST (Power On Self Test)

Recovery Console

Restore Wizard

Safe Mode

Safe Mode with Command Prompt

Safe Mode with Networking

Security log

Success Audit event

System log

Warning event

Windows 2000 Backup

Windows 2000 boot disk

Windows 2000 Professional Setup Boot Disks

Review Questions

1. Your network has just been struck by a virus. The virus checker you ran on your computer reported that the NTLDR file was infected and could not be cleaned, so it was removed. When you reboot your computer, you receive a message that the NTLDR file is missing or corrupt and the Windows 2000 operating system will not load. Your initial reaction is pure panic, but then you remember how this can be easily corrected. Which Windows 2000 repair option will provide the quickest way to recover from this failure?

   A. Safe Mode

   B. Emergency Repair Disk

   C. Dr. Watson

   D. System File Recovery utility

2. Your computer uses a SCSI adapter that supports a SCSI drive, which contains your Windows 2000 system and boot partitions. After updating the SCSI driver, you restart your computer and Windows 2000 will not load. You need to get this computer up and running as quickly as possible. Which of the following repair strategies should you try first to correct your problem?

   A. Restore your computer's configuration with your last backup.

   B. Boot your computer with the Last Known Good Configuration.

   C. Boot your computer with the Safe Mode option.

   D. Boot your computer to the Recovery Console and manually copy the old driver back to the computer.

3. You recently updated your video driver. When you restart the computer, the video display isn't working properly. You now want to load a generic video driver so that you can correct the video problem. Which configuration file includes an option that allows you to load a standard VGA video driver?

   A. BOOT.INI

   B. BOOT.VID

   C. VIDEO.INI

   D. CONFIG.SYS

4. Catherine is using a third-party application that is generating errors. Which utility is used within Windows 2000 to help diagnose application errors?

   A. Dr. Watson

   B. Sherlock

   C. Application Manager

   D. Application Event Viewer

5. Conrad wants to use his Windows 2000 Emergency Repair Disk. He does not have the Windows 2000 Professional Setup Boot disks. He does have the Windows 2000 Professional CD and access to a computer that is running the Windows 2000 operating system. Which command should he use to create the Windows 2000 Professional Setup Boot Disks from the CD?

   A. MAKEBT32

   B. BOOTPRO

   C. BOOT32

   D. WINNT32 /BOOT

6. You are the network administrator of a 50-computer Windows 2000 network. You want to update all the Emergency Repair Disks for each computer. Which of the following commands or utilities can be used to create or update an ERD?

A. ERD

B. RDISK

C. RDISK32

D. The Backup utility

7. After you updated Stuart's ERD recently, his boot files became corrupt due to a virus and now need to be restored. What process should you use to initiate a repair using an ERD?

A. Boot with the ERD.

B. Use the Windows Backup utility.

C. Use the Windows 2000 boot disk.

D. Use the Windows 2000 Professional Setup Disks.

8. Your engineering department uses Windows 2000 as the primary operating system on their development computers. Because these computers are mission critical, you want to facilitate any recovery process that may be required. You decide to install the Recovery Console on each computer. Which of the following commands should you use to install the Recovery Console?

A. RECCON

B. RECCON32

C. WINNT32 /RC

D. WINNT32 /CMDCONS

9. Which recovery option can you use to correct configuration errors or to repair system files that might be keeping your computer from starting, and that stores portions of the Registry, the system files, a copy of your partition boot sector, and information that relates to the startup environment?

   A. Last Known Good

   B. Windows Safe Mode

   C. Emergency Repair Disk

   D. Recovery Console

10. When you booted Windows 2000 Professional, you noticed that an error appeared during the startup sequence. You need the exact error code that was generated, but can't remember what the error code was. Where can you find this information?

    A. *Windir*\error.log file

    B. *Windir*\System32\error.log file

    C. *Windir*\System32\startup.log file

    D. Event Viewer System log

11. You are unable to boot your Windows 2000 Professional computer, so you decide to boot the computer to Safe Mode. Which of the following statements regarding Safe Mode is false?

    A. When the computer is booted to Safe Mode, there is no network access.

    B. Safe Mode loads all the drivers for the hardware that is installed on the computer.

    C. When you run Safe Mode, boot logging is automatically enabled.

    D. When you run Safe Mode, the Enable VGA Mode is automatically enabled.

12. You have been having problems with your Windows 2000 Professional computer. You decide to start the computer using the Enable
Boot Logging option on the Advanced Options menu. Where can you
find the log file that is created?

    A. *Windir*\ntbtlog.txt

    B. *Windir*\System32\ntbtlog.txt

    C. *Windir*\ntboot.log

    D. *Windir*\System32\ntboot.log

13. Which Advanced Options menu item can you use during the system
boot to enable and run the Kernel Debugger utility if it's installed on
your computer?

    A. Run Kernel Debugger

    B. Run Advanced Troubleshooting

    C. Debugging Mode

    D. Boot to Troubleshooting Mode

14. Your computer is configured to dual-boot between Windows 98 and
Windows 2000. How would you configure the computer so that Windows 98 would be the default selection if the user did not make a
choice within the specified amount of time?

    A. Through the STARTUP.INI file

    B. Through the SYSTEM.INI file

    C. Through Control Panel, Startup Options

    D. Through Control Panel, System, Startup and Recovery

15. You are using the Windows 2000 Backup utility and have decided to
back up the system state data. Which of the following items is not
backed up when you choose this option?

    A. Registry

    B. COM+ registration database

    C. Windows 2000 OLE database

    D. System boot files

Answers to Review Questions

1. B. You can easily restore the system boot files from the Windows 2000 Professional Setup Disks or from an Emergency Repair Disk.

2. B. In the event that you need to get a stalled computer up and running as quickly as possible, you should start with the Last Known Good Configuration option. This option is used when you've made changes to your computer's hardware configuration and are having problems restarting. The Last Known Good Configuration will revert to the configuration used the last time the computer was successfully booted. (Although this option helps overcome configuration errors, it will not help for hardware errors.)

3. A. The BOOT.INI file specifies the location of the boot partition, the boot menu, and the default operating system that should be loaded. This file can also be configured with switches that specify how the operating system should load (for example, with a standard VGA video driver).

4. A. The Dr. Watson utility is used to diagnose application errors. Windows 2000 Professional does not ship with a utility called Sherlock, Application Manager, or Application Event Viewer.

5. A. You use the command-line utility MAKEBT32 to create Windows 2000 Professional boot disks. The BOOTPRO and BOOT32 commands do not exist. There is no switch for WINNT32 called /BOOT.

6. D. The only utility that can be used to create an Emergency Repair Disk (ERD) is the Backup utility. ERD, RDISK, and RDISK32 do not exist in Windows 2000 Professional.

7. D. In order to restore the system using an ERD, you must use the Windows 2000 Professional Setup Disks.

8. D. Options A, B, and C do not exist. You use WINNT32 /CMDCONS to install the Recovery Console.

9. C.   The Emergency Repair Disk (ERD) contains the files that can be used to correct configuration errors or repair system files.

10. D.   The Event Viewer utility is used to track information about your computer's hardware and software. The System log includes any error messages that have been generated.

11. B.   When you run your computer in Safe Mode, you simplify your Windows 2000 configuration. Only the drivers that are needed to get the computer up and running are loaded.

12. A.   When you enable boot logging, the file created is *Windir*\\ ntbtlog.txt. This log file is used to troubleshoot the boot process.

13. C.   If you select Debugging Mode and have the Kernel Debugger installed, the Kernel Debugger can be used for advanced troubleshooting.

14. D.   Through the System icon in Control Panel, you can access Startup and Recovery options. The Default Operating System option lets you specify which operating system will load if no user selection is made.

15. C.   When you back up system state data, you back up the Registry, the COM+ registration database, and the system boot files.

Glossary

A

access control entry (ACE) An item used by the operating system to determine *resource* access. Each *access control list (ACL)* has an associated ACE that lists the permissions that have been granted or denied to the users and groups listed in the ACL.

access control list (ACL) An item used by the operating system to determine *resource* access. Each object (such as a folder, network share, or printer) in Windows 2000 has an ACL. The ACL lists the *security identifiers* (SIDs) contained by objects. Only those identified in the list as having the appropriate permission can activate the services of that object.

access token An object containing the *security identifier (SID)* of a running *process*. A process started by another process inherits the starting process's access token. The access token is checked against each object's *access control list (ACL)* to determine whether or not appropriate permissions are granted to perform any requested service.

Accessibility Options Windows 2000 Professional features used to support users with limited sight, hearing, or mobility. Accessibility Options include special keyboard, sound, display, and mouse configurations.

Accessibility Wizard A Windows 2000 Professional Wizard used to configure a computer based on the user's vision, hearing, and mobility needs.

account lockout policy A Windows 2000 policy used to specify how many invalid *logon* attempts should be tolerated before a user

account is locked out. Account lockout policies are set through *account policies*.

account policies Windows 2000 policies used to determine password and *logon* requirements. Account policies are set through the *Microsoft Management Console (MMC) Local Computer Policy* snap-in.

ACE See *access control entry*.

ACL See *access control list*.

ACPI See *Advanced Configuration and Power Interface*.

Active Desktop A Windows 2000 feature that makes the *Desktop* look and work like a Web page.

Active Directory A directory service available with the Windows 2000 Server platform. The Active Directory stores information in a central database and allows users to have a single user account (called a *domain user account* or *Active Directory user account*) for the network.

Active Directory user account A user account that is stored in the Windows 2000 Server *Active Directory's* central database. An Active Directory user account can provide a user with a single user account for a network. Also called a *domain user account*.

adapter Any hardware device that allows communications to occur through physically dissimilar systems. This term usually refers to peripheral cards that are permanently mounted inside computers and provide an interface from the computer's bus to another medium such as a hard disk or a network.

Administrator account   A Windows 2000 special account that has the ultimate set of security permissions and can assign any permission to any user or group.

Administrators group   A Windows 2000 local built-in group that consists of *Administrator accounts*.

Advanced Configuration and Power Interface (ACPI)   A specification that controls the amount of power given to each device attached to the computer. With ACPI, the operating system can turn off peripheral devices when they are not in use.

Advanced Graphics Port (AGP)   A type of expansion slot supported by Windows 2000. AGP is used by video cards and supports very high-quality video and graphics performance.

Advanced Power Management (APM)   A Windows 2000 feature designed to reduce the power consumption of a computer, which is especially important for laptops that are running on battery power.

AGP   See *Accelerated Graphics Port*.

alert   A system-monitoring feature that is generated when a specific *counter* exceeds or falls below a specified value. Through the *Performance Logs and Alerts* utility, administrators can configure alerts so that a message is sent, a program is run, or a more detailed log file is generated.

Anonymous Logon group   A Windows 2000 *special group* that includes users who access the computer through anonymous logons. Anonymous logons occur when users gain access through special accounts, such as the IUSR_ *computername* and TsInternetUser user accounts. Normally, a password is not required, so that anyone can log on.

answer file   An automated installation script used to respond to configuration prompts that normally occur in a Windows 2000 Professional installation. Administrators can create Windows 2000 answer files with the *Setup Manager* utility.

APM   See *Advanced Power Management*.

Application layer   The seventh (top) layer of the *Open Systems Interconnection (OSI)* model that interfaces with application programs by providing high-level network services based on lower-level network layers.

Application log   A log that tracks events that are related to applications that are running on the computer. The Application log can be viewed in the *Event Viewer* utility.

assigned applications   Applications installed with *Windows Installer packages*. Assigned applications are automatically installed when the user selects the application on the Programs menu or by document invocation (by the document extension).

audit policy   A Windows 2000 policy that tracks the success or failure of specified security events. Audit policies are set through *Local Computer Policy*.

Authenticated Users group   A Windows 2000 *special group* that includes users who access the Windows 2000 operating system through a valid username and password.

authentication   The process required to log on to a computer locally. Authentication requires a valid username and a password that exists in the local accounts database. An *access token* will be created if the information presented matches the account in the database.

automated installation   The process of installing Windows 2000 using an unattended setup method such as *Remote Installation Services (RIS)*, *unattended installation*, or *disk images*.

B

backup   The process of writing all the data contained in online mass-storage devices to offline mass-storage devices for the purpose of safekeeping. Backups are usually performed from hard disk drives to tape drives. Also referred to as archiving.

Backup Operators group   A Windows 2000 built-in group that includes users who can back up and restore the *file system*, even if the file system is *NTFS* and they have not been assigned permissions to the file system. The members of the Backup Operators group can only access the file system through the *Windows 2000 Backup* utility. To be able to directly access the file system, the user must have explicit permissions assigned.

backup type   A *backup* choice that determines which files are backed up during a backup process. Backup types include *normal backup*, *copy backup*, *incremental backup*, *differential backup*, and *daily backup*.

Backup Wizard   A Wizard used to perform a backup. The Backup Wizard is accessed through the *Windows 2000 Backup* utility.

baseline   A snapshot record of a computer's current performance statistics that can be used for performance analysis and planning purposes.

Basic Input/Output System (BIOS)   A set of routines in firmware that provides the most basic software interface drivers for hardware attached to the computer. The BIOS contains the boot routine.

basic storage   A disk-storage system supported by Windows 2000 that consists of *primary partitions* and *extended partitions*.

Batch group   A Windows 2000 *special group* that includes users who log on as a user account that is only used to run a batch job.

binding   The process of linking together software components, such as network *protocols* and *network adapters*.

BINL   See *Boot Information Negotiation Layer*.

BIOS   See *Basic Input/Output System*.

boot   The process of loading a computer's operating system. Booting usually occurs in multiple phases, each successively more complex until the entire operating system and all its services are running. Also called bootstrap. The computer's *BIOS* must contain the first level of booting.

Boot Information Negotiation Layer (BINL) The Boot Information Negotiation Layer (BINL) service responds to client requests for files from the RIS server. It is responsible for management of the RIS environment.

BOOT.INI A file accessed during the Windows 2000 *boot* sequence. The BOOT.INI file is used to build the operating system menu choices that are displayed during the boot process. It is also used to specify the location of the *boot partition*.

Boot Normally option A Windows 2000 Advanced Options menu item used to boot Windows 2000 normally.

boot partition The *partition* that contains the system files. The system files are located in C:\WINNT by default.

BOOTSECT.DOS An optional file that is loaded if the user chooses to load an operating system other than Windows 2000. This file is only used in *dual-boot* or *multi-boot* computers.

bootstrap image The bootstrap image is the fundamental network software that allows a remote client to get access to the *RIS* server via the *TFTP* protocol.

bottleneck A system *resource* that is inefficient compared with the rest of the computer system as a whole. The bottleneck can cause the rest of the system to run slowly.

C

cacheing A speed-optimization technique that keeps a copy of the most recently used data in a fast, high-cost, low-capacity storage device rather than in the device on which the actual data resides. Cacheing assumes that recently used data is likely to be used again. Fetching data from the cache is faster than fetching data from the slower, larger storage device. Most cacheing algorithms also copy data that is most likely to be used next and perform *write-back cacheing* to further increase speed gains.

CD-based image A type of image configured on a *Remote Installation Services (RIS)* server. A CD-based image contains only the Windows 2000 Professional operating system.

CDFS See *Compact Disk File System*.

central processing unit (CPU) The main *processor* in a computer.

Check Disk A Windows 2000 utility that checks a hard disk for errors. Check Disk (chkdsk) attempts to fix file-system errors and scans for and attempts to recover bad sectors.

CIPHER A command-line utility that can be used to encrypt files on *NTFS volumes*.

cipher text Encrypted data. Encryption is the process of translating data into code that is not easily accessible. Once data has been encrypted, a user must have a password or key to decrypt the data. Unencrypted data is known as plain text.

clean install   A method of *Windows 2000 Professional* installation that puts the operating system into a new folder and uses its default settings the first time the operating system is loaded.

client   A computer on a network that subscribes to the services provided by a server.

COM port   Communications port. A serial hardware interface conforming to the RS-232C standard for low-speed, serial communications.

Compact Disk File System (CDFS)   A *file system* used by Windows 2000 to read the file system on a CD-ROM.

compression   The process of storing data in a form that takes less space than the uncompressed data.

Computer Management   A consolidated tool for performing common Windows 2000 management tasks. The interface is organized into three main areas of management: *System Tools*, Storage, and Services and Applications.

computer name   A *NetBIOS* name used to uniquely identify a computer on the network. A computer name can be from 1 to 15 characters in length.

connection-oriented service   A type of connection service in which a connection (a path) is established and acknowledgments are sent. This type of communication is reliable but has a high overhead.

connectionless service   A type of connection service that does not establish a connection (path) before transmission. This type of communication is fast, but it is not very reliable.

Control Panel   A Windows 2000 utility that allows users to change default settings for operating system services to match their preferences. The *Registry* contains the Control Panel settings.

CONVERT   A command-line utility used to convert a *partition* from *FAT16* or *FAT32* to the *NTFS* file system.

copy backup   A *backup type* that backs up selected folders and files but does not set the archive bit.

counter   A performance-measuring tool used to track specific information regarding a system resource, called a performance object. All Windows 2000 system resources are tracked as performance objects, such as Cache, Memory, Paging File, Process, and Processor. Each performance object has an associated set of counters. Counters are set through the *System Monitor* utility.

CPU   See *central processing unit*.

Creator Group   The Windows 2000 *special group* that created or took ownership of the object (rather than an individual user). When a regular user creates an object or takes ownership of an object, the username becomes the *Creator Owner*. When a member of the *Administrators group* creates or takes ownership of an object, the Administrators group becomes the Creator Group.

Creator Owner group   The Windows 2000 *special group* that includes the account that created or took ownership of an object. The account, usually a user account, has the right to modify the object, but cannot modify any other objects that were not created by the user account.

D

daily backup   A *backup type* that backs up all of the files that have been modified on the day that the daily backup is performed. The archive attribute is not set on the files that have been backed up.

data compression   The process of storing data in a form that takes less space than the uncompressed data.

data encryption   The process of translating data into code that is not easily accessible to increase security. Once data has been encrypted, a user must have a password or key to decrypt the data.

Data Link layer   In the *Open Systems Interconnection (OSI) model*, the layer that provides the digital interconnection of network devices and the software that directly operates these devices, such as *network adapters*.

Debugging Mode   A Windows 2000 Advanced Option menu item that runs the Kernel Debugger, if that utility is installed. The Kernel Debugger is an advanced troubleshooting utility.

default gateway   A *TCP/IP* configuration option that specifies the gateway that will be used if the network contains routers.

Desktop   A directory that the background of the Windows Explorer shell represents. By default, the Desktop includes objects that contain the local storage devices and available network *shares*. Also a key operating part of the Windows 2000 graphical interface.

device driver   Software that allows a specific piece of hardware to communicate with the Windows 2000 operating system.

Device Manager   A Windows 2000 utility used to provide information about the computer's configuration.

DHCP   See *Dynamic Host Configuration Protocol*.

DHCP server   A server configured to provide *DHCP* clients with all of their *IP* configuration information automatically.

dial-up networking   A service that allows remote users to dial into the network or the Internet (such as through a telephone or an ISDN connection).

Dialup group   A Windows 2000 *special group* that includes users who log on to the network from a dial-up connection.

differential backup   A *backup type* that copies only the files that have been changed since the last *normal backup* (full backup) or *incremental backup*. A differential backup backs up only those files that have changed since the last full backup, but does not reset the archive bit.

Digital Versatile Disc (DVD)   A disk standard that supports 4.7GB of data per disk. One of DVD's strongest features is backward compatibility with CD-ROM technology, so that a DVD drive can play CD-ROMs. Formerly known as Digital Video Disk.

directory replication   The process of copying a directory structure from an export computer to an import computer(s). Anytime changes are made to the export computer, the import computer(s) is automatically updated with the changes.

Disk Cleanup   A Windows 2000 utility used to identify areas of disk space that can be deleted to free additional hard disk space. Disk Cleanup works by identifying temporary files, Internet cache files, and unnecessary program files.

disk defragmentation   The process of rearranging the existing files on a disk so that they are stored contiguously, which optimizes access to those files.

Disk Defragmenter   A Windows 2000 utility that performs *disk defragmentation*.

disk image   An exact duplicate of a hard disk, used for *automated installation*. The disk image is copied from a reference computer that is configured in the same manner as the computers on which Windows 2000 Professional will be installed.

Disk Management   A Windows 2000 graphical tool for managing disks and *volumes*.

disk partitioning   The process of creating logical *partitions* on the physical hard drive.

disk quotas   A Windows 2000 feature used to specify how much disk space a user is allowed to use on specific *NTFS volumes*. Disk quotas can be applied for all users or for specific users.

distribution server   A network server that contains the Windows 2000 distribution files that have been copied from the distribution CD. Clients can connect to the distribution server and install Windows 2000 over the network.

DNS   See *Domain Name System*.

DNS server   A server that uses *DNS* to resolve domain or host names to *IP addresses*.

domain   In Microsoft networks, an arrangement of client and server computers referenced by a specific name that shares a single security permissions database. On the Internet, a domain is a named collection of hosts and subdomains, registered with a unique name by the InterNIC.

domain name   A name that identifies one or more *IP addresses*, such as sybex.com. Domain names are used in *URLs* to identify particular Web hosts.

domain name server   An Internet host dedicated to the function of translating fully qualified domain names into *IP addresses*.

Domain Name Service (DNS)   The *TCP/IP* network service that translates fully qualified domain names (or host names) into *IP addresses*.

domain user account   A user account that is stored in the Windows 2000 Server *Active Directory's* central database. A domain user account can provide a user with a single user account for a network. Also called an Active Directory user account.

drive letter   A single letter assigned as an abbreviation to a mass-storage *volume* available to a computer.

driver   A program that provides a software interface to a hardware device. Drivers are written for the specific devices they control, but they present a common software interface to the computer's operating system, allowing all devices of a similar type to be controlled as if they were the same.

driver signing   A digital imprint that is Microsoft's way of guaranteeing that a driver has been tested and will work with the computer.

Dr. Watson   A Windows 2000 utility used to identify and troubleshoot application errors.

DRWTSN32   The command used to access the *Dr. Watson* utility.

dual-booting   The process of allowing a computer to *boot* more than one operating system.

DVD   See *Digital Versatile Disc*.

dynamic disk   A Windows 2000 disk-storage technique. A dynamic disk is divided into dynamic *volumes*. Dynamic volumes cannot contain *partitions* or *logical drives*, and they are not accessible through DOS. You can size or resize a dynamic disk without restarting Windows 2000. Dynamic disks are accessible only to Windows 2000 systems.

Dynamic Host Configuration Protocol (DHCP)   A method of automatically assigning *IP addresses* to client computers on a network.

dynamic storage   A Windows 2000 disk-storage system that is configured as *volumes*. Windows 2000 Professional dynamic storage supports *simple volumes*, *spanned volumes*, and *striped volumes*.

E

EB   See *exabyte*.

effective rights   The rights that a user actually has to a file or folder. To determine a user's effective rights, add all of the permissions that have been allowed through the user's assignments based on that user's username and group associations. Then subtract any permissions that have been denied the user through the username or group associations.

EFS   See *Encrypting File System*.

Emergency Repair Disk (ERD)   A disk that stores portions of the *Registry*, the system files, a copy of the partition boot sector, and information that relates to the startup environment. The ERD can be used to repair problems that prevent a computer from starting.

Enable Boot Logging option   A Windows 2000 Professional Advanced Options menu item that is used to create a log file that tracks the loading of *drivers* and *services*.

Enable VGA Mode option   A Windows 2000 Professional Advanced Options menu item that loads a standard VGA driver without starting the computer in *Safe Mode*.

Encrypting File System (EFS)   The Windows 2000 technology used to store encrypted files on *NTFS partitions*. Encrypted files add an extra layer of security to the *file system*.

encryption   The process of translating data into code that is not easily accessible to increase security. Once data has been encrypted, a user must have a password or key to decrypt the data.

ERD   See *Emergency Repair Disk*.

Error event   An *Event Viewer* event type that indicates the occurrence of an error, such as a driver failing to load.

Ethernet   The most popular Data Link layer standard for local area networking. Ethernet implements the Carrier Sense Multiple Access with Collision Detection (CSMA/CD) method of arbitrating multiple computer access to the same network. This standard supports the use of Ethernet over any type of media, including wireless broadcast. Standard Ethernet operates as 10Mbps. Fast Ethernet operates at 100Mbps.

Event Viewer   A Windows 2000 utility that tracks information about the computer's hardware and software, as well as security events. This information is stored in three log files: the *Application log*, the *Security log*, and the *System log*.

Everyone   A Windows 2000 *special group* that includes anyone who could possibly access the computer. The Everyone group includes all of the users (including *Guests*) who have been defined on the computer.

exabyte   A computer storage measurement equal to 1,024 *petabytes*.

extended partition   In *basic storage*, a *logical drive* that allows you to allocate the logical partitions however you wish. Extended partitions are created after the *primary partition* has been created.

F

Failure Audit event   An *Event Viewer* entry that indicates the occurrence of an event that has been audited for failure, such a failed logon when someone presents an invalid username and/or password.

FAT16   The 16-bit version of the *File Allocation System (FAT)* system, which was widely used by DOS and Windows 3.*x*. The file system is used to track where files are stored on a disk. Most operating systems support FAT16.

FAT32   The 32-bit version of the *File Allocation System (FAT)* system, which is more efficient and provides more safeguards than *FAT16*. Windows 95 OCR2, Windows 98, and Windows 2000 all support FAT32. Windows NT does not support FAT32.

fault tolerance   Any method that prevents system failure by tolerating single faults, usually through hardware redundancy.

fax modem   A special modem that includes hardware to allow the transmission and reception of facsimiles.

File Allocation Table (FAT)   The *file system* used by *MS-DOS* and available to other operating systems such as Windows (all versions) and OS/2. FAT, now known as *FAT16*, has become something of a mass-storage compatibility standard because of its simplicity and wide availability. FAT has fewer fault-tolerance features than the *NTFS* file system and can become corrupted through normal use over time.

file attributes   Bits stored along with the name and location of a file in a directory entry. File attributes show the status of a file, such as archived, hidden, and read-only. Different operating systems use different file attributes to implement services such as *sharing*, *compression*, and *security*.

file system   A software component that manages the storage of files on a mass-storage device by providing services that can create, read, write, and delete files. File systems impose an ordered database of files on the mass-storage device. Storage is arranged in *volumes*. File systems use hierarchies of directories to organize files.

File Transfer Protocol (FTP)   A simple Internet protocol that transfers complete files from an FTP server to a client running the FTP client. FTP provides a simple, low-overhead method of transferring files between computers but cannot perform browsing functions. Users must know the *URL* of the FTP server to which they wish to attach.

frame   A data structure that network hardware devices use to transmit data between computers. Frames consist of the addresses of the sending and receiving computers, size information, and a checksum. Frames are envelopes around packets of data that allow the packets to be addressed to specific computers on a shared media network.

frame type   An option that specifies how data is packaged for transmission over the network. This option must be configured to run the *NWLink IPX/SPX/NetBIOS Compatible Transport* protocol on a Windows 2000 computer. By default, the frame type is set to

Auto Detect, which will attempt to automatically choose a compatible frame type for the network.

FTP   See *File Transfer Protocol*.

G

GB   See *gigabyte*.

GDI   See *Graphic Device Interface*.

gigabyte   A computer storage measurement equal to 1,024 *megabytes*.

Graphical User Interface (GUI)   A computer shell program that represents mass-storage devices, directories, and files as graphical objects on a screen. A cursor driven by a pointing device such as a mouse manipulates the objects.

Graphics Device Interface (GDI)   The programming interface and graphical services provided to *Win32* for programs to interact with graphical devices such as the screen and printer.

Group Policy Object (GPO)   Group Policy comprises Windows 2000 configuration settings, administered through the use of Group Policy Objects (GPOs). GPOs are data structures that are attached in a specific hierarchy to selected Active Directory Objects. You can apply GPOs to Sites, Domains, or Organizational Units.

groups   Security entities to which users can be assigned membership for the purpose of applying the broad set of group permissions to the user. By managing permissions for groups and assigning users to groups, rather than assigning permissions to users, administrators can more easily manage security.

Guest account A Windows 2000 user account created to provide a mechanism to allow users to access the computer even if they do not have a unique username and password. This account normally has very limited privileges on the computer. This account is disabled by default.

Guests group A Windows 2000 built-in group that has limited access to the computer. This group can access only specific areas. Most administrators do not allow Guest account access because it poses a potential security risk.

GUI See *Graphical User Interface.*

H

HAL See *Hardware Abstraction Layer.*

hard disk drive A mass-storage device that reads and writes digital information magnetically on discs that spin under moving heads. Hard disk drives are precisely aligned and cannot normally be removed. Hard disk drives are an inexpensive way to store *gigabytes* of computer data permanently. Hard disk drives also store the software installed on a computer.

Hardware Abstraction Layer (HAL) A Windows 2000 service that provides basic input/output services such as timers, interrupts, and multiprocessor management for computer hardware. The HAL is a *device driver* for the motherboard circuitry that allows different families of computers to be treated the same by the Windows 2000 operating system.

Hardware Compatibility List (HCL) A list of all of the hardware devices supported by Windows 2000. Hardware on the HCL has been tested and verified as being compatible with Windows 2000.

hardware profile A file that stores a hardware configuration for a computer. Hardware profiles are useful when a single computer (a laptop that can be docked or undocked) has multiple hardware configurations.

HCL See *Hardware Compatibility List.*

hibernation The storage of anything that is stored in memory on the computer's hard disk. Hibernation ensures that none of the information stored in memory is lost when the computer is shut down. When the computer is taken out of hibernation, it is returned to its previous state.

home folder A folder where users normally store their personal files and information. A home folder can be a local folder or a network folder.

host An Internet server. A host is a node that is connected to the Internet.

hot swapping The ability of a device to be plugged into or removed from a computer while the computer's power is on.

HTML See *Hypertext Markup Language.*

HTTP See *Hypertext Transfer Protocol.*

hyperlink   A link within text or graphics that has a Web address embedded in it. By clicking the link, a user can jump to another Web address.

Hypertext Markup Language (HTML)   A textual data format that identifies sections of a document such as headers, lists, hypertext links, and so on. HTML is the data format used on the World Wide Web for the publication of Web pages.

Hypertext Transfer Protocol (HTTP)   An Internet protocol that transfers HTML documents over the Internet and responds to context changes that happen when a user clicks a *hyperlink*.

I

IEEE   See *Institute of Electrical and Electronic Engineers*.

IIS   See *Internet Information Services*.

incremental backup   A *backup type* that backs up only the files that have changed since the last normal or incremental backup. It sets the archive attribute on the files that are backed up.

Indexing Service   A Windows 2000 service that creates an index based on the contents and properties of files stored on the computer's local hard drive. A user can then use the Windows 2000 Search function to search or query through the index for specific keywords.

Industry Standard Architecture (ISA)   The design standard for 16-bit Intel-compatible motherboards and peripheral buses. The 32/64-bit *PCI* bus standard is replacing the ISA standard. Adapters and interface cards must conform to the bus standard(s) used by the motherboard in order to be used in a computer.

Information event   An *Event Viewer* entry that informs you that a specific action has occurred, such as when a system shuts down or starts.

inherited permissions   Parent folder permissions that are applied to (or inherited by) files and subfolders of the parent folder. In Windows 2000 Professional, the default is for parent folder permissions to be applied to any files or subfolders in that folder.

initial user account   The account that uses the name of the registered user and is created only if the computer is installed as a member of a workgroup (not into the *Active Directory*). By default, the initial user is a member of the *Administrators group*.

Institute of Electrical and Electronic Engineers (IEEE)   A professional organization that defines standards related to networks, communications, and other areas.

Institute of Electrical and Electronic Engineers (IEEE) 1394 standard   A standard that supports data transfer at speeds up to 400Mbps. Some of the trademark names for this standard are FireWire, I-link, and Lynx.

Integrated Services Digital Network (ISDN)   A direct, digital, dial-up connection that operates at 64KB per channel over regular twisted-pair cable. Up to 24 channels can be multiplexed over two twisted pairs.

Intel architecture   A family of microprocessors descended from the Intel 8086, itself descended from the first microprocessor, the Intel 4004. The Intel architecture is the dominant microprocessor family. It was used in the original IBM PC microcomputer adopted by the business market and later adapted for home use.

Interactive group   A Windows 2000 *special group* that includes all the users who use the computer's resources locally.

interactive logon   A *logon* when the user logs on from the computer where the user account is stored on the computer's local database. Also called a *local logon*.

interactive user   A user who physically logs on to the computer where the user account resides (rather than over the network).

internal network number   An identification for *NetWare* file servers. An internal network number is also used if the network is running File and Print Services for NetWare or is using IPX routing. This option must be configured to run the *NWLink IPX/SPX/NetBIOS Compatible Transport* protocol on a Windows 2000 computer. Normally, the internal network number should be left at its default setting.

Internet connection sharing   A Windows 2000 feature that allows a small network to be connected to the Internet through a single connection. The computer that dials into the Internet provides network address translation, addressing, and name resolution services for all of the computers on the network. Through Internet connection sharing, the other computers on the network can access Internet resources and use Internet applications, such as Internet Explorer and Outlook Express.

Internet Explorer   A World Wide Web browser produced by Microsoft and included with Windows *9x*, Windows NT 4, and now Windows 2000.

Internet Information Services (IIS)   Software that serves Internet higher-level protocols like *HTTP* and *FTP* to clients using Web browsers. The IIS software that is installed on a Windows 2000 Server computer is a fully functional Web server and is designed to support heavy Internet usage.

Internet Print Protocol (IPP)   A Windows 2000 protocol that allows users to print directly to a *URL*. Printer- and job-related information are generated in *HTML* format.

Internet printer   A Windows 2000 feature that allows users to send documents to be printed through the Internet.

Internet Protocol (IP)   The Network layer protocol upon which the Internet is based. IP provides a simple connectionless packet exchange. Other protocols such as TCP use IP to perform their *connection-oriented* (or guaranteed delivery) services.

Internet service provider (ISP)   A company that provides dial-up connections to the Internet.

Internet Services Manager   A Windows 2000 utility used to configure the protocols that are used by *Internet Information Services (IIS)* and *Personal Web Services (PWS)*.

internetwork   A network made up of multiple network segments that are connected with some device, such as a router. Each network segment is assigned a network address. *Network layer protocols* build routing tables that are used to route packets through the network in the most efficient manner.

InterNIC   The agency that is responsible for assigning *IP addresses*.

interprocess communications (IPC)   A generic term describing any manner of client/server communication protocol, specifically those operating in the *Application layer*. IPC mechanisms provide a method for the client and server to trade information.

interrupt request (IRQ)   A hardware signal from a peripheral device to the microcomputer indicating that it has input/output (I/O) traffic to send. If the microprocessor is not running a more important service, it will interrupt its current activity and handle the interrupt request. IBM PCs have 16 levels of interrupt request lines. Under Windows 2000, each device must have a unique interrupt request line.

intranet   A privately owned network based on the *TCP/IP* protocol suite.

IP   See *Internet Protocol*.

IP address   A four-byte number that uniquely identifies a computer on an IP *internetwork*.

IPC   See *interprocess communications*.

IPCONFIG   A command used to display the computer's *IP* configuration.

IPP   See *Internet Print Protocol*.

IRQ   See *interrupt request*.

ISA   See *Industry Standard Architecture*.

ISDN   See *Integrated Services Digital Network*.

ISP   See *Internet service provider*.

K

kernel   The core process of a preemptive operating system, consisting of a multitasking scheduler and the basic security services. Depending on the operating system, other services such as virtual memory drivers may be built into the kernel. The kernel is responsible for managing the scheduling of *threads* and *processes*.

L

Last Known Good Configuration option   A Windows 2000 Advanced Options menu item used to load the control set that was used the last time the computer was successfully booted.

LLC sublayer   See *Logical Link Control sublayer*.

Local Computer Policy   A *Microsoft Management Console (MMC) snap-in* used to implement account policies.

local group   A group that is stored on the local computer's accounts database. These are the groups that administrators can add users to and manage directly on a Windows 2000 Professional computer.

Local Computer Policy   A *Microsoft Management Console (MMC) snap-in* used to implement local group policies, which include computer configuration policies and user configuration policies.

local logon   A *logon* when the user logs on from the computer where the user account is stored on the computer's local database. Also called an interactive logon.

local policies   Policies that allow administrators to control what a user can do after logging on. Local policies include *audit policies, security option policies*, and *user rights policies*. These policies are set through *Local Computer Policy*.

local printer   A printer that uses a *physical port* and that has not been shared. If a printer is defined as local, the only users who can use the printer are the local users of the computer that the printer is attached to.

local security   Security that governs a local or interactive user's ability to access locally stored files. Local security can be set through *NTFS permissions*.

local user account   A user account stored locally in the user accounts database of a computer that is running Windows 2000 Professional.

local user profile   A profile created the first time a user logs on, stored in the Documents and Settings folder. The default user profile folder's name matches the user's logon name. This folder contains a file called NTUSER.DAT and subfolders with directory links to the user's *Desktop* items.

Local Users and Groups   A utility that is used to create and manage local user and group accounts on Windows 2000 Professional computers and Windows 2000 member servers.

locale settings   Settings for regional items, including numbers, currency, time, date, and input locales.

logical drive   An allocation of disk space on a hard drive, using a *drive letter*. For example, a 5GB hard drive could be partitioned into two logical drives: a C: drive, which might be 2GB, and a D: drive, which might be 3GB.

Logical Drives   A Windows 2000 utility used to manage the logical drives on the computer.

Logical Link Control (LLC) sublayer   A sublayer in the *Data Link layer* of the *Open Systems Interconnection (OSI)* model. The LLC sublayer defines flow control.

logical port   A port that connects a device directly to the network. Logical ports are used with printers by installing a network card in the printers.

logical printer   The software interface between the *physical printer* (the *print device*) and the operating system. Also referred to as just a *printer* in Windows 2000 terminology.

logoff   The process of closing an open session with a Windows 2000 computer or network.

logon   The process of opening a session with a Windows 2000 computer or a network by providing a valid authentication consisting of a user account name and a password. After logon, network resources are available to the user according to the user's assigned *permissions*.

logon script   A command file that automates the *logon* process by performing utility functions such as attaching to additional server resources or automatically running different programs based on the user account that established the logon.

M

MAC (media access control) address   The physical address that identifies a computer. *Ethernet* and Token Ring cards have the MAC address assigned through a chip on the network card.

MAC sublayer   See *Media Access Control sublayer*.

Magnifier   A Windows 2000 utility used to create a separate window to magnify a portion of the screen. This option is designed for users who have poor vision.

MAKEBT32.EXE   The command used to create *Windows 2000 Professional Setup Boot Disks*.

mandatory profile   A *user profile* created by an administrator and saved with a special extension (.man) so that the user cannot modify the profile in any way. Mandatory profiles can be assigned to a single user or a group of users.

mapped drive   A shared network folder associated with a drive letter. Mapped drives appear to users as local connections on their computers and can be accessed through a drive letter using My Computer.

Master Boot Record (MBR)   A record used in the Windows 2000 *boot* sequence to point to the active partition, which is the partition used to boot the operating system. This is normally the C: drive. Once the MBR locates the active partition, the boot sector is loaded into memory and executed.

MB   See *megabyte*.

MBR   See *Master Boot Record*.

Media Access Control (MAC) sublayer   A sublayer in the *Data Link layer* of the *Open Systems Interconnection (OSI)* model. The MAC sublayer is used for physical addressing.

megabyte   A computer storage measurement equal to 1,024 kilobytes.

member server   A Windows 2000 server that has been installed as a non-domain controller. This allows the server to operate as a file, print, and application server without the overhead of account administration.

memory   Any device capable of storing information. This term is usually used to indicate volatile *random-access memory (RAM)* capable of high-speed access to any portion of the memory space, but incapable of storing information without power.

Microsoft Disk Operating System (MS-DOS) A 16-bit operating system designed for the 8086 chip that was used in the original IBM PC. MS-DOS is a simple program loader and *file system* that turns over complete control of the computer to the running program and provides very little service beyond file system support and that provided by the *BIOS*.

Microsoft Installer (MSI) A standard that is used to automatically deploy applications with *Windows Installer packages*.

Microsoft Management Console (MMC) The Windows 2000 console framework for management applications. The MMC provides a common environment for *snap-ins*.

MMC See *Microsoft Management Console*.

modem Modulator/demodulator. A device used to create an analog signal suitable for transmission over telephone lines from a digital data stream. Modern modems also include a command set for negotiating connections and data rates with remote modems and for setting their default behavior.

MS-DOS See *Microsoft Disk Operating System*.

MSI See *Microsoft Installer*.

multi-booting The process of allowing a computer to *boot* multiple operating systems.

My Computer The folder used to view and manage a computer. My Computer provides access to all local and network drives, as well as *Control Panel*.

My Documents The default storage location for documents that are created. Each user has a unique My Documents folder.

My Network Places The folder that provides access to shared resources, such as local network resources and Web resources.

N

Narrator A Windows 2000 utility used to read aloud on-screen text, dialog boxes, menus, and buttons. This utility requires some type of sound output device.

NetBEUI See *NetBIOS Extended User Interface*.

NetBIOS See *Network Basic Input/Output System*.

NetBIOS Extended User Interface (NetBEUI) A simple *Network layer transport protocol* developed to support *NetBIOS* installations. NetBEUI is not routable, and so it is not appropriate for larger networks. NetBEUI is the fastest transport protocol available for Windows 2000.

Net PC The Net PC standard for PCs uses industry-standard components for the PC, including *processor, memory, hard disk*, video, audio, and an integrated *network adapter* and *modem*, in a locked case with limited expandability capabilities. Net PCs cost less to purchase and to manage.

NET USE A command-line utility used to map network drives.

NetWare   A popular network operating system developed by Novell in the early 1980s. NetWare is a cooperative, multitasking, highly optimized, dedicated-server network operating system that has client support for most major operating systems. Recent versions of NetWare include graphical client tools for management from client stations. At one time, NetWare accounted for more than 70 percent of the network operating system market.

network adapter   The hardware used to connect computers (or other devices) to the network. Network adapters function at the *Physical layer* and the *Date Link layer* of the *Open System Interconnection (OSI) model.*

Network Basic Input/Output System (NetBIOS)   A client/server *IPC* service developed by IBM in the early 1980s. NetBIOS presents a relatively primitive mechanism for communication in client/server applications, but its widespread acceptance and availability across most operating systems make it a logical choice for simple network applications. Many of the network *IPC* mechanisms in Windows 2000 are implemented over NetBIOS.

Network group   A Windows 2000 *special group* that includes the users who access a computer's resources over a network connection.

Network layer   The layer of the *Open System Interconnection (OSI) model* that creates a communication path between two computers via routed packets. *Transport protocols* implement both the Network layer and the *Transport layer* of the OSI stack. For example, *IP* is a Network layer service.

network printer   A *printer* that is available to local and network users. A network printer can use a *physical port* or a *logical port.*

New Technology File System (NTFS)   A secure, transaction-oriented file system developed for Windows NT and Windows 2000. NTFS offers features such as *local security* on files and folders, *data compression, disk quotas,* and *data encryption.*

normal backup   A *backup type* that backs up all selected folders and files and then marks each file that has been backed up as archived.

NTBOOTDD.SYS   A file accessed in the Windows 2000 *boot* sequence. NTBOOTDD.SYS is an optional file (the *SCSI* driver) that is used when the computer has a SCSI adapter with the on-board *BIOS* disabled.

NTDETECT.COM   A file accessed in the Windows 2000 *boot* sequence. NTDETECT.COM is used to detect any hardware that is installed and add information about the hardware to the *Registry.*

NTFS   See *New Technology File System.*

NTFS permissions   Permissions used to control access to *NTFS* folders and files. Access is configured by allowing or denying NTFS permissions to users and groups.

NTLDR   A file used to control the Windows 2000 *boot* process until control is passed to the *NTOSKRNL.EXE* file.

NTOSKRNL.EXE   A file accessed in the Windows 2000 *boot* sequence. NTOSKRNL.EXE is used to load the *kernel.*

NTUSER.DAT The file that is created for a *user profile*.

NTUSER.MAN The file that is created for a *mandatory profile*.

NWLINK IPX/SPX/NetBIOS Compatible Transport Microsoft's implementation of the Novell IPX/SPX protocol stack.

O

offline files and folders A Windows 2000 feature that allows network folders and files to be stored on Windows 2000 clients. Users can access network files even if the network location is not available.

On-Screen Keyboard A Windows 2000 utility that displays a keyboard on the screen and allows users to enter keyboard input by using a mouse or other input device.

Open Systems Interconnection (OSI) model A reference model for network component interoperability developed by the International Standards Organization (ISO) to promote cross-vendor compatibility of hardware and software network systems. The OSI model splits the process of networking into seven distinct services, or layers. Each layer uses the services of the layer below to provide its service to the layer above.

optimization Any effort to reduce the workload on a hardware component by eliminating, obviating, or reducing the amount of work required of the hardware component through any means. For instance, file *cacheing* is an optimization that reduces the workload of a hard disk drive.

organizational unit (OU) In *Active Directory*, an organizational unit is a generic folder used to create a collection of objects. An OU can represent a department, division, location, or project group. Used to ease administration of AD objects and as a unit to which group policy can be deployed.

OSI model See *Open Systems Interconnection model*.

owner The user associated with an *NTFS* file or folder who is able to control access and grant permissions to other users.

P

page file Logical memory that exists on the hard drive. If a system is experiencing excessive paging (swapping between the page file and physical RAM), it needs more memory.

partition A section of a hard disk that can contain an independent *file system volume*. Partitions can be used to keep multiple operating systems and file systems on the same hard disk.

password policies Windows 2000 policies used to enforce security requirements on the computer. Password policies are set on a per-computer basis, and they cannot be configured for specific users. Password policies are set through *account policies*.

PB See *petabyte*.

PC Card A special, credit-card-sized device used to add devices to a laptop computer. Also called a PCMCIA card.

PCI See *Peripheral Connection Interface.*

PCMCIA card See *Personal Computer Memory Card International Association card.*

Performance Logs and Alerts A Windows 2000 utility used to log performance-related data and generate *alerts* based on performance-related data.

Peripheral Connection Interface (PCI) A high-speed, 32/64-bit bus interface developed by Intel and widely accepted as the successor to the 16-bit *ISA* interface. PCI devices support input/output (I/O) throughput about 40 times faster than the ISA bus.

permissions Security constructs used to regulate access to resources by username or group affiliation. Permissions can be assigned by administrators to allow any level of access, such as read-only, read/write, or delete, by controlling the ability of users to initiate object services. Security is implemented by checking the user's *security identifier (SID)* against each object's *access control list (ACL).*

Personal Computer Memory Card International Association (PCMCIA) card A special, credit-card-sized device used to add devices to a laptop computer. Also called a *PC Card.*

Personal Web Manager A Windows 2000 utility used to configure and manage *Peer Web Services (PWS).* This utility has options for configuring the location of the home page and stopping the Web site, and displays statistics for monitoring the Web site.

petabyte A computer storage measurement that is equal to 1,024 *terabytes.*

Physical layer The first (bottom) layer of the *Open Systems Interconnection (OSI)* model, which represents the cables, connectors, and connection ports of a network. The Physical layer contains the passive physical components required to create a network.

physical port A serial (COM) or parallel (LPT) port that connects a device, such as a printer, directly to a computer.

PING A command used to send an Internet Control Message Protocol (ICMP) echo request and echo reply to verify that a remote computer is available.

Plug and Play A technology that uses a combination of hardware and software to allow the operating system to automatically recognize and configure new hardware without any user intervention.

policies General controls that enhance the *security* of an operating environment. In Windows 2000, policies affect restrictions on password use and rights assignments, and determine which events will be recorded in the *Security log.*

POST See *Power On Self Test.*

Power On Self Test (POST) A part of the Windows 2000 *boot* sequence. The POST detects the computer's *processor,* how much memory is present, what hardware is recognized, and whether or not the *BIOS* is standard or has *Plug and Play* capabilities.

Power Users group   A Windows 2000 built-in group that has fewer rights than the *Administrators group*, but more rights than the *Users group*. Members of the Power Users group can perform tasks such as creating local users and groups and modifying the users and groups that they have created.

Pre-Boot Execution Environment (PXE)   A technology that allows a client computer to remotely boot and connect to a *Remote Installation Service (RIS)* server.

Presentation layer   The layer of the *Open Systems Interconnection (OSI) model* that converts and translates (if necessary) information between the *Session layer* and *Application layer*.

primary partition   A part of *basic storage* on a disk. The primary partition is the first partition created on a hard drive. The primary partition uses all of the space that is allocated to the partition. This partition is usually marked as active and is the partition that is used to *boot* the computer.

print device   The actual physical printer or hardware device that generates printed output.

print driver   The specific software that understands a *print device*. Each print device has an associated print driver.

print processor   The process that determines whether or not a print job needs further processing once that job has been sent to the *print spooler*. The processing (also called *rendering*) is used to format the print job so that it can print correctly at the *print device*.

print queue   A directory or folder on the *print server* that stores the print jobs until they can be printed. Also called a print spooler.

print server   The computer on which the printer has been defined. When a user sends a print job to a *network printer*, it goes to the print server first.

print spooler   A directory or folder on the *print server* that stores the print jobs until they can be printed. Also called a print queue.

printer   In Windows 2000 terminology, the software interface between the physical printer (see *print device*) and the operating system.

printer pool   A configuration that allows one printer to be used for multiple *print devices*. Printer pooling can be used when multiple printers use the same *print driver* (and are normally in the same location). With a printer pool, users can send their print jobs to the first available printer.

priority   A level of execution importance assigned to a *thread*. In combination with other factors, the priority level determines how often that thread will get computer time according to a scheduling algorithm.

process   A running program containing one or more *threads*. A process encapsulates the protected memory and environment for its threads.

processor   A circuit designed to automatically perform lists of logical and arithmetic operations. Unlike microprocessors, processors may be designed from discrete components rather than be a monolithic integrated circuit.

processor affinity   The association of a *processor* with specific *processes* that are running on the computer. Processor affinity is used to configure multiple processors.

protocol   An established rule of communication adhered to by the parties operating under it. Protocols provide a context in which to interpret communicated information. Computer protocols are rules used by communicating devices and software services to format data in a way that all participants understand.

PXE   See *Pre-Boot Execution Environment*.

published applications   Applications installed with *Windows Installer packages*. Users can choose whether or not they will install published applications through the Control Panel Add/Remove Programs icon. Administrators can choose to have published applications installed when the applications are invoked.

R

RAM   See *random-access memory*.

random-access memory (RAM)   Integrated circuits that store digital bits in massive arrays of logical gates or capacitors. RAM is the primary memory store for modern computers, storing all running software processes and contextual data.

RAS   See *Remote Access Service*.

real-time application   A *process* that must respond to external events at least as fast as those events can occur. Real-time *threads* must run at very high priorities to ensure their ability to respond in real time.

Recovery Console   A Windows 2000 option for recovering from a failed system. The Recovery Console starts Windows 2000 without the graphical interface and allows the administrator limited capabilities, such as adding or replacing files and enabling and disabling services.

Recycle Bin   A folder that holds files and folders that have been deleted. Files can be retrieved or cleared (for permanent deletion) from the Recycle Bin.

REGEDIT   A Windows program used to edit the *Registry*. It does not support full editing, as does the *REGEDT32* program, but it has better search capabilities than REGEDT32.

REGEDT32   The primary utility for editing the Windows 2000 *Registry*.

Regional Options   A *Control Panel* utility used to enable and configure multilingual editing and viewing on a localized version of Windows 2000 Professional.

Registry   A database of settings required and maintained by Windows 2000 and its components. The Registry contains all of the configuration information used by the computer. It is stored as a hierarchical structure and is made up of keys, hives, and value entries.

Remote Access Service (RAS)   A service that allows network connections to be established over a modem connection, an *Integrated Services Digital Network (ISDN)* connection, or a null-modem cable. The computer initiating the connection is called the RAS client; the answering computer is called the RAS server.

remote installation Installation of Windows 2000 Professional performed remotely through *Remote Installation Services (RIS)*.

Remote Installation Preparation (RIPrep) image A type of image configured on a *Remote Installation Services (RIS)* server. A RIPrep image can contain the Windows 2000 operating system and applications. This type of image is based on a preconfigured computer.

Remote Installation Services (RIS) A Windows 2000 technology that allows the remote installation of Windows 2000 Professional. A RIS server installs Windows 2000 Professional on RIS clients. The RIS server can be configured with a *CD-based image* or a *Remote Installation Preparation (RIPrep) image*.

Removable Storage A Windows 2000 utility used to track information on removable storage media, which include CDs, DVDs, tapes, and jukeboxes containing optical discs.

rendering The process that determines whether or not a print job needs further processing once that job has been sent to the spooler. The processing is used to format the print job so that it can print correctly at the *print device*.

Replicator group A Windows 2000 built-in group that supports *directory replication*, which is a feature used by domain servers. Only *domain user accounts* that will be used to start the replication service should be assigned to this group.

Requests for Comments (RFCs) The set of standards defining the Internet protocols as determined by the Internet Engineering Task Force and available in the public domain on the Internet. RFCs define the functions and services provided by each of the many Internet protocols. Compliance with the RFCs guarantees cross-vendor compatibility.

resource Any useful service, such as a *shared folder* or a *printer*.

Restore Wizard A Wizard used to restore data. The Restore Wizard is accessed through the *Windows 2000 Backup* utility.

RFC See *Request For Comments*.

RIPrep image See *Remote Installation Preparation image*.

RIS See *Remote Installation Services*.

roaming profile A *user profile* that is stored and configured to be downloaded from a server. Roaming profiles allow users to access their profiles from any location on the network.

router A *Network layer* device that moves packets between networks. Routers provide *internetwork* connectivity.

S

Safe Mode A Windows 2000 Advanced Options menu item that loads the absolute minimum of *services* and *drivers* that are needed to start Windows 2000. The drivers that are loaded with Safe Mode include basic files and drivers for the mouse (unless a serial mouse is attached to the computer), monitor, keyboard, hard drive, standard video driver, and default system services. Safe Mode is considered a diagnostic mode. It does not include networking capabilities.

Safe Mode with Command Prompt A Windows 2000 Advanced Options menu item that starts Windows 2000 in *Safe Mode*, but instead of loading the graphical interface, it loads a command prompt.

Safe Mode with Networking A Windows 2000 Advanced Options menu item that starts Windows 2000 in *Safe Mode*, but it adds networking features.

SCSI See *Small Computer Systems Interface*.

security The measures taken to secure a system against accidental or intentional loss, usually in the form of accountability procedures and use restriction, for example through *NTFS permissions* and *share permissions*.

security identifier (SID) A unique code that identifies a specific user or group to the Windows 2000 security system. SIDs contain a complete set of *permissions* for that user or group.

Security log A log that tracks events that are related to Windows 2000 auditing. The Security log can be viewed through the *Event Viewer* utility.

security option policies Policies used to configure security for the computer. Security option policies apply to computers rather than to users or groups. These policies are set through *Local Computer Policy*.

separator page A page used at the beginning of each document to identify the user who submitted the print job. When users share a printer, separator pages can be useful for distributing print jobs.

serial A method of communication that transfers data across a medium one bit at a time, usually adding stop, start, and check bits.

service A *process* dedicated to implementing a specific function for another process. Most Windows 2000 components are services used by user-level applications.

Service group A Windows 2000 *special group* that includes users who log on as a user account that is only used to run a *service*.

service pack An update to the Windows 2000 operating system that includes bug fixes and enhancements.

Session layer The layer of the *Open Systems Interconnection (OSI) model* dedicated to maintaining a bi-directional communication connection between two computers. The Session layer uses the services of the *Transport layer* to provide this service.

Services A Windows 2000 utility used to manage the *services* installed on the computer.

Setup Manager (SETUPMGR) A Windows 2000 utility used to create automated installation scripts or unattended *answer files*.

SETUPMGR See *Setup Manager*.

share A *resource* such as a folder or printer shared over a network.

share permissions Permissions used to control access to shared folders. Share permissions can only be applied to folders, as opposed to *NTFS permissions*, which are more complex and can be applied to folders and files.

shared folder   A folder on a Windows 2000 computer that network users can access.

Shared Folders   A Windows 2000 utility for managing *shared folders* on the computer.

shortcut   A quick link to an item that is accessible from a computer or network, such as a file, program, folder, printer, or computer. Shortcuts can exist in various locations including the *Desktop*, the *Start menu*, or within folders.

SID   See *security identifier*.

Simple Mail Transfer Protocol (SMTP)   An Internet protocol for transferring mail between Internet hosts. SMTP is often used to upload mail directly from the client to an intermediate host, but can only be used to receive mail by computers constantly connected to the Internet.

simple volume   A *dynamic disk* volume that contains space from a single disk. The space from the single drive can be contiguous or non-contiguous. Simple volumes are used when the computer has enough disk space on a single drive to hold an entire volume.

SIS   See *Single Instance Store*.

SIS Groveler   This service works in conjunction with files used for automated installation when using disk images. The *SIS* Groveler service scans the SIS volume for files that are identical. If identical files are found, this service creates a link to the duplicate files instead of storing duplicate files.

Single Instance Store   The Single Instance Store (SIS) manages duplicate copies of disk images by replacing duplicates with a link to the original files. This service works in conjunction with disk images used for Windows 2000 automated installations.

slipstream technology   A Windows 2000 technology for *service packs*. With slipstream technology, service packs are applied once, and they are not overwritten as new services are added to the computer.

Small Computer Systems Interface (SCSI)   A high-speed, parallel-bus interface that connects hard disk drives, CD-ROM drives, tape drives, and many other peripherals to a computer. SCSI is the mass-storage connection standard among all computers except IBM compatibles, which use SCSI or IDE.

smart card   A special piece of hardware with a microchip, used to store public and private keys, passwords, and other personal information securely. Can be used for other purposes, such as telephone calling and electronic cash payments.

SMTP   See *Simple Mail Transfer Protocol*.

snap-in   An administrative tool developed by Microsoft or a third-party vendor that can be added to the *Microsoft Management Console (MMC)* in Windows 2000.

spanned volume   A *dynamic disk* volume that consists of disk space on 2 to 32 dynamic drives. Spanned volume sets are used to dynamically increase the size of a dynamic volume. With spanned volumes, the data is written sequentially, filling space on one physical drive before writing to space on the next physical drive in the spanned volume set.

special group A group used by the system, in which membership is automatic if certain criteria are met. Administrators cannot manage special groups.

spooler A service that buffers output to a low-speed device such as a printer, so the software outputting to the device is not tied up waiting for the device to be ready.

Start menu A Windows 2000 *Desktop* item, located on the *Taskbar*. The Start menu contains a list of options and programs that can be run.

stripe set A single *volume* created across multiple hard disk drives and accessed in parallel for the purpose of optimizing disk-access time. *NTFS* can create stripe sets.

striped volume A *dynamic disk* volume that stores data in equal stripes between 2 to 32 dynamic drives. Typically, administrators use striped volumes when they want to combine the space of several physical drives into a single logical volume and increase disk performance.

subnet mask A number mathematically applied to *IP addresses* to determine which IP addresses are a part of the same subnetwork as the computer applying the subnet mask.

Success Audit event An *Event Viewer* entry that indicates the occurrence of an event that has been audited for success, such as a successful logon.

Sysprep See *System Preparation Tool.*

System group A Windows 2000 *special group* that contains system processes that access specific functions as a user.

System Information A Windows 2000 utility used to collect and display information about the computer's current configuration.

System log A log that tracks events that relate to the Windows 2000 operating system. The System log can be viewed through the *Event Viewer* utility.

System Monitor A Windows 2000 utility used to monitor real-time system activity or view data from a log file.

system partition The active *partition* on an Intel-based computer that contains the hardware-specific files used to load the Windows 2000 operating system.

System Preparation Tool (Sysprep) A Windows 2000 utility used to prepare a *disk image* for disk duplication.

System Tools A Computer Management utility grouping that provides access to utilities for managing common system functions. The System Tools utility includes the *Event Viewer*, *System Information*, *Performance Logs and Alerts*, *Shared Folders*, *Device Manager*, and *Local Users and Groups* utilities.

T

Task Manager A Windows 2000 utility that can be used to start, end, or prioritize applications. The Task Manager shows the applications and *processes* that are currently running on the computer, as well as *CPU* and *memory* usage information.

Task Scheduler   A Windows 2000 utility used to schedule tasks to occur at specified intervals.

Taskbar   A Windows 2000 *Desktop* item, which appears across the bottom of the screen by default. The Taskbar contains the *Start menu* and buttons for any programs, documents, or windows that are currently running on the computer. Users can switch between open items by clicking the item in the Taskbar.

TB   See *terabyte*.

TCP   See *Transmission Control Protocol*.

TCP/IP   See *Transmission Control Protocol/Internet Protocol*.

TCP/IP port   A *logical port*, used when a printer is attached to the network by installing a network card in the printer. Configuring a TCP/IP port requires the IP address of the network printer to connect to.

terabyte (TB)   A computer storage measurement that equals 1,024 *gigabytes*.

Terminal Server User group   A Windows 2000 *special group* that includes users who log on through Terminal Services.

TFTP   See *Trivial File Transfer Protocol*.

thread   A list of instructions running in a computer to perform a certain task. Each thread runs in the context of a *process*, which embodies the protected memory space and the environment of the threads. Multithreaded processes can perform more than one task at the same time.

Transmission Control Protocol (TCP)   A *Transport layer* protocol that implements guaranteed packet delivery using the *IP* protocol.

Transmission Control Protocol/Internet Protocol (TCP/IP)   A suite of Internet protocols upon which the global Internet is based. TCP/IP is a general term that can refer either to the *TCP* and *IP* protocols used together or to the complete set of Internet protocols. TCP/IP is the default protocol for Windows 2000.

Transport layer   The *Open Systems Interconnection (OSI) model* layer responsible for the guaranteed serial delivery of packets between two computers over an *internetwork*. *TCP* is the Transport layer protocol in *TCP/IP*.

transport protocol   A service that delivers discreet packets of information between any two computers in a network. Higher-level, *connection-oriented services* are built on transport protocols.

Trivial File Transfer Protocol (TFTP)   A network application that is simpler than the *File Transfer Protocol (FTP)* but less capable. It is used where user *authentication* and directory visibility are not required. TFTP is used to download the Windows 2000 *Client Installation Wizard* from the *RIS* server to the RIS clients. TFTP uses the User Datagram Protocol (UDP).

U

unattended installation   A method of installing Windows 2000 Professional remotely with little or no user intervention. Unattended installation uses a *distribution server* or the Windows 2000 Professional CD to install Windows 2000 Professional on a target computer.

UNC   See *Universal Naming Convention*.

Uniform Resource Locator (URL) An Internet standard naming convention for identifying resources available via various *TCP/IP* application protocols. For example, `http://www.microsoft.com` is the URL for Microsoft's World Wide Web server site, and `ftp://gateway.dec.com` is a popular *FTP* site. A URL allows easy hypertext references to a particular resource from within a document or mail message. A URL always has the *domain* name on the right and the *host* name of the left.

uninterruptible power supply (UPS) An emergency power source that can provide a limited amount of power to a computer in the event of a power outage.

Universal Naming Convention (UNC) A multivendor, multiplatform convention for identifying shared resources on a network. UNC names follow the naming convention `\\computername\sharename`.

Universal Serial Bus (USB) An external bus standard that allows USB devices to be connected through a USB port. USB supports transfer rates up to 12Mbps. A single USB port can support up to 127 devices.

upgrade A method for installing Windows 2000 that preserves existing settings and preferences when converting to the newer operating system.

upgrade pack Software in the form of a migration DLL (dynamic link library) used with applications that need to be upgraded to work with Windows 2000.

Upgrade Report A report generated by the Setup program that summarizes any known compatibility issues that you might encounter during the upgrade. The Upgrade Report can be saved as a file or printed.

UPS See *uninterruptible power supply*.

URL See *Uniform Resource Locator*.

USB See *Universal Serial Bus*.

user profile A profile that stores a user's *Desktop* configuration and other preferences. A user profile can contain a user's Desktop arrangement, program items, personal program groups, network and printer connections, screen colors, mouse settings, and other personal preferences. Administrators can create *mandatory profiles*, which cannot be changed by the users, and *roaming profiles*, which users can access from any computer they log on to.

user rights policies Policies that control the rights that users and groups have to accomplish network tasks. User rights policies are set through *Local Computer Policy*.

username A user's account name in a *logon authenticated* system.

Users group A Windows 2000 built-in group that includes end users who should have very limited system access. After a *clean installation* of Windows 2000 Professional, the default settings for this group prohibit users from compromising the operating system or program files. By default, all users who have been created on the computer, except *Guest*, are members of the Users group.

Utility Manager A Windows 2000 utility used to manage the three accessibility utilities: *Magnifier*, *Narrator*, and *On-Screen Keyboard*.

V

video adapter The hardware device that outputs the display to the monitor.

virtual memory   A *kernel* service that stores memory pages not currently in use on a mass-storage device to free the memory occupied for other uses. Virtual memory hides the memory-swapping process from applications and higher-level services.

virtual private network (VPN)   A private network that uses secure links across private or public networks (such as the Internet). When data is sent over the remote link, it is encapsulated, encrypted, and requires *authentication* services.

volume   A storage area on a Windows 2000 *dynamic disk*. Dynamic volumes cannot contain *partitions* or *logical drives*. Windows 2000 Professional dynamic storage supports three dynamic volume types: *simple volumes*, *spanned volumes*, and *striped volumes*. Dynamic volumes are accessible only to Windows 2000; they are not accessible through DOS, Windows 9*x*, or Windows NT.

VPN   See *virtual private network*.

W

Warning event   An *Event Viewer* entry that indicates that you should be concerned with the event. The event may not be critical in nature, but it is significant and may be indicative of future errors.

Web browser   An application that makes *HTTP* requests and formats the resultant *HTML* documents for the users. Most Web browsers understand all standard Internet protocols.

Win16   The set of application services provided by the 16-bit versions of Microsoft

Windows: Windows 3.1 and Windows for Workgroups 3.11.

Win32   The set of application services provided by the 32-bit versions of Microsoft Windows: Windows 95, Windows 98, Windows NT, and Windows 2000.

Windows 9*x*   The 32-bit Windows 95 and Windows 98 versions of Microsoft Windows for medium-range, Intel-based personal computers. This system includes peer networking services, Internet support, and strong support for older DOS applications and peripherals.

Windows 2000 Backup   The Windows 2000 utility used to run the *Backup Wizard*, the *Restore Wizard*, and create an *Emergency Repair Disk (ERD)*.

Windows 2000 boot disk   A disk that can be used to *boot* to the Windows 2000 Professional operating system in the event of a Windows 2000 Professional boot failure.

Windows 2000 Client Installation Wizard   The Windows 2000 Client Installation Wizard (CIW) is used with RIS to automate Windows 2000 Professional installation to provide clients with the list of available images that can be used with the *automated installation*.

Windows 2000 Deployment Tools   The Windows 2000 Deployment Tools include the *Setup Manager* utility for creating unattended *answer files*, as well as the *System Preparation Tool* utility for creating disk images. The Deployment Tools are stored on the Windows 2000 Professional CD, in \Support\ Tools, in the Deploy.cab file. You can extract these files by using the File ➤ Extract command in Windows Explorer.

Windows 2000 Multilanguage Version
The version of Windows 2000 that supports multiple-language user interfaces through a single copy of Windows 2000.

Windows 2000 Professional   The current version of the Windows operating system for high-end desktop environments. Windows 2000 Professional integrates the best features of Windows 98 and Windows NT Workstation 4, supports a wide range of hardware, makes the operating system easier to use, and reduces the cost of ownership.

Windows 2000 Professional Setup Boot Disks   Floppy disks that can used to boot to the Windows 2000 operating system. With these disks, you can use the *Recovery Console* and the *Emergency Repair Disk (ERD)*.

Windows Installer packages   Special application distribution files used to automate the installation of applications. Windows Installer packages work with applications that are in *Microsoft Installer (MSI)* format or *ZAP file* format. The use of Windows Installer packages requires a Windows 2000 Server computer with *Active Directory* installed.

Windows Internet Name Service (WINS)
A network service for Microsoft networks that provides Windows computers with the *IP address* for specified *NetBIOS* computer names, facilitating browsing and intercommunication over *TCP/IP* networks.

Windows NT   The predecessor to Windows 2000 that is a 32-bit version of Microsoft Windows for powerful Intel, Alpha, PowerPC, or MIPS-based computers. This operating system includes peer networking services, server networking services, Internet client and server services, and a broad range of utilities.

Windows Update   A utility that connects the computer to Microsoft's Web site and checks the files to make sure that they are the most up-to-date versions.

WINS   See *Windows Internet Name Service*.

WINS server   The server that runs *WINS* and is used to resolve *NetBIOS* computer names to *IP addresses*.

WMI Control   A Windows 2000 utility that provides an interface for monitoring and controlling system resources. WMI stands for Windows Management Instrumentation.

workgroup   In Microsoft networks, a collection of related computers, such as those used in a department, that do not require the uniform security and coordination of a domain. Workgroups are characterized by decentralized management, as opposed to the centralized management that domains use.

write-back cacheing   A cacheing optimization wherein data written to the slow store is cached until the cache is full or until a subsequent write operation overwrites the cached data. Write-back cacheing can significantly reduce the write operations to a slow store because many write operations are subsequently obviated by new information. Data in the write-back cache is also available for subsequent reads. If something happens to prevent the cache from writing data to the slow store, the cache data will be lost.

write-through cacheing   A cacheing optimization wherein data written to a slow store is kept in a cache for subsequent rereading. Unlike *write-back cacheing*, write-through cacheing immediately writes the data to the slow store and is therefore less optimal but more secure.

Z

ZAP files   Files that can be used with *Windows Installer packages* instead of *Microsoft Installer (MIS)* format files. ZAP files are used to install applications using their native Setup program.

Index

Note to the Reader: Throughout this index **boldfaced** page numbers indicate primary discussions of a topic. *Italicized* page numbers indicate illustrations.

E

M

Q

S

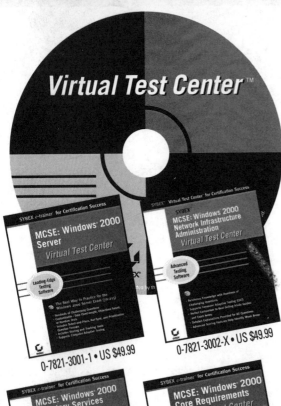

The Complete MCSE Solution

SYBEX®

Microsoft's® exam track for the Windows 2000 MCSE requires four core and three elective exams. The core, design, and additional elective exams for the Windows 2000 MCSE are listed in the table below.

For more information, visit **www.microsoft.com/trainingandservices**.

Exam #	Exam Title	Product Title	ISBN
Required Core Exams			
70-210	Installing, Configuring, and Administering Microsoft Windows 2000 Professional	MCSE: Windows 2000 Professional Study Guide	ISBN: 0-7821-2751-7
		MCSE: Windows 2000 Professional Exam Notes	ISBN: 0-7821-2753-3
		MCSE: Windows 2000 Professional Virtual Trainer	ISBN: 0-7821-5008-X
		MCSE: Windows 2000 Professional Virtual Test Center	ISBN: 0-7821-3000-3
70-215	Installing, Configuring, and Administering Microsoft Windows 2000 Server	MCSE: Windows 2000 Server Study Guide	ISBN: 0-7821-2752-5
		MCSE: Windows 2000 Server Exam Notes	ISBN: 0-7821-2754-1
		MCSE: Windows 2000 Server Virtual Trainer	ISBN: 0-7821-5009-8
		MCSE: Windows 2000 Server Virtual Test Center	ISBN: 0-7821-3001-1
70-216	Implementing and Administering a Microsoft Windows 2000 Network Infrastructure	MCSE: Windows 2000 Network Infrastructure Administration Study Guide	ISBN: 0-7821-2755-X
		MCSE: Windows 2000 Network Infrastructure Administration Exam Notes	ISBN: 0-7821-2761-4
		MCSE: Windows 2000 Network Infrastructure Administration Virtual Trainer	ISBN: 0-7821-5007-1
		MCSE: Windows 2000 Network Infrastructure Administration Virtual Test Center	ISBN: 0-7821-3002-X
70-217	Implementing and Administering a Microsoft Windows 2000 Directory Services Infrastructure	MCSE: Windows 2000 Directory Services Administration Study Guide	ISBN: 0-7821-2756-8
		MCSE: Windows 2000 Directory Services Administration Exam Notes	ISBN: 0-7821-2762-2
		MCSE: Windows 2000 Directory Services Administration Virtual Trainer	ISBN: 0-7821-5010-1
		MCSE: Windows 2000 Directory Services Administration Virtual Test Center	ISBN: 0-7821-3003-8

(Already have your MCSE for NT 4 or taken the three core "NT" exams? If so, then you qualify to take the Accelerated Windows 2000 Exam in lieu of the four new core exams in the Windows 2000 MCSE track. The MCSE: Accelerated Windows 2000 Study Guide covers all objectives sets from the four core exams in a more concise manner on the assumption that you already have a pretty good sense of what the technology is about.)

Exam #	Exam Title	Product Title	ISBN
70-240	Microsoft Windows 2000 Accelerated Exam for MCPs Certified on Microsoft Windows NT 4.0.	MCSE: Accelerated Windows 2000 Study Guide	ISBN: 0-7821-2760-6
		MCSE: Accelerated Windows 2000 Exam Notes	ISBN: 0-7821-2770-3
Choose 1 More Core Exam			
70-219	Designing a Microsoft Windows 2000 Directory Services Infrastructure	MCSE: Windows 2000 Directory Services Design Study Guide	ISBN: 0-7821-2757-6
		MCSE: Windows 2000 Directory Services Design Exam Notes	ISBN: 0-7821-2765-7
or			
70-220	Designing Security for a Microsoft Windows 2000 Network	MCSE: Windows 2000 Network Security Design Study Guide	ISBN: 0-7821-2758-4
		MCSE: Windows 2000 Network Security Design Exam Notes	ISBN: 0-7821-2766-5
or			
70-221	Designing a Microsoft Windows 2000 Network Infrastructure	MCSE: Windows 2000 Network Infrastructure Design Study Guide	ISBN: 0-7821-2759-2
		MCSE: Windows 2000 Network Infrastructure Design Exam Notes	ISBN: 0-7821-2767-3
Choose 2 Electives			
70-222	Migrating from Microsoft Windows NT 4.0 to Microsoft Windows 2000	MCSE: Windows 2000 Migration Study Guide	ISBN: 0-7821-2768-1
		MCSE: Windows 2000 Migration Exam Notes	ISBN: 0-7821-2769-X
70-224	Installing, Configuring, and Administering Microsoft Exchange 2000 Server	MCSE: Exchange 2000 Server Administration Study Guide	ISBN: 0-7821-2898-X
		MCSE: Exchange 2000 Server Administration e-trainer	ISBN: 0-7821-5012-8
		MCSE: Exchange 2000 Server Aministration Virtual Test Center	ISBN: 0-7821-3017-8
70-225	Designing and Deploying a Messaging Infrastructure with Microsoft Exchange 2000 Server	MCSE: Exchange 2000 Design Study Guide	ISBN: 0-7821-2897-1
70-227	Installing, Configuring, and Administering Microsoft Internet Security and Acceleration (ISA) Server 2000	MCSE: ISA Server 2000 Administration Study Guide	ISBN: 0-7821-2933-1
70-228	Installing, Configuring, and Administering Microsoft SQL Server 2000 Enterprise Edition	MCSE: SQL Server 2000 Administration Study Guide	ISBN: 0-7821-2921-8
		MCSE: SQL Server 2000 Administration Virtual Test Center	ISBN: 0-7821-3016-X
70-229	Designing and Implementing Databases with Microsoft SQL Server™ 2000 Enterprise Edition	MCSE: SQL Server 2000 Design Study Guide	ISBN: 0-7821-2942-0
70-244	Supporting and Maintaining a Microsoft Windows NT Server 4.0 Network	MCSE: Windows NT Server 4.0 Support and Maintenance Study Guide	ISBN: 0-7821-2992-7